# Sources of Chinese Tradition

## SECOND EDITION

## VOLUME II

INTRODUCTION TO ASIAN CIVILIZATIONS

*Introduction to Asian Civilizations*

WM. THEODORE DE BARY, GENERAL EDITOR

*Sources of Japanese Tradition*
(1958)

*Sources of Chinese Tradition*
(1960, rev. 1999)

*Sources of Indian Tradition*
(1958, rev. 1988)

*Sources of Korean Tradition*
(1997)

# Sources of Chinese Tradition

SECOND EDITION

VOLUME II

From 1600 Through the Twentieth Century

*Compiled by Wm. Theodore de Bary and Richard Lufrano*

WITH THE COLLABORATION OF
Wing-tsit Chan, Julia Ching, David Johnson,
Kwang-ching Liu, David Mungello, Chester Tan

*and contributions by*
John Berthrong, Woei Lien Chong, John Ewell, Joan Judge, Philip Kuhn,
John Lagerwey, Catherine Lynch, Victor Mair, Susan Mann, Ian McMorran,
Don Price, Douglas Reynolds, William Rowe, Lynn Struve, Burton Watson,
Tu Weiming, Pierre-Etienne Will, John D. Young, and Peter Zarrow

COLUMBIA UNIVERSITY PRESS

NEW YORK

Columbia University Press
*Publishers Since 1893*
New York Chichester, West Sussex
Copyright © 2000 Columbia University Press
All rights reserved

Library of Congress Cataloging-in-Publication Data
de Bary, William Theodore, 1919–
    Sources of Chinese tradition, vol. 2 / compiled by Wm. Theodore de Bary and
  Richard Lufrano ; with the collaboration of Wing-tsit Chan . . . [et al.]. — 2d ed.
      p.  cm. — (Introduction to Asian civilizations)
    Includes bibliographical references and index.
    ISBN 0–231–10938–5 (vol. 1 cloth) — ISBN 0–231–10939–3 (vol. 1 paper)
    ISBN 0–231–11270–X (vol. 2 cloth) — ISBN 0–231–11271–8 (vol. 2 paper)
      1. China — Civilization — Sources.   I. Lufrano, Richard.   II. Chan, Wing-tsit,
  1901–1994.   III. Title.   IV. Series.
  DS721.D37                                           1999
  951 — dc21                                   98–21762
  ∞

Casebound editions of Columbia University Press books are printed on permanent and
durable acid-free paper.
Printed in the United States of America
c  10  9  8  7  6  5  4  3  2  1
p  10  9  8  7  6  5  4  3  2

List of permissions

"Azure (Sky Blue)." *Chinese Sociology and Anthropology* (Winter 1991–92). Reprinted by permission from M.E. Sharpe, Inc., Armonk, NY 10504.

Benton, Gregor, and Alan Hunter, eds. *Wild Lily, Prairie Fire, China's Road to Democracy*. Copyright © 1995 by Princeton University Press. Reprinted by permission of Princeton University Press.

*Bringing Down the Great Wall* by Fang Lizhi. Copyright © 1991 by Fang Lizhi. Reprinted by permission of Alfred A. Knopf Inc.

"Building Socialist Spiritual Civilization." *Beijing Review*, no. 10 (March 9, 1981): 16–17.

Chan, Anita, Stanley Rosen, and Jonathan Unger, eds. *On Socialist Democracy and the Chinese Legal System*. Reprinted by permission from M.E. Sharpe, Inc., Armonk, NY 10504.

Chang, Carsun. *The Development of Neo-Confucianism*. NY: Bookman, 1962.

"The Chinese Debate on the New Authoritarianism." *Chinese Sociology and Anthropology* (Winter 1990–91 and Spring 1991). Reprinted by permission from M.E. Sharpe, Inc., Armonk, NY 10504.

Compton, Boyd. *Mao's China: Party Reform Documents*. Copyright © 1952, University of Washington Press. Reprinted with permission of publisher.

"Communique of the Third Party Plenary Session of the 11th Central Committee of the Communist Party of China." *Beijing Review*, no. 52 (December 29, 1978): 6–16.

(Permissions continued on p. 629)

This volume is dedicated to Irene Bloom in appreciation of her outstanding contributions to the study and teaching of Chinese thought and to the development of Asian Studies.

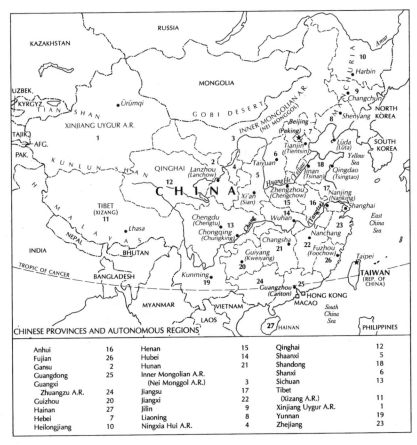

CHINESE PROVINCES AND AUTONOMOUS REGIONS

| Anhui | 16 | Henan | 15 | Qinghai | 12 |
|---|---|---|---|---|---|
| Fujian | 26 | Hubei | 14 | Shaanxi | 5 |
| Gansu | 2 | Hunan | 21 | Shandong | 18 |
| Guangdong | 25 | Inner Mongolian A.R. | | Shanxi | 6 |
| Guangxi | | (Nei Monggol A.R.) | 3 | Sichuan | 13 |
| Zhuangzu A.R. | 24 | Jiangsu | 17 | Tibet | |
| Guizhou | 20 | Jiangxi | 22 | (Xizang A.R.) | 11 |
| Hainan | 27 | Jilin | 9 | Xinjiang Uygur A.R. | 1 |
| Hebei | 7 | Liaoning | 8 | Yunnan | 19 |
| Heilongjiang | 10 | Ningxia Hui A.R. | 4 | Zhejiang | 23 |

CHINA

CONTENTS

## 34. *The Communist Revolution* 396

## 35. *Chinese Communist Praxis* 426

# EXPLANATORY NOTE

The names of contributors are indicated in the table of contents alongside the sections or selections that they are responsible for. At the end of each selection the sources of translations are rendered as concisely as possible; full bibliographical data can be obtained from the list of sources at the end of the book. Unless otherwise indicated, the author of the text is the writer whose name precedes the selection; the initials following each selection are those of the translator, as indicated in the table of contents. Where excerpts have been taken from existing translations, they have sometimes been adapted or edited in the interests of uniformity with the book as a whole.

In translating Chinese terms there is often no single equivalent in English for pivotal words that have multiple meanings in the original. Simply to transliterate the original term would be an easy way to avoid having to choose among alternatives, but it would not be a solution for the great majority of readers who are unfamiliar with Chinese. Consequently, we have adopted a standard rendering and used it wherever possible but have allowed for variants (followed by the romanized term) to be substituted when necessary. At the end of volume 1 of *Sources* is a glossary of key terms listed in romanized Chinese (*pinyin* and Wade-Giles) with alternate renderings in English; from this the reader can approximate the range of meanings that cluster around such pivotal terms.

Chinese words and names are rendered according to the *pinyin* system of romanization. For readers unfamiliar with *pinyin*, it is useful to know that the consonants *q* and *x* are to be read as *ch* and *hs*, respectively. The Wade-Giles romanization is also given for names and terms already well known in that form, as are the renderings preferred by important modern figures and in common use (such as Sun Yat-sen). A comparative table of *pinyin* and Wade-Giles romanizations may be found at the end of the book. Indic words appearing in the chapters on Buddhism as technical terms or titles in italics follow the standard system of transliteration found in Louis Renou's *Grammaire Sanskrite* (Paris, 1930), pp. xi–xiii, with the exception that here *ś* is regularly used for *ç*. To facilitate pronunciation, other Sanskrit terms and proper names appearing in roman letters are rendered according to the usage of *Webster's New International Dictionary*, second edition unabridged, except that here the macron is used to indicate long vowels and the Sanskrit symbols for *ś* (*ç*) and *ṣ* are uniformly transcribed as *sh*. Similarly, the standard Sanskrit transcription of *c* is given as *ch*.

Chinese names are rendered in their Chinese order, with the family name first and the personal name last. Dates given after personal names are those of birth and death; in the case of rulers, reign dates are preceded by "r." Generally the name by which a person was most commonly known in Chinese tradition is the one used in the text. Since this book is intended for the general reader rather than the specialist, we have not burdened the text with a list of the alternate names or titles that usually accompany biographical reference to a scholar in Chinese or Japanese historical works.

In the preparation of this volume for publication the editors have been especially indebted to the following for their expert assistance: Martin Amster, Renee Kashuba, Glenn Perkins, and Marianna Stiles.

# Sources of Chinese Tradition

SECOND EDITION

VOLUME II

# PART 5

# The Maturation of Chinese Civilization and New Challenges to Chinese Tradition

*Chapter 25*

## THE CHINESE TRADITION IN RETROSPECT

Although the Manchu conquest of China might have been expected to produce, under foreign rule, dramatic changes in Chinese life, it is a sign of the
powerful inertial force of Chinese civilization — the magnitude of the society
and the survival power of both its people and its culture — that so much of
traditional thought and institutions persisted into the new era and, in fact, even
lent stability and strength to the new regime. It is also a credit to the adaptability
of the Manchus to their new situation.

A key instance of this political and cultural survival was the early resumption
of the civil service examination system, with the same basic curriculum that
had been adopted, under Neo-Confucian influence, in the Mongol and Ming
periods. Nothing else so radically conditioned the intellectual life of Qing
China, since this curriculum based on the Four Books and Five Classics provided both the common denominator for educated discourse and the ground
for further advances in classical scholarship, which became, in the Qing period,
the greatest achievement of the cultural elite.

Although in principle education was open to all, classical learning remained
accessible only to the more leisured classes; commoners, most of them heavily
engaged in manual labor, could not indulge in such time-consuming pursuits.
True, basic literacy and popular culture shared many of the same Confucian
values on the moral level, but farmers and craftsmen could only admire, and
did not often share in, the higher forms of culture respected among the elite.

Scholar-officials, however, had their own problems. As Confucian loyalists and survivors from the Ming, their consciences kept many of them from serving the new dynasty. At the same time, as upholders of Confucian ideal standards who blamed the fall of the Ming dynasty on its own lack of political virtue, the four major thinkers represented below, instead of commemorating and eulogizing, engaged in a searching critique not just of the Ming but of dynastic rule down through the ages — a critique of unprecedented depth and incisiveness. Given, however, the unchallengeability of Qing power and authority in the late seventeenth and eighteenth centuries, the fuller significance and effect of this critique of dynastic rule was not felt until the late nineteenth and early twentieth centuries — if, indeed, it is not still to be felt.

Of these same thinkers, three (Huang Zongxi, Lü Liuliang, and Gu Yanwu) were recognized as outstanding scholars in their own time, while Wang Fuzhi worked in great isolation and became widely appreciated only much later. Lü's fate, however, was ironic. In the first decades of the Qing he was a powerful force in the revival of the Zhu Xi school and influenced leading Neo-Confucians who played a major role in the Kangxi emperor's promotion of an official Zhu Xi orthodoxy. Yet when Kangxi's successor discovered the politically subversive character of Lü's commentary on Zhu Xi's Four Books (see chapter 21) he engaged in a ruthless and almost totally successful proscription of Lü's works.

Meanwhile, alongside the promotion of the official orthodoxy, a broad movement of critical textual scholarship was developing, which, intellectually speaking, became the dominant scholarly trend (known as the Han Learning or Evidential Learning). Gu Yanwu was generally regarded as the progenitor and towering example of this movement, and his prestige endured into the twentieth century.

In terms of their official standing and formative role in shaping official orthodoxy and cultural policy, other major figures like Lu Longji, Li Guangdi, and Zhang Boxing (most of them influenced to some degree by Lü Liuliang and identified with the so-called Song Learning), would have to be mentioned, but outstanding though they were in their own day, we pass them by here in favor of others whose significance transcends their own time.

## HUANG ZONGXI'S CRITIQUE OF THE CHINESE DYNASTIC SYSTEM

Huang Zongxi (1610–1695) was the son of a high Ming official affiliated with the Donglin party who died in prison at the hands of the eunuchs. At the age of eighteen, after the fall of the chief eunuch, Wei Zhongxian, Huang avenged his father's death by bringing to justice or personally attacking those responsible for it. Thereafter he devoted himself to study, took part in a flurry of political agitation at Nanjing just before the fall of the Ming dynasty, and then engaged in prolonged, but unsuccessful, guerrilla operations against the Manchus in southeast China. There is evidence that he even took part in a mission to Japan, hoping to obtain aid. After finally giving up the struggle, Huang settled down to a career as an independent scholar and teacher, refusing all offers of employment from the Manchu regime.

Warfare being less total and intensive in those days, Huang was probably not forced to neglect his intellectual interests altogether during those unsettled years. Nevertheless, it is remarkable that his most productive years should have come so late in life. His first important work, *Waiting for the Dawn* (*Mingyi daifanglu*), was produced at the age of fifty-two. Thereafter he worked on a massive anthology of Ming dynasty prose and a broad survey of Ming thought, *Mingru xuean*, which is the first notable attempt in China at a systematic and critical intellectual history. At his death he was compiling a similar survey for the Song and Yuan dynasties. Huang's range of interests included mathematics, calendrical science, geography, and the critical study of the classics, as well as literature and philosophy. In most of these fields, however, his approach is that of a historian, and this underlying bent is reflected in the fact that his most outstanding disciples and followers in the Manchu period also distinguished themselves in historical studies. Huang was an independent and creative scholar who questioned the predominant Neo-Confucian emphasis on individual virtue as the key to governance and instead stressed the need for constitutional law and systemic reform.

Huang characterized dynastic rule as inherently "selfish," rather than conforming to the Confucian ideal of governance in the public interest or common good (*gong*), and he also reaffirmed the traditional (especially Mencian) emphasis on the critical remonstrating function of conscientious ministers. Yet he went further to insist on having a prime minister as executive head of the government (rather than the emperor, as was the case in the Ming period) and also on having schools at every level (including the capital) serve as organs of public discussion, with the emperor and his officials required to attend and listen to the airing of major public issues.

The crises of the late Ming–early Qing evoked from other scholars, like Gu Yanwu, Lü Liuliang, and Tang Zhen, similar critiques of the dynastic system based on Confucian principles. None, however, produced as systematic and comprehensive a statement, expressed in such forceful language, as Huang. Unfortunately, under the strong, efficient rule of the Qing dynasty Huang's forthright critique could be circulated only among a few scholars discreet enough not to publicize it widely or attract official repression. Only in the declining years of the Qing dynasty did reformers, both monarchist and republican, succeed in reprinting and circulating it as a native manifesto for constitutional change.

Huang's *Waiting for the Dawn* (*Mingyi daifanglu*)[1] is probably the most systematic and concise critique of Chinese imperial institutions ever attempted from the Confucian point of view. Besides dealing with the theory and structure of government, it takes up the problems of education, civil service examinations, land reform, taxation, currency, military organization, and eunuchs. Huang's views on only a few of these can be set forth here.

## On the Prince

In the beginning of human life each man lived for himself and looked to his own interests. There was such a thing as the common benefit, yet no one seems to have promoted it; and there was common harm, yet no one seems to have eliminated it. Then someone came forth who did not think of benefit in terms of his own benefit but sought to benefit all-under-Heaven and who did not think of harm in terms of harm to himself but sought to spare all-under-Heaven from harm. Thus his labors were thousands of times greater than the labors of ordinary men. Now to work a thousand or ten thousand times harder without benefiting oneself is certainly not what most people in the world desire. Therefore in those early times some men worthy of ruling, after considering it, refused to become princes — Xu You and Wu Guang[2] were such. Others undertook it and then quit — Yao and Shun, for instance. Still others, like Yu,[3] became princes against their own will and later were unable to quit. How could men of old have been any different? To love ease and dislike strenuous labor has always been the natural inclination of man.

However, with those who later became princes it was different. They believed that since they held the power over benefit and harm, there was nothing wrong in taking for themselves all the benefits and imposing on others all the harm. They made it so that no man dared to live for himself or look to his own interests. Thus the prince's great self-interest took the place of the common good of all-under-Heaven. At first the prince felt some qualms about it, but his conscience eased with time. He looked upon the world as an enormous estate to be handed on down to his descendants, for their perpetual pleasure and well-being. . . .

This can only be explained as follows: In ancient times all-under-Heaven

---

1. The Chinese title is not susceptible of literal translation; we give the general sense of it as indicated by Huang's preface to the work.

2. Legendary Daoists who refused the throne when it was offered to them.

3. Yu (or the Great Yu). During the reign of Shun he saved the country from a great flood, for which service he was ennobled and made a minister, eventually succeeding Shun on the throne as first ruler of the Xia dynasty.

were considered the master[4] and the prince was the tenant. The prince spent his whole life working for all-under-Heaven. Now the prince is master and all-under-Heaven are tenants. That no one can find peace and happiness anywhere is all on account of the prince. In order to get whatever he wants, he maims and slaughters all-under-Heaven and breaks up their families — all for the aggrandizement of one man's fortune. Without the least feeling of pity, the prince says, "I'm just establishing an estate for my descendants." Yet when he has established it, the prince still extracts the very marrow from people's bones and takes away their sons and daughters to serve his own debauchery. It seems entirely proper to him. It is, he says, the interest on his estate. Thus he who does the greatest harm in the world is none other than the prince. If there had been no rulers, each man would have provided for himself and looked to his own interests. How could the institution of rulership have turned out like this?

In ancient times men loved to support their prince, likened him to a father, compared him to Heaven, and truly this was not going too far. Now men hate their prince, look on him as a "mortal foe,"[5] call him "just another guy."[6] And this is perfectly natural. But petty scholars have pedantically insisted that "the duty of the subject to his prince is utterly inescapable."[7] . . . As if the flesh and blood of the myriads of families destroyed by such tyrants were no different from the "carcasses of dead rats."[8] Could it be that Heaven and Earth, in their all-encompassing care, favor one man and one family among millions of men and myriads of families? . . .

If it were possible for latter-day princes to preserve such an estate and hand it down in perpetuity, such selfishness would not be hard to understand. But once it comes to be looked upon as a personal estate, who does not desire such an estate as much as the prince? Even if the prince could "tie his fortune down

---

4. The term *zhu* (master) could also be translated "host," but in China, as in the West, the relationship between host and guest most often suggests that the former is obliged to accommodate the latter, in accordance with long-standing traditions of hospitality. Yet Huang obviously means that the guest has no rights, being at the mercy of the host's generosity, and thus "master" conveys better the idea of primacy, superiority, or sovereignty as Huang intends it here and "tenant" the dependence of the people on the ruler.

5. *Mencius* 4B:3.

6. *Shang shu, Taishi* B, SBCK 6:5b, and *Mencius* 1B:8 in reference to the last ruler of Shang. See n. 10.

7. The original quotation is from *Zhuangzi, Renjian shi*, SBCK, *Nanhua zhenjing* 2:16b. It is also found in the *Surviving Writings of the Cheng Brothers* (*Er Cheng yishu* 5:77, *Er xiansheng yu* in *Er Cheng ji* [Beijing: Zhonghua, 1981]), where it has a different meaning, i.e., the constant relation between prince and minister is a mutual commitment to moral principle, not an inescapable obligation to serve. If prince and minister do not agree on principles, according to Cheng Yi and Zhu Xi, the minister should leave the prince's service. See *Cuiyan, Jun chen pian*, 2:1242–1247.

8. *Zhuangzi*, "Autumn Floods," SBCK, *Nanhua zhenjing* 6:28a; Burton Watson, *The Complete Works of Chuang Tzu* (New York: Columbia University Press, 1968), p. 188.

and lock it up tight,"[9] still the cleverness of one man is no match for the greed of all. At most it can be kept in the family for a few generations, and sometimes it is lost in one's own lifetime, unless indeed the life's blood spilled is that of one's own offspring. . . .

It is not easy to make plain the position of the prince, but any fool can see that a brief moment of excessive pleasure is not worth an eternity of sorrows.

## On Ministership

Suppose there is someone who, in serving the prince, "sees [what to do] without being shown and hears without being told."[10] Could he be called a [true] minister? I say no. Suppose that he sacrifices his life in the service of his prince. Could he then be called a [true] minister? I say no. "To see without being shown and hear without being told" is "to serve [one's prince] as one's father."[11] To sacrifice one's life is the ultimate in selflessness. If these are not enough to fulfill this duty, then what should one do to fulfill the Way of the Minister?

The reason for ministership lies in the fact that the world is too big for one man to govern, so governance must be shared with colleagues. Therefore, when one goes forth to serve, it is for all-under-Heaven and not for the prince; it is for all the people and not for one family.

When one acts for the sake of all-under-Heaven and its people, then one cannot agree to do anything contrary to the Way even if the prince explicitly constrains one to do so — how much less could one do it without being shown or told! And if it were not in keeping with the true Way, one should not even present oneself to the court — much less sacrifice one's life for the ruler. To act solely for the prince and his dynasty and attempt to anticipate the prince's unexpressed whims or cravings — this is to have the mind of a eunuch or palace maid. "When the prince brings death and destruction upon himself, if one follows and does the same, this is to serve him as a mistress or some such intimate would."[12] That is the difference between one who is a true minister and one who is not.

But those who act as ministers today, not understanding this principle, think

---

9. *Zhuangzi, Quqie pian,* SBCK 6:15b; Watson, *Complete Works of Chuang Tzu,* p. 107.

10. A transposition of an expression found in the *Liji, Quli,* SBCK 1:6a, which according to the commentator Zheng Xuan enjoins upon the filial son a constant attentiveness to the behests of his parents. Legge translates it: "He should be [as if he were] hearing [his parents] when there is no voice from them, and as seeing them when they are not actually there" (*Li Ki* 1:69). Here it cannot be translated as "not actually there," because it is clear from the passage following that this is a question of discerning desires that are actually there but are simply unexpressed, unformulated.

11. *Liji, Sangfu sizhi* 63:22b.

12. *Zuozhuan,* 25th Year of Duke Xiang, *Chunqiu jingzhuan jijie,* SBCK 17:11a.

that ministership is instituted for the sake of the prince. They think that the prince shares the world with one so that it can be governed and that he entrusts one with its people so that they can be shepherded, thus regarding the world and its people as personal property in the prince's pouch [to be disposed of as he wills].

Today only if the toil and trouble everywhere and the strain on the people are grievous enough to endanger one's prince do ministers feel compelled to discuss the proper means for governing and leading the people. As long as these do not affect the dynasty's existence, widespread toil, trouble, and strain are regarded as trifling problems, even by supposedly true ministers. But was this the way ministers served in ancient times, or was it another way?

Whether there is peace or disorder in the world does not depend on the rise or fall of dynasties but upon the happiness or distress of the people. . . . If those who act as ministers ignore the "plight of the people,"[13] then even if they should succeed in assisting their prince's rise to power or follow him to final ruin, they would still be in violation of the true Way of the Minister. For governing the world is like the hauling of great logs. The men in front call out, "Heave!," those behind, "Ho!"[14] The prince and his ministers should be log-haulers working together.[15] . . .

Alas, the arrogant princes of later times have only indulged themselves and have not undertaken to serve the world and its people. From the countryside they seek out only such people as will be servile errand boys. Thus from the countryside those alone respond who are of the servile errand-boy type; once spared for a while from cold and hunger, they feel eternally grateful for his majesty's kind understanding. Such people will not care whether they are treated by the prince with due respect (lit., according to the proper rites governing such a relation) and will think it no more than proper to be relegated to a servant's status. . . .

It may be asked, Is not the term *minister* always equated with that of *child*?[16] I say no. Father and child share the same vital spirit (psycho-physical force, *qi*). The child derives his own body from his father's body. Though a filial child is a different person bodily, if he can draw closer each day to his father in vital

---

13. *Mencius* 3B:5.

14. *Huainanzi, SBCK,* sec. 1, 12:2a.

15. Reading *gong* (together) for *qi* (their). Cf. *Haishan xianguan* ed. 5a, line 8.

16. In the classics the relation of minister (*chen*) to prince, and son to father, are frequently linked, as in the *Liji:* "The ceremonies . . . of mourning and sacrifice . . . illustrate the kindly feelings of minister and son" (Legge, *Li Ki* 2:258–259. This usage is akin to the Confucian emphasis on the Five Moral Relations — between parent and child, sovereign and minister, husband and wife, elder and younger brothers, and friends (cf. *Mencius* 2B:2 and 3A:4; *Great Learning* 20:8). Mencius, however, insisted on the virtual parity of prince and minister because of their shared commitment to rightness (*yi*) and said a minister should leave a prince if they had no such agreement on what is right (2B:5, 14; 4B:3; 5B:9).

spirit, then in time there will be a perfect communion between them. An unfilial child, after deriving his body from his father's, drifts farther and farther from his parent, so that in time they cease to be kindred in vital spirit. The terms *prince* and *minister* derive from their relation to all-under-Heaven. If I take no responsibility for all-under-Heaven, then I am just another man on the street.[17] If I come to serve him without regard for serving all-under-Heaven, then I am merely the prince's menial servant or concubine. If, on the other hand, I have regard for serving the people, then I am the prince's mentor and colleague. Thus with regard to ministership the designation may change.[18] With father and child, however, there can be no such change.

## On Law

Until the end of the Three Dynasties there was Law. Since the Three Dynasties there has been no Law. Why do I say this? Because the Two Emperors and Three Kings[19] knew that all-under-Heaven could not do without sustenance and therefore gave them fields to cultivate. They knew that all-under-Heaven could not go without clothes and therefore gave them land on which to grow mulberry and hemp. They knew also that all-under-Heaven could not go untaught, so they set up schools, established the marriage ceremony to guard against promiscuity, and instituted military service to guard against disorders. This constituted Law until the end of the Three Dynasties. It was never laid down solely for the benefit of the ruler himself.

Later rulers, once they had won the world, feared only that their dynasty's lifespan might not be long and that their descendants would be unable to preserve it. They set up laws in fear for what might happen, to prevent its coming

---

17. *Mencius* 4B:3: "When the prince regards his minister as a mere dog or horse, the minister regards the prince as any other man of the country." Zhu Xi renders "man of the country" as "anyone met on the road" (*luren*), and Huang uses Zhu's term, not Mencius's. Cf. *Mengzi jizhu* 4B:3, Zixue ed. 10:15a, p. 781.

18. Zhuangzi was often quoted for his attribution to Confucius of the view that the relationship of prince and minister was as unalterable and inescapable as that of parent and child (*Zhuangzi* 2:16b). Zhu Xi agreed that the principle of a mutual commitment to rightness (*yi*) was unalterable, but there was no such relation based on blind personal loyalty. Further, he agreed with Mencius that if the ruler lacked such a commitment, the minister should leave. In other words, the underlying principle was changeless, but the personal relationship was contractual and became void if there was no agreement in principle. Huang agrees with Zhu Xi (*Mengzi jizhu* 4B:3, Zixue ed. 10:15a, p. 781. See also 2B:5, 14, and 5B:9. *Zhuzi wenji* 82:9b–10a. *Ba Song jun zhongjia ji* and *Er Cheng yishu* (Zhonghua ed.) 5:76–77, where Cheng Yi and Zhu Xi affirm the invariable principle of being in accord on what is right, but with it the obligation to withdraw if there is no such agreement.

19. The Two Emperors — Yao and Shun; the Three Kings — Yu of Xia, Tang of Shang, and Wen and Wu of Zhou together.

to pass. However, what they called "Law" was laws for the sake of one family and not laws for the sake of all-under-Heaven. . . .

The Law of the Three Dynasties "safeguarded the world for the sake of all-under-Heaven."[20] The prince did not try to seize all the wealth of the land, high or low, nor was he fearful that the power to punish and reward might fall into others' hands. High esteem was not reserved for those at court; nor were those in the countryside necessarily held in low esteem. Only later was this kind of Law criticized for its looseness, but at that time the people were not envious of those in high place, nor did they despise humble status. The looser the law was, the fewer the disturbances that arose. It was what might be called "Law without laws." The laws of later times have "safeguarded the world as if it were something in the [prince's] treasure chest."[21] It is not desired that anything beneficial should be left to those below but rather that all blessings be gathered up for those on high. If [the prince] employs a man, he is immediately afraid that the man will act in his own interest, and so another man is employed to keep a check on the other's selfishness. If one measure is adopted, there are immediate fears of its being abused or evaded, and so another measure must be adopted to guard against abuses or evasions. All men know where the treasure-chest lies, and so the prince is constantly fretting and fidgeting out of anxiety for its security. Consequently, the laws have to be made tight, and as they become tighter they become the very source of disorder. These are what one calls "un-Lawful laws."

Some say that each dynasty has its own laws and that succeeding generations of the royal house have a filial duty to follow the ancestral laws. Now "un-Lawful laws" are originally instituted because the first prince of a line is unable to curb his own selfish desires. Later princes, out of the same inability, may break down these laws. The breaking down may in itself do harm to all-under-Heaven, yet this does not mean that the original enactment of the laws did no such harm. Yet some still insist that we get involved in this kind of legalistic muck, just to gain a little reputation for upholding the regulations[22] — all of which is just the "secondhand drivel" of vulgar Confucians.[23] . . .

Should it be said that "there is only governance by men, not governance by law,"[24] my reply is that only if there is governance by law can there be governance by men. Since un-Lawful laws fetter men hand and foot, even a man

---

20. *Zhuangzi, Dazong shi, SBCK* 3:9a; Watson, *Complete Works of Chuang Tzu*, p. 81.

21. *Yanzi qunqiu, SBCK* 6:19b.

22. *Xianzhang* means to uphold the laws and institutions established by the founder of the dynasty; an expression applied to Confucius, who "elegantly displayed the regulations of Wen and Wu [founders of the Zhou dynasty], taking them as his model" (Legge, *Doctrine of the Mean,* 30:1).

23. *Liji, Quli, Shisanjing zhusu* 2:9a.

24. *Xunzi, Jundao pian, SBCK* 8:1a.

capable of governing cannot overcome inhibiting restraints and suspicions. When there is something to be done, men do no more than their share, content themselves with the easiest slapdash methods, and can accomplish nothing that goes beyond a circumscribed sphere. If the Law of the early kings were still in effect, there would be a spirit among men that went beyond the letter of the law. If men were of the right kind, all of their intentions could be realized; and even if they were not of this kind, they could not slash deep or do widespread damage, thus harming the people instead [of benefiting them]. Therefore I say that only when we have governance by Law can we have governance by men.[25]

## Establishing a Prime Minister[26]

The origin of misrule under the Ming lay in the abolition of the prime ministership by [the founder] Gao Huangdi.[27]

The original reason for having princes was that they might govern all-under-Heaven, and since all-under-Heaven could not be governed by one man alone, officials were created for the purpose of governing. Thus officials shared the function of the prince.

Mencius said, "The Son of Heaven constituted one rank, the duke one, the marquis one, and viscounts and barons each one of equal rank — five ranks in all. The ruler constituted one rank, the chief minister one, the great officers one, the scholars of the highest grade one, those of the middle grade one, and those of the lowest grade one — six ranks in all."[28] In terms of external relationships,[29] the Son of Heaven was removed from the duke to the same degree that

---

25. In Xunzi's discussion of the "Way of the Ruler," he says, "It is men that govern, not laws" (Wang Xianqian, *Xunzi jijie* 8:1a), and Zhu Xi implicitly amended this when he said in his *Commentary on the Great Learning* that it is by self-cultivation and self-discipline that the governance of men is accomplished. See ch. 21.

26. *Zhixiang*: The term that Huang uses most often for prime minister (*caixiang*) is a common, but not a formal, title in Chinese official history. At times two or three men were so designated concurrently, in which case "chief councillor" is a more appropriate translation. But to Huang's mind there should be only one such, and therefore it means here "prime minister."

27. *Gao Huangdi*: i.e., the founder of the dynasty, whose canonical name was Taizu and reign name Hongwu (1368–1398). In 1380, following the execution of Prime Minister Hu Weiyong for plotting against the throne, the prime ministership (*chengxiang*) was abolished, together with its chief agency of administration, the *zhongshu sheng*, and the Six Ministries were made directly responsible to the emperor. By this Taizu hoped to keep any one man from obtaining sufficient power to rival the throne. However, this arrangement placed a heavy administrative burden upon the emperor, too great a one for him to cope with, and led to the exercise of executive functions by members of his cabinet and eunuchs.

28. Part of Mencius's description (5B:2) of the enfeoffment system as he supposed it to have existed during the early Zhou dynasty (ca. 1000 B.C.E.). See ch. 6.

29. That is, the relationship of the emperor to the enfeoffed nobility ruling outside his own immediate domain but within the empire.

the duke, marquis, earl, and viscount and baron were in turn removed from each other. As to internal relationships,[30] the prince was removed from the chief minister to the same degree as the chief minister, great officers, and scholars were in turn removed from each other. Rank did not extend to the Son of Heaven alone and then stop, with no further degrees of rank.

In ancient times during the regencies of Yi Yin and the Duke of Zhou,[31] these men, in serving as prime ministers, acted for the emperor, and it was no different from the great officers' acting for the chief ministers, or the scholars acting for the great officers. In later times princes were arrogant and ministers servile, so that for the first time the rank of emperor fell out of line with those of the chief ministers, great officers, and scholars. . . .

In ancient times the prince treated his ministers with such courtesy that when a minister bowed to the emperor, the emperor always bowed in return.[32] After the Qin and Han this practice was abandoned and forgotten, but still when the prime minister presented himself to the emperor, the emperor rose from the throne, or, if he were riding, descended from his carriage.[33] When the prime ministership was abolished there was no longer anyone to whom respect was shown by the emperor. Thus it came to be thought that the Hundred Offices[34] were created just for the service of the prince. If a man could serve the prince personally, the prince respected him; if he could not, the prince treated him as of no account. The reason for having officials being thus corrupted, how could the reason for having princes be understood?

In ancient times the succession passed not from father to son but from one worthy man to another. It was thought that the emperor's position could be held or relinquished by anyone, as was the prime minister's. Later the emperor passed his position to his son, but the prime minister did not. Then, even though the sons of emperors were not all worthy to rule, they could still depend on the succession of worthy prime ministers to make up for their own deficiencies. Thus the idea of succession by a worthy man was not yet entirely lost to the emperors. But after the prime ministership was abolished, the moment an emperor was succeeded by an unworthy son, there was no worthy person at all to whom one could turn for help. Then how could even the idea of dynastic succession be maintained?

---

30. That is, the emperor's relationship to the officials of his court administering directly his own domain around the capital. The point of this passage is to show that in ancient times (i.e., ideally) the emperor's power and dignity were not absolute but relative to a gradually ascending hierarchy of rank, both within his own feudal domain and in China as a whole.

31. Zhou Gong: The fourth son of King Wen of Zhou and younger brother of King Wu. He served as counselor to the latter and on Wu's death assumed the regency for seven years during the minority of King Cheng. See ch. 2.

32. *Liji, Yanyi, Shisanjing zhusu* 62:19a.

33. *Han shu*, SBCK 84:3b. According to Yan Shigu's commentary, this was the Han ritual.

34. Hundred Offices: i.e., all the government officials.

It may be argued that in recent times matters of state have been discussed in cabinet, which actually amounted to having prime ministers, even though nominally there were no prime ministers. But this is not so. The job of those who handled matters in the cabinet has been to draft comments of approval and disapproval [on memorials] just like court clerks. Their function was inconsequential enough to begin with, yet worse still, the substance of the endorsement came from those closest to the emperor[35] and was then merely written up in proper form. Could you say that they had real power?

I believe that those with the actual power of prime ministers today are the palace menials. Final authority always rests with someone, and the palace menials, seeing the executive functions of the prime minister fall to the ground, undischarged by anyone, have seized the opportunity to establish numerous regulations, extend the scope of their control, and take over from the prime minister the power of life and death, as well as the power to award and confiscate, until one by one all these powers have come into their own hands. . . .

The best that could be done by the worthy men in these cabinets was to talk about "following the ancestral example." This was not because the ancestral example was always worthy to be followed but because no one took the position of these men seriously, so they were forced to use the prestige of the royal ancestors as a means of restraining their rulers and thwarting the palace menials. But the conduct of the royal ancestors was not always what it should have been, and the craftier of the palace menials could find a precedent for each of their own bad practices, saying they were "following the ancestral example." So the argument about following ancestral law became absurd. If the prime ministership had not been abolished, the practices of wise kings and ancient sages could have been used to mold the character of the ruler. The ruler would have had something to fear and respect, and he would not have dared to flout it.

*There follows a detailed discussion of how governmental business should be handled by the prime minister's office and the various ministers so as to ensure that all petitions and memorials from the people are properly acted on.*

## Schools

Schools are for the training of scholar-officials. But the sage kings of old did not think this their sole purpose. Only if the schools produced all the instrumentalities for governing all-under-Heaven would they fulfill their purpose in being created. . . . Indeed, schools were meant to imbue all men, from the highest at court to the humblest in country villages, with the broad and magnanimous spirit of the classics. What the Son of Heaven thought right was not

---

35. Literally "from inside"; i.e., from the eunuchs. See *Ming shi* 72:1730.

necessarily right; what he thought wrong was not necessarily wrong. And thus even the Son of Heaven did not dare to decide right and wrong for himself but shared with the schools the determination of right and wrong. Therefore, although the training of scholar-officials was one of the functions of schools, they were not established for this alone.

Since the Three Dynasties, right and wrong in the world have been determined entirely by the court. If the Son of Heaven favored such and such, everyone hastened to think it right. If he frowned upon such and such, everyone condemned it as wrong. . . . Rarely, indeed, has anyone escaped the evil tendencies of the times; consequently, people are apt to think the schools of no consequence in meeting the urgent needs of the day. Moreover, the so-called schools have merely joined in the mad scramble for office through the examination system, and students have allowed themselves to become infatuated with ideas of wealth and noble rank. . . .

Consequently the place of the schools has been taken by the academies.[36] What the academies have thought wrong, the court considered right and gave its favor to. What the academies have considered right, the court thought must be wrong and therefore frowned upon. When the [alleged] "false learning" [of Zhu Xi] was proscribed [in the Song][37] and the academies were suppressed [in the Ming],[38] the court was determined to maintain its supremacy by asserting its authority. Those who refused to serve the court were punished, on the charge that "they sought to lead scholar-officials throughout the land into defiance of the court."[39] This all started with the separation of the court and the schools and ended with the court and schools in open conflict. . . .

---

36. With the decline, during the late Tang, Five Dynasties, and Song periods of the official school system devoted to the preparation of men for government service through the examination system, academies grew up around some of the better private libraries, where serious and independent study could be carried on by men whose primary interest was in true learning rather than official advancement.

37. The proscription of the Zhu Xi school at the end of the twelfth century.

38. During the Ming dynasty three attempts were made to suppress the academies on the charge of heterodox and subversive teaching: in 1537–1538, when Zhan Roshui (1466–1560) was condemned; in 1579, when Zhang Juzheng attempted unsuccessfully to destroy the academies; and in 1625, when the powerful eunuch Wei Zhongxian again ordered their destruction, followed by a purge of "subversives" associated with the Donglin Academy of Wuxi. Huang has the last in mind here.

39. Huang himself cites such a case in his account of Zhuang Chang, 1437–1499 (jinshi 1466), which repeats the charge in the same language. In 1457, as a Hanlin bachelor, Zhuang, together with two colleagues, submitted memorials rebuking the emperor for his preoccupation with sexual pleasures. For this he (and they) were flogged at court in the presence of the emperor, and Zhuang was banished to Guiyang. Later rehabilitated, for some years he refused to serve and was accused by the scholar and statesman Qiu Jun (1420–1495) of "leading scholars throughout the land into defiance of the court." Qiu claimed that the Ming founder, Taizu, had made refusal to serve a punishable offense (*Mingru xuean* 45:14).

When the school system was abandoned, people became ignorant and lost all education, but the prince led them still further astray with temptations of power and privilege. This, indeed, was the height of inhumanity, but still he made people call him by what is now an empty name, "The Prince our Father, the Prince our Father." As if anyone really believed it!

The prefectural and district school superintendent (*xueguan*) should not be appointed [by the court]. Instead, each prefecture and district should, after open public discussion, ask a reputable scholar to take charge. . . .

In populous towns and villages far from the city, wherever there are large numbers of scholars, a classics teacher should also be appointed, and wherever there are ten or more young boys among the people, longtime licentiates[40] not holding office should act as elementary teachers. Thus, in the prefectures and districts there would be no students without worthy teachers.

The Libationer [Rector][41] of the Imperial College should be chosen from among the great scholars of the day. He should be equal in importance to the prime minister, or else be a retired prime minister himself. On the first day of each month the Son of Heaven should visit the Imperial College, attended by the prime minister, six ministers, and censors. The Libationer should face south and conduct the discussion, while the Son of Heaven too sits among the ranks of the students. If there is anything wrong with the administration of the country, the Libationer should speak out without reserve.

When they reach the age of fifteen, the sons of the emperor should study at the Imperial College with the sons of the high ministers.[42] They should be informed of real conditions among the people and be given some experience of difficult labor and hardship. They must not be shut off in the palace, where everything they learn comes from eunuchs and palace women alone, so that they get false notions of their own greatness.

In the various prefectures and districts, on the first and fifteenth of each month, there should be a great assembly of the local elite, licentiates, and certified students in the locality, at which the school superintendent should lead the discussion. The prefectural and district magistrates should sit with the

---

40. Certified scholars receiving official stipends.

41. Libationer (*taixue jijiu*): i.e., chancellor or rector of the Imperial College. In ancient times at great feasts the honor of offering the first libation of wine was reserved for the oldest man present. *Libationer* thus became a term of the highest respect and in the Han was applied to the most learned of the court scholars. Between 275 and 280, under the Western Jin (265–316), the head of the Imperial College was designated Libationer, a title that remained in use until the end of the Qing dynasty.

42. Here Huang follows the recommendation of the Cheng brothers and Zhu Xi. See *Er Chengji, Mingdao wenji* 1:449–450; *Yichuan wenji* 3:563; and Zhu Xi; *Daxue zhangju*, preface, pp. 1b–3a.

students, facing north and bowing twice. Then the teacher and his pupils should bring up issues and discuss them together. Those who excuse themselves on the pretext of official business and fail to attend should be punished. If minor malpractices appear in the administration of a prefectural or district magistrate, it should be the school's duty to correct them. If there are serious malpractices, the members of the school should beat the drums and announce it to the people. . . .

## The Selection of Scholar-Officials, Part 2

In ancient times the selection of scholar-officials was liberal, but the employment of them was strict. Today the selection of scholar-officials is strict, but the employment of them is liberal. Under the old system of "district recommendation and village selection,"[43] a man of ability did not have to fear that he would go unrecognized. Later on, in the Tang and Song, several types of examination were instituted, and if a man did not succeed in one, he could turn around and take another. Thus the system of selection was liberal. . . .

But today this is not so. There is only one way to become an official: through the examination system. Even if there were scholars like the great men of old . . . they would have no other way than this to get chosen for office. Would not this system of selection be called too strict? However, should candidates one day succeed, the topmost are placed among the imperial attendants and the lowest given posts in the prefectures and districts. Even those who fail [the metropolitan examinations] and yet have been sent up from the provinces[44] are given official posts without having to take examinations again the rest of their lives. Would not this system of employment be called too liberal? Because the system of selection is too confined, many great men live to old age and die in obscurity. Because the system of employment is too liberal, frequently the right man cannot be found among the many holding official rank. . . .

Therefore, I would broaden the system for selecting scholar-officials and choose men [not only] through the regular examinations [but also] through special recommendations, through the Imperial College, through the appointment of high officials' sons, through [a merit system for] junior officials in prefectures and districts, through special appointments, through specialized learning, and through the presentation of memorials. And the strictness in the employment of these men might be correspondingly elaborated upon.

---

43. A system used in the Latter Han dynasty for the selection of court officials upon the recommendation of local prefects (*junshou*) and the prime ministers of the various states (*guoxiang*).

44. Those who have passed the provincial examinations and obtained the *juren* degree.

## LÜ LIULIANG'S RADICAL ORTHODOXY

Though not considered, like Huang Zongxi, one of the Three Great Scholars of the early Qing period, Lü is without question a figure to be reckoned with. An active partisan in the unsuccessful resistance to the Manchus, Lü subsequently refused all invitations to serve them and went down in history as a symbol of unremitting hostility to China's foreign conquerors. He is known also, however, as the most articulate spokesman of the orthodox Neo-Confucian revival, which came to be identified ideologically with the very dynasty he struggled against.

Lü was born in 1629; his home, like Huang Zongxi's, was in eastern Zhejiang province, an area rich in history and culture, and especially in historians and philosophers. His family were well-established members of the educated elite who had been scholar-officials for generations and local leaders known for their philanthropy and sense of community responsibility. From an early age, instead of looking upon his study of the Neo-Confucian curriculum as routine, he described himself as deeply impressed and inspired by the works of Zhu Xi. Several scholars have noted the religious intensity with which he took to Zhu Xi as his guide in life. Along with this went a deep sense of loyalty to the Ming, despite increasing signs of the dynasty's weakness and eventual collapse. With other members of his family and the community, he took part, even at a young age, in the resistance movement carried on in his region against the Manchus, but when that proved futile, in 1647 he gave it up and returned home to a more normal pattern of life.

This pattern included passing the first level of civil service examinations, which he did in 1653, thus maintaining his family's membership in the ranks of the official literati, with the status of *shengyuan*, i.e., a stipendiary or licentiate, officially registered as a candidate for the higher examinations and some form of public service. He remained in this privileged status for thirteen years, during which he quickly made a name for himself as a scholar and in his sideline occupation as an editor of examination essays. The latter sold well, given the reading public's special orientation toward literature useful for official careers, and also given his own talents for philosophical analysis, lucid exposition, and literary style.

As a conscientious Neo-Confucian, however, Lü could not be insensitive to the ambiguities of his situation. His privileged status as a stipendiary was difficult to justify in one whose Ming loyalist, anti-Manchu sentiments, strictly held to, would seem to preclude any semblance of accepting favors from the new dynasty. Thus by 1666 he had decided to take the drastic step of renouncing his official status — no easy thing to do in a society providing few alternative careers for the educated outside of officialdom. That Lü could succeed at all in this decision testifies to his native scholarly talent and resourcefulness at commercial enterprise, and also to his continued willingness to compromise by writing model examination (eight-legged) essays, which he did more or less actively for some years thereafter.

Meanwhile Lü maintained close personal relations with some of the leading scholars of his day. Though strong-minded, irascible — and, some said, arrogant — he was respected by other prominent figures in the revival of Neo-Confucian orthodoxy, whose thinking he deeply influenced, and it was not for lack of opportunities to enjoy state patronage that he withdrew increasingly from most social involvements, and eventually, as a tactic in resisting pressure upon him to accept distinguished-scholar status at the Manchu court, he took the Buddhist tonsure. There is no indication that this represented a religious conversion or a total withdrawal from conventional society. Up until his death in 1683 Lü continued to work on scholarly projects, republishing Zhu Xi's works, editing examination essays, and meeting with his students.

Lü's later degradation at the hands of the Yongzheng emperor, during the years 1728–1733, was the outcome of the failed rebellion of one Zeng Jing (1679–1736), a scholar whose passionate antidynastic sentiments were said to have been inspired by the reading of Lü's writings. In consequence of this, Lü's remains were desecrated and an ideological campaign was mounted against him, including the publication under imperial sponsorship of *Refutation of Lü Liuliang's Discourses on the Four Books* (*Bo Lü Liuliang Sishu jiangyi*) and the subsequent banning and burning of his works in the so-called Inquisition of Qianlong.

The following selections are all from Lü's commentaries or discourses on the Four Books. Thus they are in the form of brief interlinear annotations, not separate essays. But they were read and often accepted as authoritative by many scholars preparing for the civil service examination, until banned after the Zeng Jing case.

COMMENTARIES ON THE FOUR BOOKS

## Principle in the Mind-and-Heart

Lü Liuliang rejected the view of the mind as something to be known in itself (a view he attributed to Lu Xiangshan and Wang Yangming) and emphasized instead the mind as a faculty for recognizing principle in things and affairs. In this he contributed to the reemphasis on scholarship and Evidential Learning in the Qing.

What Confucians are conscious of is principle; what heterodox teachings are conscious of is mind. One can only become conscious of principle through the investigation of things and the extension of knowledge; then with the understanding of human nature and of Heaven comes the fullest employment of the mind. If, however, one sets aside the principles of things and tries to look directly into the mind, it makes the investigation of things and extension of knowledge seem superfluous and diversionary. If one thinks of oneself as directly perceiving the substance of the mind, the principles of things amount in the final analysis to no more than useless appendages.

*Believing that rational moral principles were inherent in the mind and all things, Lü asserted that the moral consciousness and moral life were natural to human life and that freedom and spontaneity (so emphasized by the Wang Yangming school) could be attained only through the fulfillment of moral principles in action, not through any attempt at direct transcendence of the rational, moral sphere.*

Once there is Heaven [creating], human beings are necessarily born, and once there are human beings, there is sure to be the [moral] nature, and once the nature, there is sure to be this Way of what-ought-to-be. . . . So it is not only the moral imperative that is natural but the following of it. Thus both the imperative and the following of it partake of Heaven's "unceasingness" [constancy]. If there is something subtle and wondrous about this, it is that the teaching [learning] of the sage seems to be done by man and yet it is naturally and necessarily so. Since it derives from Heaven's imperative, if, in the unceasingness of the sage there is something natural and inescapable about it, this is the naturalness and inescapability of Heaven's imperative itself.

*Further, explaining Mencius's teaching concerning the "lost mind," Lü says, on the basis of Zhang Zai and Zhu Xi's view of "the mind as coordinating the nature and emotions":*

The mind coordinates the nature and emotions. The movements of the mind, their coming and going, their loss or preservation, all have to do with the spirituality of the psycho-physical [consciousness], and the subtlety of its control consists in preserving the mind of humaneness and rightness. "Losing the mind" is the loss of control by humaneness and rightness, and "seeking the lost mind" means seeking what should control the mind. If this mind is preserved, then what gives this control is preserved, and principle and the psycho-physical [consciousness] are unified. . . . If this mind is lost, then the psycho-physical consciousness runs off by itself. Wherefore it becomes imperative to employ the method of inquiry and learning to recover and nourish it through the correcting power of principle, so as to restore unity [between the mind, principle, and things]. . . .

Heterodox teachings also seek the mind, but having rejected the search for the moral principles in things-and-affairs, what they pursue is no more than the spiritual activity of a [value-free] psycho-physical consciousness, and so they cannot employ the multitude of principles in the mind to deal with things-and-affairs.

*Here Lü asserts the importance of method or process, combining moral effort and intellectual inquiry, as the requisite means for achieving and preserving the unity of the mind. Deviant teachings, such as those of Chan masters Linji and Caodong, Lu Xiangshan, Chen Xianzhang and Wang Yangming, discard this method in order to pursue the substance of the mind-in-itself, apart from things-and-affairs, thereby seeking a unity devoid of principle. This then leads also to dispensing with specific steps taught in the* Great Learning *(the Eight Items or Specifications) and the* Mean *(the five procedures of broad learning, accurate inquiry, and so on). Lü's line of analysis is clearly meant to underscore the difference between Lu Xiangshan's primary emphasis on first establishing the moral nature and Zhu Xi's on the method of inquiry and learning.*

## Principles, Desires, and Rites

Lü, like Zhu Xi, believed that human appetites and moral principles were complementary, not opposed, elements of human nature and that human desires became evil only when selfishly indulged. Rites give formal embodiment to the principles that should guide the appetites, i.e., they provide for the "measured expression" of both Heaven's principle and natural appetites.

All human hearts are the same in having desires and [their corresponding indwelling] principles. For instance, they are the same in their love of goods and sex. However, they should only get what is right for them to love. If one speaks only of their being the same in the love of goods and sex [and not having principles], then human desires can become a source of great disorder in the world. Therefore when Mencius spoke of what makes human hearts the same, he referred to principle, to what is right and proper. Filiality, brotherliness, and commiseration are common principles of what is right and proper; therefore the text [of the *Great Learning*] speaks of them as norms or standards. Rites, music, penal and administrative systems are also the common principles of what is right and proper; therefore they are called the Way. Extrapolating from these norms one projects the Way, which is the common basis for putting these principles into practice. Therefore, what is spoken of as the Way of the measuring square, refers to taking those common principles of measuring human hearts and making them the means of governance that brings peace to the world. Simply to pursue the satisfaction of the physical appetites and let everyone gratify his own desires is the naturalness and laissez-faire of the Daoists or the expedient adaptability of the Buddhists. It is not the sages' way of the measuring square.

*For Lü the quintessential "rites" were the well-field system and school systems spoken of by Mencius, the former providing for everyone's physical sustenance and the latter providing education for the moral and cultural uplift of the people.*

Some say that schools are not difficult to set up but the well-field system is far from easy to carry out, in witness whereof is the fact that today there are schools but no well-fields.[45] To this the Master [Zhu Xi] said, "They do not realize that the schools of today are not the same as the schools of antiquity. The latter were set up only after the well-fields had been instituted [to provide the material support prerequisite to education]. For the whole purpose and organization of schools was linked to the well-field system, which is not at all the case with the schools of today." So if it is easy for one [to be established], it is easy for both, and if it is difficult for one, it is equally difficult for both. There is no difference between them in this.

## The Neo-Confucian Critique of Dynastic Rule

From earliest times Confucians had invoked an idealized Age of the Sage Kings as the foil for their criticism of the status quo. Lü is even more outspoken on the point than most of his predecessors:

During the Three Dynasties every measure the sage kings took to provide for the people's livelihood and maintain the social order, including the enfeoffment, military, and penal systems, no matter how minute in detail or long-range their consequences, were only instituted for the sake of all-under-Heaven and their posterity. . . . Not a thing was done nor a law enacted simply for the ruler's own enrichment or aggrandizement, nor was their aim in the slightest to secure for their descendants an estate to be held onto forever, for fear of others trying to seize it. Thus in the *Mean* (*Zhongyong*) was the sages' humaneness acclaimed for the warmth of its earnest solicitude [for the people].

After Qin and Han [however] . . . , the underlying motive in government has been purely selfish and expedient, the fear being that otherwise one might suffer the loss of what belonged to one's family. . . . This is why Master Zhu [Xi] said that for over two thousand years the Way had not been practiced for even a single day.

*Elsewhere Lü identifies rulership with Heaven in order to emphasize both the ruler's overarching responsibility to the people and the universality of the principles that should govern the ruler's conduct: "The Son of Heaven occupies Heaven's Position (tianwei) in order to bring together the common human family within the Four Seas, not just to serve the self-interest of one family." Lü explains that during the Three Dynasties the throne was passed on to others with the idea of sharing responsibility, of doing what was best for the people. "Heaven's Imperative (tianming) and the minds-and-hearts of the people weighed heavily on them, and the world lightly. [Such being the case, as Mencius said,]*

---

45. See vol. 1, chs. 6, 11, 19.

*the sages would not commit even one unrighteous deed or kill even one person, though to do so might gain them the whole world."*

*Some scholars had justified the dynastic system as a natural extension of the parent-child relationship and had tried to promote the idea that the ruler was the loving parent of all the people. Lü dismissed this paternalism as a fraudulent claim and instead equated rulership with ministership. The original basis of rulership was no different from that of ministership; the only criteria for holding the office should be individual merit and commitment to right principles.*

Lineal succession is founded on the parent-child relationship; the passing on of rulership is founded on the ruler-minister relation. The former derives from [the principle of] humaneness; the latter, from that of rightness. On this basis these two great principles coexisted and were never confused. Thus Heaven's Position [rulership] was originally conferred on the basis of individual worth.

*Elsewhere Lü emphasizes that this basic moral relation is rooted in the nature received from Heaven:*

Heaven gives birth to the people and establishes rulers and ministers for them. Rulers and ministers are for sustaining the life of the people. The minister seeks out a ruler to head the government, and the ruler seeks out the minister to share in the governing. Together they represent Heaven's presence in the world. Thus the ruler's position is called "Heaven's position; official emoluments are called Heaven's emoluments." Heaven's order and Heaven's justice are not something the ruler and minister can take and make their own. Though there is a definite difference in the honor done to ruler and minister, it is still only a difference of one degree in the relative distance between them.

*Here Lü emphasizes the organic nature of the social order and of the moral imperatives governing human relations. Among these, he says elsewhere, the moral relation between ruler and minister is the most important of all:*

The rightness (*yi*) of the ruler-minister relation is of the first importance in the world (*yu zhong diyi shi*). It is the greatest of the human moral relations. If one does not keep to this principle, then no matter what one's accomplishments or meritorious deeds, they will count for nothing against the guilt so incurred.

*While the moral responsibility that attaches to this relation is heavy and inescapable — as fixed and unalterable as the imperatives of Heaven's mandate — this does not mean that the personal relationship between ruler and minister is similarly fixed and unalterable:*

Ruler and minister come together in agreement on what is right (*yi*). If they can agree on what is right, they can form the relation of ruler-minister; if not, they should part, as is the case in the relation between friends. It is not like father and son, or older and younger brother [i.e., a blood relation that cannot be changed]. If they do not agree, there is no need for personal resentment or recrimination. If their commitment is not the same, their Way cannot be carried out, and it is best to part.

Parting is in accordance with the rite of ruler and minister, not a departure from that relation. It was only in later times, with the abandonment of the enfeoffment system and adoption of centralized prefectures and counties, that the world came under the control of one ruler and consequently there was "advancement and retirement" [from office] but no parting. When the Qin abandoned the Way, they established the "rite" of honoring the ruler and abasing the minister, and created an unbridgeable gap between the one on high and the other below, giving the ruler complete control over the minister's advancement and retirement, while leaving him nowhere to go. That was when the relation of rightness between ruler and minister underwent a complete change.

*In consequence of this change, the conception of ministership, as well as rulership, was corrupted when Heaven's [moral] authority was no longer recognized:*

After the Three Dynasties, rulers and ministers forgot about Heaven. Rulership came to be thought of as for one's own self-gratification. Ministers thought that life and death, reward and punishment, were all at the ruler's disposal and it could not be otherwise. Thereupon the ruler became honored and the minister abased, with the two completely separated. Government, insofar as it now involved a sharing of power and prestige, could not possibly be shared. Thereupon usurpations and assassinations followed; a world of selfishness and expediency was produced. Cut off from Heaven, rulers did not understand that rites come from Heaven, ministers did not realize that fidelity [loyalty] is rooted in the moral nature, that the nature is Heaven, that Heaven is the moral imperative [and political mandate], that it is principle, and the nature is principle.

## Government: From the Top Down or Ground Up?

In Lü's view the ancient well-field system had provided the material base, and schooling the cultural support, for the people's assumption of some responsibility for maintaining the social and political order. He had this to say in commenting on Mencius's discussion of officials' emoluments as in lieu of their own cultivation of the land:

[In ancient times] the whole system of emoluments was based on the usufruct of the land, and likewise the whole system of official ranks was based on it. In

Heaven's creating of the people and providing for rulers and teachers, the basic principle was thus all-embracing. . . . Looked at from the top it might seem to some as if ranks and emoluments were projected downward to the common people; they do not realize that looked at in terms of Heaven's bestowing of life on the people, the principle originates with the people and reaches up to the ruler.

*In this emphasis on the fundamental importance of the common man we see not only a reflection of Mencius's emphasis on the people but a further application of Lü's basic doctrine that all life comes from Heaven, that all human beings are endowed with the moral nature, and that in each individual lies the imperative to act in accordance with the principles inhering in that nature. It is not a "mandate" solely for the ruler.*

*This is a point of great potential significance. Confucius and Mencius had stressed the responsibility of noble men (junzi) to provide for the needs of the common man (min), but not the responsibility of the min themselves. Here the heightened emphasis on the indwelling of principle, as the Heavenly endowed moral nature, suggests that all individuals share to some degree in this responsibility. Lü does not elaborate any new political mechanisms by which this responsibility might be actively discharged.*

Both the common man and the Son of Heaven are rooted in the same principle. Speaking of it in terms of rank from the top down, the *Great Learning* says "from the Son of Heaven down to the common man," but in terms of principle, in reality, it goes from the common man up to the Son of Heaven. The Son of Heaven's renewing of the people should proceed on the same principle, and conform to the common man's regulation of his own family.

This is not only a responsibility that weighs on the ruler. Everyone has his own self [to govern] and therefore there is no one on whom the responsibility does not lie. Just as there are the myriad things and one Supreme Ultimate, so each thing has its own Supreme Norm to follow.

*Although the matter is discussed in terms of responsibilities rather than entitlements, it is clear that each thing's having its own norm to follow confers on it a certain irreducible autonomy, which governance must take into account and respect. Thus Lü also says:*

There are many gradations from the Son of Heaven down to the common man, and each in performing his own proper function is different, but the differentiation lies in one's lot or function and not in the principle. Therefore it is said, "Principle is one and its particularizations diverse. . . ." No matter how low the commoner is, it is the same underlying principle and not a different case. The commoner may not have the official function of ordering the state and bringing peace to the world, but inherent in the fulfilling of his self-cultivation is the principle of ordering the state and bringing peace to the world.

[From de Bary, *Learning for One's Self*, pp. 291–292, 312–313, 326–330, 335–341]

## LATE CONFUCIAN SCHOLARSHIP: WANG FUZHI

Wang Fuzhi (Wang Quanshan, 1619–1692) is now widely recognized as one of the most important thinkers of the Ming-Qing period, but he was virtually unknown during his own lifetime, having been born into a strictly conservative and rather isolated family of scholars in Hengyang, Hunan. Wang's personal life and official career were shattered by the catastrophic events surrounding the collapse of the Ming dynasty. In 1642, after succeeding in the provincial (*juren*) examinations, he set off for Beijing and the *jinshi* sessions, but marauding peasant rebels forced him to turn back, and when Zhang Xianzhong's peasant army took Hengyang the following year, Wang's family became a target of the insurgents. After the fall of Beijing in 1644, Wang took an active part in anti-Manchu resistance but was defeated when he raised troops in Hunan, and though he subsequently held a minor post at the southern "imperial" court of the Yongli pretender, he soon became a victim of factional strife and was forced to resign in 1650. Still only thirty-one years old, from then until his death some forty years later, he withdrew into the hills of Hunan and a life of scholarship. Fiercely loyal to the Ming, he refused either to serve the Qing or to rally to such dubious opponents of the alien regime as Wu Sangui, when the latter proclaimed a "Zhou" dynasty in Hengyang, in 1678.

Wang never, however, relinquished his hopes of a Chinese recovery, even though he had to content himself with expressing his ideas through a prodigious amount of writing that covered the entire range of traditional Chinese scholarship. His passionate commitment to Chinese civilization and its destiny shines forth through all his studies and, along with his fiery patriotism and savage criticism of barbarians, was responsible for the vast majority of his work remaining unpublished until the latter half of the nineteenth century. (Some was banned, but most was concealed from Qing officialdom by his family.) Yet once such writings as *The Yellow Book* (*Huang shu*), *A Strange Dream* (*E meng*), *On Reading [Sima Guang's] Comprehensive Mirror* (*Du Tongjian lun*), and *On the History of the Song Dynasty* (*Song Lun*) had been published, they attracted the attention of both reformers and revolutionaries, who saw in Wang an early exponent of Chinese nationalism. Zeng Guofan, Tan Sitong, Liang Qichao, Zhang Binglin, and Mao Zedong were among those who declared their admiration for him.

Three imperatives animate Wang's writings: the crucial need to return to the sound philosophical basis provided by the "true doctrines" of the early Song Confucian Zhang Zai; an urgent necessity to learn the lessons that the study of Chinese history could reveal; and a primordial duty to preserve Chinese culture and civilization from alien encroachment and indigenous debasement.

Indeed, the philosophical basis of all Wang's thought was his own rational development of the monistic cosmology first worked out by Zhang Zai, whom he acknowledged as his master. Zhang had been one of the Song thinkers drawn upon for the great Song Neo-Confucian synthesis completed by Zhu Xi in the twelfth century, but, according to Wang, Zhang's contribution to the genuine Confucian tradition had been accorded too little importance in the Cheng-Zhu system. Moreover, Wang Yangming and his followers had subsequently perverted Confucianism, and it was their influence that had resulted in the moral anarchy and social chaos that led to the ruin of the Ming dynasty. For Wang Fuzhi the realms of philosophy (both cosmology and ethics), history, and politics were dimensions of the same universal phenomenon, evolving as integrally related parts of the one great process of change. It was doubtless his desire to understand this process of universal change and, in particular, the cataclysmic changes of his own times that led him to devote himself to an extensive study of the *Classic of Changes* and Zhang Zai, whose entire system of thought was, as Wang himself remarked, inspired by this classic.

Following Zhang Zai, Wang built his philosophy on the identification of material-force (*qi*) with the *Supreme Ultimate*, the term that had become part of the Neo-Confucian vocabulary and was generally synonymous with the Way, either as the origin of the universe, as universal laws, or as the Absolute. Zhang had preferred to use the terms *Supreme Void* (*Taixu*) to describe its aspect as original, unformed substance and *Supreme Harmony* (*Taihe*) to refer to the complex but coherent process of activity and tranquillity, agglomeration and dispersal, in the harmony of yin and yang that constitutes the Way. In this universe of continuous change, Wang emphasizes the significance of the trend of material conditions (*shi*), which are the product of the evolving material-force (*qi*) and principles (*li*), in which the importance of the time factor is crucial. His concept of *shi* (translated here as "trend" or "condition," depending on context) dominates both his historical criticism and his assessment of political institutions. It explains the rational empiricism of his proposals for reform and his firm rejection of any notion of reviving the well-field system or the enfeoffment system as anachronistic (despite his Song master's advocacy of them!).

In responding to the critical problems of Ming China, Wang's proposals were generally moderate, tempered by an awareness of what was feasible in the prevailing conditions and his conviction that change should always be gradual if the proper equilibrium (*zhen* from the *Classic of Changes*) were to be achieved and maintained. Having identified the systems of land taxation and distribution as the root of social and political disorder, he outlined original ways of improving the country's agricultural basis and restoring peasant prosperity. Perceiving the growth of commerce as a threat to the class structure of traditional Chinese society, he advocated repressive taxation on merchants. Arguing that imperial despotism had been a dominant factor in the decline of the Ming, he, like Huang Zongxi, proposed ways of restoring the balance of power shared between the emperor and his ministers — in particular, the restoration of the office of prime minister as the first step in a general decentralization throughout the administration that would put more power in the hands of scholar-officials. The latter were, according to Wang, the ultimate guarantors of the country's political health, and the Donglin activists of the late Ming had incarnated this role in their struggle with the inner court. As did such contemporaries as Huang and Tang Zhen, Wang severely criticized selfish and decadent emperors without ever calling the institution of monarchy itself into question. At the core of his proposals lay the aim to revive ministerial power and prestige, which had been dramatically eroded during the Ming.

Wang's proposals were never adopted or implemented, but he anticipated, in reply to a hypothetical critic, the objection that "at present, with the country overwhelmed and the dynasty cut off, to recount too much the errors of the past will simply arouse resentment. This is 'bolting the stable door after the horse has gone.'" Wang's answer was this: "Confucius, in writing the *Spring and Autumn Annals,* made many subtle criticisms of the reigns of Duke Ding and Duke Ai [who ruled Confucius's state of Lu during his lifetime]. At the time when one speaks, no one understands one. In setting forth what I have understood, I am also trying to advise future generations." (*Huang shu,* postface)

## COSMOLOGICAL FOUNDATIONS

In his commentary on Zhang Zai's *Zhengmeng (Discipline for Beginners),* Wang elaborates the foundations of his own system. In a cosmos of being, consisting entirely of material-force (and in which there is no room for nonbeing), the natural harmony of the complex interplay of elements in the ceaseless process of evolution depends on their orderly organization into different categories and on the normal functioning of each within its respective category. The concept of universal order based on strict observance of natural categories had, of course, significant social and political implications.

In the Supreme Void all is being; but it has not yet taken form. The *qi* (material-force) is self-sufficient through agglomeration and dispersion, change and evolution; its original substance is neither diminished nor increased. The sun and moon in their risings and settings, the four seasons in their comings and goings, the various creatures in their life and death, together with the wind and the rain, dew and thunder, flourish when the time is ripe and decline when the time is ripe. In this they are one: they are all temporary forms. . . .

. . . When the *qi* agglomerates, its existence is visible, but when it is dispersed one may suspect that it is nonexistent. Once it has agglomerated and assumed forms and images, then as regards talents (*cai*), matter (*zhi*), nature (*xing*), and feelings (*qing*), all accord with their own categories. They accept what is similar and oppose what is different; thus all things flourish in profusion and form their several categories. Moreover, the formation of each of these categories has its own organization. So it is that dew, thunder, frost, and snow all occur at their proper times, and animals, plants, birds, and fish all keep to their own species. There can be no frost or snow during the long summer days, nor can there be dew or thunder in the depths of winter. Nor can there be between man and beast, plant and tree, any indiscriminate confusion of their respective principles.

[*Quanshan yishu, Zhangzi Zhengmeng zhu* 1:2a–3a — IM]

## WANG'S "REVISION" OF ORTHODOX NEO-CONFUCIANISM

In criticizing his predecessors, Wang Fuzhi reserved his most vitriolic condemnation for Wang Yangming, but, in defending Zhang Zai's *qi*-based monism, he also took issue with Zhou Dunyi, incorporated by Zhu Xi into his Neo-Confucian synthesis as one of its founding fathers, and with Zhu Xi himself over their dualism. He attacked Zhou's notion of the Supreme Ultimate and the Way as the generative source of being together with the *qi* of yin and yang, and Zhu, for according priority to principle and the Way over material-force and actual phenomena.

Those who give a wrong explanation of the *Diagram of the Supreme Ultimate* say that in the Supreme Ultimate there was originally no yin or yang, that yang was first produced by its movement and yin from its quiescence . . . but movement and quiescence are the movement and quiescence of yin and yang. . . . It is not the case that there is first movement and afterward the yang, first quiescence and afterward the yin.

[*Quanshan yishu, Zhangzi Zhengmeng zhu* 1:6a — IM]

When the *qi* disperses, it returns to the Supreme Void and reverts to the original substance of its state of fusion. There is no destruction. When it agglomerates and brings life to various things, this arises from the eternal nature of its state of fusion. Nothing new is born or reared. . . . The agglomeration and dispersion of *qi* constitutes the life and death of things. When it emerges they come, and when it withdraws they go. All this is the natural effect of principles and conditions (*shi*). It cannot be stopped. One cannot, by according with it, become eternal. One cannot, by direction, accelerate the process of dispersion. One cannot, by intervention, delay it. This is why the gentleman is unconcerned about life and death. . . . To achieve the correct norm (*zhen*) in life and death in following out the Human Way is the outstanding doctrine of Master Zhang, who developed the heritage of earlier sages in order to refute the Buddhists and Daoists and rectify the mind of men. Because he spoke of agglomeration and dispersion and of dispersion followed by a further agglomeration, Zhu Xi criticized this as "*samsara*." My own humble opinion is that it is, on the contrary, Master Zhu's theory that is closer to what the Buddha said about *nirodha*. . . . The *Classic of Changes* also says, "Above forms it is called the Way. Below forms it is called the actual phenomenon (or concrete thing)." By the former is meant "that which is clear and penetrating and cannot take the form of images." So actual phenomena are formed and destroyed, while that which cannot take the form of images is lodged within them as their function. As it is never formed, so it is never destroyed. The actual phenomenon wears out, but its Way never ends. . . . In autumn and winter the *qi* of life is stored in the earth, and though the branches and leaves of trees are withered their roots are firm and flourishing. So it is not the case that in autumn and winter they are destroyed once and for all with nothing remaining. If a fire is made of a cartload of firewood, it is consumed in one blaze and becomes flame, smoke, and ashes. But wood reverts to wood, water to water, and earth to earth: it is simply that they become so minute and subtle that man cannot see them.

[*Quanshan yishu, Zhangzi Zhengmeng zhu* 1:3b–4b — IM]

The world consists of nothing but actual physical phenomena or concrete things. The Way is the Way (or Ways) of actual phenomena, but one cannot describe the actual phenomena as phenomena of the Way. "When the Way is nonexistent, so is the actual phenomenon" is something that anyone is capable of saying. But if the phenomenon exists, why worry about its Way not existing? The sage knows what the gentleman does not, and yet ordinary men and women can do what the sage cannot. It may be that people are not clear about the Way of some particular phenomenon, and so the thing is not perfected, but the fact that it is not perfected does not mean that it does not exist. "When the actual phenomenon is nonexistent, so is its Way" is something that few people are capable of saying, but it is really and truly so.

[*Quanshan yishu, Zhou Yi waizhuan* 5:25a — IM]

## HISTORICAL TRENDS

Wang insists on the need to understand history if one is to act appropriately in the present. In dealing with the evolution of society and its institutions, he argued, one must take the long view in order to appreciate what universal laws will work in the prevailing trends or conditions (*shi*). No trend is irreversible. Only change is inevitable. And man, who is, in Wang's phrase, "the one who controls events, as the very mind of the universe," can and must do what he can to influence it.

Wang's theory of historical development, which was an integral part of his overall cosmology, freed him from the bonds of precedent and tradition that prevented so many scholars from adapting their classical learning to the problems of their times. His own attitude to political history and the political problems of his day was an empirical one.

The ideal is to be master of the time factor. The next best thing is to anticipate it, and the next best thing after that is to accord with it. The worst thing to do is to go against it. To go against the times is fatal. When one is master of the times, the vagaries of time fluctuate in correspondence to oneself as one controls and adjusts the times. When one anticipates the times, the cardinal principle is, when one sees what is going to happen, to guide and control its realization. When one accords with the times, one complies with that which the times make inevitable in order to save oneself and so escape from disaster.

[*Quanshan yishu, Qunqiu shi lun* 5:7b — IM]

The ancient institutions were for governing the ancient world and cannot be taken as general rules applicable in the present, so the gentleman does not take them as precedents in his undertakings. One governs the world of today with what is appropriate to it today, but this will not necessarily be appropriate in the world of tomorrow, so the gentleman does not bequeath laws as precedents for posterity. This is why the institutional arrangements regarding the enfeoffment and well-field systems, the attendance of the enfeoffed lords at court, punitive expeditions, the creation of offices, and the allocation of official salaries are not discussed in the *Classic of Documents* nor by Confucius. How then can those whose virtue is less than that of Shun, Yu, or Confucius dare to state categorically that the information that they have acquired through their studies constitutes a canon valid for all time?! . . . In compiling this book I have been concerned with tracing the origins of success and failure, and [have] done my best to remain in harmony with the fundamentals of the sages' government, while I have considered each case on its merits in discussing the measures taken and have taken the time factor into consideration in assessing what was appropriate.

[*Quanshan yishu, Du Tongjian lun: quanmo* 4a–b — IM]

The discussion about the enfeoffment system is a good example of a dispute in which the proponents of two extremes engage in profitless argument. The prefectural system has survived for two thousand years without anyone being able to change it, and men of all classes have been content with it throughout that period. This being the [irresistible] trend (*shi zhi qu*), how could it possibly be so if it were not in accord with principles?! It was Heaven that made it inevitable that men should have rulers. No one caused it to happen: it was a spontaneous process. In the beginning everyone supported those whose virtue and achievements were superior to those of their fellows and served them. Subsequently, he who received overwhelming support was made emperor. All men without exception wish to be honored, and for there to be those who are honored there must be those who serve. This is in the general interest of humankind. He who is content with his position practices its Way, and so the principles behind hereditary succession were created. Though one [a ruler] might be stupid and cruel, he was nonetheless more capable than the drifting masses in the country at large. So this situation continued to exist for several thousand years, and people were content with it. But when the strong and the weak gnawed away at one another, the old ties of the enfeoffment system were completely destroyed, and by Warring States times almost nothing of it survived. How then could it possibly keep the nine regions of the empire in submission or secure the obedience of the various feudal lords and princes? Consequently the states were divided up into commanderies (*jun*) and prefectures (*xian*), and men were selected to administer them. The prefectural system existed even in pre-Qin times. All Qin destroyed was [a China that consisted of] seven states. It was not responsible for the destruction of all the fiefs established during the Three Dynasties. So how could one have made the division into commanderies and prefectures, whereby those talented and capable of ruling the people were put in positions of authority where they could exploit their talents for governing the people if this had been contrary to the general interest of all-under-Heaven? Among the ancients the feudal lords handed down their states from generation to generation, and subsequently their officials followed their example and the tenure of office became hereditary. This was a gradual development made inevitable by the prevailing trend. However, as the sons of officials always became officials, and the sons of peasants always remained peasants, and there was no selection and utilization of those who were naturally talented, there were stupid men among the officials and accomplished men among the peasants. The accomplished could not submit to the stupid indefinitely, and so there ensued a struggle between them to gain the chance to rise in the world. This was a violent development made inevitable by the prevailing conditions. The enfeoffment system was destroyed, and the selection of officials through the examination system became the practice.

[*Quanshan yishu, Du Tongjian lun* 1:1a–b  — IM]


## THE JUSTIFICATION OF SOCIAL AND
## CULTURAL DIVISIONS

Wang develops his arguments for the preservation of the distinctions between gentlemen (*junzi*) and mean men (*xiaoren*), Chinese and barbarians, in a parallel way. In both cases there is a difference in the stage of civilization attained, and the ultimate criterion is moral. Culture rather than race is still the prime consideration, even in the case of foreigners: Wang specifically declares that indigenous ethnic groups do not count as barbarians.

There are in the world two great lines of demarcation to be drawn: that between Chinese and barbarians and that between the gentleman and the mean man. It is not the case that there was originally no difference between them and that the former kings arbitrarily set up barriers between them. Barbarians and Chinese are born (live) in different lands. Since their lands are different, the climates are different too. Since their climates are different, so too are their habits, and consequently all they know and all they do is different. The noble and the inferior emerge spontaneously among them. It is simply that they are divided by physical frontiers and that their climates are different, and so there must be no confusion. If there is confusion, the destruction of (the order of) the human sector will ensue, and the people of China will suffer from the encroachments of the barbarians and be distressed. If, however, early measures are taken to ward off the barbarians, (the order of) the human sector will thereby be stabilized and human life protected. This is in accord with Heaven. As for the gentleman and the mean man, they are born of different stock. Since they are born of different stock, their physical substance is different. Since they differ in their physical substance, their habits too are different, and consequently all they know and all they do are different. The clever and the stupid emerge spontaneously among them. It is simply that they are born of different stock and have different values, and so there must be no confusion. If there is confusion, then the principles of man are contravened. The poor and weak among the people will suffer from the encroachments (of the mean men) and be distressed. If, however, one prevents the excesses of the mean men, one may thereby preserve the principles of man and enrich human life. This is in accord with Heaven. Alas, the confusion that mean men have created between themselves and gentlemen is no different from that which the barbarians have created between themselves and the Chinese! Some people may toy with the prospect, but the gravity of the harm done thereby is beyond all expectation.

Among mean men the clever and stupid divide themselves into different classes. The stupid are content to rest in their stupidity, and so bring hardship on themselves. The clever use their cleverness to wrong others. The stupid become peasants: they bring hardship on themselves but do not harm others.

The Han regarded laboring in the fields as the equivalent [among commoners] of filial virtue in selecting officials, and the result was that rites and education were gradually destroyed. This is why people say that since the Three Dynasties orderly government has never flourished. It is because confusion has been created between the peasants and gentlemen that the situation has deteriorated. This is even more true of the merchants. The merchants are the clever members of the class of mean men, and their destruction of man's nature and ruin of men's lives have already become extremely serious. Their (constitution) is such that they always frequent the barbarians, and their physical substance is such that they always get on well with the barbarians. Consequently, when the barbarians prosper, the merchants are esteemed. . . .

There are, fundamentally speaking, two great lines of demarcation to be drawn in the world, but ultimately they are one. What is this one line of demarcation? It is that between morality and profit. . . .

There are those who are born into villages of profit and grow up in the paths of profit. It is what their elders esteem, what their own flesh and blood predispose them to, and what their hearts long after. Their will and their constitution act on one another, and so too do their minds and spirits. The result is that they are so deeply sunk in profit they cannot be made to move into the stream of gentlemen and Chinese. All are men, but the barbarians are separated from the Chinese by frontiers, while the mean men are differentiated from the gentlemen by their class. One cannot but be strict in drawing the lines of demarcation.

[Quanshan yishu, Du Tongjian lun 14:2a–3a — IM]

## THE PRESERVATION OF CHINESE POLITICAL AND CULTURAL INTEGRITY

Wang's conviction that different peoples should live separately, "ignoring one another like the fish in rivers and lakes," is clearly linked to the philosophical conception outlined in his commentaries on the *Classic of Changes* and Zhang Zai. In his *Huang shu*, he develops the idea of a natural division into different species and draws out its political implications for Chinese survival. Wang's nationalism is remarkable in the history of Chinese thought not only for the violence and frequency of its expression but also for its theoretical justification.

This is why mountain creatures have cloven hoofs and those in the marshes have webbed feet; why the strengths of animals used for riding and animals used for ploughing lie in different directions; why water birds are proper to the south and cold-weather birds to the north. It is not a deliberate suppression of the state of confusion and dispersion that causes this great classification into different species: it is simply that conditions bring it about as the only way that (these creatures) can preserve themselves and ward off disaster. . . .

Therefore the sage, finding that this was true for all creatures and that each species defined its own limits, in controlling the empire and acting as its ruler separated the clever and the stupid, clarified cases where there was doubt, overcame the vicious and evil, and established lofty defensive barriers (between the groups) in order to ward off disaster and enable them to preserve themselves. . . .

Man is like other creatures insofar as he is constituted of yin and yang and eats and breathes, but he cannot be put in the same category as other creatures. The Chinese are like the barbarians insofar as their general physical characteristics are similar and they are both subject to assemblies and divisions, but the Chinese cannot be put in the same category as the barbarians. Why is this? It is because if man does not draw lines of demarcation in order to set himself apart from other creatures, the order of Heaven is violated; if the Chinese do not draw lines of demarcation in order to set themselves apart from the barbarians, terrestrial order is violated. Heaven and earth regulate mankind through such demarcations, and if men are incapable of drawing the lines of demarcation between different groups, human order is violated. This is the way the three orders control the three sectors of Heaven, earth, and humankind. . . .

Now even the ants have rulers who preside over the territory of their nests, and when red ants or flying white ants penetrate their gates, the ruler organizes all his own kind into troops to bite and kill the intruders, drive them far away from the anthill, and prevent foreign interference. Thus he who rules the swarm must have the means to protect it. If, however, a ruler fails to make long-term plans, neglects the integrity of his territory, esteems his own person more than the empire, antagonizes colleagues, creates divisions where none should exist, is driven by suspicion to exercise a repressive control, and weakens the central region, then, while he clings desperately to his privileged status and enjoys the advantages of his position without fulfilling its obligations, disaster strikes and he is incapable of overcoming it. Confronted with an external menace, he is unable to stand firm against it. He can neither keep the succession for his own descendants nor protect his own kind. Such an extinction of the Way of the true king was what the *Spring and Autumn Annals* mourned. . . .

And so, with a mind full of grief and anger, and a heart full of sorrow, I rectify what went wrong in order to restore the original divisions established by the Yellow Emperor. I look forward eagerly to the advent of an enlightened ruler, who will restore sovereignty to the country, accomplish its mission, and stabilize its frontiers, and thereby guard the central territory and drive off the barbarians forever. Once this were accomplished, then though my body may perish my soul would rejoice.

[*Quanshan yishu, Huang shu* 1a–2b, and *houxu* 1b — IM]

## GU YANWU, BEACON OF QING SCHOLARSHIP

Gu Yanwu (1613–1682), born in the last years of the Ming dynasty, had already achieved considerable reputation as a scholar when Beijing fell to the Manchus in 1644. The following year he took part in an attempt to defend his native city in Jiangnan (central China) against the invading Qing armies. With the fall of the city his foster mother, who had raised him from infancy, starved herself to death rather than live under the rule of the Manchus, on her deathbed entreating Yanwu never to serve the new dynasty in any official capacity. Gu remained true to her wishes, spending the rest of his life traveling about North China; he worked for brief periods at jobs of an unofficial but often practical nature while carrying on his researches.

During the chaotic days at the end of the Ming, Gu had already become interested in such practical subjects as economics, government, and military defense. The fall of the native dynasty before the Manchu invaders spurred him to pursue these studies with renewed vigor in an effort to find out why the old dynasty had faltered and how its mistakes could be avoided in the future. He bitterly attacked the intuitionism of the Wang Yangming school of Neo-Confucianism, which, he believed, by its subjectivity and scorn for book learning had seriously debilitated the intelligentsia of the late Ming. To combat this effete and empty speculation he insisted that scholars must undertake wide and varied research on practical subjects and return to the simple ethical precepts of early Confucianism. He likewise deplored the inordinate attention to literary elegance and belles lettres that had so often characterized scholars of earlier times, believing that such interests represented only a selfish striving for reputation. When a friend wrote a poem praising him, Gu admonished him with the advice that the writing of such eulogies was no practice for a serious gentleman. "Men must love themselves and each other in higher principles," he counseled, begging his friend to write no more such poems.[46]

His own works exemplify this new spirit of practical learning. Carrying on the systematic study of phonetics that had developed sporadically in the late Song and Ming, he perfected the inductive method of research, known as Evidential Inquiry (*kaozheng*), which was to be applied with such effect by textual critics of the later years of the Qing. Besides important works on phonetics, he produced voluminous studies on historical geography and epigraphy. But his best-known and most significant work is undoubtedly his *Rizhi lu* or *Record of Daily Knowledge,* a collection of short essays on problems in the classics, government, economics, the examination system, literature, history, and philology. Carefully composed and revised during the years of his travels and based on personal observation, wide reading, and a painstaking collection of evidence, these essays represent not simply a reworking of old material and restating of traditional views but a new and constructive contribution to the subjects dealt with. They are, as he himself said, not old coin but "copper dug from the hills."

Like many other scholars of the time, Gu believed that one of the fatal weaknesses of the Ming had been an overconcentration of power and authority in the hands of the central government. He therefore recommended a greater decentralization of authority and the strengthening of local self-government in the provinces, as well as clan organization in the local community.

The originality of his researches, and the new critical methodology and practical learning that they embodied, had a marked and beneficent influence upon the men of his age. Under his leadership the way was opened for the great movement of critical research and evaluation that characterized the best of Qing scholarship.

TRUE LEARNING: BROAD KNOWLEDGE AND A SENSE OF SHAME

It is a matter of great regret to me that for the past hundred-odd years, scholars have devoted so much discussion to the mind and human nature, all of it vague

---

46. Letter in Reply to Zide, *Tinglin shiwen ji* 4:7b.

and quite incomprehensible. We know from the *Analects* that "fate and humanity (*ren*) were things that Confucius seldom spoke of" (9:1) and that Zigong "had never heard him speak on man's nature and the Way of Heaven" (5:12). Though he mentioned the principle of human nature and fate in the appendices to the *Classic of Changes*, he never discussed them with others. When asked about the qualities of a gentleman, Confucius said, "In his conduct he must have a sense of shame" (13:20), while with regard to learning he spoke of a "love of antiquity" and "diligent seeking," discussing and praising Yao and Shun and transmitting their tales to his disciples. But he never said so much as a word about the so-called theory of "the precariousness [of the human mind] and the subtlety [of the mind of the Way] or of the [need for] discrimination and oneness" but only said, "sincerely hold fast to the Mean — if within the four seas there be distress and poverty, your Heaven-conferred revenues will come to a perpetual end."[47] Ah, this is the reason for the learning of the sage. How simple, how easy to follow! . . .

But gentlemen of today are not like this. They gather a hundred or so followers and disciples about them in their studies, and though as individuals they may be as different as grass and trees, they discourse with all of them on mind and nature. They set aside broad knowledge and concentrate upon the search for a single, all-inclusive method; they say not a word about the distress and poverty of the world within the four seas, but spend all their days lecturing on theories of "the precarious and subtle," "discrimination and oneness." I can only conclude that their doctrine is more lofty than that of Confucius and their disciples wiser than Zigong, and that while they pay honor to the school of Eastern Lu [Confucius] they derive their teachings on the mind directly from the two sage emperors Yao and Shun. . . .

What then do I consider to be the way of the sage? I would say "extensively studying all learning"[48] and "in your conduct having a sense of shame."[49] Everything from your own person up to the whole nation should be a matter of study. In everything from your personal position as a son, a subject, a brother, and a friend to all your comings and goings, your giving and taking, you should have things of which you would be ashamed. This sense of shame before others is a vital matter. It does not mean being ashamed of your clothing or the food you eat, but ashamed that there should be a single humble man or woman who does not enjoy the blessings that are his due. This is why Mencius said that "all things are complete in me" if I "examine myself and find sincerity."[50] Alas, if a scholar does not first define this sense of shame, he will have no basis as a person, and if he does not love antiquity and acquire broad knowledge, his

---

47. *Classic of Documents*, Counsels of Great Yu II.
48. *Analects* 6:25.
49. *Analects* 13:20.
50. *Mencius* 7A:4.

learning will be vain and hollow. These baseless men with their hollow learning day after day pursue sagehood, and yet I perceive that with each day they only depart further from it.

[From "A Letter to a Friend Discussing the Pursuit of Learning," *Tinglin shiwen ji* 3:1a–2b — BW]

### PREFACE TO *RECORD OF THE SEARCH FOR ANTIQUITIES*

Ever since I was young I have enjoyed wandering about looking for old inscriptions on metal or stone, although I could not understand them very well. Then when I read Ouyang Xiu's *Record of Collected Antiquities (Jigu lu)* I realized that many of the events recorded in these inscriptions are verified by works of history so that, far from being merely bits of high-flown rhetoric, they are of actual use in supplementing and correcting the histories. For the past twenty years I have traveled widely about the country, and whenever I visited some famous mountain or great commercial center, the site of an ancestral shrine or Buddhist temple, I never failed to clamber up to the steepest peak, to search the darkest valley, feeling out the toppled stone markers, tramping about the underbrush, cutting down the old tangled hedges, and sifting through the rotted earth. Anything that was legible I made a copy of by hand, and when I came across an inscription that had not been seen by my predecessors I was so overjoyed I could not sleep. I can never forget that with each day that passes more of these remaining inscriptions of the men of ancient times disappear. Most men of later times will probably not share my interest in these things, yet even if they should, in the course of several centuries how many of these inscriptions will have vanished away! . . . Thus it is still my hope that other men who share my love will carry on my work and make further recordings of their own.

[From personal preface to *Qiugulu* — BW]

### ON THE CONCENTRATION OF AUTHORITY AT COURT

That Gu shared much the same view as Huang Zongxi of the Chinese state as overcentralized is clear from this analysis of the weaknesses of local government under an administrative system more in keeping with the Legalist philosophy than the Confucian.

He who is called the Son of Heaven holds supreme authority in the world. What is the nature of this supreme authority? It is authority over all the world, which is vested in the men of the world but which derives ultimately from the Son of Heaven. From the highest ministers and officials down to the regional magistrates and petty officers, each holds a share of this authority of the Son of Heaven and directs the affairs of his charge, and the authority of the Son of

Heaven is thereby magnified in dignity. In later ages there appeared inept rulers who gathered all authority into their own hands. But the countless exigencies of government are so broad that it is quite impossible for one man to handle them all, so that authority then shifted to the laws. With this a great many laws were promulgated to prevent crimes and violations, so that even the greatest criminals could not get around them, nor the cleverest officials accomplish anything by evading them. People thereupon expended all their efforts in merely following the laws and trying to stay out of difficulty. Thus the authority of the Son of Heaven came to reside not in the officials appointed by the government but in their clerks and assistants [who were familiar with the laws]. Now what the world needs most urgently are local officials who will personally look after the people, and yet today the men who possess least authority are precisely these local officials. If local officials are not made known to the higher authorities, how can we hope to achieve peace and prosperity and prolong the life of the nation?

[From *Rizhi lu jishi* 9:15a–16a — BW]

## ON BUREAUCRATIC LOCAL ADMINISTRATION, CA. 1660

That Gu, like Huang Zongxi and Wang Fuzhi, was greatly concerned about the problem of overcentralization in the bureaucratic dynastic state is shown by a nine-part essay prominently appearing in his *Collected Writings*, from which the following excerpts are taken. But Gu, while rejecting any idea of a total return to the ancient enfeoffment system, is ready to go further in this direction than Huang, who would resort to enfeoffment only in the border commanderies. Gu called for all local administration at the county or district level to be delegated on a hereditary basis. Though a radical proposal, Gu's idea corresponds to a fairly wide perception among scholars in late imperial China that the court's attempt to impose any close control over local government was dysfunctional and self-defeating and it would be better to regularize some form of local autonomy. This has continued to be a live issue in the twentieth century.

One should also note, however, that Gu's advocacy of local autonomy is predicated on a strong belief in the local leadership role of the scholar-official class working through lineage organizations.

If one understands why the enfeoffment system (*fengjian*) was transformed into the system of centralized bureaucratic local administration (*junxian*), one can understand why the evils of the bureaucratic system must be transformed in turn. But can the bureaucratic system be transformed back into the enfeoffment system? I say not. If, however, a sage were to arise who could infuse the spirit of the enfeoffment system into the body of the bureaucratic system, all-under-Heaven would be well governed. . . . [6a]

By elevating the rank of senior local officials, giving them authority over the means of production and the regulation of the people, abolishing the posts that oversee them, making their positions hereditary, and allowing them to select subordinates by their own methods, what I have called "infusing the spirit of the enfeoffment system into the bureaucratic system" might be accomplished and order fashioned out of the evils of the past two thousand years. . . . [7a]

My proposal is to transform the county magistrate into an official of the fifth rank and change his title to "district magistrate." Those who fill this position should be natives of the area within a thousand *li* of the county in which they serve and be familiar with local customs. At first they are to be called "probationary magistrates." If after three years they show themselves to be equal to the post, their appointments are to be regularized [and if they succeed in three more three-year terms] they are to be appointed for life. Those magistrates who retire because of age or illness are to be succeeded by their sons or younger brothers. If they have no descendants, they should select their own successors. . . . Thereafter the same procedure shall be followed for the successors. . . . [7a]

Now, caring for the people is like the work of a family in raising domestic animals. One family member is assigned the task of tending the horses and oxen, and another grows the fodder. If, however, the master's hired foreman is sent to oversee them, he will not even be able to calculate the amount of fodder without consulting the master, and the horses and oxen will waste away. With my program, it would not be this way. I would select as groom one who is diligent and skillful, give him full charge of the horses and oxen, and grant him land, the produce of which would always exceed the fodder needs of the animals. If the animals grow fat and reproduce, I would reward the groom; if not, I would flog him. [8a]

The reason the empire's troubles have become so numerous is that the master, not trusting his grooms, has sent servants to oversee them. Not trusting even these, the master has become confused as to what his own eyes and ears tell him. But if one truly loves his horses and oxen, he will not calculate the cost of the fodder. If a horse is tended by a single groom, it will grow fat. If the people are governed by a single official, they will be content. . . . [8a]

Some will object: "If there are no supervisory officials, won't the magistrates serve only their own interests?" Or: "Isn't it improper that their power be passed down to their lineal descendants?" Or: "Won't men who come from within a thousand *li* of the county in which they serve tend to favor their own relatives and friends?" I say, however, that the reason so many magistrates today abuse their office for their own private gain is precisely because they come from so far away. If they were required to be residents of the same place, then even if they wanted to abuse their office for private gain, they would be unable to do so. . . . [8b]

It is every man's normal disposition to cherish his own family and to favor his own children. His feelings toward the ruler and toward all other men are inevitably not as strong as his feelings toward his own kin. It has been this way as far back as the Three Dynasties. The ancient sages availed themselves of this spirit and made use of it. Out of the self-interest of everyone throughout the empire they formed a public spirit of one accord in the ruler, and thus the empire was in good order. [9a]

Accordingly, if we let the county magistrate take a personal interest in his hundred *li* of territory, then all the people in the county will become in effect his children and kin, all the lands of the county in effect his lands, all its walls his defenses, and all its granaries his storehouses. His own children and kin he will of course cherish rather than harm; his own fields he will manage well rather than abandon; his own defenses and storehouses he will mend rather than neglect. Thus what is viewed by the magistrate as "looking out for my own" will be viewed by the ruler as "acting responsibly," will it not? The proper governance of the empire lies in this and nothing else. [9a]

[*Junxian lun*, in *Tinglin shiwen ji*, SBBY 1:6a–9a — WR]

## THE HAN LEARNING AND TEXT CRITICISM

With the firm establishment of the Qing (Manchu) dynasty in the latter half of the seventeenth century, there was a marked change in the climate of Confucian thought. The reaction against the subjectivism and idealism of the Wang Yangming school continued. At its door was laid the blame for all the weaknesses of the Ming regime, while, on the other hand, the philosophy of Zhu Xi underwent a strong revival in scholarly circles with Manchu patronage.

The most significant change, however, developed not along lines of the old philosophical rivalries but rather from those who pursued two important tendencies manifested by the thinkers just discussed, that is, the striving for breadth of learning and the insistence upon practicality of thought. Indeed, the trend toward "broad learning" and the critical study of the classics and history, as embodied in classical scholarship known as "investigative" or "evidential" learning, was itself thought of as "substantial or practical learning" (*shixue*). And in the field of classical study no movement had such influence or achieved such remarkable results as the school of Han Learning, whose name derives from the fact that this group, dissatisfied like Gu Yanwu with the metaphysical speculations of both the Song and the Ming, turned back to the studies of Han dynasty scholars and commentators as guides to the classics. In other words, by the seventeenth century Confucian thought had come around full circle; whereas the most creative minds of the Song had been ready to forgo the meticulous scholarship of the Han and Tang commentators in the interests of a more vital and expansive approach to the classical tradition, Qing scholars were now ready to return to historical and exegetical studies as a corrective to the freewheeling and often conflicting interpretations of the Neo-Confucian schools.

In this process scholars in the Han Learning movement made contributions of lasting value to our knowledge of the Confucian classics. A discovery that had important repercussions on Neo-Confucian cosmology, for instance, was that of Hu Wei (1633–1714). Following a line of investigation opened up by Huang Zongxi and his son, he demonstrated that the diagrams attached to the *Classic of Changes*, upon which the Neo-Confucians had based their theories, were late accretions of Daoist provenance rather than integral parts of the original work. Of equal significance to Confucianism as a state cult was the demonstration by Yan Roju (1636–1704) that portions of the so-called ancient text of the "Documents of the Shang Dynasty" in the *Classic of Documents*, which had been used for centuries in the official examinations, were later forgeries. Progress was also made by these and other scholars in reexamining the date and authorship of such texts as the *Great Learning*, which had been one of the Neo-Confucian Four Books, as well as in the study of historical geography, philology, phonetics, epigraphy, and other branches of knowledge having a bearing on the classics.

Considering the number of scholars who contributed to these researches (though not as a formal group), there can be no doubt that the Han Learning represented a truly broad movement in Qing thought toward a kind of critical scholarship that anticipated modern Western methods and produced a body of systematic, empirically verified knowledge. Nevertheless, it was also marked by a kind of fundamentalist urge to recover an original Confucian teaching purified of any later additions, which was bound to be less productive of new philosophical speculations.

Of these limitations in the Han school's work, other thinkers, less representative of the mainstream, were partly aware. There was, for instance, the so-called Eastern Zhejiang historical school stemming from Huang Zongxi, which stressed the value of studying recent history as well as ancient. Its leading representatives, such as Wan Sitong (1638–1702), Quan Zuwang (1705–1755), and Zhang Xuecheng (1738–1801), kept alive the Confucian view of historical studies as having a practical bearing on the conduct of government, but as they had little status or influence in the ruling regime, their efforts were devoted largely to upholding the value of private, unofficial historical writing as compared to state-sponsored projects. In this way they sought to preserve records of the Ming dynasty that might supplement or correct the Manchu version of recent events, and they drew attention to the value of local histories or gazetteers and many other types of records that might contribute to a fuller, deeper understanding of history than official accounts provided.

Another movement that stressed practicality of thought is identified with Yan Yuan (1635–1704) and Li Gong (1659–1733), who were critical of the Neo-Confucian metaphysics of the Cheng-Zhu school but equally so of their own contemporaries pursuing the Han Learning. Toward the latter their attitude was reminiscent of Wang Yangming's condemnation of book learning and classical scholarship as a distraction from the real business of life. Toward the former they had specific objections on philosophical grounds, in that they considered the Cheng-Zhu system to have been deeply influenced by Buddhist and Daoist quietism. The distinction that it had made between the physical nature of man and his Heaven-bestowed moral nature, Yan Yuan argued, had fostered the belief that one's physical desires had to be repressed so that one's ideal nature might be recovered or restored through the meditative discipline of quiet-sitting. Yan contended that this erroneous view derived from the Cheng-Zhu school's dualism between principle (*li*) and material-force (*qi*), according to which the moral nature was constant despite differences in its physical embodiment. Like Huang Zongxi and Wang Fuzhi, Yan Yuan insisted that there were no principles apart from their physical embodiment and that moral perfection could not be achieved except through the full development of the actual nature in the conduct of everyday life. True to the fundamentalist urge, however, "practicality" for him meant training in the classical arts like rites, music, archery, charioteering, writing, and arithmetic.

Dai Zhen (1724–1777), possibly the most representative thinker and scholar of the Qing dynasty, pursued Yan's line of thought further. He was especially concerned with the problem of how the truth or principles of things may be ascertained. The Neo-Confucians, by asserting that the principles of things were also contained in the mind and attainable by self-reflection, had, according to this view, led people away from the study of things into introspection and mysticism. What they called "principle" might be purely subjective, whereas in fact principle could only be found in things and studied objectively. This required careful observation and analysis, followed by submission of the results to some kind of public test in order to determine whether or not the results were confirmed by the observations of others. In practice, however, the "things" studied by Dai Zhen were for the most part the "affairs" of men with which the Confucian classics were concerned. In this respect Dai represented also the best traditions of the school of Han Learning, for he distinguished himself in the same type of classical scholarship: philology, phonology, historical geography, and mathematical history.

In the end, the very attempts of Qing Confucians to disinherit themselves from Song and Ming metaphysics demonstrated how much, after all, they were children in spirit of the Neo-Confucians. Theirs was not a movement to break the bounds of Confucian tradition and establish themselves on new intellectual ground. Their fundamental impulse was instead to return, to recover, to restore the ancient Way in its original purity. Whereas the early Neo-Confucians of the Song had thought of themselves as reviving and reconstituting the old order in its fullness, after centuries of disintegration and perversion under the Han and Tang dynasties, the critical spirit of the Han Learning became an instrument for redefining, with greater precision perhaps, the authentic tradition deriving from the Master of old. This was a slimming, paring-down process, to rediscover the Way in its irreducible, original form, stripped of all the questionable elements that the expansive Cheng-Zhu school had tried to incorporate in its new synthesis. Of even the rarest, most critical, most independent of scholars, such as Cui Shu (1740–1816), was this true. Though Cui dug deeper and deeper into the past and rejected even Han scholarship in his search for the authentic roots of Confucianism, his achievements in historical study and textual criticism only served as a testimonial of his undiminished faith in Confucius's original teaching as the source of what was worth learning.

## DAI ZHEN AND ZHANG XUECHENG

Probably in every age certain intellectuals feel frustrated or unappreciated because their best talents, most compelling interests, or deepest concerns are not in accord with the high-cultural paradigms of their day. Dai Zhen (1724–1777) and Zhang Xuecheng (1738–1801) were such figures. They often are paired in present-day discussions of Chinese scholarship because, in different ways, they exhibit a capacity for theoretical exploration and insightful generalization that has become more valued in the modern period than it was by their contemporaries of the mid-eighteenth century in China — the so-called High Qing period during which "evidential" (kaozheng) research on the concrete meanings of words and phrases in ancient texts reigned supreme.

## DAI ZHEN'S TEXT-CRITICAL MORAL PHILOSOPHY

Dai Zhen, like Zhang Xuecheng, came from an undistinguished family background and, being largely self-taught, lacked facility in writing the sorts of essays necessary to qualify for bureaucratic office through the civil service examinations. Unlike Zhang, however, he eventually attained great renown, both at court and in learned society at large, as consummate in applying knowledge of such fields as phonology, etymology, geography, mathematics, and astronomy in the comparative elucidation of classical texts. Though a paragon in this respect, Dai parted ways with contemporaneous arbiters of scholarly value in his profound realization that, having determined the authentic contents of, and lexical meanings in, those ancient canons, one still needed to theorize — albeit from a firm basis in precise, factual knowledge — in order to grasp the primordially unwritten Way of the Sages. That is, he came to feel ever more strongly that the study of archaic language in pursuit of a lost, lived reality had to proceed in tandem with deliberate moral-philosophical interpretation.

It was Dai's commitment to the latter that elicited dismay and disapproval among his peers and that inhibited the circulation of his major, philologically well-grounded but unmistakably philosophical treatises, the *Inquiry Into Goodness (Yuan shan)* completed in 1766, and the *Evidential Study of the Meaning of Terms in the Mencius* (*Mengzi ziyi shuzheng*), completed early in 1777. It also was Dai's commitment to the latter that further disquieted even those who still held some interest in speculative philosophy, because it entailed not just the fashionable dismissal, so far as solid scholarship was concerned, of metaphysically oriented "Song Learning." It led Dai into serious, penetrating criticisms of key concepts in Neo-Confucianism, especially those introduced by the core Song Learning figures, Cheng Yi (1033–1107) and Zhu Xi (1130–1200), which the Qing government (like the Yuan and Ming governments before it) maintained as its official orthodoxy but which Dai felt had widely misrepresented the outlook of the ancient sages for hundreds of years. In this, Dai resurrected, brought into sharper focus, and further developed critiques that otherwise seemed to have been left behind in the works of certain seventeenth-century thinkers.

In the first of the selections excerpted below, we find an exposition of the methods and principles of Evidential Inquiry that earned Dai such great esteem among classicists in his own time. The second encapsulates the main ideas in the endeavor that mattered most to him, his text-critical moral philosophy. Through Dai's highly allusive prose we can discern several points that were integral to his re-vision:

First, he objects that, under Buddho-Daoist influence, Confucians since the Song period have regarded Heaven (*tian*) as a vacuous, void, insubstantial state unto itself; thus, in positing principle (*li*) as that which accounts for the regularity in Heaven's Way, they have rendered both the Way and principle abstract, reified, and remote from the ordinary, corporeal lives of human beings. Especially insidious is that, as Chan Buddhism has been clothed in Confucian terms, the Way has been suspended in a state "beyond good and evil," that is, beyond valuation itself. As a consequence, Neo-Confucian urgings that the Way and principle be accessed by cultivating the mind amount to urgings that we make our minds as vacuous as their conception of Heaven.

Again succumbing to Buddho-Daoist influence, Dai Zhen charges, Neo-Confucians from the Song onward have regarded ordinary human desires, emotions, and strivings as obstructions to the union of Mind and Void and thus have disparaged them, creating a dichotomous separation between lofty *li* and the material- or vital force (*qi*) that constitutes, in their view, a spiritually impeding physical reality. Moreover, principle having been so idealized, so removed from what people can verify with their sense faculties, it had become identifiable only subjectively and thus amenable to manipulation in the self-service of any who might facilely claim the privileged insights of "learning."

Dai did not object to distinguishing intangible Heaven from the tangible world, but he thought it was fatal to true Confucianism if the two were seen as separate orders of being, rather than as two dimensions of a continuous process of transformation within a single reality, composed wholly of valid *qi*. For Dai, the unfailing *process* whereby formed, determinate things, such as human beings, are generated from the unformed dimension of reality *is* the ultimate *good*, and the regular *patterns* within that process are *principle*, fully present and discernible in all phenomena, from affairs to concrete things. Moreover, principle most assuredly is present in even the most commonplace desires, feelings, and strivings that serve — in appropriate measure — to fulfill life, which is the greatest goodness in the transformative circulation between Heaven and the phenomenal realm. Principle being objectively perceptible pattern, not subjectively assertable idea, Dai holds, it should be determined through careful, convergent study and observation by many conscientious inquirers, not through quiet contemplation or autocratic declaration by an unlearned few.

The degree to which such monistic, "materialist," anti-authoritarian views, positive valuation of the lives of ordinary people, and quasi-scientific conceptions of inquiry were regarded as radically heterodox in eighteenth-century China has perhaps been exaggerated by Dai's admirers in modern times. One can say, however, that Dai's persistence in a mode of scholarship that he knew would not please contemporaries is testimony to the enduring vitality of Confucian moral philosophy under adverse cultural conditions.

### LETTER TO SHI ZHONGMING CONCERNING SCHOLARSHIP

The recipient of this letter, Shi Jing (Zhongming) (1673–1769), was a respected Confucian scholar who had asked to see Dai Zhen's recent commentarial work on the *Classic of Odes*. Dai respectfully defers sending that unfinished exegesis but offers Shi, for the time being (1749–1750), some thoughts on why such studies cannot be rushed.

When I was young my family was poor and could not provide me with a private tutor. I heard that among the sages there had been Confucius, who set in order the Six Classics for men of later ages. Having sought out one of those classics, I opened it to read, only to find myself completely at a loss. I pondered that [experience] for a long time before making this mental note: "What the classics ultimately reach to is the Way. Their phrases are that by which the Way is made clear, and those phrases are composed of written characters. To comprehend the phrases from the [individual] characters, and then to comprehend the Way from the [discrete] phrases, must be a gradual process." In seeking the origins of what we now call "characters," I examined archaic seal-script writing and to that end obtained a copy of [the etymological dictionary] *Explanations of Writing and Characters*, by Xu Shen [ca. 100 C.E.]. For three years I studied its entries and gradually gained some insight into the beginnings and fundamentals of the ancient sages' compositions. Yet I doubted whether Mr. Xu's glosses were exhaustive, so I borrowed from a friend a set of the [ca. twelfth century] *Compendium of Commentaries to the Thirteen Classics* and read it also. Then I realized that the meaning of a character must be threaded through all the classics and grounded in the six graphic modes before it can definitely be established.

As for why, it seems, the classics are hard to understand, there are a number of matters involved. In reading aloud just a few lines into the "Canon of Yao" in the *Classic of Documents*, one comes to the phrase, "then ordered Xi and He." If one does not understand how the movements of the constellations and planets were thought to be regulated [by those two ancient astronomers], one will have to close the book without finishing. If one tries to intone even the first sections of the *Classic of Odes*, then from the first subsection onward, if one does not know the ancient rhymes and simply tries to force them, the result will be discordant, and the proper reading will be lost. Reciting from the [*Classic of*] *Etiquette and Ceremonies*, right at the beginning with the capping ceremony, if one does not know about ancient regulations concerning palace rooms and ritual garments mentioned therein, one will be disoriented and unable to distinguish their functions. If one does not know the evolution of place-names from ancient to present times, then the jurisdictions recorded in the "Tributes of Yu" in the *Documents* will lose their geographical referents. If one does not know the ancients' methods of geometric measurement, one cannot infer from the text of the "Technology" section of the *Rites of Zhou* the actual use of the implements described. And if one does not know the general characteristics and common names of birds and beasts, insects and fish, grasses and trees, then the metaphors and similes that feature them in the *Odes* will seem strange. Moreover, etymology and philology are inseparable from phonology, in which tones and sounds should be as clearly distinguishable as the vertical and horizontal of warp and weft. . . .

I have heard that in the pursuit of classical studies, generally three [things are] difficult [to attain]: broad erudition, sound judgment, and critical discernment. I certainly cannot lay claim to any of these, but I hold that the criteria of good scholarship should be rooted in them. Some of our forebears who were broadly learned and had good memories . . . wrote housefuls of books. They possessed erudition but lacked discernment. Then there have been others who slighted those qualities, saying that the Great Way can be reached by shortcuts. . . . They abandoned the practice of learned discussion and took advantage of the words "honor the moral nature" to embellish their reputations. But having discontinued the "pursuit of studies" [as really intended by these phrases in the *Mean*], they failed to reach the proper "Mean," as is well known.

Lack of attainment in the various classics and in the ancient Six Arts is cause for shame in a Confucian scholar, and I use awareness of this to guard against sloth. Fearful of forgetting what I have learned from experience in study, I have written it out in this letter. When my insight matures, I will present my *Odes* commentary to you without further delay.

[From *Dai Dongyuan ji* 9:4a–5a — JWE, LAS]

LETTER IN REPLY TO ADVANCED SCHOLAR PENG YUNCHU

The recipient of this letter, Peng Shaosheng (Yunchu) (1740–1796), was a well-known scholar who, unlike Dai Zhen, had attained the coveted *jinshi* degree in the metropolitan examinations. Somewhat unusually for a man of his position in that day, Peng took a strong, ecumenical interest in both the Song and the Ming schools of Neo-Confucianism, as well as in Buddhist and Daoist teachings. Thus, his viewpoint was the perfect foil to that of Dai's mature philosophy. Perhaps for this reason, Dai allowed Peng, who had already seen the *Inquiry Into Goodness* (*Yuan Shan*), to read the *Evidential Study of the Meaning of Terms in the Mencius* (*Mengzi ziyi shuzheng*) shortly after its completion. To points about which Peng expressed "uneasiness," Dai then responded at energetic length just one month before his death in 1777.

Before the Song, Confucius and Mencius were Confucius and Mencius, and Daoists and Buddhists were Daoists and Buddhists. Those who discoursed on Daoism and Buddhism made their words lofty and abstruse and did not attach themselves to Confucius or Mencius. Since the Song, however, the books that record the thought of Confucius and Mencius have been completely misunderstood because Confucians have randomly appropriated the theories of Daoists and Buddhists to explain them. Thus, there are those who, by reading Confucian books, slip into Daoism and Buddhism. And there are those who, lovingly immersed in Daoism and Buddhism, encounter Confucian books and delight in the support their own doctrines receive from them. So they rely on Confucian books in discussing Daoism and Buddhism. Encountering similarities with their own views, they take them as further proofs of the tradition of Mind; encountering differences, they lend their own interpretations to the Six Classics, Confucius, and Mencius, saying, "What I have attained [is] the subtle teachings and profound meanings of the sages." Crisscrossed and interlocking, such [thought]-structures have undergone repeated changes and augmentations, willy-nilly becoming seamlessly joined. . . .

Since Cheng Yi and Zhu Xi early in their lives entered into the other doctrines [i.e., of Daoism and Buddhism] and later simply turned those around to arrive at their own [Confucianism], so Cheng-Zhu ideas can be turned around again to get back to the others. "Heaven" and "Mind" having been united as one thing, the Daoists and Buddhists all invoke our doctrines to lend support to their own. Neo-Confucians having interpreted the classics in that manner, Daoists and Buddhists follow the explanation of Cheng and Zhu, citing and borrowing from the Six Classics, Confucius, and Mencius in their own behalf.

The situation is like that of a son or grandson who has never actually seen his father or grandfather and who mistakenly draws the likeness of another and serves it ritually as though it were his ancestor's true likeness. The object of his service is of course his own ancestor, and if the likeness is not true, so that in attaining the reality of filial respect he misses the pictorial likeness, what is the harm? But what if some outside person attempts to pass off a likeness of his own ancestor as a member of my patriline and actually succeeds in beguiling my family into becoming part of his? In view of this sort of situation, I have been unable to refrain from writing my *Evidential Study* to smash the wrong likeness, rectify my lineage, and protect my family. Distressed by my lineage's long decline and by my family's long dispersal among other families, I make bold to offer no quarter!

The Song Confucians merely changed the Daoist and Buddhist notion of "spiritual awareness" to designate "principle," but otherwise they left the Buddho-Daoist conceptual structures unchanged. Consequently, their explanations of the doctrines of Confucius and Mencius became similar in form and substance to Buddho-Daoist views. For example, Zhu Xi's gloss of the phrase "manifest luminous virtue" in his *Commentary on the Great Learning*, and of the phrase "what needs no display is virtue" in his *Commentary on the Mean*, are so pervaded with Buddho-Daoist views as to be almost indistinguishable from them. Thus you, sir, have felt it appropriate to cite "The work of exalted Heaven is without sound or smell" [from the *Odes*] as the great source of the tradition of Mind. Extending the Song Confucians' muddled adoption of the Daoist's esteem for "no desires" and Zhuangzi's words "return to the beginning," you have written: "To have no desires is genuineness. Tang and Wu returned to it, and this is called 'returning to the beginning.'" . . .

But in the *Great Learning*, the phrase "manifest luminous virtue" speaks of "luminous virtue" in relation to "the people." . . . All affairs are to be conducted with virtue, so that the people are struck with admiration, as if a suspended image of the sun or moon were shining brightly. . . . Since such luminous virtue accumulates, flourishes, and spreads from near to far without cease, the *Great Learning* speaks of "manifesting luminous virtue to all-under-Heaven." *Buxian* and *bucheng* [conventionally read "not manifest" and "not honored," respectively] in the *Odes*, which you cite, are the same as *pixian* and *picheng* [read "greatly manifest" and "greatly honored"] in the *Documents*. The ancient character *pi* commonly used for *bu*, meant not the negative but the "great." The *Mean* says, "His fame overspreads the middle kingdoms," and in speaking of the Way of the gentleman as "concealed," it also refers to it as "daily manifest." Why should one *not* wish it to be greatly manifest but instead prefer to take Zhu Xi's gloss, "deep, dark, mysterious, and distant," as its ultimate perfection?

When the sun is in the sky, what need is there for sound or smell for men to know it? And why, knowing this, can one not cite [as you do], "The work of exalted Heaven is without sound or smell"? But contrary to your aim, in the *Mean* this line follows upon "the virtue that transforms the people," meaning that Heaven makes no use of sound or smell to join with them. Those who talk in the manner of Laozi and the Buddhists here draw on expressions, familiar in the tradition of Mind, such as "void, psychic, undarkened," "deluded by human desires," "the brightness of the original substance," "deep and dark, mysterious and distant," "perfect virtue profound and subtle," and "the wonder of the unmanifest." This not only falls short of [understanding] the original texts of the *Great Learning* and the *Mean* by a thousand miles, even Zhu Xi's commentaries, [which use all of the expressions derisively cited above] though misinterpreting those classics, differ [from the Buddho-Daoist discussions] in basic intent.

Mencius said, "An extensive territory and a vast population are things a gentleman desires"; and "All men have the same desire to be exalted"; as well as "Fish is what I desire; bear's palm also is what I desire. . . . Life is what I desire; rightness also is what I want." . . . Song Confucians, deluded by Daoist and Buddhist talk about "desirelessness," explained the one phrase "rightness is what I want" as "the mind of the Way" and as "Heaven's principle," disparaging the rest as merely "the human mind" and as "human desire." However, desire rightly understood is the wish of one possessing life to affirm that life and protect its excellence. Feelings are spontaneous, affective responses to differences of close and distant, old and young, honored and humble [in human relationships]. Principle means the subtleties of desires and feelings being exercised to their fullest in making fine distinctions, being smoothly fulfilled, each minutely according to its proper role.

With desire, one need not worry about deficiency, only about excess. If it is excessive, one becomes habituated to selfishness and forgetful of others, one's heart becomes immersed in self-indulgence and one's actions vice-ridden. Thus Mencius said, "There is nothing better for nurturing the heart than to have *few* desires." . . . If desire does not fall into selfishness and thus constitutes humaneness; if it does not give way to self-indulgence and vice and thus constitutes rightness; if the sentiments manifest themselves in due degree and thus constitute harmony — this is what is called "Heaven's principle." If, when desires and feelings have not yet been stirred, they are limpid like still water and free of the errors that arise in activity, this is the "Heaven-bestowed nature." It is not that the Heaven-bestowed nature is an entity unto itself, nor that desire and feeling constitute a category unto themselves, nor that "Heaven's principle" itself is some thing. . . .

The *Laozi* says, "Between the flattering 'yes' and the indignant 'no,' what is the difference? Between what the world regards as 'good' and 'evil,' what is the difference?" [Mencius's antagonist] Gaozi said, "There is neither good nor bad in human nature," and "Rightness is external, not internal." The Buddhist [*Platform Sūtra* of Hui Neng] says, "Think not of good; think not of evil. At that moment recognize the original countenance." And Lu Xiangshan and Wang Yangming [by this time spoken of together as the Lu-Wang school] said, respectively, "Evil can harm the heart; good also can harm the mind-and-heart"; and "Without good and without evil — the essence of the mind and heart." What these have in common is that they do not value the good. . . .

But the *Mean* and the *Mencius* both say, "If one does not understand goodness, one cannot be true to oneself." Nowadays people disregard "understanding goodness" and regard having no desires as "being true to oneself." This is erroneous. Those who affirm the tradition of Mind thus erroneously can always take "recognizing the original countenance" as equivalent to "understanding goodness." And if one draws out the implications of this, what cannot be justified? Laozi and Gaozi held "goodness" in contempt while seeming to understand the meaning of the term. But latter-day followers of their thought treat goodness as though it were their own property while not really understanding the term at all. Nowadays, not only is what they call "morality" not what we Confucians properly call morality, *all* such terms as "the nature" and "the Way of Heaven," "sagely wisdom," "humaneness and rightness," "genuineness and clear-sightedness," and even "goodness," "decree," "principle," "knowledge," and "action" have been borrowed in name but changed in meaning. . . .

As you, Sir, have said, "In matters of scholarship nothing is more imperative than to examine the crux between good and evil and to strictly distinguish between genuineness and artificiality." Please do begin from this. If you are as diligent as Cheng and Zhu, as dedicated to the truth and as free from self-concern, then although now you agree with their early views, in your later insight you may realize that the direction in which Cheng and Zhu point is different from that of Daoism, Buddhism, Lu, or Wang. But what I myself hope you will find, Sir, is not just this. Cheng and Zhu treated "principle" as though it were a kind of thing, "received from Heaven and complete in the heart," opening the way in later generations for each person to rely on his own subjective opinion, upholding that as principle and so bringing disaster to the people. Cheng and Zhu having further admixed the doctrine of "no desires," true understanding became even more remote, the maintenance of subjective opinions ever more rigid, and the disaster to the people ever worse. How can principle bring disaster to the people? Because the arbiters thereof do not themselves realize that it is only their opinion. Taking leave of human sentiments and seeking for what purportedly is complete in the heart, how can they not mistake their mind's opinions for principle? This is what those who base all in the mind still do. . . .

Alas, one who draws a likeness of the wrong person cannot but be changed into the reality of that person. If one sincerely, conscientiously investigates the words of the Six Classics, Confucius, and Mencius to the point where one truly advances in understanding, one will see not only that their reality is vastly distant from that of Daoism and Buddhism, but that their likeness is too and cannot be falsely borrowed. What has been so borrowed are the mistaken interpretations of later scholars. Simply this is what I, in my own heart, hope that you, Sir, will find in your search.

[From *Dai Dongyuan ji* 8:8a–14a — JWE, LAS]

## ZHANG XUECHENG'S PHILOSOPHY OF HISTORY

From early in his life, Zhang Xuecheng (1738–1801) evinced a strong desire to attain greatness as an intellectual. Inconveniently, his talent and passion lay in a field that lacked prestige in his day — history. And within historical studies, his emphasis on discerning broad patterns and on an actively interpretive role for the inquirer also was out of fashion. Thus, Zhang was destined throughout his career to struggle for due respect, both for himself as a scholar who offered needful leadership and for history as a discipline that, properly pursued, could far transcend the piecemeal, philological, text-critical style of research that was ascendant precisely during his lifespan.

Among the several tactics that Zhang Xuecheng adopted to raise his own profile, along with that of historiography, was the reopening of discussion on some of the most stimulating ideas of the most revered historians in the Chinese scholarly heritage. In the two essays selectively translated below (from Zhang's extensive collection of such essays, the *Wenshi tongyi*), he explicitly does this with a well-known dictum on history-writing of the famous Tang dynasty historian and critic Liu Zhiji (661–721 C.E.), author of *Understanding History* (*Shitong*). As Zhang did on many occasions, he tries to best Liu as a philosopher of the historical challenge. To this end, he inexplicitly invokes an opaque but semi-canonical statement by the greatest of China's historians (next to Confucius, of course), Sima Qian (145?–90 B.C.E., who had been criticized by Liu) that his monumental *Records of the Grand Historian* (*Shiji*) was intended, in part, to "fathom the interface between Heaven and Humankind."

Both in belittling Liu's ideas and in implicitly claiming to share Sima Qian's grand vision, Zhang liberally employs concepts of the human condition that were fundamental to the so-called Cheng-Zhu school of Neo-Confucian philosophy: The *qi* ("ether," "material-force") of the human mind partakes of both the universality of Heaven and the partiality of human beings; its position is precariously crucial in that it enables us to empathize with and understand all things but also makes us liable to exercise favoritism and prejudice; it is the vehicle both to sagehood and to the cleverest of abominations. Therefore, one's mind must be nourished to fulfill its great potential and watched over assiduously for signs of deviance.

This set of ideas, formulated during the Song dynastic period, of course had not been part of the mental worlds of either Liu Zhiji or Sima Qian. In Zhang Xuecheng's time, Cheng-Zhu philosophy had been enshrined as state orthodoxy for several hundred years, but it had declined as a stimulus among intellectuals. So Zhang's use of this Neo-Confucian conceptual resource in attempting to enrich and elevate the historical thought of his own day did not garner much interest. One essay in Zhang's oeuvre that drew wide notice did so not because it argued the necessity to base good writing in good personal character but because it combined discussion of a current cultural issue — whether women should pursue literary repute — with acerbic, perhaps somewhat grudging criticism of the most gifted and sought-after writer of his time, Yuan Mei (1716–1798). In "Women's Learning" Zhang makes it clear that the "virtue" he looks for in historians and writers can be found in both men and women. However, in reaction to the libertine views and lifestyle of Yuan Mei, who offended many by accepting women among his poetry students and publicizing their talents, Zhang insisted that men and women should hold to their own separate spheres of virtuous expression and that women of proper social status should not ordinarily reveal their learned accomplishments outside the home. Though such opinions have struck twentieth-century readers as unprogressive, Zhang's obvious respect for the female intellect has added to the recognition that he was not a marginal oddity but an exceptional thinker who sustained the richness of Chinese historical thought during a relatively moribund phase.

### VIRTUE IN THE HISTORIAN

Talent, learning, and insight — to have one of these is not easy, but to combine them all is difficult indeed. For this reason, since earliest times there have been many literary men but few good historians. In his day Liu Zixuan [Liu Zhiji] apparently held this analysis adequate to cover all the principles of the matter. And yet, what history chiefly values is meaning, which is embodied in events, the transmission of which depends on writing. Mencius said [of the *Spring and Autumn Annals*]: "Its events are [the doings of] Duke Huan of Qi and Duke Wen of Jin"; its writing is historical [in genre], and its meaning [lies in what] Confucius himself [implied in] saying that he had selectively compiled it. Without insight, we cannot judge [history's] meaning; without [literary] talent, we cannot write it well; and without learning, we cannot marshal its events. Each of these three [abilities] of course has its approximations, as well as [abilities] that resemble them but are not the same: memorization might be called learning; colorful prose might be called talent and precipitate judgment might be called insight. But these are not the [true] talent, learning, and insight of the good historian. . . .

To possess the insight of a [true] historian, one must understand the *virtue* thereof. What is [this] "virtue"? I mean by it the [historical] writer's quality of mind. Now, a man who writes a "foul history" fouls himself thereby, and a man who writes a slanderous book slanders himself thereby. If one's general conduct makes others ashamed, how can one's writing command esteem? In the case of Wei Shou's calumnies [in the *Weishu*] and Shen Yue's concealment of evil [in the *Songshu*], readers have prior distrust of the authors, so the harm is not great. When the harm lies [rather] in [the author's] quality of mind, it means that he has the mind of a superior man, but its nourishment has not yet reached refinement. Now, having the mind of a superior man that has not been nourished to refinement is a condition one can avoid. This being the case, no [historical work] can be free of defects [arising from the author's quality of mind] except Confucius's *Spring and Autumn Annals*. Is it not indeed difficult to criticize people by such a standard? Actually not. It is [just] that he who would be a good historian should carefully distinguish between the "heavenly" and the "human," giving full play to the heavenly and not exercising too much of the human. In [so doing], if one does not get it perfect, being conscious of [the need] is enough to be regarded as having [the good historical] writer's quality of mind. But scholars of literature and history try to outdo each other in talking about talent, learning, and insight, without realizing [that they must] discern men's qualities of mind in order to discuss virtue in historians. Can this be condoned?

Now, everyone is able to say that he approves of Yao and Shun and disapproves of Jie and Zhou; and it is a well-established convention among scholars to esteem the kingly way and disparage the achievements of hegemons. As for loving good and hating evil, praising correctness and detesting wickedness, all who have wished to obtain imperishable [repute] through writing have had minds [capable of] this. But the *quality* of mind must be carefully considered, because the interpenetration of the heavenly and the human is so subtle, the petty intelligence cannot count on [discerning it].

What history records are events, and those events must avail themselves of writing to be transmitted [as historical knowledge]. Hence, all good historians work at their writing, but they fail to realize that it can suffer in thrall to events. For [historical] events must always involve success and failure, right and wrong. And when success, failure, right, and wrong are involved, then the ins and outs, the give-and-take [among them] interact vigorously [in the historian's mind]. As this vigorous interaction goes on, [the mind's] *qi* becomes concentrated. [Historical] events always involve flourishing and decline, ebb and flow. And when one contemplates such flourishing, decline, ebb, and flow, then the pathos becomes unforgettable. As this absorption goes on, feelings become profound. Most prose is not sufficiently moving; what moves people is *qi*. Most writing does not affect people much; what affects them is feeling. When *qi* accumulates, the prose is glorious; when feeling is profound, it draws the reader in. Vigorous *qi* and inviting emotion — [these are characteristics of] the best prose in the world.

But the heavenly and human elements in [these characteristics] must be differentiated. *Qi* partakes of yang's firmness, while feeling accords with the softness of yin. Human beings are subject to the [forces of] yin and yang and cannot be separated therefrom. When *qi* accords with principle, it is heavenly; in its ability to depart from principle for its own purposes, it is human. Feeling grounded in the inborn nature is heavenly; in its ability to confuse the inborn nature and indulge itself, it is human. The meaning of history issues from Heaven, but the writing of history cannot but depend on human effort for its accomplishment. When the human is afflicted with [the susceptibilities of] yin and yang, then history is written contrary to the universality of the Great Way, and its [capacity] to move or attract [people] is slight.

Now, writing cannot stand without *qi*, but *qi* is estimable [only] when in equilibrium. People's *qi* is always in equilibrium when they are at leisure. But when they respond emotively to events, their *qi* loses [its equilibrium] and becomes unsettled, aroused, or arrogant, thus adding to [the force of] yang. Writing cannot be profound without feeling, but feeling is estimable [only] if proper. People's feelings are always proper when they are unoccupied. But when they respond emotively to events, then feelings lose [their propriety] and become deviant, self-indulgent, and biased, thus adding to [the force of] yin. When the potential for disharmony in yin and yang works through [people's] physical constitutions into their minds, it insidiously subverts [their judgment such that] what seems impartial really partakes of selfish interest and what seems [as clear as] Heaven actually is beclouded by the human. When written out in prose, [the resulting viewpoints] can do violence to [history's] meaning and contravene the Way without the author himself being aware of it. Therefore I say that [the historian's] quality of mind must be regarded very seriously.

That *qi* can overbear and that feeling can take sides is to say that the movement begins with Heaven but then enters the human. [Thus, we find that] men of artistic talent become immersed in literary style, thinking that style is a manifestation of aesthetic value and not realizing how wrong [such immersion] is. The dependence of history on [good] writing is like the necessity that clothing have appearance and food have flavor. Appearance cannot be without the more decorative and the more plain; flavor cannot be without the more robust and the more bland. [But when] decorative and plain conflict, the appearance always is jarring; when robust and bland conflict, the taste always is strange. Jarring appearances that offend the eye and strange flavors that numb the palate arise from conflicts between decorative and plain, robust and bland. Among literary styles there are the skillful and the awkward, and commonplace historians go on contending over matters such as this, neglecting what is basic while pursuing the superficial. Their approach to writing has never shown superb results. And with such a view of history, how can they receive any understanding of the general conditions of the ancients?

[Zhang, "Neipian," *Wenshi tongyi* 3:1a–4b  —LAS]

### VIRTUE IN THE WRITER

In all philosophical discussions, earlier men have put forth ideas and later men have refined them, feeling compelled to explore them as far as possible. When the ancients discussed writing, they were concerned only with stylistic matters. Liu Xie used Lu Ji's basic ideas to elaborately discourse on the "literary mind," and Su Che used Han Yu's basic ideas to elaborately discourse on the "literary spirit." [But I] have not seen anyone discuss literary *virtue* — which should prompt reflection among scholars. . . .

Now in saying that I have not seen any discussion of literary virtue, I meant that in the words of the ancients, comprehensive and thorough as they are, the subject is not distinguished from that of essays by moral men. They never go into the prose itself to consider whether — besides talent, learning, and insight — literary virtue also was present. All those ancients who [were accomplished in] ancient letters had to have composure in order to effect empathy. [Let me point out that] the need for composure in beginning to write is not the same as moral cultivation [in general]; and the need for empathy in discussing ancient times is not the same as magnanimity [in general]. [Rather, specifically in writing,] empathy is the ability to put oneself in the actual situations of the ancients. Alas! Few are those who know what [the writer's] virtue is. If one understands that in commencing to write one must restrain one's *qi* and enter the lives of others, then one does understand virtue in writing. . . .

The various worthies "were such no matter where they lived" and would not necessarily recognize the trend-conscious, narrow scholarly perspectives of today. Thus, if one does not know the times of an ancient [writer], one cannot, with abandon, discourse on his literary style. Knowing his times but not knowing his personal situation, one cannot hastily [proceed] to discourse on [the substance of] his writing. Life's circumstances do undergo the vicissitudes of honor and shame, obscurity and renown, humility and boldness, sorrow and joy, and things that are said for reasons. Even You [Ruo] did not understand what [his teacher] Confucius meant [in one instance when the latter's dissatisfaction with certain recent developments crept into his reply to You's innocent query]. How much less [can it be understood by those of us] born thousands of years later? The Sage's explanation of *shu* [i.e., "empathy"] as "not putting upon others what one does not wish for oneself" is eminently to be followed. Nowadays those who would rank themselves among the literati and discuss the ancients must first establish self-[understanding], for no other reason than to exercise the empathy in the writer's virtue. . . .

Indeed, historians have three strengths in talent, learning, and insight. [To say that] the literature of ancient times did not emerge from historical writing [would be as absurd as to say that] food and drink do not ultimately derive from the cultivation of grain. Insight is born of the mind; talent comes from *qi*; and learning — that [is a matter of] concentrating the mind to nourish *qi* and forging insight to complete one's talent. A dispersed mind is not reliable; floating *qi* easily is lax. In [practicing] inner composure one continually vigilates between mind and *qi*, strictly precluding any unguarded fault or deviation. Yet, brilliant, self-composed tranquillity was that with which the sages began and ended [all affairs, thus attaining] breadth of justness. In the present [context], it is none other than to approach writing with one's mind and *qi* under supervision — the inner composure of virtue in the writer.

[Zhang, "Neipian," *Wenshi tongyi* 3:19b–20a — LAS]

WOMEN'S LEARNING

The term *women's learning* appears in the section on the ministry of state in the *Rites of Zhou*, where women's posts are listed. There it refers to "virtue, speech, decorum, and work" — a broad range of attributes. This is unlike use of the term *learning* in later times, when it came to refer to literary arts alone. . . . Zheng Xuan (127–200 C.E.) says in his commentary on these terms that "speech" means rhetoric. It follows that a woman who was not well versed in classical ritual and accomplished in letters could not be considered learned. Thus we know that in poetry recitation and mastery of the rites, the learning of women in ancient times was just slightly inferior to that of men. Although the writings of women who came later have been more inclined toward beauty and ornament, women should know their original heritage.

Pursuing the successive commentaries on the *Spring and Autumn Annals*, we find that the wives of the various feudal lords and the spouses of the chief officials were able to cite allusions and tell of the past — all in elegant prose. For example, Deng Man was able to interpret the auspicious omen in the full moon, deriving from it a detailed understanding of Heaven's Way, and Mu Jiang concisely explicated key terms in the *Classic of Changes*. The good wife of Earl Mu of Lu used canonical phrases in handing down ethical instructions, and the spouse of Minister of Education Qi was granted a nobler title because of her ritual propriety. . . . Do these classical rituals and standards of conduct, these literary hues and styles, differ in any way from those of the highest-ranking lords and statesmen?

As we see, women's behavior originally did not receive particular documentation; women simply appeared in historical records wherever they figured in specific events. If those women had appeared in later times, when histories required special treatises and a separate category for women's biographies, there would be ten times as many as in Liu Xiang's and Fan Ye's [Han period] collections who were as brilliant and distinguished as Ban Zhao (45–114? C.E.) and Cai Yuan (late Han). Thus we know that [not only the records of women's lives] but also women's learning have not been transmitted to later ages. . . .

From the Spring and Autumn period onward, when the roles of official and teacher were no longer one, learning ceased to be the domain of governmental officers, and writings came to be authorial compositions. Men of exceptional talent wrote about what affected them personally to found schools of thought. Then writing devolved into belles lettres, talent in beautiful expression counted the most, and richness of color made for renown. The fact that women of extraordinary brilliance and unusual ability, who concentrated in themselves the vital force between Heaven and Earth, were able to achieve special distinction in fine writing that was recognized in the past and is recognized today, was simply due to the circumstances of the time.

When Confucian learning flourished at the Han court, Ban Gu [32–92 C.E.] said that it was brought about via "the route to profit and fortune." That is, what official policy honored was what worthy and talented men vied for; scholars who pursued learning did so on exactly the same principle [of gain] as farmers who tilled the fields. But a woman's writing was not her vocation. Therefore when a woman excelled, it emerged from her Heaven-bestowed nature, not from vying to be fashionable or longing for fame. . . .

As for various [Han dynasty] verses and miscellanies from the inner apartments, some of which have come down to us, regardless of whether the women who wrote them were pure or dissolute, their words and phrases always are properly restrained. [Zhou] Wenjun eloped [and thus married without the proper ceremonies], yet her "Song of White Hair" only admonished [her husband, Sima] Xiangru (d. 18 C.E.), [not others]. Cai Yan lost her virtue [by remarrying as a widow], yet in writing out the works [of her father's library from memory] she steadfastly declined the services of ten official assistants [because she did not wish to seem improper in receiving things from their hands]. As for others, who were content to remain in their homes and follow accepted norms, and who became known for their purity and chastity — in every case their writings are serene like still water, wondrous like clear wind. Even though their literary eloquence arose from natural ability, the sphere of their thought did not transgress the bounds of their quarters. Thus, although women's learning was different from what it had been in ancient times, it did not conflict with civilizing instruction. . . .

When long ago the historian Ban Gu died before finishing the *History of the Former Han*, the emperor issued an edict summoning Gu's younger sister, Ban Zhao, to come in person to the imperial Dongguan Library and carry the work to completion. Thereafter, the noble lords and great ministers all brought her gifts and asked her to be their teacher. This truly can be called an extraordinary event without precedent. But it is generally the case that specialized schools of outstanding scholarship are preserved within certain families and never completely articulated in books. Without qualified persons [in the family line], there simply is no way to transmit that learning. To take another example, when the rulers of the former Jin (351–394 C.E.) first established schools and assembled a broad array of erudites and teachers of the classics, they discovered that all five classics were roughly in hand except the *Rites of Zhou*, which had been transmitted orally. The emperor declared Lady Song's home a lecture hall and appointed 120 stipended scholars to sit on the other side of a curtain and receive instruction from her, on whom was bestowed the honorary title

"Scholar of Illustrious Culture." This too was an extraordinary event with no precedent. . . .

These two mothers carried out men's tasks with women's bodies. Truly, transmitting the classics and narrating history are crucial to Heaven and humankind, the Way and the laws. Fearing that [such transmission] might be lost, the rulers of those times had no choice but to break with [bureaucratic] convention and emphasize ritual propriety [in taking women as instructors]. We cannot accuse these women of showing off their splendid talents or of suddenly deviating into vulgarity. . . .

Beginning in Tang-Song times, the only discernible talent conveys its lofty refinement through mere short poems about spring in the women's apartments, unrequited autumn love, and blooms and grasses in profusion and decay. There are notable exceptions — for instance, the *Women's Analects* by (the Tang period) Song Ruoshen and the *Women's Classic of Filial Piety* by (the Song period) Lady Zheng. Although these women's intelligence did not save them from hackneyed writing, still the general direction of their work approached refinement and correctness. When those of us in the literary world cite their writings, it is principally an acknowledgment of their praiseworthy aspirations.

As for the celebrated, "wall-toppling" courtesans, they frequently interacted with famous men of their time by exchanging poems and essays imbued with meanings appropriate to both spouses and friends. One could say that they were good at double entendre. They were like the ancient poets who, when they thought of their lords or pined for a friend, affected the sad emotions between men and women. . . . So it is that the poems of nameless lovers may approximate the perdurance of the principles of the Supreme Ultimate and yin and yang between Heaven and Earth. [In them] "the wise find wisdom, and the humane see humanity." The famous courtesans were skilled poets who also comprehended ancient meanings. They transferred these meanings and lodged them in the warm, weighty language of the poet using the realities of joy and longing between men and women. Thus, their syntax is refined and yet informed by a standard, true and yet free of lewdness. [Such works] have been transmitted for a thousand years, shining forth from the pages of books, and cannot be dismissed on account of the [fallen status of] the persons who wrote them.

But to claim a voice is to find one's proper form, and in this women are different from men. Thus a skillfully composed dirge is only appropriate for a funeral attendant to chant, and a rowing song, freewheeling and ingenious, is suitable only for a boatwoman to sing. The courtesan who presents a poem to a Mr. Li or composes verse along with a Mr. Zhang does so simply because her situation requires it. But in respectable families, the words spoken in the women's rooms are not even to be heard [in the rest of the household], so how could such words ever get into poetry exchanges on the outside? . . .

[But nowadays] one often sees printed editions of a famous scholar's poetry in which, without having read the collations through, already in the tables of contents one can scan references to rouge powders and passionate love, or mentions of poetry exchanges in the pleasure quarters. This writer adopts a chic suaveness, claiming that he is just like the ancients. He seems unaware that if a man born in this age [of strict regulations], a man of the present, can be so inept at observing official prohibitions, then he hardly can discuss any skill with words and ink. In the rituals of the Duke of Zhou, men and women from the same descent group cannot marry. Is it all right, then, to take advantage of being born after the Zhou to claim that in ancient times there was no separation between men and women, thus throwing human relationships into confusion and behaving like birds and beasts — and to further claim that the ancients were the same way?

Now talent requires learning, and in learning the premium is on insight. Talent without learning is mere cleverness; a merely clever person who has no insight has no true talent, and such a person will know no bounds. He may call a poem elegant and refined when in fact it is frivolous and shallow. He may try to make a reputation out of boastful posturing. He may show himself off to the younger generation and make outrageous displays before ladies, corrupting human hearts and mores beyond description. In ancient times frivolity was not unknown among the literati, but it never ran so far as braggadocio in front of women. To be substandard but still strive relentlessly for fame, or to be undistinguished in one's own right but trade on the reputations of others — men of high purpose should be ashamed to act in these ways. . . .

The women's learning of ancient times always emphasized mastering poetry through prior mastery of the rites. But women's learning today has turned to confounding the rites because of poetry. If the rites are shunned, we will no longer be able to discuss the human heart or social customs. Without question it is certain scholars of dubious character who, propagating heretical ideas, have subverted women's learning. Others who truly understand it look on such men as akin to excrement. How could *they* ever be fooled!

[Zhang, "Neipian," *Wenshi tongyi* 5:24b–31b — SLM, LAS]


## CUI SHU AND THE CRITICAL SPIRIT

One of the finest representatives of the integrity, critical spirit, and sound scholarship that marked the best of Qing learning is the historian Cui Shu (1740–1816). Through a long lifetime of scholarly endeavor he worked to refute not only the late Song and Ming interpretations of the classics but even the interpretations and errors of the Han Confucians, attempting by methods of historical research to restore the purity of ancient Confucianism. His most important researches are embodied in a collection of essays titled *Record of Beliefs Investigated* (*Kaoxin lu*). In addition, he wrote a brief work called *Essentials of the Record of Beliefs Investigated* (*Kaoxin lu tiyao*), in which he expounded in an informal style, interspersed with lively anecdotes, the ideals and methods that guided him in his work.

Cui avoided official life for the most part and preferred to devote himself to independent scholarly research, though this choice inevitably meant a life of hardship and poverty for himself and his faithful wife. Of his great work, *Record of Beliefs Investigated*, a famous disciple said, "Since his ideas were of no value in the examination halls, there were few who believed in him. On the contrary, there were those who seized upon his most trustworthy conclusions and on his clearest elucidations to discredit him. Within the next century there will surely be some in this broad empire who will truly understand him."[51]

### FOREWORD TO THE *ESSENTIALS OF THE RECORD OF BELIEFS INVESTIGATED*

Is it impossible to believe what other people have said? The world is very large and I cannot do and see everything in it. How much more so with the world of a thousand years ago! If I do not accept the accounts of other men, by what means can I find out about it? But is it possible to believe *everything* that others have said? . . . Tongues will grow in people's mouths and there is nothing to restrain them; brushes will find their way into men's hands and there is nothing to hold them back. Whatever comes into a man's head to say he may say, and there is no limit to how far he can go. . . .

In our prefectural town there was a Liu family who had two meteorites. According to the story that was told by everyone around the village, some shooting stars had fallen long ago on the Liu mansion and changed into stones. I was still young when I heard of this, but I already doubted it. When I was a little older I was playing once with the Liu boys and they showed me the stones and some inscriptions carved on them in seal and ordinary script. When I questioned them very closely they finally said, "That story is not really true. One of our ancestors was an official in the south, where he came across these stones. They were such an odd shape that he supposed there were no others like them in the world and so he just carved these inscriptions to give proof, and yet as you see the whole thing was a fake." How then is one to go about ascertaining the truth of what people say?

When the Zhou declined, many strange doctrines sprang up. The various schools of Yangzi, Mozi, the Logicians, the Legalists, the diplomatic alliances, and the yin and yang all made up sayings and invented incidents to fool wise men and sages. The Han Confucians were acquainted with these various teachings and, accepting them as quite reliable without even examining them carefully, proceeded to note them down in their books and commentaries. . . . After this there appeared the cults of the prophet, even more absurd, and yet [in the Han] Liu Xin and Zheng Xuan made use of them in expounding the classics so that they have been handed down for ages now. Scholars avidly study all these without ever examining their origins. They suppose only that, since the

---

51. Chen Lihe, quoted in Hummel, *Eminent Chinese*, 2:773.

Han Confucians were close to antiquity, their assertions must be based upon older traditions and not irresponsibly selected at random. Even among the Song Confucians, with all their diligence and purity, there are many who accepted these theories without alteration. . . . Mencius said, "It would be better to be without the *Classic of Documents* than to believe it all. In the 'Completion of the War' section, I select only two or three passages that I believe" [7B:3]. If a sage like Mencius is as cautious as this when reading the classics, how much more so in the case of commentaries on the classics, and even more with the various philosophical works. Mencius also said, "In learning extensively and discussing minutely what is learned, the object is to be able to go back and set forth in brief what is essential" [4B:15]. One desires a wide range of information not for the sake of extensive learning itself but only because one wishes by repeated comparisons and revisions of the data to arrive at a single truth. If one simply exhausts all learning without knowing what to select, then although he reads all the books in the world he is not so well off as a stupid and uneducated man who is yet free from serious error. . . .

The Han Confucian Dong Zhongshu once wrote a work on disasters and portents. Emperor Wu submitted the book to the court officials for their opinion. Lü Bushu, one of Dong Zhongshu's disciples, having no idea that the book was written by his teacher, expressed the opinion that it was a work of gross stupidity. As a result, Dong Zhongshu was put on trial for his life. To any book written by their own teachers men accord the fullest honor and belief; any book not by their teachers they disparage and revile the merits of the works. . . . When I read the classics I do not respect them blindly merely because they are classics. Instead I try only to discover the intentions of the sages, and thereby come to appreciate the loftiness and beauty of their writings so that I cannot be misled by forgeries. . . .

Neither in the past nor in the present has there ever been any lack of people who read books. . . . Among them have been scholars of keen intellect whose intentions were of the loftiest. And yet they were led astray by the fashions of the times. . . . As scholars who valued truth none can compare with the Song Confucians. Yet most of them concerned themselves with questions of the nature and principle of things and with moral philosophy. If one looks among them for men who devoted themselves to historical research, he will find no more than two or three out of ten. By Ming times scholarship had grown increasingly heterodox, and it became so that if one hoped to write anything important he had to be conversant with Chan doctrines and interlard his library shelves with Buddhist books. . . .

In the past centuries there have been plenty of scholars who devoted their minds to the study of antiquity. Whenever I read works such as Zhao Mingcheng's *Record of Inscriptions on Metal and Stone* (with the colophon by Hong Mai) or Huang Bosi's *Further Studies of the Dongguan*, I never fail to remark with a sigh that the breadth of learning and diligence of research of these former scholars surpass mine a hundred times. By the detail on a plate or a vase, some minute point about a goblet or a ladle, they declare, "This is Zhou," "This is Qin," "This is Han." The preface to the *Orchid Pavilion Collection* [on the ritual of the lustral sacrifices], written by Wang Xizhi, surely has no connection with the practical dos and don'ts of human affairs, and yet scholars ask, "Which is his genuine calligraphy?" "Which is forged calligraphy?" so thorough are they in their research and so discriminating in their judgments. Yet when it comes to the affairs of the rulers and sages of antiquity, which are directly concerned with morals and the human heart, people accept what others say without discriminating between truth and falsehood. Why should this be?

In order to repair some of the omissions of former scholars and supplement certain of their defects, I have written this book, *Record of Beliefs Investigated* (*Kaoxin lu*), which I hope will not be found entirely useless.

[*Kaoxin lu tiyao*, CSJC A:2–22 — BW]

## HAN LEARNING AND WESTERN LEARNING

It may seem surprising that in an age whose intellectual ideals were breadth of knowledge and practicality of thought, the new knowledge from Europe that the Jesuits brought to China in the sixteenth and seventeenth centuries did not make more of a stir. This was certainly not owing to lack of acquaintance with the new learning or lack of opportunities to learn more. The Jesuits had attracted wide attention by their scientific feats and had been installed for more than a century as the official astronomers of the Ming and Qing courts. They had even made a few important converts to their own faith among scholar-officials and a not inconsiderable number among the common people — enough to cause alarm to men like the xenophobic official Yang Guangxian (1597–1669), who saw in Western science as well as in Christianity a threat to all of Chinese civilization. Yet the net impression made on the Confucian mind was slight.

It is true that interest in mathematics and astronomy among men like Huang Zongxi, and others after him in the Han school, was greatly stimulated by the revelations of the Jesuits; in fact, a few individuals, like Mei Wending (1633–1721), were even ready to acknowledge the great value of the new scientific learning and to assimilate it. Indeed, a fair number of the best known scholars of the day were cognizant of the new Western learning, and in a few cases, most notably that of Fang Yizhi (1611–1671), it led to a significant reexamination not only of traditional Chinese astronomy but even of a central value in Neo-Confucian teaching, the "investigation of things," which he directed toward "externals" and empirical research.[52]

---

52. Willard J. Peterson, "Fang I-Chih's Western Learning," p. 401.

Yet on the whole these new speculations "did not greatly influence the general course of Qing intellectual history."[53] More typically, however, this new interest was directed toward a reexamination of China's traditional methods of astronomy, toward recovering much genuine knowledge that had been lost owing to centuries of neglect, or toward defending Chinese tradition by showing, with great ingenuity, that what was valid in the scientific learning of the West was not really new but was borrowed indirectly from the ancient Chinese, or that, on the other hand, what clearly conflicted with traditional lore must be held invalid. Ruan Yuan (1764–1849), a prodigious scholar as well as a leading official of his time, testified to the new interest in mathematics and astronomy by his biographies of notable contributors to these sciences, including even Westerners like Ptolemy. Yet his Sino-centric point of view is evident. He contends that because the knowledge of astronomy attributed to Ptolemy by the Jesuits was so far in advance of the Chinese at the same time (the Han dynasty), the Jesuits must have deliberately exaggerated it in order to deceive the Chinese concerning the accomplishments of the West.[54] Another contention of his is that the revolution of the earth around the sun must be a fallacious theory since it "departs from the classics and is contrary to the Way."[55]

We should not conclude from this that the attitude of most Confucian scholars toward Western learning was hostile or sharply defensive. More generally it was one of indifference. When in 1818 Ruan Yuan sponsored the publication of Jiang Fan's monumental survey of the school of Han Learning in the Qing dynasty (Guochao Hanxue shicheng ji), neither Jiang nor Ruan, in prefatory remarks concerning the significance of this movement, found it necessary to mention its position with respect to Western learning. The great antagonists in Ruan's mind were still the old ones — Buddhism and Daoism — and he placed much emphasis on the contribution of the Han school in purging Confucianism of Buddhist and Daoist elements that had infiltrated the original teaching.

What, then, are the reasons for this notable disinclination to pursue more vigorously contacts with the West, when by contrast many of the best minds in Europe were avidly devouring not only curious information about China but the teachings of Confucius himself as related by the Jesuits (from whom we inherit our romanization of his Chinese name, Kong Fuzi)? Much has been written on this question, and much more remains to be studied. The Jesuits themselves, from the outset, observed that the general disinterest of the Chinese in Western science was a reflection of their preoccupation with studies that led to official preferment. The Jesuit Nicholas Trigault (1577–1628), for instance, puts it this way:

---

53. John B. Henderson, Chinese Cosmology, p. 141.
54. Zhouren juan 43:6b.
55. Zhouren juan 46:19a.

It is evident to everyone here that no one will labor to attain proficiency in mathematics or in medicine who has any hope of becoming prominent in the field of [Confucian] philosophy. The result is that scarcely anyone devotes himself to these studies, unless he is deterred from the pursuit of what are considered to be the higher studies, either by reason of family affairs or by mediocrity of talent. The study of mathematics and that of medicine are held in low esteem, because they are not fostered by honors as is the study of philosophy, to which students are attracted by the hope of the glory and the rewards attached to it. This may be readily seen in the interest taken in the study of moral philosophy. The man who is promoted to the higher degrees in this field, prides himself on the fact that he has in truth attained to the pinnacle of Chinese happiness.[56]

And Jean-Baptiste Du Halde, in reporting the Jesuits' generally favorable impressions of early Qing China, notes:

The great and only Road to Riches, Honour and Employments is the study of the *jing* (or canonical books), History, the Laws and Morality; also to learn to do what they call *wenzhang*, that is, to write in a polite Manner, in Terms well chosen, and suitable to the Subject treated upon. By this means they become Doctors, and that Degree once obtained, they are possessed of such Honor and Credit, that the conveniences of life follow soon after, because they are sure to have a Government post in a short time. Even those who return into their Provinces to wait for Posts, are in great Consideration with the Mandarin of the Place; they protect their families against all vexations, and there enjoy a great many privileges. But as nothing like this is to be hoped for by those who apply themselves to the speculative Sciences, and as the Study of them is not the Road to Honours and Riches, it is no wonder that those sorts of abstract Sciences should be neglected by the Chinese.[57]

What Du Halde says here about the key role of the civil service examination system (the term *wenzhang* refers specifically to the examination essay) only confirms what Confucian reformers themselves had repeatedly pointed to: that education in China, and the capabilities of the educated class, were relatively limited by the type of examination system that controlled entrance to official life (still the most preferred of careers). Recent scholarship has tended to confirm this early judgment: namely that the new interest in scientific investigation

---

56. Gallagher, *China in the Sixteenth Century*, pp. 32–33.

57. Adapted from *A Description of the Empire of China* (London, 1741), 2:124, cited in Bernard, *Matteo Ricci's Scientific Contribution to China*, p. 20.

and cosmological speculation did not significantly deflect the mainstream of Confucian scholarship from its perennial pursuits — the central Neo-Confucian texts in the educational and examinations curriculum. As John Henderson has said: "Achievements in most other fields of learning [than Neo-Confucianism] were not so munificently rewarded or highly regarded."[58] And even among those not caught up in the examination culture, but more committed to scholarly research, like Gu Yanwu and the Han Learning, it could be said that their efforts were "largely focused on matters relating to human affairs and thus their energies were channeled into historical and textual studies, and ideally, statecraft."[59]

During the first half of the Manchu dynasty, the great influence of the state in intellectual matters was further exerted through its patronage of Confucian scholarship. In an attempt to demonstrate that though they were foreigners, their rule was based on a full appreciation of the best in Chinese culture, the Manchus lavished special honors on Confucian scholars recognized for their broad classical learning and employed large numbers of scholars and scribes in ambitious projects for the preservation, codification, and explication of the classical tradition — projects of such magnitude as the collection of the Complete Library of the Four Treasuries (*Siku quanshu*) from texts gathered all over the land and the preparation of a compendious critical bibliography for it.

The fact that this collection process also enabled the Manchus to screen out and destroy works considered subversive of their rule (a censorship process not unmixed with scholarly politics) was perhaps less significant as a negative factor than the positive support given to a type of classical research in which Chinese scholars, pursuing their own line of thought, were already diligently engaged. Nor should we overlook a more subtle and indirect contribution of the Manchus to the Chinese self-absorption in intellectual matters: the sense of well-being and complacency that was fed by the initial success of the Manchus as rulers of China in the great Kangxi and Qianlong reigns. The empire was peaceful and prosperous, the population was growing, and the arts of civilization flourished as never before. In such circumstances it was difficult to take seriously a bid from the West that had only been tendered at the hands of gentle missionaries and was not as yet backed by overwhelming force.

## THE QING VERSION OF NEO-CONFUCIAN ORTHODOXY

Compared to the wide range, fluidity, and variety of late Ming thought, the early Qing period witnessed both a conservative reaction among scholars to the

58. Henderson, *Chinese Cosmology*, p. 146.
59. Willard Peterson, *Fang I-chih's Western Learning*, p. 400.

freethinking of the late Ming and a parallel strengthening of central institutions that promoted ideological consensus and continuity. A key point in restoration of the dynastic state was the early resumption by the Qing of civil service examinations with a content and form basically similar to those of the Yuan and Ming and with Zhu Xi's version of the Four Books as the basic texts. This represented orthodoxy as an officially approved body of correct teachings, without necessarily entailing the proscription of other works or views. Simply to have the exams focus on the Neo-Confucian canon as shaped by Zhu Xi meant that, since school curricula generally aimed at preparation for the examinations, the thinking of most educated people would early be exposed to and formed by Zhu Xi's teachings.

This was not done simply by imperial fiat. In fact, as in the Yuan case earlier, the dynastic endorsement of Zhu Xi followed upon the prior recognition and acceptance of Zhu Xi's curriculum in the local academies and among independent scholars. As we have seen in volume 1, a tidal conservative reaction to Wang Yangming's liberal teachings had already shown itself at the end of the Ming, as manifested in the neo-orthodox reformism of the Donglin Academy and Fu She society, expressing the alarm of the Confucian scholar-elite over signs of political decadence and a decline in public morality.

This conservative trend carried over into the early Qing, as scholars otherwise diverse in their interests looked to Zhu Xi for their intellectual grounding and moral bearings. Even Confucian scholars identified with significant new trends, such as Gu Yanwu, a progenitor of the evidential research largely identified with Han Learning, looked up to Zhu Xi as a scholar and was strongly critical of Wang Yangming's subjectivism. Of Wang Fuzhi the same was true, though he exercised far less influence on the course of Qing scholarly thought than did Gu. Likewise turning to Zhu Xi were leading figures in the movement that stressed "practical" or "substantial" learning (*shixue*) in the early Qing (for instance, Chen Hongmou [chapter 26]), as were scholars in the closely related trend that advocated the practice of Confucian "rites" as models of political and social organization.

A central figure in all this was the Kangxi emperor (1662–1722), generally credited with high intelligence, wise judgment, and benevolent intentions. He took a special interest in Zhu Xi's teachings and had as advisers some of the leading Neo-Confucians of the day, including Lu Longji (1630–1693), the one Qing scholar esteemed enough to be enshrined in the official Confucian temple and himself an ardent champion of Zhu Xi. The continuity with late Ming neo-orthodoxy is also shown by Lu Longji's admiration for and acknowledged indebtedness to Lü Liuliang, whose radical Zhu Xi orthodoxy has been discussed above.

Yet the difference between official and scholarly orthodoxies, as well as the potential conflict between them, was sharply drawn in the next reign (Yongzheng, 1723–1735). When Lü Liuliang's challenge to dynastic rule became exposed in the course of a local revolt in 1728 inspired by Lü's ideas, Lü's works were later suppressed and even Lu Longji's collected writings were expurgated of their many favorable references to Lü Liuliang. Here the demands of dynastic loyalty overrode fidelity to Neo-Confucian tradition, while the greater tolerance of Lü shown in the Kangxi reign did not carry over to his successors.

Meanwhile, steps were taken to establish Zhu Xi as the supreme scholarly authority among the successors to Confucius and Mencius. By imperial order in 1712, his tablet was installed in the main hall of the Confucian temple along with those of Confucius's own disciples. A definitive edition of his writings (*The Complete Works of Master Zhu*, 1714) and of his recorded conversations (*The Classified Sayings of Master Zhu*) was prepared and published under imperial auspices, as well as an anthology, *The Essential Ideas of Human Nature and Principle* (1715), a selective abridgement of the official Ming collection of Neo-Confucian texts, *Great Compendium of Human Nature and Principle*.[60]

Another major project to codify orthodox teaching was undertaken by one of the Kangxi emperor's prime advisers, Zhang Boxing (1652–1725), who compiled a set of authoritative Neo-Confucian writings in *The Collected Works of the Hall of Correctness and Propriety*. As with *Essential Ideas*, referred to above, it was understood that even in such an encyclopedic collection, economy of space and selectivity of materials was called for. The perpetuation of tradition could not be achieved by indiscriminate addition and accumulation, lest the burden of received culture become unmanageable and stultifying. Hence the need for strict criteria in refining the selection, which meant, to some degree, repackaging and redefining the canon, as Zhu Xi himself had done.

In addition to these efforts to promote a scholarly orthodoxy, other major projects were undertaken in the Kangxi reign to record, preserve, and codify the larger legacy of traditional scholarship. One of these, started by an independent scholar but patronized by the court and eventually published with imperial sponsorship, was the encyclopedia *Synthesis of Books and Illustrations from Past and Present* (*Gujin tushu jicheng*, 1778). Another such was the project carried out in the Qianlong era, from 1772 to 1783, to prepare a manuscript library that would provide authoritative copies of extant works gathered throughout the empire, the Imperial Manuscript Library known as the Complete Library of the Four Treasuries (*Siku quanshu*).

Here, too, opportunity was taken to criticize or censor some offending works, while bestowing a kind of seal of approval upon others, and thus in a way defining a canon. Still, it was a vast, capacious canon, and the compilers' critical comments, many influenced by the new text criticism of the Evidential Learning, did not spare even would-be imperial sages like the Yongle emperor of the Ming, whom they castigated for promulgating his own version of authoritative

---

60. See vol. 1, ch. 22.

"sagely learning" when this would better have been left to qualified scholars.

By such official patronage of scholarship on a grand scale, the Manchu regime, especially during the long Kangxi reign (1662–1722), enlisted the services of many Confucian scholars, who, though Chinese, were more humanist than nationalist in their basic outlook and, as earlier in the Mongol period, under Khubilai, were prepared to accept non-Chinese rulers who met their universalist criteria. One of the Manchu rulers who presided over this long antecedent period of consolidation, growth, and prosperity received the posthumous title of Humane (or Benevolent) Emperor (*Renzong*), and if even European thinkers of the Enlightenment spoke of China in these years as a "benevolent despotism," it was in part a tribute to the success of the Manchus in carrying out policies that were no less effective in the cultural domain than in the military and political.

If this much be granted to the success of Qing policy and official ideology, even Neo-Confucian scholars who collaborated in this enterprise knew that it fell short of the ideals of Confucius and Zhu Xi. The aforementioned Zhang Boxing, who could be identified as well as anyone with the Qing state orthodoxy, remained conscious that the examination system, even with Zhu Xi's Four Books and commentaries installed as basic texts, failed to achieve the goals for learning set by Zhu Xi himself. In the following passage, Zhang's opening reference to the ancients evokes Confucius's, and later Zhu Xi's, basic premise that true learning should be "for the sake of one's self" and not for the pursuit of political and social success:

> In ancient times it was easy to develop one's talents to the full; today it is difficult. In antiquity scholar-officials were chosen for their [moral] substance; today they are chosen for their literary ability. In ancient times the village recommended scholars and the town selected them, so men engaged in substantial learning (*shixue*) and outdid each other in the practice of humaneness and rightness, the Way and virtue. At home they were pure scholars; at large they were distinguished officials. Today it is different. Men are chosen for their examination essays. What fathers teach their sons, and elder brothers their younger brothers, is only to compete in the writing of essays. It is not that they fail to read the Five Classics or Four Books, but that they read them only for such use as they have in the writing of the examination essays, and never incorporate them into their own hearts and lives.[61]

Thus even the official orthodoxy carried with it some seeds of its own self-examination, self-criticism, and possible renewal. Moreover, apart from, and

---

61. Zhang Boxing, personal preface to the *Chengshi . . . richeng, Zhengyi tang quanshu* 1:1.

even within, the Qing establishment there were independent scholars carrying on the critical scholarship that called into question some of the texts and doctrines closely identified with the official orthodoxy.

Yet it remains a central fact of cultural history in late imperial China, as in the educational history of East Asia as a whole, that Zhu Xi's basic texts continued to serve as the mainstays of the school curriculum down into the late nineteenth century, and to persist as the most influential force in the intellectual and moral formulation of the educated elite of China, Japan, and Korea.

## VILLAGE LECTURES AND THE SACRED EDICT

The "Sacred Edict" refers to a set of moral and governmental instructions promulgated by imperial authority for use in local rituals conducted throughout the Qing empire. First instituted by the Kangxi emperor (r. 1662–1722), it was expanded and given definitive form in Sixteen Maxims by his successor, the Yongzheng emperor (r. 1723–1735). Much ceremony attached to the recitation of these instructions, and an effort was made to popularize them through explanations in the vernacular, the telling of moral tales, and the conducting of dramatic performances to illustrate the main points of instruction.

So widespread was this educational practice that it early came to the attention of foreign observers, who noted its official character, its emphasis on compliance with the authorities, and the fact that it had tended to become a ritual routine, dutifully performed by mandarins as an official function but not taken too seriously by anyone.

What few realized was that this custom, also known as the Village Lectures, derived from the practice instituted long before by the founder of the Ming[62] and earlier spoken of as the Six Maxims [of Ming Taizu], whose "sage instructions" became increasingly thought of as a Sacred Edict, reflecting the theocratic character of the monarchy and the process of official ritualization by which the performance became endowed with a quasi-religious aura.

What fewer still realized was how this had come about as a transformation of Zhu Xi's original Community Compact promoting such communitarian values as the leadership responsibility of the local elite, consensual agreement among the members at village meetings (i.e., the "compact"), popular moral uplift, neighborly cooperation, and mutual aid, with ceremonial respect shown for age and superior wisdom but otherwise no distinctions made of rank or class. This original character is still reflected in the preservation of Zhu Xi's Six Maxims among the later Sixteen, and by the fact that, despite the aggrandizing of imperial authority in the official Ming and Qing versions, priority is still

---

62. See ch. 21.

given to the family values of filiality and brotherliness (especially as dramatized in later popular tales of heroic filial piety), while the virtue of loyalty to the throne (not mentioned in Zhu Xi's version, or even in the early Ming version, out of respect for Zhu's original formulation) is again striking for its absence from this otherwise markedly theocratic ritual.

By contrast to the Six Maxims, the Sixteen, as given below, add many items of an authoritarian and bureaucratic character that are quite foreign to the spirit of Zhu Xi's original community compact — e.g., matters pertaining to law as administered by the territorial agents of state administration; to collective security units; to the ostracizing of deserters and miscreants; to the prompt payment of taxes; to the suppression of heterodoxy — none of which are mentioned by Zhu Xi. Also striking here is the attention to scholarly achievement, which the accompanying commentary and popular expositions clearly connect with advancement through the examination system, the prime means of official recruitment. Ironically, Zhu Xi, the great scholar himself, had said nothing whatever about scholarly training in his compact; here, however, it ranks well ahead of Zhu's instructions to the young in general (item 11), which had been oriented toward moral conduct in the family, neighborhood, and village community, not to success in the state bureaucracy.

THE SACRED EDICT

1. Esteem most highly filial piety and brotherly submission, in order to give due importance to human moral relations.
2. Behave with generosity toward your kindred, in order to illustrate harmony and benignity.
3. Cultivate peace and concord in your neighborhoods, in order to prevent quarrels and litigations.
4. Give importance to agriculture and sericulture, in order to ensure a sufficiency of clothing and food.
5. Show that you prize moderation and economy, in order to prevent the lavish waste of your means.
6. Foster colleges and schools, in order to give the training of scholars a proper start.
7. Do away with errant teachings, in order to exalt the correct doctrine.
8. Expound on the laws, in order to warn the ignorant and obstinate.
9. Explain ritual decorum and deference, in order to enrich manners and customs.
10. Attend to proper callings, in order to stabilize the people's sense of dedication [to their work].
11. Instruct sons and younger brothers, in order to prevent them from doing what is wrong.

12. Put a stop to false accusations, in order to protect the honest and good.
13. Warn against sheltering deserters, in order to avoid being involved in their punishment.
14. Promptly remit your taxes, in order to avoid being pressed for payment.
15. Combine in collective security groups (*baojia*), in order to put an end to theft and robbery.
16. Eschew enmity and anger, in order to show respect for the person and life.

[Adapted and revised from Legge, "Imperial Confucianism" — dB]

# Chapter 26

## POPULAR VALUES AND BELIEFS

The vast majority of Chinese in premodern times lived in villages and small towns of a few thousand people at most. Some, such as peddlers and entertainers, traveled a great deal, but most ventured no further than the nearest market town. Their cultural horizons were also narrow, since most could not read or write. All they learned of the outside world and of the great traditions of philosophy, religion, history, and poetry had to come to them in speech or song. The few in a village who were literate generally could read only texts written in a fairly simple style; they would have had difficulty understanding the complex and allusive writings of the learned. Yet there is no question that villagers and literati shared a common culture. This does not mean that every Chinese, no matter what his or her education or social position, had the same values and attitudes and beliefs about the human and divine worlds. Yet the many class-, dialect-, and occupation-based subcultures, with all their differences, were all recognizably Chinese. What made this shared culture possible? A partial answer to this question can be discovered by thinking about the ways in which religious ideas and moral values, such as the Buddhist idea of reincarnation, or Confucian attitudes toward ritual, were communicated to ordinary people.

What we might call vernacular ideology — the largely unexamined stock of beliefs, attitudes, and values that most people in a culture share — was to a certain extent absorbed unconsciously by Chinese villagers through everyday language, customary behavior, the symbols that were used to decorate everything from houses to clothes, and the like. It was "in the air," as we say, embedded in the fabric of life. Interesting and important though this aspect of people's beliefs is, however, it is almost impossible to study historically.

Moral and religious values were also communicated intentionally, of course. Often this took the form of spontaneous responses to everyday events: the scolding of a naughty child, the quotation of a proverb to comfort a friend in distress. Extemporaneous moral guidance of this sort took place constantly in traditional China as it does everywhere, in interchanges between parents and children, teachers and students, friends and relations, and people working together. These naturally are also virtually impossible for the historian to study.

However, values and beliefs were also communicated in more structured ways, of which many written traces have been left behind that *can* be studied. These traces are of two types: first, books and pamphlets that were written for people to read to themselves or aloud, even if their formal education was fairly limited; second, opera scripts, liturgies, and other texts that served as the basis of scripted performances of one kind or another or that were directly derived from performances, like transcripts. Though we will look at both material meant for reading and material intended to be performed, the second is far more important for our purposes than the first. Our performance-related texts are divided into two broad categories, those related to ensemble performance such as ritual and opera and those related to solo/duo performance, which can be in verse, prose, or a combination of the two. These five types of performance-related text are treated in the first two sections of this chapter.

The solo/duo performance genres were generally more didactic than the ensemble genres; that is, they were often written specifically to inculcate religious beliefs or ethical standards. In this they resemble, sometimes very closely, the didactic writings aimed at a popular reading audience that are presented in the third section of this chapter.


## PART ONE: ENSEMBLE PERFORMANCE

Rituals and operas were from time to time overtly didactic, but instruction was not usually their primary purpose. Nevertheless, since the fundamental function of ritual was to order the relations of humans with the gods and with each other, the teaching of values and inculcation of beliefs was a natural and inevitable accompaniment of any ritual. By the same token, although the primary function of opera was to entertain gods and men, from the very beginning of the tradition in Jin and Yuan times almost all Chinese drama was moralistic, and therefore it taught about standards of behavior. Thus both ritual and opera, each in its own way, communicated values and beliefs. Moreover, these forms communicated with special power because they used music, dance, gesture, and costume, as well as words, and thereby involved the emotions of their audiences to a much higher degree than reading or recitation did.

By late imperial times the world of performance in China had become fantastically elaborated, with hundreds of local opera genres, probably at least as many kinds of solo performance, and an almost infinite variety of local rituals. Ritual had of course been the bedrock of Confucian thought since the time of Confucius himself and had been the core of Chinese elite culture long before that, but after the Tang dynasty theatricals of all kinds became increasingly important. By the early nineteenth century a European traveler, Father Evariste Huc, who had spent years in China, noted that the country resembled "an immense fair, where . . . you see in all quarters stages and mountebanks, jokers and comedians, laboring uninterruptedly to amuse the public. Over the whole surface of the country . . . rich and poor, mandarins and people, all the Chinese, without exception, are passionately addicted to dramatic representations. There are theaters everywhere."[1] Nevertheless, rituals of all kinds retained their central role in Chinese symbolic life, and Father Huc could with equal accuracy have characterized the country by its profusion of temples, religious processions, and family ceremonials. In short, performance — scripted performance — was central to the communication of values in traditional China, and ritual and opera were the most important forms of scripted performance.

## RITUAL

We have already seen that ritual played a central role in the life of the educated elite from the earliest times. By the late imperial era, after centuries — indeed, millennia — of indoctrination both overt and covert by the clerical elite of literati, priests, and monks, the lives of ordinary people had also come to be suffused with ritual. They experienced ritual in two settings: the community and the household. Community rituals were usually focused on a temple that had been built by the people and was maintained by them, quite independent of ecclesiastical or governmental prompting. The most important household rituals were, by contrast, focused on the family altar, at which offerings to the ancestors and to various deities were made.[2]

### Community Ritual

Rituals were celebrated collectively by villagers and townspeople at a fixed time every year (or at set intervals that could be as long as forty years) and also at times of crisis or thanksgiving. Annual festivals were generally understood to celebrate the birthday of a god who received cult in a village temple. Special

---

1. Huc, *The Chinese Empire*, pp. 263–264.

2. There was a third type of ritual, which combined features of both communal and household ritual. This was lineage ritual. Since it was important only in regions where lineage organization was strong, we will not consider it here.

rituals were held when the villagers believed themselves to be in danger or when they wished to celebrate a major accomplishment, such as the renovation of a temple.

## PROCESSIONS

Village rituals almost always began with a large procession in which the god who was being honored was carried on a palanquin, accompanied by many performers and what we would call floats. Processions served to announce the beginning of a temple festival and to identify the neighborhoods or villages that were participating in it. They were important to the people at large because — unlike many parts of the ritual proper — they were entirely public and they were exciting and entertaining to watch. Villagers from miles around would come to see them, sometimes staying with friends or relatives overnight. The very size and richness of the processions showed the degree of devotion the gods deserved, and the atmosphere of celebration and excitement taught the appropriate style in which that devotion should be expressed.

### A PROCESSION ON THE BIRTHDAY OF THE SANZONG GOD

This is a description of an unusually elaborate procession that was performed as recently as the late 1930s. It was centered on the Sanzong Temple in the Big West Gate quarter of the county capital of Zhangzi, in southeastern Shanxi province. The account was written by a native of Zhangzi County who spent many years collecting information from local residents about their temple festivals.

On the morning of the fifth day of the sixth month the traveling image of the Sanzong God [the ancient drought god known as Hou Yi, the mythical archer who shot nine suns from the sky when ten came out all at once] went out in his palanquin, carried by eight men and accompanied by music, to the Temple of the Flame Emperor [also known as Shennong, the god of farming] to quietly await the spirit tablets or palanquins of the gods of the surrounding villages who were responding to his invitation. In the afternoon around 3:00 P.M. they all returned to the Sanzong Temple. This procession was much longer and more impressive than the morning one, with many different kinds of display. It wound through the streets and alleys like a blue-green dragon writhing its tail, accompanied by loud music. The crowds of people undulated like waves, as happy as at New Year's. They came, dressed in new clothes, from twenty *li* around.

The procession began with an honor guard of old musicians. The first pair carried red banners with the words "Stand Aside!" and "Silence!" while the banners of the second pair read "Pure Way" and "Flying Tigers." The rest carried banners and weapons with fanciful names such as Golden Melons and

Big Marsh Fans. These ritual implements all came from the Laozi Temple in Nanzhuang Village, about a mile and a half away. This honor guard was an old custom, and it led the procession no matter which neighborhood was the sponsor of the temple festival that year.

After the honor guard came martial arts troupes led by strong men brandishing rope whips. They walked ahead to clear the way and were followed by men in single file, sometimes walking, sometimes dancing, who dueled with short spears, demonstrated "boxing," and wielded swords. . . . They were followed by the palanquins of the Five Honored Gods, known locally as the Little Framework Lords, led by *dharma* cymbals and altar drums. The gods, dressed in caps and robes, had clay heads, with faces painted red, white, blue, black, and yellow, and wooden framework bodies [over which they wore their robes].

Then came a troupe of flute players whose music sounded like the wind, leading the "springy four-man palanquin." This was made of padded satin quilts, folded, and padded satin mattresses. . . . In the middle of the palanquin rode two porcelain dolls, secured with cords made of colored silk floss. Antique vases, jade mirrors, and other old objects made of carved wood or carved stone were attached to each side. Through the middle of the palanquin ran springy wooden poles wrapped with colored silk. The young men carrying it . . . rhythmically bounced the palanquin up and down so that the tassels flew about.

Next came the "stiff four-man palanquin," which also was preceded by a troupe of musicians playing softly. The stiff palanquin was made of wood and was shaped like a pagoda. It was square above and below, and had brightly painted designs on each side, and was also adorned with silk, flowers, and mirrors large and small. At the top was attached an object like a feather duster, made of chicken feathers and over a yard long, to symbolize the palanquin's cloud-brushing height. Strips of colored cloth hung down all around, tangling and fluttering. . . . Each of the palanquins . . . was preceded and followed by musicians. Each was followed by several "spirit horses," fully saddled and bridled, with flowers on their heads, which were provided for the invited gods to ride.

There were any number of "lifted characters." In these, an iron frame with a long iron rod extending above it was tied securely to a strong young man and hidden under his clothes. Then an actor or actress in costume was tied to the rod in such a way that he or she could freely sing, gesture, and speak in midair, six feet or more above the ground. (They first put on their makeup, then were secured to the rods, and finally put on their costumes.)

There also were "shouldered characters." These were square platforms like tables that were about a yard on a side and were carried by two men. A specially shaped iron rod was fixed securely in the platform, and an actress was tied to its upper end while an actor stood on the table beneath her, the costumes of both concealing the rod. Each platform presented a scene from an opera. . . . The performers were all youths of about fifteen years of age.

In addition, many "little stories" were crowded in between the more elaborate creations, which were called "stories." These included "Golden Buildings," "Silver Sunshades," "Solitary Dragon Colts," "Stilt Walkers," "Double Stilt Walkers," "The Son Pulls the Basket,"[3] "Boats on Dry Land," "Two Demons Fight Over a Bushel Basket," and so on. The Golden Buildings and Silver Sunshades . . . had all sorts of women's and children's gold and silver jewelry hanging on them. As they were carried along, the natural movements of the bearers made the jewelry tinkle constantly, creating an extraordinarily attractive effect. . . .

A troupe of ten or more musicians and a group of actors dressed as generals came next. There was one generalissimo wearing a commander's helmet, green armor, a long beard, and court boots, accompanied by four bit players holding aloft fluttering banners. They rode five large horses that the acting troupe used to pull their costume and prop trunks. Behind these "generals" came the Golden Drum Banner, which had been sent by the yamen [the office of the local official]. Two yamen runners went before it, carrying big banners and beating gongs. . . .

The Master of Ceremonial and all the other officiants came next, followed by the great carriage of the Sanzong God. The traveling image of the god had a clay head with gold headdress and a wooden body clothed in dragon robes. The god sat in an eight-man dragon palanquin whose seat was covered with real tiger skin. The god was red-faced and had a long beard; he held a plaque of office in his hands. (He had been carried to his temporary palace at the Flame Emperor Temple in the morning.) His title was "Illustrious State-Protecting Spiritual-Power-Bestowing King." At the end of the procession there was a man carrying a yellow silk sunshade and another carrying a six-foot-long banner, red with black edges, on which were the words "Arbiter of Destiny of the Three Armies."

When the procession reached its destination, most of the "story" troupes took off their costumes at the foot of the outer stage. Only the musicians and the yamen runners who were crowded around the god's palanquin entered the temple grounds.

[Zhang Zhennan, "Yue ju yu sai," pp. 249–52, supplemented by his "Yue ju he sai," pp. 5–6, and his "Gu Shangdang minjian 'Ying shen sai she' su gui" — DJ]

## TEMPLE CEREMONIES ON A GOD'S BIRTHDAY

The heart of a village ceremonial, whether it was the celebration of a god's birthday or the performance of a communal thanksgiving or exorcism, was a

---

3. A traditional story in which a man, accompanied by his young son, drags his aged father out into the fields in a basket and abandons him. The man's son brings the basket along with him when they return home. When his father asks him why, he replies that he is saving it to use when the time comes to abandon *him*. The man then goes and brings the aged father back home.

ritual program that was performed in and around a specific temple. Local custom, not ecclesiastical regulations, determined what happened at a given ritual, though if the ceremonies were presided over by Daoist or Buddhist clerics, at least part of the liturgy would follow canonical forms, some very old. But many local rituals were overseen by ritual specialists who were neither Daoist nor Buddhist. They were known by such terms as "master of ceremony" (*zhuli*), "ritual master" (*lisheng*), or even "yinyang master" (*yinyang sheng*), since they sometimes also functioned as geomancers and diviners. Some of them possessed handbooks containing the texts of the prayers, invocations, and announcements that were used in the rituals of the temple festival. Most of these handbooks have been lost, but over the past ten years a few have been discovered, and more will probably come to light as work on village ritual traditions proceeds. The following two selections are taken from these rare documents.

### THE GREAT *SAI* RITUAL OF ZHANGZI COUNTY, SHANXI

The following address came at the formal beginning of the celebration of the birthday of the Sanzong God, whose procession was described in the preceding section. It was made by the Master of Ceremony to the villagers who had duties to perform during the ritual. The *shê* were precincts or neighborhoods.

To the honored god, the Jade Emperor, Supreme Thearch of Vast Heaven: Today the individuals with responsibilities in the *sai* make obeisance before you at the foot of the steps. The preliminary courtesies are finished; let every rank listen to the commands [of the Jade Emperor]. Let no one dare act on his own authority; humbly wait to learn the god's sagely intentions and receive the divine commands.

The honored god, the Jade Emperor, Supreme Thearch, issues his decrees and instructions: Let all those in the hall and at the foot of the steps, before the god and behind the god, the greater and lesser Shê Leaders, the heads of the Six Offices and the Chefs, the Pavilioners, the Attendants, the Libationers, the Servers, the Monitors, the Umbrella Men, the Grooms, the Sunshade Handlers, the Incense Elders of the Left and Right, the Platter-Bearing Pavilioners, the responsible Musicians and Actors — let all proceed to the Cinnabar Courtyard in the temple to listen to the divine commands. Bow down and attend!

I have heard that prayers in the spring and thanksgiving in the autumn, the *sai* in the summer and the sacrifices in the winter, have come down to us from ancient times. Today it is our good fortune to encounter the birthday of the honored god so-and-so. The rich mats have been spread, the umbrellas have been opened and turned. The sagely host of August Heaven has been respectfully invited to draw near the precious hall; all the gods of Sovereign Earth have descended to the incense altar. The chief Shê Leader stands respectfully in the front, all the Incense Elders are deeply reverent. Now I proclaim to you:

... Today the *Shê* Leaders so-and-so humbly and reverently make an offering in recompense for the favor of Heaven's rain and dew. [Heaven] bestows the clouds and sends the rain, and the winds that blow over all the lands. Sowing and reaping are moistened with rain, the five kinds of soil bring forth the five grains, the grasses and trees of the hills and streams flourish, the gardens and groves are verdant, all because the wind and rain have come when they should, and the yin and yang are in balance. So the people have hope for an autumn harvest, on which life depends. Without thought of personal gain they requite the gods of Heaven and Earth; they sacrifice with sincere hearts.

On the occasion of the god's birthday we respectfully invite all his subordinates to smell the incense and listen to the music. . . . The *Rites* [actually *Analects* 12.1] say: "See nothing without ritual, hear nothing without ritual, speak nothing without ritual, do nothing without ritual." These four are the ritual of man.

Wine takes pride of place: presented to kinfolk and nourishing the old, an offering to the gods, used to welcome visitors and entertain guests — how could one not have it? Warm it and let it clear, [but do not] drink to excess.

In the villages and hamlets, . . . there are neither poor nor rich, noble nor base; farmers yield on the paths between fields, travelers yield on the roads, the young make way for the old, and the poor make way for the noble. . . . Act with goodness, do not take up what is evil. The good shun [evil] as they would snakes and scorpions.

I proclaim and inform all the gentlemen of the *shê*: how can you not know your own hearts? Endure all things, do not offend even in the slightest. For those who lose their grasp on proper measure and take up evil ways, the honored god will send down heavy punishment.

*The text then goes on to exhort each of the groups of officiants in turn, starting with the* Shê *Leaders.*

[*Tang yuexing tu*, pp. 2–6 — DJ]

### COMMUNAL EXORCISM

The *sai*, like all temple-based rituals, expressed the village's devotion and gratitude toward their god. Its tone for the most part was dignified and elevated. There were other communal ceremonials that had a different purpose and a different tone: exorcisms. We can speak of two poles of popular religious ritual, the conventional and the ecstatic, and two dominant forms, sacrifice and exorcism, though very few actual ceremonies were purely one or the other. The difference between the following ritual and the *sai* is visible above all in the central role of the spirit-medium and in the atmosphere of barely contained hysteria. The liturgy has moments of considerable beauty, but the great bed of red-hot coals at the center of the ritual arena created a very different emotional ambience from a god's birthday. (Note, however, that this was an annual affair, unlike many communal exorcisms, which were performed at moments when the community felt especially threatened by demonic forces.)

### THE REFINING FIRE RITUAL OF SHENZE VILLAGE, ZHEJIANG

The Refining Fire, or Fire of Great Peace, is a great exorcistic, protective, and healing ritual featuring fire-walking that is performed in Shenze village, in central Zhejiang, every year on the ninth day of the ninth month. The central deity is Duke Hu, a native of the area who was an official early in the Song dynasty. This selection is based on documents collected in Shenze and on the report of an observer of a performance of the ritual in 1992. The ceremony began in early evening with the consecration of the altars surrounding the ritual arena, where the fire would be built. At the outset the priest chanted and sang the *Liturgy for Issuing the Great Notification*. Its opening section calls on the gods of the Daoist pantheon to take note of the commencement of the ritual and the pure intentions of those on whose behalf the priest is carrying it out.

The Great Ultimate divided Heaven from Earth,
And the light and pure ascended to assemble in Heaven.
Men are able to cultivate the Ultimate Way,
Themselves becoming true immortals. . . .
Bowing, we let the smoke of the hundred-harmonied precious incense
Wreathe through six terraces, powerfully fragrant.
We burn it in the golden censer,
Spreading it throughout the Jade Bureau.
The auspicious mist ascends to make a terrace,
The propitious clouds spread out to form a cover.
The incense communicates the supplications of earnest hearts;
It reaches to the wondrous gate of the myriad sages.
Today we thrice offer incense,
Announcing the commands everywhere.
Hearts resolved, we make the first offering of incense.
Its fragrance arrives at the Palace of Primeval Chaos;
Everywhere throughout the Palace of the Three Realms of Primeval Chaos
It becomes the flowery covering, an offering
To the Reverences of the Three Realms of Primeval Chaos.
Hearts resolved, we make the second offering of incense.
Its fragrance arrives at the Palace of the Heavenly Caverns. . . .
Hearts resolved, we make the third offering of incense.
Its fragrance arrives at the Palace of the Profound Font. . . .

*Next comes the "Incense Hymn," sung softly to the accompaniment of drums:*

> . . . Misty in the morning sun the incense smoke forms a cover,
> Turning about in the wind to transmit the sentiments of the people.
> To the marvelous fragrance before the Jade Throne, I now intone the
>     precious *gāthā*:
> The jade censer's propitious mists ascend to form the cloud canopy,
> The auspicious smoke of the cavern altar gathers at the precious terrace.
> The Golden Lad gently grasps and offers up the *garu* and sandalwood
>     incense;
> The Jade Maiden transmits and recites [the memorial] to inform the
>     Three Realms.
> This precious censer now summons,
> The Numinous Officials of the Four Shifts all descend and draw near.
> Pure feeling moves those on high, reaching the three realms,
> Where officials of Heaven, Earth, and Water are moved like reflections
>     in a mirror.

*Next, the "Water Gāthā" is intoned, during which the chanting of the priest gradually
increases in volume and becomes more excited:*

> . . . Yielding in accord with the vast expanse, the numinous spring
> Flows into the great river day and night without stopping,
> Dissolving into the vast sky as rain and fog,
> Finally returning to the billowing surf of the great ocean.
> Perfecting merit and permeating without limit,
> Of corresponding quality, Heaven and Earth exist of themselves;
> The Five Phases take it as their chief,
> The Six Bureaus revere it as immortal.
> Desiring purification of this ritual assembly,
> We intone the Water *Gāthā*:
> The Five Dragons spit forth the water of the Jasper Pool,
> It goes to the cinnabar well of the old immortal.
> The Great Emperor has depended on it for hundreds of billions of years,
> King Yu transformed it into the Hundred Rivers.
> My hands grasp the heavenly treasure seal.
> I hold it to draw from the violet and golden spring.
> One drop can disperse the beneficence of the rain and fog,
> And spread everywhere throughout the ritual assembly, purifying and
>     cleansing.

*At the climax of the Refining Fire ritual the spirit-medium and selected villagers walk
across a large circular bed of red-hot charcoal. Before they can cross the coals, however,*

*the specially constructed gates occupying the cardinal points around the Fire Altar must
be opened, activating the cosmic forces that protect the participants from injury. The
priest sounds the Dragon Horn, strikes his drum, and wields his sword as he begins the
"Opening of the Water-Fire Gates." The interchanges between the crowd, the priest, and
the spirit-medium in the following sections have been strongly influenced by the conventions of local opera.*

The Dragon Horn has sounded, and its notes rise soaring up to Heaven.
The Heavenly soldiers and spirit generals will all arrive together.
At the first summons the Heavenly Gate opens,
At the second summons the Buddha Dharma comes,
At the third summons the patriarchs arrive in person,
At the fourth summons the four great Diamond Kings appear before us,
At the fifth summons the five Thunder Generals issue orders as if they are
    right here,
At the sixth summons the Six Ding and Six Jia appear before our eyes,
At the seventh summons the seven stars of the Northern Dipper come to
    safeguard the spirits,
At the eighth summons the Eight Immortals decapitate the demons,
At the ninth summons the troops and cavalry of the Nine Continents arrive,
At the tenth summons, the Great Emperor Duke Hu comes to preside over
    the altar.
The troop-mustering First Master descends and draws nigh,
And refines the merit-making Water-Fire Altar.

Priest [speaks]: Assembled headman generals!
Participants [speak]: Here!
Priest: Who will lead the ocean troops and ocean cavalry?
Participants: We will lead the ocean troops and ocean cavalry!
Priest: Assembled generals!
Participants: Here!
Priest: Lead forth the troops and ocean cavalry!
Participants: We will lead forth the ocean troops and ocean cavalry!
Priest: What will determine it?
Participants: Thrice [casting] the divination blocks will determine it!
Priest: Thrice cast the divination blocks!

*After the divining blocks are cast, the priest leads the crowd of "generals" in a number
of circumambulations of the Altar of Heaven and performs rituals at the four gates to
seal off the sacred space. The spirit-medium and the participants assemble at the altar,
barefoot and clad only in red shorts. As the trident bearers and other participants start
to tremble and twitch, two gong bearers take up places on either side of the spirit-medium.
He too starts to writhe and twitch as the two large gongs are beaten violently close to*

*his ears. Then, when his entire body is jerking about violently in a state of extreme agitation, he calms slightly, changes demeanor, and leaps up onto the offering table of the Altar of Heaven. Looking down over the crowd, he announces himself as Duke Hu.*

Spirit-medium: Striding the cloud tops, gazing over the Nine Realms — assembled families and headmen, for what reason do you block the way of my steed with the continuous beating of drums and gongs?

Crowd: To aid you, Duke Hu, in one round of the Refining Fire of Great Peace.

Spirit-medium: Excellent! When I get to a subdistrict, I protect the subdistrict; when I get to a village, I protect the village. I bless the entire village so that the six domestic animals flourish, the five grains are harvested in abundance, the winds are mild and the rains seasonable, the country prosperous and the people at peace. I assist the yeoman tillers so that when they till the fields, the fields produce grain; so that when they till the hillsides, the hillsides produce millet. I assist the merchant gentlemen so that one coin in capital yields ten thousand in interest. I assist the gentlemen in their prime, like tigers leaping and dragons soaring, so that they may be as strong as dragons and tigers. I assist the elderly so that with ruddy complexion and white hair they turn from age and return to youth. I assist the young boys in studying their books and composing verse so that their names will be posted on the golden roll [of those who have passed the examinations]. I assist the young maidens so that they may be clever and bright, like peach blossoms in a painting.

Crowd: Many thanks for your lordship's blessing!

Spirit-medium: Assembled families and brethren, those in front and those in the back, do not contend for the front or dread the rear; I'll take you together on my mount. Headmen, assist me by sounding the gongs to open the way!

Crowd: Here!

*As the gongs sound, the spirit-medium takes up the charm-water bowl from the offering table, fills his mouth, and sprays the water out over the increasingly agitated crowd of villagers. He sprays a second time, and the crowd becomes more agitated: the spirits are descending. With the third mouthful they too are possessed and jump about violently. The spirit-medium picks up a length of iron chain from the altar table and, grasping one end with each hand, swings it over his head three times while facing the spirit tablets, then passes it down to the throng below. He repeats this procedure with a second chain, the incense burner, and a pitchfork. Finally, he grabs the charm-water bowl, leaps down from the offering table and, following the lead of the incense master, races around the Fire Altar. Arriving at the eastern Water-Fire Gate, the spirit-medium takes another mouthful from the charm-water bowl and sprays it on the fire, after which he stamps his bare foot in the coals, indicating that the gate is opened for the participants to pass through. This procedure is repeated at each of the other gates. Then the spirit-medium, followed by the villagers, strides across the coals, entering through the northern gate and exiting through the southern, then entering through the western gate and exiting through the eastern. Two or three passes through the fire is considered one "hall"; after three halls have been completed, the ritual is declared a success. Throughout this phase the on-lookers are cheering wildly while gongs and drums sound incessantly.*

*When the frenzy of the fire walking has receded, the priest captures any lingering dangerous spirits or pestilential airs, wraps them in paper, and confines them in a cooking pot filled with glowing coals and ash from incense sticks. The pot is then carried out of the village along a route that is kept secret from neighboring villagers and buried, the demons confined within it. Having returned to the site of the ceremony, the priest leads the lineage heads, the spirit-medium, the incense master, and the remaining participants around the dying embers of the fire one last time, to thank the spirits and send them on their way back to the spirit world. This is called "Thanking the Fire and Seeing Off the Gods." Finally, the many ghosts who have come to watch the ritual must be bribed with offerings so that they will leave the village. Six bowls of rice, with one stick of incense inserted in each, and three bowls of rice gruel are placed on a table that is set up near the fire altar. After the priest chants two final prayers, two gong bearers lead a procession out of the village. Incense sticks have been planted every two or three feet along the road, and people in the procession burn spirit money and sprinkle rice gruel along the ground as they go in offering to the orphaned souls. At the edge of town, any food remaining is left for wandering ghosts.*

[Adapted from Williams, "The Refining Fire," pp. 34–53 —DJ]

## Domestic Ritual

Most villagers made regular offerings at an altar, usually quite simple, in the central room of the house, on which were placed symbols of the family's ancestors and other gods. Other rituals, such as offering incense before a wood-block print of the stove god, were performed every day, and images of gods and sacred symbols could be found throughout the house in the form of woodblock prints, decorative carvings, and designs on clothing, bedding, eating utensils, and the like.[4] Of the rituals that were carried out on a regular basis, the most important were the sacrifices to the ancestors, which were supervised by the head of the family. But there also were special rituals that were performed only when required. Of these, funerals were by far the most significant, and virtually every family engaged a ritual specialist to supervise them.

Death rituals were important on two levels: first, they were an essential expression of the filial piety of the household head; not to carry out proper funeral rituals was to fail one's parents and ancestors and invite the contempt of the

---

4. For more information on the domestic cult of the Stove God, see pp. 126–27.

community. That is why families often spent more than they could afford on funerals, to the dismay of some local officials. But on another level, death rituals were needed because they protected the living against the possibly malevolent spirits of the dead. This tension between Confucian reverence toward parents and ancestors and the pre-Confucian — indeed, anti-Confucian — terror of ghosts can be traced through all Chinese popular funerary ritual. In Daoist funeral ritual, for example, this ambivalence can be seen in the simultaneous use of both priests (*daoshi*) and exorcists (*fashi*) or, as in the case of the selection that follows, by one person assuming both roles.

### THE ATTACK ON HELL, A POPULAR FUNERAL RITUAL

The Attack on Hell is only one segment of Daoist funeral ceremonial, though an intensely dramatic one that strongly engages the interest of the mourners (unlike some of the more esoteric parts). The full ceremony lasts two days and has, by one count, nineteen other segments. The ritual described below took place on November 24, 1980, in Tainan, Taiwan. The description, by an eyewitness, is supplemented by liturgical texts and information provided by the chief priest. In this performance the distinction between ritual and theater, already blurred in the Refining Fire ritual, virtually disappears. The entire central section closely resembles the popular comic dialogues called *xiangsheng*. Yet, needless to say, the whole matter was of the highest seriousness. This passage provides an almost perfect example of how ritual can teach values.

Normally, the Attack on Hell is performed before a table set up in front of the house of the deceased person. A square "fortress" representing Hell, which is made of paper and bamboo and can be large enough to hold a person, is placed at the far end of the table, and the mourners, one of them holding the soul-banner, form a semicircle behind it, facing the priest. A scroll with the character "gate" written on it is unfurled on the north side of the altar, behind the priest. The fortress is white under ordinary circumstances, red for deaths by accident or suicide. Sometimes on the front there are paper images of two infernal gate guardians, Buffalohead and Horsehead, and on the back the goddess of mercy, Guanyin, flanked by the Earth God and the City God. Inside the fortress is placed the image that represents the soul of the deceased. A small basin for washing, a change of clothing, and other items are set up in front of the table so that the soul can change and get cleaned up when it gets out of the filth of Hell.

The Attack on Hell is an exorcistic ritual. In it, the whole family crouches in a tight semicircle around the fortress, and everyone reaches out a hand to help shake it at appropriate moments. Family members are involved more directly than in any other ritual . . . [and] the tense drama of shaking the fortress often leads to tears. Clearly, to the participating family members, the Attack on

Hell involves not only the soul's rescue from Hell but also its departure from their midst. . . . The necessity of this leave-taking is the real source of the tension that manifests itself in the attack. An exorcism, its essential purpose is to ensure that the deceased *not* return to haunt the family.

After a number of invocations and libations, the priest burns a memorial and then sprays symbol-water toward the south and toward the north; then he lights a paper cone and uses it to purify a long, pronged staff and the fly-whisk. He drops the burning "old money" and steps over it. Then, as in a theater, he introduces himself by singing a verse:

> I recall that day when I was wandering in the mountains,
> I saw the tears flowing from the eyes of all mortals.
> A student of the Way on Dragon-Tiger Mountain,
> I swore my heart would not rest until I had achieved the Way.

He carries on in ordinary speech:

> I am none other than the priest of Marvelous Movement Who Saves from Distress. I come from the Mountain of the Great Net [*Daluo*, the supreme heaven beyond the Three Realms]. I have come down from my mountain this evening for no other reason than that my host has asked me to his home to invite the Three Pure Ones, Ancestors of the Way, to recite the litanies of confession and compassion and to reimburse the treasury of the underworld. The merit of the confessions has been achieved, the pardon has been proclaimed, and I have received the directives of the Ancestors of the Way to come to the fortress to save the soul of so-and-so.

The priest then mimes traveling to Hell, during which he sings a song. At the end of the song he says:

> I hear before me very distinctly the sound of drum and gongs. This must be the Gate of the Demons in the fortress of the underworld. I'll hide to one side and see what hour they are announcing.

There is a great burst of percussion, which ends with a series of drumbeats and blows to the gong announcing that it is midnight. This leads the priest to sing another song:

> The first watch has been drummed,
> The drum has been beat in the drum tower.
> Man lives a bare hundred years,
> A hundred years that pass like a distant dream.

> Begin to practice early;
> Do not wait until it is too late.

The priest then goes to the gate, shakes his staff at it, and calls on the demon general in charge that night to open up. Again there is the sound of percussion, and again the priest sings:

> The Demon Gate before the Hall of Yama opens:
> Cangues and chains are lined up on either side. . . .
> This is the place of judgment,
> Where each person gets his just deserts.

At this point a new character, the guardian of Hell's gate, enters the scene. He also begins by announcing himself:

> I have received King Yama's instructions to guard the Demon Gate. A little devil has just come in and reported that the soul of someone who has died is knocking loudly at our gate. As it is an auspicious day and the night is clear, it must be a good man or a faithful woman from the world of the living who wishes to pass through my gate.

> Priest (*impatiently*): Hurry and open up.
> Demon: Who's knocking so loud on my door at this hour?
> Priest: It's me, the priest of Marvelous Movement from the Mountain of the Great Net.
> Demon: Why isn't the priest on his mountain studying the Way, reciting scriptures, picking medicinal plants, and subliming the elixir of immortality?

The priest explains that he has come "with directives from the Ancestors of the Way" to save so-and-so, and then says:

> Priest: Sorry to bother you. Hurry and open up.
> Demon: So the priest wants to enter the gate?
> Priest: Precisely.
> Demon: That's easy enough.
> Priest: Then open up.
> Demon: Just let me ask the priest whether he brought any money or any precious gifts for us devils when he came down from his mountain?
> Priest: That's no way to talk.
> Demon: How so?
> Priest: I'm a student of the Way. I eat what others give me. I've come all alone ten thousand miles. How could I carry any money or gifts for you?
> Demon: You really have nothing?

Priest: Nothing.

Demon: Then forget it.

Priest: I'll forget it. Just open up!

Demon: Has the priest never heard the words of men of old?

Priest: Say on.

Demon: From of old there is an eight-character saying about the way to open the mandarin's gate: 'No money, don't come; with money, it's open.' If you've no money, you may as well be off. (*Laughs.*)

The demon has no need to tell him all this, replies the priest:

Priest: I knew it before you said it.

Demon: Knew what?

Priest: That all your talk is just to get some money.

The demon asks why else he should be losing sleep and exposing himself to the cold.

Priest: Well, if it's money you want, my host has given me some paper money to bring along. Wait while I burn some paper money for you demons.

The priest lights a paper cone and throws it at the drummer. The demon asks where the money has been burnt.

Priest: At the foot of the Drum Tower.

The demon doesn't want to leave his post to get it. Besides, paper money is as worthless in the underworld as it is in the land of the living; he wants "copper coins." "What about all the paper money burned on Qingming, or in the middle of the seventh month?" asks the priest. "Where does it all go?" The demon responds that Yama often sends "little devils into the world of the living to spy on sinners," and they need copper coins for such trips because merchants don't accept paper money. The priest repeats all that in the form of a question, and the demon replies, "Precisely."

Priest: I haven't a single copper coin.

Demon: Then forget it.

Priest: I'll forget it. Just open up!

Demon: Priest, are you aware that we judge the living and the dead according to their deeds here at the Demon Gate?

This judgment, he goes on to explain, is based on two books, one for those who have lived out their span of life, the other for those who have not.

Priest: How does your great King Yama judge someone who has done good and whose years are not yet up, but comes before the Demon Gate by mistake?

Demon: Someone who has done good and whose years are not yet up?

Priest: Just so.

Demon: Our great king looks in the Record of Life to see whether this person, while he was alive, worshiped the Three Treasures, was a filial child to his parents, helped build bridges and roads, took delight in good deeds, and loved alms-giving. If so, our great king sends the Golden Lad and Jade Maiden to bring him back to the other world. Such is the Great Book of Life.

Priest: And what about the bad man, how do you clerks of Yama judge such a one when he dies and comes to the Demon Gate?

Demon: Our great king sees from the Register of Death that this person, while he was alive, did not respect the Three Treasures, was disobedient to his parents, twitted his elder brother, beat his wife, killed, committed arson, and did every imaginable kind of evil deed. When he sees this, the great King Yama sends the buffaloheaded general with a pitchfork and the horseheaded general with chains to haul him into the eighteen prisons of Fengdu. . . . Such is the Great Book of Death.

Priest: So you here at the Demon Gate urge people to do good, do you?

Demon: That's right.

Priest: Good?

Demon: Good gets a good reward.

Priest: Bad?

Demon: Bad gets a bad return. Sooner or later, everyone gets what he has coming.

Priest: But you demons don't pay back everyone.

Demon: That's because their time hasn't come, it's not because we here at Demon Gate don't repay good and evil.

Priest: You say it's that their time hasn't come, not that you at Demon Gate don't judge and repay good and evil?

Demon: Just so.

Priest: Now that you devils have discussed good and evil so clearly, open the gate so I can go through.

Demon: The priest has heard that the two great Registers of Life and Death are important here. What is important to you who study the Way?

Priest: For us students of the Way, when we leave home, it's the texts and teachings of the scriptures that are most important.

Demon: Wonderful! (*Laughs.*)

Priest: Wonderful? Don't talk that demon talk!

Demon: No, that was a joyous "Wonderful!" from the heart. Priest, sing us a snatch from one of those fine scriptures from the Mountain of the Jade Capital in the Great Net that saves the souls of the deceased, and when we've heard it loud and clear, we'll let you through.

Priest: Can demons listen to scripture?

Demon: Even among brigands one finds bodhisattvas, so why shouldn't demons be able to listen to scripture?

The priest tells him to spread flowers and light incense and candles if he really wants to hear a song. When he has finished singing the song, he calls on the demon once more to open up, which at last the demon does.

Priest: We pray a path with clasped hands between life and death. We do a somersault and leap through the Demon Gate. (*Sings*)
> The road from the Demon Gate goes right through
> > to the Yellow Springs.
> I see the road is lined on both sides
> > by the flags of the demonic host.
> I hear the sound of drums and gongs.
> It is terrifying, but I must not be afraid.

After the song, the priest may go on to describe the horrors he encounters in Hell: sinners in stocks, heads split open, pools of blood on the ground. "This is the fiery road through the Yellow Springs. It's no place for a student of the Way to linger. I had better burn some paper money." Once again he demands that the Demon Gate be opened, and once again the demon asks who's disturbing the peace at such an unearthly hour. The priest identifies himself anew and repeats the name of the person he has come to save.

Demon: The priest is late.

Priest: What do you mean, late?

Demon: When Yama mounted his throne, you had not yet come. You arrived just as Yama was leaving his hall. There's nothing to be done.

Priest: Look, demon, I've come a long way over great mountain ranges. What do you mean, there's nothing to be done because I'm late?

Demon: Priest, when Yama mounted his throne, I went with him, and when he left the hall, so did I. If I let one soul go, I will be held accountable. I dare not take any such initiative.

Priest: Demon, the proverb has it that even a heart of iron softens [if it's beaten long enough].

Demon: When one word doesn't hit the mark, a thousand are of no use.

Priest: Demon, do you see the staff I have in my hand? It's the precious defense given me by order of the Ancestors of the Way. On the left it controls dragons, on the right it tames tigers. One thrust, and heaven is clear; two thrusts, and earth is potent; three thrusts, and stocks are smashed and iron locks opened.

Demon: I don't believe you.

Priest: Acolyte, beat the drum of the Law three times and have Xu Jia summon forth the divine soldiers of the Five Camps to smash the fortress.

Xu Jia is Laozi's disciple and patron saint of the "redhead" Daoists in southern Taiwan. At this point therefore, the officiant, after rattling his pronged staff menacingly in front of the fortress, comes back in front of the Table of the Three Realms, wraps a red bandanna around his black cap and trusses up his sleeves: he has become an exorcist.

The exorcist blows on his buffalo horn and burns paper money in front of the fortress. The chair-bearers, who all along have been swinging the chair off to one side, come now in front of the fortress and swing the chair back and forth violently. At the same time, and with equal violence, the family members shake the fortress, and there is furious clanging of gongs as one by one the priest lights, lets burn, and drops in the four corners and in the center five paper cones to summon the spirit soldiers of the Five Camps. Then he sprays a mouthful of symbol-water at the fortress and makes a ramming gesture. "Acolyte," he says, "beat the drum of the Law three more times, and I will smash the fortress." The mourners shake the fortress and call to the soul, "Come get your money, come wash." The priest lights the paper cones stuck on the prongs of his staff and stabs the fortress.

After breaking through the Demon Gate, he grabs the image of the deceased from inside the fortress and ties it on the back of the chief mourner. While another family member holds a parasol over the image so that it does not come in contact with the energies of the world of the living, which might bring it back to life and turn it into a wandering ghost, the family rushes with the image to the house, where a basin of water and a change of clothing have been prepared. . . . The priest returns to the altar to perform an exorcism to purify the ritual area. He removes the effigies of Guanyin and the Earth God from the remains of the fortress and brings the Earth God back to his place at the entrance to the altar. Inside the house, both the image of the deceased and the clothing are burned.

Spirit-mediums are often present for this rite. From outside the shut doors of the house, the spirit-medium is questioned about the voyage of the deceased: what does he need? Meanwhile, the remains of the fortress are given to an elderly man, who takes them to an isolated spot for burning.

[Adapted from Lagerwey, *Taoist Ritual*, pp. 216–237 — DJ]


## OPERA

The great procession in honor of the Sanzong God in Zhangzi County, Shanxi, the fire-walking ritual of Shenze village, Zhejiang, the Attack on Hell in Tainan, Taiwan — these rituals were highly dramatic, and some were in fact influenced by the conventions of opera, as we have seen. Opera was inextricably bound up with religion and ritual. Every important temple had a stage (but never a pulpit!), and every important community ritual was accompanied by the performance of opera.

Traditional Chinese drama always combined singing, declaiming, and instrumental music, hence the term *opera*, but images of chandeliers and velvet, of evening dress and limousines, should be banished from the reader's mind — in China, opera was the most democratic of arts. All but the poorest, remotest villages had their own stages, even if they sometimes were only big enough for puppets. Indeed, any social group that had the resources — family, guild, native-place association — sponsored operas to accompany the rituals that marked important occasions in its life.

There were hundreds of varieties of opera in late imperial times; along with dialect, to which it is, of course, intimately linked, opera is one of the most reliable markers of cultural difference at the village level. If illiterate people watched the same operas, in the same language, by definition they belonged to the same local culture. From operas ordinary people learned much of what they knew about gods, demons, and the world of the supernatural, and most of what they knew about Chinese history, about emperors and prime ministers, about politics, warfare, and heroism. Operas also taught them about praiseworthy and reprehensible behavior, though there the messages were less consistent, since the values inculcated ranged from the entirely orthodox to the decidedly unconventional.

As noted in the introduction, Chinese opera was moralistic from the start, and the conventions of the Chinese stage reflect this. No one was ever in doubt as to who was the hero and who the villain. Indeed, in most scripts speeches were identified by role-type, not by the name of the character. (This would be like indicating Falstaff's lines in *Henry IV* with "clown" rather than with his name.) There was minimal scenery, and the costumes, though extremely elaborate, were highly conventional. Heavy face makeup created the effect of masks, and indeed, some of the oldest opera genres frequently employed masked actors. Thus stylization, not realism, was the guiding principle. Moreover, this was stylization in the service not of the tragic vision of Greek tragedy or Japanese Nô drama but of (in most cases) the affirmation of communal values. Of course, those values varied with the community — operas for villagers were quite different from operas for literati. Then, too, in any given audience different members could, in theory at least, interpret what they were watching in different ways. Nevertheless, opera *taught*, whether intentionally or not, and taught with unique emotional power. The two works that we will look at below vividly demonstrate this.

## Religious Epic

Although opera was a part of virtually all communal religious ceremonial, relatively few operas had overtly religious themes. Among these few, the most important and impressive was *Mulian Rescues His Mother*. This Buddhist epic of temptation, damnation, filial love, and salvation has been known in China for more than a thousand years and was performed throughout the country in many versions until the middle of this century.

It tells the story of the pious young Mulian and his widowed mother, Liu Qingti, who, in one popular version, abandons at the unprincipled urging of her evil brother the Buddhist precepts she had followed faithfully while her husband was alive and sinks deeper and deeper into a life of meat-eating, violence, and blasphemy. She is condemned for these sins by the Jade Emperor, and in the scenes given below Yama, the ruler of the Underworld, sends his demon-bailiffs to seize her soul and drag it down to Hell. Madame Liu gives the demons the pretext they need when she swears falsely to her son that she has not eaten meat or done any of the other evil things she has been accused of. The rest of the opera recounts Mulian's journeys to Heaven and Hell to seek the aid of the bodhisattva Guanyin and to rescue his mother's soul, and it ends with her final enlightenment and salvation.

*Mulian* was frequently performed for the so-called Ghost Festival — the fifteenth day of the seventh lunar month — but other dates were traditional in some places. In addition, special performances of *Mulian* were staged when villagers felt that dangerous evil spirits were abroad, for example when there had been an unusual number of suicides. Some performances lasted as long as forty-nine days, but most lasted three. They usually took place at night, which made the ghosts and demons that are everywhere in the play unforgettably terrifying. A mid-seventeenth-century description of a performance in Shaoxing gives a good sense of this: "The audience was very uneasy; under the light of the lamps, the actors' faces had a demonic quality. In acts like 'Summoning the Evil Ghosts of the Five Directions' and 'Madame Liu Flees the Stage,' ten thousand people and more all screamed at once." The uproar was so great that the prefect sent a yamen officer out to see if pirates were attacking.[5]

The *Mulian* story originated in Buddhist scriptures and matured in a Chinese setting, and it taught the theology and ethics of Buddhism and Confucianism very effectively. But there is no doubt that the opera also functioned as a grand ritual whose purpose was to drive out ghosts and protect the community from evil spirits. Many versions of *Mulian* were prefaced with a scene in which five demons were driven off the stage and pursued for some distance outside the village by an actor representing a priest, a god, or the King of the Ghosts. In *Mulian*, the dividing line between opera and ritual was virtually effaced: it was an opera that had ritual functions, but one could as easily say that it was a ritual in the form of an opera. In the Qi Opera version, from which the selections below are taken, a *sūtra* recitation hall was constructed facing the stage, and an eminent Buddhist monk chanted *sūtras* in it while the opera was being performed. When Mulian's father died in the play, the monk came onstage to pray for his soul, exactly as if someone had really died. Contrariwise,

5. Zhang Dai, *Taoan mengyi* 6:47–48.

the actor who played the character of the exorcist, Master Wen, was in some cases asked by the villagers to perform an actual exorcism in their homes.

*Mulian Rescues His Mother* was the greatest of all Chinese religious operas. During its performance Buddhas, immortals, and a terrifying array of demons and ghosts swarmed over the stage, at times erupting into the audience and rushing out into the surrounding fields. It presented the mysteries of death and rebirth in scenes whose impact on audiences must have been overwhelming. It taught religious and moral values to ordinary people with incomparable force, though not always in a form that won the approval of Buddhist monks or Confucian literati.

### MULIAN RESCUES HIS MOTHER

While Mulian has been away from home after his father's death, his mother has been persuaded to break her vow to abstain from eating meat. This sin has led to others, including violence and sacrilege. When the following scene begins, accusations against her have reached the Jade Emperor, who orders Yama, King of Hell, to punish her. Yama thereupon dispatches his demon runners to apprehend her.

### SCENE 42

## The Infernal Runners Set Off

*The five demon-bailiffs enter.*

First demon-bailiff (*chants*):
> The sparrow when it pecks looks all around;
> The swallow sleeps without a care.
> For the great-hearted, blessings are naturally great,
> For the deep schemer, misfortune is deep as a well.
> Brothers!

Demon-bailiffs: Here!

First demon-bailiff: We have been ordered by Lord Yama to seize Madame Liu Qingti. We will go first to the headquarters of the City God to register, and then to the Fu house.

Demon-bailiffs: Well said!

Second demon-bailiff (*chants*): Truly,
> Demons and spirits are formless and soundless,

Third demon-bailiff:
> Inaudible and invisible to living people.
> Never forget that evil-doing is requited with evil;

Fourth demon-bailiff:
> On no account be greedy and scheming!

First demon-bailiff (*sings to the tune "Si bian jin"*):
> We're the Runners from the hall of Lord Yama.
> Carrying ropes and iron chains
> We head straight for the gate of the Fu house
> To seize the soul of Madame Liu.
> She will certainly have no place to hide,

Demon-bailiffs:
> And will find it hard to buy her way out.
> To all men we give this warning:
> Do good, don't do evil.
> To all men we give this warning:
> Do good, don't do evil.

First demon-bailiff: Let's go!

*The five demon-bailiffs exit together.*

### SCENE 43

## Life-Is-Transient Leads the Way

*The Life-Is-Transient demon, a miscellaneous role-type, dances across the stage (leading the way for the demon-bailiffs). He wears a hat about two feet tall, on which are the words "You'll come too!" He stands on stilts eight to twelve feet high and carries a palm-leaf fan.*[6]

### SCENE 44

## Ili Sweeps the Hall

[Madame Liu overhears the faithful family servant, Ili, musing to himself on the moral degradation that has overtaken the household. She is enraged and is about to begin beating him when Mulian, here called by his childhood name, Luobu, enters. She tells him to bring her a club.]

Fu Luobu: Alas, Mother, I have taken the vows!
Mme Liu: You have taken the vows, have you?

*Trembling with rage, she snatches his rosary and beats Ili with it, and overturns a chair three times.*

(*Sings*)
> Oh, Luobu!
> If I don't beat him a few times

---

6. This figure had an independent existence in the folk culture of southeastern China and Taiwan and was frequently seen in temple processions.

And curse him a few times
And if others hear of it
They will say I can't control my household at all, can't control it at all.
I must teach this evil slave a lesson
And make him examine himself.
In ordinary households
There is no confusion between right and wrong, kin and non-kin.
Honored and mean, noble and ignoble, are kept perfectly clear, kept
    perfectly clear.

*Strikes Ili, again overturns the chair three times.*

[Both Luobu and Ili do everything possible to prevent Madame Liu from beating Ili.
Eventually she relents.]

Mme Liu [*to Ili*]: Get up!
Fu Luobu: Dear Ili, just what did you say to make my mother beat you?
Ili: I just said two things I shouldn't have.
Fu Luobu: What two things?
Ili: Good deeds stay at home, but evil deeds travel a thousand leagues.
Mme Liu: Tcha!
(*Chants*)
    You two bully me with your talk;
    How could I have made any mistakes?
    If Madame Liu broke her vow of abstinence. . . .
Fu Luobu and Ili: Ai, Mother! Mother! Mistress!
Mme Liu: . . . I shall go to the garden to swear an oath, to swear an oath.

*Mme Liu exits, followed by the others.*

### SCENE 45

## The Oath in the Garden

*The five demon-bailiffs enter.*

First demon-bailiff (*chants*):
    What arises in men's hearts the demons know first;
Second demon-bailiff:
    Heaven, dark and deep, cannot be deceived;
Third demon-bailiff:
    Good and evil in the end will always be requited;
Fourth and fifth demon-bailiffs:
    The only thing uncertain is when it will occur.

First demon-bailiff: Brothers, we have been commanded by King Yama to seize Madame Liu Qingti. The Earth God says that her son serves the Buddha and so she will be difficult to take. Just now she has gone to the garden to make an oath; we will seize her there.

Second demon-bailiff: I'll wait for her here.

Others: Let's go!

First demon-bailiff: Here she comes.

Mme Liu (sings within to the tune "Hong nei yao"):

I go into the garden —

*Madame Liu enters, stumbles and falls. The five demon-bailiffs surround her. She mimes fear.*

Mme Liu: Ng-heng! Ng-heng! Ai-ya, I know this path to the garden so well — how could I have fallen down? If I can't do it this way, I'll go around. [*Exits*]

The demon-bailiffs: Wait over there.

Mme Liu (sings within):

I go into the garden —

*Madame Liu enters stage left. The five demon bailiffs surround her. She mimes fear.*

Mme Liu: Demons! Demons! Oh, I am so sorry!

(*Sings*)

Seeing the flowers
Wraps me in grief,
Makes me more ashamed.
I remember when my husband was alive
And built this flower terrace.
Truly all I hoped for was that husband would lead and wife follow,
That when our hair was dark we would stay close to each other
And when our hair was white we would part.
Who would have thought that the phoenix would depart, leaving the terrace empty,
The phoenix depart, leaving the terrace empty and the mist thickening.

*The five demon-bailiffs seize Madame Liu, and she falls to the ground. Fu Luobu enters. The five demon-bailiffs bow to him, retreat, and exit. Luobu helps Madame Liu get up.*

Mme Liu: A demon! A demon!

Fu Luobu: Mother, it's Luobu!

Mme Liu: You are Luobu?

Fu Luobu: Yes!

Mme Liu: Take my hand and lead me back.

*(Sings)*

> To raise a fine son takes all his parents' efforts —

*Ili enters.*

Mme Liu: A demon! A demon!

Fu Luobu: Dear mother, it's our Ili.

Mme Liu *(sings):*

> Ai-ya, Luobu my son!
> It is also said that slanders should not be listened to.
> If you do, disaster will befall you.
> If the lord listens to slanders, the minister will be dismissed;
> If the father listens to slanders, the son will be destroyed;
> If friends listen they will become estranged;
> If husband and wife listen they will separate.
> Imposing is a man's seven-foot frame,
> Tireless his three-inch tongue.
> The tongue is a Dragon Spring[7]
> That can kill without drawing blood.
> Don't listen to slanderous words, my son;
> They destroy the natural affection between mother and child.
> See the sunflowers —
> *[To herself]* O sunflowers,
> In the netherworld
> You are in charge of good and evil among men.
> Even if you do not know what others have done,
> You were born in my garden,
> So you must know
> The things I have done:
> Breaking my vows behind my son's back and killing living things.
> Sunflowers,
> To you sunflowers I say from the bottom of my heart,

> > It is useless to have a sincere heart,
> > It is useless to have a sincere heart,
> > You just lean toward the sun, lean toward the sun.

---

7. The name of a famous sword.

*The exploding sunflowers are set off. The five demon-bailiffs throw down the bones [that have been buried in the back garden].*


Fu Luobu and Ili *(sing):*
>Fiery red, fiery red, the flames rise up,
>Stony white, stony white, the bones fill the pit.
>Who killed all these animals?
>Why did they take the lives of all these geese and ducks?
>They buried the white bones deep in the earth.
>They must not have known that Heaven above is keeping
>    watch.
>They tried to cover it up, but only made it more obvious.
>Ai-ya, Mother!
>Why weren't they,
>Why weren't they careful from the start?

Mme Liu *(sings):*
>Whose vicious thought was this?
>Whose devilish work was this?
>Who killed the animals
>And buried white bones in the shade of flowers and trees?
>[*To herself*] When Luobu sees them he is stunned;
>When Ili sees them he is uneasy.
>[They must be feeling,] How can it not be true?
>Deception is still deception; if I deceive these two fine boys,
>When I die and go to the Yellow Springs,
>When I die and go to the Yellow Springs,
>I will not close my eyes in peace,
>I will not close my eyes in peace.


Fu Luobu: Ai-ya, Ili, Mother says she did not break her vows of abstinence, and my family has supported a *sūtra* hall for nine generations; where did these bones come from?

Ili: It is obvious.

Mme Liu *(chants):*
>[*To herself*] My son's suspicions will be difficult to deflect,
>And the old cur's words even harder to forbid.
>[*To Luobu and Ili*] If your old mother broke her vows . . .

Fu Luobu and Ili: Ai-ya, Mother, O Mother!


*Madame Liu kneels down to swear an oath.*


Mme Liu: . . . Let me suffer in Hell again and again!

*The five demon-bailiffs shackle Madame Liu's hun soul and exit. Luobu and Ili exit. . . . Madame Liu trembles, removes her shackles, exits. The five demon-bailiffs enter.*

Second demon-bailiff: The bitch has taken off!
First demon-bailiff: Pursue her closely and take care of her! . . .
*(Chants)*

> If she feels warm,
> I will use the fires of the south to make her hotter;
> And if she feels chilly,
> I will use the waters of the north to make her colder,
> To kill her and send her to King Yama, send her to King Yama.

*Madame Liu enters. The five demon-bailiffs cross the stage and shackle her. Madame Liu collapses. Luobu enters, lifts her up. Ili enters.*

Fu Luobu and Ili *(sing to melody "Yi jiang feng")*:

> She has fallen down,
> Bright blood flows from nose, mouth, ears, and eyes.
> It terrifies me.
> Her eyes and mouth are awry,
> Teeth clenched and silent,
> Hands and feet as cold as iron.
> When calamity comes you cannot fend it off.
> My bowels are being torn apart,
> I cry out but make no sound, make no sound.
> Ai-ya, dear mother, wake up!

Mme Liu *(sings the previous melody)*:

> I have hurt myself.

Fu Luobu: Mother!
Mme Liu: Demons! Demons!
Fu Luobu: Ai-ya, Mother — I am your son, Luobu.
Mme Liu: You are Luobu? Oh, I am so sorry!
*(Sings)*

> Sorry that at the start
> I did not heed, did not heed my darling boy's words.
> Ai-ya, Luobu my son!
> Just now when I was overcome with dizziness and fell down,
> I saw your father.
> He came astride a crane, riding a cloud.
> He said, "Respected wife!
> When your dear husband was nearing his end,
> I exhorted you time and again with my deathbed injunctions.

I told you to take care of Luobu and Ili,
To eat vegetarian foods, to read the *sūtras* and recite the
    Buddha's name.
Why did you send your son off to do business
And break your vows behind his back?
Why did you beat the Lamplighter Buddha
And curse the Primordial Heaven-honored One?
The Master of Fate notified Heaven,
And Heaven sent down an order
Commanding King Yama to investigate.
He despatched the Five Demons
To seize you.
Respected wife!
Heaven, dark and deep, cannot be deceived;
The spirits know your intentions before you are
    conscious of them.
Good and evil are always requited in the end,
The only thing uncertain is when it will occur.
The things that happen in the netherworld arise from
    your own actions;
The statutes of the netherworld are hard to evade.
Husband and wife are like birds in the same grove;
When the Great Limit is reached each flies away,
    each flies away.
O my wife!
I can take care of myself but I cannot take care of you;
I can take care of myself but I cannot take care of you."
Just then I was overcome by dizziness and collapsed.
I wanted to say a few words to your father,
But just then you two awakened me,
And so I wasn't able to say clearly more than a few words.
Son!
Pitiful I am, once husband and wife,
As if in a dream, now truly abandoned.
The pain in my heart like being stabbed with a knife,
    stabbed with a knife.

*The five demon-bailiffs beat the object representing Madame Liu's soul around
the stage.*

Mme Liu: Ai-yo, ai-yo, ai-yo!
Fu Luobu and Ili: Dear mother, be careful!

Mme Liu *(sings)*:

> The dark wind begins to moan,
> The hungry ghosts cluster round,
> Taking, taking your mother to Hell.

Fu Luobu: Mother!

Mme Liu: Luobu, who is that?

Fu Luobu: That's dear Ili.

Mme Liu: Tell him to come here.

Fu Luobu: Ili, Mother is calling you.

Ili: Madame, I am here.

Mme Liu *(sings)*:

> Ai-ya, my Ili!
> Ever since you left the knee of your stepmother
> I never beat you or abused you.
> Today because of a small matter
> I hit you and cursed you again and again.
> My son, never never remember it.
> O son,
> My son, quickly arrange for my journey —
> I expect that I will soon, soon go to the world below.

Fu Luobu and Ili *(sing)*:

> The winds and clouds of Heaven cannot be fathomed,
> Both blessings and calamities can come between
>     morning and evening.
> We urge you, Mother, slowly, slowly go back to the house.

Mme Liu: Demons! Demons!

Ili: Madame, please take care!

Mme Liu: Son!

Fu Luobu: Mother!

*Madame Liu looks back twice and exits, followed by Luobu and Ili.*

After Madame Liu dies, her coffin is placed on stage. The five demon-bailiffs enter, accompanied by the Pathfinder who is to lead them to Hell. The Pathfinder is played by the actor who has the role of Madame Liu. He wears a special mask and robe, under which are the makeup and costume of Madame Liu's ghost. The six of them carry the coffin off the stage and drag it to a secluded spot "an arrow's shot" away. There the five demons begin beating on the coffin lid with sticks to summon Madame Liu's soul, and at the same time the Pathfinder ducks down behind the coffin, quickly takes off his mask and robe, and then jumps up in the terrifying guise of Madame Liu's ghost. The ghost sees the five demon-bailiffs and runs wildly back up onto the stage to hide. The demons run after her, capture her backstage, and, to the shouts of the audience, drag her down to Hell.

[*Mulian zhuan*, pp. 242–259, supplemented by *Mulianxi xueshu zuotanhui lunwenxuan*, pp. 19–41 — DJ]

## Village Opera

Not all village opera was as grand and imposing as *Mulian*, of course. A typical temple festival, held on the occasion of a local god's birthday, featured a wide variety of local operas on secular themes. There were history plays that by Qing times ranged across the dynasties from antiquity to the Ming, domestic dramas, romantic comedies, and even topical farces. Although thousands of scripts of local operas still exist, those that have been published have almost invariably been revised during the editorial process and hence have lost some of their authentically popular character. Such tampering began no later than the Ming, when new and more "respectable" dialogue was provided for the dramatic masterpieces of the Yuan, and it was still being practiced in the 1950s, when "Opera Inspection Teams" sent out by the provincial Cultural Affairs Bureaus (*Wenhua ting*) collected and examined scripts of local operas in preparation for the publication of approved versions and the suppression of the rest.

There are, however, a few exceptions, and the following is one of them. It is one of forty-eight transcripts that were created when members of the Ding County Social Survey, led by Sidney Gamble, recorded the recitations (not the actual performances) of experienced village actors in Ding County, Hebei, in 1929. There were no scripts, since the performers were illiterate. The opera belongs to a genre called *yangge*, which was popular (with many local variations) throughout the provinces of Hebei, Shanxi, and Shaanxi in north China.

The *yangge* were the most popular form of entertainment in the villages of Ding County and were performed at temple fairs, New Year's and other festivals, and any other time that theatricals were called for. The actors — all men and mostly farmers — performed in and around their home villages. The plays were passed on orally from generation to generation, and thus they are true folk literature. Unlike some other forms of opera, the *yangge* were easy for the villagers to understand, both because they were in the local dialect and because information important to the plot was repeated over and over.

As one would expect given the fact that the repertoire did not undergo literati editing or government censorship, the Ding County *yangge* provide invaluable evidence of popular attitudes and values, at least in early twentieth-century Hebei. Nearly half deal with filial piety, marital fidelity, and other aspects of family relations. There are farces and romances as well, but no historical plays, and hence the themes of loyalty and political righteousness are quite absent.

## GUO JU BURIES HIS SON

One of the most striking *yangge* from the point of view of the inculcation of values is
*Guo Ju Buries His Son*, based on a brief story from a famous Confucian tract called
*The Twenty-four Exemplars of Filial Piety* (*Ershisi xiao*). (Selections from this widely
circulated text, including the story about Guo Ju, appear later in this chapter; see pp.
138–41). The *yangge* takes the familiar didactic tale, with its brutal refusal to recognize
the tragic dilemma in which Guo Ju and his wife are caught, and turns it into a
devastating critique of the arrogance of wealth and a deeply moving expression of the
irreconcilable conflict between the demands of filial piety and parental love, thus
teaching a much more complex lesson. It is given here without abridgement.

*Guo Ju enters.*

Guo (*speaks*): Mother's illness is constantly on my mind. I am Guo Ju.
　　Mother is very ill. I will go to her brother's house to borrow some rice to
　　keep us going.
Guo (*sings*):
　　　Guo Ju sits in the front room, thinking about Mother's illness.
　　　Mother is bedridden; she would like a bowlful of rice, but there
　　　　is none to give her.
　　　From her sickbed Mother tells me to go to her brother's house
　　　　and borrow some.
　　　I bow and take my leave. I tell my wife to pay attention:
　　　If our mother gets cold, build up the fire for her;
　　　If our mother is thirsty, make some tea for her.
　　　Look — here is our rice bag; I am going to Uncle's to borrow
　　　　some rice.
　　　Outside I look around; the street is filled with the well-to-do.
　　　I could take my bag into the main street to borrow rice, but the
　　　　people there help the rich, not the poor.
　　　I'll use the small lanes, not the main street;
　　　By crooked paths and devious ways I go through the *hutongs*.[8]
　　　Walking through the village and looking around, I see a temple
　　　　south of the road.
　　　The statues have only reed mats over their heads; it's open to the
　　　　sky where the ridgepole has collapsed.
　　　I see that all the walls have collapsed in ruins, and little boys are
　　　　taking the bricks away.

---

8. *Hutong* is the term used in north China for small lanes and alleys.

Showing nothing of what I am feeling, I arrive before my uncle's big gate.

I stand there and call out for him to open the gate — then call again.

Uncle *(sings)*:

I am just having a cup of wine in my inner chamber when suddenly I hear someone at the gate.[9]

I put down the cup to see who has come.

I step outside my front hall and arrive at my gate.

Opening the gate I look up and see none other than my little nephew Guo Ju.

We can't stand talking outside the gate, come with me to the front hall.

Having spoken, I enter the gate. . . .

Guo *(sings)*:

. . . Followed by Guo Ju, your little nephew.

Uncle *(sings)*:

Sit here in the front hall.

Guo *(sings)*:

He avoids me as he bows.

Having bowed, I take my seat.

May I ask whether you are well, Uncle, and Aunt also?

Uncle *(sings)*:

I answer, "Fine, fine, fine"; and is my old sister well?

Guo *(sings)*:

If you hadn't asked, it would have been all right, but now that you have asked the tears pour down.

My mother is bedridden; she would like a bowl of rice, but there is none to give her.

I wanted to make rice for her, but there is not even half a pint of rice in the house.

I wanted to ask for a loan from someone who lives on the main street, but most of them will help the rich, not the poor.

If you have rice, lend me a few pecks so I can take them home and be a filial son.

If Mother recovers, I will never forget your generosity, Uncle.

What Guo Ju has said with a pure heart about borrowing rice . . .

Uncle *(sings)*:

What you have said I greatly dislike.

Three years ago you borrowed several pecks of rice from me, and you have yet to repay half a pint.

---

9. The uncle refers to himself throughout as "the old one," which emphasizes his social superiority to Guo Ju.

You are asking again without having repaid what you owe —
    where will I find the rice to give you?
The rice I have will feed my geese, ducks, pigs, and dogs, who at
    least guard the house and announce the dawn.
The more I speak, the more I think and the angrier I get; the
    dark fire of rage burns in my heart.
I pick up my walking stick and with hatred, hatred beat you to
    death, you dog!

[Beats Guo Ju.]

Guo *(sings):*

    Hear me, Uncle, with your hateful heart. This child has
        not eaten for three meals, how can I fend off your
        great club?
    I am humiliated, you savage, and I have a few things to say to
        you!
    I wouldn't have minded your refusing to lend us the rice; but you
        ought not to have punished me so cruelly.
    On hands and knees I anxiously scramble up from the
        ground.
    I will leave having borrowed no rice, with nothing to offer
        Mother at home.
    Saying this I turn my face to tell you something else, Uncle:
    Remember when we were rich and you were poor, and you bor-
        rowed gold and silver from Guo Ju?
    Now when you are rich and I am poor, you don't treat me as a
        human being at all.
    You have rice for your geese, ducks, pigs, and dogs; is my mother
        nothing to you?
    Today the two of us will strike hands on my oath that never in my
        life will I come to your gate again.
    Guo Ju, afraid of more blows, has to retreat . . .

Uncle *(sings):*

    . . . With a blow at every step I force him out of the gate.
    Guo Ju has been forced out of the gate; turning my back, I push
        the gate closed.
    You and I will travel separate roads until we die; I will not open
        my gate to you even if you are dying.

Guo *(weeping):* I tell you, Uncle, you savage — this child has not eaten for
three meals and could [not] fend off the blows of your club. Uncle, you
savage!

*(Sings)*

    I am humiliated, you savage, and I have a few things to say to
        you!
    I have not eaten for three meals, how could I have fended off
        your great club?

> I could die by smashing my head on your gate, but what would
>    happen to Mother then?
> How hard, how hard, hard even to die, how hard it is for Guo Ju
>    to die.
> Guo Ju weeps in the main street.

Chen Zhong *(sings):*

> I'm Chen Zhong; I've been to market and now am going home.
> The people at home told me to go to market, and I've bought all
>    sorts of things.
> I've bought two nose-bags for the donkeys and two halters too.
> As I enter the village, I see Guo Ju in the middle of the street.
> Guo Ju, if you're not going to your uncle's house, why have you
>    come to the main street?

Guo *(sings):*

> You don't know, brother Chen Zhong, so let me tell you the
>    whole story from beginning to end.
> My bedridden old mother wanted a bowl of rice, but there was
>    none to be had at home.
> She told me to borrow rice from her brother.
> I wouldn't have minded if he hadn't loaned us the rice, but he
>    beat me with his stick.
> I ran away and left my rice bag behind.
> Brother Chen Zhong, when you go there, get the bag for me.
> This is the truth I've told you, and nothing false.

Chen Zhong *(sings):*

> I've twelve coins left after going to market, take them home so
>    you can be a filial son.
> I hand the coins over . . .

Guo *(sings):*

> . . . And I take them in my hand.
> Just think, there was a time when my family were wealthy gentry;
>    now twelve coins seem wonderful.
> Chen Zhong, turn around so I can prostrate myself on the
>    ground before you.
> I am paying obeisance to you for no other reason than that you
>    have saved Mother's life.
> We two will be sworn brothers, brothers in life and death.
> When your mother dies I shall wear mourning, and when my
>    mother dies you will accompany the coffin.
> I arise from the ground after kowtowing; we will each return to
>    our own home. *[Chen Zhong exits.]*

*Guo Ju does not leave after speaking, for he suddenly hears the cry of the*
*shaobing [baked sesame bun] peddler.*

You there, *shaobing* man, how much for one? If we talk price first
we won't fight later.

*Shaobing* peddler *(sings)*:

One of my buns costs six coins, two of them will cost you twelve.

Guo *(sings)*:

Twelve coins will buy only two — there is no way I can ever buy
three.

After speaking, Guo Ju turns around, and not far from the village
center he stops.

Standing outside his gate, he calls and calls again for his wife to
open it.

Suzhen *(sings)*:

Yao Suzhen is in the front room when suddenly she hears
someone at the gate.

I get down from the bed but do not leave; holding my baby I say
a few things to Mother:

Take good care of yourself here, I am going to the gate to see
who it is.

I tell Mother I am going outside, just a little ways to the front
gate.

Opening the gate, I see my husband standing there.

Outside the gate is not a place to talk; let us go into our hut and
talk.

I lead my husband through the gate, and we soon arrive at the
hut.

I give my husband a place to sit.

Guo *(sings)*:

I sit down and my tears overflow.

Suzhen *(sings)*:

As soon as my husband sits down, I can see from his expression
that something is wrong.

His hair is disheveled and his face is pale, but I don't know why.

I sit down facing him and speak respectfully:

You went to Uncle's house to borrow rice — how much did you
borrow?

Husband, please give it to me and I'll cook some, to satisfy
Mother's hunger.

Guo *(sings)*:

If you hadn't brought up borrowing rice it would have been all
right, but bringing it up is truly painful.

After I went into Uncle's house I first asked if he was well and
then brought up the matter of borrowing rice.

He said he loaned me several pecks of rice and had not yet got
back half a pint.

It would have been all right if Uncle had not loaned me the rice,
but in his rage he picked up his stick.

Because I had not eaten for three meals, I could not fend off his
stick.

He forced me out of the gate just as Chen Zhong was returning
from the market.

Cheng Zhong gave me twelve coins and I bought two *shaobing*
to be a filial son.

I hand the *shaobing* over to you . . .

Suzhen *(sings)*:

. . . And I take them in my hands.

Husband, please wait in the hut; I will go to the sick room to see
Mother and try to explain it to her.

Suzhen goes into the sick room and with one word awakens her
mother.

Mother *(sings)*:

Suddenly I hear my daughter's voice, there's nothing I can do but
open my worried eyes.

Ah, it is my son's wife, holding my grandson.

I don't crave either sour or spicy flavors — all I can think of is the
aroma of rice gruel.

I would like to have some rice right now — then I'd get better and
could leave this bed.

If there is no rice for me, then I am bound to see the King of the
Underworld.

I sent my son off to borrow some rice and bring it back here.

I tell my daughter-in-law to cook some rice, to make a bowl of
nice rice for Mother to eat.

Suzhen *(sings)*:

If you hadn't brought up borrowing rice it would have been all
right, but bringing it up is truly painful.

My husband, following Mother's request, went to Uncle's to
borrow rice.

But he said that he had loaned several pecks three years ago — let
me ask you, is he a relative or not?

If my husband hadn't asked to borrow rice Uncle wouldn't have
gotten mad, but Uncle was enraged and his stick was savage.

He drove my husband out the front gate just as Chen Zhong was
coming back from an errand.

He gave my husband twelve coins, and he used them to buy two
*shaobing* to be a filial son.

As Suzhen hands over the *shaobing* the tears pour from her eyes.

Mother *(sings)*:

As I take the *shaobing* I become angry.

I curse you, Brother, you are not human — remember the year
 when we were rich and you were poor and you borrowed gold
 and silver from us Guos?

Now when you are rich and we are poor, you don't treat our Guo
 Ju like a human being.

You said your rice was to feed your chickens, ducks, geese, and
 dogs; you did not think of what I am to you at all.

If I get better I will stand in front of your gate, you dog.

Then I'll give you what I owe you, and everything you owe me,
 principal and interest, will be taken back to my house.

She curses the old dog once more, and looks at the *shaobing* to
 see if they are real.

I will eat one of these *shaobing* and save the other to feed my
 grandson.

If I starve to death it won't matter much — I'm afraid that my
 grandson will starve to death.

If my grandson starves to death it will be very serious, for the root
 of the Guo family will be cut off.

Holding the *shaobing* I say to Daughter-in-law: Listen while I
 explain it to you.

I will eat one of the *shaobing*, and give this one to my grandson
 to eat.

I hand over the *shaobing* . . .

Yao Suzhen *(sings)*:

. . . And I take it.

Taking my leave of Mother I go outside and come to my
 husband.

Mother is going to eat one of the *shaobing* and saved this one to
 give to her grandson.

As Yao Suzhen hands over the *shaobing*, tears fall from her eyes.

Guo *(sings)*:

How painful it is to take this *shaobing*! It's like our little baby[10] is
 taking food out of Mother's mouth.

Oh, Mother! What feeling is it that makes you still want this little
 baby?

I say we should just give our little baby to someone else to raise
 and use the extra food to be filial.

---

10. Literally, "little enemy," presumably a local idiom. The literal meaning of this term of
endearment is shocking in this context, and an example of the skill of the author or authors.
Unfortunately, there is no natural-sounding English equivalent, so I have here used the bland
"little baby."

Suzhen (sings):

> You say we should give our baby to someone else to raise; but if
> that person should beat or curse him, his mother's heart would
> break.
> I say it would be better to bury him alive, and use the extra food
> to be filial.

Guo (sings):

> What you say, wife, I cannot believe.

Suzhen (sings):

> I will swear an oath to Heaven.
> I come before you and with folded hands fall to my knees.
> If I am not telling the truth about wanting to bury our baby,
> hereafter I will certainly be struck by the Five Thunders!

Guo (sings):

> As soon as I see my wife make her vow in broad daylight I know
> she is sincere.
> I was born and raised by Mother, while my wife comes from
> another family. I go forward and hurry to help her up.

Suzhen (sings):

> I get up from the ground.

Guo (sings):

> I will go and pick up my shovel and mattock;

Suzhen (sings):

> Your wife will go get our little son. [Both exit.]

*Heavenly Official Who Increases Blessings enters.*

Heavenly Official (speaks): I am the Heavenly Official Who Increases Blessings.
Guo Ju is going to bury his baby for the sake of his mother. I must go first
and bury eighteen pieces of Heavenly gold and silver. With my treasure-
sword I open the earth, open it three feet deep and bury the gold and silver.
The eighteen pieces of gold and silver I've buried Guo Ju can use to be filial
to his mother. [Exits.]

Guo (sings):

> Guo Ju shoulders his mattock and shovel;

Suzhen (sings):

> Suzhen carries the baby in her arms.

Guo (sings):

> Listen, wife, don't make any noise . . .

Suzhen (sings):

> . . . So our dozing mother won't know what we're doing.

Guo (*sings*):

If Mother should learn of this . . .

Suzhen (*sings*):

. . . There will be no way we can bury our baby.

Guo (*sings*):

Husband and wife go out their poor gate . . .

Suzhen (*sings*):

. . . And lock it behind them.

Guo (*sings*):

Husband and wife come to the main street;

Suzhen (*sings*):

There are many people in the street, making a din.

Guo (*sings*):

If we go along the main street hugging our baby . . .

Suzhen (*sings*):

. . . All our relatives will say we're so poor we are hopeless.

Guo (*sings*):

We won't go by the main street, we'll use the small lanes;

Suzhen (*sings*):

By winding ways we will go through the *hutongs*.

Guo (*sings*):

Husband and wife leave the village,

Suzhen (*sings*):

And after leaving the village head straight east.

Guo (*sings*):

Black clouds arise in the northwest;

Suzhen (*sings*):

To some wealth comes, to others poverty.

Guo (*sings*):

Can it be that Uncle has bought ten thousand years of wealth?

Suzhen (*sings*):

Can it be that our poverty is bound to a deep karmic root?

Guo (*sings*):

The Heavenly Official Who Increases Blessings has turned his
    back on us;

Suzhen (*sings*):

The hungry ghosts of the starved will not leave our house.

Guo (*sings*):

May the Heavenly Official Who Increases Blessings please come
    to our house . . .

Suzhen (*sings*):

. . . And drive away the hungry ghosts of the starved.

Guo (*sings*):

> Heavenly Official Who Increases Blessings, we invite you to our
> house;

Suzhen (*sings*):

> We will give wine and food to your heart's content.

Guo (*sings*):

> When you hit a board fence then the high is brought low;

Suzhen (*sings*):

> Of ten poor men, nine once were rich.

Guo (*sings*):

> Though the leaves of the *wutong* tree may fall, the trunk survives;

Suzhen (*sings*):

> Just get rid of the branches and twigs and wait for the spring.

Guo (*sings*):

> Even the realm of the Lord of a Myriad Years [the emperor]
> sometimes collapses and shatters;

Suzhen (*sings*):

> The affairs of this world are decided by fate, not by men.

Guo (*sings*):

> Though the fierce tiger is skin and bones, his heart is still heroic;

Suzhen (*sings*):

> Though a gentleman is poor, he is not poor in will.

Guo (*sings*):

> Liu Xiu of the Han dynasty [Emperor Wu] painted tigers and
> climbed mountains;

Suzhen (*sings*):

> Yuan Dan was bitten by a tiger while gathering firewood.

Guo (*sings*):

> All I want is that the poor do not have to be fearful.

Suzhen (*sings*):

> Shi Chong had a dream and was bitten by a scorpion.

Guo (*sings*):

> [The guests come to a rich man's door like a flood.]

Suzhen (*sings*):

> Those presenting mutton and making toasts never leave his gate.

Guo (*sings*):

> Precedence at a banquet is not determined by age;

Suzhen (*sings*):

> Those whose clothes are best are treated best.

Guo (*sings*):

> Neighbors, if you don't believe me, just you look around;

Suzhen (*sings*):

> The first ones to be toasted are the ones with lots of cash.

Guo (*sings*):

  Liu Bei could only sell straw sandals,[11]

Suzhen (*sings*):

  And Lu Zheng'en was a watchman and oil peddler.

Guo (*sings*):

  Zhang Fei had no occupation and could only sell meat,[12]

Suzhen (*sings*):

  And Zhu Maichen was a woodcutter.

Guo (*sings*):

  In the years before a *juren* passes the examinations,

Suzhen (*sings*):

  His relatives act as if he is not human.

Guo (*sings*):

  But later when he gets a regular office,

Suzhen (*sings*):

  All those who had scorned him now pay him homage.

Guo (*sings*):

  There are many ancients of whom we will not speak,

Suzhen (*sings*):

  For shortly we'll arrive at Shuangyang junction.

Guo (*sings*):

  Don't go any farther, wife!

Suzhen (*sings*):

  Is it here that we will bury him?

Guo (*sings*):

  Good wife, please climb the hill and see if there are any travelers.
  If there's a person on any of the four high roads, we won't bury
    him and will go back home.
  If there's no one on the four high roads, then we'll bury our baby
    here.

Suzhen (*sings*):

  I hear what my husband says and climb the hill to look carefully
    around.
  Suzhen has reached the hilltop, and looks off to the west, and
    then to the east.
  Can it be that our baby is fated to die? There is not a soul on the
    four roads.

---

11. Liu Bei, eldest of the three sworn brothers in the *Romance of the Three Kingdoms* and ruler of the kingdom of Shu Han in the Three Kingdoms period.

12. Zhang Fei was the youngest of the three sworn brothers of the *Romance of the Three Kingdoms* and was a butcher before he met the other heroes.

Suzhen comes down from the hill and tells her husband to hurry and dig a hole.

Guo (sings):

> I hear what my good wife says, and dig a grave for our baby.
>
> I take a shovelful, and another; I strike once with the mattock, and once again.
>
> While I am finishing the hole, keep the baby occupied as you wait by the road.

Suzhen (sings):

> I hear what my husband says, and keep the baby occupied as I wait by the road.
>
> I sit on the ground and open my ragged jacket, patches upon patches.
>
> I put the nipple in my boy's mouth, and before long his little belly is as tight as a drum.
>
> Our little baby, not knowing he is to die, gives a tiny smile and tries to stand up in his mother's arms.
>
> As our little baby is on the point of dying in the dirt, I entrust him to you.
>
> I hand over our dear baby to you . . .

Guo (sings):

> . . . And I take him in my arms.
>
> If our little baby dies in the dirt, he will lodge an accusation against me in the court of the King of the Underworld.
>
> Lord Yama will weigh your accusation, and bring your father to the Dark City.
>
> If you testify against me, I will be pitched with a trident into a vat of boiling oil.
>
> This is the punishment for anyone who buries a little baby alive, blaming us for something we were too poor to avoid.
>
> I hand over the baby to you, so I can dig the hole deeper.
>
> I can't lift another shovelful, [two characters illegible] I fall to the ground.
>
> My vision dims, my head swims — I have not eaten for three meals, how can I have the strength to dig a hole?
>
> Before long I stop digging, and tell my wife to bury our son.

Suzhen (sings):

> I crawl forward a few inches on my knees and look into the hole.
>
> But it is not just a hole in the ground, it is my baby's grave.
>
> If I put my baby in that hole he will scratch at the dirt with his hands and push at it with his feet.
>
> Your warm, breathing body, that cold dirt — all I can do is hug my baby tighter.
>
> I think you haven't dug the hole deep enough; the wolves that seize, the dogs that tear will break my heart.

I ask my husband to dig the hole deeper, to dig it deep enough to
    cover our son.

Guo (*sings*):

Guo Ju is angry, his rage pours out; he heaps curses on his wife's
    head:

Remember what you said at home? You should not have made a
    vow to Heaven.

[Because of your vow] it is impossible to not bury him, and if we
    bury him you will escape [divine punishment].

Looking toward my house in the distance I call to my old
    mother; Mother who raised me, why don't you reply?

When Mother dies I will put on deep mourning; but who will
    have a funeral for me when I die?

I turn my back on my house; gaze at my baby, gaze at the hole.

Little baby, you are a foot and a half long, but the hole is only a
    foot.

I dig out another shovelful, and another; hack out another chunk,
    and another.

Three shovelfuls, four shovelfuls — and bright silver gleams in the
    hole!

Suzhen (*speaks*): Oh, my son, I can't look at you!

Guo (*speaks*): My son! Don't cry! [*Laughs.*]

Suzhen (*speaks*): How can you laugh at such a time?!

Guo (*speaks*): There's silver!

Suzhen (*speaks*): Oh, my God! I've never seen silver!

Guo (*speaks*): Wife, embrace me! Ai-ya! Eighteen pieces of silver and gold!
    Wife, don't do anything, I'm going to take some pieces home to be filial to
    Mother!

(*Sings*)

High blue Heaven cannot be deceived.

Suzhen (*sings*):

Don't laugh at poor people wearing rags.

Guo (*sings*):

Everyone desires riches and children.

Suzhen (*sings*):

Wealth and glory are bestowed by Heaven.

Guo (*speaks*): Yes, wealth and glory are bestowed by Heaven. Now let us go
    and be filial to Mother. Husband and wife make obeisance to the sky, ha-
    ha, oh ha-ha-ha!

[Li Jinghan and Zhang Shiwen, eds., *Dingxian yangge xuan* 2:268–279[13] — DJ]

---

13. Translations of the Ding County *yangge* made by various collaborators were published by
Sidney Gamble in his *Chinese Village Plays* (Amsterdam: Philo Press, 1970). The translation
given here is a new one but remains indebted to Gamble's pioneering work.

# PART TWO: SOLO PERFORMANCE

Opera and ritual were part of a single performance complex: they took place at the same time, in the same place (except in large cities that had commercial theaters), for the same reasons. They also did not take place very often; a god's birthday or a great exorcism came no more than once a year. There were many professional entertainers, however, who did not require elaborate costumes or even a stage. Working alone or with a partner, they could perform in a villager's home, in a teahouse, on a street corner, even in the fields. These lesser performance genres — teahouse storytelling, ballad singing, streetside lecturing, *baojuan* recitation (see p. 126), and the like — in a sense filled the gaps left by ritual and opera. They brought professional performance into everyday life.

Because these genres were so personal and were performed to small audiences in relatively informal settings, they were highly effective in communicating ideas and values. Indeed, the solo genres, rather than opera and ritual, were the most effective vehicles ever devised in China for the *intentional* inculcation in ordinary people of *specific* religious ideas and ethical values. The main purpose of ritual was to bridge the gap between the human and divine worlds; opera aimed to entertain. Both taught, of course, and taught powerfully, but that was seldom their primary purpose. If you had a message to convey to people, you would not usually write an opera or a liturgy. Hence the solo genres are of great importance for this survey. There was an immense variety of them, but they can conveniently be divided into three types on the basis of literary form: verse, prose, and chantefable, a combination of verse and prose.

## *VERSE*

There were many kinds of narrative song. Some were accompanied by wooden clappers, others by drums, yet others by the *pipa*, and their subjects ranged from the romantic to the pious. Together they form a mighty stream of Chinese popular literature, and it is not surprising that many religious works can be found among them, including some, such as the following, of great dramatic power.

### WOMAN HUANG EXPLICATES THE DIAMOND *SŪTRA*

The *tanci* genre first developed during the late sixteenth century in the coastal areas of Jiangsu, Zhejiang, Fujian, and Guangdong, and by the eighteenth century it had become a largely urban art centered in cities such as Suzhou, Hangzhou, Yangzhou, and Guangzhou. "By early Qing times *tanci* had already become immensely popular, particularly with the women in large southern cities, and the stories concentrated on the theme of romantic love. . . . Late Ming and early Qing *tanci* were also closely related to the *baojuan*, which promulgated popular Buddhism and various folk religions."[14] This *tanci* gives a vivid portrayal of the tragic conflict between Woman Huang's love for her family and her desire for salvation, which requires renouncing such ties.

The text was published in Shanghai, probably in the first decade of this century; it is almost entirely in seven-syllable verse.

*The* tanci *begins with Woman Huang (we are never told her given name) attempting to persuade her husband to give up being a butcher.*

> "As a butcher you are committing sins without end,
> And the sufferings of Hell will be hard to endure."

*Her husband, Zhao Lianfang, who has previously argued that he does not believe in the karmic retribution she is warning him about, now reminds her that she herself is polluted because she has given birth to three children.*

> "When you gave birth to your children you also committed a sin:
> How many bowls of bloody water, how many bowls of fluids?
> For every child, there were three basins of water;
> Three children, and thus nine basins of fluids.
> You dumped the bloody waters into the gutters,
> And so you polluted the Sprite of the Eaves.
> Three mornings and you were already back in the kitchen,
> And so you polluted the God of the Stove.
> Before ten days were up, you went into the front hall,
> And so you polluted the household gods and ancestors.
> Before a month was up, you went out of doors,
> And so you polluted the sun, the moon, and the stars.
> You washed the bloodstained clothing in the river,
> And the tainted waters polluted the Dragon King.
> You spilled these waters onto the ground,
> And the spirits of Hell had nowhere to hide.
> After washing the clothes, you laid them on the bank to dry,
> And so you polluted the Great Yin and the Great Yang.
> In vain you rely on your reading of the *Diamond Sūtra* —
> The sins of a lifetime will not be easily redeemed."

*Woman Huang is horrified by her husband's words, and immediately dresses in simple clothing, puts away her makeup, and resolves to dedicate herself solely to her devotions,*

---

14. Wm. H. Nienhauser, ed., *The Indiana Companion to Traditional Chinese Literature* (Bloomington: Indiana University Press, 1986), 6.747B.

*in particular the recitation of the* Diamond Sūtra, *in order to purify herself. However, this also means that she must no longer share her husband's bed or do any housework. Zhao Lianfang, afraid now that the household will fall apart, pleads with her to keep the marriage vows they once made and continue to fulfill her wifely responsibilities. She, in return, replies that the love between husband and wife will not last forever.*

> "Do not say that you have a long life ahead of you,
> In a blink of an eye, your hair will turn white.
> Every life, every death, is like a spring dream. . . .
> My husband, think carefully about the life you've led,
> Why not change your ways and read the *Diamond Sūtra?*
> Here at home, I have the simple robes of a monk,
> Let's go to the *sūtra* hall and repeat the Buddha's name.
> Even if a man's life were to last a hundred thousand years,
> It would still be better to do good and not go astray.
> Whether it be riches or fame, it is all up to Heaven,
> So we must heed Heaven's will in living out our days.
> For Death cannot be bought with coins of gold and silver.
> Why then suffer so, dashing madly to and fro?"

*Zhao Lianfang is finally swayed by his wife's tears and her pleas:*

> "Today let us each live in separate rooms,
> And so avoid your lifetime being shortened.
> The three-year-old boy will go along with me,
> Cut as with a knife from his mother's milk.
> We will never again share the same bed,
> Nor think of ourselves as husband and wife."

*Woman Huang then expresses her deep gratitude for her husband's understanding and, taking her two daughters with her, goes into the* sūtra *hall and begins to recite the* Diamond Sūtra *day in and day out, leaving all of the household responsibilities to her husband. In due course, her religious zeal attracts the attention of King Yama, and he sends the Golden Lad and Jade Maiden to bring Woman Huang down to the Underworld to explicate the* sūtra *(which, of course, means her death). Woman Huang is very frightened by the sight of King Yama's messengers and attempts to bribe them to leave and come for her again after her children are grown. She is not afraid of death herself, but is reluctant to leave her children behind. She also begins to question her own faith:*

> When Woman Huang heard this, her blood ran cold,
> And the tears from her eyes rolled down her chest.
> "But reading the *sūtras* should lengthen one's life,
> Who would have known that chanting cuts it short!?

If you want me to give up my life, I don't mind,
But to leave behind my children would break my heart."


*The Underworld messengers remain unmoved, however, and Woman Huang, resigned to her fate, asks only to bid farewell to her family, which she does in a series of very moving passages. These make it clear that she is well aware of the possibility of being criticized for her negligence as both wife and mother, another indication of the sense of spiritual crisis that pervades the story.*

*After an extended tour of the Underworld and all its horrors, Woman Huang is brought before the Kings of the Ten Courts and is put through a long interrogation to test her piety (which also serves as a kind of popular catechism for the audience), all the more stringent because she is a woman, and a mother as well. The interrogation covers many different areas, including an extended section on the origin and history of the* Diamond Sūtra *and its efficacy. Woman Huang answers all the questions in great detail, breaking down only when she is reciting all the benefits of reciting the* Diamond Sūtra, *which include long life, as once again she expresses her bafflement and sense of betrayal:*


"Although the *Diamond Sūtra* can still be found in the
    world,
You will hardly find anyone who chants *sūtras* and
    Buddha's name.
I began reciting the *sūtra* at the tender age of seven;
Why then has King Yama cut my life short and summoned
    me here?"
When King Yama heard this, he smiled slightly:
"Good Woman, how very little you know.
To die early is actually a much better thing;
Why do you want to remain in a woman's body?"


*Finally, Woman Huang is asked to ascend a tall platform, built expressly for the purpose, and recite the* Diamond Sūtra. *However, before she has finished reciting it she is asked to stop, since the combined power of her piety and the* Diamond Sūtra *itself is causing havoc in the universe by bringing salvation to the evil as well as the good.*


King Yama then said, "Good Woman, please sit down;
Listen and I will explain it to you from the start.
If you recite this *sūtra* three entire times,
The Living Buddhas of the Western Heaven will appear!
The Lord on High will open up the Avici Hell,
And the Gods of the Underworld will not kill people.
The North Star will not dare determine life and death,
And the South Star will not dare determine lifespan.

Good and Evil will be difficult to distinguish,
Human kings and emperors will also be worried."

*We have here the real expression of Woman Huang's power, the power of a compassion so great that it threatens to destroy the distinction between right and wrong, not only in the Underworld but in the world of the living as well.*

*Woman Huang is reborn as the talented son of a wealthy and pious couple named Zhang. He passes the examinations and becomes an official, only to renounce his career to seek enlightenment with his parents. Earlier, this Zhang had visited Woman Huang's former family and discovered that they all were prosperous and happy. When Zhang's spiritual cultivation allows him to transcend his mortal soul, which, of course, is Woman Huang's soul, it is reborn in the second son of Woman Huang's son, bringing this tale of salvation and reincarnation almost full circle.*

[*Gailiang Huang shinü you difu dui Jingang chuan ben: Zhongyang yanjiuyuan Lishi yuyan yanjiusno cang Suqu*, microfilms reel 19. Adapted from Grant, "The Spiritual Saga of Woman Huang," pp. 266–287 — DJ]

### SONG OF GUO MOUNTAIN

This is a brief hagiography of the Honored King of Broad Compassion (*Guangze Zun Wang*), whose cult, which originated in the late tenth century, is one of the most important in the province of Fujian. The main temple is located on Guo Mountain, near Shishan in Nan'an County, Fujian, but another center of the cult is the tomb of the god's parents, about fifteen miles away. Both Daoist and Confucian rituals are used in the celebration of the cult today. This song is an excellent example of how narrative verse could be used to convey the central elements in the myth of a popular deity. According to the *Guoshan Temple Record* (1897), a collection of works relating to the home temple of the cult, our text is based on a song in an "old ballad book." Was it ever actually performed in this form? That is hard to say, but it is written in the seven-character lines standard for popular narrative verse, and the confusing quality of some of the narrative may suggest that it has not undergone significant literati editing.

Beneath Poetry Mountain in Minnan [southern Fujian] in the
   Later Tang
Master Guo had a son but no daughters. The boy had a lofty
   nature, quite uncommon;
The family was poor, there was nowhere for him to study.
At the household of Yang the Elder
They received their meals in return for looking after the livestock.
Thinking of his parents, he wept through winter and summer.
August Heaven was unkind — he lost his father;
Mother and son stood face-to-face deep in sadness.

Her dowry could not cover the costs of a grave site;
Leaving a relative unburied, they felt empty and sad.
Who should come along but an old man with white hair;
Stroking his beard by the side of the road he spoke to them.
Their misery and complete filial piety moved him;
He truly showed them a perfect grave site in the shape of a
    sleeping cow.
The boy went to Yang the Elder's home and begged for it.
"No matter how much you beg I won't give it to you."
Then he pitied this young boy of such a perfect nature;
He called him back and listened to him.
"We are in dire straits; wind and rain pierce our lonely hut.
I seek a single grave mound in which to rest the spirit of my
    ancestor.
When my father was alive, it was hard for me to leave home.
Now that my father is dead, my mother's life is even more
    difficult.
Depending on others we cannot experience good times.
We eat vegetables and drink water in the side courtyards."
From antiquity perfect sincerity could model Heaven.
The birds planting and the elephants plowing [for the filial
    paragon Shun] were no ordinary events—
How much more so such perfect conduct in one so young.
Mysteriously his conduct truly moved Heaven to feel pity.
The Heavenly Emperor said, "Ah, on the earth below there is a
    filial boy."
He ordered Wu Yang [the legendary physician] to descend and
    summon him, saying,
"Otherwise I fear he will be consumed by goblins."
In the setting sun the boy stood in a straw raincoat on the top of
    the mountain.
"Who is it that comes here?" It was the Taishen, the Messenger
    of Heaven,
In embroidered robes, riding a horse with feathered cape.
Holding jade court tablets and golden books, he proclaimed the
    emperor's words. "I don't want to go to Heaven; I want to stay
    on earth.
At home I have an old mother who relies on her only son."
But alas, how could the emperor's order be disregarded?
He sat atop an ancient vine and died with tears streaming down.
The wine was gone from his wine-jar and only the bones were
    left of his buffalo.
These strange events indeed coincide with those of antiquity.

By his side was a group of children scared half witless;
The cattle returned and pushed against the thatch fence.
His mother threw down her spinning and rushed to see what had
    happened.
His two eyes shone brilliantly and his left foot hung down.
"My son, after you are gone, how will I live on?"
The pain of his old mother could not be assuaged,
She wailed and wept in the empty mountains; her tears fell like
    the rain.
The elders knelt down by the roadside and said,
"Old woman, do not feel so bitter this night;
Your son has transformed this village with his filial piety."
These events were fully recorded.
See how the neighboring women and children brought her food.
Later Heaven sent down a jade casket;
Like the people of Lu, she was buried together with her husband.
From this time on, the power of the Honored King of Broad
    Compassion took shape.
Horses of wind and chariots of clouds came down
To express thanks to the people of the village for carrying out his
    wishes.
In his home region he drives away disaster and sweeps away
    adversity.
Beginning in the Tang and Song dynasties and lasting for so
    many springs and autumns,
His magnificent temple stands atop Phoenix Mountain.
He drove away plagues of insects and demons of drought;
With his deep red banner on his white horse, he routed rebel
    leaders.
His heavenly words are resplendent; he is worshiped in the
    Register of Sacrifices.
Living under the care of the True King, people have no worries.
His overflowing virtue and abundant deeds are difficult to
    recount in full.

> [Dai Fengyi, *Guoshan miaozhi* 7:3–4; adapted from Dean,
> *Taoist Ritual and Popular Cults*, pp. 150–151 — DJ]

## PROSE

Didactic lecturing and storytelling were quite common by Qing times. In early twentieth-century Hunan, for example, there was something called simply "lecturing," of which we have an eyewitness description: "I would often go and listen to performers reciting and singing in the alleyways and at the foot of the bridge [in my village]. . . . On the fifteenth of the first month there would also be lecturing. The lecturer would place candles and incense on the 'platform of good and evil' and, seated on it, would tell tales of good and evil." In Hubei such performances were called "morality books" (*shanshu*). "After the harvest was in, a tall platform would be erected in a clearing in the fields and decorated with candles and incense. Then a professional performer would ascend the platform and, with the help of a written text, chant the story. The atmosphere was rather somber and sad, and the performance would often elicit weeping and wailing from the women. . . . The most popular forms of entertainment among the rural villagers were local drama, shadow plays, and these *shanshu* performances."[15] There was also a fascinating type of performance known as Sacred Edict lecturing, which is the subject of the following selection.

### SACRED EDICT LECTURING

The maxims of the Qing emperors Kangxi and Yongzheng, known as the Sacred Edicts, are presented in chapter 25. They were recited and explained by men in authority on formal occasions and probably reached the ears, if not the hearts, of millions of people in that form. But discoursing on the Sacred Edict did not remain a monopoly of officials; at some point itinerant storytellers began telling moralistic but entertaining stories under the guise of "Sacred Edict lecturing." The following is a description by the great scholar Guo Moruo of Sacred Edict lecturing in rural Sichuan early in the twentieth century. (Note that the "lecturers" familiar to Guo used a combination of prose and verse.)

Sacred Edict lecturers, who recited *shanshu* about loyalty, filial piety, and fidelity, often came to our village. Most *shanshu* were nothing but our own legends or tales. In form, the narratives were a combination of speech and song, very much like *tanci*, though not identical to them. . . . At a street corner they would set up a high platform made of three square tables, one placed atop the other two. On the platform, incense and candles were lit as offerings to the plaque of the Sacred Edict. A chair was placed on the right-hand table. If two people performed together, then a chair was placed on each of the side tables. When it came time for the Sacred Edict lecturer to preach, he, dressed in the cap and gown of an official, would kowtow deeply four times to the plaque. Then he would stand up again and, drawing out his voice, would recite the ten [*sic*] maxims of the Sacred Edict. After that, he would get back up on the platform and begin his performance. As for the style of delivery, he would recite from a text quite artlessly. The sung parts were sung with drawn-out tones, to which was added the sound of weeping at tragic moments. Some of the lecturers would accompany themselves with bells, "fish tubes," bamboo clappers, and the like to help their tunes along. This artless kind of storytelling was a form of

---

15. Beata Grant, "The Spiritual Saga of Woman Huang," pp. 252–53.

entertainment that people in the villages liked very much. They would stand before the Sacred Edict platform and listen for two or three hours. The better storytellers could make their audiences weep.

[Guo Moruo, *Moruo wenji* 6:29–30; trans. adapted from Mair, "Language and Ideology," pp. 354–355 — DJ]

## CHANTEFABLE

Didactic narratives using a combination of verse and prose (chantefable) originated, at the latest, in the Tang dynasty. Manuscripts from the late Tang and Five Dynasties (eighth to tenth centuries) containing prosimetric accounts of Mulian's rescue of his mother and of the contest between Buddha's disciple Śāriputra and the heretical wizard Raudrākṣa have been discovered in Dunhuang. For the next thousand years, chantefable never lost popularity, and it eventually gave rise to many of the most important genres of popular performing literature, such as *cihua, guci, dagu, zidishu, tanci*, and *baojuan*. It is *baojuan* with which we will be concerned in this section.

The term *baojuan* was used to refer to various kinds of texts, unfortunately. Some, which clearly grew out of performance, were long narratives of the struggles of pious men and women to convert their families or to attain salvation. Since we have already looked at a text with a very similar theme, the Woman Huang *tanci*, we will not consider this type further. There were other *baojuan* that were concerned more with ethical or theological instruction than with stories that illustrate them. The Stove God *baojuan* introduced below is an example of this type.

Yet other texts labeled *baojuan* expounded, often in the words of a god, theological or eschatological doctrines, especially those of the White Lotus system, but we will postpone consideration of this type of text, which is better called "scripture," until the next section, where it properly belongs, since it was probably intended for reading or congregational recitation rather than performance.

### THE PRECIOUS SCROLL [BAOJUAN] ON THE LORD OF THE STOVE

The cult of the stove was very ancient, and by late imperial times it had become nearly universal in China. Rare was the kitchen that did not have a small shrine to "Grandfather King of the Stove" (*Zao wang ye*), with a woodblock print of the god pasted on the wall and incense burning before it. Most people believed that the god left the kitchen to make a report to the Jade Emperor on the twenty-fourth (or twenty-third) of the twelfth lunar month and returned from Heaven on New Year's Eve. There were ceremonies in the family both to send him off and to welcome him back. He functioned in theory as a divine spy in the bosom of the family, one who was particularly concerned with the behavior of the women. But people did not fear him, and the ceremonies appear to have been occasions of fun rather than religious devotion, at least in the last century or so.

A sterner version of the cult was contained in the Stove God *baojuan* and Stove God scriptures, of which there were many. The authors of both *baojuan* and scriptures wanted to popularize the idea that the god made a report to the heavenly authorities every month, and hence those texts stress the need for constant moral self-examination. They are concerned with controlling the behavior of the family's women and strengthening the structure of authority, but at the same time, somewhat unexpectedly, many also strongly advocate basic Buddhist teachings, like those we have seen in *Mulian* or the Woman Huang *tanci*, and the perennial ethics of the Chinese village, such as those we encountered in *Guo Ju Buries His Son*.

The Baojuan *on the Lord of the Stove* is firmly in the chantefable tradition and may be quite close to actual performance. From internal evidence we know that it was chanted or recited by a single person, with occasional group responses (see the opening section and the repeated response "Praise to the Bodhisattva August One of the Wheel of Fire"). It appears to have been performed at home, with the family as the audience.

Our text is an undated manuscript in the Shanghai Library, written largely in vernacular verse of seven characters per line.

*The text begins with a section in literary Chinese establishing the sanctity of the ritual arena within which it was to be performed.*

> The *baojuan* on the Lord of the Stove is now first unfolded,
> All the bodhisattvas descend.
> It is an auspicious time, the ecliptic today opens up:
> Respectfully I urge you all to recite the name of the Buddha.
> Through the hundred years [of a lifetime], thirty-six thousand days,
> If you do not constantly eat vegetarian food you are foolish.
> We bow our heads and submit, unfolding hearts of goodness,
> All the Buddhas are accordingly delighted, and all have the
>    same name.
> As I expound on the subtle and marvelous *dharma* of the
>    sacred wise ones,
> Friends with understanding will accept it and listen with
>    all their hearts.

The great masses jointly reveal that their piety and sincerity have been cultivated to completion, and first present the offering of a vegetarian repast to respectfully invite the myriad of spirits from the Ten Quarters, Three Treasures, and Ocean of Benefit to come together to witness the covenant and create a Sacred Congregation to the Lord of the Stove. Your Disciple, on behalf of the ancestors, promulgates the "Precious Scroll on the Lord of the Stove." . . . It is necessary to still the mind and listen to the promulgation, and cry out praise with one voice. The Three Karmas will be washed clean, and if one prays for good fortune, good fortune will naturally come, and if one performs exorcism to ward off disaster, disaster will be extinguished.

*There follows a section in which the listeners are urged to honor their parents, ancestors, and the patriarch masters of the three teachings of Buddhism, Daoism, and Confucianism. This ends with the exhortation "Let each of those present hail with one voice the fullness of the god's piety and sincerity." The next section recounts the origin myth of the Stove God.*

The story says: Formerly, when Undifferentiated Chaos and the world had not yet been divided, there was a Buddha named Lamplighter. He was a proper ancient Buddha. Once he was on Spirit Vulture Peak explaining the *dharma*. Then Lord Lao [i.e., Laozi], leading the Perfected One of Miraculous Action, joined Lamplighter in discussing the hour for the Opening of the Prime. Suddenly they saw a shaft of red light rush up, piercing straight through Spirit Vulture Peak. At this time the three Buddhas hurriedly mounted a cloud and followed the red light to a mountain peak. This mountain was called Mount Kunlun. On its peak was a huge tree, its roots and leaves rich and luxuriant. In its branches was a large jujube. The jujube fell onto a great rock. Then a powerful light flashing in many colors came from the inside of the rock. Immediately the rock burst open and a person appeared. His/her name was Plucking the Source. The three of them stood still on the edge of the cloud, watching. Then a girl-child appeared from inside the jujube. Lamplighter hurried down off the cloud, embraced her, and bestowed a mark upon her. Lord Lao touched the rock, and suddenly a spring of the milk of the Celestial Transcendents flowed forth. . . . Gradually the girl grew to adulthood and became the Mother of Fire. She meditated on top of the rock, waiting for the world to be complete. . . . Sitting on the high mountain she cultivated the Way for a thousand years.

> . . . Sitting upright on Kunlun the goddess refined her pneumas,
> Waiting in anticipation of the completion of the world.
> The entire body of the Old Mother was fire,
> The rock beside her was fire in solid form.
> Neither hungry nor sated,
> She drank only from the springs of Heaven;
>     the dew was not pure. . . .
> When the red sun came up the sky grew light,
> When the sun sank down again it was pitch dark.
> When hunger came people ate only the herbs and leaves
>     of the Transcendents,
> When it was cold they could only cover themselves with skins.
> People did not eat the Five Grains so they had no strength,

It was difficult for them to cultivate, plant, and be tillers
    of the land.
Though in the time of the Three August Ones they had nests,
What method did they have for getting the Source of Fire?
All in the world of the Ten Quarters were despondent
    and worried.
From the sky descended a Perfected One,
He ascended straight to the Upper Realm, summoned
    by the Jade Emperor.
He bowed down and presented his words to the Exalted One.

The Perfected One was the Perfected One of Miraculous Action. Holding his tablet in front of his breast, he memorialized: "The world below is completed, men and women are paired together. Although there are the Five Grains, there is no fire. They cannot eat raw food, thus I report to the throne."

*He goes on to recommend that the Old Mother be sent to bring fire to the world.*

When the Jade Emperor received the memorial, he exclaimed, "Good! Good! Since there is a Divine Mother Who Seeds Fire, summon her here for me so that she may rescue mortal men." Lord Lao memorialized again: "If you summon the Old Mother here, you must invest her with an official title and give her the authority to control troops. Otherwise I do not know whether she will be willing to save mortals." The Jade Emperor approved the memorial. Then he told the Golden Lad and Jade Maiden to go to the peak of Mount Kunlun and make manifest the summons to the Mother of Fire.

    . . .

The Jade Emperor transmitted his summons that she come
    at once.
The Golden Lad and Jade Maiden floated off on their cloud
To swiftly announce that the Old Mother was to go to the
    Courts of Heaven.
They hurried to the peak of Mount Kunlun;
They came before the Old Mother and said,
"The Saintly Orders have come from on high to summon you."
When the Old Mother heard this she was delighted in her heart;
She gathered up her fiery rock and mounted the cloudy road.
In less than an instant she reached the Palace of Heaven,
And walked straight up into the Basilica of the Numinous Empyrean.
Three times she called "Ten Thousand Years!" and called herself
    "Vassal."
The light of the fiery rock illuminated the entire Gate of
    Heaven. . . .

[The Old Mother said,] "If the Jade Emperor wants good fortune
    to redden the world,
I am willing to bestow fire on the mortals below."
. . .

The Jade Emperor enfeoffed her as the Lord of the Stove,
To rescue mortal men with fire,
To inspect the affairs of the world of men,
To report good and evil to the Courts of Heaven.

Praise to the Bodhisattva August One of the Wheel of Fire!

*The Old Mother then creates five subsidiary lords of fire, who are enfeoffed by the Jade
Emperor as the Emperors of the Five Directions.*

They investigate and inspect men, watch them do good and evil;
Every month on the twenty-fourth day they report to the
    Court of Heaven.
They write in two books the good and evil in the world;
Based on this, disasters and good fortune are sent down to men.

*The text next names the things that must not be done in and around the stove. Since
this list is very much shorter than in other Stove God baojuan, I include additional
prohibitions from another Stove God text.*

Lord Lao said, "All of the stoves in the homes of mortal man have prohibitions and taboos." The Perfected One of Miraculous Action said . . . "I wish to
hear the explanation of this." Lord Lao said, "The stoves in the homes of mortal
men may not be violated or offended against with chicken feathers, dog bones,
human hair, knives and axes, unclean firewood and fuel, and other foul and
filthy things. [It is forbidden to knock on the pots and stove, and throw about
and destroy implements and vessels; to expose the body, sing, cry, or weep before
the stove, or to come into the kitchen if one has recently given birth; to urinate
or defecate, and beat or curse before the stove; to turn small children loose on
the floor near the stove; to set up pigsties and privies close to the kitchen; to
put one's feet on the door of the stove, and wrap one's feet in the kitchen; to
dry dirty shoes and stockings and wet clothes in the stove; to leave things in the
kitchen or on the stove overnight.]
"If these things are done, the God of the Stove will immediately provoke
discord between men and women, entangle people in disease and ailments,
cause dimness and darkness of the eyes, reversals of dreams and waking
thoughts, barrenness of fields and silkworms, and wasting and exhaustion
among the six domestic animals. He will allow strange demons to enter into
the house fearlessly and at random, thieves and bandits to intrude and harass,
quarrels and trouble from officials to arise, and the family patrimony to be

scattered and lost. If one suffers from desperate difficulties, one should summon a true Buddhist monk who practices the precepts, or a Gentleman of the Way [Daoist priest], to set up a full Congregation of the Lord of the Stove. . . ."

Let everyone piously and sincerely praise with one voice.

*The text now describes the Stove God's reports on people's good and bad deeds.*

> First [the Stove God] made clear records in the Books of Virtue.
> The virtuous practice filial piety and burn incense,
> They maintain a vegetarian diet, keep the precepts, and chant
>     the texts of the *sūtras*.
> They carry out respectful rituals to the saints and wise men
>     and follow the Three [Buddhist] Treasures.
> They give vegetarian food to monks and nuns and those
>     who seek something to eat,
> They are filial to their parents-in-law and respect their parents.
> They honor their relatives and older and younger uncles.
> They make scriptures to distribute and install statues
>     of the Buddha.
> They support and maintain those in crisis and trouble,
>     and aid the orphaned and poor.
> They build bell towers and also temples.
> They build bridges and lay roads for people to walk on.
> In summer they give out tea and open up public wells,
> In winter they give out padded jackets and light bright lamps.
> Through all twelve periods of the day they practice great filial
>     piety.
> They are harmonious with their relatives and with all the
>     people of the neighborhood and village.

The Lord of the Stove reported the virtuous people to the Celestial Departments. When the Jade Emperor looked at the records, his dragon face was delighted. "Excellent! Excellent!" he said. "That there are such good people in the realm below! Quickly send the Lads of the Record-Books." At that time the Lord of the Stove and the Emperors of the Five Directions said, "Add to their good fortune and longevity, exempt them from disasters and calamities. . . ."

> When the household is pure and clean the gods are delighted,
> When the thought arises to do malevolent deeds the gods
>     and ghosts are enraged.
> The Stove God investigates the things that anger them,
> And makes clear notations in the Record-Books of Evil.
> The wealthy bully the poor and harm the good.

Plot to swallow up fields and get more women to marry.

The poor steal firewood and pilfer rice,
Kidnap widows and unmarried girls for licentious purposes.
They rob traveling merchants of their wealth and property,
Steal chickens, drag away dogs, and kill living things.
Birds, fish, fowls, beasts, and sparrows that fly by,
Snails, loach, and eels: they seize them, cook them, and
    gulp them down.
Killing hosts of living things is constantly in their thoughts,
They cook filthy and polluted things on the stove.
Through all twelve periods of the day they practice evil deeds.
The Lord of the Stove recorded them all clearly,
In an instant he ascended to Heaven to report to the
    Jade Emperor;
When the Jade Emperor saw the records he was furious
    and enraged.

*There follows a list of the diseases and afflictions sent down to punish sinners.*

Both good and evil are caused by oneself alone; Heaven and Hell
    one must bear oneself.
Praise to the Bodhisattva August One of the Wheel of Fire!
The spirit soldiers of the Department of Pestilence set out
    with their orders.
The guilt of those who do evil is not light.
Evil wealthy people bully the virtuous and good,
In a short time their good fortune is exhausted and disaster
    comes to life.
If they plot to take over the fields and crops of poor families,
Their children will be kidnapped and sold to others.
If they steal the property and goods of poor families,
There will be violent disasters and lawsuits; it will be hard
    for them to survive.
If they licentiously seduce the sons, wives, and daughters of
    good families,
Their own wives will run away with someone else.
If they steal chickens, geese, and ducks to cook, eat, or sell,
Their own birds will never be numerous enough to form flocks.
Those who kill living things to gulp down different flavors
Will bear the brunt of returning and repaying each one of them.
For those who love to eat the Five Non-Vegetarian Foods and
    the Three Disgusting Things,
All ten evils will be clearly noted in the record-books.

*There follows a section devoted to the sins of women, at whom much of this text is aimed. It concludes with a ritual of confession, written in literary Chinese, which ends with the following verse.*

In making confession and repentance we also seek a writ of pardon.
We cleanse our hearts and dare not commit more crimes.
The karma of a thousand forms of sin August Heaven sends away,
The punishment from ten thousand wrongs the Overseer of Destiny
    expunges.
Our bodies fill with light like the brilliant sun,
Our forms are pure and clean like glass. . . .
I urge good men and faithful women,
Return home and be filial to your parents immediately.
Do not say that Azure Heaven has no retribution or response:
Or out of the empty sky lightning will flash and you will hear
    the sound of thunder. . . .
The Earth Gods of one's locale will increase good fortune
    and longevity,
The souls of the ancestors will achieve salvation sooner.
It has all been gathered together into the Precious Scroll on the
    Lord of the Stove, which exhorts people to do good,
Exhorts mortals and the people of the world universally.
The proclamation of the Precious Scroll is ended;
We respectfully see off the Buddhas and monks of the *dharma*
    of all the heavens.
The deities and spirits of the Upper Realm return to the
    Golden Pylons,
The spirits of the Middle Realm go back to their basilicas
    and courts,
The denizens of the dim and stygian realms return to the
    Underworld,
And the good and sincere from the Ten Quarters return to
    their homes.

[*Zao huang baojuan*, MS in Shanghai Library; adapted from Chard, "Master of the Family," pp. 348–370, 321–322; and chaps. 1 and 2 — DJ]

## PART THREE: WRITTEN TEXTS

As I said in the introduction to this chapter, there were — apart from spontaneous everyday social interactions — two different ways to communicate moral and religious ideas and values to ordinary people in premodern China: scripted performances and written texts. The former, much the most important, have concerned us up to this point. But written texts also had a role to play, for not all villagers or poor townsfolk were illiterate. There was in fact a range of non-elite literacies, and books and pamphlets were written for each level in it. These varied from romantic fiction and joke books to collections of medical prescriptions, letter-writing manuals, and scriptures.

## SCRIPTURES

Of writings about ethics and religion aimed at nonelite readers we can identify three types: first, morality books (*shanshu*), which inculcated conventional ethics and are discussed at length in the first volume of *Sources of Chinese Tradition*; second, the short pamphlets closely related to *shanshu* that I call tracts; and third, books that presented the teachings of popular deities or re-counted their lives and works — that is, scriptures (*jing*). It is difficult to make a clear distinction between *jing* and *baojuan*. The terms were not used consistently, so the presence of the word *baojuan* or *jing* in the title of a work does not guarantee that it will have a specific form. It is therefore necessary to consider how the two types of texts differed, regardless of labels. The type that I have called *baojuan* was written in a combination of prose and verse, and was presented by a professional or highly skilled amateur, sometimes with musical or percussion accompaniment, to an audience. The type that I am calling *jing* or scripture contained less verse, frequently claimed to be the words of a god transmitted through a possessed spirit-medium, and was intended for private reading or for recitation by small congregations of believers.

The recitation of written scriptures was central to the many popular religious sects that became increasingly important in China after the fifteenth century. As Susan Naquin writes, "Because of the role of [scripture] recitation, these sects attracted relatively literate followers. . . . Possession of religious books was crucial to the operation of these sects. Joining a sect meant gaining an opportunity to see and hold these books, to learn to chant and to read them, and perhaps even to make handwritten copies. [Sect] teachers . . . may have lectured on the scriptures and taught reading indirectly through character-by-character explications."[16]

Clearly the *baojuan* genre, as I have defined it, shades into the scripture genre, and distinguishing between the two is difficult in the absence of information on how they were used in practice. Indeed, it can be hard to decide whether any text of the solo/duo genres was intended for performance or for reading. Yet despite the lack of a sharp boundary between *baojuan* and scriptures, the basic distinction between texts intended to be performed for audiences and those intended to be read is of great analytic significance.

---

16. Susan Naquin, "The Transmission of White Lotus Sectarianism in Late Imperial China," in David Johnson et al., ed., *Popular Culture in Late Imperial China* (Berkeley: University of California Press, 1985), pp. 260, 263.

## THE TRUE SCRIPTURE OF THE GREAT EMPEROR

The cult of Bao Sheng Da Di, the Great Emperor Who Protects Life, can be found throughout southeastern China and Taiwan. It honors Wu Dao, the Divine Doctor, a Buddho-Daoist deity who lived in the late tenth and early eleventh centuries. Kenneth Dean states that the *True Scripture* was written after the middle of the fifteenth century. The text itself states that it was composed in part by a spirit-medium in trance, and the Bao Sheng Da Di cult appears to have had especially close connections with spirit-mediumship. According to Dean, this was due to the role of medicine and exorcism in the cult.

The scripture defines itself as a text to be read and recited, not as a script to be performed: "If any man or woman obtain my true scripture with its marvelous seal, faithfully keep and worship them. Either invite Buddhist or Daoist priests to recite the scripture [as with a *sūtra* or Daoist scripture] or organize an association to read and recite it." Other internal evidence also suggests that the *True Scripture* was probably intended for private reading or congregational recitation. The fact that it was printed also suggests that its primary audience was readers.

Printed with donations collected by the Snowy Sea Studio of Mr. Yang Jun of Fujian Commandery.

Raising my head I invoke the August Heavenly Great Emperor Wu. He lived in Quanzhou Commandery but was born near Zhangzhou. His brave and valiant awesome spiritual powers arose from his merciful heart. Because he used ritual powers he became a Medicine King. To the masses of the people he brought most abundant advantages. His fulfillment of his merit moved the Jade Emperor. He was asked by imperial decree what karmic path he had followed. He replied that upon obtaining correct knowledge and perception he expanded the Dao. The Jade Emperor commanded that the great lofty title of the numinous doctor be enhanced. Also, he sent as subordinates an Immortal Medical Official named Huang, the Awesome Martial Retainer Jiang Sishi, the Perfect Man of the Green Kerchief and two pages, the Six Ding Generals who are Strong Soldiers Who Expel Evil, Maiden Qin, the Taiyi Female Physician, together with the Great Messenger Who Flies to Heaven. All of these work together to support the weak and dispel disease and misfortune.

I today with all my heart and with complete obedience, express my desire that you will be pleased to let fall your mercy at my recitation of your names.

Chant for the Opening of the Scripture:
> Great Saint, Physician Spirit, Perfected Lord Wu
> Wrote Talismans, let fall seal-script revelations,
> > and proclaimed scriptures,
> Swearing a vow that his Sacred Spell would have
> > awesome power,
> And bring auspiciousness, gather good fortune,
> > and avoid disaster.

*At an audience in the heavenly Taiqing Palace, the Most High Lord Lao makes an announcement:*

"Now when I observe the three thousand million worlds below, and the multitudes dwelling in Jambudvipa, they are all practicing the ten evils and the five disobediences, disloyal and unfilial, unmannered and unrighteous, not revering the Three Treasures, ignorant of charity, unwilling to provide assistance, frequently carrying out evil deeds, killing living beings, behaving licentiously, stealing, coveting and getting angry, entangling themselves in a web of culpability, and disrupting the nation. There both kings and men are unjust; those above do not measure by the Way, and those below do not uphold the Laws. . . .

"Today the demons have increased in number to a total of 84,000 and have suddenly raised up tornadoes and floods. The 404 diseases circulate through the seasons, bringing little good fortune to the world. The evil and rebellious masses encounter disasters and die. The Heavenly Venerable took pity on those people who had cultivated good fortune by carrying out the ten good deeds. He then extended divine protection to them. Study the words of the prophecy:

> A green dog barks,
> A wooden pig squeals.
> A rooster crows at the rabbit in the moon,
> A round moon without luster.
> Three disasters strike,
> Nine rebellions arise.

"In the *jia* and *yi* years there will be military ravages, in the *bing* and *ding* years fearful fires, in the *wu* and *ji* years locusts will spread plague, in the *geng* and *ren* years storms and flood. Thus from *jia* year to the *gui* year the first five years will have barren harvests and the last five years will have good harvests. Alas, we have come to the end of the world, the revolving sun is about to stop. All the Buddhas will attain Nirvana, saints and sages will hide away. Common men and ignorant women are unaware and do not understand; therefore I have transmitted this scripture so that it may broadly save the world, and pronounce this *gāthā*:

> The dog barks, the pig squeals,
> The bad will vanish, the good will survive.
> Take refuge in the Three Treasures,
> Uphold and recite this Scripture.
> Revere it wherever you go,
> And it will always hold down demonic soldiers.
> Heavenly spirits will protect you,
> Family and nation will be at peace.
> Widely transmit the Way of the Scripture,
> Pass it all around."

. . . In the *guiyou* year, in the fourth month, on the seventh day, the Great Emperor Who Protects Life paced the Mainstays of Heaven and sprayed out vapor. An earthquake struck three times. Then he descended into a True Medium, and pronounced this scripture.

". . . In my life I dwelt in Quanzhou commandery and left traces of my deeds near Zhangzhou. From then until now through more than three hundred years I have piled up merit in laborious deeds. Fine honors were commended and bestowed upon me. Formerly I shipped grain to save people in a drought. Also I led spirit soldiers and drove away pirate robbers. Recently I let flow a sweet spring to put an end to the sufferings of sickness. Now I transmit the methods and scriptures of the Spiritual Treasure in order to save the people of the world. If any man or woman obtain my true scripture with its marvelous seal, faithfully keep and worship it. Either invite Buddhist or Daoist priests to recite the scripture or organize an association to read and recite it. Widely order its dissemination. Then as for anything your heart desires there will be nothing that does not satisfy your wishes.

"Whensoever anyone begins to build a well or a stove, or constructs a house or a tomb, or an enclosure for pigs, sheep, oxen, horses, chickens, or ducks, and at that time there are vapors bearing sickness, they may arrange incense, flowers, lamps, and tea, offer fine fruit, recite this scripture, repeat my spell seven times successively, and write with red vermillion the talismans and recite the incantations that I have revealed, placing them upon the door. Then the demons of disaster will spontaneously dissipate and members of the family will prosper. That which I desire with all my heart is that you will all ascend to the banks of the Dao."

After the True Medium had finished speaking, he exhaled the soul and awoke.

> Perfected Lord, Perfected Lord,
> Regulate evil and behead plague demons.
> Employ your talisman, spells, and purificatory water,
> Broadly save the myriad peoples.
> Pace the Mainstays with correct *qi*,
> Forever cutting off the roots of misfortune.
> Awesome radiance shines brightly,
> Your illustrious sobriquet has been successively enhanced.
> With incense and temple sacrifices,
> Morning and night we earnestly worship you.
> The myriad spirits all pray
> That they might bathe in your divine merit.

> Recite my sacred spell,
> Sweep away the masses of evil.
> Swiftly, swiftly, in accordance with the ordinances.

It is said that this scripture specially cures periodic outbreaks of pestilence. Reciting it can liberate the masses from hardship. At the end of the original copy there was appended the Marvelous Scripture of the Immortal Maiden of Merciful Salvation Who Saves Those in Childbirth, which still awaits reprinting. Noted by Yang Jun.

[Yang Jun, Sishen zhilue, app.; trans. adapted from Dean,<br>Taoist Ritual and Popular Cults, pp. 93–97 — DJ]

## TRACTS

Tracts, short booklets written by members of the educated elite to teach ordinary people how to behave, were printed and circulated in very large numbers in late imperial times. As already mentioned, they are closely related to the "morality books" discussed in volume 1 of *Sources*. In contrast to the scripture we have just read, the values taught by tracts were what the powerful and influential thought the people should believe. They emphasized submission to constituted authority and the maintenance of traditional hierarchical relations — between parents and children, ruler and ministers, husband and wife, and so on. But this ideology was not necessarily accepted by the common people, who were more concerned about injustice than disorder and more impressed by generosity than by loyalty. This discrepancy between what the political and cultural elites wanted people to believe and what the people themselves felt was right and proper is a constant theme in Chinese history, and is still relevant today.

### SELECTIONS FROM *THE TWENTY-FOUR EXEMPLARS OF FILIAL PIETY*

*The Twenty-four Exemplars of Filial Piety* is one of the most influential tracts ever written in China. It exists in various versions, but the one most commonly seen appears to have been written during the Yuan dynasty (1279–1368). By late imperial times virtually everyone was familiar with its paragons of filial devotion, who appeared as motifs in clothing, woodblock prints, dishes, and many other items of daily use, as well as in ballads, operas, and fiction. Everyone knew the names of the filial heroes and their famous deeds. Yet the extremism of *The Twenty-four Exemplars* will leave many readers uneasy. It is a classic example of didactic literature prepared by the learned for ordinary people: it is written in literary Chinese and at times is very difficult to understand. (The edition from which the excerpts below were taken, which was certainly intended to reach a broad readership, actually has footnotes to explain difficult passages. There is no doubt that here we are firmly in the world of readers, not listeners.) Moreover, it is virtually impossible to identify with its heroes and heroines, inhumanly virtuous as they are. That *The Twenty-four Exemplars* was so influential is persuasive evidence that upper-class indoctrination could at times be highly successful.

## 3. A Bitten Finger Pains the Heart

Zeng Shen of the Zhou dynasty had the honorific name Ziyu. He served his mother with extreme filiality. One day when Shen was in the mountains gathering firewood a guest came to the house. His mother had made no preparations and she kept hoping that he would return, but he did not. Then she bit her finger, and at the same time Shen suddenly felt a pain in his heart. He shouldered his firewood and returned home; kneeling, he asked his mother what the matter was. His mother said, "A guest came unexpectedly and I bit my finger to make you aware of it."

## 8. Acting As a Laborer to Support His Mother

Jiang Ge lived in the Eastern Han dynasty. His father died when he was young, and he lived alone with his mother. Disorders broke out, so he fled, carrying his mother. Again and again they encountered bandits who wanted to force him to join them. But Ge burst into tears and told them that he had his mother with him. The bandits could not bring themselves to kill him. They took up residence in Xiapei. Impoverished and without shirt or shoes, he hired himself out as a laborer to support his mother. He gave her whatever she needed.

## 10. Breast-Feeding Her Mother-in-law

Madame Zhangsun was the great-grandmother of Cui Nanshan of the Tang dynasty. When she was old and toothless, every day Cui's grandmother, Madame Tang, after combing her hair and washing her face, entered the main hall and breast-fed her. Although the old lady did not eat a grain of rice, after several years she was still in good health. One day she fell sick, and young and old gathered about her as she announced, "There is no way that I can repay my daughter-in-law's goodness to me. If the wives of my sons and grandsons are as filial and respectful as this daughter-in-law, it will be enough."

## 11. Mosquitoes Gorged Freely on His Blood

Wu Meng of the Jin dynasty was eight years old and served his parents with extreme filiality. The family was poor, and their bed had no mosquito net. Every night in summer many mosquitoes bit him, gorging on his blood. But despite their numbers he did not drive them away, fearing that they would go and bite his parents. This is the extreme of love for parents.

## 12. Lying on Ice Seeking for Carp

Wang Xiang of the Jin dynasty was young when his mother died. His step-mother, named Zhu, was unloving toward him and constantly slandered him to his father. Because of this he lost the love of his father. His stepmother liked to eat fresh fish. Once it was so cold the river froze. Xiang took off his clothes and lay on the ice to try to get some fish. Suddenly the ice opened and a pair of carp leaped out. He took them home and gave them to his stepmother.

## 13. Burying His Son on Behalf of His Mother

The family of Guo Ju in the Han dynasty was poor. He had a three-year-old son. His mother reduced what she ate to give more food to him. Ju said to his wife, "Because we are very poor, we cannot provide for Mother. Moreover, our son is sharing Mother's food. We ought to bury this son." When he had dug the hole three feet deep he found a great pot of gold. On it were the words "Officials may not take it, commoners may not seize it."

## 16. After He Had Tasted Dung, His Heart Was Anxious

Yu Qianlou of the Southern Qi dynasty was appointed magistrate of Zhanling. He had been in the district less than ten days when suddenly he became so alarmed that he began to sweat. He immediately retired and returned home. At that time his father had been sick for two days. The doctor said, "To know whether this illness is serious or not, you only need taste the patient's dung. If it is bitter, it is auspicious." Qianlou tasted it, and it was sweet. He was deeply worried. When night came, he kowtowed to the Pole Star [the Star of Lon-gevity], begging to die in his father's place.

## 17. Playing in Colored Clothes to Amuse His Parents

Old Master Lai of the Zhou dynasty was extremely filial. He respectfully cared for his two parents, preparing delicious food for them. He was over seventy, but he never mentioned the word "old." He wore five-colored motley and played children's games at his parents' side. Often he carried water into the room and pretended to slip and fall; then he would cry like a baby to amuse his parents.

## 22. Carving Statues to Serve As Parents

When Ding Lan of the Han dynasty was young his parents passed away. He was unable to care for them, and yet was aware of how they had toiled to bring him up. So he carved wooden statues of them and served them as if they were alive. After a long time his wife ceased to revere them, and in jest she pricked one of their fingers with a needle. It bled, and when the statues saw Lan, they wept. Lan discovered the reason and brought forth his wife and divorced her.

## 23. Weeping on Bamboo Made Them Sprout

Meng Zong of the Three Kingdoms period had the honorific Gongwu. When he was young his father died, and his mother was old and very sick. In the winter she wanted to eat soup made of bamboo shoots. Zong, not knowing how to get them, went into a bamboo grove, leaned against a big bamboo, and wept. His filial piety moved Heaven-and-earth. Instantly the ground broke open and several bamboo shoots appeared. He picked them and took them home to make soup for his mother. When she had eaten it she was cured.

[Wang Miansan, ed., *Huitu Ershisi xiao* — DJ][17]

---

17. I have benefited from the translation by David K. Jordan in his "Folk Filial Piety in Taiwan."

## Chapter 27

## CHINESE RESPONSES TO

## EARLY CHRISTIAN CONTACTS

Contacts between China and Europe (known in premodern China as the "Far West" or the "Western Ocean") date from the time of the Silk Route link between Han China and the Roman Empire two thousand years ago. The two major forces that fostered Sino-Western contacts were trade and religion, and frequently the two would operate in tandem as the trade route would provide entry for Christian missionaries into China.

There is a tradition in the Christian church that Thomas, one of the Twelve Apostles of Jesus, had first carried the faith to the East. However, the first documented presence of Christianity in China is traced to missionaries of the Assyrian church. These Nestorian Christians flourished briefly during the cosmopolitan atmosphere of the Tang dynasty (618–906) and then faded. During the Yuan dynasty (1279–1368), Franciscan monks traveled across Asia and were mentioned in the account of Marco Polo. China demonstrated its ability to mount voyages to the West in the early Ming dynasty when the expeditions under the eunuch admiral Zheng He (1371–1433) reached as far as the Arabian peninsula and east Africa, but this was a short-lived interlude in Sino-Western relations and thereafter China initiated no further expeditions to the Far West.

The first substantive contact between Europe and China began in the late sixteenth century when Portuguese ships arrived in the South China Sea and their passengers established a settlement called Macao on a tiny peninsula on the southeastern coast of China. For the most part, these Portuguese sailors were acquisitive explorers whose crude and aggressive behavior alienated the Chinese officials. However, the Christian piety of the Portuguese led them to provide passage to missionaries on each of their vessels. The Catholic Reformation had produced a new order of missionaries who were as learned as they were committed to their faith. These members of the Society of Jesus, or Jesuits, initiated one of the most notable cultural exchanges in history.

Because the history of Sino-Western relations in the nineteenth and early twentieth centuries was dominated by Western imperialism with its feelings of economic, cultural, and racial superiority, the significance of the earlier sixteenth-to-eighteenth-century period of Sino-Western exchange has long been obscured. With the receding of Western colonialism, however, it has become increasingly clear that the imperialist phase was an aberration from a more typical situation of greater equality between China and the West. In spite of feelings of cultural chauvinism on both sides, there was a surprising degree of openness and receptivity, which produced attempts by Chinese to blend Christianity with Confucianism as well as attempts by Europeans to emulate Confucian principles.

As an outgrowth of their exploratory voyages, Europeans in the sixteenth through the eighteenth centuries developed a tremendous interest in foreign and exotic lands, which generated a new genre of literature focused on travel. China was an object of particular fascination for Europeans, and no group was more knowledgeable about China than the Jesuit missionaries. The Jesuits became the leading disseminators of information about China to Europeans as part of an attempt to attract support for their missionary effort. Unlike other Christian missionary orders, who had contact with the merchant and lower classes of China, the highly educated Jesuits cultivated their closest intellectual and social counterparts in China — the Confucian literati.

The Jesuits were deeply impressed by what they saw in China and communicated to Europeans a highly favorable picture of the country, including its vast size, great wealth, advanced literacy, and sophisticated governmental organization. The famous European philosopher G. W. Leibniz (1646–1716), who was in direct contact with several Jesuit missionaries in China, proposed that Europe borrow practical philosophy from the Chinese. Leibniz's understanding of China and Confucianism was remarkably deep — certainly deeper than that of his eighteenth-century successors. The cultural agenda of philosophers such as Christian Wolff (1679–1750) and Voltaire (1694–1778) exalted China as a political and ethical model of enlightened government run by literati akin to philosopher-kings.

The philosophers' appreciation of China was grounded more on enthusiasm for promoting certain ideas than on knowledge of a more dispassionate and objective sort. Their Sinophilia (love of China and things Chinese) led to European imitation of Chinese art, including ceramics, textiles, painting, architecture, and landscape gardens. European artists blended Chinese subject motifs with the rococo style to produce a new decorative style, "chinoiserie." However, eighteenth-century European Sinophilia was built on shallow foundations, which were vulnerable to the shifting tides of cultural fashion. Eventually it gave way to a reaction in the form of nineteenth-century Sinophobia (hatred and disdain of China and things Chinese) in a cyclical pattern that was to repeat itself in later Sino-Western relations. While the Jesuits supplied most of the information on China that was transformed by Europeans into Sinophobia, the Jesuits themselves did not participate in most Enlightenment currents, which were anti-religious and, in particular, anti-Christian.

One of the first Jesuit missionaries to set foot in China was the Italian Jesuit Matteo Ricci (Li Madou, 1552–1610), who formulated the model — often called "accommodation" — for the approach of Jesuits in blending Christianity with Chinese culture. Ricci was one of the most remarkable men in history — impressive in physical appearance with his blue eyes and voice like a bell, charming in manner with his facility in foreign languages and photographic memory, incisive in thinking with his ability to grasp the essentials of Chinese culture and to discern a means of entry into a sophisticated culture like that of China. Ricci, virtually on his own, developed the first romanization system for rendering the Chinese language into European script and translated the Four Books into Latin. For these and other extraordinary accomplishments, a leading European sinologue of the twentieth century has called Ricci "the most outstanding cultural mediator between China and the West of all times."[1] The times were favorable to this effort because the cultural atmosphere of the late Ming dynasty was syncretic in spirit and relatively receptive to exotic teachings. Consequently, the Jesuits achieved rapid success in baptizing a number of prominent Chinese scholar-officials, including the so-called Three Pillars of the Early Christian Church — Yang Tingyun (1557–1627), Li Zhizao (d. 1630) and Xu Guangqi (1562–1633). These three became great defenders of the Christian church in China, and it is a mark of their success that Xu's defense of this foreign teaching did not prevent him from eventually occupying one of the highest offices in the land — that of Grand Secretary.

LI ZHIZAO: PREFACE TO *THE TRUE MEANING OF THE LORD OF HEAVEN*

Li Zhizao (d. 1630), together with Xu Guangqi, was a leading Christian convert of Matteo Ricci. A scholar-official of the late Ming dynasty and holder of the highest regular literary degree (*jinshi*), Li took an early interest in Western geography and astronomy and assisted Ricci in disseminating this knowledge in China. His conversion to Christianity came later, after he had already written the following introductory note

---

1. Wolfgang Franke, in Goodrich and Fang, eds., *Dictionary of Ming Biography*, p. 1144.

(in 1607) to Ricci's basic work, *The True Meaning of the Lord of Heaven*, on the fundamentals of Christianity for the Chinese.

Note especially the attempt to identify God with the Confucian concept of Heaven as presiding over the moral order and to establish the worship of God as the culmination of the natural loyalties so much stressed in Confucian ethics. Li (and Ricci) emphasize the convergence of the Confucian moral ideal with the Christian doctrines of divine justice and self-perfection. Christ and the Cross are not in the forefront of discussion; nor, on the other hand, are the speculations of the Neo-Confucians, which Ricci found less compatible.

In ancient times when our Master [Confucius] spoke of self-cultivation, he said that one should try first to serve his parents diligently and through this come to know Heaven. Then came Mencius, who rendered the doctrine of self-cultivation and service to Heaven complete. Now to know is to serve. Serving Heaven and serving parents are one and the same thing. But Heaven is the ultimate basis of all service. In explaining Heaven, no book excels the *Classic of Changes*, the source of our written [Chinese] characters. It says that the primal power[2] that governs Heaven is the king and father of all. Furthermore, it says the Lord (Di) appears in thunder and lightning, and the master of Ziyang [Zhu Xi] identified Di as the ruler of Heaven. Thus the idea of the Lord of Heaven [God] did not begin with Mr. Li [Ricci].

The popular notion of Heaven is so unenlightened that it is not even worth discussing. The Buddhists, for their part, go too far in abandoning their homes and leaving their parents unattended; furthermore, they disregard Heaven and treat the Lord (Di) with contempt, holding only their own selves as worthy of respect. Would-be Confucians, on the other hand, are wont to discuss the Mandate of Heaven, the Principle of Heaven, the Way of Heaven, and the virtue of Heaven; but, while they are wholly immersed in these [Neo-Confucian] conceptions, the ordinary man neither knows Heaven nor holds it in awe — and it is no wonder!

The teaching of Mr. Li, which is based on serving and glorifying Heaven, explains Heaven quite clearly. Seeing that the world desecrates Heaven and venerates the Buddha, he has spoken out in repudiation of these errors. Basing his arguments on the teachings of the Master [Confucius], he has written a book in ten chapters called *The True Meaning of God* [lit. the Lord of Heaven], wherewith to instruct men in the good and ward off evil.

In this book he says that men know to serve their parents but do not know that the Lord of Heaven is the parent of all. Men know that a nation must have a rightful ruler but do not know that the Lord (Di), who alone "governs

---

2. *Qianyuan* — the primal male element identified with Heaven in the opening portion of the *Classic of Changes*.

Heaven," is the rightful ruler of all. A man who does not serve his parents cannot be a [true] son; a man who does not know the rightful ruler cannot be a [true] minister; a man who does not serve the Lord of Heaven cannot be a [true] man. This book gives particular attention to the question of good and evil, and of retribution in the form of blessings and calamities. Now goodness that is not yet complete cannot be called perfectly good;[3] and even of the slight imperfections in human nature we speak of "rectifying evils." To do good is like ascending, that is, ascending into Heaven; to do evil is like falling, that is, falling into hell. The general purpose of the book is to make men repent their transgressions and pursue righteousness, curb their passions and be benevolent toward all. It reminds men of their origin from above so as to make them fear lest they fall down into the place of punishment; it makes them consider the awful consequences and hasten to cleanse themselves of all sin. Thus they might not be guilty of any offense against the Great Heavenly Lord Above.

He [Ricci] crossed mountains and seas to bring precious gifts from a land that since ancient times has had no contact with China. At first he knew nothing of the teachings of [the ancient sages] Fu'xi, King Wen, the Duke of Zhou, or Confucius, and what he said was not based on the commentaries of [the Neo-Confucian philosophers] Zhou Dunyi, the Cheng brothers, Zhang Zai, and Zhu Xi. However, particularly in respect to his emphasis on the great importance of knowing and serving Heaven, what he says tallies with the classics and commentaries. As regards Heaven and hell, obstinate men still refuse to believe in them. Yet Confucians have always held that the rewarding of the good and the visiting of misfortune upon the wicked was a principle evident from the examination of Heaven-and-earth. To depart from good and pursue evil is like leaving the high road and plunging into steep mountains or heavy seas. Why is it that some people will not believe anything unless perhaps it concerns their most urgent duties to their rulers or parents, or unless it involves danger in the form of tigers, wolves, dragons, or crocodiles? They insist on having personal experience of everything themselves. Is this not being too stupid and unreasonable? They do not appreciate the deep sincerity that moved him to come among us. To preach the truth, of course, one need not raise the question of reward and punishment, but if it serves to frighten fools and alarm the lazy, then it is right and proper that the good should be praised and rewarded, while the wicked are berated and punished. Thus his deep and sole concern has been to instruct the people and preach sound doctrine.

I have read some of his books and found that they differ from recent scholars on many points but have an underlying resemblance to such ancient works as

---

3. That is, though the Neo-Confucians (following Mencius) spoke of human nature as good (in opposition to the Buddhists), the goodness of human nature should not be thought of as wholly perfect.

the *Suwen,*[4] *Zhoubi,*[5] *Kaogong,*[6] and Qiyuan.[7] So, it seems to me, what is spoken in truth does not contradict the truth. In self-examination and obedience to conscience he is most careful and strict with himself. He is what the world calls a "lofty teacher," and none among the Confucian scholars is more worthy of credence than he.

The mind and heart of man are the same in East and West, and reason is the same. What differs is only speech and writing. When this book appeared it was written in the same language as ours, refined and civilized, and thus could serve to open the mind for instruction. Since the purpose of the book was to promote peace and well-being, to espouse sound doctrine and improve morals, it is certainly no trifling piece, nothing to be taken lightly or to be put in the same class as the works of earlier philosophers.

My friend Mr. Wang Mengbu has reprinted this book in Hangzhou, and I have presumed to write a few words for him. Not that I would dare to publicize a foreign book in order to spread unheard-of ideas, but I am mindful of the fact that we are all under the Majesty of Heaven and owe Him homage. Perhaps, too, there are things in it that we have been accustomed to hearing but have failed to act upon, and which may now prompt us to reexamine ourselves. Moreover, it may make some contribution to our study and practice of self-cultivation.

["*Tianzhi shiyi,*" *Tianxue chuhan,* p. 1]

## XU GUANGQI: A MEMORIAL IN DEFENSE OF THE [WESTERN] TEACHING

In the fifth lunar month of 1616, the scholar-official Shen Que, vice president of the Ministry of Rites in Nanjing, initiated an anti-Christian movement by submitting a memorial to the Wanli emperor. Shen, who was disturbed by the success of the Jesuit missionaries in making converts in Nanjing, voiced his criticisms of the Jesuit missionaries in this and two other memorials to the throne in 1616 and 1617. Xu Guangqi, who had just been reinstated in his post as revisor in the Historiographical Institute in Beijing, responded with a memorial defending the Jesuit missionaries. The following excerpt from Xu's memorial demonstrates a number of salient features about Xu's thinking. It reveals, first of all, that he was deeply committed to the new teaching and willing to risk political recrimination in defending it. Second, it shows that Xu believed

---

4. One part of the *Huangdi neijing* (see vol. 1, ch. 9), the basic text of traditional Chinese medicine.

5. The *Zhoubi suanjing* was a work on mathematical astronomy traditionally ascribed to the early Zhou dynasty (c. 1000 B.C.E.).

6. The *Kaogongji* was the last section of the *Zhouli* ("Rites of Zhou"), which purported to describe how artisans were organized under the Zhou dynasty.

7. A reference to Zhuangzi, who was said to have been an official of Qiyuan.

Christianity to be in basic harmony with the teachings of the ancient sages of China (i.e., Confucianism). Third, it reveals an anti-Buddhist strain that was pervasive in the writings of Chinese Christians. Although the Jesuits also expressed anti-Buddhist sentiments, many (not all) Confucian literati drew from more traditional Chinese grounds in criticizing Buddhism. Finally, the excerpt reveals China's lack of knowledge of European history. There is a naïveté in Xu's portrayal of European history and in his exaggeration of the positive effects of Christianity in European history.

Because the teaching of the men from afar [i.e., Christian missionaries from Europe] is most correct, and because your humble servant knows from experience that it is right, he earnestly begs to memorialize the throne, to the end that blessings may last forever and peace may be handed on to all generations.

Your servant saw in the Beijing Gazette that the Ministry of Rites in Nanjing has brought charges against the Western tributary state official Pang Diwo (the Jesuit missionary Diego de Pantoja, 1571–1618) and others. The contents [of the charges] say that their doctrine has infiltrated [China] to such an extent that even among the upper classes there are those who believe it, including one, it alleges, who has dared to be an astronomer, as well as scholars who have been misled by this doctrine. The charges refer to "upper classes" and "scholars" in an anonymous manner because the ministry officials feared that they would be implicated and so named no names. However, your servant is one of these unnamed figures.

Your servant has studied principles with these tributary officials and [has aided in] printing many of their books. Thus, your servant is one of "those who believe in [this teaching]." Furthermore, I have studied calendrical methods under them and at various times have prepared memorials [on this subject] and submitted them to Your Majesty. Consequently, when the charges speak of an "astronomer," they are referring to your servant. If the tributary officials are found guilty, how would your servant dare to hope that the ministry officials might somehow not speak [of my association with them] and so in this way escape?

In fact, your servant for many years has studied with and learned from these [Western] tributary officials, and I know that they are most honest and solid. There is nothing whatsoever about them that is dubious. Truly, they are all disciples of the sages. Their way is very correct, their discipline strict, their learning very broad, their knowledge superior, their affections true, and their views very stable. In their own countries, there is not one in a thousand who is so talented, nor one in ten thousand who is so outstanding, and for this reason they were included among those who came east tens of thousands of *li*.

Now in their countries, men of the church all cultivate personal virtue in order to serve the Lord of Heaven. They heard that in China [the adherents of] the teachings of the sages also all cultivate personal virtue and serve Heaven. Because of this correspondence of principles, they [braved] hardship and difficulties and toiled through dangerous and unsafe places in order to share their truth with our truth, hoping to make everyone good, to the end that they will declare that Heaven-on-High loves men.

This teaching has as its basic tenet serving the Lord on High; to save the body and soul is the most essential principle, while one's practice should consist in loyalty, filial piety, love, and compassion. The way to begin is to choose good and repent, and the way to advance and improve is to confess and reform. True blessing in Heaven is the glorious reward of doing good, while eternal retribution in hell is the bitter recompense of doing evil. . . .

Why is it that it has been eighteen hundred years since Buddhism came east, but worldly customs and men's hearts have not yet changed? It is because their words seem right, but they are wrong. Those who advocate the Chan Buddhist sect have amplified the thoughts of [the Daoists] Laozi and Zhuangzi, [making them] abstruse and impractical. Those who practice yoga use spells and incantations that are perverse and contrary to reason. Furthermore, they desire to place the Buddha above the Lord-on-High, which is contrary to the intent of the ancient kings and sages. It causes men not to know what to follow or what to depend on. What will cause men to be utterly good is the teaching of serving Heaven transmitted by the tributary officials. Truly it is what can benefit the civilizing influence of government, aid the arts of the Confucians, and correct the law of Buddhism.

Now there are more than thirty countries in the West, and they have accepted and practiced this teaching for a thousand and several hundred years, right up to the present time, great and small living together in harmony, superior and inferior at peace with each other. The borders are not guarded, and the rulers of the states are all of the same family. Throughout all the countries there are no swindlers and liars, and they have never had the custom of licentiousness or theft. On the roads they do not pick up things that are dropped, and at night they do not lock their gates. As for revolt and rebellion, not even once has there been such a thing or such people. Indeed, there has never even been talk or writing about it. . . .

Your Majesty has supported these [Western] tributary officials for seventeen years and displayed great kindness toward them. There has been no way for these tributary officials to repay you. They tried their best to let Your Majesty know their Way and their loyalty, but to no avail. Since your servant knows them, if I were to remain silent and not speak, I should be guilty of dissimulation. For this reason, despite my ignorance, I state the case, begging Your Majesty to graciously accept it, and issue a special memorial. . . .

Your servant dares to brave Heaven's majesty. With great fear and trepidation I await your orders.

The seventh lunar month of the forty-fourth year of the Wanli reign [August 12–September 10, 1616]

[*Pianxue shugao* 1:21–28, 36 — GK, DM]

# YANG GUANGXIAN'S CRITIQUE OF CHRISTIANITY

Literati opposition to Christianity increased in the late seventeenth century. The growing opposition was only partly a reaction to the initial success of Christianity in attracting disciples. The collapse of the native Ming dynasty and the conquest of China by the Manchus in 1644 caused a slight shift in the direction of Chinese culture. The rulers of the new Qing dynasty embraced a conservative form of Confucian philosophy, while the Chinese literati recoiled from the experimental syncretism of the late Ming in a defensive return to Confucian tradition. Consequently, a foreign teaching, such as Christianity, faced greater obstacles than previously.

The growing obstacles were epitomized in writings by Yang Guangxian (1597–1669), whose intensity of feeling against Christianity stemmed as much from the sincerity and devotion of his Neo-Confucian beliefs as from xenophobic prejudice against a foreign teaching. Yang was particularly harsh in his criticism of one of the most prominent Jesuit missionaries in seventeenth-century China, Johann Adam Schall von Bell (1592–1666). Father Schall had not only been very successful in supervising calendrical work in the Chinese Bureau of Astronomy in Beijing but also had been unusually close to the youthful first Manchu ruler, the Shunzhi emperor (r. 1644–1661). Xu Guangqi was as devout a Confucian as Yang Guangxian, but while Xu believed that Confucianism and Christianity were in harmony, Yang believed that they were in irreconcilable conflict and that the adoption of Christianity by Chinese would necessarily diminish the way of the ancients (i.e., Confucianism).

Yang succeeded in having Schall and the other Jesuits dismissed from the Bureau of Astronomy and he was appointed in their place to oversee the astronomical work. He lacked the mathematical skill to lead this effort, however, and in spite of the assistance of Muslim astronomers, he could not respond effectively when the Jesuits challenged the validity of his calendar. When the Kangxi emperor disbanded the regency and assumed personal control of the government in 1668, Yang was removed form the Bureau of Astronomy and the Jesuits were reappointed in his place. Yang died in disgrace soon afterward, but the intensity of his anti-Christian views persisted among the literati.

## YANG GUANGXIAN: *I CANNOT DO OTHERWISE* (*BUDEYI*)

Beginning in 1659, Yang Guangxian wrote a series of attacks on Christianity that were collected and published in 1665 under the title *Budeyi* (*I Cannot Do Otherwise*). One of the most effective charges that he made was to cast Jesus as a rebellious figure. By doing so, Yang was attempting to damage the Christians in the eyes of the throne and Chinese scholar-officials by showing them to be a subversive sect akin to other notorious and outlawed quasi-religious sects, such as the White Lotus Society. In this same light, Mary, the mother of Jesus, was criticized by Yang for being an immoral woman who conceived Jesus by having sexual relations with a man other than her husband, Joseph.

In [the Jesuit Father] Adam Schall's own preface one can read that [the Christian scholars] Xu Guangqi and Li Zhizao both understood that they could not dare publicly to give offense to Confucian norms. Adam Schall's work says that one man and one woman were created as the first ancestors of all humankind. He was not actually so bold as to make the contemptuous assertion that all the peoples in the world are offshoots of his teaching, but according to a book by [the Christian scholar] Li Zubo,[8] the Qing dynasty is nothing but an offshoot of Judea; our ancient Chinese rulers, sages, and teachers were but the offshoots of a heterodox sect; and our classics and the teachings of the sages propounded generation after generation are no more than the remnants of a heterodox teaching. How can we abide these calumnies! They really aim to inveigle the people of the Qing into rebelling against the Qing and following this heterodox sect, which would lead all-under-Heaven to abandon respect for rulers and fathers. . . .

Our Confucian teaching is based on the Five Relationships (between parent and child, ruler and minister, husband and wife, older and younger brothers, and friends), whilst the Lord of Heaven Jesus was crucified because he plotted against his own country, showing that he did not recognize the relationship between ruler and subject. Mary, the mother of Jesus, had a husband named Joseph, but she said Jesus was not conceived by him.

Those who follow this teaching [Christianity] are not allowed to worship their ancestors and ancestral tablets. They do not recognize the relationship of parent and child. Their teachers oppose the Buddhists and Daoists, who do recognize the relationship between ruler and subject and father and son. Jesus did not recognize the relationship between ruler and subject and parent and child, and yet the Christians speak of him as recognizing these relationships. What arrant nonsense! . . .

[The Jesuit Father] M. Ricci wished to honor Jesus as the Lord of Heaven (*Tianzhu*) who leads the multitude of nations and sages from above, and he particularly honored him by citing references to the Lord-on-High (*Shangdi*) in the Six Classics of China, quoting passages out of context to prove that Jesus was the Lord of Heaven. He said that the Lord of Heaven was referred to in the ancient classical works as the Lord-on-High, and what we in the west call "the Lord of Heaven" is what the Chinese have spoken of as "the Lord-on-High." [According to Ricci] the Heaven (Tian) of the blue sky functions as a servant of the Lord-on-High, which is located neither in the east nor in the

---

8. Li Zubo, *Tianxue quankai* (*A Summary of the Propagation of Christianity*, 1665).

west, lacks a head or stomach, has no hands or feet, and is unable to be honored. How much less would earthbound land, which a multitude of feet trample and defile, be considered something to be revered? Thus Heaven and Earth are not at all to be revered. Those who argue like this are no more than beasts able to speak a human language.

Heaven is the great origin of all events, things, and principles. When principles (*li*) are established, material-force (*qi*) comes into existence. Then, in turn, numbers are created and from these numbers, images begin to take form. Heaven is Principle within form, and Principle is Heaven without form. When shape comes in to its utmost form, then Principle appears therein; this is why Heaven is Principle. Heaven contains all events and things, while Principle also contains all events and things and, as a result, when one seeks the origin of things in the Supreme Ultimate (*Taiji*) it is only what we call Principle. Beyond principle there is no other principle, and beyond Heaven there is no other Heaven [i.e., Lord of Heaven].

> [*Budeyi*, in Wu Xiangxiang, *Tianzhujiao tongjuan wenxian xubian*, pp. 1090–1122 — DM, JDY]

# ZHANG XINGYAO AND THE INCULTURATION OF CHRISTIANITY

Faced with growing opposition in the late seventeenth century, Christianity attracted less eminent disciples than previously. Nevertheless, outside the capital of Beijing there were regional pockets where talented literati converts in Fujian, Zhejiang, and Shandong provinces carried forward the difficult task of intellectually reconciling Confucianism and Christianity. They carried the process of accommodation to a deeper level, called "inculturation," in which Christianity was not simply reconciled with Confucianism but assimilated into Chinese culture to become a creative force. These Confucian Christians are less well known than earlier literati adherents, such as the Three Pillars referred to above, because of the official suppression of Christianity, which began in the early years of the eighteenth century and intensified thereafter. In addition, the situation was aggravated by the Chinese Rites Controversy emanating out of Rome, over whether it was permissible [as Ricci had said] for baptized Chinese to honor their ancestors with the traditional rites. The effect of all of this was for the government to suppress writings by the Chinese Christian literati. Works continued to be written and circulated in very limited circles, but for the most part these were never published and have been preserved only in libraries and archives in China and Europe. Notable among these late seventeenth-century writings were works by a leading literatus of the Hangzhou Christian community named Zhang Xingyao (1633–1715 + ).

Earlier Chinese Christians had attempted to reconcile Confucianism and Christianity by quoting passages from the Five Classics and Four Books that appeared to confirm that the essential ideas of Christian teaching had been present in China from antiquity. Zhang was an accomplished historian, who in addition to citing passages from the classics, drew upon his knowledge of both history and Cheng-Zhu teachings in attempting to inculturate Christianity in China. He wrote several works, most of which have remained in manuscript.

*AN EXAMINATION OF THE SIMILARITIES AND DIFFERENCES BETWEEN THE LORD OF HEAVEN TEACHING* [CHRISTIANITY] *AND THE TEACHING OF THE CONFUCIAN SCHOLARS*

This work first appeared in 1702 and was revised over the next thirteen years. The last preface was written in 1715, when Zhang Xingyao was eighty-three years old. Unlike the times nearly a century before, when Xu Guangqi wrote his memorial, the political and cultural atmosphere had turned against Christianity, and Zhang's words are a forceful expression of personal hope and religious faith.

It is clear in the China of my day that the Lord of Heaven (Tianzhu) [of the Western missionaries] is the same as the Lord-on-High (Shangdi) [of Chinese antiquity]. Since the time of the Yellow Emperor (a legendary figure dated from 2697 B.C.), officials worked together to make sacrifices to the Lord-on-High. Thereafter the words in the classics were all there for anyone to see. Thus Xue disseminated the Five Teachings [of paternal rightness, maternal compassion, friendship of an elder brother, respect of a younger brother, and filial piety of a child], and false teachings did not develop. Sagely wisdom throve; social customs were pure and beautiful. How could things have been better?

From the time the Buddha's books entered China, a teaching spread that was altogether deviant. The followers of Laozi promoted this teaching, and thereafter the minds of the people in China lost their ability to question anything. People all degenerated into a condition of merely acquiescing in what they were told, and the Buddha said, "In Heaven above and Earth below, I alone am worthy of honor." The ability to discern the Lord-of-Heaven degenerated, and it became a great and arrogant demon whom mankind no longer studied, followed, and honored. Consequently, the Three Mainstays [of ruler-minister, parent-child, and husband-wife] and the Five Constants [of Humaneness, Rightness, Ritual Decorum, Wisdom, and Trustworthiness] became hated and there was no effort to urge these on mankind. These people have all gone to hell without end and the followers of Confucius are not able to save them, because Confucius can neither reward nor punish nor judge the living and the dead.

I had known nothing of Buddhist texts, but once during a period of mourning someone said to me, "If you want to understand the meaning of life and death, why don't you take the essential Buddhist texts and meditate upon them?" Then I took up and looked through the *Lankavatara Sūtra*, the *Vimalakirti Sūtra*, and other [Buddhist] books, reading their most important passages. As a result I concluded: If these are their theories, none of them have any real meaning. I could believe what the two great Confucian scholars Cheng Yi and Zhu Xi said about the Buddhist *sūtras* being replete with half-truths, licentiousness, heterodoxy, and escape from the world. As to the teachings of the Two Heterodoxies (Daoism and Buddhism), how is it that they continue to last for even a day in these flourishing [enlightened] times?

The Western scholars came ninety thousand *li* to honor the will of the Lord of Heaven and to save the world, with many benefits to us in the Central Kingdom. Their principles are correct, their people are men of worth. How can people be inattentive to their teachings, and thus throw away the eternal life of their spiritual natures [immortal souls]. My friend, Master Zhu, styled Jinan, showed me the books of the Lord of Heaven Teaching. I had not yet finished reading them when my mind became filled with doubts about the Buddha. Then I understood that Heaven and Earth naturally possess correct principles, already present in Confucian teaching, but, with some things still not completely understood by Confucian teaching, it would not do to be without the added benefit of the teachings of the Lord of Heaven.

Therefore I have collected the books of the Lord of Heaven Teaching, explained them in the over two thousand pages of the work *Clearly Distinguishing the Lord of Heaven Teaching* [from Heterodoxy] (*Tianzhujiao mingpian*), and thus exposed the falsehoods of Buddhism and Daoism. My notes on the *Comprehensive Mirror for Aid in Governance Topically Arranged* (*Tongjian jishi benmo*),[9] filling over 1,700 pages, are so compendious and profuse that it has not been possible to get them cut and printed. However, the [Lord of Heaven Teaching] can be understood and grasped in terms of the three aspects of (1) what harmonizes with the Confucian Teaching, (2) what supplements the Confucian Teaching and finally, (3) what transcends the Confucian Teaching. The title of this work is "An inquiry into the similarities and differences between the Heavenly Lord's Teaching and the Teaching of the Confucian Scholars." . . .

Anyone today who is enlightened should comprehend my words and understand that the Lord of Heaven [of the Western missionaries] is the Lord-on-High [of Chinese antiquity] and that what I have written embodies his compassion to save the world. He knows me and brings retribution upon me. Let everyone hear me out.

Explanatory note written in the fifty-fourth year of the Kangxi emperor (1715) by the eighty-three-year-old elder Zhang Xingyao, styled Master Ziren.

[Zhang, preface, *Tianzhujiao rujiao tongyi kao*, 1a–2b — DM]

---

9. Based on Yuan Shu's rearrangement of Sima Guang's *Comprehensive Mirror for Aid in Governance* (see ch. 19).

## Chapter 28

CHINESE STATECRAFT AND THE OPENING OF CHINA

TO THE WEST

Statecraft, as represented by the Chinese term *jingshi* (world ordering), traditionally had to do with the internal affairs of the Chinese world, the "Central
Kingdom"; it was little concerned with the kind of power politics that occupied
European princes in their multistate rivalries, their international world. As such,
Chinese statecraft drew upon the age-old, voluminous record found in the
treatises of the dynastic histories from the Han and after, as well as in the
monumental institutional encyclopedias compiled from the late Tang onward
and in the local gazetteers that recorded matters of civil administration and
provincial life down through the centuries. Though we take special account of
this genre only in the Qing period, the literature concerning it was a standard
feature of Confucian, and especially Neo-Confucian, writings. Great impetus
had been given to this in the Song. As seen earlier (chapter 21), Zhu Xi's scholarship included careful attention to the ordering of economic and social institutions on the local level, and many schools of Neo-Confucian learning carried
on this work in succeeding centuries. Indeed, it was the availability of this
extensive record that enabled thinkers and scholars like Huang Zongxi and Gu
Yanwu to sum up millennia of Chinese institutional history in their magisterial
analyses, from a Confucian point of view, of China's key internal problems.

The readings in this chapter reflect developments in statecraft thinking from
the early eighteenth century to the mid nineteenth. First there are essays by
typical Confucian scholar-officials discussing traditional statecraft issues that

had been perennial problems for Chinese civil administration and remained a concern for conscientious officials even in the relatively stable and prosperous years of the early Qing. These matters command attention both for the challenges they presented to the Confucian reformist conscience and for the thoughtful, seasoned reflections they elicited from scholar-officials drawing on mature past experience.

In the second phase we encounter the accumulating problems that follow upon the high Qing's very success: the rapid economic expansion, rising affluence, and population growth that attend the long period of stable rule and secure peace under the Manchus. In the midst of spectacular advances negative factors also come into play, and complicating, limiting effects ensue. These are especially worrisome when state officials play a key role in the economy; the power of the ruler and his high officials can be checked, if at all, only by the most courageous remonstrance, and corruption becomes almost routine. In such circumstances the warnings of conscientious scholar-officials, as in the cases cited here, often go unheeded, though the warners themselves do not go unpunished. Thus the late eighteenth-century experience confirmed what Huang Zongxi had said about the ineffectiveness of even self-sacrificial protest when, in the absence of legal, systemic, constitutional restraints, there are no countervailing forces to balance the power of the ruler and his henchmen.

In the last phase, this developing statecraft emerges from its preoccupation with homegrown problems, compelled finally in the nineteenth century to turn its attention to the outside world. At this point the genre of the so-called treatise on institutional history or local gazetteer (*zhi*) is converted to new uses, as in Wei Yuan's epochal *Haiguo tuzhi* (*Illustrated Gazetteer of the Maritime Countries*). Thrust onto the world stage, Confucian "statecraft" is no longer left at home to mind and mend its own business but is forced to enter into the larger world of power politics.

## CHEN HONGMOU AND MID-QING STATECRAFT

Chen Hongmou (1696–1771) was a career provincial governor, enjoying the longest total service and the largest number of separate provincial appointments of any governor during the Qing era. Though a prolific writer, he was neither a profound original thinker nor a scholar of notable erudition. In his own lifetime he enjoyed no great influence, either intellectual or political, beyond the confines of the specific jurisdictions in which he served. Beginning shortly after his death, however, and continuing (in some circles) down to the present day, he acquired a reputation as a "model official," his well-documented administrative vigor and his reflections on the exercise of the responsibilities of office (revealed above all in his letters) serving to inspire generations of subsequent administrators.

Even more significantly, he was singled out by He Changling and Wei Yuan, the compilers of the enormously influential *Anthology of Qing Statecraft Writings* (*Huangchao jingshi wenbian*, 1826), as the foremost high Qing exemplar of the *jingshi* (statecraft) literati style: a dedication to solving the practical problems of governance based on detailed empirical observation, respect for local variation, and organizational and technological sophistication. In the anthology, Chen was the second most heavily represented figure, surpassed only by the virtually beatified Gu Yanwu.

Chen identified himself as a disciple of Zhu Xi, and the aforementioned combination of moral probity, local activism, and technical competence was a mark of the statecraft tradition stemming from Zhu Xi. Chen, however, did not follow Zhu's teachings in any slavish or partisan fashion. He took no articulated stand in the scholarly schism between the pro-Zhu "Song Learning" (see chapter 25) and the anti-Zhu "Han Learning," which was emerging during his lifetime; rather, he condemned any and all intellectual partisanship. The particular figures in the late imperial scholarly pantheon whom he most admired were Sima Guang (1019–1086) and Lü Kun (1536–1618), both of whom he identified with a deep sense of social mission and a hardheaded empiricism in developing institutional solutions to social ills. For the same reasons, beginning in midcareer Chen was increasingly attracted to the roughhewn "Shaanxi school" of Ming-Qing Confucianism (Guanxue).

## ON SUBSTANTIVE LEARNING

Chen Hongmou himself rarely used the term *jingshi*, and never in a sense suggesting that he saw himself participating in an intellectual movement by that name. He did, however, repeatedly emphasize his commitment to *shixue*, a term frequently rendered in English as "practical [as in Zhu Xi's earlier] learning," but in Chen's usage "solid" or more properly translatable as "substantive learning." Chen despised what he saw as the twin literary evils of his day: an overly aestheticized pursuit of stylistic refinement and the arcane textual scholarship of the *Kaozheng* (Evidential Learning) philological movement. Both, in his view, were irresponsible dissipations of the talent of men who ought to have been more productively engaged in solving social problems. "Substantive learning" involved something different: on the one hand, the practical quest for answers to such political-economic problems as feeding the empire's rapidly growing population and, on the other hand, the study of ethical imperatives that, when straightforwardly explained to the general population, would foster the social stability prerequisite to economic development.

The noble words and essential ideas of the sages are scattered throughout the classical canon. Only by studying these works closely can one begin to extract from them their meaning and put their ideas into practice. If one takes scholarship to be merely poetry and belles lettres, then though the craftsmanship be jewellike, it will have no relevance to one's moral nature and may indeed serve to mislead one in one's personal conduct. One will invariably end up with empty verbiage and groundless speculation, obstructing the grasp of true principle. This is of no use in personal cultivation, and still less in serving the needs of the people. Books then remain merely books, and quite separate from real life. It is because of this that so many people today dismiss book learning as no more than the repetition of conventional platitudes and scholarship as simply a way to pass the examinations.

[Letter to Depei, *Chen wengong gong shudu* 1:13 — WR]

The examination system promotes scholars on the basis of their literary achievement. But scholarly practices tend to decline over the course of time, to become less concerned with fundamentals and more with style, to substitute what simply sounds good for what one has made a genuine effort to understand. Scholars merely unthinkingly copy over the words of the past, and their vacuous phrasings have absolutely no connection to real-life affairs. Few, indeed, can even adequately explain the basic meaning of the sages' words. They simply repeat empty conventions and the world rewards them with success in the examinations. The glibness of contemporary letters, and the slovenliness of today's education, are primarily due to this.

[Letter to Wang Hao, *Chen wengong gong shudu* 1:9 — WR]

The state selects and promotes scholars above all out of the hope that they will prove useful officials in the future. In sitting for the examinations, scholars should reveal the learning they have patiently accumulated over the course of time. The examinations test first the candidate's knowledge of basic principles revealed in the classical texts, and then move on to legal and policy questions. . . .

Imperial edicts have repeatedly ordered that, in provincial-level examinations, equal weight be given to this second part, in order to scrutinize the candidates' understanding of political economy and prevent undue emphasis being accorded to facility with current literary fashions. . . . But students in fact do not diligently prepare for these practical policy questions on a day-to-day basis; instead they quickly cram for them as the examination approaches, by memorizing standardized crib book answers. . . . Since examining officials obviously do not take seriously this second half of the examination, these bad practices have become so institutionalized that even genuinely serious students no longer see this part as requiring more than last-minute cramming. Thus the study of political economy is neglected, and the court's purpose in using the examinations to select officials is defeated.

Now, the Yunnan Provincial Academy . . . has recently become quite successful in producing scholars. The only problem is that the academy's monthly tests do not include questions relevant to the second part of the examinations. Cramming at the last minute is by no means as good as studying on a protracted, regular basis. I therefore propose that, beginning with the next school term, in addition to the usual lectures on classical philosophy, a portion of each class be devoted to assignment of a passage from the Four Books, upon which the students must compose an answer in the manner of the policy questions on the exams. They should also be assigned a question in which they decide a sample legal case. The policy question should be concerned with a contemporary issue in either national or local affairs. The phrasing of this question must be clear and specific, so as to preclude giving a standard crib book response. . . . In this way, we can counter the ingrained dysfunctions of contemporary education and more fully put into practice our Sagely Dynasty's appropriate emphasis on substantive learning.

[*Peiyuantang oucun gao* 4:3–4 — WR]

Substantive learning necessarily involves painstaking immersion in texts on a routine basis. . . . It seems that today there are two major harmful trends. The first is acquisition of literary polish without penetrating the text's essential meaning. To save time, teachers lecture their students on the generalities of a passage, without making sure that they understand the precise meaning of each word and phrase. If one's reading level does not allow one to grasp the Way, one cannot employ it effectively to put the world in order. The second harmful trend is studying the classics only out of antiquarianism, without looking for applications in the world in which we live. Scholars like this may have highly refined philological skills and great bibliographic command, but by remaining mired in the past they do violence to the present. . . .

One reason why so many people today dismiss professional literati as useless is because the latter do not assiduously read the *Beijing Gazette*.[1] . . . In my opinion, all educational officials in local cities and villages ought to make the *Gazette* required reading for their students. If the students are not capable of reading it on their own, all students of the locality should be formed into study groups to read it collectively. This would be highly beneficial, yet cost very little.

[Letter to Zhang Meizhuang, *Huangchao jingshi wenbian* 2:33 — WR]

In my view, the duties of the literati are to study when dwelling at home and to serve when called to public office. By "studying," I mean to study proper moral conduct, which is the prerequisite to being of service. By "serving," I mean governing the affairs of the people, which is how the superior man puts

---

1. The *Beijing Gazette* (*Chaobao* or *Jingbao*), published in Beijing, contained transcripts of correspondence between the court and its officials regarding current conditions and policy.

into practice that which he has studied. Practical affairs and basic principles are essentially interdependent; eternal truths and functional utility are but two aspects of the same thing. Contemporary scholars treat the two as distinct, but for the ancients themselves their profound words were inseparable from positive action. . . .

There are some today who discuss classical texts but see no need to apply them to the contemporary world, or even argue that they cannot be applied to the contemporary world. This is not only a perversion of the Way but also a trivialization of the role of scholarship. . . .

Of course, just as scholarship may be correct or misdirected, substantive or vacuous, so too will those in public service inevitably include the careless and negligent as well as the judicious and skilled. There are those who acquire a reputation for scholarship and appear solid and upright, who, once selected for an official post, immediately forget all that they have previously studied. There are even those who treat their official service as a shortcut to a lavish lifestyle and an easy paycheck, behaving precisely contrary to everything they have learned in the past. It is as if the man prior to official selection and the man after selection were two different people! Official service and scholarship are mutually complementary and must be fully integrated in one's mental attitude.

[Preface to *Xueshi yigui* —WR]

## ON UNIVERSAL EDUCATION

Throughout his career, Chen campaigned vigorously to extend educational opportunities to all persons under his jurisdiction, no matter how poor or remotely located. He strove to combat the elitist cultural bias he found pervasive among his superliterate colleagues, in defense of the Confucian doctrine "In education, there are no class distinctions" (*Analects* 15:38). For Chen, education was essentially moral training. The cultivation of one's innate moral sense via literary education would enable the educated person to exercise independent moral judgment, rather than require constant discipline by external authority. In all these respects Chen carried on the educational theory and practice advocated by Zhu Xi.

Although Chen pushed his educational programs in every province in which he served, he was particularly celebrated for his efforts in frontier areas of the southwest. During an era in which the Qing was rapidly annexing border territories, Confucian schooling was an important means of promulgating Chinese cultural values (assumed by Confucian elites to be universal values) among the empire's growing numbers of non-Chinese subjects. Chen's egalitarian educational philosophy thus neatly dovetailed with the "civilizing mission" of an expanding imperial power.

Human nature is essentially good. There is no person who cannot be civilized and enlightened. Chinese and barbarians are essentially the same. There is no local custom that cannot be transformed and improved. It is the duty of those who hold local authority to ensure that schools are established in each and every locality, to see that these do not fall into neglect after they are established, and to make certain that they do not exist simply on paper. If this is done, proper guidance will be provided for the process of civilization, literacy will rise, and local customs will be excellent. . . .

I will not listen to such things as "Barbarians will always be barbarians." The transformation of frontier society is certainly not something to be achieved overnight, but processes of transformation begun today will bear results in the future.

[*Peiyuantang oucun gao* 1:33–35 — WR]

The promotion of men of talent and the improvement of popular customs are the basic tasks of education. If proper teaching methods are established, then the people will be good. If scholarship is done properly, then popular customs will be as they should be. . . .

Yunnan is a frontier region, where Chinese and barbarians dwell intermixed. Because of solicitous imperial attention, some measure of civilization has begun to take hold. However, the poor people of the province do not have the resources to educate their children, and the aboriginal people in remote rural areas have no thought of sending their children to school. If education is not applied universally, then it is very difficult to transform a population. If moral guidance is not everywhere available, then popular customs will remain uncivilized and savage. Therefore, it is even more urgent to establish schools in frontier areas than in the heartland, and more urgent in rural than in urban areas.

[*Peiyuantang oucun gao* 3:5–11 — WR]

Local officials are charged with the duty of shepherding the people and providing moral guidance. . . . Their goal must be to extend education to every locality and all persons within their jurisdiction and to improve teaching methods. In the end, there will be educated persons everywhere, and education will be under way in every remote village and marketplace. Gradually, the most capable will be able to immerse themselves in profound scholarship, while the crude masses will become imbued with respect for the rites and moral propriety. . . . Thus, the establishment of schools for elementary education is a cardinal task of local administration.

[*Peiyuantang oucun gao* 5:6–7 — WR]

## ON WOMEN'S EDUCATION

The first half of the eighteenth century witnessed a heated debate among Chinese literati over the propriety and content of women's education, prompted by the social realities of women's increasingly moving out beyond the confines of the home and of rising female literacy. Chen's anthology of historical writings on women's education, compiled in 1742 during his tenure as Jiangxi governor, was a celebrated contribution to this debate. In it, Chen did not challenge the conventional view that women ought to be restricted to occupying familial roles that subordinated them to males, but, based on his faith in human reason and in the imperative to universal education, [he] argued that women could best fulfill these roles if they had received at least an elementary classical literary education (as the Ming Empress Xu had argued earlier [see chapter 22]).

There is no uneducable person in the world. There is also no person whom it is justifiable not to educate. How then can female children alone be excepted? From the moment they grow out of infancy, they are protectively shut up deep within the women's quarters, rather than, like male children, being allowed out into the wider world, to be carefully corrected in their behavior by teachers and friends and to be cultivated by exposure to the classical literary canon. Although parents may love their daughter deeply, they give no more serious thought to her personal development than by providing her with a home, food, and clothing. They teach her to sew, prepare her dowry, and nothing more. . . . This view that female children need not be educated is a violation of Principle and an affront to the Way. . . .

Now, a woman in her parents' home is a daughter; when she leaves home she becomes a wife; when she bears a child she becomes a mother. If she is a worthy daughter, she will become a worthy wife. If she is a worthy wife, she will become a worthy mother. If she is a worthy mother, she will have worthy sons and grandsons. Thus, the process of civilization begins in the women's quarters, and the fortunes of the entire household rest on the pillar of its womenfolk. Female education is a matter of the utmost importance.

Some will object: "But women who can learn to read are few. And if they do become literate, in many cases it will actually hinder their acquisition of proper female virtue." This argument fails to recognize that all women possess a degree of natural intelligence. Even if they cannot learn to master the classics and histories, they nevertheless can get a rough idea of their message. . . . Moreover, it is evident that in today's world there are already many women with a smattering of learning. They cling fast to the half-baked ideas they have absorbed, cherishing them till their dying day and imparting them to others. Under these circumstances, would it not be better if they [learned to] recite the classical texts in order to get their message right?"

[Preface, *Jiaonü yigui* — WR]

## ON THE DUTIES OF AN OFFICIAL

Chen Hongmou's published correspondence, official and private, comprises a virtual encyclopedia of Qing techniques of governance, revealing his detailed knowledge of such diverse areas as agronomy, water conservancy, fiscal and litigation management, and communications logistics. Thus his scholarship includes the classical and the functional (as Hu Yuan had recommended in the eleventh century and Zhu Xi in the twelfth).

The selections that follow highlight his more general principles of administration. Upon transfer to office in a new province, Chen would characteristically survey both the region's potentialities and the efficacy of existing bureaucratic operations and then devise fundamental overhauls of areas he considered to be in neglect. He endeavored to gain a rapport with the local population and to convince them of his sincerity in placing priority on popular well-being. He was, however, as eager to repair perceived deficiencies of local culture as those of local economic productivity. He was also highly committed to goals of bureaucratic efficiency and the ability of the state to monitor and control all aspects of local society.

We in official service ought to look at all matters from the point of view of what is best for the people's livelihood. We must plan for the long term, rather than for the moment. We should concentrate on the substantial and practical, rather than disguising our inaction with empty words. To do otherwise would violate the court's basic principle that officials exist for the good of the people.

[Letter to Sun Quan, *Chen wengong gong shudu* 1:8 — WR]

The Way of shepherding the people involves no more than educating and nurturing them. . . . By "nurturing" I mean construction and maintenance of irrigation works, encouragement of land reclamation, and patronage of community granaries. These are all matters of great urgency. If the people can be made to produce a surplus, store it, and allow it to accumulate over the years, their well-being will be ensured. By "education" I mean promoting civilized behavior, diligently managing public schools, and widely distributing classical texts. Schools are the fountainheads of popular customs. If educational practice is correct, popular customs will be virtuous.

[Letter to the Prefect of Guangxi, *Chen wengong gong shudu* 1:4–5 — WR]

As our dynasty has ever longer exercised benevolent rule, the population has continually grown. All available natural resources have been turned into productive assets. I fear, however, that our limited supply of land cannot adequately support our growing population. Under these conditions, officials cannot sit idly by and watch as potentially useful land remains undeveloped, on the excuse that the effort involved would be too great or that their initiative would not yield immediate results. Now, feeding the people directly by the government is not as good as developing the means whereby the people can feed themselves. This always takes time, however, and results cannot be seen overnight [i.e., during an official's own tenure in a post]. Indeed, results that appear overnight almost never prove to be enduring. Therefore, officials must look to the long term, not the present, and in so doing put the interests of the people ahead of their own [career] concerns.

[Letter to the Governor of Guangxi, *Huangchao jingshi wenbian* 16:35 — WR]

In governing, good intentions and good policies alone are insufficient. There are those policies that sound admirable but that prove impossible to implement in practice. . . . If the local official truly approaches each matter from the standpoint of the people's livelihood, in carrying out any new policy he will first thoroughly canvas local public opinion on the matter. He will then consider every aspect of its implementation, noting in which aspects it is advantageous to the people and in which aspects it will cause them hardship. If the advantages outweigh the hardships, implement it. One ideally seeks a situation of absolute advantage and zero hardship, but this is seldom possible, and the possibility of hardships should not cause one to abandon a policy that will prove on balance advantageous. If the policy is a sound one, such hardships as do accrue may be redressed subsequently, so as fully to maximize the advantages.

[Letter to Wei Dingbu, *Chen wengong gong shudu* 2:4 — WR]

The court appoints officials for the benefit of the people. Officials must cherish the people and exercise their authority to the fullest in their behalf. It is no accident that the formal title of a district magistrate is "one who *knows* the district," nor that he is referred to as the "*local* official" — there should be no matter within their locality about which he does not know. The common people refer to the magistrate as their "father and mother official" and call themselves his "children." This implies that there is no suffering or pleasure on the part of the people that the magistrate does not personally share. Their relationship is exactly like that of a family. . . .

I have drawn up the following list of items a local official should keep in mind in determining how to conduct himself. Superiors are also directed to keep these points in mind when evaluating their subordinates:

1. Maintain genuine commitment. This is the basis of everything else. With genuine commitment, your energies will never flag; without it, whatever ability you possess will be wasted. Do not leave things to others, but remain personally aware of all that goes on in your district. . . . Officials without genuine commitment give prime consideration to how a policy will appear in their reports to superiors, rather than the impact it will have on the people. If local officials are truly committed to the people, all things will fall into place.

2. Be incorrupt. An official must act unselfishly and maintain the highest standards of personal integrity. Ill-gotten gains will be discovered in the end, because they will become the subject of popular gossip or because one's corruption will weigh upon one's conscience and be revealed in one's speech and

demeanor. One will therefore tend to shrink from the public gaze. . . . It may sometimes be possible to fool your superiors, but you can never fool the "ignorant populace." . . .

3. Provide exemplars of civilized behavior. Because counties are large and populous, people do not routinely see their magistrate. . . . But magistrates should make regular tours of the countryside, to investigate local customs, good and bad, and to meet with local community leaders to clarify for their benefit what is considered legal and proper. On these tours, officials should make detailed observations of conditions in villages along the way and make follow-up visits to determine if conditions have improved or deteriorated. Reward or punish community leaders accordingly. . . . Local persons who have been models of filiality or chastity, public service or philanthropy, should be rewarded with votive tablets, public rituals of praise, gifts of silver or rice, or tax exemptions. . . .

4. Endure toil and tribulations. Within my jurisdiction, what affairs do not depend on me? Among daily affairs, those that do not concern popular material well-being inevitably concern local customs and popular morale. There are so many affairs to manage that one is always plagued with anxieties that one has neglected something or that there is not enough time to do it all. How can one in such a post be the sort to shun hard work? . . .

5. Scrutinize subordinate officials carefully. . . .

6. Keep a tight rein on your clerks. . . . Failure to control their predations will inevitably generate popular resentment. . . .

7. Avoid perfunctory performance. Human beings have their own natural disposition, and events have their own natural logic. When the time is ripe for something, it cannot be avoided; discussions after the fact are fruitless. How can one suppose that the course of one's official career is due to anything other than public knowledge of one's performance? A bad habit among today's officials is to give little heed to real needs and conditions, but rather, out of selfish careerist motives, simply to imitate in a perfunctory fashion what other officials are doing. Then, when someone is promoted ahead of them, they attribute it to something having unfairly invited their superiors' enmity or someone having spread false rumors about them. Can it really be that higher-level officials do not have the public interest at heart and are led only by their partisan likes and dislikes?

8. Prevent harassment of the people. For an official to impose harassments on the people himself would be the height of stupidity. But, jurisdictions being very broad, evil government functionaries and local tyrants will inevitably come up with ways to harass the people. Consequently, no matter how hardworking the magistrate, and how well intentioned the laws, such harassments can be prevented only through constant and diligent scrutiny. . . .

9. Do not cover up your mistakes. . . . Many local officials today are unwilling to admit their mistakes in judging legal cases. Instead, they arrogantly presume

that their own superior ability will allow them to get by, and [they] figure that the people are so stupid that they will not recognize an unjust decision when they see one. . . . Such cover-ups do terrible injury to the official's own character, as well as to the locality. . . .

10. Avoid losing your temper. Officials must remain composed. . . . The way to control anger is to overcome oneself. Self-regulation is prerequisite to the regulation of others.

[*Peiyuantang oucun gao* 20:11–24 — WR]

Popular attitudes and customary practices vary from locality to locality. It is the duty of the official to promote those that are advantageous and eliminate those that are disadvantageous. . . . Magistrates are therefore directed to compile and submit to me a casebook, describing in detail the situation in their counties with regard to each of the following items:

1.  Tax and surtax assessments and collections . . .
2.  Grain tribute assessments and collections . . .
3.  Government granaries . . .
4.  Community granaries . . .
5.  Varieties of crops grown . . .
6.  Potentially reclaimable land . . .
7.  Water conservancy and irrigation works . . .
8.  Local customs regarding marriage and funerary rites and popular religious practices . . .
9.  Community libation rituals . . .
10. Exemplary cases of filiality or virtuous widowhood . . .
11. Official temples and sacrifices . . .
12. Scholarly trends and fashions . . .
13. Academies and public schools . . .
14. Incidence of feuds and capital crimes . . .
15. Incidence of theft . . .
16. Incidence of banditry . . .
17. Incidence of cattle theft and illegal slaughter . . .
18. Tax arrears . . .
19. Incidence of gambling and smuggling . . .
20. Counterfeiting or melting down of government coins . . .
21. Backlog of civil litigation . . .
22. Maintenance and security of cemeteries . . .
23. Refugees and vagrants . . .
24. Poorhouses and orphanages . . .
25. Dikes and flood-prevention measures . . .
26. Market towns and overland or water commercial routes . . .
27. Postal depots . . .

28. Historical relics . . .
29. Pettifoggers . . .
30. Leading lineages . . .
31. Sales of government salt . . .
32. Sub-officials assigned to the district . . .

[*Peiyuantang oucun gao* 12:28–32 — WR]

## ON GOVERNANCE BY LOCAL ELITES

One of the major preoccupations of Qing scholar-officials was how to achieve more effective governance of the empire's population (of whose rapid growth they were well aware) without greatly increasing government budgets or personnel. Put another way, what was the best means to bridge the widening chasm between state and society? One method, associated by most Qing thinkers with the radical anti-bureaucratism of Gu Yanwu, was to delegate various quasi-governmental tasks to members of the non-official indigenous elite. Chen Hongmou did not share Gu's deep antipathy to the state apparatus; indeed, we have just seen how he sought to order society in part by increasing the efficiency and the powers of control exercised by the bureaucracy itself. Yet he was also attracted by programs to further local self-governance, especially when these could be placed in the hands of men whose positions of authority were sanctified by ritually correct kinship bonds.

The following proposal, which Chen developed as governor of Jiangxi in the 1730s, was admiringly reprinted nearly a century later in *Huangchao jingshi wenbian*. Note, however, that despite the language of empowerment of lineage headmen that characterizes this directive, Chen's policy was at least as much aimed at asserting government control over these men, whom he knew in Jiangxi to be notoriously unmanageable, by forcing them to register with and accept subordinate status under the county magistrate.

When antisocial or illegal incidents arise among the common people, if a criminal action has occurred it must be punished accordingly. The law must be respected. Yet how much better is it to civilize and enlighten an individual before he has committed a crime than to punish him after he has already done so? The local official's primary tasks are to provide moral leadership and to uphold the law. If people nevertheless violate the law, the official must punish them. But for each person who can be reached through moral instruction, there is one more constructive member of society. For each incident or conflict that can be avoided, there is one more socially beneficial act.

Yet the local official's jurisdiction is widespread and his duties many. He simply cannot be aware of everything that goes on. This is where ancestral temples come in. Each ancestral temple has a lineage headman, and below him a number of lineage-branch headmen. These individuals naturally enjoy the respect of their lineages. They are directly on the scene and are joined to their constituencies by familial ties. Through their function of officiating at the ancestral rites, there is nothing within the lineage, good or ill, beneficial or harmful, that does not fall under their purview.

Local officials, then, should issue formal patents of authority to lineage heads, making them solely responsible for providing moral instruction and discipline to lineage members. Each and every affair within the lineage ought to be made subject to their management. If any lineage member acts unfilially or shows an inclination to violent or criminal behavior, he should be admonished by the lineage-branch headman. If he fails to respond with due respect to this admonition, he should be reported to the lineage headman and ritually disciplined in the ancestral temple before the assembled lineage members. Only if he still fails to reform should he be reported to the local official for criminal punishment.

Disputes or property transactions internal to the lineage should be mediated and resolved in an equitable way by the lineage or the branch headman. Conflicts between lineage members and outsiders should be mediated by the headmen of the two lineages and their decisions enforced. Where necessary, the local official should bring the two lineage headmen together in his office and resolve the dispute collectively and impartially. . . .

In this way, we invest the lineage headmen with the authority to enforce the laws of the government among their dependent kinsmen, with whom they collectively share the vicissitudes of life. It is only natural that they will find it far easier to scrutinize and discipline their kinsmen than will any community-compact headman or local constable who bears a different surname and is not of that family.

[*Peiyuantang oucun gao* 13:46–48  — WR]

## STATECRAFT IN THE GRAIN TRADE AND GOVERNMENT-CONTROLLED BROKERAGES

The distribution of grain, as well as government measures to control the grain market so as to maintain adequate supplies and stable prices, was a perennial problem of traditional Chinese statecraft. The following memorial is typical of the efforts of Qing officials to deal with the complexities of the problem in different times and places. It was written in 1763 by Yang Yingju, governor-general of Shaanxi and Gansu, in response to an inquiry from the court regarding the advisability of maintaining or abolishing brokerages in the grain trade. The inquiry was prompted by Yang's reported abolition of grain brokers in Guangdong, of which the court had not been informed, when he had been acting governor-general of Guangdong and Guangxi in 1754. Two of his most experienced and prestigious colleagues at the time, Fang Guancheng and Yin

Jishan, were also asked for their opinion on the proper policy toward grain brokerage.

Most remarkable in Yang's response is an acute sense of regional variation and, as a consequence, of the need for flexibility in devising policies. While his text is devoid of anti-merchant rhetoric and stresses the advantages of an open and competitive market where brokers and merchants cooperate harmoniously for the benefit of both producers and consumers, he also insists that the latter are the ones to be protected by the state and that no "abuse" should be tolerated on the part of traders. Also typical of the Qing statecraft discourse is the insistence on the necessity to curb official interference and harassment and resist the multiplication of regulations, even though state intervention appears highly desirable in the poorer areas where "traders do not go." According to Yang, practical statecraft required a combination of time-honored policies, experience in adapting them to local circumstances, accurate information, and both personal integrity and finesse on the part of officials. Excerpts from Yang's long and detailed analysis follow.

## A MEMORIAL ON GRAIN PRICES, THE GRAIN TRADE, AND GOVERNMENT-CONTROLLED BROKERAGES

I respectfully observe that in the nineteenth year of Qianlong [1754] I was appointed by imperial grace acting governor-general of Guangdong and Guangxi. Having reached my post, I thoroughly investigated the sufferings of the people and learned that Guangdong has many mountains and few rice fields and is not normally considered a rice-producing area. Year after year, its people largely depend upon the resources of [neighboring] Guangxi for their food. This is why, in the past, grain brokers were established according to quota in the provincial capital and in Foshan. Whenever grain boats from Guangxi came to Guangdong, the merchants were authorized freely to select brokers to whom they could entrust the sale, giving them a fee for their costs. For a long time things went this way peacefully.

[Then] during the tenure of former governor-general Bandi and former governor Haonian, to these brokers established by quota were added pier directorates in charge of brokering grain, one each in Canton and in Foshan, with an officially established brokerage firm [at its head]. When grain boats from Guangxi [arrived], or grain shipments from the countryside, [the merchants] were required to go to the pier directorate, and only then would they be allowed to sell. The intention was to prevent the rice brokers [already in operation] from raising or depressing market prices arbitrarily. But in fact in the past there were several established rice brokerages, and merchants were authorized freely to go to the broker [of their choice] and deal with him; if a broker was even slightly unfair, he would have to fear that the merchants would drop him and go to another one. This is why, until now, they had not dared to indulge in abuses freely. [By contrast,] the newly established pier directorate, taking advantage of the fact that they were alone in control of the situation, used their power to monopolize and manipulate [the market]. The result was that grain prices soared.

Besides, one more regulation means one more abuse; one more person means one more fee. And these fees as a rule are met out of the pockets of the small folk who buy and sell; thus as [occasions for] fleecing multiply, the costs of meeting them become more and more numerous. For this reason, the Guangxi grain boats traveling east decreased steadily in number, which was a serious obstacle to the proper nourishment of the people. . . . [The pier directorates were thereupon abolished by Yang Yingju, the new governor-general.]

When I was in Guangdong and taking care of the people's nourishment in order to meet [Your Majesty's] sagely concerns, I managed to make market prices go down, but the abolition of the grain pier directors and brokers was only one link in the process. For if the Guangxi merchants are only moved by profit, in the same way they are necessarily deterred by harassment; [from this] it follows that it is necessary both to treat them with compassion and to know how to encourage them, so as to make it clear to them that they have no harassment to fear and that there is profit to be made; then, inevitably, grain will come in a continuous flow. I [therefore] gave strict orders to the district magistrates along the route [from Guangxi], to the effect that when they have to restock grain in the [public] granaries, they should acquire it in the markets, and in no case halt the Guangxi merchants' grain boats and force them to sell, resulting in coercion and delay.

Also, [one should remember that] the precedents according to which hoarding was prohibited dealt specifically with whoever stores too much and waits for prices [to rise], or restrains [the circulation of goods] to corner the market; but in the case of those Guangxi merchant boats coming every day, one mast following the other, the situation requires that the rich local families buy and resell, which, moreover, makes it possible for the merchants rapidly to ply their oars and repeat the process (lit. "transport back and forth like a windlass"); this is exactly how grain can be circulated and prices be brought down. How could we insist on formal adherence to the precedent on hoarding and irresponsibly block their operations, so as to create difficulties for Guangxi merchants to sell, since [the latter] would get wind of it and no longer dare to make a move? There, too, I ordered the magistrates of Nan[hai] and Pan[yu] and the assistant magistrate of Foshan to examine the situation carefully and in no case provoke the least obstruction.

Again, there is the problem of the Guangxi merchants who, having sold their grain, sail back with empty boats; when the magistrates along the way happen to have assignments for them, they requisition at short notice those who pass by, and this too is something merchants and people do not happily put up with.

I consequently strictly forbade [such practices], so as to free Guangxi merchants from such anxieties and make them still more eager to move grain. . . .

Subsequently I received the [present] edict [asking] about whether or not it would be advisable generally to abolish the institution of grain brokers and [ordering] me to investigate carefully into the question, in each case taking local conditions into account. I observe that in the provinces of Shaanxi and Gansu, with the exception of some small out-of-the-way departments and counties where there have never been any grain brokers, everywhere else they have been established according to quota. Among them, some of the grain brokers of Shaanxi still are comparatively prosperous, but those of Gansu rarely have any capital. Nevertheless, they all pass [their position] on from father to son and their trade from generation to generation. [Their role] is no more than to evaluate prices and measure quantities for others, [for which] they extract [a fee of] two or three cash per peck. They are not by any means comparable to the pier directorate grain brokers that had been established in Guangdong. Furthermore, the merchants who carry grain to the market have no familiarity with the place and its people. If they do not take advantage of a broker's introduction, they will have difficulty finding purchasers to whom they can sell their wares; and, as far as the different qualities of grain and differences in price are concerned, there too they will have to avail themselves of the brokers' evaluation so as to avoid wrangles between the parties involved.

Thus, as far as the situation in Shaanxi and Gansu is concerned, the role of the brokers who are presently established is basically to help merchants and people by evaluating the price of things; it would [therefore] seem difficult to suggest their abolition. If among them there are [individuals] who deceive the country folk or arbitrarily raise and lower prices, they will have to be arrested and punished immediately; in fact, this sort of abuse is easy to eradicate. . . .

The problem is that local conditions are never the same. If one wants to prevent middlemen from using their crafty devices, and thus keep prices from soaring, it is entirely a matter of examining what fits which place at which moment; it is difficult to stick by regulations fixed once and for all. . . .

When dealing with the people's nourishment one cannot stick by a fixed set of regulations; investigating brokers and arresting stockpilers is, however, one task in the [more general program of] suppressing abuses. The edict we have now received from Our August Emperor, making inquiries and ordering careful investigations, taking account of the situation in our respective regions, truly shows the utmost wisdom and clear thinking. The only thing that high officials in the various provinces should do is deliberate on the situation in each region, according to existing circumstances, and direct their subordinates to put real energy into devising means to manage the situation, so that prices may drop and people not have to pay dearly to feed themselves; this will respond to Our Sage Ruler's utmost sense of sympathy with the distressed. Obeying the Imperial rescript, I have carefully investigated and truthfully memorialized in response.

Prostrating myself, I implore Your Majesty's astute scrutiny and instructions.

Vermilion [Imperial] rescript: One can say this is a discussion by someone who fully understands the tasks at hand.

[Memorial of 1763, QL 015160, Palace Museum Archives, Taibei — PEW]

## HONG LIANGJI: ON IMPERIAL MALFEASANCE AND CHINA'S POPULATION PROBLEM

Hong Liangji (1746–1809), a scholar-official from Changzhou in the lower Yangzi valley, advanced slowly through the civil service system (winning the final degree only at the age of forty-four) and was assigned to minor government posts and projects, in which he applied himself to a range of statecraft studies and Evidential Learning: geography, local history, government administration, and the classics. His writings show his concerns about problems spawned by the very success of stable rule in a maturing society — problems poorly coped with, in Hong's time, by an increasingly lethargic and corrupt government.

Hong's most distinguishing personal feature was his candor and conscientiousness in fulfilling the Confucian duty of political remonstrance — qualities reflecting a spirit of reformism in the New Text scholarship of his home region. His audacity in criticizing the emperor (see the letter to Prince Cheng below) led to his condemnation and exile for implicitly criticizing the emperor. To this same critical temper, perhaps, can be attributed his forthright reconsideration of a fundamental assumption in Chinese thinking: that a growing population is an index of good government and is socially desirable. Hong expressed his ideas on this subject in a few pages of miscellaneous essays, titled "Opinion," written in 1793, five years before Malthus's *Essay on the Principle of Population*. Though Hong's essential insight is the same as Malthus's, he did not think of himself as developing a new science according to rigorous methods, nor did any later Qing scholar explore his ideas further.

By Western standards China had been heavily populated since before the time of Christ — about sixty million, with considerable fluctuation during periods of extreme distress or prosperity. During the century or more before Hong wrote, however, the population began to rise rapidly toward the several-hundred-million level. No doubt, simple empirical observation and reflection sufficed to convince this acute and inquiring scholar that China was faced with a problem of new and massive proportions, pointing to an inherent contradiction in the concept of peaceful rule.

### LETTER TO PRINCE CHENG EARNESTLY DISCUSSING THE POLITICAL AFFAIRS OF THE TIME, 1799

The following excerpts are from a long letter Hong submitted to Prince Cheng (the Jiaqing Emperor) in the autumn of 1799 with the wish that it be drawn to imperial attention.

The letter specifies in detail the lack of reform following the dismissal and death of the Qianlong emperor's favorite and protégé, Heshen, who had become all-powerful at court. The letter criticizes the conduct of the Jiaqing emperor himself (for example, being late for audiences at the throne hall and spending a great deal of time with favorite courtiers, including actors) and attacks by name officials both at court and in the provinces for corruption and abuse of power. Hong also complained about the inadequate channels of communication with the throne and the generally sad state of local administration. The Jiaqing emperor was infuriated by the letter, when it was shown to him. At imperial request, the Board of Punishment recommended the death sentence for Hong, later commuted to banishment to Yili in Xinjiang.

Why do I say that the selection of personnel and the conduct of administration have not been thoroughly reformed? This is because although the man [i.e., Heshen] has been dealt with by law, it has not been objectively discussed how, in more than a decade's time, he altered the precedents established by the dynasty's ancestors and brought forward officials who were personally loyal to him. Among the current practices of the Grand Secretariat, the Six Boards, and other government offices, which are in accordance with the established statutes of the state and which are the results of Heshen's tampering with the precedents? Among the personnel of the Grand Secretariat, the Six Boards, and other government offices, who are really officials employed by the state and who, having been placed there by Heshen, were implicated in receiving bribes and shared the responsibility for corruption? The emperor is indeed humane and kind and wishes to deal with the accomplices leniently. Moreover, because so many officials were involved, it is not possible to dismiss them all. But it is my humble view that in the case of those officials whose [implication in Heshen's misdeeds] is clearly and accurately known, even if their past acts are not to be inquired into, their names ought to be put down in the registers, so that when they come up for promotion or transfer of office, the principle of encouragement for good deeds and punishment for evil deeds can be applied to them in an appropriate manner. This would make it abundantly clear to everyone that while the sagacious Son of Heaven does not act excessively, he is nonetheless aware of and is acting to make evident the distinction between right and wrong, good and evil. In this way, those who, in the past, have known only a client-patron relationship may be transformed inwardly as well as outwardly into true subjects of the state (*guojia zhi ren*). Otherwise, in the future should the court not be as orderly and above reproach as at present, if, unlikely though it might seem, someone imitated what the powerful minister [Heshen] did, many officials would again gather at the gate of such a minister [and offer themselves as clients to a patron].

Why do I say that morals and customs are deteriorating? [What I refer to is the fact that] the scholar-officials have increasingly disregarded honor and lost their sense of shame, while the common people have disregarded their socio-ethical duties [as seen in the rise of rebellion]. The common people should not be blamed for this, however; the responsibility still lies with the scholar-officials themselves. During the past dozen or more years, I have seen presidents and vice presidents of the Six Boards gladly kneel before the chief minister [Heshen]. There have been Grand Secretaries who were supervisors of the "seven courts" and who, moreover, were twice as old in age, offering themselves as disciples and clients (siren) to Heshen. Some officials befriended the servants of the chief minister and were happy to deal with them on an equal footing. The imperial academies [including the Hanlin Academy] are [supposed to be] the font of scholarly morals and morale. Now there are academicians who spend entire evenings begging pitifully to be appointed a Libationer [Rector] (jijiu), as well as those who will kneel for hours seeking appointment as Lecturer from the Classics Mat. . . . If such is the behavior of the scholar-officials, how can one criticize the common people for being deceitful and dependent on the help of others? If these things happen at the imperial court, how can one criticize the pursuit of selfish interest and corruption in the distant parts of the empire?

[Hong Liangji, appendix, *Hong Liangji nianpu*, pp. 107–108 — KCL]

### CHINA'S POPULATION PROBLEM

There has never been a people who did not delight in living under peaceful rule, nor a people not happy about living under peaceful rule that has lasted for a long time. Peaceful rule that lasts more than one hundred years is considered to have lasted a long time. But in the matter of population, it may be noted that today's population is five times as large as that of thirty years ago, ten times as large as that of sixty years ago, and not less than twenty times as large as that of one hundred years ago. Take, for example, a family that at the time of the great-great-grandfather and the great-grandfather was in possession of a ten-room house and one hundred *mou* of farmland. After the man married there were at first only the two of them; they lived in the ten-room house and upon the one hundred *mou* of land, and their resources were more than ample. Assuming that they had three sons, by the time the sons grew up, all three sons as well as the father had wives; there were a total of eight persons. Eight persons would require the help of hired servants; there would be, say, ten persons in the household. With the ten-room house and the one hundred *mou* of farmland, I believe they would have just enough space to live in and food to eat, although barely enough. In time, however, there will be grandsons, who, in turn, will marry. The aged members of the household will pass away, but there could still be more than twenty persons in the family. With more than twenty persons sharing a ten-room house and working on one hundred *mou* of farmland, I am sure that even if they eat very frugally and live in crowded quarters, their needs will not be met. Moreover, there will be great-grandchildren and great-great-grandchildren — the total number in a household will be fifty or sixty times that in the great-great-grandfather's or great-grandfather's time. For every household at the time of the great-grandfather, there will be at least ten households at the time of the great-grandson and great-great-grandson. There are families whose population has declined, but there are also lineages whose male members have greatly multiplied, compensating for the cases of decline.

Someone may say that at the time of the great-grandfather and great-great-grandfather, not all uncultivated land had been reclaimed and not all vacancies in housing available on the market had been filled. However, the amount [of available farmland and housing] has only doubled or, at the most, increased three to five times, while the population has grown ten to twenty times. Thus farmland and houses are always in short supply, while there is always a surplus of households and population. Furthermore, there are families who [have bought up or otherwise] appropriated other people's property — one person owning the houses of more than a hundred, one household occupying the farmland of a hundred households. No wonder, then, that everywhere there are people who have died from exposure to windstorm, rain, and frost, or from hunger and cold and the hardships of homelessness.

Question: Do Heaven-and-earth have a way of dealing with this situation? Answer: Heaven-and-earth's way of making adjustments lies in flood, drought, and plagues [which reduce the population]. However, people who unfortunately succumb to flood, drought, and plagues are no more than 10 or 20 percent of the total population.

Question: Do the ruler and his ministers have a way of dealing with this situation? Answer: The ruler and the ministers may make adjustments in the following ways: pursuing policies to ensure that no farmland will remain unused and that there will be no surplus labor. Migration of farmers to newly reclaimed land may be organized; heavy taxes may be reduced after a comparison is made between past and present tax rates. Extravagance in consumption may be prohibited; the wealthy household's appropriation of the property of others may be suppressed. Should there be floods, drought, and plagues, grain in the granaries may be made available, and all the funds in the government treasury may be used for relief — these are all that the ruler and his ministers can do in the way of adjustments between population and productive land.

In a word, after a long period of peaceful rule, Heaven-and-earth cannot stop the people from reproducing. Yet the resources with which Heaven-and-earth nourish the people are finite. After a period of peaceful rule, the ruler and the ministers cannot stop the people from reproducing, yet what the ruler and the ministers can do for the people is limited to the policies enumerated above. Among ten youths in a family, there are always one or two who resist being educated. Among the idle people in all the empire, how can it be expected that all will accept control from above? The housing for one person is inadequate for the needs of ten persons; how can it be sufficient for a hundred persons? The food for one person is inadequate for ten persons; how can it be sufficient for a hundred persons? This is why I am worried about peaceful rule.

[Hong, *Yiyan*, in *Juanshi geji* 1:8a–9b — KCL]

### THE DETERIORATION OF LOCAL GOVERNMENT

## Prefects and County Magistrates

Hong Liangji worried not only that the surfeit of population made subsistence difficult. The deterioration of local government in the late Qianlong period did not escape his keen attention either. The smallest unit of government traditionally was the county (*xian*), presided over by a magistrate who was responsible for collection of taxes to produce the annual quota, as well as for administration of justice. The tenure of the magistrate was often short, and the quality of his government depended largely on his control over the permanent sub-bureaucracy — the notorious yamen clerks and runners known to have tyrannized the people. In the late eighteenth century, a county magistrate could be responsible for a population as large as a hundred thousand. The direct supervisor of the county magistrate was the prefect, whose prefecture (*fu*) included a number of counties. Neither the prefect nor the magistrate could reform the local administration, especially when the central and provincial leadership was corrupt.

Prefects and county magistrates are officials close to the people. When a prefect is a good person, blessings will spread to a thousand *li*; when the magistrate is a good person, the blessings will spread to a hundred *li*. Is there any secret to the work of prefects and county magistrates? The only secret lies in the motivation of these officials. In my youth, when I attended to my grandfather and father, I remember that when someone of the neighborhood was appointed a prefect or a county magistrate, he would receive sympathy and encouragement from relatives and friends who were bound to worry as to whether the vacancy [he might then have to fill] had an excessive or a light workload and whether it was in an area known as "difficult to govern." Then during the twenty or thirty years between my coming of age and my becoming an official myself, customs and attitudes abruptly changed. When someone in the neighborhood was due to become a prefect or a county magistrate, he would receive sympathy and exhortations from friends and relatives who would worry about him as to whether the position he might fill would yield enough profit to cover what must be spent on social relations [lit. compensation and entertaining] — in other words, how much the prefect or magistrate would get for himself each year. There would no longer be any talk about the people's livelihood or the ideals of local administration.

[When the prefect or county magistrate has arrived at his post] his mind is not on the people. He must ask such questions as the amount of the customary fees (*lougui*) to be collected each year. How much will the gifts from his subordinates amount to? What surplus will there be from land and other taxes? Moreover, those who are said to be his wives, sons, brothers, other relatives, friends, servants and maidservants — all are characterized by insatiable greed and will help the prefect or the county magistrate in his pursuit of profit. When, unfortunately, the prefect or magistrate for the same area is changed several times a year, many will be in great distress — these include subordinate personnel at the boards [in Beijing][2] and, at the locality, rich merchants and common people. There may be among prefects and county magistrates those who possess self-respect and who actually have the interests of the people at heart, but it is difficult to find one or two of them among ten prefects or county magistrates. Moreover, these one or two [upright] officials will be ridiculed by the seven or eight other prefects and county magistrates as pedantic sticklers, stupid and incapable of watching out for their own interests. Even the higher officials [at the provincial level] will regard these one or two [uncorrupted local officials] as out of touch with the exigencies of the times and failing to go along with prevailing practice. If unluckily some fault is found in their conduct of official business, they will be removed as quickly as possible. . . .

## Yamen Clerks

Yamen clerks or sub-officials (*lixu*) are a subject of frequent complaint by statecraft writers from the Song on down. The latter regard the sub-bureaucracy that handles most official business as venal, grasping, and unguided by the Confucian standards that are supposedly inculcated by the classical education required of regular officials.

In present circumstances, the harm [that] officials do to the people is far less than the harm yamen clerks do to the people. How so? This is because the yamen clerks today are not the same as the clerks of antiquity . . . who were versed in classical scholarship and expert in their knowledge of laws and imperial decrees. Clerks in those times not only would not harass the people, they would even benefit the people.

This, however, is not the case today. Out of a hundred yamen clerks, not even one has advanced to become a [regular] official. Since there is no channel for promotion [to become regular officials], they concentrate on the pursuit of profit. . . .

The yamen clerks are feared by their neighbors; they are feared by scholars, farmers, artisans and merchants, and indeed by scholar-officials themselves.

---

2. This refers presumably to clerks at the Board of Civil Office, who expected gifts from local officials serving a considerable length of time.

When the especially evil-minded and cunning among them take over the actual control of the [local] administration, the government itself fears them.

Why is this so? It is because officials who themselves want to profit by exploiting the people cannot do so except through the yamen clerks. The latter know very well who is rich and who is not in the local area — these facts may be hidden from the officials but never from the yamen clerks. Whether a household is worth only one tael, or a hundred or a thousand taels, the yamen clerks know exactly, without fail. Of the amount then extracted from the people, 30 percent may go to the officials, but 50 percent will have gone to the yamen clerks.

Now among the larger counties, there could be as many as a thousand clerks; for counties of the next size, as many as seven or eight hundred; and for smaller counties, a minimum of one or two hundred. These one thousand to one or two hundred yamen clerks are not engaged in farming, and the women of their households are not engaged in weaving. Clearly, they are living off the people. Roughly speaking, the products of ten households among the people are not adequate for the demands of one yamen clerk. When there are a thousand yamen clerks in a county with a population of ten thousand, the people will be restive.

[Hong, *Yiyan*, in *Juanshi geji* 19b–22a — KCL]

### THE ROOTS OF REBELLION

The following excerpt is from Memorial on the War Against Heterodoxy, which Hong submitted in the spring of 1798 on the occasion of an imperially conducted examination for Hanlin academicians. His theme is that the "White Lotus" sectarian rebellion had broken out in Hubei, Sichuan, and other provinces because of the abuse of power by local officials, who arbitrarily added new taxes and persecuted the people. Hong believed that once local government in these areas was reformed and the military and provincial officials properly rewarded or punished, the rebellion would end of its own accord. Here he discusses the crisis in local administration.

The deterioration of the county government is a hundred times worse than ten or twenty years ago. The [county officials] have betrayed the laws of the Son of Heaven and exhausted the resources of the common people. From what I have heard, although there are heterodox sects in such places as Yichang in Hubei and Dazhou in Sichuan, the people there value their lives and property and love their wives and children too much to dare to violate the law. The county officials were not able to prevent the spread of heterodoxy by exerting good influences on the people, and when sectarianism spread, the officials would use the pretext of investigating heterodoxy to make demands on the people and threaten their lives, until the people joined the rebels. I would humbly suggest that in locations where heterodox rebellions have arisen, inquiry must be made into the causes of conflict, to see whether the rebellion was precipitated by the officials, who should be punished according to the facts of each case.

County magistrates have incriminated themselves in three ways.


1. Funds authorized by the court for disaster relief were pocketed by the officials, who would declare that the funds were intended for making up deficiencies in what was due the government — in this way, the beneficence of the court never reached the people.

2. In ordinary times, the local officials would appropriate taxes and military funds [for their own use]. But when troubles arose, they would try to conceal their failure and even claim some merit. County officials would conceal the facts from the prefects and circuit intendants; prefects and circuit intendants from the governors-general and governors; governors-general and governors from even Your Imperial Majesty. Thus the sentiments of those on the lower level have no way of reaching the higher level.

3. When there is some success, even personal servants and secretaries [of the county magistrate] claim a share of the merit. But in case of failure, the blame is fixed on the good people who are in distress as roving migrants. Failure, to be sure, is not the fault of the county officials alone. High officials at the provincial level and the high military commanders and officers all behave in this way without even making a secret of it. It is no surprise that the county officials imitate them.

[Hong, *Yiyan*, in *Juanshi geji* 10:2a–3a  — KCL]


## GONG ZIZHEN'S REFORMIST VISION

From a prominent family of scholar-officials with a rich literary background, Gong Zizhen (1792–1841) stands as a key link between the homegrown variety of statecraft thought and the later generation whose reformism responded to the challenge of the West. Though recognized as an important poet and a brilliant writer, Gong had no great success in the higher ranks of officialdom. Instead he demonstrated his talents in secretarial capacities for important state boards and in association with leading officials such as Lin Zexu and Wei Yuan, whose doings and writings, in direct confrontation with the West, continue this chapter on Chinese statecraft thinking.

Gong's writings, of which only a small portion survive, covered a wide range of intellectual interests typical of the practical, evidential learning among Qing Confucians but distinguished in his case by penetrating analyses of Qing weaknesses and prophetic warnings of dangers ahead. His independence and outspokenness no doubt account for the frustration he experienced in fulfilling his passionate desire to be of public service, while these disappointments only intensified his bitterness and sharpened his diatribes against incompetent leaders and their fawning subordinates.

Many of Gong's views bespoke hard-line resistance to the West and conservative Confucian opposition to foreign trade seen as detrimental to the basic economic interests of the Chinese people. At the same time he was a severe critic of the existing civil service examinations system, of the opium traffic, of foot binding among women, of servile conduct at court, of rituals he considered demeaning of ministers, and of superstitious practices at court. Such reformist advocacy, though unavailing at the time, won great respect for Gong among late Qing champions of radical reform.

## ON THE LACK OF MORAL FIBER AMONG SCHOLAR-OFFICIALS

The following is excerpted from an essay of Gong's titled "On Enlightened Rulers and Worthy Ministers" ("Ming liang lun"), in which the degradation of court officials in his day is contrasted to the ancient ideals of enlightened rulership and worthy ministers. The opening lines recollect Confucius's characterization of governance as depending not on coercion but on an appeal to the people's sense of shame and self-respect. Likewise, the reference to Lectures from the Classics Mat in the Song recalls Cheng Yi's insistence on the respect that rulers should show to ministers as colleagues and mentors.

When scholar-officials (*shi*) have a sense of shame, the state (*guojia*) is never shamed. For scholar-officials to know no shame, however, is a great shame for the state. Look at the scholar-officials in recent years. By the time they submit their first memorial and begin their careers, only a few among them still have a sense of shame! The longer they serve as officials, the more degraded is their spirit; the more undeserving is their reputation, the more they fawn on their superiors; and the closer they get to the throne, the more skillful flatterers they become. Once they come to fill one of the top positions at court, their position is indeed lofty, but these latter-day ministers have never seen or heard how the great ministers of antiquity conducted themselves, assuming with lofty dignity the role of teacher to the ruler — indeed, this is a role that the ministers of today have never dreamed of! Today the firm integrity of a minister is at an all-time low, and the reason for this is none other than that there is no stimulus to morals and morale at court.

How is morality at court to be stimulated? The first priority is to teach the importance of the sense of shame. . . . [In antiquity] the three high ministers of the state sat down while they discoursed with the monarch on the Way. At the height of the Tang-Song era, the high ministers and Lecturers from the Classics Mat were always asked to sit down [with the emperor] and be served tea. They would see the ruler in one of the side throne rooms, where they could discuss ancient ways at ease, and many of them became great Confucians themselves. In later times, however, when an official has an audience in the morning or evening, he has to kneel for a long period, leaving no time for anything else. I do not know why the former practices were abandoned. But with the present ritual in the throne hall, the ruler and his ministers have been increasingly separated and isolated from each other. . . .

In my humble view, nowadays all that officials engaged in politically important matters really know about are carriages and horses, proper costumes and flowery rhetoric, beyond which they are interested in nothing. All that officials in leisurely posts [such as Hanlin academicians] are good at is calligraphy and the writing of poetry, using the rhymes of other people's poems; anything else is of no concern to them. In the throne hall, officials watch for signs of imperial pleasure or displeasure as a guide to what they themselves will say. When the emperor smiles and bestows a feast on them as a present, they will be so pleased that they will immediately brag about it to their wives and children as well as to their students. If the emperor is a little displeased, they kowtow their way out of the throne hall and ponder about other ways of winning imperial favor. Are they really reverential in their hearts and in awe of the monarch? If one should ask them whether high ministers should behave in this fashion, they would give a shameful answer: "This is all we can do." Actually, one can tell what their motivation is. Those who know about carriages and horses and who are flowery in their rhetoric do not read very much. They will say, "I attend to my duties at the public office mornings and evenings. I am already worthy and industrious." Those who practice calligraphy and write poems sometimes read books, but they are not mindful of their principal responsibility. They feel that every day they remain in their position, they are honored for one more day. When their health fails, they will return to their native place and expect their sons and grandsons to rise through the examinations. This is all they wish for: that their offspring in each generation will learn to adopt passivity as a sign of maturity. Why should one's family be concerned with affairs of state?

[*Gong Zizhen quanji*, pp. 31–32 — KCL]


INSTITUTIONAL PARALYSIS AND THE NEED FOR REFORM

Gong's analysis of the evils in governmental administration closely resemble Huang Zongxi's earlier critique of governance hobbled by excessive concentration of authority, legalistic red tape, fear, distrust and suspicion, and a preoccupation with personal worries at the expense of major matters. In contrast to Huang, however, Gong reveals his susceptibility to the age-old idealistic hope of many Confucians that a wise ruler could turn everything around at once if he would just listen to a wise minister.

Laws and regulations are what the yamen clerks are concerned with, but the Son of Heaven and his officials should go beyond these and plan for the Way

of Governance (*zhengdao*). Inasmuch as the yamen clerks go by laws and regulations and do not dare to depart therefrom, they must be subordinate to the
officials and be relegated to a lowly status. The monarch and the officials, in
their pursuit of the Way of Governance, should be guided by their vision of
what they should do; this is why rulers face south [i.e., in the position of honor]
and their authority is exalted. The Son of Heaven should guide his officials to
the right way and ask them to co-govern the empire. . . .

[The practice of government today, however, is for the monarch to control
the officials closely,] to control them and to rein them in. Any morning or
evening the senior officials of the top or the second rank can be deprived of
their posts. In the *Beijing Gazette* one constantly reads of certain officials being
reviewed by the Board of Civil Service for punishment, in serious or less serious
cases. The officials of the board are skillful in comparing names and realities
[i.e., responsibility and performance]. Every month there are cases of the Board
of Civil Service deliberating on the conduct of various officials or the censorate
deliberating upon the conduct of the Board of Civil Service itself. As to local
officials at the prefectural or county level, any moment they may find that their
salaries have been reduced, or that they are demoted in rank, or that indeed
they are removed from their post. Generally [the court] is merely guessing at
what misconduct the local officials have yet to commit, and the decision is
never based on analysis of proven fact. As to those officials who were never
punished nor considered for punishment, although they may have made important contributions within the bounds of what precedent has proven feasible,
what they have accomplished is neither very harmful nor very beneficial. Is this
all that can be expected from an official in this prosperous age? I am afraid that
in a later generation, insightful writers will say that all our high ministers and
other officials are being charged to act like yamen clerks. . . .

In ancient times, the prefects and county magistrates had authority over
capital punishment, without having to report to high officials, and high officials
could appoint or dismiss subordinate officials on their own authority. This was,
of course, the source of innumerable abuses. But today, with the sagacious
wisdom of the throne, a selective adoption of the ancient methods will perhaps
not result in the officials' wanton display of power. To adopt ancient methods
may indeed provide the exact remedy for our present condition of being tied
up [by ordinances, regulations, and the red tape of clerical procedures]. To
rectify the situation without going to extremes will perhaps not yield undesirable
results. Why then should thought not be given to reform (*gengfa*)? . . .

This promises to be the awe-inspiring moment when the sagacious Son of
Heaven plans for good government such as occurs only once in a thousand
years — to do away with over-elaborate regulations, to simplify tax assessment,
to reduce the influence of the yamen clerks. The monarch will hold the principal matters of structure and discipline in his own hands, to advance or dismiss
a generation of officials. He will invest in the high officials the authority to do
what they should and ensure that all officials will adhere to their proper duties.

. . . It will be seen that from the council where the monarch meets with his officials, great and far-reaching plans will arise, and expectations will be high. In the future, in all the empire, people will say that these are purposeful actions of the monarch and ministers of a flourishing age, that these are great undertakings, reflecting generous virtue and definitely not what the yamen clerks, with their self-centered thinking and very limited vision, can ever see.

[*Gong Zizhen quanji*, pp. 34–36 — KCL]

### THE SCHOLAR-TEACHER AND SERVICE TO A DYNASTY

In this essay Gong took a courageous stance — venturing to say that a dynasty will decline and fall should it refuse to engage in reform — if it "adheres to the policies of the ancestors and shrinks from listening to the opinions of many people."

After the Xia dynasty declined, it allowed the Shang dynasty to rise — did Xia not give Shang six hundred years' time? After the Shang dynasty declined, it allowed the Zhou dynasty to rise — did Shang not give Zhou eight hundred years' time? There is never an empire that does not decline after eight hundred years. There is, to be sure, the Way that does not decline for millions of years. But by contrast, a dynasty can decline in ten or fifty years. To adhere to the policies of a single family's ancestors and shrink from listening to the opinion of many among the people is for a dynasty to allow itself to fall and wait for its successor to carry out reform (*gaidu*).

The policies of the dynastic ancestors cannot always be adequate, while the views of many among the people cannot always be heard. Rather than giving those in the future the opportunity for drastic reform, why not reform on one's own initiative? One should give some thought to this question: Wasn't the rise of one's ancestors made possible by their having revolted against the failures of the preceding dynasty? Wasn't the rise of the preceding dynasty made possible by their having revolted against the failures of the dynasty before theirs? Why is it that there are numerous ruling families in history? Why is it that Heaven needs to be displeased with one family? Why is it that the ancestral spirit needs to turn away from accepting sacrifice from one family? Bestir yourself! . . . The *Classic of Changes* says, "When all present possibilities are exhausted, change is called for. Change will lead to unimpededness, which will be of long duration." This is not a generalization concerning the six or seven [pre-Qin] dynasties beginning with the Yellow Emperor. It is meant to be an admonition for each dynasty.

[*Gong Zizhen quanji*, pp. 5–6 — KCL]

### RESPECT FOR THE GUEST

In this essay Gong argues that each dynasty may be the beneficiary of the arts of civilization and of the true Way as conveyed to it by "guests" (i.e., outsiders or survivors of other houses) who represent undying values to be respected by the ruler, intangible assets not the property of any one house. But the ruler cannot share in such moral and spiritual values or respect and employ such persons if the latter lack integrity and, instead of conducting themselves in a self-respecting way, merely act as sycophants and toadies.

In ancient times there were those who surrendered to a ruler, bringing with them sacrificial vessels, musical instruments, or maps of the surrendered country — but no one ever surrendered the Way, for the Way cannot be surrendered. In fact, regarding the skills of the artisans and the methods of the physicians and diviners, no matter how ancient their family or how ancient their office, their techniques cannot be surrendered either. This is not because the new ruler looks down upon one's skills or because he feels that the ancient Way is not worth his while. Nor is it because the king who dares to suppress an ancient people still does not dare to suppress its ritual and music, its Way and its skills. It is because the Way is indeed extraordinary; it cannot be surrendered. Ritual and music are indeed numinous and cannot be suppressed. . . .

When Confucius edited the *Six Classics*, he relied on historical sources. History, historical records, and cultivated persons living in retirement (*yimin*) [including persons who had ties with a former dynasty] were all guests from the standpoint of the Zhou house. They were different manifestations of the same reality. However, some who had the surname of a guest and belonged to the outer court, who did not hold a hereditary position nor live in the comfort of the inner chamber, would behave like servants or concubines, like actors, dogs, and horses, all in pursuit of emolument! Some such scholar-officials would merely behave in an inappropriate way; others would compromise the learning they had acquired; and in the worst cases, they would betray their ancestors. These scholar-officials placed themselves in the ranks of servants and concubines, actors, dogs, and horses — they would certainly meet with the disapproval of gentlemen of independent character.

[*Gong Zizhen quanji*, pp. 28–29 — KCL]

# WEI YUAN AND CONFUCIAN PRACTICALITY

## *THE LEARNING OF STATECRAFT*

In 1829 He Changling (1785–1848), formerly Financial Commissioner of Jiangsu, published a large anthology of Qing writings (including memorials, essays, and so on) concerning problems of government, including technical administrative matters, in a large work of 120 chapters. Wei Yuan (1794–1856) was the actual compiler of the work and was the author of its "Preface" and "Editorial Principles" (both dated 1826). A native of Hunan, Wei was a holder of the *juren* degree [who was] then serving in the personal secretariat of Commissioner He. The preface to the work sets forth the following four principles that were to mark the distinctive approach to the learning of statecraft with which both Wei and his friend Gong Zizhen are identified. These principles were (1) that practical affairs were as important as one's knowledge of one's mind-and-heart and hence as important as self-cultivation; (2) that laws and systems are important, even though governance depends on human agency; (3) that knowledge of antiquity, though of fundamental importance, must meet the needs of the present, hence the emphasis on practical affairs; and (4) that although one's knowledge of all objective beings and things inevitably is seen from the vantage point of oneself, one must still learn from the objective world and especially from the knowledge and opinions of others. Self-knowledge (so stressed by Wang Yangming) is important but not enough; knowledge of others and of external conditions is also essential. One should understand the ideas and motivations of others, so that, as a result of broad consultation and frequent discussion, simpler and more effective solutions may be found for long-standing social and administrative problems. Wei's articulation of these principles and the writings he selected for this large anthology gave new impetus to Confucian statecraft in nineteenth-century China.

### WEI YUAN: PREFACE TO *ANTHOLOGY OF QING STATECRAFT WRITINGS* (*HUANGCHAO JINGSHI WENBIAN*)

All affairs are based on [judgments of] the mind-and-heart, . . . but as in the case of a steelyard, though brass markings are needed to make measurements, it is the weight of the object that produces the [resulting] measurement, not the measuring that produces the weight. To speak properly about the mind-and-heart [in relation to affairs] one must seek verification in the facts of the matter.

Laws and systems are based on human agency. As in the case of a big-wheeled wagon that can carry a huge load over a thousand *li*, without a driver it cannot go forward at all, but even ancient craftsmen with the sharpest eyes and greatest imagination could not build a wagon behind closed doors and expect its wheels to fit the tracks in the road. To speak properly about human agency, one must recognize the need to rely on laws and systems.

Present affairs are based on past history. But as in the case of the Yellow Emperor and his minister Da Nao, before they invented the *jiazi* [sexagenary system of computing days and years] a thousand years could serve as a measure of time, but still [impressive as was their feat in improving the system], last year's calendar cannot be used for this year. The tools used by great-great-grandfather and great-grandfather are not as suitable for our use as grandfather's or father's. The more recent the time, the more telling its influence. The sages have ridden on the trends and circumstances of their times; their spiritual intelligence and statesmanship have arisen therefrom. Properly to speak of past history, one must verify in the present the lessons of the past.

External things are based on one's own observation, but when two things come together fine points emerge, when two minds come together doubts and difficulties appear, and when the doubts in two minds come together, difficulties can be easily and simply resolved.

The *Classic of Odes* says:

> Wisely arranged are the great plans —
> Sages determined them.
> What other men have in their minds,
> I can measure by reflection.[3]

Elsewhere in the *Classic of Odes* [it is said]:

> Everywhere I push my inquiries. . . .
> Everywhere I seek information and suggestions.[4]

It can thus be seen that people in antiquity did not dare to rely on their own minds alone and that, moreover, they were good at reflecting upon what was in other people's minds and emerging therefrom with their own minds enhanced. With a sense of urgency, they eagerly sought out others, even as they gave of themselves. Properly to speak of the self one must look for [opportunities presented by association with] other people and learn from them.

[*Wei Yuan ji* 1:156–157 — KCL]

## CRITERIA FOR ANTHOLOGY OF QING STATECRAFT WRITINGS

1. The criteria for selection

Every book should have its themes and purpose, while the Way is inherent in its practical application. Since the purpose is to arrive at the correct application of the Way, what is there to choose between the circuitous path and the broad thoroughfare? Since the entire collection of writings is subsumed under the theme of statecraft (*jingshi*), scholarship on this subject is the primary concern. Writings that are too lofty and subtle, or those that are so commonplace as to be submerged in mere dregs, will not be selected.

There is no time more relevant than the contemporary era, and all affairs (*shi*) are encompassed by the jurisdiction of the Six Boards. However, the source of governance lies at court; the monarch and his ministers are at the center of governmental functions. We have, therefore, prepared as prolegomena to the entire work, chapters on the "framework of governance" (*zhiti*), setting forth

---

3. Legge, *The Chinese Classics*, 4:342.
4. Legge, *The Chinese Classics*, 4:250.

the principles by which the people's affairs are to be regulated. Writings on antiquity that are inappropriate [to the present] and those that are so general as to be of no practical value will not be selected.

The *Compendium of Qing Statutes* (*Huidian*) is based on the Ming institutions, just as the *Rites of Zhou* reflect Xia and Yin [Shang] institutions. Times have changed, however, and the situation is different today; when abuses have reached an extreme, there must surely be a turning back. Policies that provided a remedy during the preceding dynasty but are of no value today likewise will not be included here. The calendar is in the charge of specialized officials, and ancient musical instruments have been a subject of controversy. These are not urgent matters and are not subjects that everyone can master. Thus such topics as astronomy and musical codes are passed over here, omitting the details.

Narrative accounts are as important to our literature as policy discussion. However, [laudatory] biographical epitaphs in stone inscriptions are hard to fit into any of our categories. What we have done is to publish only a few epitaphs that provide cases of defense against the aborigines or on the seacoast. Other such narratives are not included, despite their literary quality. Such are the boundaries of the categories adopted, so that this work will have a specific focus and theme.

## 2. The inclusiveness of the selection

Every advantage entails some disadvantage; opposing opinions may in fact complement each other. The views of the humane and the wise are equally valid; where the common destination is the Way, there is no harm in taking different paths to get there. Therefore, whether it is difficult or easy to organize the *baojia* mutual security system; whether the *jundun* military colonies are difficult to set up or not; whether the mines should be officially closed or should remain open; how one is to judge the lawsuits that began with disputes over funerary sacrifices; in the matter of the corvée service, how difficult it is to impose the levies equitably; regarding river conservancy, the contending views of south and north; regarding the salt revenue, the contrasting methods of levying through the [licensed] salt merchants or through wholesale taxes. . . . [These and numerous other questions are difficult to answer because] there are primary and secondary considerations and ramifications that are hard to determine. It is only by bringing together all views that broad interests may be served and that a middle ground may be found between extremes.

The writings collected here may be easy or difficult; the only criterion is their truthfulness — we cannot permit [the subjective preference of] white over red. It is indeed the sage's teaching that we must choose between the ardent and the cautious-minded and that we should not discard an opinion for ad hominem reasons. How much more, then, should appropriate selections be made without regard to the level of literary skill? Some selections may seem to be parochial talk and alleyway gossip, yet among them are those like fresh water that runs deep. Others are chosen from large and voluminous collections, yet among them are lonely voices, like echoes in an empty valley. We have therefore looked through everything that we have copies of, and no documentary collections have been neglected. An effort has been made to find not only the collected writings of individuals but also other versions and other works, so as to attain a comprehensive coverage. Our knowledge may have been restricted by our standpoint; we hope, however, to have profited by communications from helpful friends.

[*Huangchao jingshi wenbian, Wuli,* in *Wei Yuan ji* 1:158–159 — KCL]

## LEARNING AND THE ROLE OF SCHOLAR-OFFICIALS

Over the years, Wei Yuan compiled his own notes on moral and political philosophy in a book titled *Mogu* (*The Silent Gourd*). Published by his family in 1878, the work summarizes Wei Yuan's intellectual outlook in a crystallized form. The following selections illustrate his views on (1) the scholar-officials' need for specialized, practical knowledge and for wide consultation, (2) the ends and means of government, (3) a theory of cumulative development in Chinese history, and (4) the role of wealth in society and the potential contribution of merchants to reform efforts.

In the background of Wei Yuan's approach to statecraft are two dominant trends in Qing scholarship — Song Learning that stressed theoretical concepts of human nature and destiny and Han Learning that set great store by philological study of the texts of the classics, often ignoring the deeper meaning of the texts themselves. Wei Yuan was highly critical of both these approaches to scholarship. He urged scholars to prepare themselves for participation in government affairs — which was indeed their vocation — by devoting themselves to specialized, practical knowledge and developing a fellowship among like-minded scholars, learning from each other and indeed from people outside their social milieu — for example, merchants who operated seagoing junks. While past officials had often adopted such an approach to governance (hence the large number of early and mid-Qing writings in the anthology on statecraft that Wei compiled), he raised such issues to the level of the sages' main concern (pointing out, for instance, that agriculture and sericulture had been concerns of the *Mencius*).

### ON GOVERNANCE

In this essay, drawing on political allusions in the *Classic of Odes*, Wei, by indirection, raises fundamental issues of governance in criticism of existing political practice. Most important is the need for wide consultation instead of reliance on insiders and corrupt imperial cronies; next is to get at the actual facts and deal with them realistically. Wei is dissatisfied with many aspects of contemporary Confucian learning: the routinized examination culture, the moralistic self-satisfaction of those who engage in self-cultivation apart from actual engagement with practical affairs, and the preciosity of classical textual scholarship that is merely critical and devoid of any positive relevance to current problems. In these respects Wei anticipates many of the issues raised by late nineteenth- and early twentieth-century reformers.

There is a common phrase, "governing ability and human feelings." Governing ability is born of human feelings, and there has never been governing ability apart from human feelings. A loving mother has loving human feelings for her little son, so naturally she comes by the ability to nourish him. The hands and feet have protective feelings toward the head and eyes, so naturally they come by the ability to defend them. From antiquity to the present, there has never been a person who had no feelings for the material welfare of the common people and yet was able to use his governing ability to further their welfare. A scoundrel is indifferent and without human feelings toward his country, his sovereign, and the common people. Therefore, his intentions and intellect will be bent not on benefiting the world but on harming it. Such men truly resemble the talons and beaks of hawks and the poisonous stings of bees and scorpions. Governing ability, indeed! By contrast, in the *Classic of Odes* it is written, "When any of your people were in trouble / I went on my knees to help them."[5]

There is a common phrase, "to learn and inquire." Never has there been learning that did not benefit from inquiring. . . . Even the most extraordinary talent is necessarily inferior to long-practiced techniques in a specialized craft. A perception acquired by the sole efforts of one person is necessarily inferior to the consensus of many.[6] . . . There is no single doctrine that is absolutely correct, and no single person who is absolutely good. This is why, in the poem "Deer Call,"[7] the deer cry out to one another when foraging for food, and why, in the poem "Woodcutters,"[8] the birds call in chorus to seek their companions.

Reading the poem "Brilliant Are the Flowers,"[9] one exclaims with a sigh, "How well the author of this poem understood the governance of the empire." The first stanza has "everywhere asking for counsel," the second has "everywhere asking for instructions," the third has "everywhere asking for good plans," and the fourth has "everywhere asking for advice." There are certainly men who, even though they are widely respected pillars of rectitude, yet in public

---

5. Waley, *Songs*, no. 108.

6. The term *consensus of many* (*zhongyi*), which occurs at least as early as Western Han times, was later used by constitution writers to refer to a representative assembly, particularly the lower house in a bicameral legislature.

7. Waley, *Songs*, no. 183.

8. Waley, *Songs*, no. 195.

9. Waley, *Songs*, no. 290.

service both lose their reputations and fail in their performance. How can that be? Taking the empty theory of "abiding in one's own rectitude" and applying it to practical affairs will be effective less than three or four times out of ten. If one takes one's individual ideas and checks them with people here and there, there will be agreement in fewer than five or six cases out of ten.

The ancient and the present ages differ in what is suitable to them. North and south have different local customs. Assuredly, without getting involved personally in a particular situation, one cannot adapt oneself to it, as water does to the square or round shape of its container. And without the counsel and concurrence of many, you can hardly build a cart behind closed doors that will be able to leave your gate and fit the cart tracks outside. If you traverse mountains and rivers, merely enjoying the scenery, and fail to study strategic significance, concrete forms; if you travel through the countryside, only observing the marketplaces, and fail to investigate the local customs; if you are selecting human talent and merely choose literary polish, without judging ability and probity; then, if one day you are managing the business of the empire, you will not know what beneficial things to undertake or what harmful things to expunge. In recommending promotions or dismissals, you will not know the worthy person from the scoundrel. What is this but employing a square handle to hold a round awl? If you are a scholar and desire to take on the heavy responsibilities of the empire, you must begin with conscientious inquiry. And conscientious inquiry must begin before trouble arises. The poem "Brilliant Are the Flowers" understood this.

From ancient times, there have been wealth and power [for the state] (*fu-qiang*) that were exercised apart from the Kingly Way, but never a Kingly Way exercised apart from wealth and power. The distinction between true king and hegemon lies in their intentions, not in their overt actions. Their intentions are characterized, respectively, by principles of public good and private good, but their actions are not greatly different. The thirteenth hexagram of the *Classic of Changes* relates that when the ancient sages were forming their institutions, they began with fields and fisheries, plows and plowshares, markets and trade, sent boats and carts over long distances to link them up, and set watchmen and archers to defend them. As soon as King Yu had pacified the waters and land, he instituted the tribute and taxes and bent his efforts to military defense. The "Eight Objects of Governance" in the *Grand Model*[10] begin with food and commodities and end with the entertainment of guests of state and with military affairs. In each case, a sufficiency of food and a sufficiency of military power served as tools for governing the empire. But Confucian scholars of later ages, seizing upon Mencius's distinction between "rightness" (*yi*) and "profit" (*li*), and between "true king" (*wang*) and "hegemon" (*ba*), treated military strength

---

10. A section of the *Classic of Documents* (*Shujing*). See vol. 1, ch. 2.

and food supply as concerns pertaining only to the "five hegemons." Tabooing such things, they would not speak of them. But actually, were not Confucius and his disciples concerned with providing for the people's material welfare and managing the state's revenue? Were not "agriculture and sericulture," "trees and livestock" the very words of Mencius? . . .

The Kingly Way is finely textured and all-encompassing. Through it runs all the fine and subtle infrastructure of human life, including farming and herding, labor service, military and revenue affairs. If one's utterances are all about "mind and nature," one's personal demeanor all "rites and rightness," and one acts and speaks as if to "form one body with the myriad things," yet one does not examine the people's ills, does not study bureaucratic management, does not look into the state's revenues and border defenses, then supposing one day one enters official service; above, you will be unable to manage state revenues; outside, unable to pacify the borders; and below, unable to relieve the people's troubles. You chatter emptily about "treating the people's material welfare as one would a brother's."[11] But having reached this point, there is nothing efficacious that you can actually do for the sake of the people's material welfare! How on earth can anyone use this sort of impractical "Kingly Way"? . . .

Scholars who practice belles lettres regard a concern for farming and sericulture as vulgar. But they are unaware that the evil done by vulgar scholarship is more injurious to men than is the evil done by vulgar officials! They rely on abstruse, empty theories, considering governmental affairs as uncouth. But they are unaware that the uselessness of decadent Confucians is equivalent to heterodoxy! Certainly, account books for money and grain cannot be called scholarship. But can frivolous literary elegance and showy classical quotations really be considered sagelike learning? Buddhist and Daoist priests certainly cannot govern the kingdoms of the empire; so how can far-fetched discourse about "mind" and "nature" govern the empire itself? . . .

If those who govern fail to focus their attention on large matters, but attend merely to details, then the great principles affecting tranquillity and peril, misfortune and prosperity, will come within an eyelash of being lost. In employing men, if they fail to select persons with large understanding and merely select those with small, then the opportunity to acquire outstanding talents will slip through their hands. Therefore, to serve a ruling house by attending to a hundred details is not as good as establishing one great policy. To get a hundred efficient bureaucrats for a ruling house is not as good as getting one great statesman. The superior man is meticulously attentive to small details in regulating his own person, but not so in choosing men. Nor, however, is he abrupt or hasty in resolving complex and weighty problems. Wherever in all creation

---

11. Allusion to the Western Inscription of Zhang Zai (ch. 20).

a kingdom is located, there must be some "with whom one can collaborate in office."[12] . . .

The way later ages nourished and employed human talent has been very different [from ancient times, when men were employed for their different practical abilities]. In promoting and testing men, they use only profitless "drawing of cakes to satisfy hunger," and useless "carving of minute insects." The officials thereby recruited know nothing of military affairs and agriculture, rites and music, planning of public works, or judicial administration. When such men are given appointment, a single one may be invested with the responsibilities of all six branches of government. Or in a single year, he may traverse the distinctive regional cultures of Chinese and barbarians all over the empire. How can the authorities take up matters that the "Four Curricula" of the early Confucian school [ethics, rhetoric, government, and literature] never included, and that the "Nine Ministries" of Yao and Shun never embraced, and expect them to be handled effectively by scholars who have come up through the hack schoolroom texts of the examination system? They begin by expecting pines and junipers to produce peaches and pears, then expect official banners to spring from the peaches and pears! Then when public affairs are ill-managed, they slap their thighs and lament, "There is no talent in the empire." Alas! Is there really no talent in the empire? The *Classic of Odes* says: "The mulberry insect has young ones / And the sphex carries them away / Teach and train your sons / And they will become as good as you are."[13] . . .

This is to say, what is to be used must be nourished; and what is nourished is what is to be used. . . .

When the people of the mountains and forests want to be charitable they must give away part of their own wealth. When they want to be rid of abuses [by such as yamen runners] they must appeal to the authority of officials. Can it be that the superior man in official position has, uniquely, the power to dispense charity without using his own wealth, or to expel corrupt functionaries without relying on someone's authority? To wield a knife but not cut; to take up the oars but not row across — nobody is that stupid. Therefore, when the superior man holds a public office, he exerts his entire strength, whether in large matters or small; and it is sure that whatever he undertakes will be successful.

[*Guweitang neiji* 3:1–5b  — PAK]

## THE PURSUIT OF PROFIT

The means of governing all-under-Heaven (*tianxia*) — are they not power and authority, profit and fame? Was not the well-field system meant for the pursuit

---

12. *Analects* 9:30; Waley, *The Analects of Confucius*, p. 145.
13. Legge, *The Chinese Classics*, 4:334.

of profit? Was not the enfeoffment system based on power and authority? Were not the ancient schools meant to confer fame [on scholars]? The sage rulers shared authority, profit, and fame with all-under-Heaven. "They worried about what all-under-Heaven worried about without enjoying what all-under-Heaven enjoyed."[14] Thus the mere impulse to act was replaced by the rituals of the banquet and ceremonial greetings. In later ages, however, rulers would selfishly monopolize authority, profit, and fame. They enjoyed what was there for all-under-Heaven to enjoy and did not worry about what all-under-Heaven worried about. They were careless in guarding their own positions, and they allowed the rise of villainous strongmen who were only striving for aggrandizement. The distinction between aggressive rivalry, on the one hand, and courteous yielding, on the other, depends on how the ruler either enjoys or worries about all-under-Heaven. . . .

Wherever men are gathered together, power and authority (*shi*) arise. Wherever wealth is found, men assemble. Where the claims for fame are suppressed, order may turn into disorder. The sage ruler rides on the power factors as the dragon rides on the misty clouds. Before the morning is over, rain will fall on all-under-Heaven, and people will not know who is in possession of authority over them. Great indeed is the sacred vessel [i.e., the sage ruler]! The lives of millions of people depend on him. Is his wisdom sufficient to prevent the rise of the villainous and his strength [sufficient to suppress] covetous schemers? Only when power, gain, and fame are employed with purely moral motives will all-under-Heaven be well governed. . . .

Humankind is the kernel (*ren*/humaneness) of Heaven-and-earth. Wherever human beings are congregated, the *qi* of humaneness (*renqi*) is concentrated. . . . "Human beings are the noblest [creatures] in the nature of Heaven-and-earth." The Son of Heaven represents the aggregate of the multitude of the people — if he insults the people, is he not insulting Heaven? When the people gather together, they are strong. When the people are dispersed, their strength is dissipated. When they are pacified, the country is prosperous; when they litigate against each other, the country lies in waste; when they revolt, the country is destroyed. Therefore, when the Son of Heaven regards himself as one of the multitude of people, he regards all-under-Heaven as belonging to all-under-Heaven. The *Classic of Odes* says: "What is most powerful is the man [the monarch] / His influence will be felt in all directions."[15]

The sage rules over the superior men of all-under-Heaven by virtue of the teaching of moral norms (*mingjiao*), yet he rules over the common people by providing sources of handsome profit. Should the high ministers and officials act like petty people and seek farmland and residences, to be a merchant or to trade in oxen, they will be criticized; the little people are not expected to act

---

14. Reference to a famous saying by Fan Zhongyan; see ch. 22.
15. Cf. Legge, *The Chinese Classics*, 4:511.

like high ministers and officials. . . . In a great, flourishing age, all-under-Heaven may be expected to regard rightness as profitable.[16] The next best thing is to let the people pursue profit. The *Classic of Odes* says:

> Ordinary people's follies
> Are but sicknesses of their own.
> It is the wise man's follies.
> That are a rampant pest.[17]

When the people are forced to do what they cannot do, the statute will fail. When the people are restrained by laws that they must violate, the law cannot prevail. Moreover, even such statutes as can be established and prohibitions as are feasible may produce contrary reactions, should good government be sought in an excessively short time, should evil be dealt with in an overly strict fashion or abuses be done away with too summarily. To be too sudden in introducing new personnel, too ready to listen to advice, or too hard on oneself — all may result in starting a plan that may run out of control. Should one be able to combine the strengths of the Yellow Emperor, of Laozi, of Shen Buhai, and of Han Feizi and yet remove their weaknesses, would one not govern the country like a master cook [who combines different ingredients]? The *Odes* says:

> The tree-fellers follow the slant of the tree,
> The wood-cutters follow the direction of the grain.[18]
>
> [*Mogu xia*, sec. 3, in *Wei Yuan ji* 1:43–45 — KCL]

### ON INSTITUTIONAL PROGRESS IN HISTORY

Wei held a distinct theory of institutional progress, which contrasted the imperial era with the ancient Three Dynasties and concluded that the imperial age since the Han was indeed superior in several ways to the Three Dynasties. He affirmed the irreversible progress of institutions in serving the changing interests of the people (*bianmin*). Wei Yuan's conception of development or irreversible change (progress?) is of indigenous origin and may be compared with that of Liu Zongyuan (chapter 19) and Wang Fuzhi (chapter 25).

There are three principal ways in which the later ages were superior to the Three Dynasties. The emperor Wendi of Han abolished punishments that involved mutilation of the flesh [for example, cutting off arms and legs]. In this

---

16. Reference to the opening passage of *Mencius*, vol. 1, ch. 6.
17. Waley, *Songs*, no. 271; cf. Legge, *The Chinese Classics*, 4:511.
18. Cf. Legge, *The Chinese Classics*, 4:339.

regard the Three Dynasties were cruel and the later ages humane. [The Tang scholar-official] Liu Zongyuan was outspoken against the enfeoffment system; indeed the institutions of the Three Dynasties were particularistic (*si*) and the later ages universalistic (*gong*). The change from selection of officials from aristocratic families (*shizu*) to the rise of the examination system paralleled the transition from the enfeoffment system to the system of prefectures and districts (*junxian*). The weaknesses of the Three Dynasties' employment of men was that with aristocratic familism, high and low statuses were hereditary; this system had arisen along with enfeoffment in high antiquity and both systems were unfair. It is true that the ancient people educated their youths properly, and among the eldest sons of the dukes and ministers most were versed in the Six Arts [ritual, music, archery, charioteering, calligraphy, and arithmetic]. But how could they have been always more worthy than men from the countryside, generation after generation? It is not likely that the ancient sage kings did not clearly see the weaknesses of the system, but until the enfeoffment system gave way to change, aristocratic familism could not be expected to change. . . . If Confucius had gained an influential position and had been enabled to carry out the Way, he would have carried out great systemic reforms (*dabian qifa*) long ago and replaced aristocratic familism with [officials] trained in the Four Curricula. . . .

The [early Tang system of taxation in grain and cloth as well as corvée labor] was replaced by the Twice-a-Year Tax [in 780], and the Twice-a-Year Tax eventually by a Single Whip reform [in the sixteenth century under the Ming, when numerous taxes were consolidated into one or two annual payments in silver]. The more extensively the ancient ways were changed, the more convenient it was for the people. Even if the sage kings should return and be with us, they would not abandon the Single Whip and revive the Twice-a-Year Tax, nor abandon the latter in favor of the early Tang system. The system for selection of officials has been changed from nomination at the village and neighborhood level to recruitment from members of the prominent families, and eventually through the examination system. In the system of local services, the corvée laborer (*dingyong*) has given way to drafted laborers (*chayi*), replaced in turn by hired laborers (*guyi*). Even if the sage kings should return and be with us, they would not abandon the examination system and revive the recommendation system, nor abandon hired laborers in favor of drafted laborers. Conscript soldiers (*qiujia*) gave way to territorially administered militias (*fubing*), which in turn were replaced by cavalry and infantry battalions. Even if the sage kings should return and be with us, they would not abandon the battalion system and revive the military colonies (*duntian*) or territorially administered militias. In the affairs of all-under-Heaven, whatever changes the people have found to be inconvenient can be reversed; but whatever the people have found to be convenient cannot be reversed. . . .

[*Mogu, Zhipian*, 5, 9, in *Wei Yuan ji* 1:48–49, 60–61 — KCL]

## ON MERCHANTS AND REFORM

Although Wei Yuan was concerned with the scholar-officials' intellectual outlook and their service to society, he was sympathetic to the activities of the
merchants, who, he believed, could render vital assistance to the operation of
governmental affairs. In the period from 1826 to 1832, Wei served in the personal
secretariat of the governor of Jiangsu and also in that of the governor-general
at Nanjing. He made a thorough study of two urgent problems of state business
at the time: (1) the transport of the tribute rice to north China to meet the food-
supply needs of the Beijing area, a problem created by the very poor navigability
of the Grand Canal as a result of the flooding of the Yellow River, and (2) the
dwindling revenue of the Huaibei [i.e., north of the Huai River] salt administration, owing to the government-licensed monopoly's having to compete with
salt smugglers in distributing the salt to markets in the Yangzi provinces. In
both cases, Wei found that more merchant participation would help. While the
transport of tribute rice to north China could more safely be carried out by the
large Jiangsu seagoing junks, whose owners would be pleased with compensation smaller than the cost of the Grand Canal transport, in the case of the salt
monopoly, hitherto restricted to thirty or so principal licensed merchants, the
best way to counter smuggling was to allow many more merchants to share in
the trade, indeed to sell "salt trade tickets" to whoever might apply. Both of
Wei's proposals were adopted at the time and later more permanently.

### ON TAXATION AND THE MERCHANTS

If the people are deprived of their concern for probity and integrity, the country
will decline. If the people are made to be afraid of tending to their family affairs,
the country will be destroyed. Rulers who are good at levying revenue from the
people are like those who plant willow trees: [they] use their leaves and branches
as fuel but nourish their roots. Those who are not good at taxing people are
like those who cut scallions; they cut entire plots until all are gone. The way
to preserve wealth, according to the *Institutes of Zhou* [*Rites of Zhou*] is to
regard rich people as essential to the vitality of the area. Large-scale mobilization of funds or labor depends on the existence of rich people, as do the needs
created by a major war or famine. When the greedy rule the country, the rich
are especially exploited. When these [resources] are about to run out, they
exploit the middle classes (*zhonghu*), and when those are about to run out,
cities and homes will be in ruins. Thus, when there are no more rich people
in the land, the state itself is pauperized. When there are no middle classes in
the land, the state is in danger; by the time even the lower classes flee the land,
the state is no longer a state!

[*Mogu, Zhipian*, 14, in *Wei Yuan ji* 1:72 — KCL]

ON REFORM OF THE TRIBUTE-RICE TRANSPORT SYSTEM, 1825

My guest asks: "Is it feasible then to ship the tribute rice by sea?"

My answer: "In the affairs of all-under-Heaven, the most important thing is the actual circumstances (*shi*). The present dynasty has its capital near the sea, in contrast to earlier dynasties that had their capitals near the Yellow River or in the Kaifeng area. Jiangsu and Zhejiang are upon the seacoast, unlike other provinces remote from the sea. These are the geographical circumstances.

"During the Yuan and Ming dynasties, it was the government that promoted shipping routes by sea. Under the present dynasty, it has been merchants that developed the sea routes. Seamen are accustomed to the sea, just as river-men are accustomed to the river. These are the circumstances regarding the available resources [in transport and communications].

"When the Yellow River and the Grand Canal are unimpeded, transporting rice by way of the canal is the normal policy; when the Yellow River and the Grand Canal are not navigable, sea transport provides the alternative. Such are the circumstances of the time.

"How are we, then, to take advantage of these circumstances?

"It is not necessary to explore the [alternate] routes of transport, nor is it necessary to build new ships. It is not necessary to recruit workmen, nor to raise new revenue. To transport rice on the merchant shipping routes, to use the merchant vessels as grain transport vessels, to employ commercial personnel as military attendants, and to apply the revenue for Grand Canal transport to the sea transport . . . [these are the solutions]."

[*Zhou cao pian*, in *Wei Yuan ji* 1:404 — KCL]

ON REFORM OF THE SALT MONOPOLY

There is no institution under Heaven that is certain to promote profit [*li*] for the state. When abuses are removed, however, profit [resources] will naturally be produced. Regarding the salt trade, there is really no way to get on the trail of salt smugglers. Only when the smuggling is transmuted into [legitimate enterprise] under the government's aegis will government finances be eased.

In order to deal effectively with illicit salt, it is necessary to reduce the price of legitimate salt, which, in turn, requires that the cost of supplying salt be reduced to as little as possible. In order to reduce the cost of salt, however, it is necessary to rid the salt trade of its abuses. Profits and abuse — can they ever coexist? The smuggling trade and the trade under official auspices — are they not parts of a collusive process? If it is so difficult to remove the abuses [of the salt trade] — is this not because there are people who rely on abuse for their living?

The "ticket system for the salt trade" (*piaoyan*) has been put into practice in

Huaibei for a few years now [since 1831]. This new system, from the time it was first carried out, has transformed the illicit trade at the factories (*chang*) east of Honghu and, later, the illicit trade west of Zhengguan, involving illicit salt originally produced in Changlu in north China. . . . Now the sale price of salt under the Ticket System is only half of that under the Licensed Monopoly System. Why was it that [formerly, under the Licensed Monopoly System] the monopoly merchants allowed the ports to be undersupplied and the taxes to be in arrears, whereas there has been a big rush to ship salt in abundance under the new Ticket System? The reason is that profits under the Monopoly System were split as the corrupt middlemen's plunder. Two-tenths of the profits would go to the porters at the riverbanks and to the packaging houses; another two-tenths to the smugglers at the lakes and riverbanks [who would stay out of the market only for a fee]; still another two-tenths would go to the official levies at the salt-producing factories and riverbanks; and another two-tenths to theft by servant-carriers and to excessive and fraudulent claims [regarding the quantity of salt in each package]. The merchants therefore could not even enjoy a 10 percent profit. What the Ticket System has done is to rid itself of the corrupt middlemen's takings and give the profit to the ticketholders who applied to ship salt and paid the taxes in advance. This is why they are assured of profit even after the salt prices have been reduced by half. . . .

To sum up, abuses are usually part of a complex and difficult system, whereas it is only by making the system simple and easy that abuses can be prevented. To increase tax revenue it is necessary to reduce the cost [of salt]; heavy taxes, by increasing this cost, result in decreasing revenue. This rule applies . . . also to all fiscal affairs, including the administration of tribute rice and customs revenue.

[*Huaibei piaoyan zhi xu*, in *Wei Yuan ji* 2:438–440 — KCL]


## THE WESTERN INTRUSION INTO CHINA

The year 1839, which saw the beginning of the Opium War between Britain and China, is a milestone in Chinese foreign affairs. As a result of this and subsequent victories, Britain, followed by other Western nations and Japan, imposed a series of "unequal" treaties on China. Over the course of the nineteenth century Western powers came to control areas of China known as concessions, leaseholds, and spheres of influence; Western nationals in China came to be judged by their own laws, not China's; Chinese tariffs on exports and imports were kept low; opium was eventually legalized and missionaries allowed to proselytize in China's hinterland. All of these developments deeply affected the course of Chinese history, and Chinese attempts to reverse them led to major changes in the Chinese state, society, and culture. The new China might be slow in coming, but the outcome of this historic encounter was to ensure that eventually forces from the West would join with indigenous forces to shape a new future for China.

The outbreak of the Opium War may be attributed to three background factors. The first was the Guangzhou (Canton) trading system. For almost three centuries since the first arrival of the Portuguese off south China, the Chinese court had succeeded in dealing with Westerners on its own terms. Trade was confined to a few ports where agents of the court could regulate it strictly and skim profits off the top. Beginning in 1759, the British East India Company, a monopoly licensed by the crown, was limited to trading in the port of Guangzhou, as were other Western traders. Here, the company had to deal with a guild of Chinese traders, who were often in debt and had to be propped up by the foreign merchants. The foreigners had to obey Chinese laws (which they believed to be arbitrary), were restricted to a wharf on the river off Guangzhou, and could not communicate directly with Chinese officials. Any communication had to go through the Chinese merchant guild. Even the British superintendent of trade, the representative of the British crown in Guangzhou after the demise of the East India Company (1834), could not communicate directly with Chinese officials. Westerners, especially British traders in the early nineteenth century, remained restive under these restrictions and resentful of them. The British "free trade" philosophy that called for governments not to interfere with commerce heightened this resentment.

The second factor was the huge trade imbalance between Great Britain and China in the eighteenth century. By the middle of the century, Britons of all classes had developed the habit of tea drinking. The East India Company therefore bought massive amounts of Chinese tea but could not find products the Chinese were willing to buy in equal amounts. As a result, the British paid for the tea mostly with silver, leading to a serious bullion drain at a time when European nations considered bullion reserves to be the cornerstone of a nation's wealth and power. The Chinese economy, on the other hand, benefited from the massive influx of silver, and the commercial prosperity that China enjoyed in the eighteenth century can be attributed in part to the trade imbalance.

To remedy these problems the British dispatched a mission to China in 1793, ostensibly to offer felicitations to the Chinese emperor on his eightieth birthday. The mission, under the experienced diplomat Lord Macartney, hoped to put trade between the two empires on a solid footing, interest the Chinese in British goods, and place a representative of the British crown permanently in Beijing. Despite some progress in trade talks, the mission did not greatly advance British goals, and the Chinese court showed no inclination to establish equal relations with Western powers.

The British discovery of opium from India as a wonder drug to cure the chronic imbalance of trade with China provides the third and primary factor in the Opium War. The East India Company had a monopoly on opium in its colony in Bengal and forced the farmers to grow poppy (the plant from which opium is derived), then processed the opium in its factories. Although opium was illegal in China, private British traders bought the company's opium on credit, sold it to smugglers on the Chinese coast, and then paid the representatives of the East India Company in Guangzhou. The representatives then used the money to buy tea. This triangular trade arrangement kept the East India Company from becoming directly involved in the opium trade, but the effect was the same — trading opium for tea. As a result, the trade imbalance over the course of several decades shifted, and by the 1820s and 1830s silver began to drain out of China, creating enormous social and economic problems. The economy went into a depression, and increasing numbers of Chinese of all classes were becoming addicted to opium. Smuggling, moreover, proved lucrative not only for the direct participants but for local officials as well, who could be bribed to keep hands off the illegal traffic. These factors help to explain why it was so difficult for the government to put an end to the opium trade in spite of repeated bans on its importation and sale. The state was not merely in conflict with foreigners, but with its own members, whose self-interest led them to "squeeze" the traffic for their personal benefit rather than stamp it out for the good of all.

On the other hand, the "self-interest" of foreigners participating in the China trade was not wholly bound up with the marketing of opium, and it is possible that intelligent negotiation would have brought about gradual reduction in imports of the drug, while other articles, especially manufactured goods, took the place of opium in the trade. Unfortunately, the traditional conduct of foreign relations by the Chinese court was confined largely to tribute relations with smaller states. There was little inclination to establish regular intercourse with the Western powers that did not adhere to the pattern of ritual relations with the Chinese court. For want of a middle ground on which to meet, the means were lacking whereby to resolve the constant conflicts that arose in contacts between Chinese and foreigners over differing conceptions of justice and equity.

Under these circumstances conflict was difficult to avoid. The evils of the opium traffic were so far-reaching that the Chinese could ignore them only at great peril. Meanwhile, the British crown depended heavily on revenue from the tea trade. Any disruption of the trade would have great consequences. Some sort of showdown was imminent. After an extensive debate, during which the legalization of opium was considered, the Chinese court decided to take a hard line and put an end to the importation of opium to China. An experienced official was appointed as "drug tsar" and dispatched to Guangzhou with full powers to eradicate the opium scourge.

Here we shall concern ourselves less with the merits of the issues over which war eventually broke out than with the Chinese understanding of them and the effect on Chinese thinking of the events that followed. Instructive for this purpose are the cases of two Chinese leaders in the fields of government and scholarship: Lin Zexu (1785–1850), imperial commissioner at Guangzhou in 1839–1840, and the scholar Wei Yuan (1794–1856), who helped to interpret for Chinese minds the meaning of the fateful conflict.

## THE LESSON OF LIN ZEXU

Lin Zexu, a native of the southeast coastal province of Fujian, was an exemplary product of the Chinese educational and civil service system. After winning the *jinshi* degree in 1811, he rose rapidly through the official ranks and served with particular distinction in posts concerned with fiscal matters and public works, gaining a wide reputation for his competence, integrity, and humaneness. By the late thirties, when opium smuggling became a pressing question, Lin had already established himself as an able governor and then governor-general of rich and populous provinces in central China. In such a position a man less deeply concerned over the fate of his people might have been content to enjoy the measure of personal success that was already assured him. But Lin, having taken strong measures to end the opium traffic in his own sphere of jurisdiction, placed himself in the forefront of those who called upon the court for a full-scale assault on the opium menace. The result was his appointment as imperial commissioner at Guangzhou, with full powers to deal with the problem.

On his arrival in Guangzhou in March 1839, Lin demonstrated that he was a man of serious and inflexible purpose, not the type of official who could be wheedled, bribed, or stalled off. Within a few months he had taken such strong action against the Hong merchants [Chinese Merchant Guild] and Western traders that existing stocks of opium had been destroyed and the cessation of the traffic was all but accepted by the foreigners. It was at this time that Lin addressed his celebrated letter to Queen Victoria demanding assurances of an end to the trade.

Were opium, then, the sole or chief issue between the Chinese and British, there would presumably have been no cause for the outbreak of the first Anglo-Chinese War later that same year. To the British on the scene, however, Lin's uncompromising policies seemed not just firm or tough but arrogant and un-reasonable. Though ready to make substantial concessions with regard to the drug traffic in order not to lose all opportunities for trade, for them the lure of profits did not suffice to overcome strong feelings in what they regarded as matters of principle. The lack of treaty relations meant that there was no estab-lished procedure for the administration of justice in incidents involving Chinese and foreigners. Commissioner Lin was determined that Chinese authorities should mete out punishment for crimes on Chinese soil of which foreigners had been accused. The British were equally adamant in refusing to turn over suspects, whose guilt was by no means established, to the mercies of Chinese officials whom they considered vindictive and inhumane. When Lin countered with the breaking off of all trade and expulsion of the British from China, full-scale hostilities broke out.

The Chinese, as is well known, were pitifully unprepared on land and sea to resist the force of British arms, and it was only a matter of weeks before the underlying weakness of Lin's "get-tough" policy became fully exposed. Officially disgraced, the erstwhile viceroy and commissioner was eventually banished to Xinjiang, in the far west of the empire. In the meantime, he had become fully persuaded of the need for strengthening China through the adoption of Western arms and methods of warfare, though he could make no progress in gaining acceptance of this view at court. Even when later restored to the official ranks, partly on account of his accomplishments in flood control and land reclamation work, Lin lacked any real opportunity to influence state policy in the direction of greater realism and reform. The lesson he had learned in Guangzhou remained largely his own. It would be decades more before the court could be moved by further misfortunes to take such warnings to heart.

### LETTER TO THE ENGLISH RULER

In this celebrated letter to Queen Victoria (1839), prepared as a memorial for the emperor's endorsement, Lin argues against the opium trade with all the moral earnestness of the Confucian scholar and lofty condescension of one speaking for the imperial court. On its own terms, of course, Lin's argument is unanswerable. Yet his tone indicates how unready the Chinese were to deal with the British as diplomatic equals or to negotiate outstanding difference on other scores.

Intransigent as he appeared, Lin nonetheless compelled admiration. His likeness appeared later in Mme Tussaud's Wax Museum in London, and the distinguished British consular official and sinologist H. A. Giles said of Lin: "He was a fine scholar, a just and merciful official and a true patriot."

A communication: Magnificently our great emperor soothes and pacifies China and the foreign countries, regarding all with the same kindness. If there is profit, then he shares it with the peoples of the world; if there is harm, then he removes it on behalf of the world. This is because he takes the mind of Heaven-and-earth as his mind.

The kings of your honorable country by a tradition handed down from generation to generation have always been noted for their politeness and submissiveness. We have read your successive tributary memorials saying: "In general our countrymen who go to trade in China have always received His Majesty the Emperor's gracious treatment and equal justice," and so on. Privately we are delighted with the way in which the honorable rulers of your country deeply understand the grand principles and are grateful for the Celestial grace. For this reason the Celestial Court in soothing those from afar has redoubled its polite and kind treatment. The profit from trade has been enjoyed by them continuously for two hundred years. This is the source from which your country has become known for its wealth.

But after a long period of commercial intercourse, there appear among the crowd of barbarians both good persons and bad, unevenly. Consequently there are those who smuggle opium to seduce the Chinese people and so cause the spread of the poison to all provinces. Such persons who only care to profit themselves, and disregard their harm to others, are not tolerated by the laws of Heaven and are unanimously hated by human beings. His Majesty the Emperor, upon hearing of this, is in a towering rage. He has specially sent me, his commissioner, to come to Guangdong, and together with the governor-general and governor jointly to investigate and settle this matter. . . .

We find that your country is sixty or seventy thousand *li* [one *li* is roughly a third of a mile] from China. Yet there are barbarian ships that strive to come here for trade for the purpose of making a great profit. The wealth of China is used to profit the barbarians. That is to say, the great profit made by barbarians is all taken from the rightful share of China. By what right do they then in return use the poisonous drug to injure the Chinese people? Even though the barbarians may not necessarily intend to do us harm, yet in coveting profit to an extreme, they have no regard for injuring others. Let us ask, where is your conscience? I have heard that the smoking of opium is very strictly forbidden by your country; that is because the harm caused by opium is clearly understood. Since it is not permitted to do harm to your own country, even less should you let the harm be passed on to other countries — much less to China! Of all that China exports to foreign countries, there is not a single thing that is not beneficial to people; they are of benefit when eaten, or of benefit when used, or of benefit when resold; all are beneficial. Is there a single article from China that has done any harm to foreign countries? Take tea and rhubarb, for example; the foreign countries cannot get along for a single day without them. If China cuts off these benefits with no sympathy for those who are to suffer, then what can the barbarians rely upon to keep themselves alive? Moreover the woolens, camlets, and longells [i.e., textiles] of foreign countries cannot be woven unless they obtain Chinese silk. If China again cuts off this beneficial export, what profit can the barbarians expect to make? As for other foodstuffs, beginning with candy, ginger, cinnamon, and so forth, and articles for use, beginning with silk, satin, chinaware, and so on, all the things that must be had by foreign countries are innumerable. On the other hand, articles coming from the outside to China can only be used as toys. We can take them or get along without them. Since they are not needed by China, what difficulty would there be if we closed the frontier and stopped the trade? Nevertheless, our Celestial Court lets tea, silk, and other goods be shipped without limit and circulated everywhere without begrudging it in the slightest. This is for no other reason but to share the benefit with the people of the whole world.

The goods from China carried away by your country not only supply your own consumption and use but also can be divided up and sold to other countries, producing a triple profit. Even if you do not sell opium, you still have this threefold profit. How can you bear to go further, selling products injurious to others in order to fulfill your insatiable desire? . . .

We have further learned that in London, the capital of your honorable rule, and in Scotland, Ireland, and other places originally no opium has been produced. Only in several places of India under your control, such as Bengal, Madras, Bombay, Patna, Benares, and Malwa, has opium been planted from hill to hill and ponds have been opened for its manufacture. For months and years work is continued in order to accumulate the poison. The obnoxious odor ascends, irritating Heaven and frightening the spirits. Indeed you, O King, can eradicate the opium plant in these places, hoe over the fields entirely, and sow in its stead the five grains [i.e., millet, barley, wheat, and so on]. Anyone who dares again attempt to plant and manufacture opium should be severely punished. This would really be a great, benevolent government policy that will increase the commonweal and get rid of evil. For this, Heaven must support you and the spirits must bring you good fortune, prolonging your old age and extending your descendants. All will depend on this act. . . .

Now we have set up regulations governing the Chinese people. He who sells opium shall receive the death penalty and he who smokes it also the death penalty. Now consider this: If the barbarians do not bring opium, then how can the Chinese people resell it, and how can they smoke it? The fact is that the wicked barbarians beguile the Chinese people into a death trap. How then can we grant life only to these barbarians? He who takes the life of even one person still has to atone for it with his own life; yet is the harm done by opium limited to the taking of one life only? Therefore in the new regulations, in regard to those barbarians who bring opium to China, the penalty is fixed at decapitation or strangulation. This is what is called getting rid of a harmful thing on behalf of mankind. . . .

Our Celestial Dynasty rules over and supervises the myriad states and surely possesses unfathomable spiritual dignity. Yet the emperor cannot bear to execute people without having first tried to reform them by instruction. . . . May you, O King, check your wicked and sift out your vicious people before they come to China, in order to guarantee the peace of your nation, to show further the sincerity of your politeness and submissiveness, and to let the two countries enjoy together the blessings of peace. How fortunate, how fortunate indeed! After receiving this dispatch will you immediately give us a prompt reply regarding the details and circumstances of your cutting off the opium traffic. Be sure not to put this off. The above is what has to be communicated. [Vermilion endorsement of the emperor:] This is appropriately worded and quite comprehensive.

[From Teng and Fairbank, *China's Response to the West*, pp. 24–27]

### LETTER TO WU ZIXU ON THE NEED FOR WESTERN GUNS AND SHIPS

This letter to his friend Wu Zixu, written two years after the debacle at Guangzhou, expresses Lin's realization of the need for adopting modern weapons and methods of warfare. As one in official disgrace, however, Lin dared not speak out, nor even communicate his thoughts privately except in guarded fashion. Under such circumstances it is understandable that the advocacy of reform should have been hampered and the taking of concrete steps so long delayed.

The rebels' ships on the open sea came and went as they pleased, now in the south and now suddenly in the north, changing successively between morning and evening. If we tried to put up a defense everywhere, not only would we toil and expend ourselves without limit, but also how could we recruit and transport so many troops, militia, artillery, and ammunition, and come to their support quickly? . . .

When I was in office in Guangdong and Guangxi, I had made plans regarding the problems of ships and cannon and a water force. Afraid that there was not enough time to build ships, I at first rented them. Afraid that there was not enough time to cast cannon and that it would not be done according to the regulations, I at first bought foreign ones. The most painful thing was that when the Humen [the Bogue or "Tiger's Mouth," the entrance to the Pearl River] was broken into, a large number of good cannon fell into the hands of the rebellious barbarians. I recall that after I had been punished two years ago, I still took the risk of calling the emperor's attention to two things: ships and guns. At that time, if these things could have been made and prepared, they still could have been used with effect to fight against the enemy in Zhejiang last fall [1841]. Now it is even more difficult to check the wildfire. After all, ships, guns, and a water force are absolutely indispensable. Even if the rebellious barbarians had fled and returned beyond the seas, these things would still have to be urgently planned for, in order to work out the permanent defense of our sea frontiers. . . .

But at this time I must strictly observe the advice to seal my lips as one corks the mouth of a bottle. Toward those with identical aims and interests, however, I suddenly spit out the truth and am unable to control myself. I extremely regret my foolishness and carelessness. Nevertheless, when I turn my thoughts to the depth of your attention to me, then I cannot conceal these things from myself.

I only beg you to keep them confidential. By all means, please do not tell other persons.

[From Teng and Fairbank, *China's Response to the West*, p. 28]

## WEI YUAN AND THE WEST

Wei Yuan's *Military History of the Qing Dynasty* (*Shengwu jixu*) and *Illustrated Gazetteer of the Maritime Countries* (*Haiguo tuzhi*) are landmarks in China's modern history, for they represent the first systematic attempts by a dedicated Confucian to provide his countrymen with a realistic picture of military affairs and the outside world. A sizable compilation running to sixty chapters, the *Gazetteer* owed its inception to the pioneering work of Lin Zexu, who, while in Guangzhou, made strenuous efforts to gather information about the West, taking notes himself, collecting materials, arranging translations, and compiling a *Gazetteer of the Four Continents* (*Sizhou zhi*), which Wei used as the basis for his own work after Lin's dismissal.

In the background of the *Gazetteer* was Wei's interest in military and financial history. For most of the decade beginning in 1814, Wei had lived in Beijing, trying without success to pass the metropolitan examination; he purchased a minor official position and read voraciously on problems of statecraft. Service as a tutor in the home of a leading military commander stimulated his interest in Qing military history. He took extensive notes on archival and other sources to which he was able to gain access. During the Opium War (1839–1842), Wei, then living in Yangzhou, in the Lower Yangzi area, was stimulated enough by the events taking place to complete his book *Military History of the Qing Dynasty*, ending with chapters on the current debacle and on the need for reform. Wei traced the weaknesses of the Qing military system to the late eighteenth century — weaknesses in the system of finance, in weaponry, and above all, in low morale and the lack of vigor with which the court's orders were carried out. Wei came to realize that the "barbarians" from the maritime countries were advanced in the matter of technology, military as well as industrial. Moreover, although peace was signed at the Treaty of Nanjing (August 1842), the continuing threat from the British was implicit. Other Western countries, including France and the United States, were seeking to be recognized. Only five months after he completed *Military History of the Qing Dynasty*, Wei finished an early edition of the *Illustrated Gazetteer of the Maritime Countries*.

Wei's general thesis in the *Gazetteer* is this: the Western barbarians, bent on power and profit, have devised techniques and machines by which to subvert or conquer the civilized world. China, dedicated as she is to virtue, learning, and the ways of peace, possesses a spiritual and moral strength that can yet triumph over the enemy if only the Chinese awaken to the danger and apply themselves to the practical problems involved. Traditional military science suggests that the first requisite is intelligence of the enemy — of his strengths and weaknesses. The second requisite is to match these strengths and exploit the weaknesses. If the natural abilities of the Chinese are devoted to the study and adoption of Western military methods, and there is not too great an impatience with the achievement of immediate results, the time will come when China can reassert itself. In the meantime, it should seek to exploit the prime weakness of the West — its inherent disunity, which derives from the lack of a common moral basis and consequent anarchy of selfish ambitions among the nations. To play the Western powers off against one another is then the obvious strategy.

Despite the violent and contemptuous tone of his language, Wei is careful to state that his is a policy valid for either war or peace. He admits the possibility that China's military preparations may not enable her soon to resist or attack the West. Peace negotiations could prove necessary again, as they were in the Opium War. Yet a policy of playing the Western powers off against each other, while gaining time for reform and strengthening within, would be appropriate even in these circumstances.

Wei's *Illustrated Gazetteer of the Maritime Countries* was reprinted many times, expanded, and supplemented. Japanese editions of this work and Wei's *Military History* came to the attention of the samurai reformer Sakuma Shōzan, who spoke of Wei as a "comrade in another land." Sakuma also commented, however, that in practical matters like gunnery Wei lacked firsthand experience and his information was often inaccurate.[19]

Thus Wei's approach to the problem of national defense may be said to reflect his Confucian concern for the state, a more realistic estimate of Western power, and the Qing scholar's penchant for works of compilation based on critical, though not necessarily empirical, research. He had neither the opportunity, nor perhaps the inclination, to take up the practical art of war, which in the past had proven so uncongenial to Chinese Confucian tastes.

## PREFACE TO *MILITARY HISTORY OF THE QING DYNASTY* (*SHENGWU JIXU*), 1842

This preface indicates Wei Yuan's considerable emphasis on state power as manifested in wealth and military strength. At the same time, seeking to rouse the emperor and his ministers to action, Wei appeals to traditional Confucian moral sentiments, wherein all problems are seen as fundamentally reducible to the need for men of ability and firm will, inspired by classic ideals. It begins with an autobiographical sketch, relating the major events of his times to his own reactions to such events.

In my later years, I have lived between the Yangzi and the Huai Rivers and

---

19. Cf. Tsunoda, de Bary, and Keene, *Sources of Japanese Tradition*, ch. 24.

have frequently been disturbed by alarms from the sea and reports of war. With the sensitivity I have accumulated over the years, I can only sigh over the recent news. I have therefore opened up my files of historical sources, arranged them chronologically and topically, and gone over them many times. The sources touching on military matters as well as my comments on them are herewith presented in fourteen chapters, a total of more than 400,000 words. The work is completed in the same month [August 1842] that the maritime barbarians [i.e., the British] have accepted the peace agreement in Nanjing. . . .

Now the state is not poor when there is a deficit in its finances, it is poor when vigorous and competitive talents are wanting. The state is not weak when its decrees are not obeyed abroad, but the state is weak when its decrees are not obeyed within its own territories. Therefore the former kings did not worry about revenues but regarded human talent as the urgent matter. They did not worry about their will being thwarted by the barbarians from all directions, but they did worry about their will being thwarted anywhere within the realm. When its officials are all chosen from among human talents, the wealth of the state is assured; when none of its decrees are disregarded within its territories, the state's power is enhanced. When the state is rich and powerful, it will be effective — it deals with the traitors and they will not persist in their ways; it administers revenue and [the revenue] will not be wasted; it acquires weapons and they will not be flawed; it organizes armed forces and the troops will not be under strength. What then is there to fear about barbarians anywhere — what is there to worry about as to defense against aggression? . . .

In the *Record of Rites* it is said, "Humiliation stimulates effort; when the country is humiliated, its spirit will be aroused."[20] This is why ancient sovereigns who inherited realms that had long seen peace and security would realize that their own pronouncements were irreversible. Inspiring fear, they issued military commands so as to strengthen the morale of all-under-Heaven. In a munificent manner, they gave out military provisions to attract the talents of all-under-Heaven. With talents advanced, military affairs are in good order. When the morale of the people is stern, the state inspires great awe. When the sovereign is pleased, it will be spring in all the four seas; when he is angry, it will be autumn. The Five Senses [those of ears, eyes, mouth, nose, and heart-and-mind] are strong, and the Five Weapons [knife, sword, spear, lance, and bow and arrow] are in good supply. Prohibitions and decrees are strictly followed, and barbarians from all directions come to pay tribute to the sovereign. . . . It is thus that the later sages learn from the early sages, and later kings learn from the early kings. To learn from early sages and early kings — the closest to achieving this were our great and heroic early emperors [of the Qing dynasty]. The *Classic of Documents* says, "Have in good order also your military accoutre-

---

20. "Aigong wen," *Liji jijie* 27:93.

ments and weapons, so that you may go forth beyond the steps of Yu, and be able to travel over all the realm, even beyond the seas, everywhere meeting with submission — so shall you display the bright glory of King Wen and render more illustrious the great achievements of King Wu."[21]

I therefore am daring enough to present this military history of the sacred Qing dynasty, with folded hands and bowing my head to the ground.

[*Wei Yuan ji* v. 1, pp. 166–168 — KCL]

### PREFACE TO *ILLUSTRATED GAZETTEER OF THE MARITIME COUNTRIES* (*HAIGUO TUZHI*)

In the preface to his work, Wei, characteristically for the Qing scholar, starts with a discussion of the sources he has drawn upon. Then he explains the nature and purposes of the work and provides a conspectus of the contents, chapter by chapter. The whole is in a highly rhetorical style, replete with classical allusions and the usual assumptions in regard to Chinese cultural superiority.

The present work, *Illustrated Gazetteer of the Maritime Countries*, contains sixty chapters. Upon what is it based? It is based, on the one hand, upon the *Gazetteer of the Four Continents*, which was translated by Lin [Zexu], former governor-general of Guangdong and Guangxi, and, on the other hand, upon the histories and gazetteers of different previous dynasties, and the different series of *Island Gazetteers* published since the Ming period, and also upon many barbarian atlases and books published in recent years. They were brought together, and thoroughly searched. Many difficulties had to be worked out in order that this pioneer work might be published.

At a rough estimate, about 80 percent of the source materials used in this book covering the Southeastern Ocean [Southeast Asia] and the Southwestern Ocean [South and West Asia] and about 60 percent covering the Great Western Ocean [Western Europe], the Little Western Ocean [North Africa], the Northern Ocean [Russia and Eastern Europe], and the Outer Great Western Ocean [North and South America] are new materials supplementing the original [Lin's] book covering the same areas. They are also illustrated with maps, tables, and diagrams. A variety of opinion from different schools is presented in the interests of broad coverage.

In what respect does this work differ from the gazetteers of earlier writers? The answer is that those earlier works all described the West as it appeared to Chinese writers, while this book describes the West as it appears to Westerners.

What is the purpose of the present work? Its purpose is to show how to use barbarians to fight barbarians, how to make the barbarians pacify one another

---

21. Cf. Legge, *The Chinese Classics*, 4:521.

[to our advantage], and how to employ the techniques of the barbarians in order to bring the barbarians under control. . . . In ancient times those who succeeded in driving off the barbarians knew the enemy's position as clearly as if it were spread out upon their own desk or carpet; they were informed of the enemy's condition as intimately as if the enemy were dining or sleeping with them.

With this book in hand, then, will it be possible to drive off the barbarians?

Perhaps so, perhaps not. This book provides only military tactics, not the basic strategy. It provides the tangible means for making war, but not the intangible ones. . . .

Our present emperor, His Majesty, is benevolent and diligent. His virtue matches that of His ancestors. The operations of Heaven in time and of man through his own efforts are conjoined for our advantage. Why should we fear that the time is not ripe for extermination of the barbarians; why should we fear that there may be no chance to show our might? Thus all of our courageous people must show their eagerness for the achievement of such a task, and anyone who has not lost his senses must devise some means for its accomplishment. Away with hypocrisy! Away with all window dressing! Away with the dread of difficulty! Away with the nurturing of internal evils and the tolerating of private gain at the expense of the public interest! Then the minds of men will be aroused from their ignorant lethargy.

First of all, through practical projects we must advance practical effort; and through practical effort advance practical projects. . . . We must not try to drown ourselves in the river merely to show our heroism, nor must we try to appease our hunger by drawing picture-cakes. Then we shall no longer be plagued by a dearth of men with practical abilities.

Second, once we are rid of our ignorant lethargy, the sun will shine more brightly in the sky; once the dearth of men with practical abilities is remedied, government orders will be carried out with the speed of wind and lightning. . . .

Defensive measures may serve offensive purposes as well as purposes of peaceful negotiation. Use the barbarians to control the barbarians, so that all our borders may be strongly held. Thus the first section of this book deals with maritime defense.

Down through three thousand years [of world history], over the ninety thousand *li* of the world's circumference, both vertically in time and horizontally in space, with geographical charts and historical data, the second section presents a general survey of historical and territorial changes for all nations in the world.

Neither the barbarian religion nor the barbarian opium can penetrate the borders of our vassal states [to the south]. Alas, that they can show their will to resist [while we cannot]. So the third section deals with the nations along the coast of the Southeastern Ocean [i.e., Indochina, Thailand, and so on].

The Isles of Luzon and Java [i.e., the Philippines and Indonesia] are equal in extent to Japan, but they are either encroached upon or absorbed [by the Western barbarians]. Taking heed of the overturned cart ahead [to avert a similar disaster for ourselves], the fourth section deals with the Isles of the Southeastern Ocean [Southeastern Asia].

The religion has been changed three times [Buddhism, Hinduism, Islam] and the land cut into Five Regions. The magpies' nest is now occupied by the turtledoves,[22] which are also a threat to China. This fifth section deals with India.

Both whites and blacks are from remote and isolated areas. They are forced to serve as a vanguard, collaborating with the seafarers of the West. This sixth section deals with North Africa of the Little Western Ocean.

The western part of the Mediterranean Sea is inhabited by many barbarian tribes, who cherish only profit and power, and indeed are as treacherous as the owls. This seventh section deals with the European countries in the Great Western Ocean.

Her [Russia's] tail lies in the East and her head in the West; her northern borders extend to the sea of ice. If we make alliances with the nearby countries in order to attack those afar, she may be our friend in a land war. This eighth section deals with Russia in the Northern Ocean. [In this section Wei sets forth his hope that Russia may distract England by invading India. In the next he suggests that the United States would be a natural ally in naval warfare.]

It has effectively resisted the violent invasion of the English barbarians and faithfully guarded the central plain. If we make alliances with those afar, in order to attack those nearby, it may be of assistance in a sea war. This ninth section deals with the United States in the Outer Great [Western] Ocean.

Every man has Heaven as his source; religious teachings derive from the sages. Though the different teachings meet and part, agree and disagree, they are all orderly and logical. The tenth section deals with religions of the Western nations.

It is China alone that embraces ten thousand *li* under one sovereignty. In contrast with one another and unconnected are Europe and Arabia. This eleventh section presents a chronological table of events in China and the West.

The Chinese calendar has been supplemented by the Western; the Western calendar differs from the Chinese. As a guide for the people in their seasonal labors, ours takes the place of honor. This twelfth section presents a table of similarities and differences between the Chinese and the Western calendars.

In war topography is of first importance, however remote and wild the region. By the gathering of supplies and sketching of plans, a war can be won in the office. This thirteenth section presents a general survey of geographical conditions in each country.

Topography, important though it be, is nothing compared to cooperation

---

22. So stupid they cannot make a nest for themselves.

among men. Surprise tactics and orthodox strategy are to be used according to circumstances, so that there will be the least expenditure of force and a maximum of concerted planning. This fourteenth section presents a program for controlling the barbarians.

Knowing one's own plans and being familiar with those of the enemy, one may judge whether to wage war or negotiate peace. Without knowing the right medicine, how can one cure the disease of shortsightedness and stupidity? The fifteenth section offers a compilation of data on the barbarian situation.

Maritime warfare depends upon warships, as land warfare depends upon battlements. Without mastering the best techniques, how can the stormy seas be tamed? The sixteenth section presents a detailed discussion of warships.

The Five Phases are able to subdue one another. Among them metal and fire are the most fierce. A thunder blast from the earth can serve both offensive and defensive purposes. The seventeenth section presents a detailed discussion of firearms and their use in warfare.

The languages and conveyances of different peoples are not the same, but their currencies are similar. To make skillful use of them, one must make the utmost use of one's intelligence. The eighteenth section deals with [Western] currency, goods, and contrivances.

This preface is written by Wei Yuan of Shaoyang, Secretary to the Cabinet, on the twelfth moon of the twenty-second year of Daoguang (February 1843) at Yangzhou.

[From original preface, *Haiguo tuzhi*, 1a–6b]

*Chapter 29*

THE HEAVENLY KINGDOM OF THE TAIPINGS

In the writings of Lin Zexu and Wei Yuan we have seen the impact of the West on two men who exemplified the finest traditions of Chinese statecraft and Confucian scholarship — representatives of that elite group that had served for centuries as the custodians of the Chinese government and of Confucian values in thought and scholarship. On another level of society, in these years just after China's defeat in the Opium War, there are signs of an even more powerful and striking reaction to the West in the great Taiping Rebellion, a mass movement so remarkable that it has continued to excite and perplex historians in recent years almost as much as it did Chinese and Western observers in the mid-nineteenth century. If on closer acquaintance this popular uprising has seemed to reflect less of Western influence than of native traditions and internal unrest, it remains a fascinating example of the interplay between Chinese and Western ideas in a historical event of the first magnitude.

Hong Xiuquan (1813–1864), the leader of this rebellion that swept up like a whirlwind from the southernmost regions of China, was the son of a peasant family belonging to the Hakka minority group and living not far from Guangzhou. Hong had enough promise as a student that his family joined together in providing him with an education and sending him on to take the provincial civil service examinations. Though repeatedly unsuccessful, on one of these visits to Guangzhou (1836) Hong heard a Christian missionary preach and picked up some religious tracts. When he failed again at the examinations the following year, he seems to have suffered a nervous collapse and during his illness to have had certain visions. In one of them a fatherly old man appeared to him and complained that men, instead of worshiping him, were serving demons. In another, Confucius was scolded for his faithlessness and repented his ways. In still another, a middle-aged man appeared and instructed Hong in the slaying of demons. These apparitions he later understood as signifying that God the Heavenly Father (whom he identified with the Lord-on-High, Shangdi, of ancient Chinese tradition) and Jesus Christ, his Elder Brother, had commissioned him as the Younger Brother to stamp out demon worship. To some Hong might have appeared to be the victim of his own fevered imaginings, but others were impressed by his quiet earnestness and deep sense of conviction. Perhaps most significant from the Chinese point of view was his ability to persuade members of his own family of the rightness of the cause.

These ideas continued to ferment in Hong's mind, yet it was not until seven years later that he took the trouble to read more carefully the tracts given him in Guangzhou, containing translations and summaries from the Bible and sermons on scriptural texts. Later still, he spent two months studying in Guangzhou with the Reverend Issachar J. Roberts, an American Southern Baptist missionary, whose fundamentalist teachings provided Hong with what limited knowledge he gained of Christianity. In the meantime, Hong, who earned a livelihood teaching in village schools, had been joined by some of his relatives in idol-breaking missions that aroused local feelings and the displeasure of the authorities. Forced to shift their activities westward, these prophets without honor in their own country met with a far better reception among the Hakkas of Guangxi. By the late 1840s Hong found himself the leader of a growing band known as the God Worshipers. Here, too, however, the iconoclasm and strange teachings of the God Worshipers provoked official intervention and attempts at suppression.

It seems that in the mind of Hong the Manchu regime became identified quite early with the demonic forces that had to be destroyed in order to establish the Kingdom of Heaven on earth. But it was more than Hong's iconoclasm that led this new religious movement increasingly to take on a political and military aspect. Famine and economic depression in the late 1840s, burdensome taxation, the decline in dynastic prestige as a result of the defeat at the hands of the British, and the consequent impairment of governmental functions, especially in the more remote regions like Guangxi, contributed to a situation in which the survival of any group depended upon its ability to defend and provide for itself in the midst of confusion and lawlessness. The God Worshipers were only one such group, but they proved better organized and possessed of a greater sense of purpose than most. Under pressure of constant official harassment, Hong and his closest collaborators finally worked out a plan for full-fledged revolt. In effect, it put the God Worshipers on a total-war footing. A military organization was created that would mobilize all of the resources of the community for prosecution of the war effort. Personal property had to be turned over to a communal treasury (the "Sacred Treasury"), religious observances were strictly enforced, and a detailed code of military discipline and ethical conduct was established, with heavy penalties for any violations.

Systematically the leaders of the uprising set about consolidating their forces, making weapons, indoctrinating their followers, and training the militia. By December of 1850 the new army was able successfully to withstand a full assault by government troops, and in the flush of this first victory Hong formally proclaimed, at the start of the new year, his rebel regime, the Heavenly Kingdom of Great Peace (*Taiping Tianguo*). He himself assumed the title of Heavenly King, and others of the leaders, including several with military and organizational talents probably superior to those of Hong, were ranked as subordinate kings or princes.

The name of the new regime suggests that it was meant to fulfill the highest ideals of the Chinese political tradition (*Taiping*, or "Great Peace," designated a period of perfect peace and order invoked by earlier reformers and millenarian movements), along with the realization of a Kingdom of Heaven in which all worshiped the one True God. It was thus to be a theocratic state with military, religious, and political authority concentrated in a single hierarchy. Such an all-embracing, monolithic structure was congenial enough to the Chinese political scene and particularly suited the requirements of a revolutionary situation. As a political venture the Taiping movement appealed to anti-Manchu, ethnocentric sentiments. As a program of economic reform, it was meant to attract the overburdened and the destitute, particularly among the peasants. As a new community — indeed a great family in which all the members were "brothers" and "sisters" — it had an appeal to rich and poor alike who suffered from the social dislocation and insecurity of the times. The Taiping cause, in other words, became a rallying point for many elements that traditionally have attached themselves to a new dynastic movement.

Even in the powerful appeal of its religious mystique the Taiping Rebellion had something in common with peasant uprisings and dynastic revolutions in the past. Where it differed, however, was in the intensity and sectarian fanaticism with which Taiping religious teachings were insisted upon. Great importance was attached to the indoctrination of new recruits. Moreover, the extraordinary discipline of the Taiping armies, the heroism of many in battle, and their readiness to meet death — for which there could be no earthly reward — all suggest that this motley assemblage of malcontents and misfits, missionaries and messiahs was inspired by a deep sense of religious purpose.

From the military standpoint the rebellion enjoyed startling success in its early years. It had the advantage of tight organization, firm discipline, talented commanders, and a high degree of mobility that derived from the cutting of all personal ties to home and property. Nevertheless, if Taiping progress northward was devastatingly swift, through Hunan to the central Yangzi valley and thence eastward to Nanjing, this rapid advance came about only by the adoption of a strategy that had its own limitations — notably the bypassing of large centers of resistance. The Taipings concerned themselves little with organizing the countryside as they passed through. No permanent envelopment of these by-passed strongholds and eventual reduction of them was seriously attempted. Local opposition and temporary setbacks, instead of suggesting the need for caution and consolidation, were interpreted as signs from God that they should push on in other directions toward new and greater triumphs. The chief military commander, Yang Xiuqing, who had the title of Eastern King, frequently claimed direct revelation from God the Father in support of his strategic moves, and Taiping accounts of the campaign make it appear that the triumphal course of the rebellion reflects the direct intervention of God in history through the instrumentality of chosen deputies like Hong and Yang.

Once established in their capital of Nanjing, occupied in March 1853 and renamed "Heavenly Capital" (Tianjing), the Taipings sent out an expedition to take Beijing. The effort again made striking gains initially but was eventually slowed, isolated, and defeated. A similar expedition to the West was more successful in enlarging the area under Taiping control, but for the most part the new regime found itself engaged in a protracted struggle to maintain its position in the lower Yangzi valley, a rich and populous region that posed formidable problems of defense and administration. For ten years the fortunes of war waxed and waned, with the exploits of some Taiping commanders resulting in heavy defeats for imperial armies, while, on the other hand, increasing pressure was exerted against them by the reorganized and revitalized forces of regional Han Chinese leaders loyal to the Manchu cause — leaders such as Zeng Guofan, Zuo Zongtang, and Li Hongzhang, who were to play a dominant role in the subsequent history of the dynasty.

A significant loss for the Taipings was their failure to enlist the support of the West. There was early sympathy for the rebel cause on the part of some Westerners in the treaty ports, based on a favorable impression of Taiping morale and discipline, as well as the hope that the Taiping religion might prove to be genuinely Christian. Contacts with the leaders of the revolt soon disillusioned and alienated them, however. The fanaticism, ignorance, and arrogant pretensions of the revolutionaries to a special divine commission, to which even foreigners must submit, quickly dispelled any illusions that the Taipings would be easier for the Western powers to deal with than the Manchus. Subsequently, Taiping moves threatening Shanghai brought the active intervention of the West against them.

A far more serious weakness of the movement was internal — a failure in political leadership. The Taiping "kings" paid little attention to systematic organization of the countryside, preferring to establish themselves in the larger towns and cities. Moreover, educated men with experience in civil administration, whose services might have been highly useful, were repelled by the Taipings' uncouthness, their superstitious adherence to a "foreign" faith, and their apparent repudiation of Confucianism. A civil service examination based on official Taiping literature did little to remedy the lack of trained personnel. Increasingly, too, the cohesion and capacities of the Taiping leadership were severely strained. After the capture of Nanjing, Hong steadily withdrew from active direction of affairs and assumed a role reminiscent of the Daoist sage emperor who ruled by his magic potency — in this case his divine virtue. Yet, in fact, Hong's whole personality disintegrated rapidly, as he devoted himself more and more to the pleasures of the palace. There, in violation of the strict sexual morality and monogamy enjoined upon the Taipings, the Heavenly King kept a virtual harem.

In the meantime, the Eastern King, Yang Xiuqing, steadily arrogated greater powers to himself and even aspired to the imperial dignity before he lost his life in the first of a series of bloodbaths that deprived the regime of several top leaders and many of their adherents. Thereafter, Hong tended to place his own relatives in key positions, being more concerned about trustworthiness than ability. One such relative was Hong Ren'gan, prime minister in the last years of the regime, who had far more acquaintance with Christianity and the West than the other "kings" but who proved unable to effectuate any of his plans for the reorganization of the regime along more Western lines.

One of the great ironies of the Taiping Rebellion was revealed at the time of its final collapse in the summer of 1864. Nanjing had been in danger for months when Li Xiucheng, an able general whose military successes had not turned his head from a devoted loyalty to Hong, advised abandonment of the capital and escape to the south. The Heavenly King chose to remain, insisting that God would protect and provide for the Taipings. Yet by June 1864 Hong had himself despaired of his cause, apparently taken poison, and died; his body was found later, draped in imperial yellow, in a sewer under the palace. Hong's faithful followers held out another month in the midst of the worst privation and suffering, and when finally overwhelmed by the Manchu forces, gave up their lives in a great slaughter rather than submit. Zeng Guofan, leader of the victorious armies, is the authority for the statement that not one surrendered.

In the religious faith of the Taiping movement, the most distinguishing feature was its monotheism. In the past, China had not lacked for popular religious movements, nor had the imperial court been without its own cult linking dynastic rule to the authority of Heaven. But it was Hong who first proclaimed a belief in one God who was the Father of all, a God who was at once accessible to the prayers of the individual and actively concerned with the governing of the world. In Taiping documents, as will be seen from the selections that follow, this point is particularly stressed: whereas the old cult of Heaven was, ritualistically, a one-family affair, jealously guarded by the ruling house, the True God of the Taipings was the ruler, father, and friend of all. His direct accessibility to men, however, proved both a boon and a bane to the Taipings. For if this conception stimulated a genuine piety in many, it also provided a dangerous weapon to a few of their leaders who claimed divine inspiration for their actions and God's sanction for their own ambitions.

Western influence can be seen in some of the practices adopted by the Taipings, such as a calendar with a seven-day week and observance of the sabbath. It may have been responsible in part also for the greater equality accorded to women, the condemnation of polygamy and adultery, and the bans on slavery, foot binding, gambling, wine, and tobacco. The coincidence, however, of a straitlaced Protestant fundamentalism and a degree of native puritanism among the Chinese peasantry (the latter reflected also in the avowedly anti-Christian Communist movement of the mid-twentieth century) suggests that convergence more than simple external influence is at work here.

The peasant Chinese who so largely made up the forces of Hong Xiuquan were already deeply imbued with ethical and religious traditions rooted in the past. Moreover, the Taipings were compelled, in spite of their early hostility to Confucianism, to compromise with many of its customs and values or — more likely — unconsciously to accept them without sensing any incompatibility between traditional ethics and the new faith. Such accommodations, nonetheless, proved insufficient to bridge the gap between Taiping ideology and the Chinese tradition or to equip the revolutionary leadership for the stupendous task of ruling a mature and complex society. In the end it was the defenders of tradition and those schooled in Chinese statecraft who emerged victorious to guide China's destinies for another half-century.

## THE BOOK OF HEAVENLY COMMANDMENTS (TIANTIAO SHU)

This text, officially promulgated by the Taipings in 1852, was probably written several years earlier to serve as a basic statement of the God Worshipers' creed and religious practice when they were first organized. It bespeaks a simple and unpretentious faith, constantly reiterating the hope of Heaven and fear of hell. Much of it is devoted to forms that are to be used in the saying of prayers, grace at meals, and so on, and to an explanation of the Ten Commandments. In the last category we find provisions for segregation of the sexes and prohibitions against opium smoking and gambling.

When a translation of this work by W. H. Medhurst appeared in the English-language *North China Herald* on May 14, 1853, the editor commented: "We cannot help thinking that this is a most extraordinary document, and can see in it little to object against. Two things strike us on reading it carefully through: the one is that with the exception of occasional references to redemption by Christ and apparent extracts from the Lord's Prayer, the ideas seem to be generally taken from the Old Testament, with little or nothing from the New; the other is that it appears to be mainly a compilation drawn up by the rebels themselves, for if a Christian missionary had had anything to do with it, he certainly would not have directed the offering up of animals, wine, tea, and rice even though these offerings were presented to the Great God. As it is, we repeat it is a most extraordinary production, and were the rebels to act up to everything therein contained, they would be the most gentle and moral set of rebels we ever met with."

The translation given here is adapted and revised from that of Medhurst as emended on the basis of other early editions of the text by members of the Modern Chinese History Project, Far Eastern and Russian Institute, University of Washington, as a part of *The Taiping Rebellion: History and Documents*, by Franz Michael, published in 1971.

Who in this mortal world has not offended against the Heavenly Commandments? If one was not aware of his offense in former times, he can still be excused; now, however, as the Lord God has already issued a gracious proclamation, henceforth whoever knows how to repent of his sins in the presence of the Lord God, not to worship false spirits, not to practice perverse things, and not to transgress the Heavenly Commandments, shall be permitted to ascend to Heaven and to enjoy dignity and honor without end. Whoever does not know how to repent of his sins . . . will most certainly be punished by being sent down to hell to suffer bitterness, and for thousands and myriads of years to suffer sorrow and pain without end. Which is gain and which is loss, we ask you to think over. Our brothers and sisters throughout the mortal world, ought not all of you to awaken from your lethargy? If, however, you continue unroused, then are you truly base-born, truly deluded by the devil, and truly is there bliss that you do not know how to enjoy. [1a]

Now, those whose minds have been deluded by the demons always say that only the monarch can worship the Lord God. However, the Lord God is the universal Father of all in the mortal world. Monarchs are his able children, the good his filial children, the commoners his ignorant children, and the violent and oppressive his disobedient children. If you say that monarchs alone can worship the Lord God, we beg to ask you, as for the parents of a family, is it only the eldest son who can be filial and obedient to his parents?

Again it has been falsely said that to worship the Great God is to follow barbarians' ways. They do not know that in the ancient world monarchs and subjects alike all worshiped the Lord God. As for the great Way of worshiping the Lord God, from the very beginning, when the Lord God created in six days Heaven and earth, mountains and seas, man and things, both China and the barbarian nations walked together in the great Way; however, the various barbarian countries of the West have continued to the end in the great Way. China also walked in the great Way, but within the most recent one or two thousand years, China has erroneously followed the devil's path, thus being captured by the demon of hell. Now, therefore, the Lord God, out of compassion for humanity, has extended his capable hand to save the people of the world, deliver them from the devil's grasp, and lead them out to walk again in the original great Way. [1a–b]

## A Form to Be Observed in Repenting Sins

Let the suppliant kneel down in the sight of Heaven and pray to the Lord God to forgive his sins. He may use a written form of prayer, and when the prayer is over, he may either take a basin of water and wash his whole body clean, or he may perform his ablutions in the river, which will be still better. After repenting his sins, let him morning and evening worship the Lord God, beseeching that the Lord God look after him, and grant him His Holy Spirit to transform his heart. When taking his meals, he should give thanks to God, and every seventh day worship and praise God for His grace and virtue. Let him also constantly obey the ten Heavenly Commandments. Do not on any account let him worship all the false spirits that are in the world, still less let him do any of the corrupt things of the world. In this manner, the people may become the sons and daughters of the Lord God. While in the world the Lord God will look after them, and after ascending to Heaven the Lord God will graciously love them, and in high Heaven they will eternally enjoy bliss. [2a–b]

## The Ten Heavenly Commandments

1. Honor and worship the Lord God. . . .[1]
2. Do not worship false gods. . . .
3. Do not take the name of the Lord God in vain. . . .
4. On the seventh day, worship and praise the Lord God for his grace. . . .
5. Be filial and obedient to thy Father and Mother. . . .
6. Do not kill or injure men. . . .
7. Do not indulge in wickedness and lewdness.

    In the world there are many men, all brothers; in the world there are many women, all sisters. For the sons and daughters of Heaven, the men have men's quarters and the women have women's quarters; they are not allowed to intermix. Men or women who commit adultery or who are licentious are considered monsters; this is the greatest possible transgression of the Heavenly Commandments. The casting of amorous glances, the harboring of lustful imaginings about others, the smoking of opium, and the singing of libidinous songs are all offenses against the Heavenly Commandment.

---

1. The commentary of the Taiping expositor has been omitted except for the last four commandments.

8. Do not steal or rob.

Poverty and riches are granted by the Lord God, and whosoever steals or plunders the property of others transgresses the Heavenly Commandment.

9. Do not tell [or spread] falsehoods.

All those who speak wildly, falsely, or treacherously, and those who use coarse and vile language transgress against the Heavenly Commandment.

10. Do not think covetous thoughts.

When a man looks upon the beauty of another's wife or daughter and then covets that man's wife or daughter; when a man looks upon the richness of another man's possessions and then covets that man's possessions; or when a man engages in gambling and buys lottery tickets and bets on names,[2] all these are transgressions of the Heavenly Commandment. [6b–8a]

[Xiao Yishan, *Taiping Tianguo congshu*, ser. 1, *ce* 1, pp. 1a–2b, 6b–8a]

### A PRIMER IN VERSE (YOUXUE SHI)

This official text, first published in 1851, offers simple and concise formulations — easily put to memory — of basic religious and moral principles that the Taiping leaders wished to inculcate in their followers. Although opposed to Confucianism insofar as it was identified with the established regime or took on the appearance of a religious cult, the Taipings accepted much that is readily recognizable as Confucian in social and political ethics.

## Praising God

The Lord God-on-High, the divine Being
Is respectfully worshiped in all countries.
Men and women throughout the world,
Pay homage to Him morning and evening.
All that we see, above and below,
Basks in the Lord's favor.
In the beginning it took only six days
For the creation of all things to be completed.
Is there anyone, circumcised or uncircumcised,
Not created by God?

---

2. It was a common practice of the time, especially in Guangdong, to bet on who would succeed in the state examinations. Gambling clubs were established for this purpose. The Guangdong government first fined such gambling and later collected a gambling tax from the clubs.

Give thanks [to Him] for the Heavenly favor
That you may obtain everlasting glory.

## Praising Jesus Christ

Jesus was a Crown Prince,
Whom God sent to earth in ancient times.
He sacrificed His life for the sins of men,
Being the first to offer meritorious service.
It was hard to bear the Cross;
Grieving clouds darkened the sun.
The noble Prince from Heaven,
Died for you — men and women.
Having returned to Heaven after His resurrection,
In His glory, He holds all power.
Upon Him we are to rely —
Be saved and enter Paradise!

## Praising Parents

[Just as] the storing up of grain provides against starvation,
[So] the raising up of children provides against old age.
He who is filial to his parents will have filial sons.
Thus, mysteriously, is recompense made.
You should ask yourself,
How you were able to grow up.[3]
Respect the teaching of the Fifth Heavenly
    Commandment;
Honor and wealth will shower down on you from the
    Heavenly Court.

## The Imperial Court

The imperial court is an awesome place.
With fear and trembling heed the imperial authority as if
    it reached into your very presence.
The power of life and death belongs to the Son-of-Heaven.
Among the officials none should oppose Him.

---

3. Through the loving care of your parents.

## The Way of a King

If one man, aloft, upholds the Right,
The myriad states all enjoy repose.[4]
Let the king alone hold power;
And all slander and depravity will disappear forever.

## The Way of the Minister

The more virtuous the master, the more honest
   will be His ministers. Wise kings produce good officials.
Yi [Yin] and [Duke] Zhou have set the example [for ministers].
Upholding justice, they maintained discipline at court.

## The Way of the Family

Kinsfolk within the household —
Be cheerful and happy!
Be harmonious and united as one body,
Blessings will shower down upon you from Heaven.

*There follow similar maxims for eleven other family relationships from mother and son to older and younger sister-in-law, as well as injunctions with regard to sexual chastity and fidelity and disciplining of the senses. For the most part these are of a traditional Chinese character, and largely Confucian, like the verses above. Finally the primer concludes with the following:*

## Paradise

Whether to be noble or mean is for you to choose.
To be a real man you must make an effort to improve yourself.
Follow the teaching of the Ten Commandments;
You will enjoy the blessings of Paradise.

[Xiao Yishan, *Taiping Tianguo congshu*, ser. 1, *ce* 4, pp. 1a–5b, 14a–b]

# THE TAIPING ECONOMIC PROGRAM

The following selection is taken from *The Land System of the Heavenly Kingdom* (*Tianchao tianmu zhidu*), which was included in the list of official Taiping publications promulgated in 1853. Its precise authorship is uncertain, and there is no evidence of a serious attempt having been made to put this system into effect in Taiping-controlled areas. Nevertheless, as a statement of Taiping aims, the document carried

---

4. These two lines are adapted from the opening passage of the *Classic of Changes*.

with it all the weight of Hong Xiuquan's authority and that of the Eastern King, Yang Xiuqing, then at the height of his power. It reflects one of the chief appeals that the movement made to the Chinese peasantry.

The plan set forth here amounts to a blueprint for the total organization of society, and especially of its human resources. If its initial concern is with the land problem, as the title indicates, it quickly moves on to other spheres of human activity and brings them under a single pattern of control. The basic organization is military in nature, reminiscent of the farmer-soldier militia of earlier dynasties. In its economic egalitarianism, totalitarian communism, authoritarian hierarchy, and messianic zeal, this Taiping manifesto foreshadows aspects of the Chinese Communist movement of the twentieth century, while at the same time it echoes reformers and rebels of the past. Most typically it recalls the fondness of earlier Chinese thinkers for a neat, symmetrical system embodying the supreme values of Chinese thought: order, balance, and harmony.

Nevertheless, we can appreciate how conservative Confucians would have recoiled at the thought of so much economic regimentation. Zeng Guofan, leader in the struggle against the Taipings, commented, "The farmer cannot till his own land and [simply] pay taxes on it; the land is all considered to be the land of the Heavenly King [and all produce goes directly to the communal treasury]. The merchant cannot engage in trade for himself and profit thereby; all goods are considered to be the goods of the Heavenly King."

The organizational note is struck at the outset with an explanation of the system of army districts and military administration (omitted here). We reproduce below only the basic economic program.

All officials who have rendered meritorious service are to receive hereditary stipends from the court. For the later adherents to the Taiping cause, every family in each military district (*jun*) is to provide one man to serve as a militia man. During an emergency they are to fight under the command of their officers to destroy the enemy and to suppress bandits. In peacetime they are to engage in agriculture under the direction of their officers, tilling the land and providing support for their superiors.

All land [in the country] is to be classified into nine grades. . . .

*The classification of the land into nine grades that follows is based on that found in the "Tribute of Yu" section of the* Classic of Documents (Shujing); *the general method of land allocation follows the principle set forth in the* Rites of Zhou, Di guan, xia, SBBY 4:24.

The distribution of all land is to be based on the number of persons in each family, regardless of sex. A large family is entitled to more land, a small one to less. The land distributed should not be all of one grade but mixed. Thus for a family of six, for instance, three are to have fertile land and three barren land — half and half of each.

All the land in the country is to be cultivated by the whole population together. If there is an insufficiency [of land] in this place, move some of the people to another place. If there is an insufficiency in another place, move them to this one. All lands in the country are also to be mutually supporting with respect to abundance and scarcity. If this place has a drought, then draw upon the abundant harvest elsewhere in order to relieve the distress here. If there is a drought there, draw upon the abundant harvest here in order to relieve the distress there. Thus all the people of the country may enjoy the great blessings of the Heavenly Father, Supreme Ruler and Lord God-on-High. The land is for all to till, the food for all to eat, the clothes for all to wear, and money for all to spend. Inequality shall exist nowhere; none shall suffer from hunger or cold. . . .

Mulberry trees are to be planted along the walls [of villages] throughout the country. All women are required to grow silkworms, to do weaving, and to make clothes. Every family of the country is required to raise five hens and two hogs, in keeping with the proper breeding seasons.[5]

During the harvest season, the Group Officer[6] should direct [the grain collection by] the sergeants. Deducting the amount needed to feed the twenty-five families until next harvest season, he should collect the rest of the produce for storage in state granaries. The same method of collection is applicable to other kinds of products, such as barley, beans, ramie fiber, cotton clothes, silk, domestic animals, silver and copper cash, and so on, for all people under Heaven are of one family belonging to the Heavenly Father, the Supreme Ruler, the Lord God-on-High. Nobody should keep private property. All things should be presented to the Supreme Ruler, so that He will be enabled to make use of them and distribute them equally to all members of his great world-family. Thus all will be sufficiently fed and clothed. . . .

The Group Officer must keep a record of the amount of grain and cash he has collected and report them to the Treasurers and Receiving and Disbursing Tellers. A state treasury and a church are to be established among every twenty-five families, under the direct administration of the Group Officer. All expenditures of the twenty-five families for weddings, births, or other festival occasions are to be paid for out of the state treasury. But there is to be a fixed limit; not a penny is to be spent beyond that. . . . Thus, throughout the land in the contracting of marriages, wealth need be no consideration.

In the twenty-five family units pottery-making, metalworking, carpentry, masonry, and other such skilled work should be performed by the sergeants and militiamen in the off-seasons from farming and military service.

In conducting the different kinds of festival ceremonies for the twenty-five families under his administration, the Group Officer should hold religious ser-

---

5. A paraphrase of *Mencius* 1A:7.
6. The *liang sima*, official in charge of each twenty-five-family group.

vices to pray to the Heavenly Father, the Supreme Ruler and Lord God-on-High. All the bad customs of the past must be completely abolished.

[Xiao Yishan, *Taiping Tianguo congshu*, ser. 1, *ce* 4, pp. 1a–3a]

## THE PRINCIPLES OF THE HEAVENLY NATURE (*TIANQING DAOLISHU*)

This official work, dated 1854, was written after the Taipings had established their capital at Nanjing and the first flush of victory had given way to a seeming letdown in morale, discipline, and zeal for the cause. It served to restate the religious creed of the Taipings and emphasize those qualities — self-sacrifice, loyalty, and solidarity — that had contributed to their amazing successes. The appeal throughout is to a dedicated and crusading military elite.

Another important purpose of the book was to enhance and consolidate the position of the Taiping leadership, especially that of the Eastern King, Yang Xiuqing, who was virtual prime minister of the regime and the one who inspired the writing of this document. We see here in a strange new garb the old conception of the ruler as commissioned with divine powers to unite the world and establish peace. Both Hong and Yang are thus represented as in some degree sharing the role of Jesus Christ as saviors of the world. Since it would not have done for any of the "kings" to engage openly in such self-glorification, nominal authorship is attributed to the "marquises" and "chancellors" who constituted the next-highest ranks in the Taiping hierarchy.

Extant editions of the text appear to date from about 1858, by which time rivalries and mistrust had split the leadership, Yang had been assassinated, and his assassin, the Northern King, murdered by Hong. Though there are many direct and indirect evidences of dissension, the text has not been amended or adjusted to these later developments except to strip the Northern King of his rank.

The translation here has been adapted from that of C. T. Hu for the documentary history of the Taiping Rebellion prepared by the Modern Chinese History Project of the Far Eastern and Russian Institute, University of Washington.

We marquises and chancellors hold that our brothers and sisters have been blessed by the Heavenly Father and the Heavenly Elder Brother, who saved the ensnared and drowning and awakened the deluded; they have cast off worldly sentiments and now follow the true Way. They cross mountains and wade rivers, not even ten thousand *li* being too far for them to come, to uphold together the true Sovereign. Armed and bearing shield and spear, they carry righteous banners that rise colorfully. Husband and wife, men and women, express common indignation and lead the advance. It can be said that they are determined to uphold Heaven and to requite the nation with loyalty. [2a–b]

In the ten thousand nations of the world everyone is given life, nourished, protected, and blessed by the Heavenly Father, the Supreme Ruler and Lord God-on-High. Thus the Heavenly Father, the Supreme Ruler and Lord God-on-High, is the universal father of man in all the ten thousand nations of the world. There is no man who should not be grateful, there is no man who should not reverently worship Him. . . . [4a–5a]

*There follow citations from the Confucian classics referring to the Lord-on-High (Shangdi), which are taken here as showing that God was known to and worshiped by the ancient Chinese. Subsequently, however, various forms of idolatry arose.*

However, worldly customs daily degenerated. There were even those who likened themselves to rulers, and, being deluded in heart and nature, arrogant yet at fault, and falsely self-exalted, forbade the prime minister and those below to sacrifice to Heaven. Then [these men] competed in establishing false gods and worshiping them, thus opening up the ways of the devilish demons. The people of the world all followed in like fashion, and this became firmly fixed in their minds. Thereupon, after a considerable time, they did not know their own errors. Hence the Heavenly Father, the Lord God, in view of mortal man's serious crime of disobedience, at his first anger, sent down forty days and forty nights of heavy rain, the vast waters spreading in all directions and drowning mortal man. Only Noah and his family had unceasingly worshiped the Heavenly Father, the Supreme Ruler and Lord God-on-High; therefore, relying on the Heavenly grace, they were fortunate and they alone were preserved. In this, the first instance of the Heavenly Father's great anger, was the great proof of his great powers displayed.

After the Flood, the devilish king of Egypt, whose ambition was mediocrity and who was possessed by the demons, envied the Israelites in their worship of God and bitterly persecuted them. Therefore, the Heavenly Father in his great anger led the Israelites out of Egypt. In this, the second instance of the Heavenly Father's great anger, was the great proof of his great powers displayed.

However, the rulers and people of that time still had not completely forgotten the Heavenly grace. But since the emergence of Daoism in the [Chinese] Qin [dynasty] and the welcoming of Buddhism in the Han [dynasty], the delusion of man by the demons has day by day increased, and all men have forgotten the grace and virtue of the Heavenly Father. . . . The Heavenly Father once again became greatly angered; yet if he were to annihilate them completely, he could not bear it in his heart; if he were to tolerate them, it would not be consonant with righteousness. At that time, the elder son of the Heavenly Father, the Heavenly Elder Brother Jesus, shouldered the great burden and willingly offered to sacrifice his life to redeem the sins of the men of the world.
. . .

Let us ask your elder and younger brothers: formerly the people sacrificed only to the demons; they worshiped the demons and appealed to the demons only because they desired the demons to protect them. Yet how could they think that the demons could really protect them? . . . To worship them is of no avail. However, the men of the world sank even deeper, not knowing how to awaken themselves. Therefore, the Heavenly Father again became angry.

In the *dingyou* year [1837], our Heavenly Father displayed the heavenly grace and dispatched angels to summon the Heavenly King up to Heaven. There He clearly pointed out the demons' perversities and their deluding of the world. He also invested the Heavenly King with a seal and a sword; He ordered the Savior, the Heavenly Elder Brother, Jesus, to take command of the Heavenly soldiers and Heavenly generals and to aid the Heavenly King, and to attack and conquer from Heaven earthward, layer by layer, the innumerable demons. After their victory they returned to Heaven and the Heavenly Father, greatly pleased, sent the Heavenly King down upon the earth to become the true Taiping Sovereign of the ten thousand nations of the world and to save the people of the world. He also bade him not to be fearful and to effect these matters courageously, for whenever difficulties appeared, the Heavenly Father would assume direction and the Heavenly Elder Brother would shoulder the burden. [8a–9a]

*Several instances are then given of the way in which God's power was manifested in the triumphant campaigns of the Taiping forces and of how His will was made known to them. After describing their progress from Guangxi through Hunan to Wuchang on the Yangzi, the account tells of their drive down the river to Nanjing.*

From Wuchang to Jinling [Nanjing] the land extends as far as a thousand *li*; how strategic and important are the passes and river crossings, and how strong and firm are the cities and moats! To attack and capture the cities seemed difficult; even if victory could have been secured, it appeared that it would take a very long time. Yet in not more than one month's time, we had followed the stream eastward from Wuchang, passing Jiangxi, crossing Anhui, and pushing directly up to Jinling, without the least resistance. After reaching this provincial capital, we found the height and thickness of the city walls and the vastness of the land to be indeed twice that of other provincial cities; to attack it seemed far more difficult. Who would have known that within ten days one single effort would bring success? Jinling was captured with our hands hanging at our sides. Had it not been for our Heavenly Father's power, how could things have been so quick and easy? From this we can again see the Heavenly Father's power to predetermine things. [12b–14a]

*There follow accounts of the individual Taiping leaders showing how each triumphed over adversities and suffered great hardships in order to advance the cause.*

Even the Eastern King in his holiness and the several kings in their eminence had to undergo cleansing and polishing and repeatedly demonstrate great fortitude before they could enjoy true happiness. How much more must we elder and younger brothers preserve our fortitude in order that we may seek abundant blessings. . . .

Recollecting the past, from the righteous uprising in Jintian to the capture of Jinling, we have received great mercy from our Heavenly Father and Heavenly Elderly Brother; we have established our Heavenly capital and in a few years we have been able to enjoy the great happiness of our Heavenly Father. All this has been due to the work of our Heavenly Father and our Heavenly Elder Brother, who alone can bring such speedy results. Hence, if, with additional efforts toward improvement and perfection, we, with united hearts, combine our strength for the immediate extermination of the demons, our Heavenly Father will display his great powers and instantaneously the seas and lands will be cleared and the hills and rivers united under one command. Then our younger brothers and sisters will be reunited with their families, and blood relations will again be together. How fortunate that will be! [19a–b]

*There follows a long section dealing with disobedient and traitorous officers who serve as object lessons of the futility of deserting or betraying the Taiping cause. It is shown how God, who knows and sees all, revealed their wicked designs to the Taiping leaders. Thus their cowardice and self-seeking brought them only the most severe punishment.*

We brothers and sisters, enjoying today the greatest mercy of our Heavenly Father, have become as one family and are able to enjoy true blessings; each of us must always be thankful. Speaking in terms of our ordinary human feelings, it is true that each has his own parents and there must be a distinction in family names; it is also true that as each has his own household, there must be a distinction between this boundary and that boundary. Yet we must know that the ten thousand names derive from the one name, and the one name from one ancestor. Thus our origins are not different. Since our Heavenly Father gave us birth and nourishment, we are of one form though of separate bodies, and we breathe the same air though in different places. This is why we say, "All are brothers within the four seas."[7] Now, basking in the profound mercy of Heaven, we are of one family. . . .

We brothers, our minds having been awakened by our Heavenly Father, joined the camp in the earlier days to support our Sovereign, many bringing parents, wives, uncles, brothers, and whole families. It is a matter of course that we should attend to our parents and look after our wives and children, but when one first creates a new rule, the state must come first and the family last, public interests first and private interests last. Moreover, as it is advisable to avoid suspicion [of improper conduct] between the inner [female] and the outer [male] and to distinguish between male and female, so men must have male

---

7. *Analects* 12:5.

quarters and women must have female quarters; only thus can we be dignified and avoid confusion. There must be no common mixing of the male and female groups, which would cause debauchery and violation of Heaven's commandments. Although to pay respects to parents and to visit wives and children occasionally are in keeping with human nature and not prohibited, yet it is only proper to converse before the door, stand a few steps apart and speak in a loud voice; one must not enter the sisters' camp or permit the mixing of men and women. Only thus, by complying with rules and commands, can we become sons and daughters of Heaven. [29a–30a]

At the present time, the remaining demons have not yet been completely exterminated and the time for the reunion of families has not yet arrived. We younger brothers and sisters must be firm and patient to the end, and with united strength and a single heart we must uphold God's principles and wipe out the demons immediately. With peace and unity achieved, then our Heavenly Father, displaying his mercy, will reward us according to our merits. Wealth, nobility, and renown will then enable us brothers to celebrate the reunion of our families and enjoy the harmonious relations of husband and wife. Oh, how wonderful that will be! The task of a thousand times ten thousand years also lies in this; the happiness and emoluments of a thousand times ten thousand years also lie in this; we certainly must not abandon it in one day. [37b–38a]

[From Xiao Yishan, *Taiping Tianguo congshu*, *ce* 5, pp. 1–38]

PART 6

*Reform and Revolution*

## Chapter 30

## MODERATE REFORM AND THE
## SELF-STRENGTHENING MOVEMENT

The defeat of the Taipings was only one of the more hopeful signs for the Manchus in the early 1860s, after two decades of losses and near-disaster for the dynasty. The foreign occupation of Beijing in 1860 had been followed by a reorganization of leadership at court, with stronger and more flexible men rallying forces loyal to the dynasty and working toward better relations with the foreign powers. The new diplomatic missions established in the capital and foreign concessions in treaty ports up and down the coast, though forced upon the court originally, had now made it both necessary and possible for the Chinese to come into closer contact with Westerners — contact that slowly and imperceptibly widened their horizons on the world. In the provinces, able commanders like Zeng Guofan, Zuo Zongtang, and Li Hongzhang, who had shown great personal resourcefulness and determination in suppressing the rebels and had even demonstrated a readiness to adopt Western guns and naval vessels for use against the Taipings, continued individually to promote modernization projects that would strengthen their military positions and enhance the basis of their own regional power.

If, to Western observers, these developments suggested some hope for China's future, to the Chinese there were other grounds for encouragement — enough to justify calling this period a "revival" or "restoration" in the life of the nation and the ruling dynasty. In foreign relations, the Chinese could at most be gratified by a respite from the constant pressure of the Western powers. In internal affairs, however, they could observe with satisfaction the restoring of peace and stability after several major revolts (besides the Taipings, the Nian rebellion in Anhui and Shandong in 1853–1868, and the Muslim rebellions in both the southwestern provinces, in 1855–1873, and the northwestern provinces, in 1862–1877); so, too, a gradual improvement in local administration and steps taken to rehabilitate the economy along more or less traditional lines — the encouragement of agriculture, land reclamation and development, irrigation, flood control, tax reform, and so on. The genuine effectiveness of such time-honored measures can be appreciated in terms of their contribution to the traditional agrarian economy (upon which, obviously, so many millions of Chinese depended for their daily life), even if such methods fell far short of meeting the economic challenge of the West.

To conservative Confucians there was reassurance in all this, not only that age-old methods and institutions seemed to stand the test of these times but that men of ability and character had appeared who could make them effective. It was leadership, rather than the techniques or institutions themselves, in which the Confucians placed hope. It was the "noble man," pursuing virtue and learning rather than power and profit, who would save China. From such a point of view, no more basic or radical a change could take place than that which transformed the people inwardly and united them in support of worthy rulers. To talk of drastic changes in social or political institutions was almost unthinkable, and certainly uncalled for.

On this fundamental point there was virtually unanimous agreement, even among those who felt that the danger from the West prompted fundamental reexamination and reform. They might believe it necessary to adopt Western guns and ships — even to master the languages, the knowledge, the techniques required for the production and use of these weapons — but such measures would be indispensably linked to a regeneration of the national life, a reassertion of traditional values in government, a renewed concern for the livelihood of the people, and a kind of moral rearmament based on self-cultivation and tightened social discipline. A reexamination in these terms tended, therefore, to focus on two types of weakness: military inferiority to the West, which called for the employment of new methods, and moral inadequacy with respect to traditional ideals, which called for self-criticism and an intensified effort to uphold old standards.

Reform along these lines was most strikingly exemplified in the so-called self-strengthening movement. Its immediate objective was a buildup in military power; its ultimate aim was to preserve and strengthen the traditional way of life. In the following selections are presented the views of men prominently identified as exponents of reform on this basis: namely, that the adoption of Western arms could be justified on grounds of utility and practicality, as a means of defending China and preserving Chinese civilization. These reform ideas emerged naturally from the statecraft scholarship discussed in earlier chapters.

Self-strengthening itself appealed to one of the heroic ideals in Neo-Confucian teaching: self-reliance, self-discipline, and taking responsibility for the Way and the world on oneself.

### FENG GUIFEN: ON THE MANUFACTURE OF FOREIGN WEAPONS

Feng Guifen (1809–1874), a classicist, teacher, and official, came to recognize the need for modernization and the importance of scientific studies when he was forced to take refuge in Shanghai from the Taipings and came into contact with Westerners defending the city. Later, as an adviser to some of the leading statesmen of his time, Feng demonstrated an acute grasp of both state and foreign affairs. His essays advocating a wide variety of reforms were highly regarded by some leaders and became increasingly influential toward the end of the century. It was at his suggestion that a school of Western languages and sciences was established in Shanghai in 1863.

Feng had few illusions regarding the ease with which China might undertake reform. He appreciated the difficulty of adopting weapons that presupposed a considerable scientific knowledge and technological development. Even more, he recognized the disturbing fact that Western superiority lay not in arms alone but also in leadership. In his eyes, however, the qualities of character and mind displayed by Westerners were simply those long recognized as essential to leadership within the Chinese tradition. The foreigners' example might be edifying, and indeed a reproach to the deplorable state of Chinese public life, but it was not a lesson in the sense that China had anything new to learn from the West. The lesson was simply that it had more to make of its own learning.

Such is the two-pronged attack by Feng on Chinese complacency, as expressed in these excerpts from his book of essays, *Protests from the Study of Jiaobin* (1861). Note again that when a Confucian reformer seeks to make changes, he must come to grips with the civil service system, which was so pervasive an influence on educated Chinese.

According to a general geography compiled by an Englishman, the territory of China is eight times that of Russia, ten times that of the United States, one hundred times that of France, and two hundred times that of Great Britain. . . . Yet we are shamefully humiliated by the four nations, not because our climate, soil, or resources are inferior to theirs, but because our people are inferior. . . . Now, our inferiority is not due to our allotment [i.e., our inherent nature] from Heaven, but is rather due to ourselves. If it were allotted us by Heaven, it would be a shame but not something we could do anything about. Since the inferiority is due to ourselves, it is a still greater shame but something we can do something about. And if we feel ashamed, there is nothing better than self-strengthening. . . .

Why are the Western nations small and yet strong? Why are we large and yet weak? We must search for the means to become their equal, and that depends solely upon human effort. With regard to the present situation, several observations may be made: in not wasting human talents, we are inferior to the barbarians; in not wasting natural resources, we are inferior to the barbarians; in allowing no barrier to come between the ruler and the people, we are inferior to the barbarians; and in the matching of words with deeds, we are also inferior to the barbarians. The remedy for these four points is to seek the causes in ourselves. They can be changed at once if only the emperor would set us in the right direction. There is no need to learn from the barbarians in these matters. [58b–59a]

We have only one thing to learn from the barbarians, and that is strong ships and effective guns. . . . Funds should be allotted to establish a shipyard and arsenal in each trading port. A few barbarians should be employed, and Chinese who are good in using their minds should be selected to receive instruction so that in turn they may teach many craftsmen. When a piece of work is finished and is as good as that made by the barbarians, the makers should be rewarded with an official *juren* degree and be permitted to participate in the metropolitan examinations on the same basis as other scholars. Those whose products are of superior quality should be rewarded with the *jinshi* degree [ordinarily conferred in the metropolitan examinations] and be permitted to participate in the palace examinations like others. The workers should be paid double so that they will not quit their jobs.

Our nation's emphasis on civil service examinations has sunk deep into people's minds for a long time. Intelligent and brilliant scholars have exhausted their time and energy in such useless things as the stereotyped examination essays, examination papers, and formal calligraphy. . . . We should now order one-half of them to apply themselves to the manufacturing of instruments and weapons and to the promotion of physical studies. . . . The intelligence and ingenuity of the Chinese are certainly superior to those of the various barbarians; it is only that hitherto we have not made use of them. When the government above takes delight in something, the people below will pursue it further: their response will be like an echo carried by the wind. There ought to be some people of extraordinary intelligence who can have new ideas and improve on Western methods. At first they may take the foreigners as their teachers and models; then they may come to the same level and be their equals; finally they may move ahead and surpass them. Herein lies the way to self-strengthening. [60a–61a]

It may be argued: "Guan Zhong repelled the barbarians and Confucius acclaimed his virtue; the state of Chu adopted barbarian ways and [Confucius in] the *Spring and Autumn Annals* condemned them. Is not what you are proposing contrary to the Way of the sages?" No, it is not. When we speak of repelling the barbarians, we must have the actual means to repel them, and not just empty bravado. If we live in the present day and speak of repelling the barbarians, we should ask with what instruments we are to repel them. . . . [The answer is that] we should use the instruments of the barbarians but not adopt the ways of the barbarians. We should use them so that we can repel them.

Some have asked why we should not just purchase the ships and man them with [foreign] hirelings, but the answer is that this will not do. If we can manufacture, repair, and use them, then they are our weapons. If we cannot manufacture, repair, and use them, then they are still the weapons of others. . . . In the end the way to avoid trouble is to manufacture, repair, and use weapons by ourselves. Only thus can we pacify the empire; only thus can we become the leading power in the world; only thus can we restore our original strength, redeem ourselves from former humiliations, and maintain the integrity of our vast territory so as to remain the greatest country on earth. [61a–62b]

[*Jiaobinlu kangyi, Zhiyangqi yi*, pp. 58b–63a —CT]

### ON THE ADOPTION OF WESTERN LEARNING

Western books on mathematics, mechanics, optics, light, and chemistry contain the best principles of the natural sciences. In the books on geography, the mountains, rivers, strategic points, customs, and native products of the hundred countries are fully listed. Most of this information is beyond the reach of the Chinese people. . . .

If we wish to use Western knowledge, we should establish official translation bureaus in Guangzhou and Shanghai. Brilliant students not over fifteen years of age should be selected from those areas to live and study in these schools on double allowances. Westerners should be appointed to teach them the spoken and written languages of the various nations, and famous Chinese teachers should be engaged to teach them classics, history, and other subjects. At the same time they should learn mathematics. (Note: All Western knowledge is derived from mathematics. . . . If we wish to adopt Western knowledge, it is but natural that we should learn mathematics). . . . China has many brilliant people. There must be some who can learn from the barbarians and surpass them. [67b–68a]

It is from learning that the principles of government are derived. In discussing good government, the great historian Sima Qian said (following Xunzi), "Take the latter-day kings as your models." This was because they were nearer in time; their customs had changed from the past and were more similar to the present; and their ideas were not so lofty as to be impracticable. It is my opinion that today we should also take the foreign nations as our examples. They live at the same time and in the same world with us; they have attained prosperity and power by their own efforts. Is it not fully clear that they are similar to us and that their methods can easily be put into practice? If we let Chinese ethics and Confucian teachings serve as the foundation, and let them be supplemented by the methods used by the various nations for the attainment of prosperity and power, would it not be the best of all solutions?

Moreover, during the past twenty years since the opening of trade, a great number of foreign chiefs have learned our written and spoken language, and the best of them can even read our classics and histories. They are generally able to speak on our dynastic regulations and civil administration, on our geography and the condition of our people. On the other hand, our officials from the governors down are completely ignorant of foreign countries. In comparison, should we not feel ashamed? The Chinese officials have to rely upon stupid and preposterous interpreters as their eyes and ears. The mildness or severity of the original statement, its sense of urgency or lack of insistence, may be lost through their tortuous interpretations. Thus frequently a small grudge may develop into a grave hostility. At present the most important political problem of the empire is to control the barbarians, yet the pivotal function is entrusted to such people. No wonder that we understand neither the foreigners nor ourselves and cannot distinguish fact from untruth. Whether in peace negotiations or in deliberating for war, we are unable to grasp the essentials. This is indeed the underlying trouble of our nation. [69a–70a]

[*Jiaobinlu kangyi, Cai xixue yi*, pp. 67b–70 — CT]

## Principle Versus Practicality?

One of the first projects of the Self-Strengtheners was to set up schools for the study of Western languages, sciences, and technologies, the first an interpreters school in Beijing in 1861, subsequently expanded to include mathematics and technology. This set off a debate (1867) in which the Self-Strengtheners' proposals were opposed on grounds of principle by Confucians at court, of whom a Mongol grand secretary, Woren, was the leader. For him Western technology was no substitute for classical humanistic learning and China would be corrupted by doctrines of expediency.

Mathematics, one of the six arts, should indeed be learned by scholars as indicated in the imperial decree, and it should not be considered an unworthy subject. But according to the viewpoint of your servant, astronomy and mathematics are of very little use. If these subjects are going to be taught by Westerners as regular studies, the damage will be great. . . . Your servant has learned that the way to establish a nation is to lay emphasis on rites and rightness, not on power and plotting. The fundamental effort lies in the minds of people, not in techniques. Now, if we seek trifling arts and respect barbarians as teachers . . . all that can be accomplished is the training of mathematicians. From ancient down to modern times, your servant has never heard of anyone who could use mathematics to raise the nation from a state of decline or to strengthen it in time of weakness. . . .

Since the conclusion of the peace, Christianity has been prevalent, and half of our ignorant people have been fooled by it. The only thing we can rely on is that our scholars should clearly explain to the people the Confucian tenets, which may be able to sustain the minds of the ignorant populace. Now if these brilliant and talented scholars, who have been trained by the nation and reserved for great future usefulness, have to change from their regular course of study to follow the barbarians, then the correct spirit will not be developed, and accordingly the evil spirit will become stronger. After several years it will end in nothing less than driving the multitudes of the Chinese people into allegiance to the barbarians.

## The Self-Strengtheners' Rebuttal, 1867

In response to Woren's challenge, the Self-Strengtheners at court countered that he had no practical way to deal with Western power and, moreover, that the pursuit of Western studies need not be at the expense of traditional ones.

Your ministers have examined the memorial of Woren: the principles he presents are very lofty and the opinion he maintains is very orthodox. Your ministers' point of view was also like that before they began to manage foreign affairs; and yet today they do not presume to insist on such ideas, because of actual difficulties that they cannot help. . . .

From the beginning of foreign relations to the present there have been twenty or thirty years. At first the officials inside and outside the capital did not grasp the crux of the matter, and whether they negotiated peace or discussed war, generally these were empty words without effect. . . . Therefore your ministers have pondered a long-term policy and discussed the situation thoroughly with all the provincial officials. Proposals to learn the written and spoken languages of foreign countries, the various methods of making machines, the training of troops with foreign guns, the dispatching of officials to travel in all countries, the investigation of their local customs and social conditions, and the establishment of six armies in the area of the capital in order to protect it — all these painstaking and special decisions represent nothing other than a struggle for self-strengthening. . . .

We too are afraid that the people who are learning these things will have no power of discrimination and are likely to be led astray by foreigners, as Woren fears. Therefore we have deliberated and decided that those who participate in the examinations must be persons from regular scholastic channels. It is indeed those students who have read widely and who understand right principles and have their minds set upon upright and grand purposes — and the present situation is just what causes the scholars and officials to feel pain in heart and head — who would certainly be able to lie on faggots and taste gall [i.e., nurse vengeance] in order to encourage each other vigorously to seek the actual achievement of self-strengthening. They are different from those who have vague, easygoing, or indifferent ideas.

Even though we run the risk of receiving the criticism of the empire, we will not try to avoid it. But the grand secretary [Woren] considers our action a hindrance. Certainly he should have some better plans. If he really has some marvelous plan that can control foreign countries and not let us be controlled by them, your ministers should certainly follow in the footsteps of the grand secretary, exhausting their mean abilities in careful discussions with him, in order to show our harmony and mutual help and to console your imperial anxiety. If he has no other plan than to use loyalty and sincerity as armor, and rites and rightness as a shield, and such similar phrases, and if he says that these words could accomplish diplomatic negotiations and be sufficient to control the life of our enemies, your ministers indeed do not presume to believe it.

[Adapted from Teng and Fairbank, *China's Response to the West*, pp. 76–79]

## ZENG GUOFAN AND LI HONGZHANG: ON SENDING YOUNG MEN ABROAD TO STUDY

Zeng Guofan (1811–1872) and his protégé Li Hongzhang (1823–1901) were, in the practical sphere, the outstanding exponents of "self-strengthening" during the latter half of the nineteenth century. Acclaimed as the conqueror of the Taipings, and long governor-general in central China, Zeng was also admired as a scholar in the classical tradition and a Confucian "gentleman" who exemplified the traditional virtues in government: industry, frugality, honesty, and integrity in office and loyalty to the dynasty. He was the type of "noble man" whose learning and personal character inspired the devotion of his subordinates and gave Confucians a confidence that such personal qualities could meet the challenge of the times. Intellectually an eclectic, Zeng minimized doctrinal differences and sought agreement on the ethical bases of action. His support of certain types of modernization for purposes of national defense also reflected a readiness to make compromises for the achievement of practical ends.

In this letter, submitted in March 1871 to the Zongli Yamen, a new but minor institution that handled foreign affairs, Zeng and Li emphasize not only China's practical need to learn from the West but also the preeminent practicality of the Westerners. They are convinced that Western methods can be mastered only through prolonged and intensive study abroad, and they propose sending a select group of young men for this purpose. In Japan at this time the top leaders were themselves visiting the West and preparing to reeducate a whole nation. The aims of Zeng and Li are much more circumscribed—to train an elite corps with a combination of classical Chinese and Western studies, carefully directed and controlled in the interests of the state. Yet even so modest a proposal met with strong opposition at court before it was put into effect in 1872.

Last autumn when I [Zeng] was at Tianjin, Governor Ding Richang frequently came to discuss with me proposals for the selection of intelligent youths to be sent to the schools of various Western countries to study military administration, shipping administration, infantry tactics, mathematics, manufacturing, and other subjects. We estimated that after more than ten years their training would have been completed and they could return to China so that other Chinese might learn thoroughly the superior techniques of the Westerners. Thus we could gradually plan for self-strengthening. . . . After Mr. Bin Chun and two other gentlemen, Zhigang and Sun Jiagu, had traveled in various countries at imperial command, they saw the essential aspects of conditions overseas, and they found that cartography, mathematics, astronomy, navigation, shipbuilding, and manufacturing are all closely related to military defense. It is the practice of foreign nations that those who have studied abroad and have learned some superior techniques are immediately invited upon their return by academic institutions to teach the various subjects and to develop their fields. Military administration and shipping are considered as important as the learning that deals with the mind and body, and nature and destiny of man. Now that the eyes of the people have been opened, if China wishes to adopt Western ideas and excel in Western methods, we should immediately select intelligent young men and send them to study in foreign countries. . . .

Some may say, "Arsenals have been established in Tianjin, Shanghai, and Fuzhou for shipbuilding and the manufacture of guns and ammunition. The Tongwen College [for foreign languages] has been established in Beijing for Manchu and Chinese youths to study under Western instructors. A language school has also been opened in Shanghai for the training of young students. It seems, therefore, that a beginning has been made in China and that there is no need for studying overseas." These critics, however, do not know that to establish arsenals for manufacturing and to open schools for instruction is just the beginning of our effort to rise again. To go to distant lands for study, to gather ideas for more advantageous use, can produce far-reaching and great results. Westerners seek knowledge for practical use. . . . If we Chinese wish to adopt their superior techniques and suddenly try to buy all their machines, not only will our resources be insufficient to do so but we will be unable to master the fundamental principles or to understand the complicated details of the techniques, unless we have actually seen and practiced them for a long time. . . .

We have heard that youths of Fujian, Guangdong, and Ningbo also occasionally have gone abroad to study, but they merely attempted to gain a superficial knowledge of foreign written and spoken languages in order to do business with the foreigners for the purpose of making a living. In our plan, we must be doubly careful at the beginning of selection. The students who are to be taken to foreign countries will all be under the control of the commissioners. Specializing in different fields, they will earnestly seek for mastery of their subjects. There will be interpreters, and instructors to teach them Chinese learning from time to time, so that they will learn the great principles for the establishment of character, in the hope of becoming men with abilities of use to us.

[*Zeng Wenzhong gong quanji, Yishu hangao* 1:19b–21b — CT]

## XUE FUCHENG: ON REFORM

A onetime secretary and adviser to both Zeng Guofan and Li Hongzhang, Xue Fucheng (1838–1894) achieved no high rank or position in the bureaucracy (not having competed in the examinations for the higher civil service degrees). He did, however, become an influential advocate of reform through the circulation of his essays and memorials in official circles and, besides assisting in the negotiation of the Chefoo Convention (1876), helped to draft plans for a new Chinese navy.

This excerpt is taken from Xue's *Suggestions on Foreign Affairs* (*Chouyang chuyi*), which was submitted to Li in 1879 and forwarded by him to the Zongli Yamen. Xue argues for reform on the ground that change is inevitable and nothing new to Chinese history. But if he is tempted to accept the idea of progress as a law of history, there is no indication of it here. Rather, his premise is the thoroughly traditional one of cyclical or pulsatory change at calculable intervals, which may be for good or ill but in any case must be coped with, as indeed even the sage kings had to cope with it. A great change in circumstances, therefore, calls for a great change in methods (*fa*, which can also be understood as "laws" or "institutions").

Xue nevertheless contends that changes in method do not mean abandonment of the "immutable" Way of the sages. Indeed, it is the use of new methods that will preserve that Way inviolate. Thus a dichotomy is established between ends and means. Here the means Xue has in mind adopting is "the study of machines and mathematics." Consequently the dichotomy is between the Way and "instruments" (*fa*, as in the sense of methods). How far he would go toward changing *fa* in the sense of basic institutions is left unclear.

It is the Way of Heaven that within several hundred years there are small changes and within several thousand years great changes. . . . In several thousand years [under the early sage kings] there was change from a primitive world to a civilized world. From the age of the sage kings through the Three Dynasties there were most truly peace and order. Then the First Emperor of the Qin swallowed up the feudal states, abolished the enfeoffed lords, broke up the well-fields, and destroyed the laws of the early kings. Thus it was two thousand years from the time of [the sage kings] Yao and Shun that the feudal world was changed into a world of [centrally administered] prefectures and districts. . . . As we come down to the present, the European states suddenly rise up and assert themselves overseas because of their knowledge of machinery and mathematics. . . . In ninety thousand *li* around the globe there is no place where they do not send their envoys and establish trade relations. Confronted with this situation, even Yao and Shun would not have been able to close the doors and rule the empire in isolation. And this likewise is now two thousand years from the time of Qin and Han. Thus there has been a change from a world in which the Chinese and barbarians were isolated from each other to a world in which China and foreign countries are in close contact. . . . When change in the world is small, the laws governing the world will accordingly undergo small change; when change in the world is great, the laws will accordingly undergo great change. [46B]

Sometimes in the succession of one sage to another there cannot but be changes in the outward forms of government. Sometimes when a sage has to deal with the world, sooner or later there must be changes made. . . . Now there is rapid change in the world. It is my opinion that with regard to the immutable Way we should change the present so as to restore the past [the Way of the sages]; but with regard to changeable laws, we should change the past system to meet present needs. Alas! If we do not examine the differences between the two situations, past and present, and think in terms of practicability, how can we remedy the defects? [47a]

Western nations rely on intelligence and energy to compete with one another. To come abreast of them, China should plan to promote commerce and open mines; unless we change, the Westerners will be rich and we poor. We should excel in technology and the manufacture of machinery; unless we change, they will be skillful and we clumsy. Steamships, trains, and the telegraph should be adopted; unless we change the Westerners will be quick and we slow. . . . Unless we change, the Westerners will cooperate with each other and we shall stand isolated; they will be strong and we shall be weak. [47b]

Some may ask: "If such a great nation as China imitates the Westerners, would it not be using barbarian ways to change China?" Not so. For while in clothing, language, and customs China is different from foreign countries, the utilization of the forces of nature for the benefit of the people is the same in China as in foreign countries. The Western people happen to be the first in adopting this new way of life, but how can we say that they alone should monopolize the secrets of nature? And how do we know that a few decades or a hundred years later China may not surpass them? . . . Now if we really take over the Westerners' knowledge of machinery and mathematics in order to protect the Way of our sage kings Yao and Shun, Yu and Tang, Wen and Wu, and the Duke of Zhou and Confucius, and so make the Westerners not dare to despise China, I know that if they were alive today, the sages would engage themselves in the same tasks, and their Way would also be gradually spread to the eight bounds of the earth. That is what we call using the ways of China to change the barbarians.

Some may also say, "In making changes one should aim to surpass others and not pursue them. Now the Western methods are superior, and we imitate them; if we follow others helplessly, by what means then are we to surpass them?" This, too, is not so. If we wish to surpass others, it is necessary to know all their methods before we can change; but after we have changed, we may be able to surpass them. We cannot expect to surpass others merely by sitting upright in a dignified attitude. . . . Moreover, they have concentrated the ability and energy of several million people, have spent millions of dollars, and have gone through prolonged years and generations before they acquired their knowledge. If we want to excel them, is it really possible to do so in one morning or is it not impossible? . . . Mathematics began in China,[1] and yet it has reached its highest development in Western countries. If we compare the ability and wisdom of the Chinese with those of the Westerners, there is no reason to think that we should be unable to surpass them. It all depends on how we exert ourselves.

Alas! There are endless changes in the world, and so there are endless variations in the sages' way of meeting these changes. To be born in the present age but to hold fast to ancient methods is to be like one who in the age of Shen nong [when people had learned how to cook] still ate raw meat and drank blood. . . . Such a one would say, "I am following the methods of the ancient sages." But it is hardly possible that he should not become exhausted and fall. Moreover, the laws [or methods] that ought to be changed today can still [in their new form] embody the essence of the laws of the ancient sages. [48a–49a]

[*Chouyang chuyi*, in *Yongan quanji, ce* 12, 46b–49a — CT]

### ZHANG ZHIDONG: *EXHORTATION TO LEARN*

Zhang Zhidong (1837–1909) was one of the leading figures in the empire during the last days of the Manchus. A brilliant scholar and official, widely esteemed for his personal integrity and patriotism, he was an early supporter of reform and as a provincial administrator promoted many industrial, railway, educational, and cultural projects. When his *Exhortation to Learn* (*Quanxue pian*) was published in 1898, it was hailed by the reformers then in power and given official distribution by the emperor.

Basically Zhang was a moderate who coupled gradual reform with a stout adherence to Neo-Confucianism, defense of monarchical institutions, and loyalty to the dynasty. Avoiding extremes, he backed away from the radical measures of Kang Youwei (see pp. 260–273), on the one hand, and from the reactionary policies that led to the Boxer catastrophe in 1900, on the other. A combination of moderation and shrewdness thus helped him survive politically to play an influential role at court in the first decade of the new century. During this period he was instrumental both in the enactment of educational and civil service reforms (including abolition of the famous eight-legged essay) and in the attempt to revive Confucianism as a state cult.

Zhang's position is summed up in the catch-phrase "Chinese learning for substance, Western learning for function" (*Zhongxue wei ti, xixue wei yong*). The terms *substance* (*ti*) and *function* (*yong*) Zhang drew from the philosophical lexicon of Song metaphysics, in which they stood for the ontological and functional aspects of the same reality. Zhang, following the example of earlier reformers who distinguished between the Chinese "Way" (or Chinese moral "principles") and Western instruments, used *substance* in reference to traditional Chinese values and *function* (i.e., utility,

---

1. A widely held view, of which Ruan Yuan was a leading exponent.

practical application) in reference to the Western methods by which China and its traditional way of life were to be defended in the modern world. In this new formulation *substance* and *function* bore no intrinsic relationship to one another as they had philosophically for Zhu Xi, but they were no more incompatible than was Hu Yuan's combining of classical studies and more specialized, technical studies in his educational curriculum (see chapter 19), of which the Chengs and Zhu approved.

Zhang, who was not naive about the lengths to which Westernization would go (he insisted, for instance, that Western methods of administration were as essential as Western technology) nor wholly mistaken about the difficulties of establishing political democracy in China, may have underestimated the frictions that modernization would create within the new order and the extent to which his liberal reforms would increasingly generate revolutionary pressures. This was especially true among the educated elite, whose common bond was now no longer classical learning but Western-style education. Two years after the death of this venerable statesman in October 1909, the Manchu dynasty itself collapsed.

The crisis of China today has no parallel either in the Spring and Autumn period [i.e., the time of Confucius] or in all the dynasties from the Qin and Han down through the Yuan and Ming. . . . Our imperial court has shown the utmost concern over the problem, living in anxiety and worry. It is ready to make changes and to provide special opportunities for able ministers and generals. New schools are to be established and special examinations are to be held. All over the land men of serious purpose and sincere dedication have responded with enthusiasm and vigor. Those who seek to remedy the present situation talk of new learning; those who fear lest its acceptance should destroy the true Way hold fast to the teachings of the ancients. Both groups are unable to strike the mean. The conservatives resemble those who give up all eating because they have difficulty in swallowing, while the progressives are like a flock of sheep who have arrived at a road of many forks and do not know where to turn. The former do not know how to accommodate to special circumstances; the latter are ignorant of what is fundamental. Not knowing how to accommodate to special circumstances, the conservatives have no way to confront the enemy and deal with the crisis; not knowing the fundamental, the innovators look with contempt upon the teachings of the sages. Thus those who hold fast to the old order of things despise more and more the innovators, and the latter in turn violently detest the conservatives. As the two groups are engaged in mutual recriminations, impostors and adventurers who do not hesitate to resort to falsification and distortion pour out their theories to confuse the people. Consequently students are in doubt as to which course to pursue, while perverse opinions spread all over the country. [202:1a–b]

## United Hearts

I have learned of three things that are necessary for saving China in the present crisis. The first is to maintain the state. The second is to preserve the doctrine of Confucius. And the third is to protect the Chinese race. These three are inseparably related. We must protect the state, the doctrine, and the race with one heart, and this is what we mean by united hearts.

In order to protect the race we must first preserve the doctrine, and before the doctrine can be preserved, we must preserve the state and the race. How is the race to be preserved? If we have knowledge, it will be preserved; and by knowledge we mean the doctrine. How is the doctrine to be maintained? It is to be maintained by strength, and strength lies in armies. Thus, if the empire has no power and prestige, the doctrine will not be followed; and if the empire does not prosper, the Chinese race will not be respected. [202:2b–3a]

### The Three Mainstays or Bonds

Here Zhang's understanding of the Three Mainstays (*San gang*) or Bonds (i.e., strictly hierarchical relations) reflects the increasingly authoritarian view of this concept in late Imperial China, somewhat in contrast to the Han dynasty versions (see chapter 10), which emphasized complementarity more than mere subordination. These formulations had no canonical status in the Five Classics or Four Books but were simply accretions to later Confucian tradition in the imperial age.

The minister is bound to the sovereign, the child is bound to the parent, and the wife is bound to the husband. . . . What makes a sage a sage, what makes China China, is just this set of bonds. Thus, if we recognize the bond of minister to sovereign, the theory of people's rights cannot stand. If we recognize the bond of child to parent, then the theory that father and son are amenable to the same punishment and that funeral and sacrificial ceremonies should be abolished cannot stand. If we recognize the bond of wife to husband, then the theory of equal rights for men and women cannot stand. [202:13a–b]

Our sage represented the highest ideal of human relationships. He established in detail and with clarity rules of ritual decorum based on human feelings. Although Westerners have such rules only in abbreviated form, still foreigners have never abandoned the idea of decorum. For the norm of Heaven and the nature of man are about the same in China and in foreign countries. Without these rules of decorum no ruler could ever govern a state, and no teacher could ever establish his doctrine. [202:14b]

### Rectifying Political Rights

Nowadays scholars who become vexed with the present order of things are angry at the foreigners for cheating and oppressing us, at the generals for being unable to fight, at the ministers for being unwilling to reform, at the educational authorities for not establishing modern schools, and at the various officials for not seeking to promote industry and commerce. They therefore advocate the theory of people's rights in order to get the people to unite and exert themselves. Alas, where did they find those words that would lead to disorder!

The theory of people's rights will bring us not a particle of good but a hundred evils. Are we going to establish a parliament? Among Chinese scholar-officials and among the people there are still many today who are obstinate and uneducated. They understand nothing about the general situation of the world, and they are ignorant of the affairs of state. They have never heard of important developments concerning the schools, political systems, military training, and manufacture of machinery. Suppose the confused and tumultuous people are assembled in one house, with one sensible man there out of a hundred who are witless, babbling aimlessly, and talking as if in a dream — what use would it be? Moreover, in foreign countries the matter of revenue is mainly handled by the lower house, while other matters of legislation are taken care of by the upper house. To be a member of parliament the candidate must possess a fairly good income. Nowadays Chinese merchants rarely have much capital, and the Chinese people are lacking in long-range vision. If any important proposal for raising funds comes up for discussion, they will make excuses and keep silent; so their discussion is no different from nondiscussion. . . . This is the first reason why a parliament is of no use. . . .

At present China is indeed not imposing or powerful, but the people still get along well with their daily work, thanks to the dynastic institutions that hold them together. Once the theory of people's rights is adopted, foolish people will certainly be delighted, rebels will strike, order will not be maintained, and great disturbances will arise on all sides. Even those who advocate the theory of people's rights will not be able to live safely themselves. Furthermore, as the towns will be plundered and the Christian churches burned, I am afraid the foreigners, under the pretext of protecting [their nationals and interests], will send troops and warships to penetrate deeply and occupy our territories. The whole country will then be given to others without a fight. Thus the theory of people's rights is just what our enemies would like to hear spread about. [202:23a–24a]

Recently those who have picked up some Western theories have gone so far as to say that everybody has the right to be his own master. This is even more absurd. This phrase is derived from the foreign books of religion. It means that God bestows upon man his nature and soul and that every person has wisdom and intelligence that enable him to do useful work. When the translators interpret it to mean that every person has the right to be his own master, they indeed make a great mistake.

Western countries, whether they are monarchies, republics, or constitutional monarchies, all have a government, and a government has laws. Officials have administrative laws, soldiers have military laws, workers have labor laws, and merchants have commercial laws. The lawyers learn them; the judges administer them. Neither the ruler nor the people can violate the law. What the executive recommends can be debated by the parliament, but what the parliament decides can be vetoed by the throne. Thus it may be said that nobody is his own master. [202:24b–25a]

## Following the Proper Order

If we wish to make China strong and preserve Chinese learning, we must promote Western learning. But unless we first use Chinese learning to consolidate the foundation and to give our purpose a right direction, the strong will become rebellious leaders and the weak, slaves. The consequence will be worse than not being versed in Western learning. . . .

Scholars today should master the classics in order to understand the purpose of our early sages and teachers in establishing our doctrine. They must study history in order to know the succession of peace and disorder in our history and the customs of the land, read the philosophers and literary collections in order to become familiar with Chinese scholarship and fine writing. After this they can select and utilize the Western learning that can make up for our shortcomings and adopt those Western governmental methods that can cure our illness. In this way, China will derive benefit from Western learning without incurring any danger. [202:27a–b]

## [On Reform]

It is the human relationships and moral principles that are immutable, but not legal systems; the Way of the sage, not instruments; the discipline of the Mind-and-heart, not technology.

Laws and institutions are that with which we meet changing situations; they therefore need not all be the same. The Way is that upon which we establish the foundation; it therefore must be uniform. . . . What we call the basis of the Way consists of the Three Bonds and the four Cardinal Virtues.[2] If these are abandoned, great disorder will occur even before the new laws can be put into effect. But as long as they are preserved, even Confucius and Mencius, if they were to come back to life, could hardly condemn the reforms. [203:19b, 22a]

If we do not change our habits, we cannot change our methods (*fa*); and if we cannot change our methods, we cannot change our instruments. . . . In Chinese learning the inquiry into antiquity is not important; what is important is knowledge of practical use. There are also different branches of Western learning; Western technology is not important; what is important is Western administration. [202:iiia]

There are five important factors in the administration of the new schools.

---

2. Decorum, rightness, integrity, sense of shame.

First, both the old and the new must be studied. By the old we mean the Four Books, the Five Classics, Chinese history, government, and geography; by the new we mean Western administration, Western technology, and Western history. The old learning is to be the substance; the new learning is to be for application [function]. Neither one should be neglected. Second, both administration and technology should be studied. Education, geography, budgeting, taxes, military preparations, laws and regulations, industry and commerce, belong to the category of Western administration. Mathematics, drawing, mining, medicine, acoustics, optics, chemistry, and electricity belong to the category of Western technology. [203:9b]

> [*Quanxue pian*, in *Zhang Wenxiang gong quanji, ce* 202:ia–b, iiia–b,
> 2b–3a, 13a–14b, 23a–25a, 27a–b; 203:9b, 19b, 22a  — CT]

# Chapter 31

## RADICAL REFORM AT THE END OF THE QING

When we attempt to assess the aims and accomplishments of Chinese reformers in the 1870s and 1880s, the comparison to Meiji Japan is almost inevitable. In aims there is a strong general resemblance between the two; in the scope and effectiveness of their reforms a striking difference. Where the Chinese Self-Strengtheners sought to preserve the Confucian Way through the adoption of Western techniques, Japanese modernizers talked of combining "Eastern ethics and Western science" or spoke of preserving their distinctive "national polity" (*kokutai*) in the midst of an intense program of modernization. Yet, given this general similarity of aims, the process of change in Japan went further and faster than in China, and to a very different result. In the one case there was rapid industrialization, political centralization, educational reform, and social change — all of these involving a much fuller participation of the Japanese people in the national effort, contributing to a degree of unity and strength unprecedented in Japanese history. In China by the 1890s it was evident not only that the Self-Strengtheners had failed to achieve such an effective national unity and concerted action, but also that the very strength they found in local and regional initiatives tended to detract from central leadership and control. The imperial structure was there, as well as nominal allegiance to it, but its effective outreach was limited.

If to Wang Tao in the first selection below, a great nemesis of reform lay in the "multiplicity of governmental regulations and endless number of directives," his complaint represented not only a recognition that bureaucratic red tape left little room for reform but at the same time, paradoxically, that unless the court exercised its authority in the direction of reform, local initiatives, lacking such leadership from above, could not contribute to any overall result.

Under these circumstances, reformers might propose change for the empire as a whole, but individual Self-Strengtheners in positions of limited authority could hardly plan for a truly national program of reform. Within their own spheres of jurisdiction or influence they might inaugurate projects for the modernizing of their personal armies, the manufacturing of arms, the building of ships, the promoting of business, the opening of schools for technical and language training, as well as for the improvement of the more traditional functions of government in China; yet the tendency was for even these worthwhile ventures to take on a strongly bureaucratic character — to become part of an official sub-empire — without, however, enjoying any of the benefits of centralized planning or coordination. The net result is typified by the utter failure of Li Hongzhang's new army and navy, owing to "squeeze," corruption, and inefficiency in the supply system, when put to the test by the Japanese in the war of 1894–1895. It was this failure that led directly to demands for more drastic change.

China's humiliating defeat in the Sino-Japanese War and the seeming danger of her imminent partition by the foreign powers would have been cause enough for an outcry of alarm and protest. To these factors was added a growing sense of dissatisfaction and frustration among the younger generation of students, who by now had been exposed to reformist writings and had their eyes opened to the outside world. This group was by no means large. The educated class had always constituted a small minority of Chinese, and those affected by new ideas represented a still smaller fraction. Thus, rather than their numbers, it was their role as recruits or members of the bureaucratic elite that gave them influence. Significantly, among the leaders of the reform group were several from the Guangdong region, where, like Hong Xiuquan before them and Sun Yat-sen after, they were stimulated by close contact with the West in Hong Kong and Guangzhou. Increasingly, toward the end of the century, these young men were being challenged and inspired by the brilliant journalism of a writer like Wang Tao. Youthful impressions, once wholly formed by the Confucian classics and native tradition, were now being formed also by the translations of men like Yan Fu (1853–1921), who made available in Chinese the works of Thomas Huxley, John Stuart Mill, Herbert Spencer, and Adam Smith.

## WANG TAO ON REFORM

Wang Tao (1828–1897) represents a new type of reformer on the Chinese scene. In contrast to the great reformers of the past (e.g., Wang Mang, Wang Anshi) who were scholar-officials, and in contrast also to his contemporaries Feng Guifen and Xue Fucheng, who wrote as officials and worked closely with statesmen like Zeng Guofan and Li Hongzhang, Wang Tao was an independent scholar and journalist. Sometimes, indeed, he is referred to as "the father of Chinese journalism." His work was done mainly in the ports of Hong Kong and Shanghai, under foreign protection and in close touch with foreigners. For years he assisted the eminent British sinologue James Legge in his translations from the Chinese classics, and with Legge's help he visited England and Western Europe, observing and writing on developments there. Later, too, Wang visited Japan, where he was well received as a scholar and reformer. When finally he settled down to a career as a journalist, he did so as a man with foreign contacts, a wide knowledge of the outside world, and the kind of freedom to express himself that had been unknown in the past — when not only the right to criticize but even the means (a public press) and the audience (an influential public opinion) were lacking.

The following is taken from an essay of Wang's written about 1870, which reiterates many of the earlier reformers' basic points but carries them even further. There is the argument from cyclical change to the need for adapting to the current situation. There is the assertion that Confucius himself would have advocated change under such circumstances. There is the distinction between the Way of the sages, which must be preserved, and the instruments (weapons, methods) of the West, which should be adopted for its defense. At the same time, Wang insists that change must go deeper and further than mere imitation of the West in externals and suggests, however vaguely, that a thorough renovation of society is necessary. Though his specific recommendations here relate primarily to education, eventually he advocated basic governmental change as well. Consequently the ambiguity in Wang's use of the term *bianfa* for "reform" is even more pronounced than in Xue Fucheng's essay. Though he speaks of adopting from the West only "instruments," he intends that change should extend not only to technology ("methods") but to *fa* in the sense of "basic institutions." Wang therefore presages, intellectually, the transition from reformism conceived in terms of immediate utility to a more radical view of institutional change. It is still, however, change to be directed from the top down, to be initiated by the imperial court.

The following excerpt is preceded by a discussion of previous changes in Chinese history that we have already seen echoed by Xue. Here, however, Wang is consciously reexamining Chinese history to refute the assertion of "Western scholars that China has gone unchanged for 5,000 years." Contending in effect, that China's stagnation was a comparatively recent development, he then goes on to deal with the present situation.

I know that within a hundred years China will adopt all Western methods and excel in them. For though both are vessels, a sailboat differs in speed from a steamship; though both are vehicles, a horse-drawn carriage cannot cover the same distance as a locomotive train. Among weapons, the power of the bow and arrow, sword and spear, cannot be compared with that of firearms; and among firearms, the old types do not have the same effect as the new. Although it be the same piece of work, there is a difference in the ease with which it can be done by machine and by human labor. When new methods do not exist, people will not think of changes; but when there are new instruments, to copy them is certainly possible. Even if the Westerners should give no guidance, the Chinese must surely exert themselves to the utmost of their ingenuity and resources on these things.

However, these are all instruments; they are not the Way, and they cannot be called the basis for governing the state and pacifying the world. The Way of Confucius is the Human Way. As long as humankind exists, the Way will remain unchanged. The Three Mainstays [Bonds] and the Five Moral Relations began with the birth of the human race. When one fulfills one's duty as a human being, one need have no regrets in life. On this is based the teaching of the sages. [1:11a]

I have said before that after a few hundred years the Way will achieve a grand unity. As Heaven has unified the south, north, east, and west under one sky, it will harmonize the various teachings of the world and bring them back to the same source. . . .

Alas! People all understand the past, but they are ignorant of the future. Only scholars whose thoughts run deep and far can grasp the trends. As the mind of Heaven changes above, so do human affairs below. Heaven opens the minds of the Westerners and bestows upon them intelligence and wisdom. Their techniques and skills develop without bound. They sail eastward and gather in China. This constitutes an unprecedented situation in history, and a tremendous change in the world. The foreign nations come from afar with their superior techniques, contemptuous of us in our deficiencies. They show off their prowess and indulge in insults and oppression; they also fight among themselves. Under these circumstances, how can we not think of making changes? Thus what makes it most difficult for us not to change is the mind of Heaven, and what compels us unavoidably to change is the doings of men. [1:11b–12a]

If China does not make any change at this time, how can it be on a par with the great nations of Europe and compare with them in power and strength? Nevertheless, the path of reform is beset with difficulties. What the Western countries have today is regarded as of no worth by those who arrogantly refuse to pay attention. Their argument is that we should use our own laws to govern the empire, for that is the Way of our sages. They do not know that the Way of the sages is valued only because it can make proper accommodations according to the times. If Confucius lived today, we may be certain that he would not cling to antiquity and oppose making changes. . . .

But how is this to be done? First, the method of recruiting civil servants should be changed. The examination essays, coming down to the present, have gone from bad to worse and should be discarded. And yet we are still using them to select civil servants. . . .

Second, the method of training soldiers should be changed. Now our army units and naval forces have only names registered on books, but no actual persons enrolled. The authorities consider our troops unreliable, and so they recruit militia who, however, can be assembled but cannot be disbanded. . . . The arms of the Manchu banners and the ships of the naval forces should all be changed. . . . If they continue to hold on to their old ways and make no plans for change, it may be called "using untrained people to fight,"[1] which is no different from driving them to their deaths. . . .

Third, the empty show of our schools should be changed. Now district directors of schools are installed, one person for a small town and two for a large city. It is a sheer waste of government funds, for they have nothing to do. The type of man in such posts is usually degenerate, incompetent, senile, and with little sense of shame. [1:12a–14a]

Fourth, the complex and multifarious laws and regulations should be changed. . . . The government should reduce the mass of regulations and cut down on the number of directives; it should be sincere and fair and treat the people with frankness and justice. . . .

After the above four changes have been made, Western methods could be used together with others. But the most important point is that the government above should exercise its power to change customs and mores, while the people below should be gradually absorbed into the new environment and adjusted to it without their knowing it. This reform should extend to all things — from trunk to branch, from inside to outside, from great to small — and not merely to Western methods. . . . [1:14b]

The advantage of guns lies in the techniques of discharging them; that of ships in the ability to navigate them. The weapons we use in battle must be effective, but the handling of effective weapons depends upon people. . . . Yet those regarded as able men have not necessarily been able, and those regarded as competent have not necessarily been competent. They are merely mediocrities who accomplish something through the aid of others. Therefore, the urgent task of our nation today lies primarily in the governance of the people, and next in the training of soldiers. And in these two the essential point is to gather men of abilities. Indeed, superficial imitation in concrete things is not so good as arousing intellectual curiosity. The forges and hammers of the factories cannot be compared with the apparatus of people's minds. [1:15a–b]

[*Bianfa*, in *Taoyuan wenlu waibian* 1:11a–15b — CT]

## YAN FU ON EVOLUTION AND PROGRESS

Yan Fu (1854–1921) was best known as an interpreter of Western liberal thought at the end of the Qing dynasty. His translations, which bent the originals to his

---

1. *Mencius* 4B:8.

own reformist agenda, included Thomas Henry Huxley's *Evolution and Ethics* (1898), Adam Smith's *Wealth of Nations* (1901–1902), Herbert Spencer's *A Study of Sociology* (1903), John Stuart Mill's *On Liberty* (1903), and Montesquieu's *Spirit of the Laws* (1909).

Having received a classical education until age twelve, when his father died, Yan Fu was reduced by his family's impoverishment to the pursuit of further learning on a stipend at the Fuzhou Arsenal School of Navigation. There he acquired English and developed a strong admiration for the scientific rigor of the technical curriculum. In 1877 he was sent to England for two years' further study, and there his quest for the basis of Western military power shifted from technology to politics, economics, and culture. He enthusiastically embraced Herbert Spencer's social Darwinism and found in it the key to the difference between Victorian England — the epitome of Western civilization — and China.

Returning to China, Yan failed repeatedly to pass the traditional examinations and seemed to be stuck in the position of superintendent of the Beiyang Naval School. After 1905 he rose to a number of advisory and consulting positions, and then in 1911 to the Naval General Staff, but the influence of his publications on currents of thought remained greater than his influence in government. His career as publicist had begun in the immediate aftermath of the disastrous Sino-Japanese War (1894–1895). From 1895 to 1897, amid the flood of reform writings that began to inform educated Chinese about the realities of the modern world, Yan published four powerful essays, including one translated in part here, introducing his new understanding of the world and China's perilous position in it. His preoccupation with national strength and survival and his embrace of Western learning and institutions as a means to achieve them both influenced and mirrored the tide of emerging Chinese nationalism. In one of the early essays, "Refutation of Han Yu,"[2] Yan Fu attacked the power of Chinese emperors as a kind of booty acquired by theft and asserted that an emperor truly concerned to advance the country would allow his people the freedom to do as they pleased so long as they did not harm their fellow citizens. Elsewhere, he pointed out that modern science had discredited the monarchy's claims to natural legitimacy. His condemnation of the irrationality, exploitation, and paternalism of the imperial institution did not, however, lead to political radicalism. Rather, his sense that China's survival and progress would require a profound transformation of her people's ingrained habits and values inclined him to reject political revolution as a remedy. A political upheaval, he believed, would only hinder the real task. Indeed, after the Revolution of 1911, Yan Fu became deeply troubled by the chaos into which China fell. Advocating monarchical government under strongman Yuan Shikai as the only way to preserve minimal order, he also called for the establishment of Confucianism as a state religion. Further disillusioned by the destructiveness

2. See Han Yu's idealization of the ruler, ch. 18.

of World War I in Europe, he lost faith in the entire project of modernization and rejected the whole New Culture Movement in the May 4 period (see chapter 33).


ON STRENGTH

Yan's most important influence on Chinese thinking at the turn of the century was his view of material progress as driven by Darwinian struggle, especially by competition among nations, which, following Spencer, he conceived as large-scale organisms. Such a conception of cosmic struggle differed radically from the idealistic, universalistic, harmony-oriented tradition of the Chinese elite, whose ideal lay in the past, not the future. In this, his new vision, at once frightening and exhilarating, Yan contrasted the pragmatic dynamism of Western society to the stagnation and formalism of China — a contrast quickly echoed in the widely popular reform writings of Liang Qichao and his colleagues, and later in the New Culture iconoclasm of Chen Duxiu. Yan's appreciation of Western progress was deeply colored by his belief, shared by reformers and revolutionaries alike, that liberty was the factor most responsible for Western strength and progress.

Such was the message of his essay "On Strength," originally published in an unfinished, serialized version in the newspaper *Zhibao* in 1895. A revised version appeared subsequently in 1901, in a collection of Yan's writings, and it seems to have been republished at least five times by 1915. The translation below is based on this later version, which had a wider circulation than the first and added a more extensive analysis of the citizens' strengths and virtues, as well as more concrete recommendations for reform.


Darwin is an English biologist. Heir to his family's scholarly traditions, he traveled around the world as a young man, amassing a rich collection of rare and curious plants and animals. After several decades' exhaustive and subtle reflection upon them, he wrote *The Origin of Species*. Since the publication of this book, of which nearly every household in Europe and America now has a copy, there has been a tremendous change in the scholarship, politics, and religion of the West. The claim that the revolution in outlook and intellectual orientation occasioned by Darwin's book exceeds that of Newtonian astronomy is hardly an empty one.

His book says that for all their diversity, the species originated from a single source and that their differences developed slowly, for the most part in connection with changes in the environment and an abiding biological tendency toward incremental differentiation. Eventually divergence from the remote source led to vast and irreversible differences, but these were brought about by natural processes in later ages and were not inherent in life at its origins.

Two chapters of the book are particularly noteworthy. . . . One is called

"Competition" and the other, "Natural Selection." "Competition" refers to the struggle of things to survive, and "Natural Selection" is the retention of the fit. The idea is that people and things exist in profusion, surviving on what the natural environment provides, but when they encounter others, peoples and things struggle over the means of survival. At first species struggled with species, and when they advanced somewhat, one group (*jun*) struggled with another. The weaker regularly became the prey of the stronger, and the more stupid were dominated by the more intelligent. Those who survived to perpetuate their kind were inevitably the strong and ruthless, the quick and clever, as well as those best adapted to the times and the natural human circumstances. This kind of struggle is not necessarily a matter of slaughter by fang and claw. Those accustomed to repose when forced to labor, or those familiar with mountains when forced to dwell in a marsh will, in competition with those accustomed to labor in marshes, die out in a few generations. Such is the competition among things. . . .

So it is with animals and plants and likewise with humans. Humankind is indeed a kind of animal. Encompassing all living things, this is the general idea of Darwin's thesis. . . .

Spencer, likewise an Englishman, is a contemporary of Darwin, and his book, which appeared earlier than Darwin's *Origin of Species*, adopts the evolutionary methodology to give a general account of morality and politics. He calls his field of study "sociology." It is the ability to form societies, in terms of which Xunzi explains the superiority of man to animals, that gives rise to the term *sociology*. The various ways in which people contribute to each other's lives and nourishment, easing their tasks and coordinating their efforts, ultimately developing into the major institutions of law, government, rites, and music, all arise from this ability to form societies. And now, the latest principles and techniques of science are employed further to develop personal cultivation, the regulation of society, the governance of the state, and the ordering of the world. His command of [scholarship on] the peoples of the five continents, from savages in their wilderness to respectable civilized states, gives him a masterful and exhaustive comparative perspective, and as the causes of the prosperity or debility, strength and weakness of particular states, and the reasons for the health or disarray of the people's morale, he addresses these questions over and over. . . . His thesis is fully presented in his first book, called *First Principles*, in which he scrutinizes all the life-forms in the universe to uncover the principles that encompass them all, from their beginnings in primordial matter to all their manifold manifestations. He then takes up the principles of biology and psychology to join them in the study of society. It is truly a masterpiece. . . .

In its constitution, the structure and functions of a social body are no different from those of an animal's body; despite the difference in size, there is a coordination of the faculties, so that if we understand how life is maintained in our bodies we can understand how societies can exist; if we understand longevity in individuals, we can understand how the vitality of a state can endure. Within the individual, body and spirit support each other. Within a society, power and virtue complement each other. The individual values his freedom, the state values its autonomy. The similarity of life-forms to societies consists precisely in the fact that both are conscious organisms. Thus all learning converges on sociology and only when sociology is understood can political order and chaos, prosperity and debility, be understood, and personal cultivation, the regulation of society, the governance of the state, and the ordering of the world be effective. . . .

Now there are three essential elements in sustaining the life of the people, and their vigor and survival depend on them. The first is vitality and physical strength, the second, intellectual capacities, the third, virtue and ethics. Hence Western students of history and government always evaluate races in terms of the people's strength, intelligence, and virtue. Without all three, the people's livelihood will not be abundant, and without all three, a country will not be able to assert itself. To the contrary, if a people is dispirited and stupid, each pursuing private ends, then the society will disintegrate, and when a society in disintegration encounters an aggressive, intelligent, patriotic people, it will be dominated at best, and at worst, exterminated, and not necessarily by force of arms and slaughter. . . . Hence Western students of culture and government recognize that self-preservation is the individual organism's highest priority, and preservation of the species the second, but hold that when the two are compared, the individual life should be sacrificed for the preservation of the species. He who follows this path is regarded as a martyr and a hero. And in the realm of laws and decrees, Western students' overall criterion is the people's strength, intelligence, and virtue. Everything that promotes these three is vigorously implemented, and everything that diminishes them is to be abolished. . . .

Months and years slip by, and with rapacious neighbors all around, I fear that we will be too late, that we will follow upon Poland and India, providing an example of Darwin's [elimination] before we have been able to implement Spencer's methods. . . . Alas, our individual lives are not worth the worry, but what of our descendants, and the 400,000,000 of our race? . . .

[Against those who argue that China has survived conquest by alien races before,] the Manchus, Mongols, and Han today are all of the yellow race. . . . Hence China since antiquity has been under rulers of one race and has never fallen under the domination of another. . . . [Moreover, such a view] misunderstands the two reasons for the comparative strengths of races: there is expansive, aggressive strength, and there is the strength of virtue, intellect, and skill. . . . Those who excelled in raw power were herdsmen and hunters. The rulers and people of those countries were close as members of a family, sharing their abundance and facing peril together. Their rules of communal life were few and simple, they rode and shot from horseback, gathering and dispersing . . .

thus the people were fond of war and scorned death. If a strong man organized and led them, their power could dominate the world, but although dominant, they could not go on to change it. . . . A country that excels in civilization plants, weaves, and dwells in cities. It governs with rituals, music, and penalties, and has a learning promoted by examinations and schools. . . . Hence the people delight in life and respect regulations. Those who govern by using this way correctly can easily maintain peace and order; if they fail to do so, they can easily fall into corruption. Hence the culmination of this process often leads to domination by those who excel in raw power. . . .

As for today's Westerners, they are altogether different. How so? They both use and dispense with regulations, and in both ways they excel us. With respect to their liberty and equality, they reject taboos, discard onerous obligations, and eliminate cover-ups. People pursue their aims and speak their minds. There is no great gulf between the power of rulers and ruled; monarchs are not overly honored nor are the people too lowly. Rather, they are linked as in one body. This is how they excel by dispensing with regulations. But from the standpoint of clear and complete rules regarding officials, workmen, soldiers, and merchants, everyone knows his job and does it without monitoring, and the most minute tasks are all completed according to the proper sequence. Orders issued from far or near are acted upon within the day, and no one finds it oppressive. This is how they excel in using regulations. . . .

In all their affairs they rely on learning, and all their learning is based on direct consideration of the facts, building up layer on layer of knowledge to develop the best-considered and most-extensive course of action. Hence there is no matter in which their theories cannot be put into practice. The reason is that they take freedom as the essential principle and democracy as its application. The peoples of one continent have spread over seven or eight, vying with each other as they advance together, honing each other's skills, beginning as adversaries but ending in mutual development, each employing his intelligence to the fullest, so that one's daily progress is matched by another's monthly innovations. Thus they can use regulations without being hampered by their defects. This is what is awe-inspiring. . . .

Thus the strength, prosperity, and stability of a country reflects its people's strength, wisdom, and virtue. Only after all three are established will its politics and law follow. . . . Were one to say, " . . . Our plan today is simply to pursue wealth and power. The West is truly wealthy and powerful, therefore in today's policies we can have no other teacher than the West, so within the government we must establish democracy and true ministerial government, and in the country at large, build railways, open mines, train a national army, create a navy with hundreds of ships," this would be but an unsuccessful approximation of the idea of strengthening. . . .

In essence, wealth and power mean benefiting the people. But policies to benefit people must start with the people's ability each to benefit himself, and the ability to benefit oneself starts with each one's enjoyment of freedom. If each is to have freedom, this must begin with the ability of each to control himself. Otherwise there is chaos. And those who can control themselves in freedom are those whose strength, wisdom, and virtue are truly superior. Hence the essential policies today are summed up in three principles: promote the people's strength, expand their knowledge, and revive their virtue.

[*Shiwen*, in *Yan Fu yi*, ed. Wang Ji, 1:15–32 — DP]

# KANG YOUWEI AND THE REFORM MOVEMENT

More even than by such ideas as evolution, progress, and liberty — radically new though these were and certain to stir intellectual ferment — this generation was disturbed, and profoundly so, just by the shock of events, especially the defeat by Japan in 1894–1895. Not only the handful of active reformers but officialdom in general found its pride and self-confidence shaken. This loss of poise and self-assurance may have helped to provide the rare, if momentary, opportunity that innovators seized upon in the famous Hundred Days of Reform in 1898. Yet it also created a deeply felt need among educated Chinese somehow to be reassured that China's cultural identity would not be wholly lost amid these changes — a need that the reformers themselves felt more acutely even than those who opposed them.

Kang Youwei (1858–1927), the dominant figure of the reform movement, was born near Guangzhou (Canton) into a world of crisis. The Taiping Rebellion raised up by Kang's fellow provincial was still agonizing the empire from within, while from without the British and French, who had moved again into Guangzhou only the year before, were pressing a campaign that would lead to the occupation of Beijing itself in 1860.

As the scion of a distinguished scholar-official family, Kang was provided with an education along traditional lines, but at the age of fifteen he made known his distaste for the business of mastering the eight-legged essay so indispensable to success in the civil service examinations. Two years later he was reading about Western geography and in time became a voracious reader of Chinese books on the history and geography of the West. Probably the chief influence on Kang in these early years was exerted by a teacher of the old school, who aroused in him a passion for classical scholarship and a sense of complete dedication to the Confucian ideals of personal virtue and service to society. An episode recounted in Kang's *Life Chronology* shows, nevertheless, that his independence and iconoclasm were already quite marked:

My Master praised highly the writings of Han Yu and so I read and studied the collected works of Han [Yu] and Liu [Zongyuan], emulating him in this as well. By this time I had read the books of the philosophers and had learned [that] the [various] methods of [seeking] the Way were shallow, and that in searching for concrete substance in the writings of all the great names in scholarship down through the Song, Ming and the present dynasty, [I had found that] they were all empty and lacking in substance. I ventured to say that when one spoke of the Way, it should be like Zhuangzi or Xunzi; when one spoke of governing, it should be like Guanzi or Hanfeizi; while as regards medicine, the *Su wen* would constitute a separate subject. But as to Han Yu, he was no more than a literary craftsman skilled in the undulation of broad and sweeping cadences that, while they appealed to the ear, had nothing to do with the Way. Thus his *Essentials of the Moral Way (Yuandao)* was extremely superficial. . . . The Master, who was usually correct and stern, in this case laughingly chided me for being wrongheaded. From the time he had first seen me he had often cautioned me about my undue feelings of superiority, and after this I was [more] humble, but nevertheless my fellow students came to be shocked at my intractability.

With the arrival of autumn and winter, I had learned in their broad outlines the general meaning of the important books in the four divisions [of literature]. My intelligence and comprehension became confused, for every day I was buried amid piles of old papers, and I developed a revulsion for them. Then one day I had a new idea. I thought: scholars engaged in textual research, such as Dai Zhen, filled their homes with the books that they had written, but in the end what was the use of all this? Thus I gave it up and in my own heart I fancied seeking a place where I might pacify my mind and decide my destiny. Suddenly I abandoned my studies, discarded my books, shut my door, withdrew from my friends, and sat in contemplation, nurturing my mind. My schoolmates thought me very queer, for there had been no one who had done this, inasmuch as the Master upheld the individual's actual practice [of the Confucian virtues] and detested the study of Chan [Buddhism]. While I was sitting in contemplation, all of a sudden I perceived that Heaven, earth, and the myriad things were all of one substance with myself, and in a great release of enlightenment I beheld myself a sage and laughed for joy; then suddenly I thought of the sufferings and hardships of all living beings, and I wept in melancholy; abruptly I thought: why should I be studying here and neglecting my parent? and that I should pack up immediately and go back to the thatched hut over my grandfather's grave. The students, observing that I sang and wept for no apparent reason, believed that I had gone mad and was diseased in mind.[3]

This experience of Kang's was not unusual in the Neo-Confucian tradition. Others, like Wang Yangming before him, had suddenly found themselves suf-

---

3. *Kang Nanhai zibian nianpu* 4:113–114, as translated by Richard Howard.

focated and overburdened by the kind of broad learning Zhu Xi had encouraged — scholarship that often exhausted one's mind and spirit before one began to exhaust the sources. Still others, like Wang Gen (see chapter 24), had had a kind of mystical experience in which they felt themselves, in their very "humanity," to be of "one substance with Heaven, earth, and all things," an experience that inspired them with a sense of a heroic vocation to save all mankind.

After Kang spent a few months in lonely isolation and reflection, this sense of a special destiny to save mankind through active involvement in the affairs of the world took command of him. Subsequent visits to Hong Kong and Shanghai impressed him with the orderliness and prosperity of Western civilization. Intensifying his pursuit of Western learning, he also became involved in efforts toward practical reform, like his movement to abolish foot binding. Meanwhile, the young reformer had by no means abandoned classical Confucian studies but had begun to identify himself with the so-called New Text school of textual criticism. The purpose of this, for Kang, was not so much to determine by critical methods what must have been the original teaching of Confucius but, whether consciously or not, to justify his new view of the sage as essentially a reformer and to discredit all else that passed for Confucianism.

By the mid-1880s Kang, still only twenty-seven, had already formulated in his mind the ideas that became the basis of his two most famous works, the *Grand Commonality* (*Datong shu*) and *Confucius As a Reformer* (*Kongzi gaizhi kao*). By 1887 he had succeeded, after an earlier failure, in winning the second degree in the civil service examinations, and by 1895, the highest regular (*jinshi*) degree. He had also begun to attract talented students, who helped in the revising and publishing of his works and later in the organizing of reformist societies that spread his ideas and made him the center of violent controversy. Japan, whose defeat of China created an atmosphere of crisis and imminent catastrophe in the late 1890s, now became Kang's model of reform. He urged the court to follow the example of Meiji Japan and openly advocated a basic change from absolute monarchy to constitutional rule. Finally an opportunity to put his ideas into effect came when the Guangxu emperor asked him to take charge of the government in June 1898.

During Kang's few months of tenure a stream of edicts issued forth from the court, aimed at transforming China into a modern state. The old bureaucracy was to be thoroughly revamped. Education and recruitment would be based on Western studies as well as Chinese; bureaucratic functions would be reorganized to serve modern needs. There would be a public school system and a public press. These, together with popularly elected local assemblies, would prepare the people to take part in eventual parliamentary government. In the economic sphere, too, Kang had ambitious plans. Bureaus were set up to promote commerce, industry, modern banking, mining, and agricultural development. Last, and most important, Kang attempted to reorganize and strengthen the armed forces. Here, however, he ran into serious difficulty trying to bring under central control armies that for decades had been virtually autonomous units loyal to their own commanders.

Had he not failed in this last respect, Kang might have survived the bitter opposition that his reforms provoked from the entrenched bureaucracy. It was perhaps characteristic of his dogged adherence to principle, if not indeed indicative of a self-righteous and egocentric character, that Kang reckoned little with such hostility and even less with the surprise and bewilderment felt by many who were simply unaccustomed to rapid change and unable to cope with his radically new ideas. Before many of his plans could take effect, a coup d'état restored the more conservative Empress Dowager to active control of affairs and drove Kang's group from power. Some died as martyrs to the cause of reform; others, like Kang, escaped to become exiles.

Until the dynasty itself collapsed, Kang continued to write and raise funds overseas on behalf of the movement. After the Revolution of 1911, however, Kang's "cause" became more and more a personal one. In a little more than a decade the trend of events and ideas had left him behind. As a constitutional monarchist who still protested his loyalty to the Manchu dynasty, Kang was now swimming against a strong Republican tide; as a reformer who had always insisted on his fidelity to Confucius, he found himself suddenly surrounded by progressives — a generation that no longer needed to be won over to reform and could not now be won back to Confucius.

The significance of Kang Youwei as a thinker lies in his attempt to provide a Confucian justification for basic institutional reforms. The so-called Self-Strengtheners had urged reform on the grounds of immediate utility, thinking that Western weapons and techniques could be adopted without proceeding further to basic changes in Chinese government and society. They spoke of preserving the Confucian Way (Dao) through the use of Western "instruments" (*qi*) or "methods" (*fa*). Yet, as men like Wang Tao came to appreciate, Western power and prosperity rested on something more than technology. To bring China abreast of the modern world, therefore, would require changes that were more radical. Thus reform began to take on a new meaning for them. Change would now extend to *fa* in the sense of institutions as well as *fa* in the sense of methods.

It was here that real trouble arose. According to a hallowed principle of Chinese dynastic rule, the life of a dynasty was bound up with its adherence to the constitution laid down by its founding father (the first emperor). Supporters of Manchu rule could be counted on to resist any such tampering with its institutions. For those more concerned about the Chinese way of life than the fate of the Manchus, the problem was even more acute. How far could one go in changing basic institutions while still keeping the Way intact? Would not Confucianism be reduced to a mere set of pious platitudes once its social integument had been destroyed?

Kang's resolution of this dilemma was a bold one. Rather than permit the sphere occupied by the Confucian Way in Chinese life to be further narrowed and displaced by Western "methods," he would redefine the Way and enlarge its scope so as virtually to include the latter. Instead of making more room for Western institutions alongside Confucianism, he would make room for them inside it. This he did by exploiting to the fullest two ideas already put forth by Wang Tao. The first of these was that the Way of the Sages was precisely to meet change with change; Confucius himself had done so, and if he were alive today he would do so again. Kang provided this theory with an elaborate scriptural justification through his studies of the so-called forged classics and his sensational tract *Confucius As a Reformer*. In terms of its historical influence this was undoubtedly Kang's main contribution — though not an original one — to the thinking of his times.

Implicit in his notion of reform, however, was a still more momentous idea, since it ran more directly counter to the age-old Confucian view of history and tradition: the idea of progress. It was one thing to assert that the Confucian sage, when faced by one of those cyclically recurring cycles of degeneration spoken of by Mencius or the *Classic of Changes*, took appropriate steps to reform the times, reassert the Way, and restore the institutions of the sage kings. It was quite another to offer, in place of a return to the Golden Age of the past, a utopia beckoning in the future.

Here again the idea was, among Chinese, originally Wang Tao's. He had glimpsed a future stage in which the Way would make all things one, a natural result of the process going on around him by which the different nations in the world and their respective ways of life were being brought together by technological progress. He had even referred to it in terms taken from the Confucian *Record of Rites* as the age of Grand Unity or Commonality (*Datong*). What the *Record of Rites* had spoken of as a golden age at the dawn of history, however, Wang Tao saw as a vision of the future. And Kang Youwei, in his *Grand Commonality*, made this vision the center of his whole worldview. Henceforth, "reform" would not mean what it had in the past — an adaptation of laws and methods to cyclical change. It was now a wholesale launching of China into the modern world and, beyond that, into a glorious future.

Feng Guifen and Xue Fucheng, in their writings on reform, had shown deference to China's age-old pretensions to cultural superiority by reassuring their readers that it need not merely follow along behind the Western powers but could overtake and surpass them. Kang, in the *Grand Commonality*, took the lead for China himself by pointing the way into the One World of the future. If China suffered humiliation now for its backwardness, looking ahead, he would be satisfied with nothing less for it than the ultimate in progress. In his world of the future there were to be no social, provincial, and national barriers. Government would virtually cease to exist except in local units fixed arbitrarily on the basis of square degrees of longitude and latitude. Within these units life would be completely communal and egalitarian. All distinctions of race, class, clan, and family would disappear, since they could no longer serve any valid social function. And in place of the differentiated loyalties that had bound men to their particular social group, there would be only an undifferentiated feeling of human-kindness or love, which he identified with the Confucian virtue of humanity (*ren*).

Those who recall the layout of Mencius's well-fields, of which Kang's polity based on square degrees of longitude and latitude are so reminiscent; or the neat symmetrical organization of society set forth so early in the *Rites of Zhou* and so late in the plans of the Taiping rebels; or the Chinese fondness for political geometry, reflected even in the plan of capital cities like Changan and Beijing, will recognize in Kang's grand design a quality by no means foreign to native tradition.

If in this respect, then, Kang's vision of the future still reflects something of the past, what can be said of his Confucianism? The ostensible claims for placing him still within the Confucian tradition are his emphasis upon the cardinal virtue of humaneness (*ren*), his universalistic humanism (in contrast to ethnic nationalism), and his efforts to preserve Confucianism as the state religion. Against this, most obviously, is his decisive rejection of the Confucian family system along with other structural elements in culture and society that he considered divisive.

Whatever abuses may have appeared in the family system as it was formulated and practiced down through the centuries, it would seem difficult to disassociate Confucius completely from it or to preserve Confucianism entirely without it. Without the family virtues and obligations, certainly, the concept of *ren* loses much of its tangible significance and approaches more nearly — if it does not exactly coincide with — Mozi's principle of undifferentiated universal love or Buddhist undifferentiated compassion. Since Mozi's social ideals resemble Kang's so closely, the comparison is all the more pointed.

Furthermore, in Kang's attempt to preserve Confucianism as a kind of national religion, there is something foreign to the spirit of Confucianism itself. The sage's teaching had been offered, and accepted by many peoples, as something universal. Its humanistic values were rooted in the nature of man and human relationships. Kang's defense of it now as a religion and as the focus of a new state ideology, while testifying no doubt to his belief that China must have something comparable to the Christianity of the West or state Shinto in Japan, nevertheless sacrifices the substance of tradition for the trappings of modern nationalism. Henceforth Confucianism is to be valued not on its own terms but as a state ritual.

What remains as unquestionably Confucian is Kang's own sense of dedication to the service of society, his aim of "putting the world in order." Yet even this is not exclusively a Confucian concern (certainly Mozi shared it), nor does his favorite expression for it, "saving the world," hark back only to the sage — there may be overtones here, too, of the Buddhist saviors (bodhisattvas) and of Jesus Christ.

After the collapse of the 1898 reform movement, Kang spent much of his life in exile. The final statement of his vision of the Grand Commonality was completed in India in 1902. Kang had been a fugitive from the Qing while still professing loyalty to it and after 1911 was enough of a "Confucian" monarchist to survive only as an anachronism in republican times; his utopian vision of the Grand Commonality had little influence on China's turbulent political course, except paradoxically, by the sweep of its universalism and egalitarian leveling of all social distinctions, to clear the way for the revolutionary jugger-naut to follow. The excerpts given here from the introduction and conclusion of Kang's *Grand Commonality* convey the totalistic vision of a world order and human perfectibility so reminiscent of earlier Chinese idealisms that would still lend themselves, in a chaotic age, to simplistic revolutionary solutions and enthusiasms.

In the light of history, Kang and the reform movement may well appear as the great turning point between old and new in Chinese thought. In his hands, China was being launched on a perilous journey, in the course of which much baggage might have to be jettisoned if anything at all was to survive. Confucian traditionalists saw the dangers perhaps better than Kang did. Dropping him as pilot, however, was not the same thing as steering a safe course homeward. The storm now drove all before it, and there was no turning back.

CONFUCIUS AS A REFORMER

Kang's *Kongzi gaizhi kao* (lit., study of Confucius's reforms) was started in 1886 and finally published in 1897. It provides an extended analysis of the innovations that Kang believed to have been advocated by Confucius. The following are taken from section introductions that present his general argumentation. As Kang's subheadings indicate, they purport to show that Confucius's greatness derives from his having written the Six Classics to promote reform in his own time.

## How Confucius Founded His Teaching in Order to Reform Institutions

Every founder of doctrine in the world reformed institutions and established laws. This is true with Chinese philosophers in ancient times. Chinese princi-ples and institutions were all laid down by Confucius. His disciples received his teachings and transmitted them so that they were carried out in the country and used to change the old customs. [9:1a]

## The Six Classics Were All Written by Confucius to Reform Institutions

Confucius was the founder of a doctrine. He was a godlike sage king. He com-plements Heaven and earth and nurtures the myriad things. All men, things, and principles are embraced in the Great Way of Confucius. He is, therefore, the most accomplished and perfect sage in the history of mankind. And yet, concerning the Great Way of Confucius, one would search in vain for a single word [under the master's own name]. There are only the *Analects*, which was a record of the master's sayings taken down by his disciples, and the *Spring and Autumn Annals*, which was a kind of old-fashioned gazette copied from ancient documents relative to public events and ceremonies. As to the *Classics of Odes, Documents, Rites, Music*, and *Changes*, they are regarded as the ancient records of Fu Xi, the Xia and Shang dynasties, King Wen and the Duke of Zhou; thus they have nothing to do with Confucius. If this were true, Confucius would have been merely a wise scholar of later times, no better than Zheng Kangcheng [127–200] or Zhu Xi [1130–1200, who wrote commentaries on the Confucian classics]. How, then, could he have been called the only model of the human race and the perfect sage of all generations? . . . Before the Han dynasty it was known to all that Confucius was the founder of the doctrine and the reformer of institutions and that he was the godlike sage king. . . . Wherein lies the reason for this? It lies in the fact that scholars knew the Six Classics were written by Confucius. This was the opinion of all before the Han dynasty. Only when a scholar recognizes that the Six Classics were written by Confucius can he understand why Confucius was the great sage, the founder of the doctrine, and the model for all ages; and why he alone was called the supreme master. [10:1a–b]

[*Kongzi gaizhi kao* 9:1a; 10:1a–b  — CT]

### THE THREE AGES

Kang's theory of progress is set forth in terms of the Three Ages, a concept of the New Text school for which he derived classical sanction from the *Gongyang Commentary* on the *Spring and Autumn Annals*, the "Li yun" section of the *Record of Rites*, and commentaries by the Han scholars Dong Zhongshu and He Xiu. Here we see the earlier view of the devolution of history adapted to the modern evolutionary view, by a process of rationalization and idealization that bears little resemblance to the traditional account in the *Record of Rites*.

The meaning of the *Spring and Autumn Annals* consists in the evolution of the Three Ages: the Age of Disorder, the Age of Order, and the Age of Great Peace. . . . The Way of Confucius embraces the evolution of the Three Sequences and the Three Ages. The Three Sequences were used to illustrate the Three Ages, which could be extended to a hundred generations. The eras of Xia, Shang, and Zhou represent the succession of the Three Sequences, each with its modifications and accretions. By observing the changes in these three eras one can know the changes in a hundred generations to come. For as customs are handed down among the people, later kings cannot but follow the practices of the preceding dynasty; yet, since defects develop and have to be removed, each new dynasty must make modifications and additions to create a new system. The course of humanity progresses according to a fixed sequence. From the clans come tribes, which in time are transformed into nations. And from nations the Grand Commonality comes about. Similarly, from the individual man the rule of tribal chieftains gradually becomes established, from which the relationship between ruler and subject is gradually defined. Autocracy gradually leads to constitutionalism, and constitutionalism gradually leads to republicanism. Likewise, from the individual the relationship between husband and wife gradually comes into being, and from this the relationship between parent and child is defined. This relationship of parent and child leads to the loving care of the entire race, which in turn leads gradually to the Grand Commonality, in which there is a reversion to individuality.

Thus there is an evolution from Disorder to Order, and from Order to Great Peace. Evolution proceeds gradually and changes have their origins. This is true with all nations. By observing the child, one can know the adult and the old man; by observing the sprout, one can know the tree when it grows big and finally reaches the sky. Thus, by observing the modifications and additions of the three successive eras of Xia, Shang, and Zhou, one can by extension know the changes in a hundred generations to come.

When Confucius prepared the *Spring and Autumn Annals*, he extended it to embrace the Three Ages. Thus, during the Age of Disorder he considers his own state as the center, treating all other Chinese feudal states as on the outside. In the Age of Order he considers China as the center, while treating the outlying barbarian tribes as on the outside. And in the Age of Great Peace he considers everything, far or near, large or small, as if it were one. In doing this he is applying the principle of evolution.

Confucius was born in the Age of Disorder. Now that communications extend through the great earth and changes have taken place in Europe and America, the world is evolving toward the Age of Order. There will be a day when everything throughout the earth, large or small, far or near, will be like one. There will no longer be any nations, no more racial distinctions, and customs will be everywhere the same. With this uniformity will come the Age of Great Peace. Confucius knew all this in advance.

[From *Lunyu zhu* 2:11a–12b — CT]

The methods and institutions of Confucius aim at meeting with the particular times. If, in the Age of Disorder, before the advent of civilization, one were to put into effect the institutions of Great Peace, this would certainly result in great harm. But if, in the Age of Order, one were to continue to cling to the institutions of the Age of Disorder, this too would result in great harm. The present time, for example, is the Age of Order. It is therefore necessary to propagate the doctrines of self-rule and independence, and to discuss publicly the matter of constitutional government. If the laws are not reformed, great disorder will result.

[From *Zhongyong zhu* 36b —CT]

### THE NEED FOR REFORMING INSTITUTIONS

This memorial to the throne, submitted January 29, 1898, and titled Comprehensive Consideration of the Whole Situation, gives the arguments by which Kang attempted to persuade the Guangxu emperor to inaugurate reforms, which he did a few months later. Note Kang's equivocation on the question of "ancestral institutions," while he has no reservations about taking Meiji Japan as the model for China.

A survey of all states in the world will show that those states that undertook reforms became strong while those states that clung to the past perished. The consequences of clinging to the past and the effects of opening up new ways are thus obvious. If Your Majesty, with your discerning brilliance, observes the trends in other countries, you will see that if we can change, we can preserve ourselves; but if we cannot change, we shall perish. Indeed, if we can make a complete change, we shall become strong, but if we only make limited changes, we shall still perish. If Your Majesty and his ministers investigate the source of the disease, you will know that this is the right prescription.

Our present trouble lies in our clinging to old institutions without knowing how to change. In an age of competition between states, to put into effect methods appropriate to an era of universal unification and laissez-faire is like wearing heavy furs in summer or riding a high carriage across a river. This can only result in having a fever or getting oneself drowned. . . .

It is a principle of things that the new is strong but the old weak; that new things are fresh but old things rotten; that new things are active but old things static. If the institutions are old, defects will develop. Therefore there are no institutions that should remain unchanged for a hundred years. Moreover, our present institutions are but unworthy vestiges of the Han, Tang, Yuan, and Ming dynasties; they are not even the institutions of the [Manchu] ancestors. In fact, they are the products of the fancy writing and corrupt dealing of petty officials rather than the original ideas of the ancestors. To say that they are the ancestral institutions is an insult to the ancestors. Furthermore, institutions are for the purpose of preserving one's territories. Now that the ancestral territory cannot be preserved, what good is it to maintain the ancestral institutions? . . .

Although there is a desire to reform, yet if the national policy is not fixed and public opinion not united, it will be impossible for us to give up the old and adopt the new. The national policy is to the state just as the rudder is to the boat or the pointer is to the compass. It determines the direction of the state and shapes the public opinion of the country. [1b–2b]

Nowadays the court has been undertaking some reforms, but the action of the emperor is obstructed by the ministers, and the recommendations of the able scholars are attacked by old-fashioned bureaucrats. If the charge is not "using barbarian ways to change China," then it is "upsetting the ancestral institutions." Rumors and scandals are rampant, and people fight each other like fire and water. To reform in this way is as ineffective as attempting a forward march by walking backward. It will inevitably result in failure. Your Majesty knows that under the present circumstances reforms are imperative and old institutions must be abolished. I beg Your Majesty to make up your mind and to decide on the national policy. After the fundamental policy is determined, the methods of implementation must vary according to what is primary and what is secondary, what is important and what is insignificant, what is strong and what is weak, what is urgent and what can wait. . . . If anything goes wrong, no success can be achieved.

After studying ancient and modern institutions, Chinese and foreign, I have found that the institutions of the sage kings and Three dynasties [of Xia, Shang, and Zhou] were excellent, but that ancient times were different from today. I hope Your Majesty will daily read Mencius and follow his example of loving the people. The development of the Han, Tang, Song, and Ming dynasties may be learned, but it should be remembered that the age of universal unification is different from that of sovereign nations. I wish Your Majesty would study *Guanzi*[4] and follow his idea of managing the country. As to the republican governments of the United States and France and the constitutional governments of Britain and Germany, these countries are far away and their customs are different from ours. Their changes occurred a long time ago and can no longer be traced. Consequently I beg Your Majesty to adopt the purpose of Peter the Great of Russia as our purpose and to take the Meiji Reform of Japan as the model for our reform. The time and place of Japan's reform are not remote and her religion and customs are somewhat similar to ours. Her success is manifest; her example can be easily followed. [3a–b]

[From *Yingchao tongchou quanjuzhe*, in *Wuxu zougao*, 1b–3b  — CT]

## THE GRAND COMMONALITY

In these excerpts from Kang's magnum opus, he first professes his humanitarian motivations and aspirations, combining the bodhisattva's unlimited compassion for the sufferings of humankind with the Neo-Confucian sense of a heroic vocation to save the world. His final messianic vision is of a world totally liberated from all limits and

---

4. Early book on political and economic institutions that foreshadows Legalist doctrines. See ch. 7.

bounds, as if history and inevitable progress assured a millennial outcome. Although Kang himself opposed revolutionary violence, in the absence of any realistic process or structure his anarchistic "no hands" approach to a total solution of human ills lent itself to the illusions of a revolutionary idealism, echoed later by the founders of the Chinese Communist Party.

Having been born in the Age of Disorder, I have been struck by the sufferings [of this age], and I have wondered if there could be a way to save it. "Bewildered, I have pondered." [The solution lies] only in following the Way of the Grand Commonality of Complete Peace-and-Equality. If we look at all the ways of saving the world through the ages, to discard the Way of Grand Commonality and yet to hope to save men from suffering and to gain their greatest happiness is next to impossible. The Way of the Grand Commonality is [the attainment of] utmost peace-and-equality, utmost justice, utmost humaneness, and the most perfect government. Even though there be [other] Ways, none can add to this. . . .

We see that the whole world is but a world of grief and misery, all the people of the whole world are but grieving and miserable people, and all the living beings of the whole world are but murdered beings. The azure Heaven and the round Earth are nothing but a great slaughter yard, a great prison.

Being that I was born on the earth, then mankind in the ten thousand countries of the earth are from the same womb but of different bodily types. Being that I have knowledge of them, then I have love (*qin*) for them. All that is finest and best of the former wisdom of India, Greece, Persia, Rome, and of present-day England, France, Germany, and America, I have lapped up and drunk, rested on, pillowed on; and my soul in dreams has fathomed it. With the most ancient and noted savants, famous scholars, and great men, I have likewise often joined hands.

Being that I am a creature of all the heavens, would it be better if I could abandon the world and the heavens, cut [myself] off from my kind, flee from the social relationships (*lun*), and be happy all by myself? Those whose perceptiveness and awareness are small, their loving-mind is also small; those whose perceptiveness and awareness are great, their humane heart-and-mind is also great. Boundless love goes with boundless perceptiveness.

But if we look at the miseries of life, [we see that] the sources of all suffering lie only in nine boundaries. What are the nine boundaries?

The first is called national boundaries: [this is] division by territorial frontiers and by tribes.

The second is called class boundaries: [this is] division by noble and base, by pure and impure.

The third is called racial boundaries: [this is] division by yellow, white, brown, and black [skin types].

The fourth is called gender boundaries: [this is] division by male and female.

The fifth is called familial boundaries: [that is] the private relationships of parent and child, husband and wife, elder and younger brother.

The sixth is called property boundaries: [this is] the private ownership of agriculture, industry, and commerce.

The seventh is called disorder boundaries: [this is] the existence of unequal, unthorough, dissimilar, and unjust laws.

The eighth is called species boundaries: [this is] the existence of a separation between man, and the birds, beasts, insects, and fish.

The ninth is called suffering boundaries: [this means,] by suffering, giving rise to suffering. The perpetuation [of suffering] is inexhaustible and endless — beyond conception.

(The remedy for suffering lies, therefore, in abolishing these nine boundaries. The following nine parts of the book thus deal in detail with each of the boundaries, with the substitution of the Grand Commonality of Complete Peace-and-Equality in their place.) . . .


## [The Historical Evolution of] Democracy, from Less to More, Presages One World

The progress of democracy from less to more is a natural principle. Hence after the United States had been established, a great revolution in laws took place, and other countries followed this. Thereupon constitutions were set up everywhere, republican[ism] flourished, communist theories appeared, and labor parties were started up every day. . . . Hence the arising of democracy, the flourishing of constitutions, the talk about unions and communism, all are the first signs (lit., sounds) of One World. As for constitutional monarchy, [since the monarch] is already powerless, it is just the same as a democratic [form of government]. Some day monarchy will certainly be abolished and discarded, and [all states] will only belong to the One World [government]. . . .


## If We Wish to Attain One World of Complete Peace-and-Equality, We Must Abolish the Family

Now, we desire that men's natures shall all become perfect, that men's characters shall all become equal, that men's bodies shall all be nurtured. [That state in which] men's characters are all developed, men's bodies are all hale, men's dispositions are all pacific and tolerant, and customs and morals are all beautiful, is what is called Complete Peace-and-Equality. But there is no means whereby to bring about this Way [and yet] to avoid abolishing the family. . . . To have the family and yet to wish to reach Complete Peace-and-Equality is to be afloat on a blocked-up stream, in a sealed-off harbor, and yet to wish to reach an open waterway. To wish to attain Complete Peace-and-Equality and yet to have the family is like carrying earth to dredge a stream, or adding wood to put out a fire: the more done, the more the hindrance. Thus, if we wish to attain the beauty of complete equality, independence, and the perfection of [human] nature, it can [be done] only by abolishing the state, only by abolishing the family.

## The Abolition of Boundaries

In the Grand Commonality there will be no states, therefore there will be no severe military laws. There will be no rulers, and so there will be no cases of opposing the superior and creating rebellion. There will be no husbands and wives, and so there will be no fighting over sexual desire, no provisions against sexual immorality, no repressive regulations or bearing of grievances, no resentment or hatred, no divorces, no miseries of punishment and killing. There will be no family relationships, and so there will be no need to support [one's family members], no compulsion to do the right thing [by them], no wrangling over [property shares]. There will be no nobility, and so there will be no depending upon intimidation or coercion, no oppression, no grabbing, no intriguing for position, no toadying. There will be no private property, so there will be no litigation over fields and houses, over industry and commerce, or over production. There will be no burial of the dead, and so there will be no litigation over the cemetery. There will be no customs barriers, and so there will be no crimes of evasion and smuggling. There will be no class divisions, and so there will be no mistreatment or oppressive laws [on the part of the superior class], and their violation or opposition [by the inferior classes].

Aside from this, then, what crimes will still exist, what punishments will still exist? I think that in the time of the Grand Commonality, while there may be faults (or, mistakes), there cannot be sins (or, crimes). What will these faults be? In a job or in official position, there may be negligence or mistakes, or discourtesy or gossip. Through the influence of twenty years' schooling, conduct and customs will be excellent, human nature will have become perfected, and [men's] energies will also be abundant; with this, even faults and mistakes should just about be eliminated.

[Adapted from Thompson, *One World*, pp. 72, 74–75, 86, 253 — LGT]

*For the relevance of the above to the revolutionary and millenarian thinking that inspired the founding of the Chinese Communist movement, compare the foregoing with Li Dazhao's "The Victory of Bolshevism" (chapter 34).*

# CONSERVATIVE REACTIONS

The great momentum attained by the reform movement after the Sino-Japanese War of 1894–1895 also provoked strong conservative reactions. A stormy debate ensued in which the reformers were charged with subverting the established order and destroying Chinese culture. In Hunan province, where reformers like Tan Sitong had organized an academy for the spreading of their ideas, the reaction was particularly forceful. Eminent scholars such as Wang Xianqian (1842–1918), outstanding classicist and compiler of the monumental *Dong hua lu* (*Imperial Documents of the Qing Dynasty*), and Ye Dehui (1864–1927), famous bibliophile, rallied to the defense of Chinese traditions and Confucianism. In Beijing powerful figures led by Rong Lu (1836–1903) fought the reformers with logic and invective until, with the help of the Empress Dowager, they succeeded in bringing the reform movement of 1898 to an abrupt end. Still another brand of opposition was encountered in the statesman Zhang Zhidong, who, though himself something of a reformer, wished to hold the line against drastic changes and tried to preserve intact the earlier distinction between traditional Confucian ethics and the Western techniques, which should serve only as means for defending the Chinese Way.

Resistance to reform took three main lines. First, conservatives argued that ancestral institutions should never be changed under any conditions. Said Zeng Lian, one of the conservative writers: "The state (dynasty) belongs to the ancestors; the emperor merely maintains the dynasty for them. He cannot change the permanent laws laid down by the ancestors." This argument, founded upon the tradition of filial piety, was in fact the most formidable obstacle to the reformers, one that Kang Youwei tried to overcome again and again in his memorials to the throne. It was this same argument that the Grand Councilor, Rong Lu, used so effectively against Kang.

Second, conservatives argued, on traditional Confucian lines, a good government depended upon men rather than upon laws. It was the moral state of the people and their leaders that needed improvement, not legal or political institutions. Rather than try to change institutions, one should seek to change or win over the minds of the people. Without men exemplifying superior virtue in the government, this could never be achieved, and in default of it, institutional changes would only bring harm to the country.

Third, as regards the cultivation of these virtues, the traditional teachings of China were definitely superior to those of the West. The Westerners, caring only for money, might build a strong and wealthy country but would be unable to achieve harmony and unity. Western governments were based upon power; the Chinese government, upon humanity and rightness. Calculating and self-centered, the Westerners neglected the ethical bases of government and could offer no sound alternative for the establishment of a harmonious social order.

All three of these conservative arguments were conventional insofar as they assumed the legitimacy of the established order and identified Confucianism with preservation of the dynastic state, which some earlier Neo-Confucians had questioned (in writings suppressed by the dynasty; see chapter 25). Understandably, this kind of conservatism provoked a more radical response from others later, who attacked both Confucianism and the dynastic order as inseparable evils.

The memorial of the censor Chu Chengbo, submitted in 1895 after China's disastrous defeat by Japan, analyzes that failure in a manner different from the institutional reformers. It is not a failure to change laws and institutions that accounts for the defeat, but precisely that such changes were made without remedying the basic weakness — the incompetence and venality of officials. Since, in fact, graft and corruption among army and navy officers had rendered China's modern weapons useless in battle, Chu was on strong ground in arguing the need for official probity and integrity. The implication of this for him was that in the training and recruitment of officials traditional ethical values and moral character should be emphasized over technical qualifications and scientific training (which would have involved still further changes in methods and institutions). Thus, though not wholly opposed to change or to the reforms already undertaken, Chu resisted the reform movement's tendency toward progressive displacement of Chinese values — the Confucian Way — by Western methods and institutions.

In the present world our trouble is not that we lack good institutions but that we lack upright minds. If we seek to reform institutions, we must first reform men's minds. Unless all men of ability assist each other, good laws become mere paper documents; unless those who supervise them are fair and enlightened, the venal will end up occupying the places of the worthy. . . .

At the beginning of the Tongzhi reign (1862–1874), Zeng Guofan, Zuo Zongtang, Shen Baozhen, Li Hongzhang, and others, because the danger from abroad was becoming daily more serious, strongly emphasized Western learning. In order to effect large-scale manufacture, they built shipyards and machine factories; in order to protect our commercial rights, they organized the China Merchants Steam Navigation Company and cotton mills; in order to educate persons of talent, they founded the Tongwen College and other language schools; in order to strengthen training, they established naval and military academies. Countless other enterprises were inaugurated, and an annual expenditure amounting to millions was incurred. Truly no effort was spared in the attempt to establish new institutions after the pattern of the West.

When these enterprises were first undertaken, the regulations and systems were thoroughly considered so as to attain the best. It was asserted then that although China at the outset had to imitate the superior techniques of the West, eventually she would surpass the Western countries. But [in fact] perfunctory execution of these reforms has brought us to the point now where the island barbarians [the Japanese] have suddenly invaded us, and the whole situation of the nation has deteriorated. Was it because there were no reforms or because the reforms were no good? The real mistake was that we did not secure the right men to manage the new institutions. [18a–19a]

In some cases the authorities knew only how to indulge in empty talk; in other cases the officials succeeding those who originated the reforms gradually became lax and let the projects drop. Generally the initial effort was seldom maintained to the end; and while there was much talk, there was little action. . . . If the proposals had been carried out gradually and persistently, China would have long ago become invincible. But these far-reaching plans failed because we only put up an ostentatious facade behind which were concealed the avarice and selfishness [of the officials]. [19b]

In order to create a new impression in the country and to stimulate the lax morale of the people, it is necessary to distinguish between meritorious and unworthy men and to order rewards and punishments accordingly. . . . If this fundamental remedy is adopted, the raising of funds will bring in abundant revenues, and the training of troops will result in a strong army. Institutions that are good will achieve results day by day, while institutions that are not so good can be changed to bring out their maximum usefulness. Otherwise, profit-seeking opportunists will vie with each other in proposing novel theories . . . and there will be no limit to their evil doings. [20b–21a]

As to the present institutions and laws, although in name they adhere to past formulations "respectfully observed," in fact they have lost the essence of their original meaning. If we cling to the vestiges of the past, it will be conforming to externals while departing from the spirit. But if we get at the root, a single change can lead to complete fulfillment of the Way. . . . We should, therefore, make the necessary adjustments in accordance with the needs of the time. If we secure the right persons, all things can be transformed without a trace; but if we do not obtain the right persons, laws and institutions will only serve the nefarious designs of the wicked. [21a–22a]

[*Jianzheng tang zhegao* 2:18a–22a —CT]

### ZHU YIXIN: FOURTH LETTER IN REPLY TO KANG YOUWEI

Zhu Yixin (1846–1894), an official who withdrew from the government to teach and pursue classical studies, prided himself on his Confucian orthodoxy and made no compromises with Westernization. He opposed even the introduction of machines on the ground that, though useful in countries with vast resources and a shortage of manpower, they would only create unemployment in China and thus drive people to desperation and violence.

Zhu correctly discerned that the effect of Kang's ideas (as expressed in *Confucius As a Reformer*) would be not only to change the outward forms of Chinese life but ultimately to undermine traditional Confucian morality itself. The "way" of the West could not be adopted piecemeal: its values and institutions were inseparably related, as were those of China. On the other hand, it was both impossible and undesirable for the Chinese to surrender their own Way — the basis of their whole civilization — for that of the West. The only solution was a return to fixed principles, rejecting expediency and utilitarianism. It is significant, however, that Zhu's appeal is to the leadership class, who should set a good example for the people as a whole. If even a few superior men adhere to principle, the masses will follow.

Since ancient times there have been no institutions that might not develop defects. When a true king arises, he makes small changes if the defects are small and great changes if the defects are great. . . . Thus Confucius said, "Let there be the [right] men and the government will flourish; but without the [right] men, the government will decay and cease."[5] The defects of a government are due to the failings of those who manage the institutions rather than of those who establish them. Now by referring to Confucius as a reformer, your real intention is to facilitate the introduction of new institutions. The accounts of Confucius as a reformer come from apocryphal texts and cannot be wholly believed. But even if the sage has spoken thus, he was only taking a simple pattern and elaborating upon it in order to return to the ancient institutions of the Three Dynasties and sage kings. How could he have intended to use "barbarian ways to reform China"? [1:11a]

I have heard of "daily renovating one's virtue,"[6] but I have never heard of daily renovating one's moral principles. The scholars of the Qianlong [1736–1795] and Jiaqing [1796–1820] periods regarded moral principle as something one should not talk about.[7] Now, in order to rescue us from the degeneration and loss [that resulted] you do not seek a return to fixed principles, but instead, you talk about changing principles. The barbarians do not recognize the moral obligations between ruler and minister, parent and child, elder brother and younger brother, husband and wife. There is your change in principles. Do you mean that the classics of our sages and the teachings of our philosophers are too dull and banal to follow, and that we must change them so as to have something new? Only if we first have principles can we then have institutions. Barbarian institutions are based on barbarian principles. Different principles make for different customs, and different customs give rise to different institutions. Now, instead of getting at the root of it all, you talk blithely of changing institutions. If the institutions are to be changed, are not the principles going to be changed along with them?

---

5. *Mean* 20.
6. *Classic of Changes*, Hexagram no. 26 (*Dachu*).
7. That is, the Han Learning pursued text criticism at the expense of moral principle.

The manufacture of instruments by the workers involves techniques, not principles. As the minds of the people become more and more artful, clever contrivances will daily increase. Once started, there is no resistance to it. Why, therefore, need we fear that our techniques will not become sufficiently refined?

Now, because our techniques have not yet attained the highest level of skill-fulness, it is proposed that we should seek to achieve this by changing our institutions as well as our principles. . . . Is this not like rescuing a person from being drowned by pushing him into a deep abyss? Is this not going much too far?

Men's minds are corrupted by utilitarianism. Those who run the institutions will utilize them for self-interest. One institution established only means one more evil added. Consequently, the path to good government is, above all, the rectification of the people's minds-and-hearts, and the establishment of virtuous customs. The perfecting of institutions should come next.

Moreover, our institutions are by themselves clear and complete, and it is not necessary to borrow from foreign customs. How can we blame later mistakes on our ancestors and let the theory of utilitarianism be our guide?

Of course, the pitiably stupid people who only follow shadows and listen to echoes cannot be made to understand this. But even a few well-intentioned scholars, going to extremes and believing that the *Classics of Odes, Documents, Rites,* and *Music,* which have been handed down to us by the sages, are not adequate to meet the changing circumstances, take to what is strange and novel and maintain that therein lies the path to wealth and power. But does the reason for the foreigners' being rich and powerful lie in this? Or does it not lie in their having a way that is the source and basis [of their institutions]? And is it not true that a way that is basic and original with them can never be practiced in China, and furthermore that it should absolutely not be practiced by our descendants? [12b–13a]

Mencius said, "The noble man seeks simply to bring back the unchanging standard, and that being rectified, the masses are roused to virtue. When they are so roused, forthwith perversities and wickedness disappear."[8] A review of our history since ancient times will show that herein lies the key to order and disorder. [13b]

[Su Yu, ed., *Yijiao congbian* 1:11a–13b — CT]

### YE DEHUI: THE SUPERIORITY OF CHINA AND CONFUCIANISM

In his criticism of the reformers in the late 1890s, Ye Dehui (1864–1927) attempted to defend not only Confucian ethical ideals but existing institutions. While acknowledging that the West had its points of excellence, worthy of selective emulation, for him

---

8. *Mencius* 7B:37.

they were few indeed compared to what China had to offer. Instead, therefore, of claiming for her simply moral superiority over the West, and thus seeming to retreat from vulnerable institutions into an unimpeachable tradition, Ye tended to justify the whole existing order — the monarchy, rule by an elite, the civil service examination system, and so on — against democracy and Westernization. Government by the masses will lead to chaos. With regard to institutions, however, he claimed no more than China's right to keep her own because they were peculiarly suited to her, while in regard to Confucianism he did not hesitate to proclaim its universality and ultimate adoption by the West.

Conservatism of this type, which sanctified the status quo and identified Confucianism so closely with it, helped convince Chinese of the next generation that to overthrow the old dynastic order required the destruction of Confucianism too.

Of all countries in the five continents China is the most populous. It is situated in the north temperate zone, with a mild climate and abundant natural resources. Moreover, it became civilized earlier than all other nations, and its culture leads the world. The boundary between China and foreign countries, between Chinese and barbarians, admits of no argument and cannot be discussed in terms of their strength or our weakness.

Of the four classes of people, the scholars are the finest. From the beginning of the present dynasty until today there have been numerous great ministers and scholars who rose to eminence on the basis of their examination essays and poems. Although special examinations have been given and other channels of recruitment have been opened, it is mostly from the regular civil service examinations that men of abilities have risen up. The Western system of election has many defects. Under that system it is difficult to prevent favoritism and to uphold integrity. At any rate, each nation has its own governmental system, and one should not compel uniformity among them. [4:78b–79a]

An examination of the causes of success and failure in government reveals that in general the upholding of Confucianism leads to good government while the adoption of foreignism leads to disorder. If one keeps to kingly rule [relying on virtue], there will be order; if one follows the way of the overlord [relying on power], there will be disorder. . . .

Since the abdication of Yao and Shun, the ruling of China under one family has become institutionalized. Because of China's vast territory and tremendous resources, even when it has been ruled under one monarch, still there have been more days of disorder than days of order. Now, if it is governed by the people, there will be different policies from many groups, and strife and contention will arise. [4:12a–13a]

[Mencius said,] "The people are the most important element in a nation,"[9]

---

9. *Mencius* 7B:14.

not because the people consider themselves important but because the sovereign regards them as important. And it is not people's rights that are important. Since the founding of the Qing dynasty our revered rulers have loved the people as their own children. Whenever the nation has suffered from a calamity such as famine, flood, and war, the emperor has immediately given generous relief upon its being reported by the provincial officials. For instance, even though the treasury was short of funds recently, the government did not raise any money from the people except for the *likin*[10] tax. Sometimes new financial devices are proposed by ministers who like to discuss pecuniary matters, but even if they are approved and carried out by order of the department concerned, they are suspended as soon as it is learned that they are troubling the people. How vastly different is this from the practice of Western countries where taxes are levied in all places, on all persons, for all things and at all times? [4:31a]

Confucianism represents the supreme expression of justice in the principles of Heaven and the hearts of men. In the future it will undoubtedly be adopted by civilized countries of both East and West. The essence of Confucianism will shine brightly as it renews itself from day to day.

Ethics is common to China and the West. The concept of blood relations and respect for parents prevails also among barbarians. To love life and hate killing is rooted in the human heart. The Confucian ideal is expressed in the *Spring and Autumn Annals*, which aims at saving the world from disorder and treason; proper conduct is defined in the *Classic of Filial Piety*, which lays down the moral principles and obligations for all generations to come. And there is the *Analects*, which synthesizes the great laws of the ancient kings. Zengzi, Zixia, Mencius, and others who transmitted the teaching all mastered the Six Arts and knew thoroughly the myriad changes of circumstances. All that the human heart desires to say was said several thousand years ago. [3:31a]

Chinese scholars who attack Western religion err in false accusation, while those who admire it err in flattery. Indeed, only a superficial Confucian would say that Westerners had no moral principles, and yet only fools would say that Western religion excels Confucianism. Insofar as there is morality, there must be Confucianism. [3:33b]

> [Su Yu, ed., *Yijiao congbian* 3:32b–33a, *Ming jiao*; 4:12a–13a, *Youxian jinyu*; 31a, *Zheng jie pian*; 78b–79a, *Fei youxue tongyi* — CT]

# TAN SITONG

Tan Sitong (1865–1898) is one of the most striking figures of the reform movement. The nonconformist son of a high official, he loved both independent

---

10. Internal customs duties.

study and the active life — now delving in books and writing poetry, now practicing swordsmanship, serving as a military officer in the Far West, or traveling
about as he pleased in search of historic sites and boon companions. He was
disinclined toward an official career and might never have sought office had
he not, from his unorthodox studies (embracing Christianity and Buddhism as
well as Confucianism and Daoism), developed a passionate interest in the Western world and the modernization of China. Active leadership in the reform
movement and study under Kang Youwei led eventually to participation at court
in the Hundred Days of Reform. With its failure, he died a "martyr" at the age
of thirty-three, risking death in hopes of rescuing the young Guangxu emperor
from his enemies.

Not only his martyrdom but also his extreme idealism made Tan a far greater
hero to the new generation of Chinese than his master, Kang, was. Accepting
many of Kang's basic ideas, he became an immediate and outspoken champion
of some that Kang regarded only as future possibilities. He openly advocated
republicanism instead of the monarchical system that Kang would have retained and merely reformed. Here Tan cited Huang Zongxi (as did other reformers and revolutionaries of the time) as native authority for his anti-dynastic
views. As against loyalty to the Manchus he proclaimed Chinese nationalism,
pointing in this case to Wang Fuzhi as its exemplar in the past. Tan also attacked
directly and unqualifiedly the traditional Confucian virtues based on specific
human relationships, which Zhang Zhidong had upheld as the essence of Confucianism and the Chinese way of life. It was these ideas — republicanism,
nationalism, and opposition to the Chinese family system — that anticipated
main trends in the early twentieth century.

### THE STUDY OF HUMANITY

Tan's chief work, *The Study of Humanity* (*Renxue*, 1898), might more accurately be
called *On Humanitarianism*. It offers an eclectic philosophy with elements drawn
ostensibly from Confucianism, Buddhism, and Christianity. The central conception
of *ren* differs little from that of Kang: a generalized feeling of goodwill toward men,
which suggests most the "liberty, equality, and fraternity" of the French Revolution,
somewhat less Christian "charity" and Buddhist "compassion," and perhaps least of
all, the Confucian virtue of "humaneness" (*ren*). Though akin, in certain respects, to
the Neo-Confucian concept of *ren* as a cosmic empathy that unites man to Heaven
and earth, its ethical character is radically altered by Tan's repudiation of the obligations of human relationship,[11] the relationships between ruler and minister, parent
and child, husband and wife, elder brother and younger brother, and friends, which

---

11. The relationships between ruler and minister, parent and child, husband and wife, elder
brother and younger brother, and friends.

in the past had given practical significance to *ren* for Confucians and Neo-Confucians alike. Indeed, the "Confucius" of Tan Sitong bears little resemblance to the Confucius of the *Analects* but freely represents the sage in the image of a modern radical reformer.

When Confucius first set forth his teachings, he discarded the ancient learning, reformed existing institutions, rejected monarchism, advocated republicanism, and transformed inequality into equality. He indeed applied himself to many changes. Unfortunately, the scholars who followed Xunzi forgot entirely the true meaning of Confucius's teaching but clung to its superficial form. They allowed the ruler supreme, unlimited powers and enabled him to make use of Confucianism in controlling the country. The school of Xunzi insisted that duties based on human relationships were the essence of Confucianism, not knowing that this was a system applicable only to the Age of Disorder. Even for the Age of Disorder, any discussion of the human relationships without reference to Heaven would be prejudicial and incomplete, and the evil consequences would be immeasurable. How much worse, then, for them recklessly to have added the Three Bonds (Mainstays),[12] thus openly creating a system of inequality with its unnatural distinctions between high and low and making men, the children of Heaven and earth, suffer a miserable life. . . .

For the past two thousand years the ruler-minister relationship has been especially dark and inhuman, and it has become worse in recent times. The ruler is not physically different or intellectually superior to man: on what does he rely to oppress 400 million people? He relies on the formulation long ago of the Three Bonds and Five Moral Relations, so that, controlling men's bodies, he can also control their minds. As Zhuangzi said, "He who steals a belt buckle pays with his life; he who steals a state gets to be a feudal lord."[13] When Tian Chengzi stole the state of Qi, he also stole the [Confucian] system of humaneness, rightness, and sage wisdom. When the thieves were Chinese and Confucians, it was bad enough; but how could we have allowed the unworthy tribes of Mongolia and Manchuria, who knew nothing of China or Confucianism, to steal China by means of their barbarism and brutality! After stealing China, they controlled the Chinese by means of the system they had stolen, and they shamelessly made use of Confucianism, with which they had been unfamiliar, to oppress China, to which they had been strangers. But China worshiped them as Heaven and did not realize their guilt. Instead of burning the books in order to keep the people ignorant [as did the Qin], they more cleverly used the books to keep the people under control. Compared with them, the tyrannical emperor of the Qin dynasty was but a fool! [A:37a–38a]

---

12. The Han dynasty conception otherwise known as the Three Mainstays: the relations of ruler/minister, parent/child, husband/wife.

13. *Zhuangzi*, ch. 10. Trans. from Watson, *Chuang Tzu*, p. 110.

At the beginning of the human race, there were no princes and subjects, for all were just people. As the people were unable to govern each other and did not have time to rule, they joined in raising up someone to be the prince. Now "joined in raising up" means not that the prince selected the people [as for civil service][14] but that the people selected the prince; it means that the prince was not far above the people but rather on the same level with them. Again, by "joined in raising up" the prince, it means that there must be people before there can be a prince: the prince is therefore the "branch" [secondary] while the people are the "root" [primary]. Since there is no such thing in the world as sacrificing the root for the branch, how can we sacrifice the people for the prince? When it is said that they "joined in raising up" the prince, it necessarily means that they could also dismiss him. The prince serves the people; the ministers assist the ruler to serve the people. Taxes are levied to provide the means for managing the public affairs of the people. If public affairs are not well managed, it is a universal principle that the ruler should be replaced. . . .

The ruler is also one of the people; in fact, he is of secondary importance as compared to ordinary people. If there is no reason for people to die for one another, there is certainly less reason for those of primary importance to die for one of secondary importance. Then, should those who died for the ruler in ancient times not have done so? Not necessarily. But I can say positively that there is reason only to die for a cause, definitely not reason to die for a prince. [B:1a–b]

In ancient times loyalty [fidelity] meant actually being loyal. If the subordinate actually serves his superior faithfully, why should not the superior actually wait upon his subordinate also? Loyalty signifies mutuality, the utmost fulfillment of a mutual relationship. How can we maintain that only ministers and subjects should live up to it? Confucius said, "The prince should behave as a prince, the minister as a minister." He also said, "The father should behave as a father, the son as a son, the elder brother as an elder brother, the younger brother as a younger brother, the husband as a husband, the wife as a wife." The founder of Confucianism never preached inequality. [B:2b]

As the evils of the ruler-minister relationship reached their highest development, it was considered natural that the relationships between parent and child and between husband and wife should also be brought within the control of categorical morality.[15] This is all damage done by the categorizing of the three bonds. Whenever you have categorical obligations, not only are the

---

14. Tan's account has some resemblance to Huang Zongxi's, but Huang speaks of the sage rulers of antiquity only as men who stood forth to undertake a heroic, self-sacrificial role as servants of the people. As such they were accepted by the people, but not raised up in the sense of being elected.

15. Under the influence of Buddhism and perhaps utilitarianism, Tan viewed the traditional moral values as mere "names" or empty concepts (*ming*) in contrast to reality or actuality (*shi*).

mouths of the people sealed so that they are afraid to speak up but their minds are also shackled so that they are afraid to think. Thus the favorite method for controlling the people is to multiply the categorical obligations. [B:7b–8a]

As to the husband-wife relationship, on what basis does the husband extend his power and oppress the other party? Again it is the theory of the Three Bonds that is the source of the trouble. When the husband considers himself the master, he will not treat his wife as an equal human being. In ancient China the wife could ask for a divorce, and she therefore did not lose the right to be her own master. Since the inscription of the tyrannical law [against remarriage] on the tablet at Kuaiji during the Qin dynasty, and particularly since its zealous propagation by the Confucians of the Song dynasty — who cooked up the absurd statement that "To die in starvation is a minor matter, but to lose one's chastity [by remarrying] is a serious matter" — the cruel system of the Legalists has been applied to the home, and the ladies' chambers have become locked-up prisons. [B:7–8]

Among the Five Moral Relations, the one between friends is the most beneficial and least harmful to life. It yields tranquil happiness and causes not a trace of pain — so long as friendships are made with the right persons. Why is this? Because the relationship between friends is founded on equality, liberty, and mutual feelings. In short, it is simply because friendship involves no loss of the right to be one's own master. Next comes the relationship between brothers, which is somewhat like the relationship between friends. The rest of the Five Relationships that have been darkened by the Three Bonds are like hell. [B:9a]

The world, misled by the conception of blood relations, makes erroneous distinctions between the nearly related and the remotely related and relegates the relationship between friends to the end of the line. The relationship between friends, however, not only is superior to the other four relationships but should be the model for them all. When these four relationships have been brought together and infused with the spirit of friendship, they can well be abolished. . . .

People in China and abroad are now talking of reforms, but no fundamental principles and systems can be introduced if the Five Moral Relations remain unchanged, let alone the Three Bonds. [B:9b–10a]

[From *Renxue, Tan Liuyang quanji* A:37a–b, B:1a–10a — CT]


# REFORM EDICT OF JANUARY 29, 1901

After China's defeat by Japan in 1895, the Empress Dowager had been amenable to conservative or moderate reform. What she opposed in 1898 was radical reform of the kind associated with Kang Youwei. The Reform Edict of January 29, 1901, charged Kang and his "rebels" with propounding "less reform of the laws than lawlessness," but this same edict committed the court and its officials to its own bold and precarious course — a full review of public and governmental affairs, both foreign and Chinese, in order "to blend together the best of what is Chinese and what is foreign."

This shift in thinking was impelled by the Boxer disaster and the evacuation of the court to distant Xi'an in August 1900. It was meant to save the Qing dynasty from extinction, as the court entered into protracted negotiations for a Boxer peace settlement. Yet for all these pressures of the moment, it launched a process that brought the abandonment of the old-style civil service examinations (with the school curriculum geared toward them) and the adoption of many modern elements, chiefly from Japan, laying the foundation for new institutions that outlasted the dynasty. The reforms embraced Western-style education (new curriculum, new textbooks, new concepts, and vocabulary mostly imported from Japan), the military, modern police, the law (civil, criminal, and commercial), the judiciary, administrative organs of government, banking and currency, and economic regulations. The Revolution of 1911, far from abandoning these changes, kept them in place. Carried forward by Yuan Shikai, they continued with modifications on into the warlord period, the Nanjing decade, and beyond.

The 1901 edict, in contrast to the Reform Edicts of 1895 and 1898, openly invited and legitimated borrowing from foreign countries, exposing China intellectually and institutionally to the outside world. In this it is comparable to the imperial Five-Article Charter Oath of Meiji Japan, 1868, which more than thirty years earlier had committed Japan to a similar course.

The Chinese government that issued the edict and orchestrated the reforms was a centralized, authoritarian regime, heir to a long-established tradition. It provided firm and coordinated leadership at court, continuing through multiple administrative layers on down to the people. With such direction and coordination from the top, it was possible to effect sweeping institutional changes with remarkable speed.

In 1908 the Empress Dowager and the Guangxu emperor died. The court, having grown dependent on the Empress Dowager for unified direction, found itself increasingly adrift and divided. Imprudent actions and policies by Manchus at court alienated non-Manchu elites whose support was needed. At the end of 1911, in rapid succession and with some turmoil and bloodshed, one province after another declared for a republic, and the isolated Manchu center collapsed.

Certain principles of morality (*changjing*) are immutable, whereas methods of governance (*zhifa*) have always been mutable. The *Classic of Changes* states that "when a measure has lost effective force, the time has come to change it." And the *Analects* states that "the Shang and Zhou dynasties took away from and added to the regulations of their predecessors, as can readily be known."

Now, the Three Mainstays (Bonds) [ruler/minister, parent/child, and husband/wife] and the Five Constant Virtues [humaneness, rightness, ritual decorum, wisdom, and trustworthiness] remain forever fixed and unchanging, just as the sun and the stars shine steadfastly upon the earth. . . .

Throughout the ages, successive generations have introduced new ways and abolished the obsolete. Our own august ancestors set up new systems to meet the requirements of the day. . . . Laws and methods (*fa*) become obsolete and, once obsolete, require revision in order to serve their intended purpose of strengthening the state and benefiting the people. . . .

It is well known that the new laws propounded by the Kang rebels were less reform laws (*bianfa*) than lawlessness (*luanfa*). These rebels took advantage of the court's weakened condition to plot sedition. It was only by an appeal to the Empress Dowager to resume the reins of power that the court was saved from immediate peril and the evil rooted out in a single day. How can anyone say that in suppressing this insurrectionary movement the Empress Dowager declined to sanction anything new? Or that in taking away from and adding to the laws of our ancestors, we advocated a complete abolition of the old? We sought to steer a middle course between the two extremes and to follow a path to good administration. Officials and the people alike must know that mother and son [the Empress Dowager and the Guangxu emperor] were activated by one and the same motive.

We have now received Her Majesty's decree to devote ourselves fully to China's revitalization, to suppress vigorously the use of the terms *new* and *old*, and to blend together the best of what is Chinese and what is foreign. The root of China's weakness lies in harmful habits too firmly entrenched, in rules and regulations too minutely drawn, in the overabundance of inept and mediocre officials and in the paucity of truly outstanding ones, in petty bureaucrats who hide behind the written word and in clerks and yamen runners who use the written word as talismans to acquire personal fortunes, in the mountains of correspondence between government offices that have no relationship to reality, and in the seniority system and associated practices that block the way of men of real talent. The curse of our country (Ch. *guojia*, J. *kokka*) lies in the one word *si*, or "private advantage"; the ruin of our realm lies in the one word *li*, or "narrow precedent."

Those who have studied Western methods up to now have confined themselves to the spoken and written languages and to weapons and machinery. These are but surface elements of the West and have nothing to do with the essentials of Western learning. Our Chinese counterparts to the fundamental principles upon which Western wealth and power are based are the following precepts, handed down by our ancestors: "to hold high office and show generosity to others," "to exercise liberal forbearance over subordinates," "to speak with sincerity," and "to carry out one's purpose with diligence." But China has neglected such deeper dimensions of the West and contents itself with learning a word here and a phrase there, a skill here and a craft there, meanwhile hanging on to old corrupt practices of currying favor to benefit oneself. If China disregards the essentials of Western learning and merely confines its studies to surface elements that themselves are not even mastered, how can it possibly achieve wealth and power?

To sum up, administrative methods and regulations must be revised and abuses eradicated. If regeneration is truly desired, there must be quiet and reasoned deliberation.

We therefore call upon the members of the Grand Council, the Grand Secretaries, the Six Boards and Nine Ministries, our ministers abroad, and the governors-general and governors of the provinces to reflect carefully on our present sad state of affairs and to scrutinize Chinese and Western governmental systems with regard to all dynastic regulations, state administration, official affairs, matters related to people's livelihood (*minsheng*), modern schools, systems of examination, military organization, and financial administration. Duly weigh what should be kept and what abolished, what new methods should be adopted and what old ones retained. By every available means of knowledge and observation, seek out how to renew our national strength, how to produce men of real talent, how to expand state revenues and how to revitalize the military. . . .

The first essential, even more important than devising new systems of governance (*zhifa*), is to secure men who govern well (*zhi ren*).[16] Without new systems, the corrupted old system cannot be salvaged; without men of ability, even good systems cannot be made to succeed. . . . Once the appropriate reforms are introduced to clear away abuses, it will be more than ever necessary to select upright and capable men to discharge the functions of office. Everyone, high and low: take heed!

The Empress Dowager and we have long pondered these matters. Now things are at a crisis point where change must occur, to transform weakness into strength. Everything depends upon how the change is effected.

[From *Guangxu chao Donghualu* 4:4601–4602 — DR]

## LIANG QICHAO

Liang Qichao (1873–1929), disciple of Kang Youwei and his coworker in the reform movement, escaped to Japan after the failure of Kang's brief regime and there became perhaps the most influential advocate of reform in the years before the Revolution of 1911. His writings, in a lucid and forceful style, dealt with a wide range of political, social, and cultural issues. To thousands of young Chinese studying abroad (most of them in Japan) or reading his books and pamphlets on the mainland, he became an inspiration and an idol — a patriotic hero, whose command of Chinese classical learning together with a remarkable sensitivity to ideas and trends in the West, gave him the appearance of an intellectual giant joining Occident and Orient, almost a universal man.

The fortnightly journal *Renewing the People* (*Xinmin congbao*), which Liang published in Yokohama from 1902 to 1905, showed a great change in his think-

---

16. Cf. Huang Zongxi, ch. 25.

ing. He was now exposed far more to Western influences and enormously impressed by Japan's progress in contrast to China's repeated failures. Sensing the power of nationalism as the force that galvanized the Western peoples and the Japanese into action and realizing too the apathy and indifference of China's millions toward the abortive palace revolution of 1898 (as, indeed, toward most public issues on the higher policy levels), Liang became fully convinced that popular education and the instillment of nationalism were China's greatest needs. In these years everything in its past culture that seemed an obstacle to national progress was to be cast aside.

Instead of reinterpreting Confucianism to find a sanction for progress, as he and Kang had done earlier, Liang now put forward a new view of world history strongly colored by social Darwinism: a struggle for survival among nations and races. Evolution of this fierce, competitive sort, rather than an optimistic view of inevitable progress toward the Grand Commonality, became the spur to drastic reform. In the 1890s he and Kang had urged going beyond the mere adoption of Western "methods" and "instruments" to basic institutional reform; now he argued that institutional change itself could only be effected through a more thoroughgoing transformation of the Chinese way of life — particularly its morals, always considered the very essence of Confucianism.

While the Qing regime lasted, Liang remained in favor of constitutional monarchy, but after 1911 he accepted the new republican order. Thus when Yuan Shikai attempted a restoration of the monarchy in 1916 Liang refused to support it, contending consistently that the need to respect the established constitutional order transcended the claims of any authority figure. As many early advocates of modernization, like Yan Fu, in later years experienced some disillusionment with the West and a loss of faith in wholesale Westernization, Liang sought increasingly to ground the modernization process in a strengthening of the rule of law and the building of a civil infrastructure, conducive to greater, informed participation of the people in government but also congenial to the more liberal of Chinese humanistic traditions.

## RENEWING THE PEOPLE

Anyone familiar with the Neo-Confucian curriculum ubiquitous in premodern East Asia would recognize that Liang's title draws upon the key expression "renewing the people" in Zhu Xi's formulation of the Three Main Guidelines (*san gangling*) in the *Great Learning*, first in order of his Four Books. Liang thereby establishes his own doctrine squarely in relation to the dominant philosophy of education in traditional China, but he invests it with a new meaning. For Zhu Xi, *xinmin* meant renewing the people through universal self-cultivation, as the basis of the whole social, political, and cultural order. Individual self-renewal would transform "the people" (*min*) and lift them up from an illiterate, undisciplined, inarticulate mass. Thus Zhu's key slogan: "Self-cultivation for the governance of men" (*xiuji zhiren*).

Here Liang's sense of "a people" is of a "nation" informed by the Western (and Japanese) sense of nationalism: "a" people as a nation (not just "the people" as commoners) would become an organic group with a consciousness of its own identity, actively participating in the determination of its national destiny in a world of many contending peoples. To this end he sees a need for corporate organization, an educational system and communication media, bridging the gap between educated elite and illiterate masses. This involves not just individual self-understanding and self-cultivation but one's own group learning from other peoples and their cultures.

Since the appearance of mankind on earth, thousands of countries have existed on the earth. Of these, however, only about a hundred still occupy a place on the map of the five continents. And among these hundred-odd countries there are only four or five great powers that are strong enough to dominate the world and to conquer nature. All countries have the same sun and moon, all have mountains and rivers, and all consist of people with feet and skulls; but some countries rise while others fall, and some become strong while others are weak. Why? Some attribute it to geographical advantages. But geographically, America today is the same as America in ancient times; why then do only the Anglo-Saxons enjoy the glory? Similarly, ancient Rome was the same as Rome today; why then have the Latin people declined in fame? Some attribute it to certain heroes. But Macedonia once had Alexander, and yet today it is no longer seen; Mongolia once had Chinggis Khan, and yet today it can hardly maintain its existence. Ah! I know the reason. A state is formed by the assembling of people. The relationship of a nation to its people resembles that of the body to its four limbs, five viscera, muscles, veins, and corpuscles. It has never happened that the four limbs could be cut off, the five viscera wasted away, the muscles and veins injured, the corpuscles dried up, and yet the body still live. Similarly, it has never happened that a people could be foolish, timid, disorganized, and confused and yet the nation still stand. Therefore, if we wish the body to live for a long time, we must understand the methods of hygiene. If we wish the nation to be secure, rich, and honored, we must discuss the way for "renewing the people." [13:36b]

## The Meaning of "Renewing the People"

The term *renewing the people* does not mean that our people must give up entirely what is old in order to follow others. There are two meanings of *renewing*. One is to improve what is original in the people and so renew it; the other is to adopt what is originally lacking in the people and so make a new people. Without both of these, there will be no success. . . .

When a nation can stand up in the world its citizens must have a unique character. From morality and laws to customs, habits, literature, and the arts, these all possess a certain unique spirit. Then the ancestors pass them down and their descendants receive them. The group becomes unified and a nation is formed. This is truly the wellspring of nationalism. Our people have been established as a nation on the Asian continent for several thousand years, and we must have some special characteristics that are grand, noble, and perfect, and distinctly different from those of other races. We should preserve these characteristics and not let them be lost. What is called preserving, however, is not simply to let them exist and grow by themselves and then blithely say, "I am preserving them, I am preserving them." It is like a tree: unless some new buds come out every year, its withering away may soon be expected. Or like a well: unless there is always some new spring bubbling, its exhaustion is not far away. [12:40a]

Is it enough merely to develop what we already have? No, it is not. The world of today is not the world of yesterday. In ancient times, we Chinese were people of villages instead of citizens. This is not because we were unable to form a citizenry but due to circumstances. Since China majestically used to be the predominant power in the East, surrounded as we were by small barbarian groups and lacking any contact with other large states, we Chinese generally considered our state to encompass the whole world. All the messages we received, all that influenced our minds, all the instructions of our sages, and all that our ancestors passed down qualified us to be individuals on our own, family members, members of localities and clans, and members of the world. But they did not qualify us to be citizens of a state. Although the qualifications of citizenship are not necessarily much superior to these other characteristics, in an age of struggle among nations for the survival of the fittest while the weak perish, if the qualities of citizens are wanting, then the nation cannot stand up independently between Heaven and earth.

If we wish to make our nation strong, we must investigate extensively the methods followed by other nations in becoming independent. We should select their superior points and appropriate them to make up for our own shortcomings. Now with regard to politics, academic learning, and technology, our critics know how to take the superior points of others to make up for our own weakness; but they do not know that the people's virtue, the people's wisdom, and the people's vitality are the great basis of politics, academic learning, and techniques. If they do not take the former but adopt the latter, neglect the roots but tend the branches, it will be no different from seeing the luxuriant growth of another tree and wishing to graft its branches onto our withered trunk, or seeing the bubbling flow of another well and wishing to draw its water to fill our dry well. Thus, how to adopt and make up for what we originally lacked so that our people may be renewed should be deeply and carefully considered. [12:40b]

All phenomena in the world are governed by no more than two principles: the conservative and the progressive. Those who are applying these two principles are inclined either to the one or to the other. Sometimes the two arise simultaneously and conflict with each other; sometimes the two exist simultaneously and compromise with each other. No one can exist if he is inclined only to one. Where there is conflict, there must be compromise. Conflict is the forerunner of compromise.

Those who excel at making compromises become a great people, such as the Anglo-Saxons, who, in a manner of speaking, make their way with one foot on the ground and one foot going forward, or who hold fast to things with one hand and pick up things with another. Thus, what I mean by "renewing the people" does not refer to those who are infatuated with Western ways and, in order to keep company with others, throw away our morals, learning, and customs of several thousand years' standing. Nor does it refer to those who stick to old paper and say that merely embracing the morals, learning, and customs of these thousands of years will be sufficient to enable us to stand upon the great earth. [12:41a]

## On Public Morality

The main deficiency in our citizens is their lack of public morality. "Public morality" simply refers to that which allows people to form groups and nations. Humans are the species of animal who can best establish themselves through this morality (as the Western philosopher Aristotle noted). . . .

Among our people there is not one who looks on national affairs as if they were his own affairs. The significance of public morality has not dawned on us. Examining into it, however, we realize that the original basis for morality lies in its serving the interests of the group. As groups differ in their degree of barbarism or civilization, so do their appropriate morals vary. All of them, however, aim at consolidating, improving, and developing the group. . . . In ancient times some barbarians considered it moral to practice sharing of women or to treat slaves as if they were not human beings. And modern philosophers do not call it immoral because under the particular situation at the time that was the proper thing to do in the interests of the group. Thus morality is founded on the interests of the group. If it is against this principle, even the perfect good can become an accursed evil. Public morality is therefore the basis of all morals. What is beneficial to the group is good; what is detrimental to the interests of the group is bad. This principle applies to all places and to all ages.

As to the external features of morality, they vary according to the degree of progress in each group. As groups differ in barbarism or civilization, so do their public interests and their morals. Morality cannot remain absolutely unchanged. It is not something that could be put into a fixed formula by the ancients several thousand years ago, to be followed by all generations to come. Hence, we who live in the present group should observe the main trends of the world, study what will suit our nation, and create a new morality in order to solidify, benefit, and develop our group. We should not impose upon ourselves a limit and refrain from going into what our sages had not prescribed. Search for public morality and there will appear a new morality, there will appear "a people renewed." [12:47a–b]

## On Progress

Generally, those who talk about a "renewal" may be divided into two groups. The lower group consists of those who pick up others' trite expressions and assume a bold look in order to climb up the official hierarchy. Their Western learning is stale stuff, their diplomacy relies on bribes, and their travels are moving in the dark. These people, of course, are not worth mentioning. The higher group consists of those who are worried about the situation and try hard to develop the nation and to promote well-being. But when asked about their methods, they would begin with diplomacy, training of troops, purchase of arms, and manufacture of instruments; then they would proceed to commerce, mining, and railways; and finally they would come, as they did recently, to officers' training, police, and education. Are these not the most important and necessary things for modern civilized nations? Yes. But can we attain the level of modern civilization and place our nation in an invincible position by adopting a little of this and that, or taking a small step now and then? I know we cannot. [13:32b]

Let me illustrate this by commerce. Economic competition is one of the big problems of the world today. It is the method whereby the powers attempt to conquer us. It is also the method whereby we should fight for our existence. The importance of improving our foreign trade has been recognized by all. But in order to promote foreign trade, it is necessary to protect the rights of our domestic trade and industry, and in order to protect these rights, it is necessary to issue a set of commercial laws. Commercial laws, however, cannot stand by themselves, and so it is necessary to complement them with other laws. A law that is not carried out is tantamount to no law; it is therefore necessary to define the powers of the judiciary. Bad legislation is worse than no legislation, and so it is necessary to decide where the legislative power should belong. If those who violate the law are not punished, laws will become void as soon as they are proclaimed; therefore, the duties of the judiciary must be defined. When all these are carried to the logical conclusion, it will be seen that foreign trade cannot be promoted without a constitution, a parliament, and a responsible government. Those who talk about foreign trade today blithely say, "I am promoting it, I am promoting it," and nothing more. I do not know how they are going to promote it. The above is one illustration, but it is true with all other cases. Thus I know why the so-called new methods nowadays are ineffectual. Why? Because without destruction there can be no construction. . . . What, then, is the way to effect our salvation and to achieve progress? The answer is that we must shatter at a blow the despotic and confused governmental system of some thousands of years; we must sweep away the corrupt and sycophantic learning of these thousands of years. [13:33a–b]

[*Xinmin shuo*, in *Yinbing shi wenji* 12:36b, 40a–b, 41a, 47a–b; 13:32b–33b — CT]

### THE CONSCIOUSNESS OF RIGHTS

Liang Qichao considered that the "new citizenry" possessed rights both individually and collectively. The term here translated as "rights" is *quanli*, a more literal rendering of which would be "power and profit." The earliest use of the compound *quan-li* occurs in the Confucian classic *Xunzi*, where we read that when one has perfected one's learning and self-cultivation, "*quan-li* cannot move one [to do wrong]" (*Xunzi Index*, 3/1/49). In other words, Xunzi considered *quan-li* to be something that we should not allow to influence us. Liang's essay is representative of a movement toward reinterpreting and reevaluating *quanli*, propelled both by internal Confucian developments and by Western writings (translated into Chinese terms by the Japanese) that emphasized rights as empowerment.

All people have responsibilities toward others that they ought to fulfill, and all people have responsibilities to themselves that they ought to fulfill. Not fulfilling one's responsibility to others is indirectly to harm the group, while not fulfilling one's responsibility to oneself is directly to harm the group. How is this? Not fulfilling one's responsibilities to others is like killing another; not fulfilling one's responsibilities to oneself is like killing oneself. If someone kills himself, then the group is decreased by one person. If there were a group all of whose members killed themselves, that would mean no less than the entire group's suicide.

What are one's responsibilities to oneself? In giving birth to things, Heaven endowed them with innate abilities to defend and preserve themselves; all living things are examples of this. The reason why humans are superior to the other myriad things is that they have not only a "physical" existence but also a "metaphysical" one. There is more than one requirement for metaphysical existence, but the most important of them is rights.

Thus animals have no responsibilities toward themselves other than preserving their lives, while in order for those who are called "human" to completely fulfill our self-responsibilities, we must preserve both our lives and our rights, which rely on one another. If we do not do this, we will immediately lose our qualifications to be human and will stand in the same position as animals. Thus all laws of Rome that saw slaves as equivalent to animals were, according to logical theory, perfectly correct. (If we used a logical syllogism to make the reasoning explicit, it would look like this: (1) those without rights are animals; (2) slaves have no rights; (3) therefore, slaves are animals.)

Thus while in a "physical" suicide, only one person is killed, in the case of a "metaphysical" suicide, a whole society is turned into animals. Furthermore, their descendants will reproduce endlessly. This is why I say that not fulfilling one's responsibility to oneself is to directly harm the group. Alas! I really do not understand why so many of my fellow Chinese are willing to kill themselves!

Where do rights originate? Rights originate in strength. Lions and tigers always have first-class, absolute rights with respect to the myriad animals, as do chieftains and kings with respect to the common people, aristocrats with respect to commoners, men with respect to women, large groups with respect to small, and strong nations with respect to weak ones. This is not due to the violent evil of the lions, tigers, chieftains, and so on. It is Heaven's nature that all humans desire to extend their own rights and never be satisfied with what they have attained. Thus it is the nature of rights that someone must first give them up before someone else can snatch them away.

For a human to be committed to strengthening himself through preserving his rights is an unparalleled method for firmly establishing and improving his group. In ancient Greece there were those who made offerings to the god of justice. The statue of this god held a scale in its left hand and a sword in its right. The scale was for weighing rights, and the sword was for protecting the practice of rights. To have a sword but no scale would be mean and wicked, but to have a scale without a sword is to make "rights" empty talk and ultimately futile. . . .

If considering only humane government will not do, it goes without saying that cruel government is still worse. In general, that humans possess rights consciousness is due to innate good knowing and good ability. But why is it that there are great inequalities — some are strong while others are weak, some dormant while others disappear? Such differences always follow the history of a nation and the gradual influence of political circumstances. Mencius said it before me: "It is not that there were never sprouts [on the mountainside], but cattle and sheep continuously graze there, so that it becomes barren." If one observes the histories of nations that have been destroyed — whether Eastern or Western, ancient or contemporary — one sees that in the beginning, there has always been some resistance against tyrannical rule to seek liberty. But as the government seeks repeatedly to eradicate opposition, the resistance gets steadily weaker, more despondent, and melts away until eventually the rigorous, intoxicating consciousness of rights comes increasingly under control and is increasingly diluted, to the point that any hope of its restoration is lost and the people come to accept repression. As the situation continuously worsens over the decades and centuries, rights consciousness completely disappears. . . .

The citizenry is an assemblage of individual persons. The rights of the state are composed of the rights of individuals. Therefore, the thoughts, feelings, and actions of a citizenry will never be obtainable without the thoughts, feelings, and actions of each individual member. That the people is strong means that the state is strong; that the people is weak means that the state is weak; that the people is rich means that the state is rich; that the people is poor means that the state is poor; that the people possesses rights means that the state possesses rights; and that the people is without shame means that the state is without shame. Is it rational to hope to establish the nation on the basis of the three characters "nation without shame"? Is it rational? . . .

The state is like a tree, and the consciousness of rights is like its roots. If the roots are destroyed, the tree will wither and die no matter how strong its trunk or vigorous its leaves. If fierce winds and rains come, it will be smashed all the sooner. Or else the scorching heat of a drought will soon cause it to completely decay away. When a citizenry that lacks rights consciousness is confronted with foreign pressures, it is like a withered tree in a storm. Or if there are no foreign pressures, such a citizenry is like the tree in a drought. I see that of all the millions of inhabitants of the earth, except for the black savages of India, Africa, and Southeast Asia, no one has a weaker sense of rights than do we Chinese.

[*Xinmin shuo*, ch. 8, pp. 31–32, 38–39 — PZ]

## THE CONCEPT OF THE NATION

Liang Qichao's concept of a "new citizenry" and "public morality" was directly correlated to his new conviction concerning the nation as the irreducible core of social organization and civilized life. In contrast to his former mentor Kang Youwei, whose universalistic, cosmopolitan ideal would subsume all human loyalties in the "Grand Commonality," Liang argued the need for national loyalty. Like Zhang Binglin and Sun Yat-sen, he believed that the Chinese lacked a sense of nationalism; traditional Chinese loyalties had been more to self, family, and local community. This left China without the solidarity and cohesion needed to survive in the struggle among nations. A conscious effort was therefore needed to develop a sense of nationhood and to inculcate national loyalty among the people.

During the primitive stage of "human grouping," there are only tribal peoples and no national citizens. The evolution from tribal peoples to national citizens divides barbarism from civilization. How different are tribal peoples and national citizens from one another! Groups of people who form clans to live together and naturally create their own customs are called tribal peoples. People who have a concept of the nation and can participate in politics themselves are termed "citizens." Nowhere on earth can nations be established without citizens.

What is the concept of the nation? First, being aware of the nation in relation to the individual. Second, being aware of the nation in relation to the court. Third, being aware of the nation in relation to foreigners. Fourth, being aware of the nation in relation to the world.

What does "being aware of the nation in relation to the individual" mean?

Humanity is superior to other creatures in that people can form groups. If individuals stood alone in nature, since they cannot fly as well as birds nor can they run as well as animals, the human race would have perished a long time ago. Therefore, in regard to the internal domain, in the age of Great Peace, cooperative efforts make things easy and the division of labor benefits everybody, in that it is impossible for individuals to do everything by themselves. In regard to the outside world, at a time of crisis, the group combines all their wisdom and strength and defends the walls against invasion, while it is totally impossible for individuals to protect themselves. Thus did nations arise.

The establishment of nations was inevitable. That is to say, everyone understood that only to rely on the individual was not feasible, thus leading them instead to associate together, to assist each other, to protect one another, and to benefit each other; they wanted the associations never to fall apart, the assistance never to fade, the protection never to miscarry, and the benefits never to fail. Therefore, everyone must realize that above the individual is something larger and more important. Whenever they have a thought, make an utterance, or undertake a task, they always pay attention to what is said to stand above the individual self. (There is nothing wrong even with considering this principle of impartial love as "egotism," because it is a universal truth that without benefiting the group one cannot benefit oneself.) Otherwise, associations will never be formed and humanity will nearly disappear. This is the first principle of the concept of the nation.

What does "awareness of the nation in relation to the court" mean? If the nation is like a corporation, then the court is the corporate headquarters while those who control the court are the general managers. If the nation is like a town or a city, then the court is the lodge of fellow townsmen while those who control the court are its superintendents. The question whether the headquarters is established for the sake of the corporation or the corporation for the headquarters, or whether the lodge of fellow townsmen is established for the sake of the city or the city for the lodge, does not need to be debated to be clear. The natures of the two [nation and court] are different, and so their spheres of importance cannot be violated. Therefore, the remark of the French king Louis XIV, "L'état c'est moi," is still today considered to be the words of a traitor. Whenever children in the West hear of this, they all condemn him, while from the Chinese point of view there may be nothing strange in the remark. At the same time, consider this analogy: if the manager of a corporation says, "I am the corporation" or the superintendent of a city [lodge of fellow townsmen] says, "I am the city," could the stockholders or the citizens accept this?

It is certain that a nation cannot exist without a court, and so it is necessary always to extend love of country to love of court. . . . Those who understand the concept of the nation generally love the court, but those who love the court do not necessarily possess the concept of the nation. Those courts that are established legally are the courts that represent the nation, and thus to love the court is to love the nation. Those courts that are not established legally are courts that betray the nation. Only if the court is legitimated can one speak of love of country. This is the second principle of the concept of the nation.

What does "awareness of the nation in relation to alien peoples" mean? The term "nation" appears in relation to the outside world. If the world consisted of just one nation, then the "nation" would not have been named. So "myself" appears when two selves stand side by side, "my family" appears when two families are adjacent, and "my nation" appears when two nations confront each other. For millions of years the human race has multiplied in separate places, and each people prospered. From language and customs to even concepts and legal systems, all differed in form and substance as well as in spirit, and thus peoples inevitably developed their own nations. Since under the universal law of the struggle for survival and natural selection, conflicts are unavoidable between people and between nations, "nations" were established to deal with other groups. Therefore, even if there were saintly wise men in foreign countries, true patriots would never be willing to live under the sovereignty of foreigners. They would rather make the people of the entire nation sacrifice life and limb until no one was left, rather than grant even the slightest of their rights to another people. Otherwise, the capacity for making the nation would soon collapse. Consider the analogy to a family. Even if one's home is completely deserted, one still does not want anyone else to use it. Awareness of oneself leads to one's survival. This is the third principle of the concept of the nation.

What does "awareness of the nation in relation to the world" mean? . . . Competition is the mother of civilization, and if competition ceased even for a single day, the progress of civilization would halt at once. Through competition, families arise out of individuals, villages arise out of families, and nations arise out of villages. Nations are the largest units of association and the peak of competition.

If boundaries were abolished as nations merged — this is actually unattainable, but if it *did* happen — competition would cease, and so would not civilization soon vanish as well? Even more to the point is the fact that human nature is unable to exist without competition. That being so, after the Grand Commonality was established, it would not be long before something inevitably gave rise to competition in the Heavenly Kingdom, and then at that time the world would return to tribal competition instead of national competition. This would lead the people of the world back to barbarism. Those who study about such things today all know the excellence of this doctrine [of the abolition of national boundaries] but regard its excellence as pertaining to spiritual boundaries rather than historical ones. Therefore, it is with good reason that they remain content with the nation and not the world as the highest form of human association. However, for those who advocate universal love, the sacrifice of the interests of the individual for the sake of love for the family is permissible; and to sacrifice the interests of the family for the sake of love for the village is permissible; and to sacrifice the interests of the individual, the family, or the village for the sake of love of the nation is permissible. The nation is the standard of partial love; that the ultimate standard of universal love is therein either fallen short of or gone beyond is barbarism. Why? Because both situations are characteristic of tribal peoples instead of citizens of a nation. This is the fourth principle of the concept of the nation.

Alas, how diminished we are! We Chinese lack the concept of the nation. Inferior people care only about the prosperity of the individual and the family, while superior people airily deliberate philosophical truths, turning their backs on practical things. . . .

[However,] the search for how to truly benefit oneself, as well as how to preserve one's benefits without ever losing them, cannot be successful without cultivating the concept of the nation. My compatriots! Don't say that it is enough to rely on the great size of our territory. At its zenith, the extent of the Roman Empire was no smaller than China today. Don't say that it is enough to rely on the population. There are billions of natives in India. Don't say that it is enough to rely on civilization. In the past, when Athens in Greece was an independent state, it claimed that its culture was the best in the world until it became subservient to other peoples, was unable to rise up, and eventually was shattered. And during the barbarian Yuan dynasty in China, the literati all learned Mongol (the "Notes on the Twenty-Two Histories" records this in detail), and learning nearly ceased.

Only the nation is our father and mother.

Without a father, what can be relied on? Without a mother, what can be relied on?

[If we are] Alone and desolate, who will pity us?

As soon as the opportunity is lost, we are finished.

Reflecting on this, so far we still have a chance. [*Chuci*]

[*Xinmin shuo*, ch. 6, pp. 16–18, 22–23  — PZ]

## LIANG QICHAO AND THE NEW PRESS

Liang Qichao was active in the development of the late Qing political press and became a prime molder of public opinion in the late nineteenth and early twentieth centuries. In form these late Qing journals were most directly influenced by the Western missionary and commercial press that had operated in China from 1815. By the late nineteenth century, a number of foreign-managed Chinese-language commercial newspapers such as *Shenbao* (*Shanghai Journal*, founded 1872) were already in existence. In contrast, the new political press, which would become increasingly influential in the late 1890s, distinguished itself from these commercial newspapers in two ways: it was owned and managed by Chinese nationals, and its main emphasis was on political commentary. While the origins of such political commentary can be traced back to newspapers founded by Western-influenced Chinese merchants, officials, and intellectuals in the 1870s through the 1890s (including Wang Tao's *Xunhuan ribao*, founded in Hong Kong in 1873), the real turning point in late Qing press history came in 1895. In the wake of China's defeat by Japan and its acceptance of the humiliating terms of the Treaty of Shimonoseki, Kang Youwei and several of his students, including Liang Qichao, founded China's first new-style political journals. The most important of these was *Shiwu bao* (*China Progress*, 1886).

The changes in the late Qing press initiated by the events of 1895 were both qualitative and quantitative. Whereas in the early and mid-1890s about a dozen newspapers were published in the chief port cities, between 1895 and 1898 some sixty newspapers were established, many of them outside of the foreign-dominated centers. The Guangxu emperor himself recognized the importance of this early reform press and encouraged its development during the Hundred Days of Reform. After the Empress Dowager's coup on September 21, 1898, however, Kang, Liang, and the reform press were forced into exile in Japan.

This forced exile gave rise to one of the most important chapters in the development of late Qing political journalism. Two of the most influential reform organs were founded in Japan by Liang Qichao during this period: *Qingyi bao* (*The China Discussion*, 1898), and *Xinmin congbao* (*Renewing the People*, 1902). Thus young intellectuals who later became major actors in the early twentieth-century China-based press had an opportunity to develop their skills as reformists and publicists — skills that proved invaluable once reform was put back on the official agenda in Beijing, through the aforementioned Imperial Edict of January 29, 1901, which announced administrative reforms and opened up the possibility of more-substantial political reforms. Taking advantage of this opening, from the year 1904 reformists began to create newspapers and periodicals in China advocating the establishment of a constitutional monarchy. Their mission was to monitor the depth of the government's commitment to reform, encourage the development of politically aware constitutional citizens, and guide China to a position of strength in the world through legal and institutional reform.

The *Eastern Times* (*Shibao*) became the most important of these new reform journals. Its history began in the early spring of 1904 when Liang Qichao, still in exile, risked a visit to Shanghai in order to guide the preparations for its establishment. He chose the newspaper's name, outlined its general regulations, and wrote the inaugural statement for its first edition (translated below). Eventually, it distanced itself from the Kang-Liang faction, but by 1909 it was the most widely circulated newspaper in the Shanghai region. Thus, in the absence of political parties and representative bodies, the new press became the institutional base of late Qing reformers and their principal mouthpiece.

## INAUGURAL STATEMENT FOR THE *EASTERN TIMES* (*SHIBAO*)

Conscious of the need to raise people's awareness of national issues and create active public opinion in regard to national policy, Liang joined in establishing this newspaper as a forum for the discussion of such issues. He wrote this inaugural statement for its first issue, June 12, 1904, to set forth its purposes and functions. It is a manifesto of reform, combining intellectual eclecticism with calls for a political middle course between conservatism and radicalism. Intent on finding a synthesis between Western learning — in this text specifically the ideas of Charles Darwin and Herbert Spencer — and the truths of the classical Confucian tradition, the editors attempted to forge a new constitutional course for China, seeing their role as mediators between old elites who opposed reform, young revolutionaries who advocated total Westernization, and impractical intellectuals whom Liang indirectly faulted for the failure of the Hundred Days of Reform.

Why publish the *Eastern Times* (*Shibao*)? The *Record of Rites* says, "A gentleman acts according to the golden mean."[17] It also says, "A man of profound self-cultivation and high learning uses his knowledge appropriately."[18] Therefore, in regulating the state and ordering society, nothing is more valuable than timeliness. It is not the Chinese teachings alone that emphasize this. In the West, Darwin first developed the principle of natural selection and the triumph of the strong. Spencer later replaced this principle with the theory of survival of the fittest. According to this theory, which constitutes the field of victory and defeat, that which is of superior quality but not adapted to the environment will eventually become inferior and that which is of inferior quality but adapted to the environment will eventually become superior. Therefore, although the fur of a fox is very warm, it is of no use in the heat of summer, and although fine satin is very beautiful, it cannot protect against the cold of winter. That which is not appropriate to the time will certainly fail.

In China today, those in lofty and powerful positions and those who are reclusive hermits are all unaware of the general world situation. They believe that thousand-year-old politics and thousand-year-old learning are appropriate to the changes of today. According to an assessment of present conditions, however, this is not possible; one could knit one's brow in worry for a whole day and still not be able to solve today's problems with yesterday's methods. As a result, when heroic young activists hear that Western nations have such and such a method of regulating chaos, such and such a method of self-strengthening, they all run and shout, "We too must do it this way! We too must do it this way!" While no one would deny that these methods are the reason the West can regulate chaos

---

17. *Mean* 2.
18. *Mean* 25.

and strengthen itself, we simply do not know if these methods are appropriate to our times. As Confucius said, "To go beyond is as wrong as to fall short."[19] To fall short and apply methods that are no longer fitting to the times is a waste; every day corruption would increase and there would be no way to save the nation. At the same time, to go beyond the present situation and apply methods that are too advanced for the times, to yell and shout and wildly push forward, would not accomplish anything either. Moreover, proceeding in this way could give rise to new problems, and the nation would become unsalvageable. In sum, if the country should be lost, both kinds of people [conservatives and Western-oriented radicals] would be equally responsible.

There are also intelligent, broad-minded, and steadfast individuals who are committed to listening to both sides but choosing the middle course in order to plan the orderly progress of the people. It seems, however, that because their general knowledge is insufficient, their understanding of scientific theory weak, and their concrete investigations of the current situation lacking, when they speak in terms of general principles they have no tangible proof, when they try to manage matters they cannot manage them successfully, and when they want to implement their ideas they are bewildered and do not know how to proceed. They vigorously apply themselves to do one or two things but because their methods are mistaken, they incessantly fail. Because everyone is aware of this and admonished by it they do not dare speak of reform again.[20] Alas! Although there are numerous kinds of publicists and politicians in the nation, upon scrutiny all of them follow one of these three paths [of conservatives, radicals, or impractical reformists].

Alas! This is a dangerous time and we are deeply concerned. Therefore in founding this newspaper, we have named it *shi* — *The Times* (*Shibao*).[21] While we of course wish to revere the essence of the nation, we believe that that which is not appropriate to the present should be put aside and forgotten. And while we of course admire Western civilization, we believe that that which is not appropriate to the level of Chinese development must be temporarily put aside. We will exert our knowledge to the highest possible level in order to resolve the major political and scholarly problems that arise in China and abroad. Using fair and honest discussions, we will analyze the positive and negative, advantageous and disadvantageous aspects of these problems. We will also investigate methods for delivering the nation from danger and coping with the current situation, while cooperating with the government and conferring with the citizens.

---

19. *Analects* 11:15; Legge, *The Chinese Classics*, p. 242.

20. Liang is referring to the failed Hundred Days of Reform.

21. The character *shi* can be translated as time or an era, but in this context, "timely" or "the opportune moment" is close to the meaning.

It is the duty of newspapers in advanced nations[22] to report on the facts in the news, to follow the trend of international public opinion, to investigate conditions in the interior of the nation, to develop knowledge of politics and the arts, to introduce new ideas, and to provide materials for leisurely reading. We must drive ourselves on. We will use our writings to define and convey the will of the nation. We must also, however, take note of the saying of Western philosophers that "perfect things must be produced in perfect times." Today, given that our nation is still young in terms of development, I realize that it is not appropriate for us to wish to place ourselves among the great newspapers of all of the nations in the world. But by taking one step after another, a distance of one thousand miles can eventually be overcome, and by joining together one hundred streams, the four seas could eventually be formed. It is certain that, sooner or later, our newspaper's trajectory will not only follow but parallel the progress of the nation. This is what we will assiduously work toward every day.

Our nation can take the highest position among the nations of the world. Therefore, this newspaper must seek to take the highest position among all of the newspapers in the world. The favor that the people of our nation will owe us is unlimited! The favor that the people of our nation will owe us is unlimited!

[*Shibao*, June 12, 1904; *Xinmin congbao*, #44–45 —JJ]

## ADVOCATES OF SCRIPT REFORM

Among the important radical reform issues in the late Qing was the proposal to replace Chinese characters by an alphabetic script. This was by no means the first time the question had been raised. In the Song, the encyclopedic scholar Zheng Qiao (see chapter 19), from his study of Sanskrit, had already noted the cumbersomeness of Chinese characters and the advantages of an alphabetic script. Then in 1605, the Jesuit missionary Matteo Ricci published *The Miracle of Western Letters* (*Xizi qiji*) in Beijing. This was the first book to use the Roman alphabet to write a Sinitic language. Twenty years later, another Jesuit in China, Nicolas Trigault, wrote on the same subject in his *Aid to the Eyes and Ears of Western Literati* [*Xiru ermu zi*] at Hangzhou. Neither book had much immediate impact on the way in which the Chinese people thought about their writing system, and the romanizations they described were intended more for Westerners than for the Chinese, but their eventual impact on China was enormous.

One of the earliest Chinese thinkers to react to and evaluate Western alpha-

---

22. *Wenming guo* is translated here as "advanced nations," according to the new meaning the term *wenming* took on in Meiji Japan in the late nineteenth century rather than in its classical meaning as a civilized cultural condition.

bets was the late Ming, early Qing scholar-official Fang Yizhi (1611–1671). A progressive, scientifically minded individual, he criticized the sinographs for being too numerous and too complicated, in contrast to Western systems of writing that were more economical and elegantly analytical in their mode of composition.

Fang Yizhi understood well the implications that these complicated and ambiguous methods of character formation had for the script as a whole: "The confusion of characters is due to their interchangeability and borrowing but, if a concept pertained to a single word and each word had a single meaning, as in the distant West where sounds are combined in accordance with concepts, and words are formed in accordance with sounds, so that there would be neither duplication nor sharing, wouldn't that be superior?" (*Tongya* 1:96–97).

It was not until more than two hundred years later that the concept of spelling planted in China by the Jesuits had sufficiently matured for the Chinese themselves to begin proposing its application for the design of new and more efficient scripts for their own languages.

SONG SHU: ILLITERACY IN CHINA

The first late Qing reformer to propose that China adopt a system of spelling was Song Shu (1862–1910). A student of the great scholars Yu Yue and Zhang Taiyan, Song had been to Japan and observed the stunning effect of the *kana* syllabaries and Western learning there. This galvanized him into activity on a number of fronts, one of the most important being reform of the script. While Song did not himself actually create a system for spelling Sinitic languages, his discussion of the idea proved fertile and led to a proliferation of schemes for phonetic scripts in the following years. The following is excerpted from an essay, "Civilizing," in a tract by Song titled "Accommodating to Circumstances."

Among men and women of white nations who can read, in cases where they are many they amount to more than nine out of ten, and in cases where they are few they still amount to almost two out of ten. Among yellow peoples, Japan has the largest number of people who can read. India . . . today also has four out of a hundred.

In China, . . . if we compute those who can read today, among men there are approximately one out of a hundred and among women roughly one out of every forty thousand. This is far removed from India, not to mention Japan and the white nations. With so few individuals able to read, how will the people ever be liberated from their accumulated distress? Now, we should emulate Japan and issue orders for education. Orders should be given that all boys and girls between the ages of six and thirteen should enter school. The parents of those who do not would be fined. Every county, village, settlement, and hamlet would uniformly establish one boys' and one girls' school for each district. The expenses for the schools would be paid for by the counties, villages, settlements, and hamlets themselves. Textbooks would give consideration to the merits of foreign nations, while readers would exclusively use Chinese characters. (Note: According to the laws governing Japanese schools today, instruction is given first in *kana* and only later in sinographs. If we learn from this example, then we need to devise many spelling systems for the [dialects of the] area south of the Yangzi and Huai Rivers to facilitate the studies of our children. The implications of this matter are so great that I dare not discuss them here.)

[Song Shu, *Liuzhai beiyi*, in *Song Shu ji* 1:135–136 — VM]

## LU ZHUANGZHANG'S ATTEMPT AT ROMANIZATION

The first Chinese to propose a system of spelling for Sinitic languages was Lu Zhuang-zhang (1854–1928). Lu was from Fujian and he grew up in Xiamen, where romanized writing of the local language was used widely after it was introduced by Christian missionaries (a romanized Chinese translation of the Bible had already been made in 1852). At age twenty-one, Lu moved to Singapore, where he studied English. After he returned to Xiamen four years later, he assisted an English missionary in compiling a Chinese-English dictionary.

Lu's *First Steps in Being Able to Understand at a Glance* (*Yimu liaoran chujie*), published in Xiamen in 1892, was the first book written by a Chinese that presented a potentially workable system of spelling for a Sinitic language. His script was based on the Roman alphabet with some modifications. Among other improvements over the sinographs that Lu's alphabet possessed was the linking up of syllables into words and their separation by empty spaces. Although he believed that all of the local languages should be written out with phonetic scripts, Lu advocated that the speech of Nanjing be adopted as the standard for the whole nation as it was when Matteo Ricci had come to China three centuries earlier. Altogether, Lu worked for forty years to bring an efficient system of spelling to China. He is now viewed by Chinese language workers as the father of script reform in their country.

Chinese characters are perhaps the most difficult of all characters in the whole world today. Tracing them back to the time of the Yellow Emperor, Cang Jie[23] created characters as pictographs, indicatives, associative compounds, figurative extensions, pictophonograms, and phonetic loans. Up to today, successive transformations of the forms of the characters have already been taking place for more than forty-five hundred long years. In antiquity, they used "cloud writing" and "bird tracks." Later, they used the tadpole script and pictographs. Still later

---

23. In Chinese mythology, he is held to be the inventor of writing.

there were the seal script, the clerkly script, and the eight divisions. By the Han, they had changed to the eight methods and, in the Song, they changed to the Song style. All these changes have been in the direction of replacing the difficult with the easy. . . .

In the *Kangxi Dictionary* (1716), there are 40,919 [*sic*, > 47,043] separate symbols. . . . Normally, when one writes poems and essays, one uses only a little over 5,000 of these characters. But if one wants to recognize these several thousand characters, even the most intelligent person will have to spend more than ten years of hard work. Herein lies the suitability of spelling.

In my humble opinion, the wealth and strength of a nation are based on science;[24] the advancement of science is based on the desire for learning and understanding principle of all men and women, young and old. Their being able to desire learning and understand principle is based on the spelling of words. Once they have become familiar with the letters and the methods of spelling, they can read any word by themselves without a teacher. Because the written and spoken words are the same, when they read with their mouths they comprehend in their hearts. Furthermore, because the strokes of the letters are simple, they are easy to recognize and easy to write, saving more than ten years of a person's life. This time may be dedicated to mathematics, physics, chemistry, and all kinds of practical learning. What worry would there then be for the wealth and strength of the nation?

In the whole world today, except for China, all the other nations mostly use twenty or thirty letters for spelling. . . . Therefore, in the civilized nations of Europe and America, all men and women over the age of ten, even in remote villages and isolated areas, are able to read. . . . What is the reason for this? It is because they spell their words, because the written and the spoken word are the same, and because the strokes of the letters are simple. Japan also has been using Chinese characters, but more recently some particularly intelligent person devised letters for spelling that are forty-seven simple graphs. Consequently, culture and education have flourished greatly there. . . . That men and women of foreign nations all can read is due to spelling.

[Lu, preface, *Yimu liaoran chujie* — VM]

## SHEN XUE'S UNIVERSAL SCRIPT

In 1896, Shen Xue's (1871–c. 1900) brilliant "Original Sounds for a Flourishing Age" ("Shengshi yuanyin") was published in two Shanghai newspapers. These were the *Shanghai Journal* (*Shenbao*), the oldest newspaper of modern China founded in 1872

---

24. *Gezhi* (an abbreviation of "the investigation [of things] and the extension [of knowledge]"in the *Great Learning*). This term was also used as an equivalent of "physics" in the early days of contact with the modern West.

by an English merchant, and *China Progress*, whose publisher was Huang Zunxian (1848–1905). The editor of the latter was Liang Qichao (1873–1929) and another of Kang Youwei's (1858–1927) disciples was its manager. Shen, a medical student, had originally written the work in English under the title "Universal System," but it was never published. The Chinese version is but a partial translation of the English work. Shen's original preface begins as follows:

Those who discuss the affairs of the times nowadays either call for the restoration of the old Zhou rituals or for renewal through Western learning. Although what they speak of seems different, their determination is the same. They all cherish accommodation to circumstances, just as with officialdom, military strategy, agricultural policy, commercial affairs, manufacturing, mining, and schools. I, however, consider the accommodation of script to circumstances to be primary.

Script is an instrument of intelligence, conveying as it does the language and thoughts of antiquity and the present. The difficulty or ease of a script is that which separates the intelligent from the stupid, the strong from the weak. . . .

From the time when Cang Jie created the characters until today, it has been more than forty-five hundred years. There are three different ways to divide up the characters into groups: by category, by rhyme, and by strokes. Radicals may be as many as 544 or as few as 214. Altogether, we may count more than 40,900 character forms. Those commonly used by scholars are only 4,000 or 5,000. Unless you earnestly read the thirteen classics, you cannot be considered smart, and unless you spend more than a decade, you cannot do it. How many decades does a person have available for use in one life? Consequently, those who read books are few, while those who embrace the ancient and the modern or survey China and abroad are even fewer!

At this deeply painful juncture when civil affairs are in disarray and foreign calamities are raging, everyone wishes to devise a plan for self-strengthening. The first is that of the strength of the separate nations of Europe. After Rome lost the Way, Europe broke up into separate nations. The reason why the separate nations of Europe are strong is because they have Roman letters for spelling. This makes it easy for people to read, and thus it is easy for them to understand principle. Having understood principle, they can distinguish clearly between advantage and disadvantage. Those above and those below share the same intention to seek wealth and strength.

The second is that of the strength of America. The reason why America is strong is because the Europeans moved there and planted the seeds of reading on a large scale. Now, American's sciences, wealth, and strength are running abreast of Europe's. This, too, is because they have letters for spelling. Letters for spelling make it easy to communicate one's innermost feelings to each other so that there are no barriers between those above and those below.

The third is that of the strength of Russia and Japan. The Russian czar, Peter the Great, set about studying Europe when he was young. All affairs pertaining to wealth and strength were imprinted in his heart and written in his books. When he ascended to the throne, his new government was magnificent, and now Russia is feared throughout the world. In the twenty years since Japan has been engaged in trading, it has vigorously flourished because it is courageous in learning from others. . . .

The Chinese people occupy one-third of the whole world. Since the people are so numerous, it is appropriate that the method for becoming literate should be all the more convenient. Otherwise, the vast majority of them would be a bunch of blockheads. Although they have eyes and ears, it is as though they have no vision or hearing. . . .

In the present situation where the Chinese script is compelled to change but the conditions are such that the change cannot be too abrupt, what can be done? There is no principle in the world that cannot be investigated and there is nothing in the world that cannot be done. Through clarification of form and function (*tiyong*), I have obtained these eighteen letters, which constitute the Original Sounds for a Flourishing Age. They can be presented to the whole world and can spell all the sounds in the world. . . . Obtaining the shortcut of script is the fountainhead of self-strengthening.

[Preface to "Shengshi yuanyin" — VM]

## WANG ZHAO'S "MANDARIN LETTERS"

Another influential late Qing script reformer was Wang Zhao (1859–1935?), who hailed from Hebei province. As a boy, he liked to read translated books that were popular in China at the time. This penchant was one of the reasons his relatives and neighbors said that he was possessed by strange spirits. Nonetheless, he became a high-ranking scholar and official in the Qing government, and in 1897 he founded the first modern primary school at the district level in China. After the failure of the 1898 reforms, in which he had taken part, he fled to Japan. He stayed there for two years, during which he created a sort of *kana*-like syllabary for Chinese in imitation of the native Japanese syllabic writing system. It was called Mandarin Letters (*Guanhua zimu*). In 1900 he returned to China and published his first book introducing this new system of phonetic writing. It was titled *Letters for Combining the Sounds of Mandarin* (*Guanhua hesheng zimu*). In the preface he wrote:

The Chinese script was among the earliest created. In my view, the earliest is the foremost. For explaining essences and revealing secrets, it would seem that the Chinese script is far superior to those of other nations. Although the scripts of the other nations are shallow, however, each of the people throughout those nations is thoroughly conversant with them because language and script are consistent. Their letters are simple and convenient and, for even the dullest youths, the age they can speak is the age when they become conversant with writing. . .

But not even one out of a hundred of the people in our nation can comprehend the meaning of a text. After they have spent ten years, if you ask them what they've learned, they say, "I've learned how to read characters." The dullards may study for half their lives without being able to write a letter because it is so difficult. . . .

The literati and the commoners are like two different worlds. Whatever may be the grand intention of the government, the general outlines of geography, the connections between above and below or the vicissitudes of China and other countries, there is no way to make them comprehend even the rudiments.

No matter how trenchantly the officials issue their orders, the common people are obtusely ignorant. Should one attempt to exhort the people to learning, to manage finances, to drill troops and so forth, in contrast with other nations east and west, one becomes aware of the vast disparity between the difficulty for us and the ease for them. . . .

Now, in the various nations [of the West], education prospers greatly, the arts of government flourish day by day, and even in Japan commands are unified and changes are rapid. Surely there are reasons for this in each case. The identity of speech and writing and the simplicity of their scripts are actually the most important factors.

An administration that leads to wealth and strength lies in each of the common people becoming adept in his career, broadening his knowledge, and knowing his position, not in having an outstanding elite.

[Preface to *Guanhua hesheng zimu*, pp. 1–3 — VM]

*The debate over the fate of the traditional writing system is still waged to this day. In their early revolutionary days, the Chinese Communists were champions of romanization, for reasons similar to those presented in the foregoing, but after coming to power they contented themselves with adopting a system of simplified characters for words in common use. Nevertheless, if the role of simplified characters expands and the applications of spelling increase, the future of the sinographs may become more doubtful. It is certain, however, that calligraphers will continue to practice them and classicists will always study them. The dawning of the information age may radically alter the way Chinese communicate with each other, but it cannot completely eradicate the heritage of the sinographs.*

## ZHANG BINGLIN'S REVOLUTIONARY NATIONALISM

Zhang Binglin (1868–1936) is often spoken of as the father of Chinese nationalism. Born into a once wealthy but declining gentry family in the lower Yangzi region, he was one of the last great classicists of the Chinese tradition, equally at home amid philosophical, historical, and literary texts. Unlike Wei Yuan and Kang Youwei, who favored the New Text school, Zhang's scholarly allegiance lay with the Old Text school, especially with the *Zuozhuan*, but he was increasingly anti-Confucian and became a leader in the movement to rediscover the noncanonical pre-Qin texts.

In the mid- and late 1890s, Zhang supported the reform movement, but in the years after the debacle of the 1898 Hundred Days of Reform and the Boxer Rebellion of 1900, which resulted in Western and Japanese troops occupying Beijing, he moved toward an explicitly revolutionary call to overthrow the Manchu Qing government and as a symbolic act of defiance cut off his queue (the braid of hair that signaled allegiance to the Qing dynasty). On issues such as modernization and democratic politics, the differences between the radical reformers and the revolutionaries were often slight, but Zhang did much to magnify the issue of overthrowing the Manchu dynasty and building Chinese nationalism on the basis of Han ethnicity. Kang Youwei, on the other hand, still promoted the cause of gradual reform, hoping the Empress Dowager could be retired and the deposed Guangxu emperor restored to power. Kang criticized anti-Manchu racism, pointing out that China had been composed of numerous peoples and that the Manchus had identified themselves with Confucian humanist universalism. He warned that revolution would result in bloodshed, dictatorship, and foreign invasion.

The passages below are translated from Zhang's open letter to Kang written in 1903. Zhang explicitly espoused revolution and attacked the Manchus. His nationalism cannot be called "racist" in the ethnic sense of being based on "blood." Rather, he insisted (as had Wang Fuzhi) that long historical experience produced deep cultural differences among peoples, implying that these were for all practical purposes as impassable as biological determinism, and he emphasized the right of self-determination of all peoples (in this regard, Zhang acknowledged that the Manchus had a right to Manchuria but not to rule the Chinese).

Zhang's letter is both erudite and deliberately provocative. He was arrested for calling the emperor a little clown and using his tabooed personal name, Zaitian. Released from prison in 1906, he continued to agitate for an anti-Manchu revolution, sometimes working with and sometimes estranged from Sun Yat-sen. After the Revolution of 1911, Zhang briefly engaged in politics, was put under house arrest for three years, and increasingly turned toward traditional scholarship in the 1920s and 1930s.

## LETTER OPPOSING KANG YOUWEI'S VIEWS ON REVOLUTION

This open letter was written in 1903 not long after the failure of the Boxer Rebellion, at a time when the Qing regime was belatedly moving toward a constitutional process. It is a lengthy and powerful diatribe against Kang as a champion of constitutionalism and against the Manchus as foreign conquerors. Much of it consists of stinging personal ridicule of both Kang and the deposed Emperor Guangxu, as well as of conflicting readings by Kang and Zhang of events in Chinese or world history.

Following are excerpts that illustrate three main themes of Zhang: nationalism as a basic human instinct, Manchu rule as inherently repressive and exploitative, and revolution as the only means to achieve effective change.

Though opposed in their views on Confucianism and nationalism and equally unsuccessful politically, Kang and Zhang contributed to two major trends of the times: millenarian expectations of a total solution to China's problems, and on Zhang's part, revolution as the necessary course of action.

Dear Changsu [Kang Youwei],

I have read the letter you wrote to the Chinese merchants in the Americas in which you say that China should only have a constitutional monarchy and not a revolution. You long-windedly cite endless historical precedents. Alas, Changsu, how can you be happy doing this? You are desperately trying to get recalled into government service after a restoration [of Guangxu to power], and so first you write this nonsense to get the attention of the Tungusic beasts [Manchus], hoping that by some chance you will be amnestied. You weren't writing to merchants — you were writing to the Manchus!

For a moment's wealth and prestige, you dare everything that is wrong and won't quit. Your tricky rhetoric has confused the nation to the point where you set the example for evil Confucians and vicious culprits. You are respected as a sage and you call yourself a religious leader, but it seems that your fanciful lies here mean you are doing nothing but cunningly buttering up the Manchus. However, the way you have fooled the world far surpasses that which comes out of the mouths of the evil Confucians and vicious culprits. Can I let this nonsense go by without a word of correction?

Your basic idea is that one should ground a theory only on truth and results and not talk about whether races are the same or not. Although nationalism was a firmly rooted potentiality even among primitive peoples in ancient times, it began to develop only as we approached modern times. It is a natural human sentiment.[25]

Today, have the Manchus assimilated to the Han people? Or have they conquered the Han people? Manchu shamanism is not the orthodox imperial religion; queues and jeweled necklaces are not the Chinese caps; and the documents of the Qing in its own language are not traditional Chinese characters. The Manchus merely respected Confucius, followed the ways of Confucianism, and presented a false picture as a technique for claiming the emperorship and fooling the people. Their talk of the "same race" is not to turn the Manchus into Han people but to make the Han people Manchus!

---

25. The natural knowledge or good knowing (*liang zhi*) of Mencius and Wang Yangming.

You have admitted that the Grand Commonality (*Datong*) and universal principles are not practical in our times. Rather, since ours is certainly the age of nationalism, your confounding together Manchus and Han is like mixing fragrances and stinks in the same bowl. . . .

As for clothing and queues, [you argue that] the Han people have become accustomed to Manchu fashion, and even if we could go back to Song and Ming fashions, we would feel uncomfortable with them. But do you people not know that these queues are a barbarian fashion instituted by force? How can we become accustomed to them? When King Yu went to the kingdom of the naked peoples, he wore his hair long and tattooed his body; when Mozi went to Chu, he wore embroidered clothes and played the *sheng*. They did not enjoy doing these things. After being forced to be a particular way for a long time, one becomes accustomed to it, but this is certainly no way to determine right and wrong.

*Kang Youwei's letter had defended Manchu rule as more enlightened than the Ming, especially for the Manchu's professing of Confucian egalitarian and meritocratic ideals whereby worthy Chinese, including the successful scholar-official-generals Zeng Guofan and Zuo Zongtang, had risen to high positions under the Qing. Zhang belittled all this.*

Although General Zeng, General Zuo, and others were given wonderful titles, they really just commanded tiny local forts and never had real power. Yet, as soon as Fukangan [a Manchu general] suppressed an uprising in Taiwan he was ennobled as a Beile Commandery Prince, while Zeng and Zuo, who managed to destroy the Taipings and restore the emperorship to Manchus, were merely made marquises and assigned only nominal positions. While Zeng was still alive he had to fawn upon [the Qing bannerman] Guanwen to protect his life. How can we compare them in terms of importance or accomplishments! Lately, the leading members of the Council of State have all been imperial relatives. The ruler does nothing yet controls everything, and his subordinates are mere servants. [The Manchu] Prince Gong and Prince Chun succeeded while doing nothing, while [the Han Chinese] Shen, Li, Weng, and Sun worked hard, which shows that the former were masters while the latter were slaves. . . .

Now the reasons why you do not admit that we are slaves, and why you promote constitutional monarchy in order to destroy the sprouts of revolution, are simply that you have twisted your own heart and bent your will too long, and have turned yourself into a slave. In promoting constitutional monarchy, you had to make the emperor into a sage. . . .

After 1895, what worried this "sagely emperor" most was that he would not stay on the throne long just because the Empress Dowager wanted to abdicate. Saddened by internal problems, [Guangxu] planned to reach out externally. He knew that without reform there was no way to get the support of the foreign powers; without the support of the foreign powers there was no way to shore up his strength and take away the Empress Dowager's powers. The little clown Zaitian [the taboo personal name of the Guangxu emperor] couldn't even distinguish between beans and wheat, and he marched into danger. He certainly was not planning for the Manchus as a whole. . . .

Today five million Manchus rule over more than four hundred million Han only because rotten traditions make the Han stupid and ignorant. If the Han people should one day wake up, then the Manchus would be totally unable to rest peacefully here, like the Austrians in Hungary or the Turks in the former Eastern Roman Empire. It is human nature to love one's own race and to seek gain for oneself. The so-called Sagely Emperor is not far from this human nature. Can he really discard his position, and forsake everything to benefit the Han people? . . .

Moreover, the so-called constitutional system must have a bicameral legislature. The lower house would make laws while the upper house would have a veto power over them. But who would comprise the members of the upper house? If it is to be the imperial clan, then it will simply consist of the emperor's relatives and princes. If it is to be the nobility, then it will simply consist of the Eight Banners and the princes of Inner and Outer Mongolia. If it is to be the important religious leaders, then it will simply consist of the Dalai Lama and the Panchen Lama of Tibet. Of all these groups, none includes any Han people in their number — there are only people of other races — and so parliamentary rights will still not be given to Han people. . . .

You believe that "blood will flow like water and the dead will lie everywhere in the disaster of revolution, and its goals will in the end still be left incomplete." However, can a constitutional system ever be achieved without bloodshed? England, Austria, Germany, and Italy all first won their rights to liberty and parliaments through revolts. Were these insurrections just a matter of debate, or did they involve spears and bows and flying bullets? Closer to us lies the example of Japan. Although their constitutionalist movement first arose in peaceful discussion, it had been preceded by armies devoted to expelling the foreigners and overthrowing the Bakufu. There would have been no constitutional system without the violent struggle that preceded it.

Men of spirit [self-sacrificing activists] who would take responsibility for the world are originally without real power; we cannot discuss them in terms of success and failure. The emperor, however, must be judged in terms of success and failure. Why so? Because to possess power but not be able to use it is simply to clothe oneself with the empty title of "emperor." He cannot protect even himself, yet he wishes to share the concerns of the country! He cannot control even his own ministers, yet he wishes to make the people follow the laws! . . .

You suppose, "The Chinese people today are incapable of understanding universal principles or abolishing old customs; thus, after a revolution violence would continue unabated and bare survival would be difficult. How then could one reform the country and save the people and reorder politics!" But how could a people who cannot understand universal principles and [who] persist in following old customs be incapable of revolution but capable of constitutionalism? How can there be a constitutional order with a single sage at the top while the rest of the population are the most primitive of barbarians?

In your "The Destruction of India" ("Lun Yindu wangguo shu") you said that Indian literature and craftsmanship were vastly superior to Chinese, and you cited a number of writings as evidence. But you forget that tropical zones do not have to worry about cold and hunger and so their people become lazy. Various objects quickly rot in the heat, and so the people have little idea of ownership. This is why Hinduism and Buddhism could arise nowhere but in India. Precisely because they lack the idea of ownership, they think that everything is impermanent and they cannot hold on to anything. Sociologists have proved this beyond any doubt. Since their idea of possession is weak, Indians have generally not cared if their national territory is lost or if their race declines. When the Buddha was born, a number of Indian kingdoms had already been turned into provinces of Persia. The Buddhist scriptures show that they only thought about the various kingdoms and never the Persian emperor, as if they didn't know that the nation was lost to the Persians. Only King Asoka roused himself to maintain the independence of his kingdom. . . . The Chinese terrain and national spirit are vastly superior to those of India. The land is not fragmented and the people are possessive. Ever since the Manchu conquest, we have been enraged by the sheep stink of these lesser races. Chinese determination is stronger than the Indian, and we can foresee that Chinese accomplishments will certainly surpass those of the Indians. . . .

If the Manchus are not expelled, however, we cannot expect that the scholars will perform well or that the people will share a bitter hatred of the enemy in order to reach a realm of freedom and independence. If the situation continues to decline, we will simply become the slaves of the Westerners. If bad seeds are not removed, the good ones will not grow. If bad people are not removed, the good ones will not flourish, and naturally if we do not personally take a large broom to sweep away the rotten customs of the ancestors, then how can we hope to foster the ideal China?

[*Bo Kang Youwei lun geming shu*, in *Zhang Taiyan quanji* 4:173–184 — PZ]

*Chapter 32*

## THE NATIONALIST REVOLUTION

The Chinese Revolution of 1911, which led to the overthrow of the Manchus the following year, was complex in its origins and confused as to its outcome. There is no single trend of thought or political action with which it can be identified. Nevertheless, amid the shifting currents of ideas and events in the two decades following, nationalism and republicanism emerged as perhaps the leading slogans in the political arena; and in the popular mind (if we may so speak of a political consciousness still somewhat inchoate), it was Sun Yat-sen (1866–1925) and his Nationalist (Guomindang) followers who stood out as the most eloquent, though not always the most effective, spokesmen for these concepts. In the post-Mao era many Chinese returned to these ideas as having a continuing relevance to the process of modernization under Deng Xiaoping. To express their basic aims and hopes is the purpose of the selections that follow. The next chapter will illustrate the extraordinary intellectual ferment and vitality during this same republican era.

## SUN YAT-SEN AND THE NATIONALIST REVOLUTION

The origins of the revolutionary movement may be traced back to 1895, when Sun, convinced that the Manchu regime was beyond hope of reforming, attempted his first abortive coup in Canton. As a practitioner of revolution Sun was never a great success; nor, on the other hand, did he stand out as a brilliant political philosopher. It was rather as a visionary that Sun eventually caught the imagination of Chinese youth — as a man of intense convictions and magnetic personality, who, through his crusading and somewhat quixotic career, dramatized ideas and catalyzed forces that outlived him. The first clear sign of this came just after the Russo-Japanese War, which gave great impetus to revolutionary nationalism throughout Asia. Japan was a hotbed of agitation among Chinese in exile and students sent abroad for study under official auspices. Sun, in 1905, united his secret revolutionary society with other extremist groups to form the League of Common Alliance (*Tongmeng hui*, sometimes loosely translated as the Revolutionary Alliance), out of which later grew the Nationalist Party (Guomindang). Through its party organ, the *People's Report* (*Minbao*), this group published a manifesto that stated the aims of the movement, including three from which evolved the Three People's Principles.

One significant feature of this new movement is that it derived its inspiration largely from Western sources. We have already seen how the thinking of the late nineteenth-century reformers was often decisively influenced by the West, either through its ideas or through the alternatives it presented. In most cases, however, these reformers had been trained in the classical culture and had prepared themselves for entry into the old elite. Even as reformers they felt a need somehow to reconcile the new with the old. Sun Yat-sen's case is different. His training was almost entirely in Western schools (including secondary education at a mission school in Hawaii). In contrast to generations of office seekers who had passed through the examination halls, this prospective leader of the new China aspired first to a military career and then went to medical school in Hong Kong. Knowing little of classical studies, and inclined at first to think them useless, he inspired respect or enthusiasm more by what seemed his practical grasp of world trends than by any Chinese erudition. Moreover, his knowledge of China itself was limited, since his life was mostly spent in a few port cities, in Western outposts like Hong Kong and Macao, or in exile abroad.

This is not to say that Sun was wholly Westernized. One whose early years had been spent in a peasant household, whose boyhood hero had been the Taiping leader Hong Xiuquan, and whose associations in later life were for the most part with overseas Chinese could be cut off from the official tradition and Confucian orthodoxy without ceasing in many ways to be Chinese. But it does mean that Sun's aims, primarily political in character and suggested by prevailing modes of thought in the West, were little adapted at the outset either to traditional Chinese attitudes or to the realities of Chinese life. They were inspired rather by a belief that, with the progress of civilization and the advance of science, Western ideas and institutions could be adopted quickly and easily by the Chinese, without regard to their past condition. Yet the bridging of this gap, between what revolutionaries perceived to be China's sluggish past and

Sun's high-speed future, proved to be the great despair of the nationalist movement. As events after 1911 showed, China could not be remade overnight. Sun was forced to modify his own program, and others after him still faced an enormous task of adjustment and reevaluation.

# HU HANMIN

### THE SIX PRINCIPLES OF THE PEOPLE'S REPORT

The basic platform of the League of Common Alliance (*Tongmeng hui*) was set forth in a manifesto issued in the fall of 1905. It reiterated Sun's early anti-Manchu and republican aims, as well as a third, equalization of land rights, which showed a developing interest in socialist ideas. The manifesto also stated Sun's plan of revolution in three stages: (1) military government, (2) a provisional constitution granting local self-government, and (3) full constitutional government under a republican system.

A somewhat fuller statement of the league's basic principles was written for the third issue of the party organ, *People's Report*, in April 1906, by its editor, Hu Hanmin (1879–1936). The statement carried Sun Yat-sen's endorsement. Three of the six principles are set forth here — nationalism, republicanism, and land nationalization — corresponding roughly to Sun's famous *Three People's Principles*. The other three, not reproduced below, dealt with problems of immediate concern to the revolutionists in Yokohama, as affecting their relations with others, especially the Japanese. The fourth principle asserts the indispensability of a strong, united China to the maintenance of world peace, since it is China's weakness that encourages the great powers to contend for special advantages and risk a catastrophic war. Here the influence of the Japanese statesman Ōkuma Shigenobu, a liberal leader upon whose support the revolutionists counted heavily, is evident. The fifth and sixth principles advocate close collaboration between the Chinese and Japanese and urge other countries also to support the revolution. Nationalism, at this point, is thus not opposed to foreign intervention but in fact welcomes it — if it is on the right side.

While the Manchu regime is the prime target of the revolutionists' indignation, their actual antagonists in the political struggle are not so much those in power at home as reformers in exile (like Kang Yuwei and Liang Qichao, then also active in Yokohama) who remain loyal to the dynasty and favor constitutional monarchy. During the first decade of the twentieth century the contest between these two groups, reformist and revolutionary, for the support of Chinese students in Japan was bitter and sometimes violent.

## 1. Overthrow of the Present Evil Government

This is our first task. That a fine nation should be controlled by an evil one and that, instead of adopting our culture, the Manchus should force us to adopt theirs, is contrary to reason and cannot last for long. For the sake of our independence and salvation, we must overthrow the Manchu dynasty. . . . Those who advocate assimilation of the Manchus without having them overthrown merely serve as tools of the tyrannical dynasty and are therefore shameless to the utmost. Our nationalism is not to be mixed with political opportunism. What distresses us sorely and hurts us unceasingly is the impossible position of subjugation we are in. If we recover our sovereignty and regain our position as ruler, it is not necessary to eliminate the evil race in order to satisfy our national aspirations. . . . But unless their political power is overthrown, the Chinese nation will forever remain the conquered people without independence and, being controlled by a backward nation, will finally perish with it in the struggle with the advanced foreign powers. . . .

The Manchu government is evil because it is the evil race that usurped our government, and their evils are not confined to a few political measures but are rooted in the nature of the race and can neither be eliminated nor reformed. Therefore, even if there are a few ostensible reforms, the evils will remain just the same. The adoption of Western constitutional institutions and law [by the Manchu dynasty] will not change the situation . . . [contrary to the view of Liang Qichao]. [pp. 446–447]

## 2. Establishment of a Republic

That absolute monarchy is unsuitable to the present age requires no argument. It is but natural therefore that those who propose new forms of government in the twentieth century should aim at rooting out the elements of absolutism. Revolutions broke out in China one after another in the past, but because the political system was not reformed, no good results ensued. Thus the Mongol dynasty was overthrown by the Ming, but within three hundred years the Chinese nation was again on the decline. For although foreign rule was overthrown and a Chinese regime was installed in its place, the autocratic form of government remained unchanged, to the disappointment of the people. . . .

The greatest difficulty in establishing a constitutional government, as experienced by other countries, is the struggle of the common people against both the monarch and the nobility. Constitutional government was established without difficulty in America because after its independence there was no class other than the common people. One of the great features of Chinese politics is that since the Qin and Han dynasties there has existed no noble class (except for the Mongol and Manchu dynasties when a noble class was maintained according to their alien systems). After the overthrow of the Manchus, therefore, there will be no distinction between classes in China (even the United States has economic classes, but China has none). The establishment of constitutional government will be easier in China than in other countries. . . .

We agree with Herbert Spencer, who compared the difficulty of changing an established political system to that of changing the constitution of an organism after its main body has been formed. Since constitutional democracy can be established only after a revolution, it is imperative that following our revolution, only the best and the most public-spirited form of government should be adopted so that no defects will remain. As to constitutional monarchy, the demarcation between ruler and ruled is definite and distinct, and since their feelings toward each other are different, classes will arise. Constitutional democracy will have none of these defects, and equality will prevail. We can overthrow the Manchus and establish our state because Chinese nationalism and democratic thought are well developed. When we are able to do this, it is inconceivable that, knowing the general psychology of the people, we should abandon the government of equality and retain the distinction between ruler and ruled. [pp. 447–449]

*Sun, during his exile in the West, had been influenced by a variety of socialistic ideas as divergent as German state socialism and Henry George's single-tax theories. While Sun's own thinking (and that of his associates) was still somewhat fluid and vague, the provision for "equalization of land rights" in the original League of Common Alliance* (Tongmeng hui) *manifesto was clearly an adaptation of the ideas of Henry George and John Stuart Mill, calling for state appropriation of all future increases in land value but recognizing its present value as the property of the owner. Hu Hanmin's version is more extreme. It represents a violent attack on landlordism and calls for complete socialization of the land.*

*In the preceding section, however, Hu has already asserted that China, in contrast to the West, has no economic classes but only a ruling elite that must be overthrown. Therefore rural landlordism was not, presumably, the primary target in his mind. Whether as an accommodation to Sun or not, it is the urban landlordism attacked by Henry George in the West that appears to be Hu's major concern. In the port cities of China he sees a process developing like that in the West, and his object is to prevent its spread when China modernizes after the coming revolution.*[1]

*Note in the following that Hu takes as his point of departure the economic evils of modern society, rather than age-old abuses in China. Note also the sanction for land nationalization that he finds in the ancient well-field system — a symbol for Hu of primitive communism — though it actually came closer to a mix of equal private landholding and public land.*

---

1. On this point, see further Harold Schiffrin, "Sun Yat-sen's Land Policy," *Journal of Asian Studies* 16, no. 4 (August 1957): 549–564.

## 3. Land Nationalization

The affliction of civilized countries in the modern age is not political classes but economic classes. Hence the rise of socialism. There are many socialist theories, but they all aim at leveling economic classes. Generally speaking, socialism may be divided into communism and collectivism, and nationalization of land is part of collectivism. Only constitutional democracies can adopt collectivism, for there the ruling authority resides in the state and the state machinery is controlled by a representative legislature. . . .

Not all collectivist theories can be applied to China at her present stage of development. But in the case of land nationalization we already have a model for it in the well-field system of the Three Dynasties, and it should not be difficult to introduce land nationalization as an adaptation of a past system to the present age of political reform. Nationalization of land is opposed to private ownership. It is based on the theory that since land is the essential element in production and is not man-made, any more than sunshine or air, it should not be privately owned. . . .

The evil consequences of landlordism are that the landlord can acquire absolute power in society and thereby absorb and annex more land, that the farmers can be driven out of work, that people may be short of food and thus have to depend on outside supply, and that the entire country may be made poorer while capital and wealth all go to the landlords.

Land in China today, as affected by commercial development in the coastal ports, may in ten years have its value increased more than ten times what it was formerly. We can see from this that after the revolution with the progress of civilization, the same process would be accelerated in the interior. If a system of private monopoly is reestablished, then the economic class will perpetuate itself as a political class, but if we make adequate provision against this at the beginning, we can easily plan so that the evil never arises.

There are various measures for carrying out land nationalization, but the main purpose is to deprive people of the right of landownership. . . . In this way the power of the landlord will be wiped out from the Chinese continent. All land taxes levied by the state must have the approval of parliament; there will be no manipulations for private profit, nor heavy taxes detrimental to the farmers' interests. Profit from land will be high, but only self-cultivating farmers can obtain land from the state. In this way people will increasingly devote themselves to farming and no land will be wasted. Landlords who in the past have been nonproductive profiteers will now be just like the common people. They will turn to productive enterprises and this will produce striking results for the good of the whole national economy. [pp. 449–450]

[Zou Lu, ed., *Zhongguo Guomindang shi gao* 25:446–450]

# SUN YAT-SEN

## THE THREE PEOPLE'S PRINCIPLES

After the Revolution of 1911 Sun Yat-sen reluctantly allowed his secret revolutionary society to be converted into an open political party, the Nationalist Party (Guomindang). It accomplished little through parliamentary politics, however, and even when Sun reverted to revolutionary tactics the lack of military support and his failure to obtain sufficient help from Japan or the West kept him from registering any substantial progress. Nevertheless, Sun was impressed and encouraged by the success of the Russian Revolution, and offers of Soviet help induced him in 1923 to reorganize the Guomindang along Leninist organizational lines and to enter upon a period of collaboration with the Soviets and the recently founded Chinese Communist Party. Even so, while making certain tactical adjustments in his propaganda line and adopting a more anti-Western tone, Sun was steadfast in his repudiation of Marxism as such.

The *Three People's Principles* (*San min zhuyi*), which served as the basic text of the nationalist movement, was given its final form in a series of lectures by Sun to party members in 1924, after the Nationalists' reorganization with Soviet help the year before. It attempted to reformulate the principles put forward in 1905, modifying them in accordance with Sun's subsequent experience and the altered circumstances in which he was making a bid for military and political unification of the country.

Sun's nationalism, in 1905, had been directed mainly against the Manchus. Events after the Revolution of 1911, however, proved that ridding China of foreign rule was not enough to assure its future as a nation. Even with the Manchus gone, China was as weak as ever, and still more disunited. Consequently, by 1924 foreign rule had been superseded in Sun's mind by two other issues. First was the Chinese people's need for national solidarity; though possessing all the other requisites of a great nation, they still lacked a capacity for cohesion. Second (and this was perhaps one means of generating the first), Sun found a new target of national indignation: foreign economic imperialism. This was an issue to which Sun acknowledged the Chinese people were not yet alive. Yet it had assumed new significance for him now as the basis for collaboration with the Communists in a national revolution against imperialism. And it reflected Sun's increasing bitterness toward the West for its failure to support him.

The lack of national solidarity Sun saw as partly the legacy of long foreign rule. It was aggravated, however, by a growing cosmopolitanism and internationalism resulting from the West's disenchantment with nationalism after World War I. Sun, who had once represented the vanguard of nationalism from the West, now found himself fighting a rear guard action in defense of his old cause. He spoke more and more in deprecation of the modern West — its materialism especially — and increasingly sought in Chinese tradition the basis for a nationalism that it had never been made to serve before. In this, Sun's political instinct was undoubtedly sound, for nationalism remained in fact a potent issue, in China as in the rest of Asia.

[*China as a Heap of Loose Sand*]. For the most part the four hundred million people of China can be spoken of as completely Han Chinese. With common customs and habits, we are completely of one race. But in the world today what position do we occupy? Compared to the other peoples of the world we have the greatest population and our civilization is four thousand years old; we should therefore be advancing in the front rank with the nations of Europe and America. But the Chinese people have only family and clan solidarity; they do not have national spirit. Therefore, even though we have four hundred million people gathered together in one China, in reality they are just a heap of loose sand. Today we are the poorest and weakest nation in the world and occupy the lowest position in international affairs. Other men are the carving knife and serving dish; we are the fish and the meat. Our position at this time is most perilous. If we do not earnestly espouse nationalism and weld together our four hundred million people into a strong nation, there is danger of China's being lost and our people being destroyed. If we wish to avert this catastrophe, we must espouse nationalism and bring this national spirit to the salvation of the country. [pp. 4–5, lecture 1]

[*China as a "Hypo-colony"*]. Since the Chinese Revolution, the foreign powers have found that it was much less easy to use political force in carving up China. A people who had experienced Manchu oppression and learned to overthrow it would now, if the powers used political force to oppress it, be certain to resist, and thus make things difficult for them. For this reason they are letting up in their efforts to control China by political force and instead are using economic pressure to keep us down. . . . As regards political oppression, people are readily aware of their suffering, but when it comes to economic oppression, most often they are hardly conscious of it. China had already experienced several decades of economic oppression by the foreign powers, and so far the nation had for the most part shown no sense of irritation. As a consequence China is being transformed everywhere into a colony of the foreign powers.

Our people keep thinking that China is only a "semi-colony" — a term by which they seek to comfort themselves. Yet in reality the economic oppression we have endured is not just that of a "semi-colony" but greater even than that of a full colony. . . . Of what nation then is China a colony? It is the colony of every nation with which it has concluded treaties; each of them is China's master. Therefore China is not just the colony of one country; it is the colony of many countries. We are not just the slaves of one country, but the slaves of many countries. In the event of natural disasters like flood and drought, a nation that is sole master appropriates funds for relief and distributes them, thinking this its own duty; and the people who are its slaves regard this relief work as something to which their masters are obligated. But when North China suffered drought several years ago, the foreign powers did not regard it as their responsibility to appropriate funds and distribute relief; only those foreigners resident in China raised funds for the drought victims, whereupon Chinese observers remarked on the great generosity of the foreigners who bore no responsibility to help. . . .

From this we can see that China is not so well off as Annam [under the French] and Korea [under the Japanese]. Being the slaves of one country represents a far higher status than being the slaves of many, and is far more advantageous. Therefore, to call China a "semi-colony" is quite incorrect. If I may coin a phrase, we should be called a "hypo-colony." This is a term that comes from chemistry, as in "hypo-phosphite." Among chemicals there are some belonging to the class of phosphorous compounds but of lower grade, which are called phosphites. Still another grade lower, and they are called hypophosphites. . . . The Chinese people, believing they were a semi-colony, thought it shame enough; they did not realize that they were lower even than Annam or Korea. Therefore we cannot call ourselves a "semi-colony" but only a "hypocolony." [pp. 15–16, lecture 2]

[*Nationalism and Cosmopolitanism*]. A new idea is emerging in England and Russia, proposed by the intellectuals, which opposes nationalism on the ground that it is narrow and illiberal. This is simply a doctrine of cosmopolitanism. England now and formerly Germany and Russia, together with the Chinese youth of today who preach the new civilization, support this doctrine and oppose nationalism. Often I hear young people say, "The Three Principles of the People do not fit in with the present world's new tendencies; the latest and best doctrine in the world is cosmopolitanism." But is cosmopolitanism really good or not? . . . Theoretically, we cannot say it is no good. Yet it is because formerly the Chinese intellectual class had cosmopolitan ideas that, when the Manchus crossed China's frontier, the whole country was lost to them. . . . [pp. 28–29, lecture 3]

[*Nationalism and Traditional Morality*]. If today we want to restore the standing of our people, we must first restore our national spirit. . . . If in the past our people have survived despite the fall of the state [to foreign conquerors], and not only survived themselves but been able to assimilate these foreign conquerors, it is because of the high level of our traditional morality. Therefore, if we go to the root of the matter, besides arousing a sense of national solidarity uniting all our people, we must recover and restore our characteristic, traditional morality. Only thus can we hope to attain again the distinctive position of our people.

This characteristic morality the Chinese people today have still not forgotten. First comes loyalty and filial piety, then humanity and love, faithfulness and duty, harmony and peace. Of these traditional virtues, the Chinese people still speak, but now, under foreign oppression, we have been invaded by a new culture, the force of which is felt all across the nation. Men wholly intoxicated by this new culture have thus begun to attack the traditional morality, saying that with the adoption of the new culture, we no longer have need of the old morality.² . . . They say that when we formerly spoke of loyalty, it was loyalty to princes, but now in our democracy there are no princes, so loyalty is unnecessary and can be dispensed with. This kind of reasoning is certainly mistaken. In our country princes can be dispensed with, but not loyalty. . . . If indeed we can no longer speak of loyalty to princes, can we not, however, speak of loyalty to our people? [pp. 51–52, lecture 6]

[*Zhongshan quanshu* 1:4–5, 15–16, 28–29, 51–52 — CT]

## THE PRINCIPLE OF DEMOCRACY

In 1905 Sun had proclaimed the principle of democracy mainly against the advocates of constitutional monarchy whom he identified with "absolutism." In 1924 his notion of the forms that this democracy should take is given more explicit expression, against a background of personal experience that confirmed Sun's long-standing belief in the need for strong political leadership. The result is a plan of government that he believed would ensure popular control through electoral processes, yet give a strong executive wide powers to deal with the business of government. The emphasis is on leadership now, not liberty. In fact, argues Sun (thinking again of the Chinese people as a "heap of loose sand"), the struggle of the Chinese people is not for individual liberty, of which they have had an excess, but for the "liberty of the nation." Consequently, he attempts to distinguish between sovereignty, which the people should retain, and the ability to rule, which should be vested in an elite group of experts.

A distinctive feature of Sun's constitutional order is his five branches or powers of the government. These would include the three associated with the American government — executive, legislative, and judicial — along with two that were intended as a check on elected officials and their powers of appointment, and for which Sun believed Chinese political tradition provided a unique precedent: a censorate or supervisory organ, and an independent civil service system. These latter he spoke of as if they had indeed been independent organs of the traditional Chinese state, thus enabling him as a nationalist not only to offer a constitution that represented a unique Chinese synthesis but also to redeem Chinese tradition and place it on at least a par with the West.

[*Separation of Sovereignty and Ability*]. How can a government be made all-powerful? Once the government is all-powerful, how can it be made responsive to the will of the people? . . . I have found a method to solve the problem. The method that I have thought of is a new discovery in political theory and is a fundamental solution of the whole problem. . . . It is the theory of the distinction between sovereignty and ability. [pp. 117–118, lecture 5]

---

2. See ch. 24.

After China has established a powerful government, we must not be afraid, as Western people are, that the government will become too strong and that we will be unable to control it. For it is our plan that the political power of the reconstructed state will be divided into two parts. One is the power over the government; that great power will be placed entirely in the hands of the people, who will have a full degree of sovereignty and will be able to control directly the affairs of state — this political power is popular sovereignty. The other power is the governing power; that great power will be placed in the hands of the government organs, which will be powerful and will manage all the nation's business — this governing power is the power of the government. If the people have a full measure of political sovereignty and the methods for exercising popular control over the government are well worked out, we need not fear that the government will become too strong and uncontrollable. . . .

Let the people in thinking about government distinguish between sovereignty and ability. Let the great political force of the state be divided into two: the power of the government and the power of the people. Such a division will make the government the machinery and the people the engineer. The attitude of the people toward the government will then resemble the attitude of the engineer toward his machine. The construction of machinery has made such advances nowadays that not only men with mechanical knowledge but even children without any knowledge of machinery are able to control it. [pp. 139–140, lecture 6]

[*The Four Powers of the People*]. What are the newest discoveries in the way of exercising popular sovereignty? First, there is suffrage, and it is the only method practiced throughout the so-called advanced democracies. Is this one form of popular sovereignty enough in government? This one power by itself may be compared to the earlier machines, which could move forward only but not back.

The second of the newly discovered methods is the right of recall. When the people have this right, they possess the power of pulling the machine back.

These two rights give the people control over officials and enable them to put all government officials in their positions or to remove them from their positions. The coming and going of officials follows the free will of the people, just as the modern machines move to and fro by the free action of the engine. Besides officials, another important thing in a state is law; "with men to govern there must also be laws for governing."[3] What powers must the people possess in order to control the laws? If the people think that a certain law would be of great advantage to them, they should have the power to decide upon this law and turn it over to the government for execution. This third kind of popular power is called the initiative.

---

3. Probably a reference to Huang Zongxi, whose writings on rulership and law Sun had reprinted and widely distributed. See ch. 25.

If the people think that an old law is not beneficial to them, they should have the power to amend it and to ask the government to enforce the amended law and do away with the old law. This is called the referendum and is a fourth form of popular sovereignty.

Only when the people have these four rights can we say that democracy is complete, and only when these four powers are effectively applied can we say that there is a thoroughgoing, direct, and popular sovereignty. [pp. 141–142, lecture 6]

[*The Five-Power Constitution*]. With the people exercising the four great powers to control the government, what methods will the government use in performing its work? In order that the government may have a complete organ through which to do its best work, there must be a five-power constitution. A government is not complete and cannot do its best work for the people unless it is based on the five-power constitution [i.e., a government composed of five branches: executive, legislative, judicial, civil service examination, and censorate]. . . .

All governmental powers were formerly monopolized by kings and emperors, but after the revolutions they were divided into three groups. Thus the United States, after securing its independence, established a government with three coordinate departments. The American system achieved such good results that it was adopted by other nations. But foreign governments have merely a triple-power separation. Why do we now want a separation of five powers? What is the source of the two new features in our five-power constitution?

The two new features come from old China. China long ago had the independent systems of civil service examination and censorate, and they were very effective. The imperial censors of the Manchu dynasty and the official advisers of the Tang dynasty made a fine censoring system. The power of censorship includes the power to impeach. Foreign countries also have this power, only it is placed in the legislative body and is not a separate governmental power.

The selection of real talent and ability through examinations has been characteristic of China for thousands of years. Foreign scholars who have recently studied Chinese institutions highly praise China's old independent examination system. There have been imitations of the system for the selection of able men in the West. Great Britain's civil service examinations are modeled after the old Chinese system, but they are limited to ordinary officials. The British system does not yet possess the spirit of the independent examination of China. In old China, [however], . . . the powers of civil service examination and the censorate were independent of the Throne. . . .

Hence, as for the separation of governmental powers, we can say that China had three coordinate departments of government just as the modern democracies. China practiced the separation of autocratic, examination, and censorate powers for thousands of years. Western countries have practiced the separation of legislative, judicial, and executive powers for only a little over a century. However, if we now want to combine the best from China and the best from other countries and guard against all kinds of abuse, we must take the three Western governmental powers — the executive, legislative, and judicial — add to them the Chinese powers of examination and censorate and make a perfect government of five powers. Such a government will be the most complete and the finest in the world, and a state with such a government will indeed be of the people, by the people, and for the people. [pp. 143–145, lecture 6]

[*Zhongshan quanshu* 1:117–118, 139–145; adapted from Price, *San min chu i*, pp. 345–346, 350–358]

## THE PEOPLE'S LIVELIHOOD

The "People's Livelihood" (*minsheng zhuyi*) joined nationalism and democracy to make up Sun Yat-sen's Three People's Principles in 1906. It was meant to cover the economic side of Sun's program broadly enough so as to embrace a variety of social and economic theories that had attracted Sun's attention. Often he and his followers used *minsheng zhuyi* as an equivalent for socialism, drawing upon the popularity of this idea in general, while retaining the freedom to interpret it as they chose. For Sun in 1924 its most essential component was still Henry George's single tax. Though paying tribute to Marx as a "social scientist," Sun rejected entirely Marx's theory of class struggle and cited a work little known in the West, *The Social Interpretation of History*, by a Brooklyn dentist, Maurice William, as a conclusive refutation of Marx's economic determinism. Sun also disputed Marx's belief in the steady impoverishment of the worker under capitalism and the latter's imminent collapse. American experience (e.g., Henry Ford) showed that capitalist success and rising living standards for the worker were not mutually exclusive.

Sun exhibited great confidence in China's future, in her ability to catch up with the West and yet avoid its economic woes. China's problem was one of production, not of distribution, and the inequality of wealth need never arise if economic development were based on Sun's land tax program, which would prevent "unearned increments" from accruing to individuals at the same time that it provided revenues for state investment in industry. Sun envisaged a kind of mixed economy, permitting small-scale capitalist enterprise to exist alongside nationalized industries and utilities. But the immediate need was to encourage China's infant industries. Here Sun stressed her emancipation from foreign economic imperialism, the main point of which was to gain customs autonomy, lost through the unequal treaties, and to erect protective tariffs. Foreign investment he was only too ready to promote. His program for agriculture involved mainly technological improvement.

Although Sun did not live to see it, years later, after the failure of Mao Zedong's economic program, the Communist leadership in the eighties and nineties adopted policies for a mixed economy, foreign investment, and economic development in China similar to those advocated under Sun.

[*The Principle of Livelihood*]. The Nationalist Party some time ago in its party platform adopted two methods by which the principle of livelihood is to be carried out. The first method is equalization of landownership; the second is regulation of capital. [p. 166]

Our first method consists in solving the land question. The methods for solution of the land problem are different in various countries, and each country has its own peculiar difficulties. The plan that we are following is simple and easy — equalization of landownership. . . .

If our landowners were like the great landowners of Europe and had developed tremendous power, it would be very difficult for us to solve the land problem. But China does not have such big landowners, and the power of the small landowners is still rather weak. If we attack the problem now, we can solve it; but if we lose the present opportunity, we will have much more difficulty in the future. . . . We propose that the government shall levy a tax proportionate to the price of the land and, if necessary, buy back the land according to its price.

But how will the price of the land be determined? I would let the landowner himself fix the price. . . . According to this plan, if the landowner makes a low assessment, he will be afraid lest the government buy the land at the declared value and make him lose his property; if he makes too high an assessment, he will be afraid of the government taxing according to the value and his losing through heavy taxes. Comparing these two serious possibilities, he will certainly not want to report the value of his land too high or too low; he will strike the mean and report the true market price to the government. In this way neither the landowner nor the government will lose.

After the land values have been fixed we should have a regulation by law that from that year on, all increase in land value, which in other countries means heavier taxation, shall revert to the community. This is because the increase in land value is due to improvement made by society and to the progress of industry and commerce. . . . The credit for the progress and improvement belongs to the energy and enterprise of all the people. Land increment resulting from that progress and improvement should therefore revert to the community rather than to private individuals. [pp. 175–176, lecture 2]

[*Capital and the State*]. China cannot be compared to foreign countries. It is not sufficient for us to regulate capital. Other countries are rich while China is poor; other countries have a surplus of production while China is not producing enough. So China must not only regulate private capital, but it must also develop state capital. . . .

First, we must build means of communication, railroads, and waterways on a large scale. Second, we must open up mines. China is rich in minerals, but alas, they are buried in the earth! Third, we must hasten to develop manufacturing. Although China has a multitude of workers, it has no machinery and so cannot compete with other countries. Goods used throughout China have to be manufactured and imported from other countries, with the result that our rights and interests are simply leaking away. If we want to recover these rights and interests, we must quickly employ state power to promote industry, use machinery in production, and see that all workers of the country are employed. When all the workers have employment and use machinery in production, we will have a great, new source of wealth. If we do not use state power to build up these enterprises but leave them in the hands of private Chinese or of foreign businessmen, the result will be the expansion of private capital and the emergence of a great wealthy class with consequent inequalities in society. . . .

China is now suffering from poverty, not from unequal distribution of wealth. Where there are inequalities of wealth, the methods of Marx can, of course, be used; a class war can be advocated to destroy the inequalities. But in China, where industry is not yet developed, Marx's class war and dictatorship of the proletariat are impracticable. [pp. 177–179]

[*Zhongshan quanshu* 1:166, 175–179; adapted from Price, *San min chu i*, pp. 431–434, 437–441]

## THE THREE STAGES OF REVOLUTION

The significance of Sun's "Three Stages of Revolution" lies mainly in his doctrine of political tutelage, which represents perhaps the first conscious advocacy of "guided democracy" among the leaders of Asian nationalism. When first enunciated in 1905, it seems to have been Sun's answer to those who argued that the Chinese people, long accustomed to political absolutism and unaccustomed to participation in government, were unprepared for democracy. Sun acknowledged that a period of adjustment or transition would be required, but his early confidence in the people's ability to "learn" democracy is shown by the exact time schedule he had worked out for this process — political tutelage would last just six years.

The following explanation of the Three Stages is taken from *A Program of National Reconstruction*, prepared in 1918, and follows in the main his earlier ideas, though it stresses the difficulties of reconstruction encountered after the revolution. Sun's awareness of these difficulties led to increasing emphasis on the importance of strong leadership in the period of tutelage, somewhat less on the readiness of the people for democracy. In his *Outline of National Reconstruction*, written in 1924 just before his death, he omitted reference to a definite time schedule, as if to concede that the period of tutelage might extend beyond his original expectations.

[*The Three Phases of National Reconstruction*]. As for the work of revolutionary reconstruction, I have based my ideas on the current of world progress and followed the precedents in other countries. I have studied their respective advantages and disadvantages, their accomplishments and failures. It is only after mature deliberation and thorough preparation that I have decided upon the Program of Revolution and defined the procedure of the revolution in three stages. The first is the period of military government; the second, the period of political tutelage; and the third, the period of constitutional government.

The first stage is the period of destruction. During this period martial law is to be enforced. The revolutionary army undertakes to overthrow the Manchu tyranny, to eradicate the corruption of officialdom, to eliminate depraved customs, to exterminate the system of slave girls, to wipe out the scourge of opium, superstitious beliefs, and geomancy, to abolish the obstructive *likin* trade tax and so forth.

The second stage is a transitional period. It is planned that the provisional constitution will be promulgated and local self-government promoted to encourage the exercise of political rights by the people. The *xian*, or district, will be made the basic unit of local self-government and is to be divided into villages and rural districts — all under the jurisdiction of the district government.

The moment the enemy forces have been cleared and military operations have ceased in a district, the provisional constitution will be promulgated in the district, defining the rights and duties of citizens and the governing powers of the revolutionary government. The constitution will be enforced for three years, after which period the people of the district will elect their district officers. . . .

In respect to such self-governing units the revolutionary government will exercise the right of political tutelage in accordance with the provisional constitution. When a period of six years expires after the attainment of political stability throughout the country, the districts that have become full-fledged self-governing units are each entitled to elect one representative to form the National Assembly. The task of the assembly will be to adopt a five-power constitution and to organize a central government consisting of five branches, namely, the Executive Branch, the Legislative Branch, the Judicial Branch, the Examination Branch, and the Control Branch [Censorate]. . . .

When the constitution is promulgated and the president and members of the National Assembly are elected, the revolutionary government will hand over its governing power to the president, and the period of political tutelage will come to an end.

The third phase is the period of the completion of reconstruction. During this period, constitutional government is to be introduced, and the self-governing body in a district will enable the people directly to exercise their political rights. In regard to the district government, the people are entitled to the rights of election, initiative, referendum, and recall. In regard to the national government, the people exercise the rights of suffrage, while the other rights are delegated to the representatives to the National Assembly. The period of constitutional government will mark the completion of reconstruction and the success of the revolution. This is the gist of the Revolutionary Program. [pp. 37–38]

[*The Necessity of Political Tutelage*]. What is meant by revolutionary reconstruction? It is extraordinary destruction and also rapid reconstruction. It differs from ordinary reconstruction, which follows the natural course of society and is affected by the trend of circumstances. In a revolution extraordinary destruction is involved, such as the extermination of the monarchical system and the overthrow of absolutism. Such destruction naturally calls for extraordinary reconstruction.

Revolutionary destruction and revolutionary reconstruction complement each other like the two legs of a man or the two wings of a bird. The republic after its inauguration weathered the storm of extraordinary destruction. This, however, was not followed by extraordinary reconstruction. A vicious circle of civil wars has consequently arisen. The nation is on the descendent, like a stream flowing downward. The tyranny of the warlords together with the sinister maneuvers of unscrupulous politicians is beyond control. In an extraordinary time, only extraordinary reconstruction can inspire the people with a new mind and make a new beginning of the nation. Hence the Program of Revolution is necessary. . . .

It is not to be denied that the Chinese people are deficient in knowledge. Moreover, they have been soaked in the poison of absolute monarchy for several thousand years. . . . What shall we do now? Men of the Yuan Shikai type argue that the Chinese people, deficient in knowledge, are unfit for republicanism. Crude scholars have also maintained that monarchy is necessary.

Alas! Even an ox can be trained to plow the field and a horse to carry man. Are men not capable of being trained? Suppose that when a youngster was entering school, his father was told that the boy did not know the written characters and therefore could not go to school. Is such reasoning logical? It is just because he does not know the characters that the boy must immediately set about learning them. The world has now come to an age of enlightenment. Hence the growing popularity of the idea of freedom and equality, which has become the main current of the world and cannot be stemmed by any means. China therefore needs a republican government just as a boy needs school. As a schoolboy must have good teachers and helpful friends, so the Chinese people, being for the first time under republican rule, must have a farsighted revolutionary government for their training. This calls for the period of political tutelage, which is a necessary transitional stage from monarchy to republicanism. Without this, disorder will be unavoidable. [p. 42]

[*Zhongshan quanshu* 2, *Jianguo fanglue*, part 1 (also titled *Sun Wen xueshuo*), ch. 6, pp. 37–42 —CT]

# DEMOCRACY AND ABSOLUTISM: THE DEBATE OVER POLITICAL TUTELAGE

Sun Yat-sen's concept of political tutelage, a key doctrine of the Nationalists (Guomindang) after his death, also remained a continuing issue in Chinese politics. With all the talk about a constitution and preparation for the adoption of democratic institutions, party tutelage still provided the working basis of the new regime and the rationale for Chiang Kai-shek's increasingly strong role as Sun's heir to Nationalist leadership. The party itself, however, was by no means unanimous in support of this idea. The middle-class and considerably Westernized Chinese whom it represented, especially in the commercial ports, included numerous individuals educated abroad or exposed to Western ideas of political democracy. Many of them were poorly reconciled to what seemed a reactionary and dictatorial system of party leadership. Others not identified with the party itself, but active in educational institutions or in journalism, did not hesitate to attack this fundamental premise of the Nanjing regime.

The debate that ensued on this issue in the 1930s illustrates a basic dilemma of Nationalist rule. Though the party was committed to a kind of limited democracy on the theory that the building of national unity must take priority over the extension of political freedom, the achieving of national unity was long postponed by civil war, the Japanese invasion and occupation of the 1930s and 1940s, and still more civil war thereafter.

### LUO LONGJI: WHAT KIND OF POLITICAL SYSTEM DO WE WANT?

Luo Longji (1896–1965), a Western-trained educator and journalist, wrote this criticism of Sun Yat-sen's doctrine of political tutelage shortly after his return to China after studying at the University of Wisconsin, at the London School of Economics under Harold Laski, and for the doctorate at Columbia University (1928). He later served as editor of influential newspapers in North China, became a leader of the left-wing Democratic League, and was active politically under the Communists. He suffered condemnation as a "rightist," however, during the "Hundred Flowers" campaign in 1957. Luo's objections to party tutelage would also have applied to Mao's "party dictatorship."

By the time Luo wrote this article, communism already offered an important political alternative to the Nationalists, and Marxist doctrines, such as the withering away of the state, had become a part of his intellectual frame of reference.

We may sincerely say that we do not advocate any high-sounding theory of eliminating the state. We recognize that "to abolish the state through the party" is a blind alley in the twentieth century. In the present world the only road we can take is to maintain the state. *But in taking this road, we want to have the kind of state we cherish and the kind of governmental system we can support. . . .*

Let us first discuss with those who talk of "saving" and "reconstructing" the state the following problems: (1) What is the nature of the state? (2) What is the purpose of the state? (3) What should be the strategy for the reconstruction of the state?

Frankly, in the entire *Complete Works of Sun Yat-sen*, no mention has ever been made about such fundamental problems of political philosophy as the nature of the state and the purpose of the state. What concerned Dr. Sun most was the strategy for "national salvation" and "national reconstruction."[4] His weakness — which at the same time was his strength — lay in the fact that in the selection of a strategy his main concern was the attainment of his objectives, not the evaluation of the means. Because he paid no attention to the purpose of the state, he often took "national salvation" or "national reconstruction" for that purpose. Because he was concerned with the end rather than the means, often in the matter of strategy he took a road that was opposed to the nature and purpose of the state. *The strategy of "party above the state" is an illustration.* . . .

The great trouble of China today is that, on the one hand, the Communists consider the state an instrument of class war and, on the other, those who cry for "national salvation" and "national reconstruction" regard the state as the ultimate purpose itself. For those who consider the state as an end, the people exist for the sake of the state rather than the state for the sake of the people. They do not ask what benefits the state offers the people but maintain that "national salvation" and "love for the state" are the unconditional duties of the people. And they do not hesitate to employ those weighty words of "national salvation" and "national reconstruction" to silence the people. Thus the people may not be aided in time of famine and calamity, but burdensome taxes must be collected; local peace may not be maintained, but civil war must be fought. Because the state is an end, people become the means for "national salvation" and "national reconstruction." And so the state need not protect the life and property of the people, who become the slaves of the "principle of national salvation"; nor need it support freedom of thought, for schools should become propaganda agencies for the "principle of national salvation." In short, as soon as the banner of "national salvation" and "national reconstruction" is hoisted, all burdensome taxes and levies and all fighting and wars receive new significance. The people can only surrender unconditionally. . . .

When the party is placed above the state, the state becomes the instrument of the party rather than the instrument of the entire people for the attainment of the common purpose. . . . Let us examine whether or not the system of "party above the state" can achieve the purpose of the state.

The political systems of other countries today are founded on two different principles: dictatorship and democracy. Dictatorship refers to the political system under which the political power of the state is held by one person, one

---

4. Sun Yat-sen had argued the need for nationalism on the grounds that the Chinese had hitherto lacked a conception of nationhood and had known only loyalty to family or to dynastic state. After the fall of the Qing dynasty, however, he spoke of "state and nation" in almost one breath. The character for state and nation being the same in Chinese, these slogans also had the meaning of "the state's salvation" and "the state's reconstruction." The emotional appeal of nationalism was used, in this case, for the strengthening of the state.

party, or one class. Democracy refers to the political system under which political power resides in the people as a whole and *all citizens of age can participate directly or indirectly in politics on an equal basis.* The system of "party above the state" or "party authority above state authority" is certainly a dictatorship rather than a democracy.

We must emphatically declare here that we are *absolutely opposed to dictatorship, whether it be dictatorship by one person, one party, or one class. Our reason is very simple: dictatorship is not the method whereby the purpose of the state can be achieved.* Let us explain briefly as follows:

First, the state is the instrument of the people for the attainment of their common purpose through mutual constraint and cooperation. Its function is to protect the rights of the people. We believe that the rights of the people are secure only to the extent that the people themselves have the opportunity to protect them. In the present society, man's public spirit has not developed to such a perfection that we can entrust entirely our political rights to a person, a group, or a class and depend upon him or it to be the guardian of our rights. In practical politics, *he who loses political power will lose all protection of his rights. . . .*

Second, . . . The function of the state is to tend and develop the people. In a dictatorship the function of tending and developing is lost. Take, for instance, the cultivation and development of the thought of the people. A dictatorship, whether enlightened or dark, will consider freedom of thought its greatest enemy. The first task it sets itself is to reshape the mind of the people in a single mold by a so-called thought-unification movement. . . . After oppression and persecution under a dictatorship, the people's thought necessarily becomes timid, passive, dependent, senile, and the people themselves may even become pieces of thoughtless machinery.

Third, the state is the instrument of the entire people for the attainment of the common purpose of happiness for all through mutual restraint and cooperation. In order to achieve this purpose the state must furnish the people with an environment of peace, tranquillity, order, and justice. A dictator, be it an individual, a party, or a class, occupies a special position in national politics. This fundamentally rejects political equality as well as justice. The special position of the dictator inevitably incurs the indignation and hatred of the people for their governors, and indignation and hatred are the source of all revolutions. In a society of recurrent revolutions, peace, tranquillity, and order are naturally not to be found. . . .

The Nationalists themselves recognized the inherent evils of dictatorship, but they use such words as *temporary* and *transitional* to cover the system. The word *temporary* or *transitional* often designates the so-called period of political tutelage. . . .

We believe that the saying "The more you learn, the more there is to learn" applies equally to politics as to other callings. Man seeks experience and progress in politics unceasingly because there is no limit to them. If the people must have reached a certain ideal stage before they can participate in political activities, then the British and the Americans should also be under political tutelage now. To obtain experience from trial and error, to effect progress from experience — this is the political method of the British and Americans, and this also is the reason why we are opposed to political tutelage. If political tutelage is ever necessary, we believe the rulers — the present tutors — are more urgently in need of training than the people.

["Women yao shenmayang de zhengzhi zhidu?" in Xin yue 2,<br>no. 12, pp. 4–13 — CT]

## JIANG TINGFU: "REVOLUTION AND ABSOLUTISM"

The Nationalist system of one-party rule under a strong leader found a defender rather than a critic in another Western-trained (Oberlin College and Columbia University) scholar, Jiang Tingfu (1895–1965). A college professor and an authority on political and diplomatic history at the time he wrote this essay, Jiang became increasingly active as a Nationalist official, as ambassador to the USSR, and later as the Nationalists' permanent representative on the United Nations Security Council (known there as T. F. Tsiang).

Mr. Hu Hanmin has recently said that not a single good thing has been done by the government during the past two years. His statement is both overdrawn and inadequate. It is overdrawn because the government did do some good things, but they were of no avail and probably did not outweigh the bad things it had done. The statement is inadequate because the situation described applies not only to the government in the past two years but to the government in the past twenty years. Actually, while China did not have a very good government in the past twenty years, there was no extremely evil government either. Extremely good or extremely bad governments existed at the local level, but not at the national. For even if the central government had intended to do something good, it did not have the capacity to do anything very good. Similarly, even if it had intended to do something bad, it did not have the capacity to do anything bad. This is generally true with the past twenty years during which groups and individuals of various kinds, including Yuan Shikai and Chiang Kai-shek, assumed control of the government. In my opinion, even northern warlords such as Yuan Shikai, Duan Qirui, Wu Peifu, and Zhang Zuolin were all desirous of doing good, but no good results come out of them. This is because all their energy was spent in dealing with their political enemies. When engaged in dealing with their enemies, they had to sacrifice reconstruction to maintain an army and resort to any dubious means in order to win. The problem is therefore not that of personality but that of circumstances. Given the circumstances, no one could achieve good results. The basic situation of China may be summarized in one sentence: Without a unified political power, there can be no good government. . . .

Viewed from the standpoint of history, this phenomenon is quite natural, and no nation is an exception to it. Advanced Western countries such as England, France, and Russia resembled China in their early stages of development when there was only internal order but not revolution. In England the Wars of the Roses raged in the fifteenth century, but no results were achieved. It was toward the end of the fifteenth century that Henry VII unified England and began a century of absolutism under the name of the Tudor dynasty. During these hundred years the British people had a good rest and rehabilitation; as a result, the national state was formed. The seventeenth century saw the culmination of political conflicts in a genuine revolution. Historians are agreed that had there been no Tudor autocracy in the sixteenth century there could not have been any revolution in the seventeenth century. . . . [Jiang goes on to cite the Bourbons and the French Revolution, the Romanovs and the Russian Revolution as illustrations of the same point.]

The present situation in China is similar to that of England before the Tudor absolutism, or that of France before the Bourbon absolutism, or that of Russia before the Romanov absolutism. The Chinese, too, can have only internal disturbance but not genuine revolution. Although we had several thousand years of absolute government, unfortunately our absolute monarchs, because of environmental peculiarities, did not fulfill their historic duty. The heritage left to the republic by the Manchu dynasty was too poor to be revolutionary capital. In the first place, our state is still a dynastic state, not a national one. Chinese citizens are generally loyal to individuals, families, or localities rather than to the state. Second, our absolute monarchs did not leave us a class that could serve as the nucleus of a new regime. In fact, the historic task of the Chinese monarchies was to destroy all the classes and institutions outside the royal family that could possibly become the center of political power. As a result, when the royal family was overthrown, the nation became a "heap of loose sand." Third, under the absolutist regime our material civilization lagged far behind. Consequently, when the foreigners took advantage of our trouble after the outbreak of the revolution, we were unable to offer any effective resistance.

In sum, the political history of all countries is divided into two phases: first, the building of a state, and second, the promotion of national welfare by means of the state. Since we have not completed the first phase, it is idle to talk of the second. As a Western saying goes, "The better is often the enemy of the good." The so-called revolution of China today is a great obstacle to our national reconstruction. The Chinese people should adopt an objective attitude and view the civil war as a historical process, just as physicians study physiology. We should foster the unifying force, because it is the vital power of our state organism. We should eliminate the anti-unification force, because it is the virus in our state organism. Our present problem is the existence of our state, not what type of state we should have.

["Kaiming yu zhuanzhi," pp. 2–5 — CT]

### HU SHI: "NATIONAL RECONSTRUCTION AND ABSOLUTISM"

A direct rejoinder to Jiang Tingfu's defense of Nationalist party tutelage came from one of the intellectual leaders of republican China, Hu Shi (1891–1962). Like Luo and Jiang, he had been educated in the United States (Cornell University and Columbia University) and became a thoroughgoing exponent of Westernization or modernization in many fields. As such he was often critical of the Nationalists and of attitudes expressed by Sun Yat-sen or Chiang Kai-shek. Nevertheless, his personal standing as a scholar and thinker was so high both in China and in the West that the Nationalist government entrusted important diplomatic and educational assignments to him and later in Taiwan awarded him the presidency of its top academic institution, the Academia Sinica.

### 1. Is Absolutism a Necessary Stage for National Reconstruction?

In regard to this problem, there is a basic difference between Mr. Jiang Tingfu's views and mine. As I see it, the history of England, France, and Russia as cited by Mr. Jiang is only the history of national reconstruction in the three countries. But the scope of national reconstruction is very broad, and the factors involved are complex. We cannot single out "absolutism" as the only cause or condition. We may say that the three dynasties (the Tudors of England, the Bourbons of France, and the Romanovs of Russia) were the periods during which their respective states were built, but we cannot prove that the formation of the state in these three countries was due to absolute rule. . . . The birth and propagation of the new English language and literature, the circulation of the English Bible and the Book of Common Prayer, the influence of Oxford and Cambridge universities, the impact of London as England's political, economic, and cultural center, the rapid development of the textile industry, the rise of the middle class — all of these were important factors in the formation of the English national state. Most of these factors did not first appear under the Tudor dynasty; their origins may be traced to the time before the Tudors, although their development was particularly rapid in that century of unity and peace.

What Mr. Jiang probably means to say is that a unified political power is indispensable to the building of the state. However, his use of the term *absolutism* to describe the unity of political power easily leads the people to think of a dictatorship with unlimited power. The reign of Henry VIII was the period in which parliamentary power began to rise: members of Parliament were secure from arrest, and the king established the new church upon the support of

Parliament. Therefore, instead of asserting that absolutism is an indispensable stage for the building of the state, we had better say that unity of political power is the condition. And unity of political power does not depend on completely following the dictatorship of the Romanov dynasty.

### 2. Why Did Centuries of Absolute Government Fail to Create a National State in China?

Concerning this question, my views are again different from those of Mr. Jiang. Generally speaking, China had long since become a national state. What we now find defective is that the solidarity and unity of the Chinese national state have proved inadequate for a modern national state. In national consciousness, in unity of language, in unity of history and culture, in unity and continuity of governmental system (including examination, civil service, law, etc.) — in all these, China in the past two thousand years was qualified to be a national state. It is true that there were periods of foreign rule, but during those periods national consciousness became more vigorous and enduring so that eventually there arose national heroes such as Liu Yu, Zhu Yuanzhang, Hong Xiuquan, and Sun Yat-sen, who led the national revolutions. Indeed, all of the capital for national reconstruction that we have today is the national consciousness passed on to us by our forebears through two thousand years. . . .

As to the three defects pointed out by Mr. Jiang, they prove only the evil consequences of the former social and political order, but not the lack of a national state in China. First, Mr. Jiang said, "Chinese citizens are generally loyal to individuals, families, or localities rather than to the state." This is because in the old days the power of the state did not extend directly to the people. When "the emperor was as remote as the sky [from the people]," how could anyone bypass his family, which exerts an immediate influence on his life, and profess loyalty to the state in the abstract, unless he was highly educated? The famous Burke of eighteenth-century England said, "In order that the people love the state, the state must first be lovable." Can we then say that England in the eighteenth century had not become a national state? The reason the masses of the people today do not love the nation is partly that they are inadequately educated and therefore unable to imagine a state and partly that the state has not bestowed any benefits upon the people.

[Jiang, "Jianguo yu zhuanzhi," pp. 3–5 — CT]

## CHIANG KAI-SHEK: NATIONALISM AND TRADITIONALISM

Chiang Kai-shek (Jiang Jieshi, 1887–1975), who took over leadership after Sun Yat-sen's death, was a devoted follower and admirer of Dr. Sun. He was also a very different man from his mentor. For one thing, Chiang had virtually no

Western education and, knowing no foreign language well, was dependent upon others to interpret the West for him. Consequently, his ideas were formed much more within the Chinese tradition and found their most typical expression in the language and formulas of the past. His experience of foreign lands was also much more limited. The net effect even of his relatively brief travel and study in Japan and later in Soviet Russia was only to increase his consciousness of being a Confucian Chinese. Throughout life this consciousness deepened as a result of intensive and prolonged study of Chinese classical literature.

Understandably, then, it was the first of Sun's Three Principles, nationalism, which had the most significance for Chiang. Others of his contemporaries, however, no less intensely nationalistic than he and no less limited in their experience of the outside world, still showed by their eager acceptance of Western standards that the new nationalism could be quite divorced from any strong attachment to the values of the past. The contact zone of East and West, in which such a cultural hybrid as Dr. Sun had been produced just a generation before, had moved from Honolulu, Hong Kong, Macao, and Yokohama into the very classrooms of provincial China, where Western-style education now prevailed. Chiang himself, in a certain sense, had moved with it. He had, for instance, become a devout Methodist, married a Wellesley-educated woman, attempted to learn English, adopted Western standards of personal hygiene, and made considerable use of Western advisers. All this notwithstanding, his own philosophy of life drew more and more upon Chinese sources of inspiration, and in offering it to the Chinese people as a national way of life, he cut across the Westernizing trend of the times.

What Chiang found so essential in Chinese tradition — Confucian ethics — actually represented an important link between him and Dr. Sun. The latter, in his long struggle to organize and lead a national revolution, had come to a new appreciation of the traditional Confucian virtues for which earlier he had found little use. They could serve as a means of achieving social discipline and national cohesion among a people who were otherwise just a "heap of loose sand." Chiang himself had no less reason, politically, to adopt the same view. He confronted all the same problems of leadership as Sun had and felt the same need for disciplined loyalty among his followers. Moreover, as a man who had received military training in Japan, he no doubt had a keener sense than most men of the importance of discipline.

With Chiang, however, it was more than a question of simply exploiting traditional attitudes that could serve present purposes. It had become a deep personal conviction of his (as it never seems to have been of Sun's) that moral values were the ultimate basis of human life. His own experience seems to have taught him the value of self-discipline to the individual, as much as the importance of social discipline to the nation.

These convictions manifested themselves early in Chiang's public career, and he never abandoned them. In 1924, as superintendent of the Nationalist

(Guomindang) military academy at Whampoa, where Soviet influence was strong and the revolutionary fever ran high, Chiang did not hesitate to base military indoctrination on a text compiled from the moral teachings of the nineteenth-century Neo-Confucian and Restoration hero Zeng Guofan. Thus, in contrast to Sun's glorification of the Taiping leader Hong Xiuquan as a national revolutionary figure, Chiang acclaimed the very suppressor of the Taipings as the finest exemplar of national tradition. In this way the cultivation of personal virtue and nobility of character was stressed over revolutionary fervor. [For this, Western liberals criticized Chiang as a reactionary, but later in the eighties and nineties, under the Deng and Jiang regimes, Zeng came back into official favor, on terms similar to Chiang Kai-shek's estimation of him.]

Ten years later, when Chiang launched his New Life Movement as a program for the strengthening of national morale, the Confucian virtues of decorum, rightness, integrity, and a sense of shame provided the chief catchwords and main content of this campaign of mass education. Significantly, the first of these virtues, *li*, implied an acceptance of social discipline, of law and authority, in opposition to the trend from the West toward unfettered individualism. Again, in 1943 when Chiang published his *China's Destiny* to serve as a primer for the party and its Youth Corps, he declared that, with the approaching end of foreign rule and exploitation in China, the great task would be one of internal reconstruction through moral rearmament, Confucian-style. Then in the 1950s, after the retreat to Taiwan, courses in Confucian ethical philosophy became compulsory for all students under the Nationalist regime.

It would be a distortion of Chiang's social philosophy and program to sum it up in terms only of nationalism and Neo-Confucian ethics. He remained committed to Dr. Sun's Three Principles, including a large measure of economic planning as well as eventual political democratization. And if he did not pursue with equal vigor these other aspects of Sun's original program, his justification for the delay in achieving the objectives of People's Rule and People's Livelihood was one provided by Sun himself in the doctrine of political tutelage. Military unification had to come first.

It must be allowed that Chiang's traditionalism was more than a personal idiosyncrasy, a quixotic gesture. As we will see, there were other Chinese at this time — including erstwhile advocates of Westernization, now disillusioned — who joined him in attacking Western individualism and materialism as a threat to the spiritual and moral values of Chinese civilization. Indeed, subsequent developments in the People's Republic under Deng Xiaoping and Jiang Zemin confirm this as a broad, long-term trend of Chinese politics.

Nor was this a purely Chinese phenomenon. Nationalists in India and Japan often shared a revulsion for those aspects of Western life that Chiang found so distasteful in treaty ports like Shanghai. Commercialism, cynicism, soft-living, and self-indulgence seemed to typify the bourgeois culture of the West as transplanted to the soil of Asia. Was this all the West had to offer in place of the traditional values it was destroying? On this point, Chiang's rejection of Western moral decadence linked him in spirit with an Indian nationalist like Gandhi, while his *Essentials of the New Life Movement* (from which excerpts are given below) showed at the same time some close kinship with the authors of *Fundamentals of Japan's National Polity* (*Kokutai no hongi*), the official credo of Japanese nationalists in the 1930s, who decried as he did the individualism and class antagonisms of the West, while extolling the social virtues of Confucianism.[5]

Chiang's traditionalism, it is true, was never conceived as a total opposition to Westernization. The Three People's Principles — nationalism, democracy, and the people's livelihood — were basically Western in inspiration, and however much he or Dr. Sun adapted them to their own tastes, the use of such slogans constituted a recognition on their part that certain Western ideals had an irresistible attraction for twentieth-century Asia.

Moreover, this attraction to Western ways, far from being a passing fancy, has proved a long-term trend in East Asia throughout the twentieth century. Yet, no less persistent are reactions to it similar to Chiang's. As the last chapter shows, even in a China long subjected to the anti-Confucian polemics of a Communist regime, there have more recently been conscious and concerted efforts by official organs to resurrect Confucian morality as an antidote to the "spiritual pollution" and "rampant individualism" charged once again to the cultural influence of the modern West. Thus, to dismiss Chiang Kai-shek's type of moral rearmament as merely the passing predilection of a reactionary generalissimo would be to underestimate the problem. Underlying this phenomenon are deep-seated issues of cultural conflict and identity that persist through political upheavals and revolutionary change.

### CHIANG KAI-SHEK: *ESSENTIALS OF THE NEW LIFE MOVEMENT*

The New Life Movement was inaugurated by Chiang in a speech at Nanchang in September 1934. Its immediate purpose was to rally the Chinese people for a campaign against the Communists in that region, but a more general aim was to tighten discipline and build up morale in the Nationalist regime and the nation as a whole. Laxity in public life, official corruption, lack of discipline in the ranks of party and army, and apathy among the people were among the weaknesses Chiang tried to overcome by a great moral reformation emphasizing Confucian self-cultivation, a life of frugality, and dedication to the nation. There were also exhortations on behalf of personal hygiene and physical training, as well as injunctions against smoking tobacco and opium, dancing, spitting on the floor, and leaving coats unbuttoned. In these respects, however, Chiang thought of himself as promoting progress — cleaning up and dressing

---

5. This is not to say, of course, that the three did not differ considerably in other respects.

up China in answer to the type of Westerner who complained about its untidiness and lack of sanitation.

An important influence on the New Life ideology was exerted by Chiang's close adviser and minister of education, Chen Lifu, a Western-educated exponent of a modernized Neo-Confucianism. Often stigmatized as an arch reactionary in Chiang's regime, he later appeared as an honored guest of the People's Republic at the celebration of Confucius's birthday in Beijing. He has been reputed to be the "ghost writer" of the following text, but he personally denied any part in it, and Chiang remains the accepted author.

## The Object of the New Life Movement

### WHY IS A NEW LIFE NEEDED?

The general psychology of our people today can be described as spiritless. What manifests itself in behavior is this: lack of discrimination between good and evil, between what is public and what is private, and between what is primary and what is secondary. Because there is no discrimination between good and evil, right and wrong are confused; because there is no discrimination between public and private, improper taking and giving [of public funds] occur; and because there is no distinction between primary and secondary, first and last are not placed in the proper order. As a result, officials tend to be dishonest and avaricious, the masses are undisciplined and calloused, youth become degraded and intemperate, adults are corrupt and ignorant, the rich become extravagant and luxurious, and the poor become mean and disorderly. Naturally it has resulted in disorganization of the social order and national life, and we are in no position either to prevent or to remedy natural calamities, disasters caused from within, or invasions from without. The individual, society, and the whole country are now suffering. . . . In order to develop the life of our nation, protect the existence of our society, and improve the livelihood of our people, it is absolutely necessary to wipe out these unwholesome conditions and to start to lead a new and rational life.

## The Content of the New Life Movement

### 1. THE PRINCIPLES OF THE NEW LIFE MOVEMENT

The New Life Movement aims at the promotion of a regular life guided by the four virtues, namely, *li, yi, lian,* and *chi.*[6] Those virtues must be applied to

---

6. Standard translations for these terms are *li*, ritual/decorum; *yi*, rightness or duty; *lian*, integrity or honesty; *chi*, sense of shame. Since Chiang defines the terms in what follows, we have kept the romanized forms here.

ordinary life in the matter of food, clothing, shelter, and action. The four virtues are the essential principles for the promotion of morality. They form the major rules for dealing with men and human affairs, for cultivating oneself, and for adjustment to one's surroundings. Whoever violates these rules is bound to fail, and a nation that neglects them will not survive.

There are two kinds of skeptics:

First, some hold that the four virtues are merely rules of good conduct. No matter how good they may be, they are not sufficient to save a nation whose knowledge and technique are inferior to others.

Those who hold this view do not seem to understand the distinction between matters of primary and secondary importance. People need knowledge and technique because they want to do good. Otherwise, knowledge and technique can only be instruments of dishonorable deeds. *Li, yi, lian,* and *chi* are the principal rules alike for the community, the group, or the entire nation. Those who do not observe these rules will probably utilize their knowledge and ability to the detriment of society and ultimately to their own disadvantage. Therefore, these virtues not only can save the nation but also can rebuild the nation.

Second, there is another group of people who argue that these virtues are merely formal refinements that are useless in dealing with hunger and cold. . . . [Yet] when these virtues prevail, even if food and clothing are insufficient, they can be produced by human labor; or, if the granary is empty, it can be filled through human effort. On the other hand, when these virtues are not observed, if food and clothing are insufficient, they will not be made sufficient by fighting and robbing; or, if the granary is empty, it will not be filled by stealing and begging. The four virtues, which rectify the misconduct of men, are the proper methods of achieving abundance. Without them, there will be fighting, robbing, stealing, and begging among men. . . .

## 2. THE MEANING OF LI, YI, LIAN, AND CHI

Although *li, yi, lian,* and *chi* have always been regarded as the foundations of the nation, yet the changing times and circumstances may require that these principles be given a new interpretation. As applied to our life today, they may be interpreted as follows:

*Li* means "regulated attitude."

*Yi* means "right conduct."

*Lian* means "clear discrimination."

*Chi* means "real self-consciousness."

The word *li* (decorum) means *li* (principle). It becomes natural law when applied to nature; it becomes a rule when applied to social affairs; and it signifies discipline when used in reference to national affairs. A man's conduct is considered regular if it conforms with the above law, rule, and discipline. When one conducts oneself in accordance with the regular manner, one is said to have the regulated attitude.

The word *yi* means "proper." Any conduct that is in accordance with *li* — i.e., natural law, social rule, and national discipline — is considered proper. To act improperly, or to refrain from acting when one knows it is proper to act, cannot be called *yi*.

The word *lian* means "clear." It denotes distinction between right and wrong. What agrees with *li* and *yi* is right, and what does not agree is wrong. To take what we recognize as right and to forgo what we recognize as wrong constitute clear discrimination.

The word *chi* means "consciousness." When one is conscious of the fact that his own actions are not in accordance with *li*, *yi*, *lian*, and *chi*, one feels ashamed.

From the above explanations, it is clear that *chi* governs the motive of action, that *lian* gives the guidance for it, that *yi* relates to the carrying out of an action, and that *li* regulates its outward form. The four are interrelated. They are dependent upon each other in the perfecting of virtue.

## Conclusion

In short, the main object of the New Life Movement is to substitute a rational life for the irrational, and to achieve this we must observe *li*, *yi*, *lian*, and *chi* in our daily life.

1. By the observance of these virtues, it is hoped that rudeness and vulgarity will be got rid of and that the life of our people will conform to the standard of art. By art we are not referring to the special enjoyment of the gentry. We mean the cultural standard of all the people, irrespective of sex, age, wealth, and class. It is the boundary line between civilized life and barbarism. It is the only way by which one can achieve the purpose of man, for only by artistically controlling oneself and dealing with others can one fulfill the duty of mutual assistance. . . . A lack of artistic training is the cause of suspicion, jealousy, hatred, and strife that are prevalent in our society today. . . . To investigate things so as to extend our knowledge, to distinguish between the fundamental and the secondary, to seek the invention of instruments, to excel in our techniques — these are the essentials of an artistic life, the practice of which will enable us to wipe out the defects of vulgarity, confusion, crudity, and baseness.

2. By the observance of these virtues, it is hoped that beggary and robbery will be eliminated and that the life of our people will be productive. The poverty of China is primarily caused by the fact that there are too many consumers and too few producers. Those who consume without producing usually live as parasites or as robbers. They behave thus because they are ignorant of the four virtues. To remedy this we must make them produce more and spend less. They

must understand that luxury is improper and that living as a parasite is a shame.

3. By the observance of these virtues, it is hoped that social disorder and individual weakness will be remedied and that people will become more military-minded. If a country cannot defend itself, it has every chance of losing its existence. . . . Therefore our people must have military training. As a preliminary, we must acquire the habits of orderliness, cleanliness, simplicity, frugality, promptness, and exactness. We must preserve order, emphasize organization, responsibility, and discipline, and be ready to die for the country at any moment.

[*Xin shenghuo yundong gangyao*, in *Zongzai yanlun xuanji* 2:403–414 — CT]

## CHINA'S DESTINY

*China's Destiny* appeared in March 1943, during the darkest period of the war with Japan, when Chinese morale badly needed boosting. Chiang explained at length how his country's difficulties in the past arose from foreign oppression and the consequent deterioration of national life. The recent abrogation of the unequal treaties by Britain and the United States, however, heralded a new era of independence and self-respect for China once the Japanese were defeated. Chiang's great goal was still political and military unification. To achieve this he outlined a five-point program of national reconstruction, emphasizing pride in China's past, a return to Confucian virtues, restoration of the traditional system of group responsibility and mutual aid, and a long-range program of economic development along lines laid down by Sun Yat-sen — industrialization, land equalization, and state capitalism in a planned and controlled economy.

A prime target of Chiang's indignation was the prevalence of foreign ideologies and attitudes among intellectuals, who were accused of yielding and pandering to popular trends, especially in the Westernized treaty ports. Decadent trends from the West, almost as much as communism, came under his fire for encouraging moral anarchy, the pursuit of selfish ambitions, and the quest for private profit or class domination. Yet Chiang also insisted that these negative tendencies represented not Western civilization itself, properly understood, but only a superficial imitation of the West by shallow-minded Chinese.

## Social Effects [of the Unequal Treaties]

During the last hundred years, under the oppression of unequal treaties, the life of the Chinese people became more and more degenerate. Everyone took self-interest as the standard of right and wrong, and personal desires as the criterion of good and evil; a thing was considered right if it conformed to one's self-interest or good if it conformed to one's personal desires. Rascals became influential in the villages, rogues were active in the cities, sacrificing public safety and the welfare of others to satisfy their own interest and desires. In the meantime, extravagant and irresponsible ideologies and political doctrines were freely advanced, either to rationalize self-interest and personal desires or to exploit them for ulterior motives. The rationalizers idolized them as an expression of the self, and the exploiters utilized them as a means of fomenting disturbances in the community, in order to fish in troubled waters. The practice of following in the footsteps of the sages or emulating the heroes and being "friends with the ancients" not only tended to disappear but was even considered mean and despicable. [p. 72]

## Moral Effects

For five thousand years China had always stressed the importance of honest work and frugality. Her people were noted for their simplicity in food and clothing; women occupied themselves with their looms and men with their plows. These good habits, however, were swept away by the prevalence in the [foreign] concessions of the vices of opium smoking, gambling, prostitution, and robbery.

China's ancient ethical teachings and philosophies contained detailed and carefully worked out principles and rules for the regulation and maintenance of the social life of man. The structure of our society underwent many changes, but our social life never deviated from the principles governing the relationship between parent and child, husband and wife, brother and brother, friend and friend, superior and inferior, man and woman, old and young, as well as principles enjoining mutual help among neighbors and care of the sick and weak.

During the past hundred years, wherever the influence of the foreign concessions was felt, these principles were not only neglected but also despised. Between parent and child, husband and wife, brothers and friends, superiors and inferiors, old and young, and among neighbors the old sentiments of respect and affection and the spirit of mutual help and cooperation were disappearing. Only material interests were taken into consideration, and everywhere there was a general lack of moral standards by which to judge oneself. Whenever duty called, people tried to shirk it; whenever there was material profit to be gained, they struggled for it. . . . A country that had hitherto attached the greatest importance to decorum and rightness was now in danger of losing its sense of integrity and honor. What harm these unequal treaties had caused!

The deterioration of national morality also tended to affect the physique of our people. The physical strength of the numberless unemployed in the cities was easily impaired. The health of those merchants who abandoned themselves to a life of extravagance and dissoluteness could not but break down. The most serious thing, however, was the effect upon the health of the youth in the schools. Physical training was not popularized in most of the schools; moral education was also neglected by school masters and teachers. In the meantime, the extravagant and dissolute life outside the school attracted the students, caused them to indulge in evil habits, and resulted in the deterioration of their moral character. Infectious and venereal diseases, too, which were rampant in the cities, further undermined their physical constitution. How could these young men, who were unsound in body and mind, help to advance learning, reform social customs, render service to the state, and promote enterprises after their graduation? The inevitable result of such a state of affairs was the steady disintegration of our country and the further demoralization of the Chinese nation. [pp. 75–77]

## Psychological Effects

After the Student Movement of May 4, 1919, two currents of thought, ultra-individualistic liberalism and class-struggle communism, found their way into Chinese academic circles and later became widespread in the country. On the whole, Chinese academic circles desired to effect a change in our culture, forgetting that it had certain elements that are immutable. With respect to different Western theories they imitated only their superficial aspects and never sought to understand their true significance in order to improve China's national life. The result was that a large number of our scholars and students adopted the superficialities and nonessentials of Western culture and lost their respect for and confidence in our own culture. [pp. 81–82]

## The Decisive Factor in China's Destiny

The work of reforming social life and carrying out the program of national reconstruction is one of paramount importance in the process of national revival — a task that requires persistent effort. Individuals, striving singly, will not achieve great results nor lasting accomplishments. Consequently, all adult citizens and promising youths, whether in a town, a district, a province, or in the country at large, should have a common organization, with a systematic plan for binding the members together and headquarters to promote joint reconstruction activities and also personal accomplishments. . . .

In the past our adult citizens have been unable to unite on a large scale or for a long period. They have been derisively compared to "a heap of loose sand" or spoken of as having "only five minutes' enthusiasm." Now, incapacity to unite is a result of selfishness, and the best antidote for selfishness is public spirit. That unity does not last is due to hypocrisy and the best antidote for hypocrisy is sincerity. With a public spirit, one can take "all men as one's kin and all things as one's company." With sincerity, one can persevere and succeed in the end. . . .

The principal fault of our youth today and the cause of their failure and ineffectual living lie essentially in the unsound education they have received.

Since they do not follow the guidance of their teachers or realize the importance of organization as a factor in the success or failure of their life, and since they do not understand what freedom and discipline mean, they are irresponsible in their conduct and unrealistic in their thinking. As soon as they enter society, they feel the lack of ability and confidence to take up any practical work, let alone the task of social and national reconstruction. . . . [pp. 212–214]

To avoid the mistake of living a misguided and regrettable life, they should never again allow themselves to be led astray by blind and impulsive following of others as in the past. We must realize that the Three Principles represent not only the crystallization of China's time-honored civilization and of her people's highest virtues but also the inevitable trend of world affairs in this modern age. The San Min Zhu Yi Youth Corps is the central organization of all Chinese youths who are faithful adherents of the Three Principles. All young men and women must therefore place themselves under the guidance of the Corps in order to keep their aims true and to avoid doing harm to themselves and to the nation. It is only by working within the framework of the Corps' program that they can make decisions about their life work in the right direction. . . . It will be their mission to save the country from decline and disorganization, to wipe out national humiliation, to restore national strength, and to show loyalty to the state and filial devotion to the nation. They should emulate the sages and heroes of history and be the lifeblood of the people and the backbone of the nation.

To sum up, the Nationalist Party and the San Min Zhu Yi Youth Corps are organic parts of the nation. . . . Considering the state as an organism as far as its life is concerned, we may say that the Three Principles constitute the soul of our nation, because without these principles our national reconstruction would be deprived of its guiding spirit. . . . Without the Nationalist Party, China would be deprived of its pivot. If all the revolutionary elements and promising youths in the country really want to throw in their lot with the fate of the country, if they regard national undertakings as their own undertakings and the national life as their own life — then they should all enlist in the party or in the Youth Corps. By so doing, they can discharge the highest duties of citizenship and attain the highest ideal in life. Then and only then can our great mission of national reconstruction be completed. [pp. 219–221]

[Adapted from *China's Destiny*, trans. by Wang Chung-hui, pp. 72–84, 212–221]

## JIANG JINGGUO (CHIANG CHING-KUO): THE REPUBLIC OF CHINA IN TAIWAN

After the Nationalists' withdrawal from the mainland to Taiwan in 1949, Sun Yat-sen's *Three People's Principles* remained the basic ideological text of the Taiwan regime under Chiang Kai-shek and his son, Jiang Jingguo (Chiang

Ching-kuo), with the latter taking successive steps to implement the transition to representative government under a constitution modeled on Sun's ideas. A practical and rather unpretentious person rather than a dynamic leader or brilliant theoretician, Jiang Jingguo left no great body of doctrine, but the following brief excerpts explain in rather simple terms his view of how the Nationalists moved to implement Sun's goals.

Although the local inhabitants, who suffered repression in the early years of mainlander rule, and the political opposition would question whether the process was as gentle and benign as Jiang describes it below, most observers would grant the substance of his claims: that economic reform led to rapid and substantial prosperity; that the new wealth became widely shared among the population, rather than accruing only to the benefit of an upper class; that this shared affluence became the basis of a greatly expanded modern educational and training system; and that the latter supported the quick development of efficient, high-tech industry. Finally, the lifting of martial law, freeing of the press, and holding of elections for the executive and legislative branches completed the transition to representative democracy, which contrasts with the Communists' declared opposition to any such "peaceful evolution" to democracy.

Not mentioned in Jiang's statements for a Western audience is a notable feature of Nationalist policy: its defense and promotion of Chinese cultural traditions during the same period when Communist China was engaged in the great Cultural Revolution directed especially against Confucianism. It has remained a question just how these traditions, including Confucianism, religious Daoism, and Buddhism, would adapt to rapid modernization, but toward the end of the century they remained shared cultural links to mainland China, once the latter abandoned its anti-traditionalism in the eighties.

THE EVOLUTION OF CONSTITUTIONAL DEMOCRACY IN TAIWAN

The following excerpt is from "The Struggle with the Communists Is a Struggle Over Lifestyle," an interview with Hong Kong English-language reporters on February 5, 1987.

Since the founding of the Republic of China [in 1912], implementing democratic, constitutional government has been the goal of our nation. Unfortunately, because of frequent domestic and foreign turmoil, constitutional government could not be realized until 1947. It had not been in force for even two years when the Communists seized the mainland. In order to prevent Communist military invasion and subversion after the government moved to Taiwan in 1949, we declared martial law on Taiwan and [the offshore islands of] Penghu, Jinmen, and Mazu to protect national security and guarantee a secure environment for the constitution. The facts clearly show that the scope of martial law was extremely limited and had little effect on the people's daily life and basic rights. Moreover, the government on Taiwan, Penghu, Jinmen, and Mazu worked steadily and vigorously to promote democratic, constitutional government.

The recent decision by the government to end martial law and lift the ban on political activities seeks to realize policies to promote democracy and the rule of law adopted at the beginning of the republic. With more than thirty years of work [on Taiwan], the political situation is stable, the economy flourishing, and education universal. Consequently, the government, after carefully researching social change and the needs of the people, has decided to end martial law, lift the ban on political activities, and expand democratic, constitutional government in the near future.

[*Jiang Jingguo xiansheng wenji* 15:196 — RL]

### IMPLEMENTING "THE THREE PEOPLE'S PRINCIPLES"

The following are excerpts from an interview with an editor of America's *Readers Digest*, December 11, 1985.

*Question:* How did the Republic of China achieve its remarkable economic development?

*Answer:* The basic reasons for the success of our nation's economic development are:

1. We advocate freedom and democracy and hold fast to a constitutional system. The government and the people trust one another and are harmoniously united, providing for democracy and a stable political environment.

2. Our policy of a free economy with planned characteristics encourages private enterprise and stimulates the diligence of the people and the creativity of entrepreneurs.

3. The implementation of an excellent, universal educational system with everyone having equal access to education and the promotion of the development of science and technology have raised the productive power of the people.

4. [By] adhering to a policy of [providing] equal [access to] wealth, we have lessened the gap between rich and poor, enhanced social well-being, raised the quality of life, and created an equal and harmonious society.

*Question:* What specific policies did your government adopt to promote this economic development?

*Answer:* These can be divided into several stages:

1. In the early 1950s we first carried out currency reform, encouraging saving and successfully stabilizing the value of the currency and the price of com-

modities. Next, we implemented equitable land reform and adopted the strategy of developing both agriculture and industry equally, [thus] smoothly solving the unemployment problem.

2. At the end of the 1950s we successively reformed foreign exchange, trade, financial administration, and banking and encouraged light industry, which already had a foundation to open up export markets. [All of these measures] caused industrial production and foreign trade to soar in the 1960s.

3. In the 1970s we methodically developed heavy industry and the chemical industry while improving basic infrastructure such as transportation and electricity, [thus] establishing an excellent foundation for economic growth and development. In addition, successive administrative reform measures such as extending compulsory education to nine years beginning in 1968 and actively encouraging foreign-trained students to return and serve the nation greatly enhanced the human resources needed for economic growth.

4. Now in the 1980s our policy is to emphasize the development of high-tech industry and the implementation of the requisite social and economic systemic reforms. At the same time, we strive to maintain the good quality of the environment to become a truly modern nation.

*Question:* If the regime on the mainland were not communist, could it reach the same economic level as the Republic of China?

*Answer:* I must first stress that as long as the Communists occupy the mainland, no matter what economic reforms they carry out they will be unable to become a noncommunist regime. Therefore, if the mainland wants to reach our economic level, it must abandon communism and adopt "The Three People's Principles." If it can do this, considering the size and great human and material resources of the mainland, it would of course be able to attain the economic level of the Republic of China on Taiwan. This is why we have raised the slogan "Unite China with 'The Three People's Principles.' "

[*Jiang Jingguo xiansheng wenji* 15:154–159 — RL]

# Chapter 33

## THE NEW CULTURE MOVEMENT

As its name implies, the New Culture Movement was an attempt to destroy what remained of traditional Confucian culture in the republican era and to replace it with something new. The collapse of the old dynastic system in 1911 and the failure of Yuan Shikai's Confucian-garbed monarchical restoration in 1916 meant that, politically, Confucianism was almost dead. It had, however, been much more than a political philosophy. It had been a complete way of life, which nationalism and republicanism supplanted only in part. There were some even among republicans who felt that certain aspects of the old culture, Confucian ethics especially, should be preserved and strengthened, lest the whole fabric of Chinese life come apart and the new regime itself be seriously weakened. Others, with far more influence on the younger generation, drew precisely the opposite conclusion. For them, nothing in Confucianism was worth salvaging from the debris of the Manchu dynasty. In fact, whatever vestiges of the past remained in the daily life and thinking of the people should be rooted out; otherwise the young republic would rest on shaky foundations, and its progress would be retarded by a backward citizenry. The new order required a whole new culture. The political revolution of 1911 had to be followed by a cultural revolution. In this conflict of views many issues surfaced that reappeared in the 1980s and 1990s between those who advocated a return to Confucianism and those who saw "modernization" as requiring liberation from the past.

During and just after World War I the intellectual spearhead of this cultural revolution went on the offensive, launching a movement that reached out in many directions and touched many aspects of Chinese society. Roughly, it may be divided into six major phases, presented below in more or less chronological order. They are (1) the attack on Confucianism, (2) the Literary Revolution, (3) the proclaiming of a new philosophy of life, (4) the debate on science and the philosophy of life, (5) the "doubting of antiquity" movement, and (6) the debate on Chinese and Western cultural values. Needless to say, these phases overlapped considerably, and certain leading writers figured prominently in more than one phase of the movement.

From the movement's anti-traditionalist character one may infer that its leaders looked very much to the West. Positivism was their great inspiration, science and materialism were their great slogans, and — in the early years especially — John Dewey and Bertrand Russell were their great idols. The leaders themselves were in many cases Western-educated, though not necessarily schooled in the West, since Western-style education was by now established in the East, in Japan, and in the new national and missionary colleges of China. Often college professors themselves, the leaders now had access to the lecture platform, as well as to the new organs of the public journalism and the intellectual and literary reviews that were a novel feature of the modern age. Above all, they had a new audience — young, intense, frustrated by China's failures in the past, and full of eager hopes for the future.

## THE ATTACK ON CONFUCIANISM

The open assault on Confucianism, which began in 1916, was led by Chen Duxiu (1879–1942), editor of a magazine titled *The New Youth*. Earlier reformers had attacked certain of the concepts of Confucianism, often in the name of a purified and revitalized Confucian belief or, with less obvious partisanship, combining criticism of certain aspects with praise of others. Chen, by contrast, challenged Confucianism from beginning to end, realizing as he did so that he struck at the very heart of the traditional culture. For him, a partisan of "science" and "democracy," Confucianism stood simply for reaction and obscurantism. He identified it with the old regime, with Yuan Shikai's attempt to restore the monarchy, with everything from the past that, to his mind, had smothered progress and creativity.

Such an uncompromising attack was bound to shock many — those who had taken Confucianism as much for granted as the good earth of China or those who still held to it consciously, and with some pride, as an expression of cultural nationalism. But there were others upon whom Chen's bold denunciations had an electrifying effect — those, particularly young teachers and students, for whom Confucianism had come to hold little positive meaning as their own education became more Westernized; those for whom, in fact, it was now more likely to be felt in their own lives simply as a form of unwanted parental or societal constraint. Young people of this group, with Beijing as their center, *The New Youth* as their mouthpiece, and Chen as their literary champion, were glad to throw themselves into a crusade against this bugbear from the past and to proclaim their own coming of age in the modern world by shouting, "Destroy the old curiosity shop of Confucius!"

### CHEN DUXIU: "THE WAY OF CONFUCIUS AND MODERN LIFE"

Through articles such as this, which appeared in December 1916, Chen Duxiu established himself as perhaps the most influential writer of his time. His popular review, *Xin qingnian (The New Youth)*, had for its Western title *La Jeunesse nouvelle*, reflecting the avant-garde character of its editor, who had obtained his higher education first in a Japanese normal college and later in France. Here the Westernized and "liberated" Chen directs his fire at social customs and abuses that seemed to have Confucian sanction but have no place in the modern age. Here the man who was to found the Chinese Communist Party five years later speaks as an individualist, who attributes the lack of individualism in China to the traditional view of property as family-owned and -controlled rather than belonging to an individual.

The pulse of modern life is economic, and the fundamental principle of economic production is individual independence. Its effect has penetrated ethics. Consequently, the independence of the individual in the ethical field and the independence of property in the economic field bear witness to each other, thus reaffirming the theory [of such interaction]. Because of this [interaction], social mores and material culture have taken a great step forward.

In China, the Confucians have based their teachings on their ethical norms. Sons and wives possess neither personal individuality nor personal property. Fathers and elder brothers bring up their sons and younger brothers and are in turn supported by them. It is said in chapter 30 of the *Record of Rites*: "While parents are living, the son dares not regard his person or property as his own" [27:14]. This is absolutely not the way to personal independence. . . .

In all modern constitutional states, whether monarchies or republics, there are political parties. Those who engage in party activities all express their spirit of independent conviction. They go their own way and need not agree with their fathers or husbands. When people are bound by the Confucian teachings of filial piety and obedience to the point of the son not deviating from the father's way even three years after his death[1] and the woman not only obeying

---

1. Referring to *Analects* 1:11.

her father and husband but also her son,[2] how can they form their own political party and make their own choice? The movement of women's participation in politics is also an aspect of women's life in modern civilization. When they are bound by the Confucian teaching that "To be a woman means to submit,"[3] that "The wife's words should not travel beyond her own apartment," and that "A woman does not discuss affairs outside the home,"[4] would it not be unusual if they participated in politics?

In the West some widows choose to remain single because they are strongly attached to their late husbands and sometimes because they prefer a single life; they have nothing to do with what is called the chastity of widowhood. Widows who remarry are not despised by society at all. On the other hand, in the Chinese teaching of decorum, there is the doctrine of "no remarriage after the husband's death."[5] It is considered to be extremely shameful and unchaste for a woman to serve two husbands or a man to serve two rulers. The *Record of Rites* also prohibits widows from wailing at night [27:21] and people from being friends with sons of widows. For the sake of their family reputation, people have forced their daughters-in-law to remain widows. These women have had no freedom and have endured a most miserable life. Year after year these many promising young women have lived a physically and spiritually abnormal life. All this is the result of Confucian teachings of ritual decorum.

In today's civilized society, social intercourse between men and women is a common practice. Some even say that because women have a tender nature and can temper the crudeness of man, they are necessary in public or private gatherings. It is not considered improper even for strangers to sit or dance together once they have been introduced by the host. In the way of Confucian teaching, however, "Men and women do not sit on the same mat," "Brothers- and sisters-in-law do not exchange inquiries about each other," "Married sisters do not sit on the same mat with brothers or eat from the same dish," "Men and women do not know each other's name except through a matchmaker and should have no social relations or show affection until after marriage presents have been exchanged,"[6] "Women must cover their faces when they go out,"[7] "Boys and girls seven years or older do not sit or eat together," "Men and women have no social relations except through a matchmaker and do not meet until after marriage presents have been exchanged,"[8] and "Except in religious sacrifices, men and women do not exchange wine cups."[9] Such rules of decorum

2. *Record of Rites* 9:24.
3. Ibid.
4. Ibid. 1:24.
5. Ibid. 9:24.
6. Ibid. 1:24.
7. Ibid. 10:12.
8. Ibid. 10:51.
9. Ibid. 27:17.

are not only inconsistent with the mode of life in Western society; they cannot even be observed in today's China.

Western women make their own living in various professions such as that of lawyer, physician, and store employee. But in the Confucian Way, "In giving or receiving anything, a man or woman should not touch the other's hand,"[10] "A man does not talk about affairs inside [the household] and a woman does not talk about affairs outside [the household]," and "They do not exchange cups except in sacrificial rites and funerals."[11] "A married woman is to obey" and the husband is the mainstay of the wife.[12] Thus the wife is naturally supported by the husband and needs no independent livelihood.

A married woman is at first a stranger to her parents-in-law. She has only affection but no obligation toward them. In the West, parents and children usually do not live together, and daughters-in-law, particularly, have no obligation to serve parents-in-law. But in the way of Confucius, a woman is to "revere and respect them and never to disobey day or night,"[13] "A woman obeys, that is, obeys her parents-in-law,"[14] "A woman serves her parents-in-law as she serves her own parents,"[15] she "never should disobey or be lazy in carrying out the orders of parents and parents-in-law." "If a man is very fond of his wife, but his parents do not like her, she should be divorced."[16] (In ancient times there were many such cases, like that of Lu Yu [1125–1210].) "Unless told to retire to her own apartment, a woman does not do so, and if she has an errand to do, she must get permission from her parents-in-law."[17] This is the reason why cruelty to daughters-in-law has never ceased in Chinese society.

According to Western customs, fathers do not discipline grown-up sons but leave them to the law of the country and the control of society. But in the Way of Confucius, "When one's parents are angry and not pleased and beat him until he bleeds, he does not complain but instead arouses in himself the feelings of reverence and filial piety."[18] This is the reason why in China there is the saying, "One has to die if his father wants him to, and the minister has to perish if his ruler wants him to." . . .

Confucius lived in a feudal age. The ethics he promoted is the ethics of the feudal age. The social mores he taught and even his own mode of living were teachings and modes of a feudal age. The objectives, ethics, social norms, mode of living, and political institutions did not go beyond the privilege and prestige

---

10. Ibid. 27:20.
11. Ibid. 10:12.
12. Ibid. 9:24.
13. *I-li*, ch. 2; Steele, 1:39.
14. *Record of Rites* 41:6.
15. Ibid. 10:3.
16. Ibid. 10:12.
17. Ibid. 10:13.
18. Ibid. 10:12.

of a few rulers and aristocrats and had nothing to do with the happiness of the great masses. How can this be shown? In the teachings of Confucius, the most important elements in social ethics and social life are the rules of decorum, and the most serious thing in government is punishment. In chapter 1 of the *Record of Rites*, it is said, "The rules of decorum do not go down to the common people and the penal statutes do not go up to great officers" [1:35]. Is this not solid proof of the [true] spirit of the Way of Confucius and the spirit of the feudal age?

[From Chen, "Kongzi zhi dao yu xiandai shenghuo," pp. 3–5 — WTC]

## THE LITERARY REVOLUTION

Paralleling the attack on Confucianism was the attack on the classical literary language — the language of Confucian tradition and of the old-style scholar-official. With the abandonment of the "eight-legged essay" examinations for the civil service in 1905, the discarding also of the official language, so far removed from ordinary speech, might have seemed inevitable. This was a time of rising nationalism, which in the West had been linked to the rise of vernacular literatures; an era of expanding education, which would be greatly facilitated by a written language simpler and easier to learn; a period of strong Westernization in thought and scholarship, which would require a more flexible instrument for the expression of new concepts. No doubt each of these factors contributed to the rapid spread of the literary revolution after its launching by Hu Shi, with the support of Chen Duxiu in 1917. And yet it is a sign of the strong hold that the classical language had on educated men, and of its great prestige as a mark of learning, that until Hu appeared on the scene with his novel ideas, even the manifestos of reformers and revolutionaries had kept to the classical style of writing as if there could be no other.

Hu Shi (1891–1962) had studied agriculture at Cornell on a Boxer Indemnity grant and philosophy at Columbia under John Dewey, of whom he became the leading Chinese disciple. Even before his return home he had begun advocating a new written language for China, along with a complete reexamination and reevaluation of the classical tradition in thought and literature. Chen Duxiu's position as head of the department of literature at Beijing National University, and his new political organ, *The New Youth*, represented strong backing for Hu's revolutionary program — a program all the more commanding of attention because its aim was not merely destructive of traditional usage but, ambitiously enough, directed to the stimulation of a new literature and new ideas. Instead of dwelling solely upon the deficiencies of the past, Hu's writings were full of concrete and constructive suggestions for the future. There was hope here, as well as indignation.

Hu's program thus looked beyond the immediate literary revolution, stress-

ing the vernacular as a means of communication, to what came to be known
as the literary renaissance. There can be no doubt that this movement stimulated literary activity along new lines, especially in the adoption of forms and
genres then popular in the West. Yet there is real doubt whether this new literary
output was able to fulfill all of Hu's expectations, given the political constraints
to which it was later subjected. It excelled in social criticism and so contributed
further to the processes of social and political disintegration. Also — and this is
particularly true of Hu's own work — it rendered great service in the rehabilitation of popular literature from earlier centuries, above all, the great Chinese
novels. But whether it produced in its own right a contemporary literature of
great distinction and creative imagination is a question that must be left to
historians and critics of the future with a better perspective on these troubled
times.

### HU SHI: "A PRELIMINARY DISCUSSION OF LITERARY REFORM"

Many people have been discussing literary reform. Who am I, unlearned and
unlettered, to offer an opinion? Nevertheless, for some years I have studied the
matter and thought it over many times, helped by my deliberations with friends;
and the conclusions I have come to are perhaps not unworthy of discussion.
Therefore I shall summarize my views under eight points and elaborate on
them separately to invite the study and comments of those interested in literary
reform.

I believe that literary reform at the present time must begin with these eight
items: (1) Write with substance. (2) Do not imitate the ancients. (3) Emphasize
grammar. (4) Reject melancholy. (5) Eliminate old clichés. (6) Do not use
allusions. (7) Do not use couplets and parallelisms. And (8) Do not avoid popular expressions or popular forms of characters.

1. *Write with substance.* By *substance* I mean: (a) Feeling. . . . Feeling is the
soul of literature. Literature without feeling is like a man without a soul. . . .
(b) Thought. By *thought* I mean insight, knowledge, and ideals. Thought does
not necessarily depend on literature for transmission, but literature becomes
more valuable if it contains thought, and thought is more valuable if it possesses
literary value. This is the reason why the essays of Zhuangzi, the poems of Tao
Qian [365–427], Li Bo [689–762], and Du Fu [717–770], the *ci* of Xin Jiaxuan
[1140–1207], and the novel of Shi Naian [that is, the *Shuihu zhuan* or *Water
Margin*] are matchless for all times. . . . In recent years literary men have
satisfied themselves with tones, rhythm, words, and phrases and have had neither lofty thoughts nor genuine feeling. This is the chief cause of the deterioration of literature. This is the bad effect of superficiality over substantiality,
that is to say, writing without substance. To remedy this bad situation, we must

resort to substance. And what is substance? Nothing but feeling and thought.

2. *Do not imitate the ancients.* Literature changes with time. Each period from Zhou and Qin to Song, Yuan, and Ming has its own literature. This is not my private opinion but the universal law of the advancement of civilization. Take prose, for example. There is the prose of the *Classic of History*, the prose of the ancient philosophers, the prose of [the historians] Sima Qian and Ban Gu, the prose of the [Tang and Song masters] Han Yu, Liu Zongyuan, Ouyang Xiu, and Su Xun, the prose of the *Recorded Conversations* of the Neo-Confucians, and the prose of Shi Naian and Cao Xueqin [d. ca. 1765, author of *The Dream of Red Mansions*]. This is the development of prose. . . . Each period has changed in accordance with its situation and circumstance, each with its own characteristic merits. From the point of view of historical evolution, we cannot say that the writings of the ancients are all superior to those of modern writers. The prose of Zuo Qiuming [sixth century B.C., author of the *Zuozhuan*] and Sima Qian is wonderful, but compared to the *Zuozhuan* and *Records of the Historian*, wherein is Shi Naian's *Water Margin* (*Shuihu zhuan*) inferior? . . .

I have always held that colloquial stories alone in modern Chinese literature can proudly be compared with the first-class literature of the world. Because they do not imitate the past but only describe the society of the day, they have become genuine literature. . . .

3. *Emphasize grammar.* Many writers of prose and poetry today neglect grammatical construction. Examples are too numerous to mention, especially in parallel prose and the four-line and eight-line verses.

4. *Reject melancholy.* This is not an easy task. Nowadays young writers often show passion. They choose such names as "Cold Ash," "No Birth," and "Dead Ash" as pen names, and in their prose and poetry they think of declining years when they face the setting sun, and of destitution when they meet the autumn wind. . . . I am not unaware of the fact that our country is facing many troubles. But can salvation be achieved through tears? I hope all writers become Fichtes and Mazzinis and not like Jia Yi [201–169 B.C.], Wang Can [177–217], Qu Yuan [343–277 B.C.], Xie Gaoyu [1249–1295], and so on [who moaned and complained]. . . .

5. *Eliminate old clichés.* By this I merely mean that writers should describe in their own words what they personally experience. So long as they achieve the goal of describing things and expressing the mood without sacrificing realism, that is literary achievement. Those who employ old clichés are lazy people who refuse to coin their own terms of description.

6. *Do not use allusions.* I do not mean *allusion* in the broad sense. These are of five kinds: (a) analogies employed by ancient writers, which have a universal meaning . . . ; (b) idioms; (c) references to historical events . . . ; (d) quoting from or referring to people in the past for comparison . . . ; and (e) quotations. . . . Allusions such as these may or may not be used.

But I do not approve of the use of allusions in the narrow sense. By *using allusions* I mean that writers are incapable of creating their own expressions to portray the scene before them or the concepts in their minds, and instead muddle along by borrowing old stories or expressions that are partly or wholly inapplicable. . . .

7. *Do not use couplets and parallelisms.* Parallelism is a special characteristic of human language. This is why in ancient writings such as those of Laozi and Confucius, there are occasionally couplets. The first chapter of the *Daodejing* consists of three couplets. *Analects* 1:14, 1:15, and 3:17 are all couplets. But these are fairly natural expressions and have no indication of being forced or artificial, especially because there is no rigid requirement about the number of words, tones, or parts of speech. Writers in the age of literary decadence, however, who had nothing to say, emphasized superficiality, the extreme of which led to the development of the parallel prose, regulated *ci*, and the long regulated verse. It is not that there are no good products in these forms, but they are, in the final analysis, few. Why? Is it not because they restrict to the highest degree the free expression of man? (Not a single good piece can be mentioned among the long regulated verse.) To talk about literary reform today, we must "first establish the fundamental"[19] and not waste our useful energy in the nonessentials of subtlety and delicacy. This is why I advocate giving up couplets and rhymes. Even if they cannot be abolished, they should be regarded as merely literary stunts and nothing to be pursued seriously.

There are still people today who deprecate colloquial novels as trifling literature, without realizing that Shi Naian, Cao Xueqin, and Wu Jianren [1867–1910][20] all represent the main line of literature while parallel and regulated verse are really trifling matters. I know some will keep clear of me when they hear this.

8. *Do not avoid popular expressions or popular forms of characters.* When Buddhist scriptures were introduced into China, because classical expressions could not express their meanings, translators used clear and simple expressions.

---

19. *Mencius* 6A:15.

20. Author of *Ershi nian mu du zhi guai xianzhuang* (*Strange Phenomena Seen in Two Decades*).

Their style already approached the colloquial. Later, many Buddhist lectures and dialogues were in the colloquial style, thus giving rise to the "conversation" style. When the Neo-Confucians of the Song dynasty used the colloquial in their *Recorded Conversations*, this style became the orthodox style of scholarly discussion. (This was followed by scholars of the Ming.) By that time, colloquial expressions had already penetrated rhymed prose, as can be seen in the colloquial poems of Tang and Song poets. From the third century to the end of the Yuan, North China had been under foreign races and popular literature developed. In prose there were such novels as *Water Margin* (*Shuihu zhuan*) and *Journey to the West* (*Xiyou ji*). In drama the products were innumerable. From the modern point of view, the Yuan period should be considered as a high point of literary development; unquestionably it produced the greatest number of immortal works. At that time writing and colloquial speech were the closest to each other, and the latter almost became the language of literature. Had the tendency not been checked, living literature would have emerged in China, and the great work of Dante and Luther [who inaugurated the substitution of a living language for dead Latin] would have taken place in China. Unfortunately, the tendency was checked in the Ming when the government selected officials on the basis of the rigid "eight-legged" prose style and at the same time literary men like the "seven scholars" including Li [Mengyang, 1472–1529] considered "returning to the past" as highbrow. Thus the once-in-a-millennium chance of uniting writing and speech was killed prematurely, midway in the process. But from the modern viewpoint of historical evolution, we can definitely say that the colloquial literature is the main line of Chinese literature and that it should be the medium employed in the literature of the future. (This is my own opinion; not many will agree with me today.) For this reason, I hold that we should use popular expressions and words in prose and poetry. Rather than using dead expressions of three thousand years ago, it is better to employ living expressions of the twentieth century, and rather than using the language of the Qin, Han, and the Six Dynasties, which cannot reach many people and cannot be universally understood, it is better to use the language of the *Water Margin* (*Shuihu zhuan*) and *Journey to the West* (*Xiyou ji*), which is understood in every household.

[Hu, "Wenxue gailiang chuyi," in *Hu Shi wencun*, collection 1, ch. 1, pp. 5–16; original version in *Xin qingnian* 2, no. 5 (January 1917): 1–11 — WTC]

## CHEN DUXIU: "ON LITERARY REVOLUTION"

The movement of literary revolution has been in the making for some time. My friend Hu Shi is the one who started the revolution of which he is the vanguard. I do not mind being an enemy of all old-fashioned scholars in the country and raising to great heights the banner of "the Army of Literary Revolution" to support my friend. On this banner shall be written these three fundamental principles of our revolutionary army: (1) Destroy the aristocratic literature, which is nothing but literary chiseling and flattery, and construct a simple, expressive literature of the people. (2) Destroy the outmoded, showy, classical literature and construct a fresh and sincere literature of realism. (3) Destroy the obscure and abstruse "forest" literature[21] and construct a clear and popular literature of society. . . .

At this time of literary reform, aristocratic literature, classical literature, and forest literature should all be rejected. What are the reasons for attacking these three kinds of literature? The answer is that aristocratic literature employs embellishments and depends on previous writers and therefore has lost the qualities of independence and self-respect, that classical literature exaggerates and piles word after word and has lost the fundamental objective of expressing emotions and realistic descriptions; and that "forest" literature is difficult and obscure and is claimed to be lofty writing but is actually of no benefit to the masses. The form of such literatures is continuous repetition of previous models. It has flesh but no bones, body but no spirit. It is an ornament and is of no actual use. With respect to their contents, their horizon does not go beyond kings and aristocrats, spiritual beings and ghosts and personal fortunes and misfortunes. The universe, life, and society are all beyond their conception. These defects are common to all three forms of literature. These types of literature are both causes and effects of our national character of flattery, boasting, insincerity, and flagrant disregard of truth and facts. Now that we want political reform, we must regenerate the literature of those who are entrenched in political life. If we do not open our eyes and see the literary tendencies of the world society and the spirit of the time but instead bury our heads in old books day and night and confine our attention to kings and aristocrats, spiritual beings and ghosts and immortals, and personal fortunes and misfortunes, and in so doing hope to reform literature and politics, it is like binding our four limbs to fight Meng Ben [an ancient strong man].

[Chen, "Wenxue geminglun," pp. 1–4 — WTC]

HU SHI: "CONSTRUCTIVE LITERARY REVOLUTION —
A LITERATURE OF NATIONAL SPEECH"

## A National Speech of Literary Quality

Since I returned to China last year, in my speeches on literary revolution in various places, I have changed my "eight points" [in the previous selection] into something positive and shall summarize them under four items:

---

21. An expression of Chen's for esoteric literature.

1. Speak only when you have something to say. (A different version of the first of the eight points.)

2. Speak what you want to say and say it in the way you want to say it. (Different version of points 2–6.)

3. Speak what is your own and not that of someone else. (Different version of point 7.)

4. Speak in the language of the time in which you live. (Different version of point 8.)

The literary revolution we are promoting aims merely at the creation of a Chinese literature of national speech. Only when there is such a literature can there be a national speech of literary quality. And only when there is a national speech of literary quality can our national speech be considered a real national speech. A national speech without literary quality will be devoid of life and value and can be neither established nor developed. This is the main point of this essay. . . .

Why is it that a dead language cannot produce a living literature? It is because of the nature of literature. The function of language and literature lies in expressing ideas and showing feelings. When these are well done, we have literature. Those who use a dead classical style will translate their own ideas into allusions of several thousand years ago and convert their own feelings into literary expressions of centuries past. . . . If China wants to have a living literature, we must use the plain speech that is the natural speech, and we must devote ourselves to a literature of national speech. . . .

Someone says, "If we want to use the national speech in literature, we must first have a national speech. At present we do not have a standard national speech. How can we have a literature of national speech?" I will say, this sounds plausible but is really not true. A national language is not to be created by a few linguistic experts or a few texts and dictionaries of national speech. . . . The truly effective and powerful text of national speech is the literature of national speech — novels, prose, poems, and plays written in the national speech. The time when these works prevail is the day when the Chinese national speech will have been established. Let us ask why we are now able simply to pick up the brush and write essays in the plain-speech style and use several hundred colloquial terms. Did we learn this from some textbook of plain speech? Was it not that we learned from such novels as the *Water Margin* (*Shuihu zhuan*), *Journey to the West* (*Xiyou ji*), *Dream of Red Mansions* (*Hongloumeng*) and *Unofficial History of the Scholars* (*Rulin waishi*)? This type of plain-speech literature is several hundred times as powerful as textbooks and dictionaries. . . . If we want to establish anew a standard national speech, we must first of all produce numerous works like these novels in the national speech style. . . .

A literature of national speech and a national speech of literary quality are our basic programs. Let us now discuss what should be done to carry them out.

I believe that the procedure in creating a new literature consists of three

steps: (1) acquiring tools, (2) developing methods, and (3) creating. The first
two are preparatory. The third is the real step to create a new literature.

1. *The tools.* Our tool is plain speech. Those of us who wish to create a
literature of national speech should prepare this indispensable tool right away.
There are two ways to do so:

(a) Read extensively literary works written in the plain speech that can serve
as models, such as the works mentioned above, the *Recorded Conversations* of
the Song Neo-Confucians and their letters written in the plain speech, the plays
of the Yuan period, and the stories and monologues of the Ming and Qing
times. Tang and Song poems and *ci* written in the plain speech should also be
selected to read.

(b) In all forms of literature, write in the plain-speech style. . . .

2. *Methods.* I believe that the greatest defect of the literary men who have
recently emerged in our country is the lack of a good literary method. . . .

Generally speaking, literary methods are of three kinds:

(a) The method of collecting material. . . . I believe that for future literary
men the method of collecting material should be about as follows: (i) Enlarge
the area from which material is to be collected. The three sources of material,
namely, officialdom, houses of prostitution, and dirty society [from which present novelists draw their material], are definitely not enough. At present, the
poor man's society, male and female factory workers, rickshaw pullers, farmers
in the interior districts, small shop owners and peddlers everywhere, and all
conditions of suffering have no place in literature [as they should]. Moreover,
now that new and old civilizations have come into contact, problems like family
catastrophes, tragedies in marriage, the position of women, the unfitness of
present education, and so on, can all supply literature with material. (ii) Stress
actual observation and personal experience. . . . (iii) Use broad and keen imagination to supplement observation and experience.

(b) The method of construction. . . . This may be separated into two steps,
namely, tailoring and laying the plot. . . . While tailoring is to determine what
to do, laying the plot is to determine how to do it. . . .

(c) The method of description. . . .

3. *Creation.* The two items, tools and methods, discussed above are only
preparations for the creation of a new literature. . . . As to what constitutes the
creation of a new literature, I had better not say a word. In my opinion we in
China today have not reached the point where we can take concrete steps to
create a new literature, and there is no need of talking theoretically about the
techniques of creation. Let us first devote our efforts to the first two steps of
preparatory work.

[Hu, "Jianshe di wenxue geminglun," *Xin qingnian* 4, no. 4 (April 1918): 290–306;
*Hu Shi wencun*, collection 1, pp. 56–73 — WTC]

# THE DOUBTING OF ANTIQUITY

Another significant trend of the New Culture Movement that owes its inception to Hu Shi is the new historical and critical approach to the study of Chinese philosophy and literature begun by Hu with his doctoral studies at Columbia. His *Outline of the History of Chinese Philosophy* (*Zhongguo zhexue shi dagang*), published in 1919, is permeated with a spirit of doubt that led him to reject tradition and to study Chinese thought historically and critically. This spirit soon penetrated the whole New Culture Movement. Hu's friend Qian Xuantong (1887–1939) and pupil Gu Jiegang (1895–1980) took it up as a concerted "debunking" movement in the early 1920s, which resulted in an almost complete rejection of traditional beliefs in regard to ancient Chinese history, as well as to the loss by the Confucian classics of whatever sacredness, prestige, or authority they still retained.

The attacks of reformers in recent decades had already undermined belief in the political and social ethics of Confucianism among young Chinese. As nationalists, however, these same reformers had often felt a pride in Chinese antiquity that inclined them to spare it the devastating scrutiny to which they subjected the recent past. Now ancient history too — a domain in which Confucians had always excelled and that was so vital to their whole worldview — was invaded and occupied by modern skepticism.

## GU JIEGANG: PREFACE TO *DEBATES ON ANCIENT HISTORY* (1926)

In those years [1918 ff.] Dr. Hu Shi published many articles. Those articles often provided me with the methods for the study of history. . . . If I can do what Dr. Hu has done in his investigations for the novel *Water Margin* (*Shuihu zhuan*), discovering the stages through which the story developed and going through the story systematically to show how these stages changed, wouldn't it be interesting! At the same time I recalled that this past spring Dr. Hu published an article on the "well-field" system in the periodical *Construction* (*Jianshe*), using the same critical method of investigation. It shows that ancient history can be investigated by the same method as the investigation of the novel. [p. 40]

As is well known, the history of China is generally considered to be five thousand years old (or 2,276,000 years according to the apocryphal books!). Actually it is only two thousand years old if we deduct the history recorded in spurious works and also unauthenticated history based on spurious works. Then we have only what is left after a big discount! At this point I could not help arousing in my mind an ambition to overthrow unauthentic history. At first I wanted only to overthrow unauthentic history recorded in unauthentic books. Now I wanted also to overthrow unauthentic history recorded in authentic works. Since I read the first section of [Kang Youwei's] *Confucius As a Reformer*

[*Kongzi gaizhi kao*], my thought had been germinating for five or six years, and now for the first time I had a clear conception and a definite plan to overthrow ancient history. What is this plan? Its procedure involves three things to be done. First, the origin and the development of the events recorded in unauthentic histories must be investigated one by one. Second, every event in the authentic histories must be investigated to see what this and that person said about it, list what they said, and compare them, like a judge examining evidence so that no lie can escape detection. Third, although the words of liars differ, they follow a certain common pattern, just as the rules governing plots in plays are uniform although the stories themselves differ. We can detect the patterns in their ways of telling falsehood. [pp. 42–43]

My only objective is to explain the ancient history transmitted in the tradition of a certain period by the circumstances of that period. . . . Take Boyi [c. 1122 B.C.?, who according to tradition preferred starving to death to serving another king]. What was the man really like? Was he the son of the Lord of Guzhu? We have no way of knowing. But we do know that in the Spring and Autumn period people liked to talk about moral cultivation and upheld the "gentleman" as the standard of molding personal character. Consequently, when Boyi was talked about in the *Analects*, he was described as "not keeping in mind other people's former wickedness" [5:22] and "refusing to surrender his will or degrade himself" [18:8]. We also know that in the Warring States period, rulers and prime ministers liked to keep scholars in their service and scholars desperately looked for rulers to serve. For this reason, the book of *Mencius* says of Boyi that, having heard King Wen was in power, his hopes were aroused and he declared, "Why should I not go and follow him? I hear King Wen is hospitable to the old" [4a:13, 7a:22]. We also know that after the Qin united the empire, the concept of absolute loyalty to the ruler became very strong and no one could escape from the mutual obligation between the ruler and minister. For this reason, in the *Records of the Historian* he is recorded as one who bowed before King Wu of Zhou to admonish him [not to overthrow King Zhou of Shang] and, having failed in this mission, chose to follow what he believed to be right, refusing to eat the food produced under the Zhou and starving to death in the Shouyang Mountain.[22] After the Han dynasty the story, which had undergone many changes before, became stabilized; books had become common and as a result the personality of Boyi no longer changed in accordance with the varying circumstances of time. We therefore should treat ancient history in the same way as we treat the stories of our own day, for they have all passed from mouth to mouth.

[Gu and Luo, *Gushi bian*, vol. 1, pt. 1, pp. 40–66 —WTC]

---

22. *Shiji*, ch. 61.

# A NEW PHILOSOPHY OF LIFE

The energetic assault on traditional thought and literature focused attention on what should replace Confucianism as a way of looking at the world and at life. Here again, during the years 1918–1919, Chen Duxiu and Hu Shi manifested their role as leaders of the whole New Culture Movement. At a time that saw the introduction and lively discussion of the philosophies of Kant, Hegel, Marx, Nietzsche, Bergson, James, Dewey, Russell, and others, Chen and Hu bespoke the dominant belief in science and social progress. In these days Chen, reacting strongly against what he conceived to be the social conformism and authoritarianism of Confucian thought, emphasized individualism as the basis of his philosophy. Yet his belief in science and materialism also inclined him strongly to the study of Marxism — an inclination checked to some degree by his interest in the ideas of John Dewey, who lectured widely in China in 1919 and 1920. Hu Shi, for his part, identified himself unequivocally with pragmatism. Nevertheless, in the movement as a whole, philosophical allegiances were less clearcut. It was a period of fermentation and transition, producing also strong countercurrents to trends from the West (as shown in succeeding sections). We can say, however, that the prevailing trend among the educated was toward acceptance of such ideas as individualism, freedom, progress, democracy, and science.

### CHEN DUXIU: THE TRUE MEANING OF LIFE

What is the ultimate purpose in life? What should it be, after all? . . . From ancient times not a few people have offered explanations. . . . In my opinion, what the Buddha said is vague. Although the individual's birth and death are illusory, can we say that humanity as a whole is not really existent? . . . The teachings of Christianity, especially, are fabrications out of nothing and cannot be proved. If God can create the human race, who created Him? Since God's existence or nonexistence cannot be proved, the Christian philosophy of life cannot be completely believed in. The rectification of the heart, cultivation of the person, family harmony, ordering of the state, and world peace that Confucius and Mencius talked about are but some activities and enterprises in life and cannot cover the total meaning of life. If we are totally to sacrifice ourselves to benefit others, then we exist for others and not for ourselves. This is definitely not the fundamental reason for man's existence. The idea [of altruism] of Mozi is also not free from one-sidedness. The doctrines of Yang Zhu [fourth century B.C.?] and Nietzsche fully reveal the true nature of life, and yet if we follow them to their extremes, how can this complex, organized, and civilized society continue? . . .

Because we Chinese have accepted the teachings [of contentment and laissez-faire] of Laozi and Zhuangzi, we have to that extent been backward. Scientists say that there is no soul after a man's death. . . . It is difficult to refute these words. But although we as individuals will inevitably die, it is not easy for the whole race or humanity to die off. The civilization created by the race or humanity will remain. It is recorded in history and will be transmitted to later generations. Is this not the consciousness or memory of our continuation after death? From the above, the meaning of life as seen by the modern man can be readily understood. Let me state it briefly as follows:

1. With reference to human existence, the individual's birth and death are transitory, but society really exists.

2. The civilization and happiness of society are created by individuals and should be enjoyed by individuals.

3. Society is an organization of individuals — there can be no society without individuals. . . . The will and the happiness of the individual should be respected.

4. Society is the collective life of individuals. If society is dissolved, there will be no memory or consciousness of the continuation of the individual after he dies. Therefore social organization and order should be respected.

5. To carry out one's will and to satisfy his desires (everything from food and sex to moral reputation is "desire") are the basic reasons for the individual's existence. These goals never change. (Here we can say that Heaven does not change and the Way does not change either.)

6. All religions, laws, moral and political systems are but necessary means to preserve social order. They are not the individual's original purpose of enjoyment in life and can be changed in accordance with the circumstances of the time.

7. People's happiness in life is the result of their own effort and is neither the gift of God nor a spontaneous natural product. If it were the gift of God, how is it that He was so generous with people today and so stingy with people in the past? If it is a spontaneous, natural product, why is it that the happiness of the various peoples in the world is not uniform?

8. The individual in society is comparable to the cell in the body. Its birth and death are transitory. New ones replace the old. This is as it should be and need not be feared at all.

9. To enjoy happiness, do not fear suffering. Personal suffering at the moment sometimes contributes to personal happiness in the future. For example, the blood shed in righteous wars often wipes out the bad spots of a nation or mankind. Severe epidemics often hasten the development of science.

In a word, what is the ultimate purpose in life? What should it be, after all? I dare say:

*During his lifetime, an individual should devote his efforts to create happiness and to enjoy it, and also to keep it in store in society so that individuals of the future may also enjoy it, one generation doing the same for the next and so on unto infinity.*

[From Chen, "Rensheng zhenyi," pp. 90–93 — WTC]

HU SHI: "PRAGMATISM"

There are two fundamental changes in basic scientific concepts that have had the most important bearings on pragmatism. The first is the change of the scientific attitude toward scientific laws. Hitherto, worshipers of science generally had a superstition that scientific laws were unalterable universal principles. They thought that there was an eternal, unchanging "natural law" immanent in all things in the universe and that when this law was discovered, it became scientific law. However, this attitude toward the universal principle has gradually changed in the last several decades. Scientists have come to feel that such a superstitious attitude toward a universal principle could hinder scientific progress. Furthermore, in studying the history of science they have learned that many discoveries in science are the results of hypotheses. Consequently, they have gradually realized that the scientific laws of today are no more than the hypotheses that are the most applicable, most convenient, and most generally accepted as explanations of natural phenomena. . . . Such changes of attitude involve three ideas: (1) Scientific laws are formulated by men. (2) They are hypotheses — whether they can be determined to be applicable or not entirely depends on whether they can satisfactorily explain facts. (3) They are not the eternal, unchanging natural law. There may be such a natural law in the universe, but we cannot say that our hypothecated principles are this law. They are no more than a shorthand to record the natural changes known to us. [pp. 291–294]

Besides this, there was in the nineteenth century another important change that also had an extremely important bearing on pragmatism. This is Darwin's theory of evolution. . . . When it came to Darwin, he boldly declared that the species were not immutable but all had their origins and developed into the present species only after many changes. From the present onward, there can still be changes in species, such as the grafting of trees and crossing of fowls, whereby special species can be obtained. Not only do the species change, but truth also changes. The change of species is the result of adaptation to environment, and truth is but an instrument with which to deal with environment. As the environment changes, so does truth accordingly. . . . The knowledge that mankind needs is not the way or principle that has an absolute existence but the particular truths for here and now and for particular individuals. Absolute truth is imaginary, abstract, vague, without evidence, and cannot be demonstrated. [pp. 294–295]

## The Pragmatism of James

What we call truth is actually no more than an instrument, comparable to this piece of paper in my hand, this chalk, this blackboard, or this teapot. They are all our instruments. Because this concept produced results, people in the past therefore called it truth, and because its utility still remains, we therefore still call it truth. If by any chance some event takes place for which the old concept is not applicable, it will no longer be truth. We will search for a new truth to take its place. . . . [pp. 309–310]

## The Fundamental Concepts of Dewey's Philosophy

Dewey is a great revolutionist in the history of philosophy. . . . He said that the basic error of modern philosophy is that modern philosophers do not understand what experience really is. All quarrels between rationalists and empiricists and between idealists and realists are due to their ignorance of what experience is. [p. 316]

Dewey was greatly influenced by the modern theory of biological evolution. Consequently, his philosophy is completely colored by bio-evolutionism. He said that "experiencing means living; and that living goes on in and because of an environing medium, not in a vacuum. . . . The human being has upon his hands the problem of responding to what is going on around him so that these changes will take one turn rather than another, namely, that required by his own further functioning. . . . He is obliged to struggle — that is to say, to employ the direct support given by the environment in order indirectly to effect changes that would not otherwise occur. In this sense, life goes on by means of controlling the environment. Its activities must change the changes going on around it; they must neutralize hostile occurrences; they must transform neutral events into cooperative factors or into an efflorescence of new features."[23]

This is what Dewey explained as experience. [p. 318]

The foregoing are the basic concepts of Dewey's philosophy. Summarized, they are (1) Experience is life and life is dealing with environment; (2) In the act of dealing with environment, the function of thought is the most important. All conscious actions involve the function of thought. Thought is an instrument to deal with environment; (3) True philosophy must throw overboard the previous toying with "philosophers' problems" and turn itself into a method for solving human problems.

[Hu, "Shiyan zhuyi," *Hu Shi wencun*, collection 1, ch. 2, pp. 291–320; originally published in *Xin qingnian* 6, no. 4 (April 1919): 342–358 — WTC]

---

23. John Dewey, *Creative Intelligence* (New York: Henry Holt, 1917), pp. 8–9.

# THE DEBATE ON SCIENCE AND THE
# PHILOSOPHY OF LIFE

The prevailing glorification of science prompted a reaction in some quarters, which pointed to the inadequacy of science when conceived as a philosophy for dealing with some of the fundamental questions of human life. The debate was touched off by a lecture at Qinghua College, near Beijing, by Dr. Zhang Junmai (Carsun Chang, 1886–1969), who insisted upon the need for a metaphysics as the basis for a genuine philosophy of life. In the controversy that followed (also known as the controversy between metaphysics and science), Zhang drew some support from his teacher Liang Qichao, now much disillusioned with Western materialism and scientism, and from the professional philosopher and translator of Bergson, Zhang Dongsun (1886–1973). A far larger number of writers, however, immediately rose to attack metaphysics and defend science. Zhang's chief opponent was Ding Wenjiang (1888–1936), a geologist by profession, who stigmatized metaphysics as mere superstition and insisted that there were no genuine problems of philosophy or psychology that lay outside the domain of science or to which science, with the progress of civilization, would not eventually find an answer. Many others with a basically materialistic view, from Chen Duxiu (now a Marxist and Communist) to Hu Shi and Wu Zhihui (1865–1953), a writer closely identified with the Nationalists (Guomindang), joined in the battle. Altogether the writings that dealt with this issue, later compiled in book form, amounted to more than 250,000 words. In the end, as far as majority opinion was concerned, the "anti-metaphysics, pro-science" group carried the day. The controversy thus served to underscore the overwhelming acceptance of pragmatism and materialism among the younger generation of writers and students.

## ZHANG JUNMAI: "THE PHILOSOPHY OF LIFE"

Zhang Junmai was a young professor of philosophy when he delivered this controversial lecture on February 14, 1923. Like so many others of his generation, he had received his higher education in Japan (Waseda University) and Europe. A follower of Liang Qichao and a believer in the "spiritual" civilization of China, he combined Bergsonian intuitionism with the Neo-Confucian teachings of Wang Yangming. In later years Zhang was also politically active as the leader of a "third force" advocating nationalism and socialism, which had some influence among intellectuals but little mass following.

The central focus of a philosophy of life is the self. What is relative to it is the nonself. . . . But all problems of the nonself are related to human life. Now human life is a living thing and cannot so easily be governed by formulae as can dead matter. The unique character of a philosophy of life becomes especially clear when we compare it with science.

First of all, science is objective, whereas a philosophy of life is subjective. The highest standard of science consists in its objective efficacy. Mr. A says so, Mr. B says so, and C, D, E, F all say so. In other words, a general law is applicable to the entire world. . . . A philosophy of life is different. Confucius's doctrine of firm action and Laozi's doctrine of Doing Nothing represent views. . . . Darwin's theory of struggle and survival and Kropotkin's theory of mutual aid represent different views. All these have their pros and cons, and no experiment can be conducted to determine who is right and who is wrong. Why? Because they are philosophies of life; because they are subjective.

Second, science is controlled by the logical method whereas a philosophy of life arises from intuition. . . . Science is restricted by method and by system. On the other hand, philosophies of life — whether the pessimism of Schopenhauer and Hartmann or the optimism of Lambert, Nietzsche, and Hegel; whether Confucius's doctrine of personal perfection and family harmony or Buddha's doctrine of renunciation; and whether the Confucian doctrine of love with distinctions or the teaching of universal love of Mozi and Jesus — are not restricted by any logical formula. They are not governed by definitions or methods. They are views held according to one's conscience for the sake of setting a norm for the world and for posterity. This is the reason why they are intuitive.

Third, science proceeds from an analytical method, whereas a philosophy of life proceeds from synthesis. The key to science is analysis. . . . A philosophy of life, on the other hand, is synthetic. It includes everything. If subjected to analysis, it will lose its true meaning. For example, the Buddha's philosophy of life is to save all living beings. If one seeks his motive and says that it is due to the Indian love of meditation or to India's climate, to some extent such analysis is reasonable. But it would be a mistake to conclude that Buddhism and all it contains can be explained in terms only of the motives just analyzed. Why? Motives and a philosophy of life are different things. A philosophy of life is a whole and cannot be discovered in what has been divided or mutilated. . . .

Fourth, science follows the law of cause and effect whereas a philosophy of life is based on free will. The first general law governing material phenomena is that where there is cause, there is effect. . . . Even the relation between body and mind . . . is also the result of cause and effect. But purely psychological phenomena are different, and a philosophy of life is much more so. Why is it that Confucius did not even sit long enough to warm his mat [before hurrying off to serve society] or that Mozi's stove did not have a chance to burn black [before he did likewise]? Why was Jesus crucified, and why did Shakyamuni devote his life to asceticism? All these issued from the free action of conscience and were not determined by something else. Even in an ordinary person, such things as repentance, self-reform, and a sense of responsibility cannot be explained by the law of cause and effect. The master agent is none other than the person himself. This is all there is to it, whether in the case of great men like Confucius, Mozi, the Buddha, and Jesus, or in the case of an ordinary person.

Fifth, science arises from the phenomenon of uniformity among objects, whereas a philosophy of life arises from the unity of personality. The greatest principle in science is the uniformity of the course of nature. Plants, animals, and even inorganic matter can all be classified. Because of the possibility of classification, there is a principle running through all changes and phenomena of a particular class of objects, and therefore a scientific formula for it can be discovered. But in human society some people are intelligent while others are stupid, some are good and some are bad, and some are healthy while others are not. . . . The distinction of natural phenomena is their similarity, while that of mankind is its variety. Because of this variety there have been the "first to be enlightened" and the "hero," as they are called in traditional Chinese terminology, and the "creator" and "genius," as they are called in Western terminology. All these are merely intended to show the unique character of human personality.

From the above we can see that the distinguishing points of a philosophy of life are subjectivity, intuitiveness, synthesizing power, free will, and personal unity. Because of these five qualities, the solution of problems pertaining to a philosophy of life cannot be achieved by science, however advanced it may be, but can be achieved only by people themselves.

[Zhang Junmai, "Rensheng guan," in Zhang et al.,
*Kexue yu rensheng guan* 1:4–9 — WTC]

### DING WENJIANG: "METAPHYSICS AND SCIENCE"

Ding Wenjiang (V. K. Ting, 1888–1936) was a professor of geology at the University of Beijing when he responded to Zhang Junmai with this article, published in April 1923. Trained at Cambridge and Glasgow Universities, he was widely respected for his writings in such fields as geology, mining, and geography but became known also as a leading political pamphleteer. In 1919, a few years before this controversy arose, he had accompanied Liang Qichao, Zhang Junmai, and others on an inspection trip to Europe, from which Zhang returned much disillusioned with the materialism of the West. Though Ding's basic outlook was not altered by this experience, from it developed his interest in a wider range of questions — political and philosophical — than his scientific studies had embraced earlier.

Metaphysics is a bewildered specter that has been haunting Europe for twenty centuries. Of late it has gradually lost its treacherous occupation and all of a sudden come to China, its body swinging, with all its banners and slogans, to lure and fool the Chinese people. If you don't believe me, look at Zhang Junmai's "Philosophy of Life." Zhang is my friend, but metaphysics is an enemy of science. . . .

Can a philosophy of life and science be separated? . . . Zhang's explanation is that philosophies of life are "most diversified" and therefore science is not applicable to them. But it is one thing to say that at present philosophies of life are not unified and quite another thing to say that they can never be unified. Unless you can advance a reason to prove why they can never be unified, we are obliged to find the unity. Furthermore, granted that at present "there are no standards of right and wrong, truth or falsity" [as Zhang said], how can we tell that right and wrong and truth and falsity cannot be discovered? Unless we discover them, how are we going to have standards? To find right and wrong and truth and falsity, what other method is there aside from the scientific? . . . [p. 6]

Zhang says that a philosophy of life is not controlled by the logical method. Science replies: "Whatever cannot be studied and criticized by logic is not true knowledge. He claims that "purely psychological phenomena" lie outside the law of cause and effect. Science replies: Psychological phenomena are at bottom materials of science. If the phenomena you are talking about are real, they cannot go beyond the sphere of science. He has repeatedly emphasized individuality and intuition, but he has placed these outside the logical method and definition. It is not that science attaches no importance to individuality and intuition. But the individuality and intuition recognized by science are those that "emerge from living experience and are based on evidences of experience" [as Hu Shi has said]. Zhang has said that a philosophy of life is a synthesis — "It is a whole and cannot be discovered in what has been divided and mutilated." Science replies: We do not admit that there is such a confused, undifferentiated thing. Furthermore, he himself has distinguished the self and the nonself and listed nine items under the latter. Thus he has already analyzed it. He says that "the solution of problems pertaining to a philosophy of life cannot be achieved by science." Science replies: Anything with a psychological content and all true concepts and inferences are materials for science. [pp. 14–15]

Whether we like it or not, truth is truth and falsity is falsity. As truth is revealed, metaphysics becomes helpless. Consequently, the universe that used to belong to metaphysics has been taken over by science. . . . Biology has become a science. . . . Psychology has also declared [its] independence. Thereupon metaphysics has retreated from First Philosophy to ontology, but it is still without regret and brags before science, saying: "You cannot study intuition; you cannot study reality outside of sensation. You are corporeal, I am metaphysical. You are dead; I am living." Science does not care to quarrel with it, realizing that the scientific method is all-mighty in the realm of knowledge. There is no fear that metaphysics will not finally surrender. [p. 16]

Metaphysicians talk only about their ontology. We do not want to waste our valuable time attacking them. But young people at large are fooled by them and consider all problems relating to religion, society, government, and ethics to be really beyond the control of the logical method. They think there is really no right or wrong, no truth or falsity. They believe that these problems must be solved by what they call a philosophy of life, which they say is subjective, synthesizing and consisting of free will.

If so, what kind of society will ours be? If so, there will be no need to read or learn, and experience will be useless. We will need only to "hold views according to our conscience," for philosophies of life "all issue from the free action of conscience and are not dictated by something else." In that case, aren't study, learning, knowledge, and experience all a waste of time? Furthermore, there will be no room for discussing any problem, for discussion requires logical formulae, definitions, and methods, and all these are unacceptable to Zhang Junmai. . . . Moreover, everyone has his own conscience. What need is there for anyone to "enlighten" or "set an example" for us? If everyone can "hold his view" according to his irrational philosophy of life, why should he regard the philosophies of life of Confucius, the Buddha, Mozi, or Jesus as superior to his own? And there is no standard of right and wrong or truth and falsity. Thus a person's philosophy of life may be self-contradictory and he may be preaching the doctrine of equality of the sexes and practicing polygamy at the same time. All he needs to say is that it is "the free action of his conscience," and he does not have to bother whether it is logical or not. Whenever it is the free action of conscience, naturally other people must not interfere. Could we live in such a society for a single day? [pp. 18–19]

> [Ding, "Xuanxue yu kexue," in Zhang et al., *Kexue yu rensheng guan* 2:1–19 — WTC]

### WU ZHIHUI: "A NEW CONCEPT OF THE UNIVERSE AND LIFE BASED ON A NEW BELIEF"

These excerpts are from a long essay by Wu Zhihui (1865–1953), which Hu Shi hailed as "the most significant event" in the controversy over science and metaphysics. "With one stroke of the pen he ruled out God, banished the soul, and punctured the metaphysical idea that man is the most spiritual of all things." Wu, an iconoclast who had a reputation as something of a wit and satirist, is remembered for his declaration, which became a virtual battle cry among the anti-Confucianists: "All thread-bound [old-style] books should be dumped in the lavatory."

After taking the first steps up the old civil service ladder under the Manchus, Wu had become involved in the reform movement and then had studied for many years in Japan, England, and France, where he espoused anarchism. Acquaintance with Sun Yat-sen led him eventually into the revolutionary movement. He became a confidant of Sun and Chiang Kai-shek, and in his later years he was a sort of elder statesman among the Nationalists.

Zhang Junmai has mobilized his soldiers of science to protect his specter of metaphysics and engage in warfare with Ding Wenjiang. Liang Qichao has formulated for them "laws of the war of words" in preparation for stepped-up mobilization on both sides and for a prolonged struggle. . . . To some extent I feel that even if the struggle lasted for a hundred years, there would be no conclusion. [pp. 24–25]

What philosophy of life have you, oldster? Well, friends, let me tell you. . . .

We need only say that "the universe is a greater life." Its substance involves energy at the same time. To use another term, it may also be called power. From this power the will is produced. . . . When the will comes into contact with the external world, sensations ensue, and when these sensations are welcomed or resisted, feelings arise. To make sure that the feelings are correct, thought arises to constitute the intellect. When the intellect examines again and again a certain feeling to see to it that it is natural and proper or to correct the intellect's own ignorance, this is intuition. [pp. 28–30]

What is the need of any spiritual element or the so-called soul, which never meets any real need anyway? [p. 32]

I strongly believe (1) that the spirit cannot be separated from matter . . . , (2) that the universe is a temporary thing . . . , (3) that people today are superior to people in the past and that people in the future will be superior to people today . . . , (4) that they are so in both good and evil . . . , (5) that the more advanced material civilization becomes, the more plentiful will material goods be, the human race will tend more and more to unity, and complicated problems will be more and more easily solved . . . , (6) that morality is the crystallization of civilization and that there has never been a low morality when civilization reached a higher state . . . , and (7) that all things in the universe can be explained by science. [pp. 112–137]

[Wu, "Yige xinxinyang," in Zhang et al., *Kexue yu rensheng guan* 2:24–137 —WTC]

#### HU SHI: SCIENCE AND PHILOSOPHY OF LIFE

The Chinese people's philosophy of life has not yet been brought face-to-face with science. At this moment we painfully feel that science has not been sufficiently promoted, that scientific education has not been developed, and that the power of science has not been able to wipe out the black smoke that covers the whole country. To our amazement there are still prominent scholars [like Liang Qichao] who shout, "European science is bankrupt; blame the cultural bankruptcy of Europe on science, deprecate it, score the sins of the scientists' philosophy of life, and do not let science exert any influence on a philosophy of life." Seeing this, how can those who believe in science not worry? How can they help crying out loud to defend science? This is the motive that has given rise to this big battle of "science versus philosophy of life." We must understand this motive before we can see the position the controversy occupies in the history of Chinese thought. . . .

Zhang Junmai's chief point is that "the solution of problems pertaining to a philosophy of life cannot be achieved by science." In reply to him, we should make clear what kind of philosophy of life has been produced when science was applied to problems pertaining to a philosophy of life. In other words, we should first describe what a scientific philosophy of life is and then discuss whether such a philosophy of life can be established, whether it can solve the problems pertaining to a philosophy of life, and whether it is a plague on Europe and poison to the human race, as Liang Qichao has said it is. I cannot help feeling that in this discussion consisting of a quarter of a million words, those who fight for science, excepting Mr. Wu Zhihui, share a common error, namely, that of not stating in concrete terms what a scientific philosophy of life is, but merely defending in an abstract way the assertion that science *can* solve the problems of a philosophy of life. . . . They have not been willing publicly to admit that the concrete, purely materialistic and purely mechanistic philosophy of life is the scientific philosophy of life. We say they have not been willing; we do not say they have not dared. We merely say that with regard to the scientific philosophy of life, the defenders of science do not believe in it as clearly and firmly as does Mr. Wu Zhihui and therefore they cannot publicly defend their view. . . .

In a word, our future war plan should be to publicize our new belief, to publicize what we believe to be the new philosophy of life. The basic ideas of this new philosophy of life have been declared by Mr. Wu. We shall now summarize these general ideas, elaborate and supplement them to some extent, and present here an outline of this new philosophy of life:

1. On the basis of our knowledge of astronomy and physics, we should recognize that the world of space is infinitely large.

2. On the basis of our geological and paleontological knowledge, we should recognize that the universe extends over infinite time.

3. On the basis of all our verifiable scientific knowledge, we should recognize that the universe and everything in it follow natural laws of movement and change — "natural" in the Chinese sense of "being so of themselves" — and that there is no need for the concept of a supernatural Ruler or Creator.

4. On the basis of the biological sciences, we should recognize the terrific wastefulness and brutality in the struggle for existence in the biological world, and consequently the untenability of the hypothesis of a benevolent Ruler who "possesses the character of loving life."

5. On the basis of the biological, physiological, and psychological sciences, we should recognize that man is only one species in the animal kingdom and differs from the other species only in degree but not in kind.

6. On the basis of the knowledge derived from anthropology, sociology, and the biological sciences, we should understand the history and causes of the evolution of living organisms and of human society.

7. On the basis of the biological and psychological sciences, we should recognize that all psychological phenomena are explainable through the law of causality.

8. On the basis of biological and historical knowledge, we should recognize

that morality and religion are subject to change and that the causes of such change can be scientifically discovered.

9. On the basis of our newer knowledge of physics and chemistry, we should recognize that matter is not dead or static but living and dynamic.

10. On the basis of biological and sociological knowledge, we should recognize that the individual — the "small self" — is subject to death and extinction, but humanity — the "Large Self" — does not die and is immortal and [we] should recognize that to live for the sake of the species and posterity is religion of the highest kind and that those religions that seek a future life either in Heaven or in the Pure Land are selfish religions.

This new philosophy of life is a hypothesis founded on the commonly accepted scientific knowledge of the last two or three hundred years. We may confer on it the honorable title of "scientific philosophy of life." But to avoid unnecessary controversy, I propose to call it merely "the naturalistic philosophy of life."

[ Hu, *Hu Shi wencun*, collection 2, ch. 1, pp. 121–139 — WTC]

## THE CONTROVERSY OVER CHINESE AND WESTERN CULTURES

Intimately related to the debate on science and metaphysics was the controversy over Chinese and Western cultures, which arose from the apparent disillusionment with the West of some who not long before had been the strongest champions of Westernization. In 1919 Liang Qichao returned from Europe, where he had observed the aftermath of World War I. The picture he proceeded to give of the West was much in contrast to his early view of it as the vanguard of social progress and enlightened civilization. Now he saw it as sick and declining, the victim of its own obsession with science, materialism, and mechanization. The notion of inevitable progress, which had once inspired his belief that China could rise above its past and move forward to new greatness, was now bankrupt. Its bankruptcy, however, was all the West's, not Liang's. If Europe fell victim to its own shattered illusions, neither he nor China need suffer in the catastrophe, for the failure of science and materialism served only to vindicate China and its "spiritual" civilization.

Liang was by no means ready to forgo completely the benefits of science and material progress. The failure of the West he saw as resulting from its proclivity toward extremes, its current overemphasis on materialism being an excessive reaction to the exaggerated idealism and spirituality of medieval Europe. China's historical mission had been to preserve a balance between the two, and in the modern world it was specially equipped to reconcile these divergent forces in a new humanistic civilization. Thus Liang arrived at a new synthesis. Whatever was of value in Western science and material progress China could claim for herself and blend with her own spiritual traditions.

Strong support for this view came from Liang Shuming (1893–1988), who likewise saw the superiority of Chinese civilization as lying in its capacity for harmonizing opposing extremes. As in the debate over science and metaphysics, however, the voices of those who spoke for progress and modernism — with Hu Shi again among the leaders — prevailed against the neo-traditionalists. The latter might appeal to national pride or self-respect and thus swell a growing sense of nationalism, but they could not arrest the steady disintegration of traditional Chinese civilization, which Liang himself had done much to hasten.

## LIANG QICHAO: "TRAVEL IMPRESSIONS FROM EUROPE"

What is our duty? It is to develop our civilization with that of the West and to supplement Western civilization with ours so as to synthesize and transform them to make a new civilization. . . .

Recently many Western scholars have wanted to import Asian civilization as a corrective to their own. Having thought the matter over carefully, I believe we are qualified for that purpose. Why? In the past, the ideal and the practical in Western civilization have been sharply divided. Idealism and materialism have both gone to the extreme. Religionists have one-sidedly emphasized the future life. Idealistic philosophers have engaged in lofty talk about the metaphysical and mysterious, far, far removed from human problems. The reaction came from science. Materialism swept over the world and threw overboard all lofty ideals. Therefore I once said, "Socialism, which is so fashionable, amounts to no more than fighting for bread." Is this the highest goal of mankind?

Now pragmatism and evolutionism are being promoted, the aim being to embrace the ideal in the practical and to harmonize mind and matter. In my opinion, this is precisely the line of development in our ancient systems of thought. Although the schools of the sages — Confucius, Laozi, and Mozi — are different, their common goal is to unify the ideal and the practical. . . . Also, although Buddhism was founded in India, it really flourished in China. . . . Take Chinese meditation Buddhism [Chan, Zen]. It can truly be considered as practical Buddhism and worldly Buddhism. Certainly it could have developed only outside India, and certainly it can reveal the special characteristics of the Chinese people. It enables the way of renouncing the world and the way of remaining in the world to go hand in hand without conflict. At present, philosophers like Bergson and Eucken want to follow this path but have not been able to do so. I have often thought that if they could have studied the works of the Buddhist Idealistic School, their accomplishments would surely have been greater, and if they could have understood Meditation Buddhism, their accomplishments would have been still greater.

Just think. Weren't the pre-Qin philosophers and the great masters of the Sui and the Tang eras our loving and sagely ancestors who have left us a great heritage? We, being corrupted, do not know how to enjoy them and today we suffer intellectual starvation. Even in literature, art, and the rest, should we yield to others? Of course we may laugh at those old folks among us who block their own road of advancement and claim that we Chinese have all that is found in Western learning. But should we not laugh even more at those who are drunk with Western ways and regard everything Chinese as worthless, as though we in the last several hundred years have remained primitive and have achieved nothing? We should realize that any system of thought must have its own period as the background. What we need to learn is the essential spirit of that system and not the conditions under which it was produced, for once we come to the conditions, we shall not be free from the restrictions of time. For example, Confucius said a great deal about ethics of an aristocratic nature, which is certainly not suitable today. But we should not take Confucius lightly simply because of this. Shall we cast Plato aside simply because he said that the slavery system should be preserved? If we understand this point, we can study traditional Chinese subjects with impartial judgment and accept or reject them judiciously.

There is another very important matter. If we want to expand our civilization, we must borrow the methods of other civilizations because their methods of study are highly refined. . . . I therefore hope that our dear young people will, first of all, have a sincere purpose of respecting and protecting our civilization; second, that they will apply Western methods to the study of our civilization and discover its true character; third, that they will put our own civilization in order and supplement it with others' so that it will be transformed and become a new civilization; and fourth, that they will extend this new civilization to the outside world so that it can benefit the whole human race.

[Liang, in *Yinbing shi heji*, vol. 5, *juanji* no. 23, part i, sec. 13, pp. 35–37 — WTC]

## LIANG SHUMING: CHINESE CIVILIZATION VIS-À-VIS EASTERN AND WESTERN PHILOSOPHIES

At a time when Confucianism was being decried as decadent and outmoded, Liang Shuming (1893–1988), originally a Buddhist, endorsed Confucianism as the basis for a reconstruction of Chinese civilization and later for world civilization as well. In the first passage translated below, written in 1922, he is quite negative with regard to "Indian attitudes," but later he saw them as still relevant to the evolution of the world at large.

Though not unappreciative of certain Western values, such as individualism and science, which might be embraced in a synthesis with China's own humanistic values, he condemned wholesale Westernization as impractical and undesirable. Instead he believed that underlying traditional values and orientations would constitute a more practical basis for building a cohesive modern society, as well as the basis for a future human culture.

According to Liang, the underlying bases of Western democracy — material, social, and spiritual — were totally lacking in China. Consequently, political democracy of the Western type could not possibly succeed there. Reformers and revolutionaries who tried arbitrarily to superimpose Western institutions on China failed to recognize the essentially rural and agrarian character of Chinese society. A sound program of reconstruction, Liang believed, could start only at the grass roots and slowly evolve a new socialist society, avoiding the excesses of both capitalism and communism.

To promote such reconstruction of agriculture and rural life, Liang founded the Shandong Rural Reconstruction Institute. He was one of the founders of the Democratic League and was prominent in the attempt to mediate between the Nationalist and Communist parties after World War II. Later, under the pressure of Communist ideological campaigns, he steadfastly refused to confess any errors.

There are three ways in human life: (1) to go forward; (2) to modify and to achieve harmony, synthesis, and the mean in the self; and (3) to go backward. . . . The fundamental spirit of Chinese culture is the harmony and moderation of ideas and desires, whereas that of Indian civilization is to go backward in ideas and desires [and that of the West is to go forward]. [pp. 54–55]

Generally speaking, Westerners have been too strong and too vigorous in their minds and intellect. Because of this they have suffered spiritually. This is an undeniable fact since the nineteenth century. [p. 63]

Let us compare Western culture with Chinese culture. First, there is the conquest of nature on the material side of Western culture — this China has none of. Second, there is the scientific method on the intellectual side of Western culture — this also China has none of. And third, there is democracy on the social side of Western culture — this, too, China has none of. . . . This shows negatively that the way of Chinese culture is not that of the West but is the second way [mentioned above — namely, achieving the mean]. . . . As to Indian culture . . . religion alone has flourished, subordinating to it philosophy, literature, science, and art. The three aspects of life [material, intellectual, and social] have become an abnormal spiritual development, and spiritual life itself has been an almost purely religious development. This is really most extraordinary. Indian culture has traveled its own way, different from that of the West. Needless to say, it is not the same as that of Chinese culture. [pp. 64–66]

In this respect Chinese culture is different from that of India, because of the weakness of religion, as we have already said. For this reason, there is not much to be said about Chinese religions. The most important thing in Chinese culture is its metaphysics, which is applicable everywhere. . . . Chinese metaphysics is different from that of the West and India. It is different in its problems. . . . The problems discussed in the ancient West and ancient India have in fact not existed in China. While the problems of the West and India are not really identical, still they are the same insofar as the search for the reality of the universe is concerned. Where they are the same is exactly where they are decidedly different from China. Have you heard of Chinese philosophers debating monism, dualism, or pluralism, or idealism and materialism? The Chinese do not discuss such static problems of tranquil reality. The metaphysics handed down from the greatest antiquity in China, which constituted the fundamental concept of all learning — great and small, high and low — is that completely devoted to the discussion of change that is entirely nontranquil in reality. [pp. 114–115]

The first point of the Confucian philosophy of life arising out of this type of Chinese metaphysics is that life is right and good. Basically, this metaphysics speaks in terms of "the life of the universe." Hence it is said that "change means reproduction and reproduction."[24] Confucius said many things to glorify life, like "The great characteristic of Heaven and earth is to give life,"[25] and "Does Heaven speak? All the four seasons pursue their course and all things are continually being produced." . . .[26] Human life is the reality of a great current. It naturally tends toward the most suitable and the most satisfactory. It responds to things as they come. This is change. It spontaneously arrives at centrality, harmony, and synthesis. Hence its response is always right. This is the reason why the Confucian school said, "What Heaven has conferred is what we call human nature. To fulfill the law of human nature is what we call the Way."[27] As long as one fulfills his nature, it will be all right. This is why it is said that it can be understood and put into practice even by men and women of the simplest intelligence. This knowledge and ability are what Mencius called the knowledge possessed by man without deliberation and the ability possessed by him without having been acquired by learning.[28] [pp. 121–125]

What attitude should we Chinese hold now? What should we select from the three cultures? We may say:

1. We must reject the Indian attitude absolutely and completely.

2. We must accept Western culture as a whole [including conquest of nature, science, and democracy] but make some fundamental changes. That is to say, we must change the Western attitude somewhat [from intellection to intuition].

3. We must renew our Chinese attitude and bring it to the fore, but do so critically. [p. 202]

[Liang, *Dongxi wenhua ji qi zhexue*, pp. 54–202  — WTC]

---

24. *Changes, Xizi* 1, ch. 5; Legge, *Yi King*, p. 356.
25. Ibid. 2, ch. 1; Legge, *Yi King*, p. 381.
26. *Analects* 17:19.
27. *Mean* ch. 1.
28. *Mencius* 7a:15.

RECONSTRUCTING THE COMMUNITY

The following excerpt is from Liang's "Reconstruction of the Village Community." In it he addresses the problem of community organization by reference to the original community compact (*xiangyue*) advocated by Zhu Xi on the basis of his reconstruction of the earlier compact of the Lü family in the eleventh century (chapter 21). In the form recommended by Zhu and adapted later by Wang Yangming and other sixteenth-century Neo-Confucian reformers, Liang saw a type of voluntary, cooperative organization that could be adapted to modern needs but would avoid the passivity of the authoritarian, bureaucratic "village lecture" system officially established under the Ming and Qing (chapter 25). In this he reflected a consciousness shared by many earlier twentieth-century reformers that traditional China was riven by a gap between the top-heavy power structure above and a fragmented, individualistic, politically inert society below. In other words, he was addressing the lack of a more active and involved infrastructure such as more recently has been referred to as "civil society." What he says reverses the claims made in some quarters that the "individualism" of the West stands in contrast to the "communitarianism" of Asia.

In simple terms, we can indicate two points: one, the question of science and technology and two, the question of group organization. As for science and technology, everyone has seen how the West is superior and how we are deficient. . . . What I want to discuss now is the question of group organization.

Westerners have always had everywhere group life, beginning from religion on to economics and government. Whereas Chinese have always lacked group life; everywhere it seems the whole is broken into parts. . . . [p. 51]

What is meant by construction is nothing but the construction of a new structure of social organization; that is, to construct new customs. Why? Because in the past our structure of social organization was shaped out of social customs; it was not shaped out of national laws. . . . [p. 40]

In the contemporary world, if the Chinese do not move toward group organization, in the future they will not be able to exist. Reality compels us toward organization, to turn in the direction of the West . . . but might the turn be incompatible with our old spirit? . . . Although Chinese lack group organization, they are not opposed to group organization; hence there is no necessary conflict. [p. 145]

This is a time of great distress for the Chinese, a time caught in contradiction on either side, coming and going. That is to say, on the one hand the Chinese lack group organization, and at the same time they lack the establishment of individual liberty and equality; the two [deficiencies] both urgently await being made up. But if we emphasize the aspect of liberty and equality . . . then it will be very difficult for us to attend to the aspect of combining into groups and will cause the Chinese to be even more dispersed. If we take care of the aspect of group organization, emphasizing the West's most recent tendency, then liberty and equality cannot be given enough play. . . . Relational ethics should allow both aspects to be established. As a result of giving play to ethical relations, the individual will necessarily respect the group, fulfilling the requisite obligation; the group will necessarily respect the individual, according it due liberty and equality. . . .

[R]egarding the group organization we have just discussed, the principle of this organization is based in China's idea of ethics. It is as if, to the five relationships of father-son, ruler-minister, husband-wife, friends, and elder brother-younger brother, there were added a relationship of group toward member, member toward group. . . .

Once we have resolved the several conflicts and difficulties between [the spirits of] China and the West, then we can discover a new social organization. This social organization will still take ethical sentiments as its source and take the upward movement of human life [*rensheng xiangshang*] as its aim. . . . This is purely a rational [*lixing*] organization; it fully gives play to humanity's spirit (reason) and fully absorbs the strengths of the Westerners. Westerners' strengths are four: first is group organization — this sets right our being dispersed; second is the active participation in group life by the members of the group — this sets right our defect of being passive; third is respect for the individual — this furthers the position of the individual relative to before, completes the character of the individual; fourth is the socialization of wealth — this enhances social relations. This organization of ours completely encompasses these four Western strengths without any omission, hence we say that this organization takes China's ancient spirit as its basis and absorbs Westerners' strengths. . . . [T]his organization is one that humanity has never known before. [pp. 174–176]

Above we discussed two aspects of our organization: one is to seek organization from reason [*lixing*], one is to start with the villages. . . . These two were originally the root of Chinese society. . . . What we are about now is to grow new sprouts from this root. . . . This new organization is just the supplementation and transformation of what earlier Chinese called "the community compact" [*xiangyue*]. . . . But the community compact referred to here is not the community compact promoted in the Ming and Qing dynasties by the government using political force; rather it refers to the community compact launched in the beginning by villagers themselves at the outset in the Song dynasty. That village covenant was the creation of Mr. Lü Heshu. [pp. 187–188]

[O]ur transformation is not strange; if the ancients were born today, they would certainly want to transform the community compact, and, further, the result of their transformation might be similar to ours. Because people are alive, they adapt; those living in today's society are certainly like this. The direction of supplementation and transformation is all one — to transform inactive into active. And supplementation and transformation can be divided for purposes of discussion.

First: Turn inactive mutual relief into active undertaking. . . . We do not wait for disaster to come before providing relief; we want to be more active. For example, poverty is a large problem for the Chinese; we want to form producing and marketing cooperatives. We do not want merely to relieve poverty; we will actively make [society] unimpoverished. . . . The community compact is a bit inactive; we want to change it to be active, to add an active flavor; rather than wait until the last minute and give aid, the best would be not to let things come to this pass. . . . Earlier the Chinese did not much look for progress in their mode of life. For example, having hand carts and ox and horse carts, they could neglect to strive for cars and trains. This kind of attitude is also evident in the community compact. We, on the other hand, will change it into some-thing active, encompassing the sense of striving for progress in active under-takings. . . .

Second: Note that in the community compact there is an upward movement of human life [rensheng xiangshang], the stirring up of aspiration [zhichi, am-bition]. This is basic to the community compact. . . . Aspiration is most impor-tant; without aspiration everything will be fruitless. This is the original idea of the community compact. Our supplementation and transformation [are as follows]:

Our judgment is that earlier Chinese, in the community compact, over-emphasized the goodness [shan] of the individual, how to perfect the moral character of the individual. Regarding the ideal of goodness, they seem a bit limited, as if goodness were not in an endless course of unfolding. That is to say, in the compact of the Chinese earlier, one can discern that they harbor a standard custom and think that it is enough to reach this standard. In fact goodness is inexhaustible, always in the course of unfolding. Yet in the com-munity compact it is as if there is a set standard and as if it leans toward indi-vidual goodness. Its defects are leaning toward the individual and having limits. Our supplementing transformation is to regard society in place of the emphasis on the individual, to see an endless unfolding in place of what is limited. In other words, when we organize villages, right from the beginning we want to stir up aspiration, expand hopes. Expand what hopes? Just this: to transform society, create a new culture, create an ideal society, establish a new organiza-tion. . . .

Third: This is a concrete question. . . . Our community compact is not just the compact of a single village; it is not that those in one village can encourage each other to goodness and that is sufficient. We want to move outward, to connect with outside places, near and far. Although the past community com-pact also had this idea, it was not active. From connecting village with village, we want gradually to reach to the connection of county with county, province with province; to make connections everywhere, to have mutual intercourse, to communicate information. Why do we want this? Because we want to transform society, create a new culture; it is not merely to make the individual good.

Merely to make the individual good, it would not be necessary to do all this. If we want to transform society, then we as individuals are unable to transform it; it is necessary to make connections. One point is to engage in making connections, and another point is to establish an organ to promote progress. Not only do we want mutual encouragement toward goodness, but we want to stress progress in the mode of life, the area that was not stressed earlier.

Fourth: This idea is something that was originally part of the community compact . . . but it is easily overlooked and forgotten by people, easily gotten wrong. What is this point? That the community compact organization cannot be practiced by relying on political power. . . . [pp. 199–202]

In the practice of the community compact, relying on political power will not work, promotion by private individuals also will not work; hence, although in history many times there has been the intention to initiate it, however in reality none of these can be considered successful. I am afraid success could only be seen today. We understand that to rely on political power to do things — to use the power of command and coercion, if this kind of power is used, in each step it all is mechanical. . . . Each time it goes down a level, the further by a step it is from the place where it was initiated, the more it is passive, the more it becomes mechanical, the more it lacks vitality, the more it lacks energy, the more it is unable to fit the problems. . . . The more it is unable to fit problems, the more it loses its meaning, the more it becomes useless. . . .

Our village construction [rural reconstruction] is the construction of social organization, and we often like to say that this social organization is something that grows, something that gradually unfolds, that grows from sprouts, that unfolds from hints. Its sprouts and hints are in the village and from the village will slowly unfurl to form a whole society. This unfolding or growth must wait on the progress in reality (the reality of how we go about living in society). Organization grows out of the needs of social life; it cannot be tacked on suspended in thin air, cannot be arbitrarily tacked on. Whatever is really in the midst of unfolding must be a need of actual reality, hence we say that the unfolding of organization must await the progress in reality. More specifically, it must await economic progress. Once progress gradually unfolds in the techniques of economic production, methods of management, and economic relations, then it will be possible to have a new social organization unfold. . . . Economic progress awaits people, and if people are not enlivened, then the economy . . . cannot progress. How can people be enlivened? It is necessary to set in motion the Chinese people's spirit. How can the Chinese people's spirit be set in motion? It is necessary to rely on the strength of life's upward motion, to stir up aspiration. Otherwise Chinese people will become even more narrow, more unable to move ahead. We want to stir up aspiration, place economics in this kind of human life, allow human life to drive economics, control economics, enjoy the use of economics, not to cause economics to control human life.

(Among Westerners, it is economics that controls human life.) If we want to accomplish this, then it is all the more a question of spirit, a question of human life, or, we could say, a question of culture. [pp. 205–206]

[Liang, *Xiangcun jianshe lilun*, pp. 51, 140–145, 174–177, 187–188, 199–202, 205–106 — CL]

## HU SHI: OUR ATTITUDE TOWARD MODERN WESTERN CIVILIZATION

The most surprising rejoinder to the critics of the West came from Hu Shi, who defended the "materialistic" West on the ground that it was indeed more spiritual than China.

At present the most unfounded and more harmful distortion is to ridicule Western civilization as materialistic and worship Eastern civilization as spiritual. . . . The modern civilization of the West, built on the foundation of the search for human happiness, not only has definitely increased material enjoyment to no small degree, but can also satisfy the spiritual needs of mankind. In philosophy it has applied highly refined methods to the search for truth and to investigation into the vast secrets of nature. In religion and ethics, it has overthrown the religion of superstitions and established a rational belief, has destroyed divine power and established a humanistic religion, has discarded the unknowable Heaven or paradise and directed its efforts to building a paradise among men and Heaven on earth. It has cast aside the arbitrarily asserted transcendence of the individual soul, has utilized to the highest degree the power of man's new imagination and new intellect to promote a new religion and new ethics that are fully socialized, and has endeavored to work for the greatest amount of happiness for the greatest number of people.

The most outstanding characteristic of Eastern civilization is to know contentment, whereas that of Western civilization is not to know contentment.

Contented Easterners are satisfied with their simple life and therefore do not seek to increase their material enjoyment. They are satisfied with ignorance and "not understanding and not knowing"[29] and therefore have devoted no attention to the discovery of truth and the invention of techniques and machinery. They are satisfied with their present lot and environment and therefore do not want to conquer nature but merely [to] be at home with nature and at peace with their lot. They do not want to change systems, but rather to mind their own business. They do not want a revolution, but rather to remain obedient subjects.

The civilization under which people are restricted and controlled by a material environment from which they cannot escape, and under which they can-

---

29. *Book of Odes*, Da ya, Wen wang 7.

not utilize human thought and intellectual power to change environment and improve conditions, is the civilization of a lazy and nonprogressive people. It is truly a materialistic civilization. Such civilization can only obstruct but cannot satisfy the spiritual demands of mankind.

[Hu, *Hu Shi wencun*, collection 3, ch. 1, pp. 1–13 — WTC]

## SA MENGWU, HE BINGSONG, AND OTHERS: "DECLARATION FOR CULTURAL CONSTRUCTION ON A CHINESE BASIS"

The increasing pace of Westernization in the early 1930s, especially in the universities, prompted further expressions of fear that Chinese culture might be wholly submerged. This 1935 declaration by ten university professors in the magazine *Cultural Construction* deplored the prevailing trend and, in the general vein of Liang Qichao and Liang Shuming, called for a synthesis of Chinese and Western cultures that would nevertheless be distinctively Chinese. Vague though this syncretism was, it attracted enough attention throughout the country that Hu Shi felt compelled to protest, as he did in the piece that follows the declaration here, this kind of "conservatism . . . hiding under the smoke screen of compromise."

Some people think we should return to the past. But ancient China is already history, and history cannot and need not be repeated. Others believe that China should completely imitate England and the United States. These viewpoints have their special merits. But China, which is neither England nor the United States, should have its own distinctive characteristics. Furthermore, China is now passing from an agricultural feudal society to an industrial society and is in a different situation from England and the United States, which have been completely industrialized. We therefore definitely oppose complete imitation of them. Besides the proponents of imitating England and the United States, there are two other schools of thought, one advocating imitation of Soviet Russia, the other, of Italy and Germany. But they make the same mistake as those promoting the imitation of England and the United States; they likewise ignore the special spatial and temporal characteristics of China. . . .

We demand a cultural construction on the Chinese basis. In the process of reconstruction, we should realize that:

1. China is China, not just any geographical area, and therefore has its own spatial characteristics. At the same time, China is the China of today, not the China of the past, and has her own temporal characteristics. We therefore pay special attention to the needs of here and now. The necessity to do so is the foundation of the Chinese basis.

2. It is useless merely to glorify ancient Chinese systems and thought. It is equally useless to curse them. We must examine our heritage, weed out what

should be weeded out, and preserve what should be preserved. Those good systems and great doctrines that are worthy of praise should be brought to greater light with all our might and be presented to the whole world, while evil systems and inferior thoughts that are worthy of condemnation should be totally eliminated without the slightest regret.

3. It is right and necessary to absorb Western culture. But we should absorb what is worth absorbing and not, with the attitude of total acceptance, absorb its dregs also.

4. Cultural construction on the Chinese basis is a creative endeavor, one that is pushing ahead. Its objective is to enable China and the Chinese, who are backward and have lost their unique qualities in the cultural sphere, not only to keep pace with other countries and peoples but also to make valuable contributions to a world culture.

5. To construct China in the cultural sphere is not to abandon the idea of the world as a Grand Commonality. Rather, it is first to reconstruct China and make her a strong and complete unit so that she may have adequate strength to push forward the Grand Commonality of the world.

Essentially speaking, China must have both self-recognition and a world perspective, and must have neither any idea of seclusion nor any determination to imitate blindly. Such recognition is profound and precise recognition. Proceeding on such recognition, our cultural reconstruction should be not to adhere to the past, nor to imitate blindly, but to stand on the Chinese basis, keep a critical attitude, apply the scientific method, examine the past, hold on to the present, and create a future.

> [Sa, He et al., "Zhongguo benwei di wenhua jianshe xuanyan,"
> *Wenhua jianshe* 1, no. 4 (January 1935): 3–5 —WTC]

## HU SHI: CRITICISM OF THE "DECLARATION FOR CULTURAL CONSTRUCTION ON A CHINESE BASIS"

At the beginning of the year [1935] ten professors, Sa Mengwu, He Bingsong et al., issued a declaration on "cultural construction on a Chinese basis." Considerable popular attention in the country has been attracted to it in the last several months. . . . I can't help pointing out that while the ten professors repeatedly uttered the phrase "Chinese basis" and while they declared in so many words that they were "not conservatives," in reality it is their conservative thinking that has been fooling them. The declaration is a most fashionable expression of a reactionary mood prevalent today. Of course, it is out of fashion for people conscientiously to advocate returning to the past and therefore their conservative thinking takes refuge under the smoke screen of compromise. With respect to indigenous culture, the professors advocated discarding the dregs and preserving the essence, and with respect to the new culture of the world, they advocated accepting the good and rejecting the bad and selecting what is best. This is the most fashionable tune of compromise. . . .

The fundamental error of Professors Sa, He, and others lies in their failure to understand the nature of cultural change. . . . Culture itself is conservative. . . . When two different cultures come into contact, the force of competition and comparison can partially destroy the resistance and conservatism of a certain culture. . . . In this process of survival of the fittest, there is no absolutely reliable standard by which to direct the selection from the various aspects of a culture. In this gigantic cultural movement, the "scientific method" the ten professors dream of does not work. . . . There is always a limit to violent change in the various spheres of culture, namely, that it can never completely wipe out the conservative nature of an indigenous culture. This is the "Chinese basis" the destruction of which has been feared by numerous cautious people of the past as well as the present. This indigenous basis is found in the life and habits produced by a certain indigenous environment and history. Simply stated, it is the people — all the people. This *is* the "basis." There is no danger that this basis will be destroyed. No matter how radically the material existence has changed, how much intellectual systems have altered, and how much political systems have been transformed, the Japanese are still Japanese and the Chinese are still Chinese. . . . The ten professors need not worry about the "Chinese basis." . . . Those of us who are forward-looking should humbly accept the scientific and technological world culture and the spiritual civilization behind it. . . . There is no doubt that in the future the crystallization of this great change will, of course, be a culture on the "Chinese basis."

[Hu, *Hu Shi wencun*, collection 4, ch. 4, pp. 535–540 — WTC]

# RADICAL CRITIQUES OF TRADITIONAL SOCIETY

The radical critique of traditional culture led directly to the spawning of new political movements, often inspired by trends in the West and Japan, to remedy what were seen as social injustices and oppressive institutions in China. These were essentially intellectual movements, without popular support, but they had a profound influence on members of the educated elite who became leaders of revolutionary parties. Among these, anarchist, egalitarian, and feminist movements in the early decades of the twentieth century contributed to the ferment and discontent that stirred the founders of the Chinese Communist Party. In the essays that follow, the close association of feminism and liberationist ideals with anarchism and communism is evident.

### HE ZHEN: "WHAT WOMEN SHOULD KNOW ABOUT COMMUNISM"

The early anarchist movement in China produced a rigorous critique of the family system and the place of women in traditional society. Chinese feminism had been a distinct current since at least the 1880s, when Kang Youwei had organized a society against foot binding, and again in the 1890s, when Liang Qichao argued that women should become productive members of society and that as the first educators of China's children, they needed to become educated themselves. The woman revolutionary Qiu Jin also eloquently spoke of the plight of women.

The essay below is by He Zhen, of whom little is known beyond the fact that she was the wife of Liu Shipei (1884–1917), a leader of the anarchist movement. The essay, probably originally a speech or lecture, was published in the journal *Natural Justice* (*Tianyi bao*), founded by He and Liu after they fled to Tokyo in 1907. Circulated for the most part on a monthly basis among the growing exile and student community in Tokyo, copies of the journal were also smuggled back to the mainland. Along with *New Century* (*Xin shiji*), published by Chinese exiles in Paris, it propagated anarcho-communism while advocating revolutionary action; it may be said to represent the most radical wing of the growing revolutionary movement. In this essay, He Zhen refused to justify feminism on grounds of its subserving the nationalist movement, instead demanding "women's liberation" as an absolute right. Further, she argued that the state and society oppressed both men and women and that both would continue to be oppressed as long as capitalism survived. Revolutionary change was thus needed to create a new society on truly egalitarian principles; for a few women to join ruling-class men at the top of society would still leave the majority of women mired in misery at the very bottom.

What is the most important thing in the world? Eating is the most important. You who are women: what is it that makes one suffer mistreatment? It is relying on others in order to eat. Let us look at the most pitiable of women. There are three sorts. There are those who end up as servants. If their master wants to hit them, he hits them. If he wants to curse them, he curses them. They do not dare to offer the slightest resistance, but slave for him from morning to night. They get up at four o'clock and do not go to bed until midnight. What is the reason for this? It is simply that the master has money and you depend on him in order to eat.

There are also women workers. Everywhere in Shanghai there are silk factories, cotton mills, weaving factories, and laundries. I don't know how many women have been hired by these places. They too work all day into the evening, and they too lack even a moment for themselves. They work blindly, unable to stand straight. What is the reason for this? It is simply that the factory owner has money and you depend on him in order to eat.

There are also prostitutes. Every day they are beaten by their pimps. Whatever the customer is like, they must service him if he wants to be serviced, or they must gamble with him if he wants to gamble. People despise them. The "wild chickens" of Shanghai have to stand in the streets waiting for customers at midnight in the wind and snow. What is the reason for this? It is simply that since your family is poor you must sell yourself in this way in order to eat.

Aside from these three kinds of people, there are also concubines. They must swallow their resentment no matter how the first wife mistreats them. This too is because they depend on men in order to eat. As for widows, a very few who are from rich families will die to protect their virtue. Very many who are from poor families will die because they have no children [to support them] and cannot remarry. This too is because they have nothing to eat. But even if they survive, their lives are still bitter and so they actively seek to die. As for women who farm the fields or raise silkworms, their lives are also very bitter. The things they have to do are just enough to let them scrape by. Moreover, women who marry are beaten and cursed by their husbands or else ignored, and they dare not make trouble. [This is] not because they want to gaze upon their husband's face but because they want to gaze upon a bowl of rice.

Thus those of us who are women suffer untold bitterness and untold wrongs in order to get hold of this rice bowl. My fellow women: do not hate men! Hate that you do not have food to eat. Why don't you have any food? It is because you don't have any money to buy food. Why don't you have any money? It is because the rich have stolen our property. They have forced the majority of people into poverty and starvation. Look at the wives and daughters in the government offices and mansions. They live extravagantly with no worries about having enough to eat. Why are you worried every day about starving to death? The poor are people just as the rich are. Think about it for yourselves; this ought to produce some disquieting feelings.

There is now a kind of person who says that if women only had a profession, they would not fear starvation. Middle-class families, for example, are sending their daughters to school, either to study a general course or to learn a little of handicrafts. Then if they get married they can become teachers. They won't need to rely on men in order to survive. Likewise, families that are very poor are sending their daughters and daughters-in-law to work in factories. As long as they stay there day after day, they will have a way of making a living. They won't have to become maids or prostitutes. This point of view has some truth in it. However, as I see it, schools too are owned and operated by certain people, and if you teach in a school, then you are depending on those people in order to eat. Factories too are built by investors, and if you work in a factory, you are depending on its owners in order to eat.

As long as you depend on others, you cannot be free. This is not much different from those who depended on others in previous ages and thus were subject to oppression. How could they be called independent? Moreover, when you depend on a school or a factory for your living, won't you end up jobless if they close down or if your boss decides he has too many workers or if no one wants your skills? Therefore, in the final analysis depending on others is dangerous and not at all a good idea. . . .

I have a good idea that will exempt you from relying on others while still finding food naturally. How? By practicing communism. Think of all the things in the world. They were either produced by nature or by individual labor. Why can rich people buy them but poor people cannot? It is because the world trades with money. It is because people seize the things they have bought with money for their exclusive use. If every single woman understands that nothing is more evil than money, and they all unite together to cooperate with men to utterly overthrow the rich and powerful and then abolish money, then absolutely nothing will be allowed for individuals to own privately. Everything from food to clothes and tools will be put in a place where people — men and women alike, as long as they perform a little labor — can take however much of whatever they want just like taking water from the ocean. This is called communism.

At this time, not only will we be free of depending on others for food to eat, but also the food will all be good to eat. It will be possible to have good things to wear, good things to use, and good things to play with. Think about it: will this be a better future or not? I am not lying to you. If we only unite together, with this method [communism] we can naturally have a good future. There is no doubt about it. As we say colloquially, "the good times are coming." This is what I have to say today.

[He, "Lun nüzi dangzhi gongchan zhuyi," pp. 229–232 — PZ]

WOMEN'S REVENGE

The learning of Confucianism has tended to be oppressive and to promote male selfishness. Therefore, Confucianism marks the beginning of justifications for polygamy and chastity. People of the Han dynasty studied Confucianism and felt free to twist the meaning of the ancient writings as they pertained to women in order to extend their own views. The *Discourses in the White Tiger Hall* is a good example of this. The people who proposed these doctrines were simply pursuing their selfish interests. For example, from Wang Mang, who dressed up the *Rites of Zhou* to have more imperial concubines, ordinary wives, and empresses, down to the likes of Zhang You and Ma Rong, everyone increased the number of their wives and concubines.

Song dynasty Confucians continued [these doctrines]. They further supported this system of oppression and denigrated women, placing them outside of the "human way." Ever since, every single man of learning has praised the theories of the Han and the Song as priceless beyond jade and gold. These attitudes have reinforced each other, and the faults of the theory have never been understood. Cunning people have dressed up these theories to their own advantage. Stupid people believe in these theories with a superstitious force impregnable to skepticism. I don't know how many of us women have died as a result. Therefore, the entire learning of Confucianism is a murderous learning. . . .

The ancients said that the relationship between the wife and her husband was like that of the minister and his ruler, and so men took precedence over women and men were honorable while women were contemptible. From this, every evil theory designed to keep women from having freedom followed; for example, the theories that the yang force leads while the yin force follows and that men take action while women follow. Precisely because of the theory that men were honorable while women were contemptible, every evil theory making men into Heaven followed: men were to Heaven as women were to earth and men were yang while women were yin. An absolute inequality was accordingly formed between men and women. Alas! . . .

Since men practiced polygamy and feared that women would want more than one husband, they therefore made women's morality a matter of diligence, chastity, and purity. They also feared that women would not be able to control themselves and so guided them with doctrines of prudence and staying at home, treating women like prisoners. Men also feared that after they died, their women would no longer be theirs. So "honoring chastity" is simply a euphemism [for preventing remarriage]. This is like an autocrat encouraging loyalty and constancy to himself because he wants his ministers to be willing to die for him. The subtlety of these phrases is magnificent. However, the women of ancient times did not regard remarriage as taboo. The *Rites* therefore spoke of the mourning required after the death of a father, and the prohibition against remarriage after the death of a husband arose. Later, the Confucians of the Song dynasty all in a great wave agreed that starving to death was but a small matter compared to the loss of a woman's virtue [through remarriage]. Is this not treating women like private property?

Aside from "virtuous wives" they spoke also of "chaste women." Virtuous wives have to protect their virtue for their husbands. Chaste women have to protect their chastity for their fiancés, once they are betrothed. . . . Jiao Xun also advocated virtue in women. He said a virtuous woman did not change her name (remarry), just as men loyal to a fallen dynasty went into hiding. Women should die faithful to their deceased husbands, like a loyalist giving his life to his dynasty. . . . Thus are women driven to their deaths with this empty talk of virtue. We can see that the Confucian insistence on ritual decorum is nothing more than a tool for murdering women. . . .

This proves that women have duties but no rights. Because household responsibilities cannot be assumed by men, all the tasks of managing the household are given to women. Out of fear that women might interfere with their concerns, men made up the theory that women had no business outside of the home. By doing so, they deprived women of their natural rights. Giving women duties without rights allowed men to live in idleness while condemning women to work. Keeping women at home allowed men to pursue education while women were trapped in ignorance. Isn't this the greatest of injustices? . . .

This proves that the right of a woman to leave her husband resides with men.

A husband can leave his wife, but a wife cannot leave her husband. Therefore, no matter how badly a husband treats his wife, there is nothing she can do about it. But if a wife behaves badly toward her husband, she becomes subject to the seven grounds for divorce. Isn't this how the ancients augmented the rights of males? . . .

How did this poison fill the entire world? It can be traced to the doctrines of Ban Zhao of the Eastern Han. These have been taken as the last word on the subject ever since then, though they are completely ridiculous. An examination of her *Admonitions for Women* [chapter 23] shows that first of all she emphasizes the ignoble and weak nature of women. She says women are inferiors and should be humble and yielding as well as respectful and deferential. They should place others before themselves and must accept all insults and hardships, as if ever kneeling in fear.

Ban Zhao also said that if a wife did not serve her husband proper order would collapse and that the female principle of yin found its function in gentleness while women found their beauty in weakness. Women were prohibited from insulting their husbands, while virtue lay in their being pure and quiet. Alas! Once this doctrine was propagated women were subjected to men by a set of rules. This was called the doctrine of propriety, but it is nothing but humiliation! It was called "proper order" but is nothing but shamelessness! Isn't this [actually] the Way of the concubine? . . .

This traitor Ban was herself a woman, but she was deluded by the false notions of Confucianism. . . . The reason why women's rights never developed lay in the fact that everybody was reciting the books of the traitor Ban. People followed what was already written and the writings of the traitor Ban closely followed the Confucian books, also following what was already written. Thus the crime of the traitor Ban in fact originated in Confucianism.

Therefore, since this doctrine has been propagated by the Confucians, not only have men enjoyed and followed it but also women have sincerely believed in it. Not only has it harmed scholarship but it has also harmed the law. Look at recent laws. If a woman kills her husband, she is put to death by slow torture. If a woman is promised in marriage and betrothal gifts are received, but later the family changes its mind, they are flogged fifty times. The laws are based on the doctrine that men are superior while women are base. The law was thus based on scholarship while scholarship was based on Confucian writings. If we do not utterly abolish the false doctrines of the Confucian writings, the truth will never again be heard.

[He, "Nüzi fuzhou lun," pp. 7–23 —PZ]

### HAN YI: "DESTROYING THE FAMILY"

This essay, published in 1907 under the pseudonym Han Yi ("a member of the Han race"), was possibly written by Liu Shipei, who favored a Han Chinese revolution against the Manchu oppressors. It reflects a view radical for the time, but one already anticipated by Kang Youwei's as yet unpublished *Grand Commonality* (*Datong shu*), which was equally critical of the family system, proposed one-year marriage contracts, and advocated public nurseries for the raising of children. Liu here attacks the family as the source of partiality, which he implicitly contrasts to the ideal of the public good.

All of society's accomplishments depend on people to achieve, while the multiplication of the human race depends on men and women. Thus if we want to pursue a social revolution, we must start with a sexual revolution — just as if we want to reestablish the Chinese nation, expelling the Manchus is the first step to the accomplishment of other tasks. . . . Yet, whenever we speak of the sexual revolution, the masses doubt and obstruct us, which gives rise to problems. In bringing up this matter then we absolutely must make a plan that gets to the root of the problem. What is this plan? It is to destroy the family.

The family is the origin of all evil. Because of the family, people become selfish. Because of the family, women are increasingly controlled by men. Because of the family, everything useless and harmful occurs (people now often say they are embroiled in family responsibilities while in fact they are all just making trouble for themselves, and so if there were no families, these trivial matters would instantly disappear). Because of the family, children — who belong to the world as a whole — are made the responsibility of a single woman (children should be raised publicly since they belong to the whole society, but with families the men always force the women to raise their children and use them to continue the ancestral sacrifices). These examples constitute irrefutable proof of the evils of the family. . . .

Moreover, from now on in a universal commonwealth, everyone will act freely, never again will they live and die without contact with one another as in olden times. The doctrine of human equality allows for neither forcing women to maintain the family nor having servants to maintain it. The difficulties of life are rooted in the family. When land belongs to everyone and the borders between here and there are eradicated, then there will be no doubt that the "family" itself definitely should be abolished. As long as the family exists, then debauched men will imprison women in cages and force them to become their concubines and service their lust, or they will take the sons of others to be their own successors. If we abolish the family now, then such men will disappear. The destruction of the family will thus lead to the creation of public-minded people in place of selfish people, and men will have no way to oppress women. Therefore, to open the curtain on the social revolution, we must start with the destruction of the family.

[Han Yi [pseud.], "Huaijia lun" — PZ]

## Chapter 34

### THE COMMUNIST REVOLUTION

On the surface, Chinese Communism would seem to have little to do with Chinese tradition. From the outset—from the party's founding in 1921 under the leadership of the iconoclast Chen Duxiu—it was blatantly hostile to Confucian tradition and unashamedly committed to violent overthrow of the old order. Mao Zedong, too, though he recognized a kind of native tradition in the peasant rebellions and popular "revolutionary" literature of earlier dynasties, did not thereby acknowledge any debt to the past. For him, recurrent rebellions showed only how the Chinese masses had suffered and protested. They did not show a way out of the historical impasse: the constant reestablishment of dynasticism and warlordism after futile outbursts of popular discontent.

For such an abortive revolutionary tradition Mao could feel pity, but if any lesson was to be learned—and this was Mao's real point—it was the uniqueness of Marxism-Leninism and of the victory that the Communist Party alone was able to achieve over such an oppressive past. Whereas earlier failures demonstrated only the need for something totally new to break a deadlock that had spelled frustration and stagnation for centuries, the ideology and organization of Communism had for the first time given China a revolution worthy of the name.

Yet if, in Communist eyes, the successful Chinese revolution has been so peculiarly a product of superior Marxist science and leadership, Chinese Communism has been also, in the perspective of history, an unmistakable product of the Chinese revolution. For almost a century this revolution had been in the making — perhaps even for longer, if it is taken as part of a much older process, as the latest issue from the ancient womb of dynastic change. But conjoined to the familiar processes of dynastic decay, which might have led to a rebellion typical of the past, was a world revolution of which Communism itself must be considered only one manifestation.

It is not our purpose here to assess the forces and factors that contributed to the triumph of Communism in China. The circumstances in which the party took its rise, however, have a bearing on the relation between Communism and the Chinese tradition. By 1921 the course of revolutionary change was already well advanced. Not only had the Manchu dynasty fallen, but every attempt to restore the old monarchical and dynastic system had met with insuperable resistance. If, therefore, the republican era still looked much like earlier periods of warlordism and disorder, the possibility had nevertheless vanished of this phase's yielding inexorably to another period of dynastic rule.

With it, however, had not vanished the need for a government strong enough to cope with the enormous problems of China's adjustment to the modern world. In the answers to that need proposed by Sun Yat-sen, anti-Marxist though he was, it is not difficult to discern tendencies with a close affinity to Communism. Whatever Dr. Sun's own intentions, the popularity of his People's Principles (which went almost unchallenged from either left or right long after his death) helped create an atmosphere conducive to the acceptance of Communist aims: the people's livelihood or socialism, of a state-controlled economy; the "freedom of the nation" (rather than of the individual) and party tutelage as Sun interpreted it, of rule by a party elite under a strong leader; and nationalism as adapted by Sun to the Leninist struggle against imperialism and colonialism, of resistance to, and hostility toward, the West.

While republican politics floundered in a sea of warlordism and economic dislocation, the estrangement of Chinese intellectuals from traditional ideals and institutions deepened. This process, which began with concessions to Westernization by even would-be defenders of Confucianism, had reached a climax well before the republican revolution with the abandonment of the traditional curriculum for the civil service, long the institutional stronghold of Confucian ideology. If a new political elite were ever to regain the power of the old centralized bureaucracy, it would be as unlikely to consist of Confucian scholar-officials as the regime itself would be to take the form of monarchy. Instead now of intellectuals serving as defenders of tradition, they had become its most implacable critics. Thus Confucianism had lost not only its bureaucratic function but even the basis of its intellectual life in the school.

As we have seen in the preceding chapter, the dominant trend of thought in the New Culture Movement was toward Westernization. This was expressed in certain general attitudes that won increasing acceptance among the educated and especially among the younger generation: (1) positivism, as a belief in the value and universal applicability of methods of inquiry developed for the natural sciences; (2) pragmatism, in the sense that the validity of an idea was to be judged primarily by its effectiveness; and (3) materialism, especially as a denial of traditional religious and ethical systems. While each of these attitudes might be held by as liberal a scholar and as eloquent an anti-Communist as Hu Shi, for many others they represented transitional stages on a road that led naturally and easily to Communism — to an acceptance of Marxism as the science of society, of Leninism as the effective method for achieving social revolution, and of dialectical materialism as a philosophy of life.

More than any such intellectual trends, however, what created a receptivity to revolutionary change among the Chinese people as a whole was attitudes of a more general and pervasive character. First among these was the desire for and expectation of a better life, which the material progress of the West had seemed to bring within hope of realization. Second was a new view of history as dominated by forces that would either crush those who fell behind or guarantee a bright future to those who understood and utilized them. Third was the prevailing frustration over China's failure to keep pace with these forces and to fulfill the high expectations of her modern political prophets.

Each of these attitudes contributed to a climate of opinion that called for wholesale change and in which nothing that was not "revolutionary" could hope to arouse popular enthusiasm. Of this, the revolutionary aims of the Nationalists themselves are an eloquent example. We have already seen how quick Western-educated and "liberal-minded" Chinese were to find fault with the Nationalist regime for its failure to exemplify liberal principles and establish political democracy. Yet toward the Communists, whose political aims were still more authoritarian and totalitarian, these same "liberals" sometimes showed far more indulgence. In the revolutionary context of the times it was not difficult for the Communists to gain acceptance as fellow "progressives" — a little extreme, perhaps, but nonetheless devoted to the cause of social and economic revolution, to science and technological progress, and above all to the fulfillment of the millennial ideal.

Westernized intellectuals like Hu Shi had joined hands with Chen Duxiu in the attack on traditional values, but nothing pragmatism had to offer in the way of scientific analyses or solutions to the specific problems of modern Chinese society proved intelligible or acceptable to the great masses of Chinese as a substitute for the old value system. Thus as the weakening of traditional ethics left a vacuum to be filled, Communist ideology appealed to many as a comprehensive and systematic answer to China's urgent problems.

In the selections that follow, the presentation of these aims and principles is guided by two basic criteria. First, this is not intended as a documentary history of Chinese Communism, and questions of primarily historical significance are not emphasized. Questions of strategy and tactics, though of fundamental importance to an understanding of the Communists' actual rise to power, cannot properly be evaluated except through a more detailed analysis of historical factors than is possible within the scope of these readings. Second, this chapter centers upon the most important pronouncements of Mao Zedong, as the chief exponent of Chinese Communism in his day.

Within these limits, the readings attempt to answer three main questions:

1. In what intellectual and historical context did the Chinese Communist movement arise?

2. How did Mao Zedong analyze the problems of the revolution, especially the role of the Communist Party in relation to the Chinese peasantry, the new role of the "people" in the modern age, and the stages by which Mao's economic and political goals might be attained?

3. How did Mao and his lieutenants carry out the indoctrination and training of the party cadres for the class struggle that was seen as the heart of the revolutionary movement, and how did Mao deal with intellectuals whose cooperation was needed to pursue the regime's economic and social aims?

## THE SEEDBED OF THE COMMUNIST REVOLUTION: THE PEASANTRY AND THE ANARCHO-COMMUNIST MOVEMENT

A significant forerunner of the Communist revolution was the anarchist movement that appeared in the early 1900s, a part of the radicalism that contributed to the downfall of the Qing dynasty in 1911. The first generation of anarchists were exiles who published extensively in Paris and Tokyo, especially between 1907 and 1910. They shared a great many assumptions with the other revolutionaries and reformers of their day: they were not an intellectually isolated fringe, though critics felt they were too idealistic. Men like Wu Zhihui (1865–1953), Liu Shipei (1884–1919), and Li Shizeng (1881–1973) offered a critique of authority and especially of imperial pretensions, a condemnation of China's cultural tradition (including Confucianism and the family), support for feminism, and a radical interpretation of liberty and equality. Although later Chinese anarchists specifically attacked Marxist notions of class struggle and proletarian hegemony, the first generation of anarchists were among those who introduced Marxism to China. Furthermore, they were the first to explore the possibility of a class-based revolution. Thus, although they tended to envision the whole of society rising up against the state and capitalism, in contrast to the elitism of most early twentieth-century Chinese revolutionaries, anarchists such as Liu Shipei analyzed the capacity of "oppressed" people to make revolution. He thought workers and peasants need not simply play supporting roles but could themselves lead and define the revolution.[1]

---

1. Cf. Mao on this point, in his Hunan report, pp. 408–409.

Anarchist interest in workers and peasants owed less to Marxism, however, than to Russian populism and European anarchism, which had been in vogue during the late nineteenth century. In retrospect, the anarchist appreciation of the peasants' capacity to support a revolution that would change the entire sociopolitical system, not just rebel against specific injustices, seems prescient. The following essay was probably written by Liu Shipei or by Liu together with his wife, He Zhen.

LIU SHIPEI: "ANARCHIST REVOLUTION AND PEASANT REVOLUTION"

Liu Shipei's essay reflects the intermingling of anarchist and communist ideas in the early revolutionary movement, as well as the importance of the peasantry as the main proletarian force in China, drawing on the peasants' capacity for broad cooperative organization.

What methods can those who want to spread anarchist revolution in China really adopt? This is truly the biggest question of the day. We can try to analyze it by noting that if Chinese peasants really revolt, this will accomplish anarchist revolution. Therefore, the anarchist revolution must start with peasant revolution. "Peasant revolution" is simply a matter of resistance to taxes and opposition to the government and landlords. Let us list its causes below.

1. Landlords comprise the majority of China's big capitalists. When the landlord system is overthrown, the majority of the capitalist class will have been overthrown, and so resistance to the landlords constitutes resistance to most of the capitalists.

2. Peasants comprise the majority of China's people. A peasant revolution would constitute a revolution of the majority of the people of the whole nation. Results would quickly be obtained from the resistance of the majority to a minority.

3. The land tax comprises the main part of the revenue of the Chinese government. If the peasants refuse to pay taxes, the government would lose the main part of its annual income, it would certainly be unable to maintain itself, and the collapse of the government would be easy to bring about.

4. The basis of a communitarian property system must begin with the sharing of land. Since most of the land is farms, if the peasants just put a system of sharing the land into effect, then it will be easy to institute a communist system of property.

The above points are in truth easy to understand; further comments are not necessary to explain them. However, opponents of these theories think that Chinese peasants lack the predisposition to form groups or the strength to resist, and even that peasants cannot understand anarcho-communism. They conclude that peasants do not have the wherewithal to make revolution. However, we can refute this influential attitude:

1. Peasants are prone to forming groups. The associations of the Chinese upper classes are all organized formalistically, while the associations of peasants are more natural. Look at the villages in any province. The number of households ranges from thousands to a few dozen. They treat each other as friends, and they help each other on occasions of trouble, just as in former times. If a family has an emergency, the whole village will come to help; if something unfair happens to one family, the whole village will make plans to help it. Moreover, the various jobs like dredging ponds and building roads are all managed through cooperative labor; people come together spontaneously. Even questions over whether to invite teachers in or to stage operas to thank the gods are settled by people assembling in public places (such as temples) to determine the general sentiment. If a thief comes to bother a family, everyone hurries to help when they beat the gong. When people are resisting the government's runners, they also get universal and instant assistance. When several villages are close together, people from the various villages join together to help each other; some form cooperative groups (the *baojia* falls into this category). These associations all stem from the attitude of sharing benefits and injuries.

Let us look at the urban population. Few people in a neighborhood may be well known to each other, but villagers live in the same place, and they overflow with love and concern for each other. It is therefore clear that of all the social classes in China, the one that is richest in the capacity for unification is the peasantry.

2. The peasantry includes anarchists. Peasants are people who have no faith in government, who think that rulership can be abolished. According to an ancient proverb, "We go to work when the sun rises, and we rest when the sun sets. We dig wells to drink, and we tend our fields to eat: what does the emperor have to do with us?" This demonstrates the traditional view of the peasants. Tao Qian's "Peach Blossom Spring" imagines the happiness of a people in a village beyond rulership. Liu Zongyuan's account "Hunchback Guo Plants a Tree" also warns against interfering with peasants.

This all proves that peasants detest being bothered. A common saying of peasants today has it that "good commoners will not see the faces of officials" and "without fear of officials, without fear of officiousness." Thus, aside from escaping rulership, the ideal shared by all peasants is to have nothing to do with the state. A proverb of Guizhou peasants goes: "Barking dogs will not rest when the government agent comes." The peasants of the Huainan region have a saying "When government agents arrive in the village, the commoners meet the king." Agents are the claws and fangs of government bureaus. As the people hate agents, they do not wish to fall under government supervision. In all of China's counties only rarely is even one portion of one field measured correctly, and many fields are kept off the tax rolls altogether. This shows how peasants escape from rulership. Moreover, in all the villages of the provinces of north China, countless people escape the census registration. There are several rural districts in the eastern parts of Fengtai and Shouzhou in Anhui province that have never paid their taxes. Officials from the highest to the lowest do not dare to enter this area. This represents the practice of anarchism. Therefore the peasants are the weakest element in the political thought of nationalism. Anarchism is equivalent to second nature for the peasants, and it is built out of ordinary customs.

3. The peasantry sustains a communist system. Although peasants possess land privately, aside from land, all of their other systems resemble communism. We have observed that in various villages in the Huainan region, people unite in order to dredge irrigation ponds. Then the ponds belong to everyone. . . . Aside from this, sometimes several families will share ownership of a cow. When we examine other provinces, most are like this. Moreover, when old cripples and childless couples live in a village, the villagers all give them help. In northern villages when a traveler spends the night, everyone offers him food and drink, which does not have to be repaid. In the provinces of the north and the southwest, in bad years the people without food divide up the grain stored by rich families. . . . In the past most people supported the poor. Surely this resembles a communist system being anciently practiced in the villages. . . .

4. The peasantry possesses the capacity for resistance. Let us examine Chinese history. Chen She led agricultural workers in revolt, Liu Xiu led peasants, and in the beginning of the Tang, Liu Heita, all of whose followers were peasants, revolted in Chang'an. This is clearly the case. Aside from this, during the Western Qin, refugees who made trouble were also all starving peasants. During the Ming, Deng Maoqi led a force of bond-servants in Fujian. During the disturbances at the end of the Ming, there was also an enormous number of starving peasants. More recently, the Nian bandits spread into all the northern provinces. However, all the memorials of Zeng Guofan and such men call them "bandit rebels" (*fei*) when they are assembled together and "farmer peasants" (*nong*) when they are scattered. This is another proof that revolutionaries emerge out of the peasantry. . . . All around China few of the attacks on officials and other big cases come at the hands of urbanites. It should be abundantly clear that the powers of resistance of the peasants vastly outweigh those of urbanites. . . .

If the revolution occurs, then it will tend to progress from small organizations to larger organizations, from minimal resistance to great resistance, and from primitive anarcho-communism to a high level of anarcho-communism. Since the peasants display a rich capacity for forming organizations, it is clear that their small organizations may easily become larger organizations. Since the peasants display the courage to resist the government, it is clear that their minor resistance movements may easily become major rebellions. Since anarcho-communism is already practiced in the villages, it is clear that anarcho-communism is most suitable for peasants. The beginning of this peasant revolution lies in the anarchist revolution. The methods of peasant revolution are:

a. Tax resistance. Peasants everywhere have banded together and sworn not to pay taxes. When tenant farmers get their own land, they no longer regard the fields as the landlord's. When the landlord demands the rent, they refuse. If he brings them up on charges, then when the government agents come to take them, they unite to resist them. Farmers who own their own fields also swear not to pay taxes. If the tax collectors come, they beat them; village heads and the like who demand payment are expelled. . . .

b. Grain theft. Vast quantities of grain are collected by major landlords in the villages [and] they wait to sell it in bad years to gain great profits. At this point the peasants break into their storehouses to divide up the grain.

When these methods are practiced, officials will inevitably send troops to suppress the peasants. But this is nothing to worry about. Why is this? The power of workers is concentrated, while the power of peasants is diffuse. Workers are assembled in a single city and a single factory, but since soldiers are concentrated in cities also, the bosses can easily bring in troops to suppress strikes. Peasants, however, are dispersed in their villages, and since there is nowhere to concentrate soldiers, the troops will always arrive late. . . . Even if several thousand soldiers are dispatched, they will have to be scattered among several districts, amounting to no more than ten soldiers per village. Moreover, the government offices and rich people in the cities will need military protection, thus further decreasing the military power that can be deployed against the peasants. . . .

Most soldiers today are recruited from the peasantry, and some of them maintain their community ties with the peasants. Who would be willing to fight his own people?

All this conclusively proves that the peasants can be victorious. . . . The result of the peasant revolution will therefore inevitably end in an anarchist world. As for what happens after the revolution, there are still two questions regarding the peasantry:

a. Communal ownership of land. When the revolution begins, tenants will escape from the shackles of the landlords, while those who farm their own land will escape from the fetters of the government. This is completely a system of individual ownership. Thus once the revolution is complete, then they will extend the system of primitive communism to the point where no one owns their own land but rather land is communal and finally labor is shared to produce commodities that will be shared equally. Please consult Kropotkin's "The Conquest of Bread" for a detailed description.

b. Agrarian reform. The agricultural methods used in China are extremely labor-intensive. Only by using scientific methods can labor be minimized and output maximized, greatly benefiting humankind. These methods can also be found in Kropotkin's "The Conquest of Bread." Please consult his "The creation of fields into factories" for a detailed explanation. ("If agriculture were reformed now, it would benefit only the capitalists, but if it is reformed in the future, the benefits will flow to the people.")

According to this essay, all our hope for the peasants is that they may rise up. "Sow seed — but let no tyrant reap the harvest!" — Shelley.

[*Hengbao*, in Ge et al., *Wuzhengfu*, pp. 158–162 — PZ]

### LI DAZHAO: THE VICTORY OF BOLSHEVISM

Li Dazhao (1888–1927) was a Beijing University professor and librarian who joined in the intellectual ferment that found expression in Chen Duxiu's *New Youth* magazine. He exerted an especially profound influence on his student and library assistant, the youthful Mao Zedong. Marxism had attracted comparatively little attention among Chinese, until the success of the October revolution inspired Li to hail it enthusiastically in this article for the November 15 issue of *New Youth* in 1918. Thereafter he launched a Marxist study club, from which recruits were drawn for the founding of the Communist Party in 1921. One of the cofounders of the party, along with Chen Duxiu, Li later was captured in a raid on the Soviet Embassy compound in Beijing and executed. Since Chen, the original chairman of the party, was subsequently expelled and disowned by it, Li came to be honored in his place and to be revered posthumously as the party's founding father.

Although not yet a convinced Marxist at this time, in this article Li bespeaks a widespread feeling of hope and expectation aroused by the Bolshevik revolution among Chinese bitterly disappointed with the outcome of the revolution of 1911. Note how he specifically acclaims it as a potent new religion offering messianic hope for the future.

"Victory! Victory! The Allies have been victorious! Surrender! Surrender! Germany has surrendered!" These words are on the national flags bedecking every doorway, they can be seen in color and can be distinctly heard in the intonation of every voice. . . .

But let us think carefully as small citizens of the world, to whom exactly does the present victory belong? Who has really surrendered? Whose is the achievement this time? And for whom do we celebrate? . . .

For the real cause of the ending of the war was not the vanquishing of the German military power by the Allied military power but the vanquishing of German militarism by German socialism. . . . The victory over German militarism does not belong to the Allied nations; even less does it belong to our factious military men who used participation in the war only as an excuse [for engaging in civil war], or to our opportunistic, cunningly manipulative politicians. It is the victory of humanitarianism, of pacifism; it is the victory of justice and liberty; it is the victory of democracy; it is the victory of socialism; it is the victory of Bolshevism [Chinese text inserts "Hohenzollern" by error]; it is the victory of the red flag; it is the victory of the labor class of the world; and it is the victory of the twentieth century's new tide. Rather than give Wilson and others the credit for this achievement, we should give the credit to Lenin [these names appear in romanization], Trotsky, Collontay [Alexandra Kollontai], to Liebknecht, Scheidemann, and to Marx. . . .

Bolshevism is the ideology of the Russian Bolsheviki. What kind of ideology is it? It is very difficult to explain it clearly in one sentence. If we look for the origin of the word, we see that it means "majority." An English reporter once asked Collontay, a heroine in that [Bolshevik] party, what the meaning of "Bolsheviki" was. The heroine answered . . . "Its meaning will be clear only if one looks at what they are doing." According to the explanation given by this heroine, then, "Bolsheviki means only what they are doing." But from the fact that this heroine had called herself a Revolutionary Socialist in western Europe, and a Bolshevika in eastern Europe, and from the things they have done, it is clear that their ideology is revolutionary socialism; their party is a revolutionary socialist party; and they follow the German socialist economist Marx as the founder of their doctrine. Their aim is to destroy the national boundaries that are obstacles to socialism at present and to destroy the system of production in which profit is monopolized by the capitalist. Indeed, the real cause of this war was also the destruction of national boundaries. Since the present national boundaries cannot contain the expansion of the system of production brought about by capitalism, and since the resources within each nation are inadequate for the expansion of its productive power, the capitalist nations all began depending on war to break down these boundaries, hoping to make of all parts of the globe one single, coordinated economic organ.

So far as the breaking down of national boundaries is concerned, the socialists are of the same opinion with them. But the purpose of the capitalist governments in this matter is to enable the middle class in their countries to gain benefits; they rely on world economic development by one class in the victor nations and not on mutual cooperation among humanitarian, reasonable organizations of the producers of the world. This war will cause such a victor nation to advance from the position of a great power to that of a world empire. The Bolsheviki saw through this point; therefore they vigorously protested and proclaimed that the present war is a war of the tsar, of the kaiser, of kings and emperors, that it is a war of capitalist governments, but it is not their war. Theirs is the war of classes, a war of all the world's proletariat and common people against the capitalists of the world. While they are opposed to war itself, they are at the same time not afraid of it. They hold that all men and women should work. All those who work should join a union, and there should be a central administrative soviet in each union. Such soviets then should organize all the governments of the world. There will be no congress, no parliament, no president, no prime minister, no cabinet, no legislature, and no rule. There will be only the joint soviets of labor, which will decide all matters. All enterprises will belong to those who work therein, and aside from this no other possessions will be allowed. They will unite the proletariat of the world, and create global freedom with their greatest, strongest power of resistance: first they will create a federation of European democracies, to serve as the foundation of a world federation. This is the ideology of the Bolsheviki. This is the new doctrine of the twentieth-century revolution.

In a report by Harold Williams in the *London Times*, Bolshevism is considered a mass movement. He compares it with early Christianity and finds two points of similarity: one is enthusiastic partisanship, the other is a tendency to revelation. He says, "Bolshevism is really a kind of mass movement, with characteristics of religion." . . . Not only the Russia of today but the whole world of the twentieth century probably cannot avoid being controlled by such religious power and swayed by such a mass movement. . . .

Whenever a disturbance in this worldwide social force occurs among the people, it will produce repercussions all over the earth, like storm clouds gathering before the wind and valleys echoing the mountains. In the course of such a world mass movement, all those dregs of history that can impede the progress of the new movement — such as emperors, nobles, warlords, bureaucrats, militarism, capitalism — will certainly be destroyed as though struck by a thunderbolt. Encountering this irresistible tide, these things will be swept away one by one. . . . Henceforth, all that one sees around him will be the triumphant banner of Bolshevism, and all that one hears around him will be Bolshevism's song of victory. The bell is rung for humanitarianism! The dawn of freedom has arrived! See the world of tomorrow; it assuredly will belong to the red flag! . . . The revolution in Russia is but the first fallen leaf warning the world of the approach of autumn. Although the word *Bolshevism* was created by the Russians, the spirit it embodies can be regarded as that of a common awakening in the heart of each individual among mankind of the twentieth century.

[Teng and Fairbank, *China's Response to the West*, pp. 246–249]

# MAO'S REVOLUTIONARY DOCTRINE

### REPORT ON AN INVESTIGATION OF THE HUNAN PEASANT MOVEMENT

Under the early leadership of Chen Duxiu the Chinese Communist Party followed a policy of collaboration with the Nationalists dictated by the Comintern. Since this ended in near disaster for the party in 1927 and brought about Chen's fall from leadership, Chen's writings and ideas do not figure prominently today in the orthodox tradition of Chinese Communist doctrine. By contrast, this report on the Hunan peasant movement by Mao Zedong (1893–1976), who was then of much less importance in the party hierarchy, came to be seen, after his rise to supremacy, as a document of the greatest significance to the development of the revolution.

After taking part in the formation of the Communist Party, Mao had been assigned in 1925 to the organizing of peasants in his native Hunan, where he became convinced of the enormous revolutionary potential of the peasantry. In this report, prepared early in 1927, Mao describes the methods used by the peasant associations and reveals with undisguised satisfaction the campaign of terror waged against local landlords and officials. These terror tactics became a feature of Mao's program of class warfare in areas taken over by the Red Army. Such a condoning of extremism is contrary to the dominant strain in Chinese thought, which favors moderation, compromise, and harmony, but has ample precedent in Chinese political practice and in peasant revolutions like the Taiping movement. Curiously enough, among the great deeds of the peasants that Mao lists (including the organizing of peasants' associations and cooperatives, tax reduction, price control, and so on) we find prohibitions on gambling, smoking opium, feasting, and drinking wine, which reflect the strain of native puritanism already encountered in Taiping teaching.

More significant is the relation of the party to the peasantry. Mao emphasizes the party's need to recognize the revolutionary potential of the peasants, but it is for the party, not the peasants themselves, to assume the leadership role. Peasant rebellions in the past had come to nothing because they lacked educated leadership and organization. This the party can now provide if it frees itself from academic ways of thinking taught in the new Western-style schools and identifies with the peasant mentality. Those ready to learn from the peasants, whatever their class origins (i.e., whether peasant themselves or not), can assume the leadership as the vanguard of the revolution, and it is this party vanguard that will be entitled to claim for itself the exclusive right to rule as the "dictatorship of the proletariat" (later spoken of as "the people").

In the passages that follow, there is ample evidence of Mao's capacity to see things through the eyes of the peasant, but there are signs also of the new revolutionary expectations proclaimed in the foregoing declaration by Li Dazhao.

## The Importance of the Peasant Problem

During my recent visit to Hunan[2] I conducted an investigation on the spot into the conditions in the five counties of Xiangtan, Xiangxiang, Hengshan, Liling, and Changsha. In the thirty-two days from January 4 to February 5, in villages

---

2. Hunan was then the storm center of the peasant movement in China. Unless otherwise noted, footnotes in these selections are from the official text. [Ed.]

and in county towns, I called together for fact-finding conferences experienced peasants and comrades working for the peasant movement, listened attentively to their reports, and collected a lot of material. Many of the hows and whys of the peasant movement were quite the reverse of what I had heard from the gentry in Hankou and Changsha. And many strange things there were that I had never seen or heard before. I think these conditions exist in many other places.

All kinds of arguments against the peasant movement must be speedily set right. The erroneous measures taken by the revolutionary authorities concerning the peasant movement must be speedily changed. Only thus can any good be done for the future of the revolution. For the rise of the present peasant movement is a colossal event. In a very short time, in China's central, southern, and northern provinces, several hundred million peasants will rise like a tornado or tempest, a force so extraordinarily swift and violent that no power, however great, will be able to suppress it. They will break all trammels that now bind them and rush forward along the road to liberation. They will send all imperialists, warlords, corrupt officials, local bullies, and bad gentry to their graves. All revolutionary parties and all revolutionary comrades will stand before them to be tested and to be accepted or rejected as they decide.

To march at their head and lead them? Or to follow at their rear, gesticulating at them and criticizing them? Or to face them as opponents?

Every Chinese is free to choose among the three alternatives, but circumstances demand that a quick choice be made. [pp. 21–22]

### Down with the Local Bullies and Bad Gentry!

All Power to the Peasant Association!

The peasants attack as their main targets the local bullies and bad gentry and the lawless landlords, hitting in passing against patriarchal ideologies and institutions, corrupt officials in the cities, and evil customs in the rural areas. In force and momentum, the attack is like a tempest or hurricane; those who submit to it survive and those who resist it perish.

### "An Awful Mess!" and "Very Good Indeed!"

The revolt of the peasants in the countryside disturbed the sweet dreams of the gentry. When news about the countryside reached the cities, the gentry there immediately burst into an uproar. When I first arrived in Changsha, I met people from various circles and picked up a good deal of street gossip. From the middle strata upward to the right-wingers of the Nationalists, there was not a single person who did not summarize the whole thing in one phrase: "An awful mess!" . . .

But the fact is . . . that the broad peasant masses have risen to fulfill their historic mission, that the democratic forces in the rural areas have risen to overthrow the rural feudal power. [pp. 23–25]

## The Question of "Going Too Far"

There is another section of people who say, "Although the peasant association ought to be formed, it has gone rather too far in its present actions." This is the opinion of the middle-of-the-roaders. But . . .

The opinion of this group, reasonable on the surface, is erroneous at bottom.

First, the things described above have all been the inevitable results of the doings of the local bullies and bad gentry and lawless landlords themselves.

Second, a revolution is not the same as inviting people to dinner, or writing an essay, or painting a picture, or doing fancy needlework; it cannot be anything so refined, so calm and gentle, or so mild, kind, courteous, restrained, and magnanimous.[3] A revolution is an uprising, an act of violence whereby one class overthrows another. A rural revolution is a revolution by which the peasantry overthrows the authority of the feudal landlord class. If the peasants do not use the maximum of their strength, they can never overthrow the authority of the landlords, which has been deeply rooted for thousands of years. In the rural areas, there must be a great fervent revolutionary upsurge, which alone can arouse hundreds and thousands of the people to form a great force. [pp. 26–27]

## Vanguard of the Revolution

The main force in the countryside that has always put up the bitterest fight is the poor peasants. Throughout both the period of underground organization and that of open organization, the poor peasants have fought militantly all along. They accept most willingly the leadership of the Communist Party. [p. 31]

## Overthrowing the Clan Authority of the Elders and Ancestral Temples, the Theocratic Authority of the City Gods and Local Deities, and the Masculine Authority of the Husbands

A man in China is usually subjected to the domination of three systems of authority: (1) the system of the state (political authority), ranging from the national, provincial, and county government to the township government; (2) the system of the clan (clan authority), ranging from the central and branch ancestral temples to the head of the household; and (3) the system of gods and

---

3. These were the virtues of Confucius, as described by one of his disciples.

spirits (theocratic authority), including the system of the netherworld ranging from the King of Hell to the city gods and local deities, and that of supernatural beings ranging from the Emperor of Heaven to all kinds of gods and spirits. As to women, apart from being dominated by the three systems mentioned above, they are further dominated by men (the authority of the husband). These four kinds of authority — political authority, clan authority, theocratic authority, and the authority of the husband — represent the whole ideology and institution of feudalism and patriarchy and are the four great cords that have bound the Chinese people and particularly the peasants. We have already seen the peasants are overthrowing the political authority of the landlords in the countryside. The political authority of the landlords is the backbone of all other systems of authority. Where it has already been overthrown, clan authority, theocratic authority, and the authority of the husband are all beginning to totter.

Theocratic authority begins to totter everywhere as the peasant movement develops. In many places the peasant associations have taken over the temples of the gods as their offices. Everywhere they advocate the appropriation of temple properties to maintain peasant schools and to defray association expenses, calling this "public revenue from superstition." . . . In places where the power of the peasants is predominant, only the older peasants and the women still believe in gods, while the young and middle-aged peasants no longer do so. Since it is the young and middle-aged peasants who are in control of the peasant association, the movement to overthrow theocratic authority and eradicate superstition is going on everywhere.

As to the authority of the husband, it has always been comparatively weak among the poor peasants, because the poor peasant women, compelled for financial reasons to take more part in manual work than women of the wealthier classes, have obtained more right to speak and more power to make decisions in family affairs. In recent years the rural economy has become even more bankrupt and the basic condition for men's domination over women has already been undermined. And now, with the rise of the peasant movement, women in many places have set out immediately to organize the rural women's association; the opportunity has come for them to lift up their heads, and the authority of the husband is tottering more and more every day. In a word, all feudal and patriarchal ideologies and institutions are tottering as the power of the peasants rises. [pp. 45–49]

## Cultural Movement

With the downfall of the power of the landlords in the rural areas, the peasants' cultural movement has begun. And so the peasants, who hitherto bitterly hated the schools, are now zealously organizing evening classes. The "foreign-style schools" were always unpopular with the peasants. In my student days I used to stand up for the "foreign-style schools" when, upon returning to my native place, I found the peasants objecting to them. I was myself identified with the "foreign-style students" and "foreign-style teachers" and always felt that the peasants were somehow wrong. It was during my six months in the countryside in 1925, when I was already a Communist and had adopted the Marxist viewpoint, that I realized I was mistaken and that the peasants' views were right. The teaching materials used in the real primary schools all dealt with city matters and were in no way adapted to the needs of the rural areas. . . . As a result, the peasants wanted old-style rather than modern schools — "Chinese classes," as they call them, rather than "foreign classes" — and they preferred the masters of the old-style school to the teachers in the primary schools.

Now the peasants are energetically organizing evening classes, which they call peasant schools. The county education boards wanted to use these public funds for establishing primary schools, that is, "foreign-style schools" not adapted to the needs of the peasants, while the peasants wanted to use them for peasant schools. . . . As a result of the growth of the peasant movement, the cultural level of the peasants has risen rapidly. [pp. 56–57]

[Mao, *Selected Works*, 1:21–57]

THE QUESTION OF LAND REDISTRIBUTION

The Chinese Communist Party viewed relations between landlords and tenants as the main contradiction in Chinese rural areas. When Mao and his Red Army established their own government in a mountainous region in central China, they immediately tackled the issue of land distribution. This issue has concerned Chinese thinkers and officials for millennia, and the Chinese Communist Party's efforts resonate with features of earlier plans and designs for land redistribution. In the long run, the significance of the so-called land reform movement lay less in giving land to the peasants (since eventually they had to surrender it to the collectives and communes) than in the techniques of class warfare and political mobilization developed in these campaigns on the local level.

There are a few methods for distributing land. The major one is equal redistribution per capita. Only 20 percent of the land in the county was not redistributed. Of the land already redistributed, 80 percent of the land was reallotted on the basis of equal redistribution per capita, regardless of age or gender. At the beginning of the land struggle, no law existed that could be applied to this situation. The Xunwu County Revolutionary Committee (the county government) suggested the following four methods, asking that the district and township soviets summon mass meetings to discuss and choose one method:

1. Equal redistribution per capita.
2. Redistribution according to productivity. Those who have greater produc-

tivity receive more land and those who have less productivity receive less land. In other words, anyone over 4 years old and under 55 is regarded as one labor unit and receives one share; those who are under 4 or over 55 receive only one-half share.

3. Redistribution according to financial resources. Artisans get less land, and those who do not have an occupation get more.

4. Redistribution according to soil fertility. Those who receive poorer lands receive more; those who get fertile lands get less.

In the event, most places chose the first method. Later on, the Xunwu County Communist Party applied the first method to all districts and was supported by the majority of the poor peasants and the masses. At present about 80 percent of the areas that redistributed land used this method. Within these areas, regardless of age, gender, or productivity, the total amount of land was divided by the number of persons. Some villages did not redistribute the land to people under four. Among those over four years old, regardless of their productivity, some got a 50 percent share or a 70 percent share, the rest received a full share. This was the method practiced in Liuche, Fengshan, Shangqi, and Datong townships, which have a population of about 10,000.

Some areas redistributed the land equally by the number of persons and then had those who were incapable of farming return part of their share to the soviet; this land was then added to the share of those with greater productivity. (The amount of shares returned were unequal; each person decided individually.) In the end, persons capable of greater physical labor got more land and those not as capable got less. This method is similar to the second method suggested by the county government. The difference is that peasants returned some part of the land of their own accord after the land was redistributed instead of redistributing the land according to productivity from the beginning. Longtu Township followed this method. In another township, Huangsha, a similar situation occurred, except this time the land was not returned by the peasants on their own accord. When the government saw that some people could not farm the land they had received, it ordered them to return part of the land to the government. The peasants did not complain when asked to return part of the land unless the government forced them to return the fertile part and would not let them return the poor part, then they got upset. The combined population of Longtu and Huangsha is 2,500.

[Mao, *Report from Xunwu*, pp. 197–199]

## THE CHINESE REVOLUTION AND THE CHINESE COMMUNIST PARTY

Along with *On New Democracy*, which appeared soon after it (January 1940), *The Chinese Revolution and the Chinese Communist Party* (December 1939) is one of two basic texts prepared by Mao to provide a definitive interpretation of the nature and aims of the revolution. Together they represent an adroit analysis of the party's situation and the strategy to be pursued in the achievement of its objectives, presented in the simple catechetical style, the vigorous and unadorned prose, that are so characteristic of Mao's direct approach to mass indoctrination.

Much had happened since Mao's early days as a peasant organizer in Hunan, when he had become fired with enthusiasm for the revolutionary potentialities of the peasant masses. The lesson of early defeats and disappointments in Hunan and long experience as a practicing revolutionary leader, both in the Jiangxi Soviet and on the Long March to Yan'an, are reflected in Mao's analysis of revolutionary strategy. He had devoted much attention to military matters in the early years at Yan'an and had expressed himself at great length on such problems as guerrilla warfare, military tactics, revolutionary objectives, mass organization and discipline. Some of his main points are summarized in the selections that follow.

At the same time, Mao had been devoting himself to intensive study of Marxism-Leninism and the writings of Stalin. He had prepared texts setting forth the chief theoretical tenets of Communist orthodoxy, and he had given much attention to the proper interpretation of Chinese history and the nature of the Chinese revolution in "orthodox" terms. Indications of this, including Mao's acceptance of Stalin's periodization of Chinese history according to the classical Western pattern (from primitive communism, to slavery, to feudalism, to capitalism) rather than Marx's differentiation of it as a peculiarly Asiatic or Oriental society, are found in the writings below. They present first Mao's view of Chinese history, his characterization of the revolution, and his analysis of revolutionary strategy. Following those sections are passages from *On New Democracy*, stating the political and economic program that Mao had formulated for this stage in the revolution.

It should be remembered that these two works were written in the middle phase of the second United Front period, supposedly based on collaboration with the Nationalists against the Japanese. With the conclusion of the Moscow-Berlin Pact, signalizing Stalin's accommodation of the Axis powers, the struggle against Japan no longer rated such a high priority. Mao, though still eager to exploit anti-Japanese feeling, felt less of a need to work closely with the Nationalists in the "anti-imperialist" struggle. Accordingly, he placed greater stress on the revolution within China and on the Communist Party's leadership of it, as over against the Nationalists.

## The Chinese Nation

Developing along the same lines as many other nations of the world, the Chinese nation (chiefly the Hans) first went through some tens of thousands of years of life in classless primitive communes. Up to now approximately four thousand years have passed since the collapse of the primitive communes and the transition to class society, first slave society and then feudalism. In the history of Chinese civilization, agriculture and handicraft have always been known as highly developed; many great thinkers, scientists, military experts, men of letters, and artists have flourished, and there is a rich store of classical works. The compass was invented in China very long ago. The art of papermaking was discovered as early as eighteen hundred years ago. Block printing was invented thirteen hundred years ago. In addition, movable type was invented eight hundred years ago. Gunpowder was used in China earlier than in Europe. China, with a recorded history of almost four thousand years, is therefore one of the oldest civilized countries in the world.

The Chinese nation is famous throughout the world not only for its stamina and industriousness but also as a freedom-loving people with a rich revolutionary tradition. . . . In thousands of years of the history of the Hans, there have been hundreds of peasant insurrections, great or small, against the regime of darkness imposed by the landlords and nobility. . . . So the Chinese nation is also a nation with a glorious revolutionary tradition and a splendid historical heritage. [pp. 73–74]

## Ancient Feudal Society

Although China is a great nation with a vast territory, an immense population, a long history, a rich revolutionary tradition, and a splendid historical heritage, yet it remained sluggish in its economic, political, and cultural development after its transition from the slave system into the feudal system. This feudal system, beginning from the Zhou and Qin dynasties, lasted about 3,000 years. [p. 74]

The extreme poverty and backwardness of the peasants resulting from ruthless exploitation and oppression by the landlord class is the basic reason why China's economy and social life has remained stagnant for thousands of years. . . . [Moreover], since neither new productive forces, nor new relations of production, nor a new class force, nor an advanced political party existed in those days, and consequently peasant uprisings and wars lacked correct leadership as is given by the proletariat and the Communist Party today, the peasant revolutions invariably failed. . . . Thus, although some social progress was made after each great peasant revolutionary struggle, the feudal economic relations and feudal political system remained basically unchanged.

Only in the last hundred years did fresh changes take place. [pp. 75–76]

## Present-Day Colonial, Semi-Colonial, and Semi-Feudal Society

It was not until the middle of the nineteenth century that great internal changes took place in China as a result of the penetration of foreign capitalism.

As China's feudal society developed its commodity economy and so carried within itself the embryo of capitalism, China would of herself have developed slowly into capitalist society even if there had been no influence of foreign capitalism. The penetration of foreign capitalism accelerated this development. [pp. 76–77]

Yet this fresh change represented by the emergence and development of capitalism constitutes only one aspect of the change that has taken place since imperialistic penetration into China. There is another aspect that coexists with it as well as hampers it, namely, the collusion of foreign imperialism with China's feudal forces to arrest the development of Chinese capitalism. [p. 78]

The contradiction between imperialism and the Chinese nation and the contradiction between feudalism and the great masses of the people are the principle contradictions in modern Chinese society. . . . [pp. 81–82]

## The Chinese Revolution

The national revolutionary struggle of the Chinese people has a history of exactly one hundred years dating from the Opium War of 1840, and of thirty years dating from the revolution of 1911. As this revolution has not yet run its full course and there has not yet been any signal achievement with regard to the revolutionary tasks, it is still necessary for all the Chinese people, and above all the Chinese Communist Party, to assume the responsibility for a resolute fight. [pp. 82–83]

Since the character of present-day Chinese society is colonial, semi-colonial, and semi-feudal, then what after all are our chief targets or enemies at this stage of the Chinese revolution?

They are none other than imperialism and feudalism, namely, the bourgeoisie of the imperialist countries and the landlord class at home. . . .

Since Japan's armed invasion of China, the principal enemies of the Chinese revolution have been Japanese imperialism and all the collaborators and reactionaries who are in collusion with it, who have either openly capitulated or are prepared to capitulate.

The Chinese bourgeoisie, also actually oppressed by imperialism, once led revolutionary struggles; it played a principal leading role, for instance, in the revolution of 1911 and also joined such revolutionary struggles as the Northern Expedition and the present Anti-Japanese War. In the long period from 1927 to 1937, however, the upper stratum of the bourgeoisie, as represented by the reactionary bloc of the Nationalists, was in league with imperialism and formed a reactionary alliance with the landlord class, turning against the friends who had helped it — the Communist Party, the proletariat, the peasantry, and other sections of the petty bourgeoisie, betraying the Chinese revolution and thereby causing its defeat. [pp. 83–84]

Confronted with such enemies, the Chinese revolution must, so far as its principal means or the principal form is concerned, be an armed rather than a peaceful one. This is because our enemy makes it impossible for the Chinese people, deprived of all political freedoms and rights, to take any peaceful political action. Stalin said, "In China, armed revolution is fighting against armed counterrevolution. This is one of the peculiarities and one of the advantages of the Chinese revolution."[4] This statement is a perfectly correct formulation. The view that belittles armed struggle, revolutionary war, guerrilla war, and army work is therefore incorrect.

In these circumstances, owing to the unevenness in China's economic development (not a unified capitalist economy), to the immensity of China's territory (which gives the revolutionary forces sufficient room to maneuver in), to the disunity inside China's counterrevolutionary camp (which is fraught with contradictions), and to the fact that the struggle of the peasants, the main force in the Chinese revolution, is led by the party of the proletariat, the Communist Party, a situation arises in which, on the one hand, the Chinese revolution can triumph first in the rural districts and, on the other hand, a state of unevenness is created in the revolution and the task of winning complete victory in the revolution becomes a protracted and arduous one. It is thus clear that the protracted revolutionary struggle conducted in such revolutionary base areas is chiefly a peasant guerrilla war led by the Chinese Communist Party.

However, to emphasize armed struggle does not mean giving up other forms of struggle; on the contrary, armed struggle will not succeed unless coordinated with other forms of struggle. And to emphasize the work in rural base areas does not mean giving up our work in the cities and in the vast rural districts under the enemy's rule; on the contrary, without the work in the cities and in other rural districts, the rural base areas will be isolated and the revolution will suffer defeat. Moreover, the capture of the cities now serving as the enemy's main bases is the final objective of the revolution, an objective that cannot be achieved without adequate work in the cities.

This shows clearly that it is impossible for the revolution to triumph in both the cities and the countryside unless the enemy's principal instrument for fighting the people — his armed forces — is destroyed. Thus besides annihilating enemy troops in war, it is important to work for their disintegration.

This shows clearly that in the Communist Party's propaganda and organizational work in the cities and the countryside long occupied by the enemy and dominated by the forces of reaction and darkness, we must adopt, instead of an impetuous and adventurist line, a line of hiding the crack forces, accumulating strength, and biding our time. In leading the people's struggle against the enemy we must adopt the tactics of advancing slowly but surely . . . ; vociferous cries and rash actions can never lead to success. [pp. 84–86]

[Mao, *Selected Works*, 3:73–86]

---

4. J. V. Stalin, *On the Perspective of the Revolution in China*, as translated in *Political Affairs* (New York, December 1950), p. 29.

## THE MASS LINE

This piece explains an important aspect of Chinese Communist Party governing technique known as the mass line. While maintaining the dominance of the Leninist party and eschewing democracy, the Chinese Communist Party nevertheless involved the people to some extent in the ruling of their base areas in places such as Jiangxi and Yan'an. The main emphasis is on the leadership group activating and mobilizing those who are indifferent or resistant, following Stalin's policies for the Bolshevization of the revolution.

1. There are two methods that must be employed in whatever work we do. One is to combine the general with the particular; the other is to combine the leadership with the masses.

2. In any task, if no general and widespread call is issued, the broad masses cannot be mobilized for action. But if persons in leading positions confine themselves to a general call — if they do not personally, in some of the units, participate deeply and concretely in the application of *this call*, make a breakthrough at some single point, gain experience, and afterward use this experience for guiding other units — then they will have no way of testing the correctness or of enriching the content of their general call, and there is the danger that nothing may come of it. . . . This is the method by which the leaders combine leading and learning. No one in a leading position is competent to give general guidance to all the units unless he has *studied concrete* individuals and events in *concrete* subordinate units. This method must be promoted everywhere so that leading cadres at all levels learn to apply it.

3. . . . However active the leading group may be, its activity will be transformed into fruitless effort by a handful of people unless combined with the activity of the broad masses. On the other hand, if the broad masses alone are active without a strong leading group to organize their activity properly, such activity cannot be sustained for long, or carried forward in the right direction, or raised to a high level. The masses in any given place are generally composed of three parts — the relatively active, the intermediate, and the relatively backward. *If we compare these three groups of people, then in general the two extremes are small, while the middle group is large.* The leaders must therefore be skilled in uniting the small number of active elements to form a leading group and must rely on this leading group to raise the level of the intermediate elements and to win over the backward elements. A leading group that is genuinely united and linked with the masses can be formed only gradually in the process of mass struggle, *such as in rectification or study campaigns*, and not in isolation from it. . . . In every organization, school, or army unit, whether large or small, we should give effect to the ninth of Stalin's conditions for the Bolshevization of the party, namely that regarding the establishment of a nucleus of leadership.

The criteria for such a leading group should be with the four that Dimitrov enumerated in his discussion of cadre policy — absolute devotion to the cause, contact with the masses, capacity for independent work, and observance of discipline. . . .

5. . . . Many comrades do not see the importance of, or are not good at, drawing together the activists to form a nucleus of leadership, and they do not see the importance of, or are not good at, linking this nucleus of leadership closely with the broad masses, and so their leadership becomes bureaucratic and divorced from the masses. . . . Many comrades rest content with making a general call with regard to a task and do not see the importance of, or are not good at, following it up immediately with particular and concrete guidance, and so their call remains on their lips, or on paper, or in the conference room, and their leadership becomes bureaucratic.

[Chinese Communist Party Central Committee directive, June 1943
(attributed to Mao)]

## ON NEW DEMOCRACY

According to the established Communist (Stalinist) view, China was following in the main the path of other societies from feudalism through a bourgeois-democratic revolution to a socialist revolution led by the proletariat. During the earlier period of the Nationalist-Communist collaboration, the latter acknowledged the "bourgeois" Nationalists as the main force of the so-called democratic revolution. In 1940, however, Mao was unwilling to grant such leadership to the Nationalists, even though he conceded that the "democratic" revolution had not yet been completed and the socialist revolution still waited upon it. His *On New Democracy* — based on Leninist and Stalinist doctrines concerning the nature of the bourgeois-democratic revolution in colonial and semi-colonial countries, and its relation to the anti-imperialist struggle led by the Soviet Union — was Mao's way of ensuring Communist ("proletarian") leadership for a new type of democratic revolution.

Politically the New Democracy bore little resemblance to Western democracy but conformed rather to Leninist "democratic centralism," which ensured Communist domination of a multi-class coalition. Economically it involved a moderate program of land reform and nationalization of key industries. It was this moderate program that led some Western observers to think of the Communists as simply "agrarian reformers." Yet Mao's writings make it abundantly clear that the Communists had no intention of sharing real power and every intention of pushing on to full socialism.

## The Chinese Revolution Is Part of the World Revolution

The historical feature of the Chinese revolution consists in the two steps to be taken, democracy and socialism, and the first step is now no longer democracy

in a general sense, but democracy of the Chinese type, a new and special type —
New Democracy. How, then, is this historical feature formed? Has it been in
existence for the past hundred years, or is it only of recent birth?

If we make only a brief study of the historical development of China and of
the world, we shall understand that this historical feature did not emerge as a
consequence of the Opium War but began to take shape only after the first
imperialist world war and the Russian October Revolution. [pp. 109–110]

After these events, the Chinese bourgeois-democratic revolution changes its
character and belongs to the category of the new bourgeois-democratic revolution and, so far as the revolutionary front is concerned, forms part of the
proletarian-socialist world revolution. [pp. 110–111]

This "world revolution" refers no longer to the old world revolution — for
the old bourgeois world revolution has long become a thing of the past — but
to a new world revolution, the socialist world revolution. Similarly, to form
"part" of the world revolution means to form no longer a part of the old bourgeois revolution but of the new socialist revolution. This is an exceedingly great
change unparalleled in the history of China and of the world.

This correct thesis propounded by the Chinese Communists is based on
Stalin's theory.

As early as 1918, Stalin wrote in an article commemorating the first anniversary of the October Revolution:

The great worldwide significance of the October Revolution chiefly consists in the fact that:

1. It has widened the scope of the national question and converted it
from the particular question of combating national oppression in Europe
into the general question of emancipating the oppressed peoples, colonies, and semi-colonies from imperialism.

2. It has opened up wide possibilities for their emancipation and the
right path toward it, has thereby greatly facilitated the cause of the emancipation of the oppressed peoples of the West and the East, and has drawn
them into the common current of the victorious struggle against
imperialism.

3. It has thereby erected a bridge between the socialist West and the
enslaved East, having created a new front of revolutions against world
imperialism, extending from the proletarians of the West, through the
Russian revolution to the oppressed peoples of the East.[5]

Since writing this article, Stalin has again and again expounded the theoretical proposition that revolutions in colonies and semi-colonies have already

---

5. J. V. Stalin, *Works*, English ed. (Moscow, 1953), 4:169–170.

departed from the old category and become part of the proletarian-socialist revolution. [pp. 112–13]

The first step in, or the stage of, this revolution is certainly not, and cannot be, the establishment of a capitalist society under the dictatorship of the Chinese bourgeoisie; on the contrary, the first stage is to end with the establishment of a new-democratic society under the joint dictatorship of all Chinese revolutionary classes headed by the Chinese proletariat. Then the revolution will develop into the second stage so that a socialist society can be established in China. [p. 115]

## New-Democratic Politics

As to the question of "political structure" [in the New Democracy], it is the question of the form of structure of political power, the form adopted by certain social classes in establishing their organs of political power to oppose their enemy and protect themselves. Without an adequate form of political power there would be nothing to represent the state. . . . But a system of really universal and equal suffrage, irrespective of sex, creed, property, or education, must be put into practice so that the organs of government elected can properly represent each revolutionary class according to its status in the state, express the people's will and direct revolutionary struggles, and embody the spirit of New Democracy. Such a system is democratic centralism.[6] Only a government of democratic centralism can fully express the will of all the revolutionary people and most powerfully fight the enemies of the revolution.

The state system — joint dictatorship of all revolutionary classes. The political structure — democratic centralism. This is new-democratic government; this is a republic of New Democracy, the republic of the anti-Japanese united front, the republic of the new Three People's Principles with the three cardinal policies, and the Republic of China true to its name. [p. 121]

## New-Democratic Economy

We must establish in China a republic that is politically new-democratic as well as economically new-democratic.

---

6. According to an earlier definition of Mao's, in his report "The Role of the Chinese Communist Party in the National War," democratic centralism in the party consists in the following principles: (1) that individuals must subordinate themselves to the organization; (2) that the minority must subordinate itself to the majority; (3) that the lower level must subordinate itself to the higher level; and (4) that the entire membership must subordinate itself to the Central Committee. "Whether in the army or in the local organizations, democracy within the party is meant to strengthen discipline and raise fighting capacity, not to weaken them" (*Selected Works* 2:254–255). [Ed.]

Big banks and big industrial and commercial enterprises shall be owned by this republic.

Enterprises, whether Chinese-owned or foreign-owned, that are monopolistic in character or that are on too large a scale for private management, such as banks, railways, and airlines, shall be operated by the state so that private capital cannot dominate the livelihood of the people. This is the main principle of the control of capital.

This was also a solemn statement contained in the Manifesto of the First National Congress of the Nationalists during the period of the Nationalist-Communist cooperation; this is the correct objective for the economic structure of the new-democratic republic under the leadership of the proletariat. The state-operated industries are socialist in character and constitute the leading force in the national economy as a whole; but this republic does not take over other forms of capitalist private property or forbid the development of capitalist production that "cannot dominate the livelihood of the people," for China's economy is still very backward.

This republic will adopt certain necessary measures to confiscate the land of landlords and distribute it to those peasants having no land or only a little land, carry out Dr. Sun Yat-sen's slogan of "land to the tillers," abolish the feudal relations in the rural areas, and turn the land into the private property of the peasants. In the rural areas, rich peasant economic activities will be tolerated. This is the line of "equalization of land ownership." The correct slogan for this line is "land to the tillers." In this stage, socialist agriculture is in general not yet to be established, though the various types of cooperative enterprises developed on the basis of "land to the tillers" will contain elements of socialism. [p. 122]

## New-Democratic Culture

A given culture is the ideological reflection of the politics and economy of a given society. There is in China an imperialist culture, which is a reflection of the control of imperialism over China politically and economically. This part of culture is advocated not only by the cultural organizations run directly by the imperialists in China but also by a number of shameless Chinese. All culture that contains a slave ideology belongs to this category. There is also in China a semi-feudal culture, which is a reflection of semi-feudal politics and economy and has as its representatives all those who, while opposing the new culture and new ideologies, advocate the worship of Confucius, the study of the Confucian canon, the old ethical code, and the old ideologies. Imperialist culture and semi-feudal culture are affectionate brothers, who have formed a reactionary cultural alliance to oppose China's new culture. This reactionary culture serves the imperialists and the feudal class and must be swept away. [p. 141]

### Some Errors on the Question of the Nature of Culture

So far as national culture is concerned, the guiding role is fulfilled by Communist ideology, and efforts should be made to disseminate socialism and communism among the working class and to educate, properly and methodically, the peasantry and other sections of the masses in socialism. [p. 152]

### A National, Scientific, and Mass Culture

New-democratic culture is national. It opposes imperialist oppression and upholds the dignity and independence of the Chinese nation. . . . China should absorb on a large scale the progressive cultures of foreign countries as an ingredient for her own culture; in the past we did not do enough work of this kind. We must absorb whatever we today find useful, not only from the present socialist or new-democratic cultures of other nations, but also from the older cultures of foreign countries, such as those of the various capitalist countries in the age of enlightenment. However, we must treat these foreign materials as we do our food, which should be chewed in the mouth, submitted to the working of the stomach and intestines, mixed with saliva, gastric juice, and intestinal secretions, and then separated into essence to be absorbed and waste matter to be discarded — only thus can food benefit our body; we should never swallow anything raw or absorb it uncritically. So-called wholesale Westernization[7] is a mistaken viewpoint. China has suffered a great deal in the past from the formalist absorption of foreign things. Likewise, in applying Marxism to China, Chinese Communists must fully and properly unite the universal truth of Marxism with the specific practice of the Chinese revolution; that is to say, the truth of Marxism must be integrated with the characteristics of the nation and given a definite national form before it can be useful; it must not be applied subjectively as a mere formula. . . .

Communists may form an anti-imperialist and anti-feudal united front for political action with certain idealists and even with religious followers, but we can never approve of their idealism or religious doctrines. A splendid ancient culture was created during the long period of China's feudal society. To clarify the process of development of this ancient culture, to throw away its feudal dross, and to absorb its democratic essence is a necessary condition for the development of our new national culture and for the increase of our national

---

7. A view advanced by a number of the Chinese bourgeois scholars completely enslaved by antiquated individualist bourgeois Western culture. They recommend so-called wholesale Westernization, which means "imitating the capitalist countries of Europe and America in everything."

self-confidence; but we should never absorb anything and everything uncritically. . . . [pp. 153–155]

[Mao, *Selected Works*, 3:109–155]

## The Twofold Task of the Chinese Revolution and the Chinese Communist Party

To complete China's bourgeois-democratic revolution (the new-democratic revolution) and to prepare to transform it into a socialist revolution when all the
necessary conditions are present — that is the sum total of the great and glorious
revolutionary task of the Communist Party of China. All members of the party
should strive for its accomplishment and should never give up halfway. Some
immature Communists think that we have only the task of the democratic
revolution at the present stage but not that of the socialist revolution at the
future stage; or that the present revolution or the agrarian revolution is in fact
the socialist revolution. It must be emphatically pointed out that both views are
erroneous. Every Communist must know that the whole Chinese revolutionary
movement led by the Chinese Communist Party is a complete revolutionary
movement embracing the two revolutionary stages, democratic and socialist,
which are two revolutionary processes differing in character, and that the socialist stage can be reached only after the democratic stage is completed. The
democratic revolution is the necessary preparation for the socialist revolution,
and the socialist revolution is the inevitable trend of the democratic revolution.
And the ultimate aim of all Communists is to strive for the final building of
socialist society and communist society.

[Mao, *Selected Works*, 3:100–101]

### THE DICTATORSHIP OF THE PEOPLE'S DEMOCRACY

*The Dictatorship of the People's Democracy* was written for the twenty-eighth anniversary of the Communist Party, July 1, 1949, on the eve of the complete conquest of
mainland China. In the main it conforms to the principles laid down in *On New
Democracy*, affirming that the new government would continue to represent a coalition
of classes under the proletarian leadership of the Communist Party. The present text
is noteworthy, however, for its clear definition of what democracy and dictatorship
were to represent under the new regime — a definition based on concepts set forth by
Lenin much earlier.

After a historical résumé demonstrating the indispensability of Marxism-Leninism
and Communist leadership to the Chinese revolution, Mao takes up hypothetical
objections to Communism and answers them in his typical catechetical fashion. The
key question here concerns its dictatorial character, which Mao does not deny, and
the key distinction he draws is a political one, subsuming economic class distinctions,

between the "people" (those who accept Communist leadership) and the "reaction-aries" (those who do not).

## People's Democratic Dictatorship

"You are dictatorial." Dear sirs, you are right; that is exactly what we are. The experience of several decades, amassed by the Chinese people, tells us to carry out the people's democratic dictatorship. That is, the right of reactionaries to voice their opinions must be abolished and only the people are allowed to have the right of voicing their opinions.

Who are the "people"? At the present stage in China, they are the working class, the peasant class, the petty bourgeoisie, and national bourgeoisie. Under the leadership of the working class and the Communist Party, these classes unite together to form their own state and elect their own government [so as to] carry out a dictatorship over the lackeys of imperialism — landlord class, the bureau-cratic capitalist class, and the Nationalist reactionaries and their henchmen representing these classes — to suppress them, allowing them only to behave properly and not to talk and act wildly. If they talk and act wildly, their actions will be prohibited and punished immediately. The democratic system is to be carried out within the ranks of the people, giving them freedom of speech, assembly, and association. The right to vote is given only to the people and not to the reactionaries. These two aspects — namely, democracy among the people and dictatorship over the reactionaries — combine to form the people's demo-cratic dictatorship.

Why should it be done this way? Everybody clearly knows that otherwise the revolution would fail, and the people would meet with woe and the state would perish.

"Don't you want to eliminate state authority?" Yes, but we do not want it at present, we cannot want it at present. Why? Because imperialism still exists, the domestic reactionaries still exist, and classes in the country still exist. Our present task is to strengthen the apparatus of the people's state, which refers mainly to the people's army, people's police, and people's courts, for the defense of the country and the protection of the people's interests; and with this as a condition, to enable China to advance steadily, under the leadership of the working class and the Communist Party, from an agricultural to an industrial country, and from a new democratic to a socialist and communist society, to eliminate classes and to realize the state of universal fraternity. The army, po-lice, and courts of the state are instruments by which classes oppress classes. To the hostile classes the state apparatus is the instrument of oppression. It is violent and not "benevolent." "You are not benevolent." Just so. We decidedly will not exercise benevolence toward the reactionary acts of the reactionaries and re-actionary classes. Our benevolence applies only to the people, and not to the reactionary acts of the reactionaries and reactionary classes outside the people.

## Future of the Reactionaries

After their political regime is overthrown, the reactionary classes and the reactionary clique will also be given land and work and a means of living; they will be allowed to reeducate themselves into new persons through work, provided they do not rebel, disrupt, or sabotage. If they are unwilling to work, the people's state will compel them to work. Propaganda and educational work will also be carried out among them and, moreover, with care and adequacy, as we did among captured officers. This can also be called "benevolent administration," but we shall never forgive their reactionary acts and will never let their reactionary activity have the possibility of free development. . . .

The grave problem is that of educating the peasants. The peasants' economy is scattered. Judging by the experience of the Soviet Union, it requires a very long time and careful work to attain the socialization of agriculture. Without the socialization of agriculture, there will be no complete and consolidated socialism. And to carry out the socialization of agriculture a powerful industry with state-owned enterprises as the main component must be developed. The state of the people's democratic dictatorship must step by step solve this problem (of the industrialization of the country).

[Brandt, Schwartz, and Fairbank, *Documentary History*, pp. 456–458]

## Chapter 35

### CHINESE COMMUNIST PRAXIS

In addition to the clear projection of his revolutionary goals, Mao gave close attention to revolutionary education. Although the content of this education was mostly Leninist and Stalinist — and when he came to power a Stalinist curriculum largely replaced the so-called bourgeois education transplanted from the West in the first half of the century — the keynote of Mao's educational program was training and indoctrination for revolutionary class struggle. In that Mao consciously rejected Confucianism — and saw it (along with Western liberalism) as his nemesis to the bitter end of the Cultural Revolution in the late sixties and early seventies — his program for the ideological remolding of the Chinese people explicitly rejected Confucian humanist universalism and moral self-cultivation in favor of intense class consciousness and class struggle. Nevertheless, Mao's primary emphasis was on the training of leadership cadres, and even though this new elite was urged to keep in close touch with the masses, one can see how Mao's vision was refracted by significant inherited assumptions from the past — the crucial importance of moral education and the key role of trained leaders — as well as by influences from the more recent past, e.g., the renewing of the people in Liang Qichao's sense of their active participation in the political process (less prominent in traditional Confucianism).

Much of Mao's early success is attributable to the methodical and systematic way he went about the training and indoctrination of party cadres throughout the thirties and forties. And after the failure of his grandiose economic programs of the fifties, it was to the renewal and intensification of this naked revolutionary morality, stripped of all traditional culture, that Mao turned in a bootstrap effort to salvage his situation. Indeed, one can say, in the last years of the twentieth century, that the loss of this early revolutionary élan and discipline remains a key problem for Mao's successors in the Communist regime.

In this and the next chapter, along with the writings of Mao and his cohorts, we include certain counterpoints to their claims made by others who were skeptical of them, in order to show that all was not well at a time when much of the world was hearing only of Mao's successes. In this light, the latter may be seen primarily as the successes of a master of propaganda and systematic indoctrination: the "Great Teacher," as he was called.

### LIU SHAOQI: *HOW TO BE A GOOD COMMUNIST*

Liu Shaoqi (1900–1969), a veteran Communist who had joined the Party in 1921, the year of its founding, was one of Mao's closest coworkers and spoke with an authority second only to Mao's. When the People's Republic was established in 1949, Liu became vice-chairman of the Central People's Government, and after Mao relinquished the chairmanship in 1959, Liu succeeded to it. Subsequently, however, the two fell out, and Liu became a prime target of the Cultural Revolution.

*How to Be a Good Communist* was a basic text of indoctrination for party members, delivered first as a series of lectures in July 1939, at the Institute of Marxism-Leninism in Yan'an. It represents one aspect of the campaign for tightening party discipline and strengthening orthodoxy that was pressed in the late thirties and early forties in order to ensure the proper assimilation of new recruits, growing rapidly in number, and the maintenance of party unity along orthodox Leninist lines.

The original Chinese title of the work was literally translated as *The Cultivation of Communist Party Members*. Both the title and Liu's frequent reference to earlier Chinese concepts of self-cultivation suggest a link with Chinese tradition, most specifically with Neo-Confucian praxis based on the *Great Learning*, the *Mean*, and self-examination through quiet-sitting. Plainly, Liu aims to tap the moral idealism and self-discipline fostered by the preexisting tradition, but he also warns against the subjective individualism and spiritual autonomy implicit in the Neo-Confucian cultivation of sagehood. Hence his insistence that Communist self-criticism remain subject to group discipline and party authority. From this, self-criticism became an instrument of widespread repression and persecution in Chinese Communist Party ideological campaigns and the Cultural Revolution. For Liu, however, the passage ends on a note of complete faith in the perfecting of human society through the victory of Communism.

Comrades! In order to become the most faithful and best pupils of Marx, Engels, Lenin, and Stalin, we need to carry on cultivation in all aspects in the course of the long and great revolutionary struggle of the proletariat and the masses of the people. We need to carry on cultivation in the theories of Marxism-Leninism and in applying such theories in practice; cultivation in revolutionary strategy and tactics; cultivation in studying and dealing with various problems according to the standpoint and methods of Marxism-Leninism; cultivation in ideology and moral character; cultivation in party unity, inner-party struggle, and discipline; cultivation in hard work and in the style of work; cultivation in being skillful in dealing with different kinds of people and in associating with the masses of the people; and cultivation in various kinds of scientific knowledge, and so on. We are all Communist Party members, and so we have a general cultivation in common. But there exists a wide discrepancy today among our party members. Wide discrepancy exists among us in the level of political consciousness, in work, in position, in cultural level, in experience of struggle, and in social origin. Therefore, in addition to cultivation in general, we also need special cultivation for different groups and for individual comrades.

Accordingly, there should be different kinds of methods and forms of cultivation. For example, many of our comrades keep a diary in order to have a daily check on their work and thoughts, or they write down on small posters their personal defects and what they hope to achieve and put them up where they work or live, together with the photographs of persons they look up to, and ask comrades for criticism and supervision. In ancient China, there were many methods of cultivation. There was Zengzi,[1] who said, "I reflect on myself three times a day." The *Book of Odes* has it that one should cultivate oneself "as a lapidary cuts and files, carves and polishes." Another method was "to examine oneself by self-reflection" and to "write down some mottoes on the right-hand side of one's desk" or "on one's girdle" as daily reminders of rules of personal conduct. The Chinese scholars of the Confucian school had a number of methods for the cultivation of their body and mind. Every religion has various methods and forms of cultivation of its own. The "investigation of things, the extension of knowledge, sincerity of thought, the rectification of the heart, the cultivation of the person, the regulation of the family, the ordering well of the state and the making tranquil of the whole kingdom" as set forth in the *Great Learning*[2] also means the same. All this shows that in achieving one's progress one must make serious and energetic efforts to carry on self-cultivation and study. However, many of these methods and forms cannot be adopted by us because most of them are idealistic, formalistic, abstract, and divorced from social practice. These scholars and religious believers exaggerate the function of subjective initiative, thinking that so long as they keep their general "good

1. A disciple of Confucius. [Note in the original.]
2. The *Great Learning* is said to be "a Book handed down by the Confucian school, which forms the gate by which beginners enter into virtue." [Note in the original.]

intentions" and are devoted to silent prayer they will be able to change the existing state of affairs, change society, and change themselves under conditions separated from social and revolutionary practice. This is, of course, absurd. We cannot cultivate ourselves in this way. We are materialists, and our cultivation cannot be separated from practice.

What is important to us is that we must not under any circumstances isolate ourselves from the revolutionary struggles of different kinds of people and in different forms at a given moment and that we must, moreover, sum up historical revolutionary experience and learn humbly from this and put it into practice. That is to say, we must undertake self-cultivation and steel ourselves in the course of our own practice, basing ourselves on the experiences of past revolutionary practice, on the present concrete situation, and on new experiences. Our self-cultivation and steeling are for no other purpose than that of revolutionary practice. That is to say, we must modestly try to understand the standpoint, the method, and the spirit of Marxism-Leninism, and understand how Marx, Engels, Lenin, and Stalin dealt with people. And having understood these, we should immediately apply them to our own practice, i.e., in our own lives, words, deeds, and work. Moreover, we should stick to them and unreservedly correct and purge everything in our ideology that runs counter to them, thereby strengthening our own proletarian and Communist ideology and qualities. . . . At the same time, we must find out in what respects specific conclusions of Marxism-Leninism need to be supplemented, enriched, and developed on the basis of well-digested new experiences. That is to say, we must combine the universal truth of Marxism-Leninism with the concrete practice of the revolution. . . .

First of all, we must oppose and resolutely eliminate one of the biggest evils bequeathed to us by the education and learning in the old society — the separation of theory from practice. . . . Despite the fact that many people read over and over again books by ancient sages, they did things the sages would have been loath to do. Despite the fact that in everything they wrote or said they preached righteousness and morality, they acted like out-and-out robbers and harlots in everything they did. Some "high-ranking officials" issued orders for the reading of the Four Books and the Five Classics,[3] yet in their everyday administrative work they ruthlessly extorted exorbitant requisitions, ran amuck with corruption and killing, and did everything against righteousness and morality. Some people read the *Three People's Principles* over and over again and could recite the *Will of Dr. Sun Yat-sen*, yet they oppressed the people, opposed the nations who treated us on an equal footing, and went so far as to compro-

---

3. The Four Books and the Five Classics are nine classics of philosophy of the Confucian canon as defined in Neo-Confucianism and used in the imperial examination system. [Note in the original.]

430 REFORM AND REVOLUTION

mise with or surrender to the national enemy. Once a scholar of the old school told me himself that the only maxim of Confucius that he could observe was "To him food can never be too dainty; minced meat can never be too fine," adding that all the rest of the teachings of Confucius he could not observe and had never proposed to observe. Then why did they still want to carry on educational work and study the teachings of the sages? Apart from utilizing them for window-dressing purposes, their objects were (1) to make use of these teachings to oppress the exploited and make use of righteousness and morality for the purpose of hoodwinking and suppressing the culturally backward people; (2) to attempt thereby to secure better government jobs, make money and achieve fame, and reflect credit on their parents. Apart from these objects, their actions were not restricted by the sages' teachings. This was the attitude of the "men of letters" and "scholars" of the old society to the sages they "worshiped." Of course we Communist Party members cannot adopt such an attitude in studying Marxism-Leninism and the excellent and useful teachings bequeathed to us by our ancient sages. We must live up to what we say. We are honest and pure and we cannot deceive ourselves, the people, or our forefathers. This is an outstanding characteristic as well as a great merit of us Communist Party members. [pp. 15–18]

What is the most fundamental and common duty of us Communist Party members? As everybody knows, it is to establish communism, to transform the present world into a Communist world. Is a Communist world good or not? We all know that it is very good. In such a world there will be no exploiters, oppressors, landlords, capitalists, imperialists, or fascists. There will be no oppressed and exploited people, no darkness, ignorance, backwardness, and so on. In such a society, all human beings will become unselfish and intelligent Communists with a high level of culture and technique. The spirit of mutual assistance and mutual love will prevail among mankind. There will be no such irrational things as mutual deception, mutual antagonism, mutual slaughter and war, and so on. Such a society will, of course, be the best, the most beautiful, and the most advanced society in the history of mankind. . . . Here the question arises: Can Communist society be brought about? Our answer is "yes." About this, the whole theory of Marxism-Leninism offers a scientific explanation that leaves no room for doubt. . . . The victory of socialism in the USSR has also given us factual proof. Our duty is, therefore, to bring about at an early date this Communist society, the realization of which is inevitable in the history of mankind. . . .

At all times and on all questions, a Communist Party member should take into account the interests of the party as a whole and place the party's interests above his personal problems and interests. It is the highest principle of our party members that the Party's interests are supreme. [p. 31]

*In the following passages, quoted sayings are mostly from Confucian and Neo-Confucian sources, but by this time they survive in the collective memory only as traditional sayings without awareness of their exact provenance. They draw heavily on the Neo-Confucian ideal of heroic moral leadership.*

If a party member has only the interests and aims of the Party and communism in his ideology, if he has no personal aims and considerations independent of the Party's interests, and if he is really unbiased and unselfish, then he will be capable of the following:

1. He will be capable of possessing very good Communist ethics. Because he has a firm outlook, he "can both love and hate people." He can show loyalty to and ardent love for all his comrades, revolutionaries, and working people, help them unconditionally, treat them with equality, and never harm any one of them for the sake of his own interest. He can deal with them in a "faithful and forgiving" spirit and "put himself in the position of others." He can consider others' problems from their points of view and be considerate to them. "He will never do to others anything he would not like others to do to him." He can deal with the most vicious enemies of mankind in a most resolute manner and conduct a persistent struggle against the enemy for the purpose of defending the interests of the party, the class, and the emancipation of mankind. As the Chinese saying goes, "He will worry long before the rest of the world begins to worry, and he will rejoice only after the rest of the world has rejoiced."[4] Both in the Party and among the people he will be the first to suffer hardship and the last to enjoy himself. He never minds whether his conditions are better or worse than others', but he does mind as to whether he has done more revolutionary work than others or whether he has fought harder. In times of adversity, he will stand out courageously and unflinchingly, and in the face of difficulties he will demonstrate the greatest sense of responsibility. Therefore, he is capable of possessing the greatest firmness and moral courage to resist corruption by riches or honors, to resist tendencies to vacillate in spite of poverty and lowly status, and to refuse to yield in spite of threats or force.

2. He will also be capable of possessing the greatest courage. Since he is free from any selfishness whatever and has never done "anything against his conscience," he can expose his mistakes and shortcomings and boldly correct them in the same way as the sun and the moon emerge bright and full following a brief eclipse. He is "courageous because his is a just cause." He is never afraid of truth. He courageously upholds truth, expounds truth to others, and fights for truth. . . .

3. He will be best capable of acquiring the theory and method of Marxism-Leninism, viewing problems, and perceiving the real nature of the situation keenly and aptly. Because he has a firm and clear-cut class standpoint, he is

---

4. By Fan Zhongyan. See ch. 19.

free from personal worries and personal desires that may blur or distort his observation of things and understanding of truth. . . .

4. He will also be capable of being the most sincere, most candid, and happiest of men. Since he has no selfish desires and since he has nothing to conceal from the Party, "there is nothing that he is afraid of telling others," as the Chinese saying goes. Apart from the interests of the Party and of the revolution, he has no personal losses or gains or other things to worry about. . . . His work will be found in no way incompatible with the Party's interests no matter how many years later it is reviewed. He does not fear criticism from others, and he can courageously and sincerely criticize others. That is why he can be sincere, candid, and happy.

5. He will be capable of possessing the highest self-respect and self-esteem. For the interests of the Party and of the revolution, he can also be the most lenient, most tolerant, and most ready to compromise, and he will even endure, if necessary, various forms of humiliation and injustice without feeling hurt or bearing grudges. . . . But if for the sake of certain important aims of the Party and of the revolution he is required to endure insults, shoulder heavy burdens, and do work that he is reluctant to do, he will take up the most difficult and important work without the slightest hesitation and will not pass the buck.

A Communist Party member should possess all the greatest and noblest virtues of mankind. . . . Such ethics are not built upon the backward basis of safeguarding the interests of individuals or a small number of exploiters. They are built, on the contrary, upon the progressive basis of the interest of the proletariat, of the ultimate emancipation of mankind as a whole, of saving the world from destruction and of building a happy and beautiful Communist world. [pp. 32–34]

[Liu Shaoqi, *How to Be a Good Communist*, pp. 15–34]

## MAO ZEDONG: THE RECTIFICATION CAMPAIGN

### REPORT OF THE PROPAGANDA BUREAU OF THE CENTRAL COMMITTEE ON THE ZHENGFENG REFORM MOVEMENT, APRIL 1942

Eschewing the checks and balances used in democratic governments, Mao Zedong used the political campaign to check corruption or deviance within the party and government. The rectification (*zhengfeng*) campaign described here was the first of a long series of campaigns that would sweep through the nation after 1949. Mao's genius lay in his methodical approach to party organization and training, as well as his techniques of mass mobilization and indoctrination. His weakness lay in overconfidence in the efficacy of his own formulations and faith in the mere assertion of the revolutionary moral will. After initiating such rectification campaigns, he was often unable to control them once they started. The nation therefore underwent constant turmoil and chaos. The fear engendered by the campaigns created a mentality among officials to "lean to the left" to avoid criticism. In the end, these campaigns did little to check corruption and bureaucratism. Nevertheless, later in the eighties and early nineties many who had gone along with this kind of idealistic self-rectification looked back on this period as the "good old days" of self-sacrificing idealism.

Since July 1941, the resolutions of the Central Committee on the party spirit, investigation and research, and other resolutions, together with Comrade Mao Zedong's recent report condemning subjectivism, sectarianism, and party formalism, have caused a revolution in party thought and have served as a sharp weapon for the correction of the thought of cadres and party members and for the alteration of working styles. In order that cadres fully grasp the spirit and substance of the Central Committee resolutions and the report of Comrade Mao Zedong, and utilize these weapons in their work, it is necessary that they recognize the problem to be one of practical activity and long-term education in thought. The problem is not so simple that it can be resolved after one discussion. . . .

1. All organs and schools must engage in thorough research and lively debate on the Central Committee resolutions, Comrade Mao Zedong's report, and the other documents designated by the Central Committee. They should first of all gain a thorough comprehension of the spirit and substance of these documents and make them their weapon. With this object in view, all comrades must read each document, take notes, and afterward debate the separate documents or several documents together in small committees. When necessary, representatives of the Central Committee or representatives of this office will be dispatched to make reports. In reading and in debate, all must deliberate deeply and thoroughly, examining their own work and thought and their own life history in its entirety. In examining others, the procedure should also entail a complete examination of the man's past, so as to avoid harmful ex parte judgments. It is incorrect to calculatingly protect oneself and fail to speak out; it is also incorrect to avoid attacking one's own faults, while only attacking others. . . .

4. The objectives of research, discussion, and investigation are a thorough understanding of the contents of the Central Committee documents, the earnest and sincere reform of styles in education, the Party, and literature, the reconstruction of work, the consolidation of cadres, and the consolidation of the entire Party. Any discussion or activity contravening these objectives is incorrect. Thus, the attitude in discussion and criticism must be severe, thorough, and pointed. On the other hand, it must be sincere, straightforward, truthful, and based on fact. Cold ridicule and hidden invective, slander and calumny, abuse based on hearsay and exaggeration are all incorrect. During discussions,

Comrade Mao Zedong's warnings "Don't repeat past mistakes" and "Save men by curing their ills" should be constantly heeded. Of the comrades who commit errors, those who intend to correct themselves and progress should be encouraged and assisted, even though they are still unable to avoid error during the course of their advance. The slightest advance by a comrade should be welcomed as a starting point in the struggle for the completion of his progress. Comrades should be made to understand that it is with this objective that the weapon of criticism is used.

5. The time period for the study of documents designated by the Central Committee is stipulated to be three months for all organs and two months for schools.

[Adapted from Compton, *Mao's China*, pp. 1–5]

## WANG SHIWEI: "WILD LILY"

Wang Shiwei was a writer and translator at the main Chinese Communist Party base area at Yan'an. His views on young people differed dramatically from those of Liu Shaoqi expressed above. Although these views come out of the May 4 tradition and were popular at Yan'an, they were repressed in the Rectification Campaign. However, as early as the mid-fifties, it became clear that they prefigured student, especially college student, discontent with the party and government in the People's Republic of China.

Recently young people here in Yan'an seem to have lost some of their enthusiasm and to have become inwardly ill at ease.

Why is this? What is lacking in our lives? Some would answer that it is because we are badly nourished and short of vitamins. Others that it is because the ratio of men to women is eighteen to one and many young men are unable to find girlfriends. Or because life in Yan'an is dreary and lacks amusements.

There is some truth in all these answers. It is true that there is need for better food, for partners of the opposite sex, and for more interest in life. That is only natural. But one must also recognize that young people here in Yan'an came with a spirit of sacrifice to make revolution, and not for food, sex, and an enjoyable life. I cannot agree with those who say that their lack of enthusiasm, their inward disquiet even, are a result of our inability to resolve these problems. . . .

Young people should be treasured for their purity, their perceptiveness, their ardor, their courage, and their energy. They experience the darkness before others experience it, they see the filth before others see it; what others do not dare to say, they say. Because of this they are more critical, but this is by no means "grumbling." What they say is not always well balanced, but it is by no means "bawling." We should inquire into problems that give rise to "grumbling," "bawling," and "disquiet" and set about removing their causes in a rational way. (Yes, rational! It is completely untrue that young people are always engaged in "thoughtless clamor.") To say that Yan'an is superior to the "outside world," to tell young people not to "grumble," to describe Yan'an's dark side as some "slight disappointment" will solve no problems. Yes, Yan'an is superior to the "outside world," but it should and can be better still.

Of course young people are often hotheaded and impatient. . . . But if all young people were to be mature before their time, how desolate this world would be! In reality young people in Yan'an have already seen a great deal of the world. . . . So far from resenting "grumbling" of this sort, we should use it as a mirror in which to inspect ourselves. To say that youth "of student origin" are "coddled into adulthood, whispered to about life with love and warmth, and taught to imitate pure and beautiful emotions" is very subjectivist. Even though most Yan'an youth come from "a student background" or are "inexperienced" and have not "seen more than enough of life's hardships," most arrived in Yan'an after a whole series of struggles, and it is not true to say that they experienced nothing but "love and warmth"; on the contrary, it was precisely because they knew all about "hatred and cold" that they joined the revolutionary camp in the first place. From what the author of "Running Into Difficulties" says, all the young people in Yan'an were brought up pampered and only "grumble" because they miss their candied fruit. But it was because of "evil and coldness" that they came to Yan'an in search of "beauty and warmth," that they identified the "evil and coldness" here in Yan'an and insisted on "grumbling" about it in the hope of alerting people's attention and reducing it to a minimum.

[Wang Shiwei, "Wild Lily"]

LIU SHAOQI: "ON INNER-PARTY STRUGGLE"

This essay, delivered by Liu Shaoqi as a series of lectures to a party school in July 1941, is a kind of sequel to *How to Be a Good Communist* in the series of basic indoctrination texts used for tightening party organization and morale during the reform campaigns of the early forties. Where the earlier work focused upon the individual party member and his self-discipline, attention here is more on the relations among party members and their conduct within the organization. It is a question, then, of inner struggle for self-purification of the party, not of outward struggle for supremacy over others.

The dynamism of Chinese Communism in this early period owes no less to its concept of struggle both within and without the party than to its messianic promises for the future. As a means of keeping party members in a constant state of alertness, sensitive to the larger interests of the party rather than to their own, and as a method for overcoming the traditional weakness of hierarchical, bureaucratic organizations — factionalism and favoritism — this kind of ceaseless internal struggle was highly effective for a time, even if it exacted a heavy toll in the longer run. An essential Leninist feature was the insistence upon differences in principle as the only valid issues for such struggles. Actually, principled struggle proved far from peaceful, and serious factional infighting ensued.

## Introductory Remarks

Right from the day of its birth, our Party has never for a single moment lived in any environment but that of serious struggle. . . .

From the very day of its inception, our Party has struggled not only against enemies outside the Party but also against all kinds of hostile and nonproletarian influences inside the Party. These two kinds of struggle are different, but both are necessary and have a common class substance. If our Party did not carry on the latter type of struggle, if it did not struggle constantly within the Party against all undesirable tendencies, if it did not constantly purge the Party of every type of nonproletarian ideology and overcome both "left" and "right" opportunism, then such nonproletarian ideology and such "left" and "right" opportunism might gain ground in the Party and influence or even dominate our Party. . . . For example, it was in this manner that the Social-Democratic parties in Europe were corrupted by bourgeois ideology and transformed into political parties of a bourgeois type, thus becoming the main social pillars of the bourgeoisie.

Inner-party struggles consist principally of ideological struggles. The divergences and antagonisms among our comrades on matters of ideology and principle can develop into political splits within the Party, . . . but, in character and content, such divergences and antagonisms are basically ideological struggles.

Consequently, any inner-party struggle not involving divergences in matters of ideology and principle, and any conflict among party members not based on divergences in matters of principle, is a type of unprincipled struggle, a struggle without content. . . . It is detrimental and not beneficial to the Party. Every party member should strictly avoid such struggles. [pp. 2–4]

Comrade Stalin said:

> The question here is that contradictions can be overcome only by means of struggle for this or that principle, for defining the goal of this or that struggle, for choosing this or that method of struggle that may lead to the goal. We can and we must come to agreement with those within the Party who differ with us on questions of current policy, on questions of a purely practical character. But if these questions involve difference over principle, then no agreement, no "middle" line can save the cause. There is and there can be no "middle" line on questions of principle. The work of the Party must be based on either these or those principles. The "middle" line on questions of principle is a "line" that muddles up one's head, a "line" that covers up differences, a "line" of ideological degeneration of the Party, a "line" of ideological death of the Party. It is not our policy

to pursue such a "middle" line. It is the policy of a party that is declining and degenerating from day to day. Such a policy cannot but transform the Party into an empty bureaucratic organ, standing isolated from the working people and becoming a puppet unable to do anything. Such a road cannot be our road.

He added:

> Our Party has been strengthened on the basis of overcoming the contra-dictions within the Party. This explains the essential nature of inner-party struggle. [p. 5]

Many comrades did not understand that our inner-party struggle is a struggle over principle . . . for choosing this or that method of struggle that may lead to the goal.

These comrades did not understand that on questions of current policy, on questions of purely practical character, we can and must come to agreement with those within the Party who differ with us. They did not know or understand that on issues involving principle, on questions of defining the goal of our struggles and of choosing the methods of struggle needed to reach such goal they should wage an uncompromising struggle against those in the Party who hold divergent opinions; but on questions of current policy, on questions of a purely practical character, they should come to agreement with those within the Party who hold divergent opinions . . . so long as such questions do not involve any difference over principle. [p. 17]

## How to Conduct Inner-Party Struggle

Comrades! Now the question is very clear. It is how to conduct inner-party struggle correctly and appropriately.

On this question, the Communist Parties of the USSR and many other countries have much experience and so has the Chinese Party. Lenin and Stalin have issued many instructions and so has the Central Committee of our Party. . . .

In carrying out inner-party struggle we must first fully adopt the correct stand of the party, the unselfish stand of serving the interest of the party, of doing better work, and of helping other comrades to correct their mistakes and to gain a better understanding of the problems. . . .

Comrades must understand that only by first taking the correct stand oneself can one rectify the incorrect stand of others. Only by behaving properly oneself can one correct the misbehavior of others. The old saying has it: "One must first correct oneself before one can correct others." [pp. 55–56]

Second . . . in conducting inner-party struggle comrades must try their best to assume a sincere, frank, and positive educational attitude in order to achieve unity in ideology and principle. Only in cases where we have no alternative, when it is deemed imperative, may we adopt militant forms of struggle and apply organizational measures. All party organizations, within appropriate limits, have full right to draw organizational conclusions in regard to any party member who persists in his errors. . . . When we are eventually fully clear regarding ideology and principle, it is very easy for us to draw organizational conclusions if necessary. It does not take us a minute to expel party members or announce voluntary withdrawal from the party. [pp. 58–59]

Third, criticisms directed against party organizations or against comrades and their work must be appropriate and well regulated. Bolshevik self-criticism is conducted according to the Bolshevik yardstick. Excessive criticism, the exaggeration of others' errors, and indiscriminate name-calling are all incorrect . . . [p. 60]

Fourth, the holding of struggle meetings, either inside or outside the party, should in general be stopped. The various defects and errors should be pointed out in the course of summing up and reviewing work. We should first deal with "the case" and then with "the person." We must first make clear the facts, the points at issue, the nature, the seriousness, and the cause of the errors and defects, and only then point out who is responsible for these defects and errors and whose is the major responsibility and whose is the minor responsibility. [p. 61]

Fifth, every opportunity to appeal must be given to comrades who have been criticized or punished. . . . [p. 62]

On questions of ideology or principle, if agreement cannot be finally reached within the party organization after discussion, the matter may be settled by a majority decision. After that, the minority who still hold different opinions may have the right to reserve their opinions on condition that they absolutely abide by the decision of the majority in respect to organizational matters and in their activities. . . . [p. 63]

All in all, inner-party struggle is fundamentally a form of struggle and controversy over ideology and principles. Inside the Party everything must submit to reason, everything must be reasoned out, and everything must have some reason for it, otherwise it will not do. We can do anything without difficulty if we have reasoned it out.

Inside the Party we must cultivate the practice of submitting to reason. The yardstick for determining whether this or that reason is sound is [this]: the interests of the Party and the interests of the proletarian struggle; the subordination of the interests of the Party to those of the whole; and the subordination of the immediate interest to long-range interests. . . . [pp. 67–68]

Everything must submit to reason! It would not do if it didn't! It would not do either if we reason incorrectly! It would be even more undesirable if we indulge in empty talk! Of course, this is a rather difficult job. But only in this way can we become qualified as Bolsheviks. [p. 69]

[Liu Shaoqi, *On Inner-Party Struggle*, pp. 2–5, 17, 55–69]

## MAO ZEDONG: "COMBAT LIBERALISM"

If to Liu Shaoqi the essence of Marxism-Leninism lay in "principled struggle," to Mao Zedong the essence of liberalism was laxity in matters of principle. Liberalism he saw not as a political philosophy but as the want of one, a moral infection that arose from bourgeois individualism and produced selfishness, self-indulgence, slackness, a non-committal attitude, avoidance of struggle, and a desire for peace at any price. In this respect Mao's views resemble those of Chiang Kai-shek in *China's Destiny* (see chapter 32) (Mao's piece was actually written earlier, in September 1937), but they represent a much more severe and sweeping critique. Missing is Chiang's recognition that not all of Western liberalism conformed to this caricature of its weakness.

Ironically, Mao's position was enunciated during the early phase of the second United Front period. No doubt one of his purposes was to ensure that party members would not be contaminated and corrupted in the midst of collaboration with Westernized "liberals."

We advocate an active ideological struggle, because it is the weapon for achieving solidarity within the Party and the revolutionary organizations and making them fit to fight. Every Communist and revolutionary should take up this weapon.

But liberalism negates ideological struggle and advocates unprincipled peace, with the result that a decadent, philistine style in work has appeared and certain units and individuals in the Party and the revolutionary organizations have begun to degenerate politically.

Liberalism manifests itself in various ways.

Although the person concerned is clearly known to be in the wrong, yet because he is an old acquaintance, a fellow townsman, a school friend, a bosom companion, a loved one, an old colleague, or a former subordinate, one does not argue with him on the basis of principle but lets things slide in order to maintain peace and friendship. Or one touches lightly upon the matter without finding a thorough solution, so as to maintain harmony all around. As a result, harm is done to the organization as well as to the individual concerned. This is the first type of liberalism.

To indulge in irresponsible criticism in private, without making positive suggestions to the organization. To say nothing to people's faces but to gossip behind their backs; or to say nothing at a meeting but gossip after it. Not to care for the principle of collective life but only for unrestrained self-indulgence. This is the second type.

Things of no personal concern are put on the shelf; the less said the better about things that are clearly known to be wrong; to be cautious in order to save one's own skin, and anxious only to avoid reprimands. This is the third type.

To disobey orders and place personal opinions above everything. To demand special dispensation from the organization but to reject its discipline. This is the fourth type.

To engage in struggles and disputes against incorrect views, not for the sake of solidarity, progress, or improving the work but for personal attacks, letting off steam, venting personal grievances, or seeking revenge. This is the fifth type.

Not to dispute incorrect opinions on hearing them, and not even to report counterrevolutionary opinions on hearing them, but to tolerate them calmly as if nothing had happened. This is the sixth type.

Not to engage in propaganda and agitation, to make speeches or carry on investigations and inquiries among the masses, but to leave the masses alone, without any concern for their weal and woe; to forget that one is a Communist and to behave as if a Communist were merely an ordinary person. This is the seventh type.

Not to feel indignant at actions detrimental to the interests of the masses, not to dissuade or to stop the person responsible for them or to explain things to him, but to allow him to continue. This is the eighth type.

To work halfheartedly without a definite plan or direction; to work perfunctorily and let things drift. "So long as I remain a [Buddhist] monk, I go on tolling the bell." This is the ninth type.

To regard oneself as having performed meritorious service in the revolution and to put on the airs of a veteran; to be incapable of doing great things, yet to disdain minor tasks; to be careless in work and slack in study. This is the tenth type.

To be aware of one's own mistakes yet make no attempt to rectify them, and to adopt a liberal attitude toward oneself. This is the eleventh type.

We can name several more. But these eleven are the principal types.

All these are manifestations of liberalism.

In revolutionary organizations liberalism is extremely harmful. It is a corrosive that disrupts unity, undermines solidarity, induces inactivity, and creates dissension. It deprives the revolutionary ranks of compact organization and strict discipline, prevents policies from being thoroughly carried out, and divorces the organizations of the Party from the masses under their leadership. It is an extremely bad tendency.

Liberalism stems from the selfishness of the petty bourgeoisie, which puts personal interest foremost and the interests of the revolution in the second place, thus giving rise to ideological, political, and organizational liberalism.
. . .

Liberalism is a manifestation of opportunism and conflicts fundamentally with Marxism. It has a passive character and objectively has the effect of helping the enemy; thus the enemy welcomes its preservation in our midst. Such being its nature, there should be no place for it in the revolutionary ranks.

We must use the active spirit of Marxism to overcome liberalism with its passivity. A Communist should be frank, faithful, and active, looking upon the interests of the revolution as his very life and subordinating his personal interest to those of the revolution; he should, always and everywhere, adhere to correct principles and wage a tireless struggle against all incorrect ideas and actions so as to consolidate the collective life of the Party and strengthen the ties between the Party and the masses.

[Mao, *Selected Works*, 2:74–76]

## MAO ZEDONG: "ON ART AND LITERATURE"

The so-called *zhengfeng* movement of party "Rectification" gave particular attention to the reform of undesirable tendencies in the cultural sphere. In this speech made to a forum on literature and art in Yan'an in May 1942, Mao reasserts the orthodox Communist view that art and literature must serve the political ends of the revolution but insists that art cannot be mere propaganda. He acknowledges that aesthetic criteria are distinct from political ones, that political correctness is not enough in works of art, and that they fail if lacking in "artistic quality." He does not, however, pursue the question of how such quality is to be achieved in the aesthetic form if the ideological content is so rigidly controlled, and he suggests no remedy for the sterilizing effect that such control has usually had on artistic creativity.

Note the attention given to the special need of cadres, as an elite group, for works of art representing cultural "elevation" rather than mere popularization.

Comrades! We have met three times during this month. In the pursuit of truth, heated debates have taken place and scores of Party and non-Party comrades have spoken, laying bare the issues and making them concrete. I think this is very profitable to the whole artistic and literary movement.

In discussing any problem we should start from actual facts and not from definitions. We shall be following the wrong method if we first look up definitions of art and literature in the textbooks and then use them as criteria in determining the direction of the present artistic and literary movement or in judging the views and controversies that arise today. . . .

What, then, is the crux of our problems? I think our problems are basically those of working for the masses and of how to work for them. If these two problems are not solved, or [are] solved inadequately, our artists and writers will be ill-adapted to their circumstances and unfit for their tasks and will come up against a series of problems from within and without. My conclusion will center round these two problems, while touching upon some other problems related to them.

I

The first problem is: For whom are our art and literature intended?

This problem has, as a matter of fact, been solved long ago by Marxists, and especially by Lenin. As far back as 1905 Lenin emphatically pointed out that

our art and literature should "serve the millions upon millions of working people."⁵ [pp. 69–70]


## II


The question of "whom to serve" having been solved, the question of "how to
serve" comes up. To put it in the words of our comrades: Should we devote
ourselves to elevation or to popularization? [p. 75]

Though man's social life constitutes the only source for art and literature,
and is incomparably more vivid and richer than art and literature as such, the
people are not satisfied with the former alone and demand the latter. Why?
Because although both are beautiful, life as reflected in artistic works can and
ought to be on a higher level and of a greater power and better focused, more
typical, nearer the ideal, and therefore more universal than actual everyday life.
Revolutionary art and literature should create all kinds of characters on the
basis of actual life and help the masses to push history forward. For example,
on the one hand there are people suffering from hunger, cold, and oppression,
and on the other hand there are men exploiting and oppressing men — a contrast that exists everywhere and seems quite commonplace to people; artists and
writers, however, can create art and literature out of such daily occurrences by
organizing them, bringing them to a focal point, and making the contradictions
and struggles in them typical — create art and literature that can awaken and
arouse the masses and impel them to unite and struggle to change their environment. If there were no such art and literature, this task could not be fulfilled
or at least not effectively and speedily fulfilled.

What are popularization and elevation in art and literature? What is the
relation between the two? Works of popularization are simpler and plainer and
therefore more readily accepted by the broad masses of the people of today.
Works of a higher level are more polished and therefore more difficult to produce and less likely to win the ready acceptance of the broad masses of people
of today. The problem facing the workers, peasants, and soldiers today is this:
engaged in a ruthless and sanguinary struggle against the enemy, they remain
illiterate and uncultured as a result of the prolonged rule of the feudal and
bourgeois classes, and consequently they badly need a widespread campaign of
enlightenment, and they eagerly wish to have culture, knowledge, art, and literature that meet their immediate need and are readily acceptable to them so
as to heighten their passion for struggle and their confidence in victory, to
strengthen their solidarity, and thus to enable them to fight the enemy with one
heart and one mind. . . .

But popularization and elevation cannot be sharply separated. . . . The peo-

---

5. See Lenin, *The Party's Organization and the Party's Literature*. [Note in the original.]

ple need popularization, but along with it they need elevation too, elevation month by month and year by year. Popularization is popularization for the people, and elevation is elevation of the people. Such elevation does not take place in midair, nor behind closed doors, but on the basis of popularization. It is at once determined by popularization and gives direction to it. . . .

Besides the elevation that directly meets the need of the masses, there is the elevation that meets their need indirectly, namely, the elevation needed by the cadres. Being advanced members of the masses, the cadres are generally better educated than the masses, and art and literature of a higher level are entirely necessary to them; and it would be a mistake to ignore this. Anything done for the cadres is also entirely done for the masses, because it is only through the cadres that we can give education and guidance to the masses. [pp. 77–79]

## IV

One of the principal methods of struggle in the artistic and literary sphere is art and literary criticism. . . .

There are two criteria in art and literary criticism: political and artistic. According to the political criterion, all works are good that facilitate unity and resistance to Japan, that encourage the masses to be of one heart and one mind, and that oppose retrogression and promote progress; on the other hand, all works are bad that undermine unity and resistance to Japan, that sow dissension and discord among the masses, and that oppose progress and drag the people back. And how can we tell the good from the bad here — by the motive (subjective intention) or by the effect (social practice)? Idealists stress motive and ignore effect, while mechanical materialists stress effect and ignore motive; in contradistinction from either, we dialectical materialists insist on the unity of motive and effect of winning their approval, and we must unite the two. . . . In examining the subjective intention of an artist, i.e., whether his motive is correct and good, we do not look at his declaration but at the effect his activities (mainly his works) produce on society and the masses. Social practice and its effect are the criteria for examining the subjective intention or the motive. . . . According to the artistic criterion, all works are good or comparatively good that are relatively high in artistic quality and bad or comparatively bad that are relatively low in artistic quality. Of course, this distinction also depends on social effect. As there is hardly an artist who does not consider his own work excellent, our criticism ought to permit the free competition of all varieties of artistic works, but it is entirely necessary for us to pass correct judgments on them according to the criteria of the science of art, so that we can gradually raise the art of a lower level to a higher level, and to change the art that does not meet the requirements of the struggle of the broad masses into art that does meet them.

There is thus the political criterion as well as the artistic criterion. . . . But all classes in all class societies place the political criterion first and the artistic criterion second. The bourgeoisie always reject proletarian artistic and literary works, no matter how great their artistic achievement. As for the proletariat, they must treat the art and literature of the past according to their attitude toward the people and whether they are progressive in the light of history. Some things that are basically reactionary from the political point of view may yet be artistically good. But the more artistic such a work may be, the greater harm will it do to the people, and the more reason for us to reject it. The contradiction between reactionary political content and artistic form is a common characteristic of the art and literature of all exploiting classes in their decline. What we demand is unity of politics and art, of content and form and of revolutionary political content and the highest possible degree of perfection in artistic form. Works of art, however politically progressive, are powerless if they lack artistic quality. Therefore we are equally opposed to works with wrong political approaches and to the tendency toward so-called poster and slogan style that is correct only in political approach but lacks artistic power. We must carry on a two-front struggle in art and literature. [pp. 84–86]

[Mao, *Selected Works*, 4:69–86]

### WANG SHIWEI: "POLITICAL LEADERS, ARTISTS"

In February 1942 Wang Shiwei enthusiastically took up Mao's call for the rectification of the party and the government. In so doing, he sought to continue the independent role that intellectuals had first assumed during the New Culture Movement as critics of society and government. Although Wang was eventually purged and executed, Mao still looked to intellectuals to check the power of the bureaucracy in the abortive One Hundred Flowers Campaign of the mid-fifties.

There are two sides to the revolution: changing the social system and changing people. Political leaders are the revolution's strategists and tacticians; they unite, organize, and lead the revolution. Their main task is to transform the social system. Artists are the "engineers of the soul," and their main task is to transform people's heart, spirit, thinking, and consciousness.

The filth and darkness in people's souls are the product of an irrational social system, and the soul's fundamental transformation is impossible until the social system has been fundamentally transformed. In the process of transforming the social system, the soul too is transformed. . . . The tasks of the political leader and the artist are complementary.

The political leaders command the revolution's material forces; the artists arouse the revolution's spiritual forces. The political leaders are generally cool, collected people, good at waging practical struggles to eliminate filth and darkness, and to bring about cleanliness and light. The artists are generally more emotional and more sensitive, good at exposing filth and darkness, and at pointing out cleanliness and light. . . .

The political leaders understand that during the revolution the people in their camp will be less than perfect and things will rarely be done ideally. They take the broad view, making sure that the wheel of history advances and that the light wins. The artists, more passionate and more sensitive, long for people to be more lovable and things to be more splendid. When they write they take small things as their starting points: they hope to eliminate the darkness so far as they can so that the wheel of history can advance as fast as possible. As the practical transformers of the social system, the political leaders take things more seriously; the artists, as the soul's engineers, go even further in demanding perfection of people. In uniting, organizing, and leading the revolution and waging practical struggles, the political leaders are superior. But the artists are better at plunging into the depths of the soul to change it — transforming our side in order to strengthen it, and transforming the enemies so as to undermine them.

The political leaders and the artists each have their weak points. If the political leaders are to attack the enemy successfully, establish links with allied forces, and strengthen our side, they must understand human nature and the ways of the world, be masters of tricks and devices, and be skilled in making and breaking alliances. Their weakness springs from those very strengths. When they use them for the revolutionary cause, they become the most beautiful and exquisite "revolutionary art," but unless they are truly great political leaders they are bound to make use of them for their own fame, position, and interest, thus harming the revolution. In this respect we must insist that cat's claws be used only for catching rats and not for seizing chickens. Here we must distinguish political leaders from artists; and we must be ever on our guard against cats that are good not at catching rats but at taking chickens. The main weaknesses of most artists are pride, narrowness, isolation, inability to unite with others, and mutual suspicion and exclusion. Here we must ask the engineers of the soul to start by making their own souls clean and bright. This is hard and painful, but it is the only way to greatness. . . .

Lu Xun was a fighter all his life, but anyone who understands him will know that at heart he was lonely. He struggled because he recognized the laws of social development and believed that the future was bound to be better than the present; he was lonely because he saw that even in the souls of his own comrades there were filth and darkness. He knew that the task of transforming old China could only be carried out by the sons and daughters of old China, despite their filth and darkness. But his great heart could not help yearning for his comrades to be more lovable.

The revolutionary camp exists in old China, and the revolution's fighters have grown up in old China, which means that our souls are inevitably stained. The present revolution requires that we ally not only with the peasants and the urban petty bourgeoisie but with even more backward classes and strata, and that we make concessions to them, thus becoming contaminated with yet more filth and darkness. This makes the artist's task of transforming the soul even more important, difficult, and urgent. To boldly expose and wash away all that is filthy and dark is as important as praising the light, if not more important. Exposing and cleansing are not merely negative, because when darkness is eliminated the light can shine even brighter. Some people think that revolutionary artists must "direct their fire outside" and that if we expose our weakness we give the enemy easy targets. But this is a shortsighted view. Though our camp is now strong enough for us to have no fears about exposing our shortcomings, it is not yet fully consolidated; self-criticism is the best way of consolidating it. . . .

Some who think highly of themselves as political leaders smile sarcastically when they speak of artists. Others who pride themselves on being artists shrug their shoulders when they mention political leaders. But there is always some truth in objective reflections: each would do well to use the other as a mirror. They should not forget that they are both children of old China.

A truly great political leader must have a soul great enough to move the souls of others and cleanse them; thus a great political leader is a great artist. An artist who has a truly great soul is bound to have a part to play in uniting, organizing, and leading the forces of revolution; thus a great artist is also a great political leader.

Finally I would like to appeal warmly to artist comrades: be even more effective in transforming the soul, and aim in the first place at ourselves and our own camp. In China transforming the soul will have an even greater effect on transforming society. It will determine not only how soon but even whether the revolution succeeds.

[Wang Shiwei, "Political Leaders, Artists"]

## DING LING: "THOUGHTS ON MARCH 8, 1942"

Mao Zedong as a young man had been concerned with the plight of women, and Chinese Communist Party policy professed to bring about equality between men and women. The noted writer Ding Ling, however, took advantage of International Women's Day to point out the hypocritical attitudes and behavior of male party members and the special pressures on women revolutionaries. The article created much controversy and Ding herself became a target of criticism during the Rectification Campaign and later again in the Anti-Rightist Campaign and Cultural Revolution.

When will it no longer be necessary to attach special weight to the word *woman* and raise it specially?

Each year this day comes round. Every year on this day, meetings are held all over the world where women muster their forces. Even though things have not been as lively these last two years in Yan'an as they were in previous years, it appears that at least a few people are busy at work here. And there will certainly be a congress, speeches, circular telegrams, and articles.

Women in Yan'an are happier than women elsewhere in China. So much so that many people ask enviously, "How come the women comrades get so rosy and fat on millet?" It doesn't seem to surprise anyone that women make up a big proportion of the staff in the hospitals, sanatoria, and clinics, but they are inevitably the subject of conversation, as a fascinating problem, on every conceivable occasion.

Moreover, all kinds of women comrades are often the target of deserved criticism. In my view these reproaches are serious and justifiable.

People are always interested when women comrades get married, but that is not enough for them. It is virtually impossible for women comrades to get onto friendly terms with a man comrade, and even less likely for them to become friendly with more than one. Cartoonists ridicule them: "A departmental head getting married too?" The poets say, "All the leaders in Yan'an are horsemen, and none of them are artists. In Yan'an it's impossible for an artist to find a pretty sweetheart." But in other situations they are lectured: "Damn it, you look down on us old cadres and say we're country bumpkins. But if it weren't for us country bumpkins, you wouldn't be coming to Yan'an to eat millet!" But women invariably want to get married. (It's even more of a sin not to be married, and single women are more of a target for rumors and slanderous gossip.) So they can't afford to be choosy; anyone will do, whether he rides horses or wears straw sandals, whether he's an artist or a supervisor. They inevitably have children. The fate of such children is various. Some are wrapped in soft baby wool and patterned felt and looked after by governesses. Others are wrapped in soiled cloth and left crying in their parents' beds, while their parents consume much of the child allowance. But for this allowance (twenty-five yuan a month, or just over three pounds of pork), many of them would probably never get a taste of meat. Whoever they marry, the fact is that those women who are compelled to bear children will probably be publicly derided as "Noras who have returned home." Those women comrades in a position to employ governesses can go out once a week to a prim get-together and dance. Behind their backs there will also be the most incredible gossip and whispering campaigns, but as soon as they go somewhere, they cause a great stir and all eyes are glued to them. This has nothing to do with our theories, our doctrines, and the speeches we make at meetings. We all know this to be a fact, a fact that is right before our eyes, but it is never mentioned.

It is the same with divorce. In general there are three conditions to pay attention to when getting married: (1) political purity; (2) both parties should be more or less the same age and comparable in looks; (3) mutual help. Even though everyone is said to fulfill these conditions — as for point one, there are no open traitors in Yan'an; as for point three, you can call anything "mutual help," including darning socks, patching shoes, and even feminine comfort — everyone nevertheless makes a great show of giving thoughtful attention to them. And yet the pretext for divorce is invariably the wife's political backwardness. I am the first to admit that it is a shame when a man's wife is not progressive and retards his progress. But let us consider to what degree they are backward. Before marrying, they were inspired by the desire to soar in the heavenly heights and lead a life of bitter struggle. They got married partly because of physiological necessity and partly as a response to sweet talk about "mutual help." Thereupon they are forced to toil away and become "Noras returned home." Afraid of being thought "backward," those who are a bit more daring rush around begging nurseries to take their children. They ask for abortions and risk punishment and even death by secretly swallowing potions to produce abortions. But the answer comes back: "Isn't giving birth to children also work? You're just after an easy life; you want to be in the limelight. After all, what indispensable political works have you performed? Since you are so frightened of having children and are not willing to take responsibility once you have had them, why did you get married in the first place? No one forced you to." Under these conditions, it is impossible for women to escape this destiny of "backwardness." When women capable of working sacrifice their careers for the joys of motherhood, people always sing their praises. But after ten years or so, they have no way of escaping the tragedy of "backwardness." Even from my point of view, as a woman, there is nothing attractive about such "backward" elements. Their skin is beginning to wrinkle, their hair is growing thin, and fatigue is robbing them of their last traces of attractiveness. It should be self-evident that they are in a tragic situation. But whereas in the old society they would probably have been pitied and considered unfortunate, nowadays their tragedy is seen as something self-inflicted, as their just deserts. Is it not so that there is a discussion going on in legal circles as to whether divorces should be granted simply on the petition of one party or on the basis of mutual agreement? In the great majority of cases, it is the husband who petitions for divorce. For the wife to do so, she must be leading an immoral life, and then of course she deserves to be cursed.

I myself am a woman, and I therefore understand the failings of women better than others. But I also have a deeper understanding of what they suffer. Women are incapable of transcending the age they live in, of being perfect or of being hard as steel. They are incapable of resisting all the temptations of society or all the silent oppression they suffer here in Yan'an. They each have their own past written in blood and tears; they have experienced great emotions — in elation as in depression, whether engaged in the lone battle of life or drawn into the humdrum stream of life. This is even truer of the women comrades who come to Yan'an, and I therefore have much sympathy for those fallen and classified as criminals. What is more, I hope that men, especially those in top positions, as well as women themselves, will consider the mistakes women commit in their social context. It would be better if there were less empty theorizing and more talk about real problems, so that theory and practice would not be divorced, and better if all Communist Party members were more responsible for their own moral conduct. But we must also hope for a little more from our women comrades, especially those in Yan'an. We must urge ourselves on and develop our comradely feeling.

[Ding, *I Myself Am a Woman*, pp. 316–321]

*Chapter 36*

THE MAO REGIME

## ESTABLISHMENT OF THE PEOPLE'S REPUBLIC

In the early years of the People's Republic of China, the Communist Party unified the country militarily (except for Taiwan) and fought the United States to a standstill in Korea. Domestically, it distributed land to the peasants, accelerated industrialization, revamped education on the Soviet model, and passed a marriage law. After decades of war and chaos, peace reigned. Gangsters and drug pushers were executed; prostitutes and opium addicts were rehabilitated. Health care improved and some serious diseases were eradicated in the countryside. Infant mortality went down and life expectancy gradually rose. Patriotic Chinese educated abroad came home to participate in the reconstruction of the motherland. China became a nuclear power in 1964. In later years many people looked back nostalgically on the early days of the Mao regime, imagining it as a kind of Golden Age.

Yet there were a number of anomalies in the Communist success. Having operated for twenty years in the countryside, the Party, when it came to power, adopted the Soviet model rather than building a new order based upon peasant experience or the needs of Chinese agriculture. Although the party had ridden to power on the backs of a largely peasant army, it was the urban population that benefited the most from the policies of the new state. The term *iron rice bowl* described the cradle-to-grave support now enjoyed by a large percentage of the urban population. Many of the comrades who had sacrificed during the long years of struggle believed that now, in this new state, they were entitled to good positions and special privileges. At the same time, the party and government, now ruling the whole country, recruited new cadres on a massive scale. Many such recruits constituted a "new class," in a position to pass privileged educational, health care, and housing opportunities on to their children. Meanwhile, the party conducted one class-warfare campaign after another against landlords, reactionaries, traitors, and corrupt officials, creating an atmosphere of terror and intimidation. Much of the early goodwill and sense of security began to dissipate.

By the mid-fifties Mao had become increasingly dissatisfied, as agricultural production, counted on to support heavy industrialization, lagged. Peasants who had been glad to receive land of their own were much less eager to see it collectivized. Against the advice of fellow leaders who favored a more gradual approach, Mao pressed ahead, with the result that all farmland in China became collectivized in a remarkably short time.

Despite Mao's efforts to rein in intellectuals during the Rectification Campaign of the early forties, in the mid-fifties he still counted on them to play a role in the modernization of China. By 1957 he believed that the new regime was well established and that the majority of Chinese now accepted the socialist path. Intellectuals, he hoped, could serve as a check on corruption and privilege in the party, a concern that had originally arisen during the Rectification Campaign and now was vented again in the campaign to "Let a Hundred Flowers Bloom." Some leaders had approved the idea of opening up the party to criticism from the outside, but when criticism became vociferous and even turned anti-socialist, Mao turned on the intellectuals he had previously encouraged to speak out, purging at least 300,000 and sending them into internal exile.

Undeterred by either economic or political setbacks, Mao pressed ahead with the Great Leap Forward in order to jump-start more rapid industrialization. The movement promoted bootstrap efforts in the countryside, typified by "backyard furnaces" to boost steel production. Seeking to decentralize some of the power that had accumulated in Beijing but also to gain greater control over agricultural production, Mao began to turn the countryside into autarkic communes, declaring that China was on the verge of communism, a claim that had not even been made by the Soviet Union. As a result of this and other differences, China had a major falling-out with the Soviet Union by 1960, and the two sides almost went to war at the end of the decade. The Great Leap Forward, too, went awry; agricultural production declined further, distribution was uneven, and famine led to the deaths of tens of millions of peasants.

At this juncture new leadership under Liu Shaoqi and Deng Xiaoping came forward to espouse more-moderate policies: the expansion of private garden plots, the opening up of local markets, and the offering of material incentives for increased production. All notions of achieving full communism were shelved. Mao fumed against Liu and Deng, believing that their policies would lead to a restoration of capitalism in China. After much political maneuvering, Mao managed to launch his Great Proletarian Cultural Revolution of 1966 and called upon the students of China to lead it, bypassing and outflanking the party and state bureaucracies.

Ostensibly, the purpose of the Cultural Revolution was to destroy the remnants of past tradition (especially Confucianism) and bourgeois liberalism, but more directly it aimed at opponents in the Chinese Communist Party (CCP) who were accused of "economism" (i.e., favoring markets and incentives) and of "walking the capitalist road." Mao singled out individuals in the party who were said to have been corrupted by power and privilege. Liu and Deng, considered the top two "capitalist roaders" in China, were eventually purged from the party, along with thousands of alleged "followers." No one was immune to attack as a rightist; children were even encouraged to accuse their parents. Students, organized as Red Guards, also attacked intellectuals who, unlike members of the party, had no organization to protect themselves. Liu's and Deng's policies were reversed. The struggle between contending factions led to mass chaos and the near collapse of China.

## MAO ZEDONG: "LEANING TO ONE SIDE"

In *Dictatorship of the People's Democracy* (1949) (see chapter 34), besides making the case for Leninist "democratic centralism," Mao also stated that the Chinese Communist Revolution should be guided by the experience of the Soviet Union and, as an ally of the Soviets, should take part in the world revolutionary movement. Anticipating the objection that this meant "leaning to one side" in favor of the Soviets, he defended the policy as follows:

"You are leaning to one side." Exactly. The forty years' experience of Sun Yatsen and the twenty-eight years' experience of the Communist Party have taught us to lean to one side, and we are firmly convinced that in order to win victory and consolidate it we must lean to one side. In the light of the experiences accumulated in these forty years and these twenty-eight years, all Chinese without exception must lean either to the side of imperialism or to the side of socialism. Sitting on the fence will not do, nor is there a third road. . . .

"Victory is possible even without international help." This is a mistaken idea. In the epoch in which imperialism exists, it is impossible for a genuine people's revolution to win victory in any country without various forms of help from the international revolutionary forces, and even if victory were won, it could not be consolidated. This was the case with the victory and consolidation of the Great October Revolution as Stalin told us long ago. This was also the case with the overthrow of the three imperialist powers in World War II and the establishment of the people's democracies. And this is also the case with the present and the future of People's China.

[From Selden, *The People's Republic of China*, pp. 176–177]

MAO ZEDONG: "STALIN IS OUR COMMANDER"

This speech, actually given in 1939, was published in the *People's Daily*, the authoritative organ of the Chinese Communist Party, only after the founding of the People's Republic of China on October 1, 1949. It constituted a reaffirmation by Mao after the more-moderate "New Democracy" phase, of his earlier revolutionary commitments, and of his continuing faith in Stalin as the leader of the world revolution. Of particular significance here is Mao's assertion that all of Marxism is summed up in "the one sentence: To rebel is justified." This was later invoked repeatedly at the launching of the Great Proletarian Cultural Revolution.

At the present time, the whole world is divided into two fronts struggling against one another. On the one side is imperialism, which represents the front of the oppressors. On the other is socialism, which represents the front of resistance to oppression. . . . Who is in command of the revolutionary front? It is socialism, it is Stalin. Comrade Stalin is the leader of the world revolution. Because he is there, it is easier to get things done. As you know, Marx is dead, and Engels and Lenin too are dead. If we did not have a Stalin, who would give the orders? . . .

There are innumerable principles of Marxism, but in the last analysis they can all be summed up in one sentence: "To rebel is justified." For thousands of years everyone said: "Oppression is justified, exploitation is justified, rebellion is not justified." From the time when Marxism appeared on the scene, this old judgment was turned upside down, and this is a great contribution. This principle was derived by the proletariat from its struggles, but Marx drew the conclusion. In accordance with this principle, there was then resistance, there was struggle, and socialism was realized. What is Comrade Stalin's contribution? He developed this principle, he developed Marxism-Leninism and produced a very clear, concrete, and living doctrine for the oppressed people of the whole world. This is the complete doctrine of establishing a revolutionary front, overthrowing imperialism, overthrowing capitalism, and establishing a socialist society.

The practical aspect consists in turning doctrine into reality. Neither Marx, Engels, nor Lenin carried to completion the cause of the establishment of socialism, but Stalin did so. This is a great and unprecedented exploit. Before the Soviet Union's two five-year plans, the capitalist newspapers of various countries proclaimed daily that the Soviet Union was in desperate straits, that socialism could not be relied upon, but what do we see today? Stalin has stopped Chamberlain's mouth,[1] and also the mouths of those Chinese diehards. They all recognize that the Soviet Union has triumphed.

Stalin has helped us from the doctrinal standpoint in our war of resistance against Japan. Apart from this, he has given us material and practical aid. Since the victory of Stalin's cause, he has aided us with many airplanes, cannons, aviators, and military advisers in every domain, as well as lending us money. What other country in the world has helped us in this way? What country in the world, led by what class, party, and individual, has helped us in this way? Who is there, apart from the Soviet Union, the proletariat, the Communist Party, and Stalin?

[From Schram, *The Political Thought of Mao Tse-tung*, pp. 426–429]

### GUO MORUO: ODE TO STALIN — "LONG LIVE STALIN" ON HIS SEVENTIETH BIRTHDAY, 1949

This poem to Stalin was written by Guo Moruo (1897–1977), a major intellectual figurehead of the People's Republic, unofficial poet laureate, and president of the Chinese Academy of Sciences. Before 1949 he was prominent as a writer, historian, and left-wing activist, but not as an open Communist; after 1949 he was a supposedly "non-partisan" representative in the People's Republic Political Consultative Conference, and later vice president of the Standing Committee of the People's Congress. At his death it was revealed that he had long been a secret member of the Party, but this Ode leaves little doubt where his sentiments lay.

The "orders of nature" spoken of at the end of the ode is presumably a reference to the Lysenko theory of evolution approved by Stalin in those years.

### Long Live Stalin!

### (Stalin, Banzai!)

The Great Stalin, our beloved "Steel," our everlasting sun!
Only because there is you among mankind,
  Marx-Leninism can reach its present heights!
Only because there is you, the Proletariat can have
  its present growth and strength!
Only because there is you, the task of liberation can be
  as glorious as it is!

---

1. A reference to the pact in 1939 between Stalin and Hitler that left the latter free to deal with Chamberlain and Britain.

It is you who are leading us to merge into the stream
    flowing into the ocean of utopia.
It is you who are instructing us that the West will never
    neglect the East.
It is you who are uniting us into a force never before
    seen in history.

There is the fortress of peace of the USSR, standing firm,
    with unparalleled strength.
There are the new republics of Asia and Europe, side by side,
    growing more and more prosperous.
There is the Chinese People's Republic, turning in a new
    direction, brightening the world.

The history of mankind is opening a new chapter.
The orders of nature will also follow the direction of revolution.

The name of Stalin will forever be the sun of mankind.
Long live Great Stalin!
Long live Our Beloved "Steel"!

[Trans. by Chaoying Fang]

## JI YUN: "HOW CHINA PROCEEDS WITH THE TASK OF INDUSTRIALIZATION" (1953)

Citing Lenin, Stalin, and the Soviet Union as models for the CCP, this statement gives early priority to heavy industry and agricultural collectivization in a Soviet-style Five-Year Plan. The Communists saw large-scale projects and a planned economy as the key to the nearly century-old goal of wealth and power.

The five-year construction plan, to which we have long looked forward, has now commenced. Its basic object is the gradual realization of the industrialization of our state.

Industrialization has been the goal sought by the Chinese people during the past one hundred years. From the last days of the Manchu dynasty to the early years of the republic, some people had undertaken the establishment of a few factories in the country. But industry as a whole has never been developed in China. . . . It was just as Stalin said: "Because China did not have its own heavy industry and its own war industry, it was being trampled upon by all the reckless and unruly elements. . . ."

We are now in the midst of a period of important changes, in that period of transition, as described by Lenin, of changing "from the stallion of the peasant, the farm hand, and poverty, to the stallion of mechanized industry and electrification."

We must look upon this period of transition to the industrialization of the state as one equal in importance and significance to that period of transition of the revolution toward the fight for political power. . . .

It was through the implementation of the policies of the industrialization of the state and the collectivization of agriculture that the Soviet Union succeeded in building up, from an economic structure complicated with five component economies, a unified socialist economy; in turning a backward agricultural nation into a first-class industrial power of the world; in defeating German fascist aggression in World War II; and in constituting itself the strong bastion of world peace today.

We are looking upon the Soviet Union as our example in the building of our country. Soviet experiences in the realization of industrialization are of great value to us. . . .

The foundation of socialism is large industrial development. Lenin said, "There is only one real foundation for a socialist society, and it is large industry. If we do not possess factories of great size, if we do not possess a large industrial structure with the most advanced equipment, then we shall generally not be able to talk of socialism, much less in the case of an agricultural country."

Accordingly, in order to enable our state to progress victoriously toward socialism, we must construct large industries. . . . Numerous facts have proved that it is futile to attempt the enforcement of socialism on the foundations of small agriculture or small handicrafts. Industry must first be developed to provide possibilities for the collectivization and mechanization of agriculture, for the socialist reform of agriculture.

At the same time, only with industrialization of the state may we guarantee our economic independence and nonreliance on imperialism.

[Ji Yun, in *People's Daily*, May 23, 1953; adapted from Selden, *The People's Republic of China*, pp. 290–292]

LI FUQUN: "REPORT ON THE FIRST FIVE-YEAR PLAN FOR
DEVELOPMENT OF THE NATIONAL ECONOMY OF THE PEOPLE'S REPUBLIC
OF CHINA IN 1953–1957, JULY 5 AND 6, 1955"

Although called a "report," the following is more a restatement of the goals of the first five-year plan than an actual account of progress made. Nevertheless, these policies did succeed in establishing some industrial base by the mid-fifties. Note the heavy investment in major capital construction, reflecting a similar Soviet emphasis on large-scale state projects of great visibility.

The general task set by China's first five-year plan was determined in the light of the fundamental task of the state during the transition period.

It may be summarized as follows: We must center our main efforts on industrial construction; this comprises 694 above-norm construction projects, the core of which are the 156 projects that the Soviet Union is designing for us and on which we lay the preliminary groundwork for China's socialist industrialization; we must foster the growth of agricultural producers' cooperatives, whose system of ownership is partially collective, and handicraft producers' cooperatives, thus laying the preliminary groundwork for the socialist transformation of agriculture and handicrafts; and in the main, we must incorporate capitalist industry and commerce into various forms of state capitalism, laying the groundwork for the socialist transformation of private industry and commerce. . . .

The total outlay for the country's economic construction and cultural and educational development during the five-year period will be 76,640 million yuan, or the equivalent in value of more than 700 million taels [a little over an ounce] of gold. Such an enormous investment in national construction would have been absolutely inconceivable in the past. This is possible only for a government led by the working class and working wholeheartedly in the interests of the people.

Investments in capital construction will amount to 42,740 million yuan, or 55.8 percent of the total outlay for economic construction and cultural and educational development during the five-year period. Of the remaining 44.2 percent, or 33,900 million yuan, part will be spent on work occasioned by the needs of capital construction, such as prospecting resources, engineering surveying and designing, stockpiling of equipment and material, and so on. Part will be spent to develop industrial production, transport and posts and telecommunications, including such items as overhaul of equipment, technical and organizational improvements in production, trial manufacture of new products, purchase of miscellaneous fixed assets, and so on; another part will serve as circulating capital for the various economic departments; and still another part will go to funds allocated to all economic, cultural, and educational departments for operating expenses and for the training of specialized personnel. . . .

The industrialization that our country is striving to achieve is socialist industrialization, modeled on Soviet experience and carried out with the direct assistance of the Soviet Union and the people's democracies. It is not capitalist industrialization. Therefore, our industry, particularly those branches producing means of production, is capable of rapid development.

[Adapted from Selden, *The People's Republic of China*, pp. 295–300]

# CHANGES IN MID-COURSE

MAO ZEDONG: "THE QUESTION OF AGRICULTURAL COOPERATION,"
JULY 31, 1955

Under the Soviet model, Chinese agriculture, through the sale of grain to the Soviet Union, was to provide the resources to fund an ambitious industrialization program. By the mid-fifties, however, the leadership realized that agricultural production was lagging and the surplus derived from it was insufficient. Collectivization of the land was seen as the solution to this problem. However, farmers, having received land in the early land reform movement, could be expected to resist subsequent moves for them to surrender it. The program thus was envisioned as a long-term project that would take decades and would be done on a voluntary basis. In the following, Mao spelled out the steps by which the people could be persuaded to join in the process: building small-scale cooperatives that would then be expanded into large production units. When the farmers saw the advantages of cooperative farming, he thought, they would join the cooperatives of their own accord.

When production fell, in part on account of the farmers' noncooperation, however, Mao decided to press ahead, convinced that the masses would go along with the tide of revolutionary change and that the eventual results would confirm the rightness of his policies. Instead of taking several decades, China's land collectivization was accomplished in a year or two. Though less violent than the Soviet collectivization of the thirties, it was not without resistance and loss of life.

The following passages reveal, in the way Mao expresses himself, how easily his own thoughts are put into the minds of others — how prone he is to letting the strong conviction of his own rightness color his reading of a situation.

A new upsurge in the socialist mass movement is in sight throughout the Chinese countryside. But some of our comrades are tottering along like a woman with bound feet, always complaining that others are going too fast. They imagine that by picking on trifles, grumbling unnecessarily, worrying continuously, and putting up countless taboos and commandments, they will guide the socialist mass movement in the rural areas along sound lines.

No, this is not the right way at all; it is wrong.

The tide of social reform in the countryside — in the shape of cooperation — has already reached some places. Soon it will sweep the whole country. This is a huge socialist revolutionary movement, which involves a rural population more than five hundred million strong, one that has very great world significance. We should guide this movement vigorously, warmly, and systematically, and not act as a drag on it. . . .

It is wrong to say that the present pace of development of the agricultural producers' cooperatives has "gone beyond practical possibilities" or "gone beyond the consciousness of the masses." The situation in China is like this: its population is enormous, there is a shortage of cultivated land (only three *mou* of land per head, taking the country as a whole; in many parts of the southern provinces, the average is only one *mou* or less), natural catastrophes occur from time to time — every year large numbers of farms suffer more or less from flood, drought, gales, frost, hail, or insect pests — and methods of farming are backward. As a result, many peasants are still having difficulties or are not well off. The well-off ones are comparatively few, although since land reform the standard of living of the peasants as a whole has improved. For all these reasons there is an active desire among most peasants to take the socialist road. . . .

We have been taking steps to bring about a gradual advance in the socialist transformation of agriculture. The first step in the countryside is to call on the peasants, in accordance with the principles of voluntariness and mutual benefit, to organize agricultural producers' mutual-aid teams. Such teams contain only the rudiments of socialism. Each one draws in a few households, though some have ten or more. The second step is to call on the peasants, on the basis of these mutual-aid teams and still in accordance with the principles of voluntariness and mutual benefit, to organize small agricultural producers' cooperatives semi-socialist in nature, characterized by the pooling of land as shares and by single management. Not until we take the third step will the peasants be called upon, on the basis of these small, semi-socialist cooperatives and in accordance with the same principles of voluntariness and mutual benefit, to unite on a larger scale and organize large agricultural producers' cooperatives completely socialist in nature. These steps are designed to raise steadily the socialist consciousness of the peasants through their personal experience, to change their mode of life step by step, and so minimize any feeling that their mode of life is being changed all of a sudden.

> [Mao, *Guanyu nongye hezuohua wenti*; trans. adapted from Schram,
> *The Political Thought of Mao Tse-tung*, pp. 343–346]

## MAO ZEDONG: "ON THE CORRECT HANDLING OF CONTRADICTIONS AMONG THE PEOPLE"

This speech, popularly known by the catch-phrase "Let a Hundred Flowers Bloom," is one of Mao Zedong's most important theoretical statements after the consolidation of Communist power on the mainland of China and after the death of Stalin left Mao the senior Communist theoretician. It was occasioned in part by the shock of the uprising in Hungary late in 1956, which showed the degree of pent-up dissatisfaction possible under even a seemingly well-established Communist regime. If Mao's gesture was meant to encourage the "letting off of steam," those who took advantage of the offer found, after a brief period of forbearance by the Party, that they would be subjected to severe attack and penalized for their outspokenness.

In long-range terms the significance of this statement lay not in any liberalization or loosening of Communist ideological control but precisely in its reaffirmation of the importance that Mao attached to unity in matters of theory and doctrine. As we have seen, for Mao and for Liu Shaoqi, the principal means of preserving that unity as a dynamic force had been ideological struggle. Yet under conditions of Party dominance, the threat of stagnation was always present. Consequently for Mao, always concerned to keep his cohorts in battle-readiness, the question was how to stimulate the airing of contradictions without allowing them to become antagonistic.

Mao continued to wrestle with this problem, hoping to find a use for "nonantagonistic" criticism as an outlet for discontent. However, with the Party standing as sole judge of what was antagonistic or not, and making an object lesson of those who unknowingly overstepped the invisible line, this particular contradiction could not be easily resolved.

Mao's speech was originally delivered on February 27, 1957, before a large audience at the Supreme State Conference. When finally published at the end of June, it had been substantially revised and probably represented a much more guarded statement of policy than the original lecture. The purpose was now less to encourage "fragrant flowers" and more to identify "poisonous weeds."

## Two Different Types of Contradictions

Never has our country been as united as it is today. The victories of the bourgeois-democratic revolution and the socialist revolution, coupled with our achievements in socialist construction, have rapidly changed the face of old China. Now we see before us an even brighter future. . . . Unification of the country, unity of the people, and unity among our various nationalities — these are the basic guarantees for the sure triumph of our cause. However, this does not mean that there are no longer any contradictions in our society. . . . We are confronted by two types of social contradictions — contradictions between ourselves and the enemy and contradictions among the people. These two types of contradictions are totally different in nature. [pp. 14–15]

The contradictions between ourselves and our enemies are antagonistic ones. Within the ranks of the people, contradictions among the working people are nonantagonistic, while those between the exploiters and the exploited classes have, apart from their antagonistic aspect, a nonantagonistic aspect. Contradictions among the people have always existed, but their content differs in each period of the revolution and during the building of socialism.

In the conditions existing in China today, what we call contradictions among the people include the following:

Contradictions within the working class, contradictions within the peasantry, contradictions within the intelligentsia, contradictions between the working class and the peasantry, contradictions between the working class and peasantry on the one hand and the intelligentsia on the other, contradictions between the working class and other sections of the working people on the one hand

and the national bourgeoisie on the other, contradictions within the national bourgeoisie, and so forth. Our People's Government is a government that truly represents the interests of the people and serves the people, yet certain contradictions do exist between the government and the masses. These include contradictions between the interests of the state, collective interests, and individual interests; between democracy and centralism; between those in positions of leadership and the led; and contradictions arising from the bureaucratic practices of certain state functionaries in their relations with the masses. All these are contradictions among the people; generally speaking, underlying the contradictions among the people is the basic identity of the interests of the people.

In our country, the contradiction between the working class and the national bourgeoisie is a contradiction among the people. . . . The contradiction between exploiter and exploited that exists between the national bourgeoisie and the working class is an antagonistic one. But, in the concrete conditions existing in China, such an antagonistic contradiction, if properly handled, can be transformed into a nonantagonistic one and resolved in a peaceful way. But if it is not properly handled — if, say, we do not follow a policy of unity, criticizing and educating the national bourgeoisie, or if the national bourgeoisie does not accept this policy — then the contradictions between the working class and the national bourgeoisie can turn into an antagonistic contradiction between ourselves and the enemy. [pp. 16–18]

There were other people in our country who took a wavering attitude toward the Hungarian events because they were ignorant about the actual world situation. They felt that there was too little freedom under our people's democracy and that there was more freedom under Western parliamentary democracy. They ask for the adoption of the two-party system of the West, where one party is in office and the other out of office. But this so-called two-party system is nothing but a means of maintaining the dictatorship of the bourgeoisie; under no circumstances can it safeguard the freedom of the working people. . . .

Those who demand freedom and democracy in the abstract regard democracy as an end and not a means. Democracy sometimes seems to be an end, but it is in fact only a means. Marxism teaches us that democracy is part of the superstructure and belongs to the category of politics. That is to say, in the last analysis it serves the economic base. The same is true of freedom. Both democracy and freedom are relative, not absolute, and they come into being and develop under specific historical circumstances.

Within the ranks of the people, democracy stands in relation to centralism, and freedom to discipline. They are two conflicting aspects of a single entity, contradictory as well as united, and we should not one-sidedly emphasize one to the denial of the other. Within the ranks of the people, we cannot do without democracy, nor can we do without centralism. Our democratic centralism means the unity of democracy and centralism and the unity of freedom and discipline. Under this system, the people enjoy a wide measure of democracy and freedom, but at the same time they have to keep themselves within the bounds of socialist discipline. All this is well understood by the people. [pp. 21–22]

Marxist philosophy holds that the law of the unity of opposites is a fundamental law of the universe. This law operates everywhere — in the natural world, in human society, and in human thinking. Opposites in contradiction unite as well as struggle with each other, and thus impel all things to move and change. Contradictions exist everywhere, but as things differ in nature so do contradictions in any given phenomenon or thing; the unity of opposites is conditional, temporary and transitory, and hence relative, whereas struggle between opposites is absolute. Lenin gave a very clear exposition of this law. In our country, a growing number of people have come to understand it. For many people, however, acceptance of this law is one thing and its application, examining and dealing with problems, is quite another. . . . Many people refuse to admit that contradictions still exist in a socialist society, with the result that when confronted with social contradictions they become timid and helpless. They do not understand that socialist society grows more united and consolidated precisely through the ceaseless process of correctly dealing with and resolving contradictions. . . . [p. 26]

## On "Letting a Hundred Flowers Blossom" and "Letting a Hundred Schools of Thought Contend"

The policy of letting a hundred flowers blossom and a hundred schools of thought contend is designed to promote the flourishing of the arts and the progress of science; it is designed to enable a socialist culture to thrive in our land. Different forms and styles in art can develop freely, and different schools in science can contend freely. We think that it is harmful to the growth of art and science if administrative measures are used to impose one particular style of art or school of thought and to ban another. . . . In the past, new and correct things often failed at the outset to win recognition from the majority of people and had to develop by twists and turns in struggle. Correct and good things have often at first been looked upon not as fragrant flowers but as poisonous weeds; Copernicus's theory of the solar system and Darwin's theory of evolution were once dismissed as erroneous and had to win out over bitter opposition. Chinese history offers many similar examples. . . .

Marxism has also developed through struggle. . . . It is true that in China socialist transformation, insofar as a change in the system of ownership is concerned, has in the main been completed, and the turbulent, large-scale, mass class struggles characteristic of the revolutionary periods have in the main concluded. But remnants of the overthrown landlord and comprador classes still exist, the bourgeoisie still exists, and the petty bourgeoisie has only just begun to remold itself. Class struggle is not yet over. . . . In this respect, the question of whether socialism or capitalism will win is still not really settled. Marxists are still a minority of the entire population as well as of the intellectuals. Marxism therefore must still develop through struggle. . . . As humankind in general rejects an untruth and accepts a truth, a new truth will begin struggling with new erroneous ideas. Such struggles will never end. This is the law of the development of truth, and it is certainly also the law of development in Marxism. [pp. 44–46]

People may ask: Since Marxism is accepted by the majority of the people in our country as the guiding ideology, can it be criticized? Certainly it can. As a scientific truth, Marxism fears no criticism. If it did and could be defeated in argument, it would be worthless. In fact, are not the idealists criticizing Marxism every day and in all sorts of ways? . . . Fighting against wrong ideas is like being vaccinated — a man develops greater immunity from disease after the vaccine takes effect. Plants raised in hothouses are not likely to be robust. Carrying out the policy of letting a hundred flowers bloom and a hundred schools of thought contend will not weaken but strengthen the leading position of Marxism in the ideological field.

What should our policy be toward non-Marxist ideas? As far as unmistakable counterrevolutionaries and wreckers of the socialist cause are concerned, the matter is easy; we simply deprive them of their freedom of speech. But it is quite a different matter when we are faced with incorrect ideas among the people. Will it do to ban such ideas and give them no opportunity to express themselves? Certainly not. . . . That is why it is only by employing methods of discussion, criticism, and reasoning that we can really foster correct ideas, overcome wrong ideas, and really settle issues. [pp. 47–48]

So what, from the point of view of the broad masses of the people, should be a criterion today for distinguishing between fragrant flowers and poisonous weeds? . . .

Basing ourselves on the principles of our constitution, the will of the overwhelming majority of our people, and the political programs jointly proclaimed on various occasions by our political parties and groups, we believe that, broadly speaking, words and actions can be judged right if they:

1. Help to unite the people of our various nationalities and do not divide them
2. Are beneficial, not harmful, to socialist transformation and socialist construction
3. Help to consolidate, not undermine or weaken, the people's democratic dictatorship
4. Help to consolidate, not undermine or weaken, democratic centralism
5. Tend to strengthen, not to cast off or weaken, the leadership of the Communist Party
6. Are beneficial, not harmful, to international socialist solidarity and the solidarity of the peace-loving peoples of the world

Of these six criteria, the most important are the socialist path and the leadership of the Party. . . . When the majority of the people have clear-cut criteria to go by, criticism and self-criticism can be conducted along proper lines, and these criteria can be applied to people's words and actions to determine whether they are fragrant flowers or poisonous weeds. These are political criteria. Naturally, in judging the truthfulness of scientific theories or assessing the aesthetic value of works of art, other pertinent criteria are needed, but these six political criteria are also applicable to all activities in the arts or sciences. In a socialist country like ours, can there possibly be any useful scientific or artistic activity that runs counter to these political criteria? [pp. 49–50]

[Mao, *Let a Hundred Flowers Bloom*, pp. 14–26, 44–50]

LIU BINYAN: "A HIGHER KIND OF LOYALTY"

In this essay Liu Binyan, a prominent journalist who later became an outspoken critic of the Mao and Deng regimes, recalls how thrilled he was by Mao's original speech on the Hundred Flowers Campaign, but then how disillusioned he was by the repression that followed. Liu subsequently became convinced that the campaign was set by Mao deliberately to trap his opponents; today, not all historians are so convinced, but there is little disagreement about the chilling outcome.

I do not remember a moment in my life more exhilarating than when Mao Zedong's February 1957 speech to the State Council was released. My estimation of him soared to sublime heights. At *China Youth News* the response was equally enthusiastic; it seemed as if we were at the beginning of a new era in China.

In his speech, Mao distinguished between two basically different sets of "contradictions" — antagonistic and nonantagonistic. In so doing, he appeared to be announcing that the era of class struggle was over, that "internal contradictions" (including those between capitalists and the working class) were the main ones within our society, and the foremost among these were contradictions between the Party and the people. These were seen as nonantagonistic conflicts. This also meant that the Party must be placed under supervision of the people and that the fight against bureaucratism was a major task, requiring our full and constant attention. In that speech, Mao announced that dogmatism should not be mistaken for Marxism; he reiterated his policy of letting "a hundred flowers bloom and a hundred schools of thought contend"; he advocated open criticism and reiterated that senior party leaders should not be exempt from criticism. As for strikes by workers and students — unprecedented since the founding of the People's Republic and now taken seriously for the first time — he said the right way of dealing with them was not by force or coercion but by overcoming bureaucratism.

These issues were exactly the unspoken ones that had been weighing on me for the last few years — special privileges within Party ranks, bureaucratism, and dogmatic tendencies. Now my disquiet had been dispelled as if by magic. The political climate in Beijing cleared up; the mood of intellectuals brightened; everything seemed to take on a rosy hue. Mao was virtually advocating more democracy and liberalization in matters of ideology; as a journalist and writer, I now felt I had a free hand in pursuing my vocation.

In March I went to Harbin and Changchun, two big cities in northeast China, and I was shocked by the state of things I saw. The local Party Committee's attitude toward Mao's speech was diametrically opposed to that of the intellectuals; local officials just sat back, waiting for a change in the wind. The Party Committee in Harbin was conducting its own criticism of "bourgeois ideology." The municipal Party secretary had decided that bureaucratism was a form of bourgeois ideology, so opposing bourgeois ideology covered everything.

Another thing that shocked me was the diametrically opposed interpretations of Mao's intentions. Mao's talk was filtering down to Party cadres in these two cities, and among those who had heard and studied the talk, some felt that Mao was attacking dogmatism and leftist tendencies, while others felt differently. It is true, the latter conceded, Mao had criticized Chen Qitong's January letter in the *People's Daily* attacking liberal tendencies in art and literature. But that criticism, they argued, was leveled at Chen's ineptitude in timing and presentation, not at his basic stand.

Thirty years later, I reread Mao's speech (the original version, not the one revised for publication) and realized that at the time I had been too preoccupied with his main drift to detect hints of other tendencies hidden between the lines. For instance, he did not mince words over Stalin's dogmatism, but then insisted that Stalin must be assessed on the "three-seven" principle — that is, seven parts merit to three parts fault. Again Mao considered "democracy" as basically a tool to mobilize the people for the Party's own ends.

[Liu Binyan, A *Higher Kind of Loyalty*, pp. 69–70]

## INTELLECTUAL OPINIONS FROM THE HUNDRED FLOWERS PERIOD

After seemingly endless rectification campaigns, intellectuals had become understandably reluctant to heed the Communist Party's call to speak out freely. Gradually, however, they overcame this reluctance. Much of what they wrote was cautious and did not pose any challenge to the Party. Some of the bolder statements, however, did challenge the monopoly of power and the competence of the Communist Party, and this led eventually to the repressing of the Hundred Flowers and the purging of hundreds of thousands of intellectuals.

[From the editor of *Literary Studies*:]

No one can deny that in our country at present there are still floods and droughts, still famine and unemployment, still infectious disease and the oppression of the bureaucracy, plus other unpleasant and unjustifiable phenomena. . . . A writer in possession of an upright conscience and a clear head ought not to shut his eyes complacently and remain silent in the face of real life and the sufferings of the people. If a writer does not have the courage to reveal the dark diseases of society, does not have the courage to participate positively in solving the crucial problems of people's lives, and does not have the courage to attack all the deformed, sick, black things, then can he be called a writer?

[Huang Qiuyun, in *People's Literature* 9 (1956); adapted from Goldman,
"The Party and the Intellectuals," p. 249]

[From a factory manager:]

Learning from the Soviet Union is a royal road; but some cadres do not understand and think that it means copying. I say if we do, it will paralyze Chinese engineers. . . . I have been engaged in electrical engineering for twenty years. Some of the Soviet experiences simply do not impress me. Of course, I suffered a good deal in the Five-Anti movement [against private business and business leaders] because of these opinions.

[Sun Ding, in *Guangming Daily*, May 5; adapted from MacFarquhar,
*The Hundred Flowers Campaign*, p. 64]

[From a writer:]

I think that Chairman Mao's speech delivered at the Yan'an Forum on Literature and Art consisted of two component parts: one was composed of theories of a tactical nature with which to guide the literary and artistic campaigns at the time, the other was composed of theories involving general principles with which to guide literary and artistic enterprises over the long run. . . .

Owing to the fact that the life these works reflected belonged to a definite period and that the creative processes of the writers were hurried and brief, the artistic content of these works was generally very poor, and the intellectual content extremely limited. . . .

If we were to use today the same method of leadership and the same theories as were used in the past to supervise and guide writers' creative works, they would inevitably perform only the function of achieving "retrogression" rather than progress.

We cannot but admit that since the liberation of the country, our guiding theoretical ideas have been conservative and at the same time profoundly influenced by doctrinairism from abroad, which to a considerable degree has hindered and stunted the development and prosperity of literary and artistic enterprises. . . .

The root causes of formalization and conceptualization lie in the dogmatists mechanically, conservatively, one-sidedly, and in an exaggerated way carrying out and elaborating upon the tactical theories that Chairman Mao used to guide the literary and artistic movement at the time. . . .

Literature and art do not serve politics by mechanically serving a certain policy, nor do creative works that conform to the constitution, Party regulations, and the letter of the law; they mainly do so through the class nature of works, through encouraging people, and through the function of aesthetic education of the people's moral qualities.

> [Liu Shaotang, in *Literary Studies* 5 (1957); adapted from MacFarquhar,
> *The Hundred Flowers Campaign*, pp. 179–180]

[From the editor in chief of the *Guangming Daily*:]

After the liberation [1949], intellectuals warmly supported the Party and accepted the leadership of the Party. But in the past few years the relations between the Party and the masses have not been good and have become a problem of our political life that urgently needs readjustment. Where is the key to the problem? In my opinion, the key lies in the idea that "the world belongs to the Party." I think a party leading a nation is not the same as a party owning a nation; the public supports the Party, but members of the public have not forgotten that they are masters of the nation . . . isn't it too much that within the scope of the nation, there must be a Party man as leader in every unit, big or small, whether section or subsection. . . . For many years, the talents or capabilities of many Party men have not matched their duties. They have bungled their jobs, to the detriment of the state, and have not been able to command the respect of the masses, with the result that the relations between the Party and the masses have been tense.

> [Qu Anping, in *Guangming Daily*, June 1; adapted from MacFarquhar,
> *The Hundred Flowers Campaign*, p. 51]

[From a college professor:]

The Party members, due to their occupying positions of leadership and being favorably situated, seem to enjoy in all respects excessive privileges. Take theaters, for instance; a certain Party member pointed out in his self-examination that he was never happy unless he was offered a seat in the first ten rows. Why did he feel like that? Because he was used to seats in the first ten front rows. . . . During the past few campaigns, one by one the people have had the skin of their faces torn to pieces, and the intellectuals have had their authority knocked for six, all of which may, should, and indeed does have certain advantages. But why is it that the rectification of Party members must be done behind closed doors, and why is it that the masses are not allowed to probe into things if and when a Party member makes a mistake? . . . Never treat a person as if he were worse than dog's excreta one moment and regard him as worth ten thousand ounces of gold the next. The intellectuals cannot stomach the ice-cold, nor can they swallow the piping-hot.

[Xu Zhongyu, in *Guangming Daily*, May 1; adapted from MacFarquhar, *The Hundred Flowers Campaign*, pp. 65–66]

[From a student leader:]

True socialism is highly democratic, but the socialism we have here is not democratic. I call this society a socialism sprung from a basis of feudalism. We should not be satisfied with the Party's rectification and reformist methods and the slight concessions made to the people.

[Lin Xiling, speech at the open-air forum of Beijing University, May 23; adapted from MacFarquhar, *The Hundred Flowers Campaign*, p. 140]

## MAO ZEDONG: REMARKS AT THE BEIDAIHE CONFERENCE, AUGUST 1958

Massive work projects to expand agricultural production led to the creation of large-scale organizations in the countryside, as Mao pushed for his version of socialism through the movement known as the Great Leap Forward. Mao called the organizations themselves people's communes, even though it implied that China was moving from socialism to communism ahead of the Soviet Union, toward the elimination of all private plots and property. Mao had persuaded himself that this was a response to the spontaneous wishes of the people, but the subsequent strong resistance to the movement suggests that he misread their feelings.

Now on the problem of the people's communes: what should they be called? They may be called people's communes, or they may not. My inclination is to call them people's communes. This [name] is still socialist in nature, not at all overemphasizing communism. They're called people's communes, first [because] they're big and second [because] they're public. Lots of people, a vast area of land, large scale of production, [and] all [their] undertakings are [done] in a big way. [They] integrate government [administration] with commune [management] to establish public mess halls, and private plots are eliminated. But chickens, ducks, and the young trees in front and behind a house are still private. These, of course, won't exist in the future. [If we] have more grain, [we] can practice the supply system; [for the present] it's still reward according to one's work. Wages will be given to individuals according to their ability and won't be given to the head of the family, which makes the youth and women happy. This will be very beneficial for the liberation of the individual. In establishing the people's communes, as I see it, once again it has been the countryside that has taken the lead; the cities haven't started yet, [because] the workers' wage scales are a complicated matter. Whether in urban or rural areas, [the aim] should be the socialist system plus communist ideology. The Soviet Union practices the use of high rewards and heavy punishments, emphasizing [only] material incentives. We now practice socialism and have the sprouts of communism. Schools, factories, and neighborhoods can all establish people's communes. In a few years big communes will be organized to include everyone. . . .

The people's communes have been set up as a result of the masses' initiative; it wasn't we who advocated it. We advocated uninterrupted revolution, eradicating superstition, liberating thought, and daring to think, daring to speak, daring to act; [and] the masses have risen [to the occasion]. [We] did not anticipate this at the Nanning conference, the Chengdu conference, or the second session of the Eighth Party Congress. The spontaneity of the masses has always been an element inherent in communism. First there was utopian socialism, classical materialism, and dialetics; then came the summation [of these theories] by Marx and others. Our people's communes have been developed on the basis of the agricultural producers' cooperatives; they've not come into being from nowhere. We need to understand this clearly in order to systematize this question. The characteristics of the people's communes are (1) big and (2) public. [They have] vast areas of land and abundant resources [as well as] a large population; [they can] combine industry, agriculture, commerce, education, and military affairs, as well as farming, forestry, animal husbandry, sideline production, and fisheries — being "big" is terrific. [With] many people, there's lots of power. [We say] public because they contain more socialism than do the cooperatives, [and] they will gradually eradicate the vestiges of capitalism — for example, the eradication of private plots and private livestock rearing and the running of public mess halls, nurseries, and tailoring groups so that all working women can be liberated. They will implement a wage system and agricultural factories [in which] every single man, woman, old person, and youth receives his own wage, in contrast to the former [system of] distribution to the head of the household. Direct payment of wages is much welcomed by the youth and by women. This eradicates the patriarchal system and the system of bourgeois rights. Another advantage of [communes'] being public is that labor efficiency can be raised higher than in cooperatives.

[From MacFarquhar, Cheek, and Wu, *The Secret Speeches of Chairman Mao*, pp. 397–441]

PENG DEHUAI: "LETTER OF OPINION" TO MAO ZEDONG ON THE
GREAT LEAP FORWARD, JULY 1959

At a party meeting in the summer of 1959, the defense minister, Peng Dehuai, delivered a letter to Mao. While carefully reaffirming the general correctness of Mao's policies, Peng, writing on the basis of personal investigations, diplomatically pointed out the shortcomings of the Great Leap. This kind of frank exchange of opinion had been accepted practice at gatherings of the top leadership, but now Mao viciously lashed out at Peng and eventually purged him. Before this, Mao had already begun to realize the mistakes of the movement and had begun to modify it. Stung by Peng's criticism, however, Mao decided to press the movement forward, creating massive starvation in the countryside and causing the deaths of tens of millions of peasants. Peng, hounded, persecuted, and imprisoned for years, died a painful death, still insisting that he had always been loyal to Mao.

In the past, a lot of problems were exposed in our way of thinking and our style of work. These problems are worthy of our attention. The principal ones are as follows:

1. The habit of exaggeration bred and spread rather universally. Last year, at the time of the Beidaihe meeting, a higher estimate of grain output was made than was warranted. This created a false phenomenon. Everybody felt that the problem of food had been solved and that our hands could be freed to engage in industry. There was serious superficiality in our understanding of the development of the iron and steel industry. . . .

The habit of exaggeration spread to various areas and departments, and some unbelievable miracles were also reported in the press. This has surely done tremendous harm to the prestige of the Party.

At that time, from reports sent in from various quarters, it would seem that communism was around the corner. This caused not a few comrades to become dizzy. In the wake of the [claimed] wave of high grain and cotton output and the doubling of iron and steel production, extravagance and waste developed. . . .

2. Petty bourgeois fanaticism renders us liable to commit "left" mistakes. In the course of the Great Leap Forward of 1958, like many comrades I was bewitched by the achievements of the Great Leap Forward and the passion of the mass movement. Some "left" tendencies developed to quite an extent; we always wanted to enter into communism at one step. Our minds swayed by the idea of taking the lead, we forgot the mass line and the style of seeking truth from facts that the party had formed over a long time. . . .

For instance, the slogans raised by the chairman, such as "Grow less, produce more and reap more" and "Catch up with Britain in fifteen years," were strategic and long-range policies. But we did not study them well; we failed to give attention to and study the current concrete conditions, and we failed to arrange work on a positive, steady, and reliable basis. . . . As a result, divorced from reality, we failed to gain the support of the masses. For instance, the law of exchange of equal values was negated prematurely, and the free supply of meals was effected too early. . . .

In the view of some comrades, putting politics in command could be a substitute for everything. They forgot that putting politics in command was aimed at raising the consciousness of labor, ensuring improvement of products in both quantity and quality, and giving full play to the enthusiasm and creativeness of the masses in order to speed our economic construction. Putting politics in command is no substitute for economic principles, still less for concrete measures in economic work.

[Peng, "Letter of Opinion," July 14, 1959, *Selections from People's Republic of China Press* 4032; trans. adapted from Selden, *The People's Republic of China*, pp. 476–485]

## WU HAN: "HAI RUI SCOLDS THE EMPEROR," JUNE 19, 1959

Wu Han was a prominent historian and the author of a noted biography of the founder of the Ming dynasty, as well as a high official in the Beijing municipal government. Although Mao had originally encouraged Wu to write on the Ming official Hai Rui, these writings came to be seen as the latest manifestations of an age-old Chinese tradition — writing about the past to indict the present. Wu later developed the essay below into a play, *Hai Rui Dismissed from Office*, wherein some saw the courageous Ming official as Peng Dehuai and the autocratic emperor as Mao. A 1965 article condemning this play served as the opening salvo of the Cultural Revolution, a major onslaught on supposedly traditional values obstructing the revolutionary transformation.

In feudal times, the emperor was so inviolable that even his name was not to be used or mentioned in any manner. Violation of this taboo was regarded as a serious crime. It was not unusual for the violator to lose his arms or legs, even though he was otherwise innocent.

As to the scolding of an emperor, it was almost unheard of in history. However, it was a different matter entirely when Wu Wang of Zhou scolded the Emperor Zhou of the Shang dynasty after the latter had been defeated in 1122 B.C., or when the rebel Li Zicheng scolded the Chongzhen emperor of the Ming dynasty after [the] Ming was overthrown in 1644. In both cases it was the victor who scolded the defeated monarch.

Because it was impossible to scold an emperor in the old days, it is very gratifying to learn from history that someone really did scold an emperor. Perhaps for this reason did many people enjoy seeing the play *Empress He Scolds the Emperor*. If the people were not permitted to scold the emperor when they wanted to, they might do it on the stage and get tremendous satisfaction out of it. . . .

In any event, there was a man who really did scold an emperor. This man was the famous Ming dynasty statesman Hai Rui. According to the *Ming History*, volume 226, some of the bitter words used by Hai Rui to scold the Jiajing emperor were: "You have been increasing taxes, bankrupting the state treasury, and neglecting state affairs for more than ten years, and now the matter becomes even worse. People are now using your imperial title 'Jiajing' to signify 'Every house is empty' [a pun, because both phrases have the same pronunciation in Chinese]. . . ."

The Jiajing emperor of the Ming dynasty became so lazy toward the end of his reign that he lived in the Western Park doing nothing but worshiping and writing Daoist charms. A charm is a letter to God, and it must be well written. Both Grand Secretaries Yan Gao and Xu Jie had written beautiful charms and because of this talent only, they had each become prime minister. During their premiership the government was extremely corrupt. Anyone who dared to speak out in the royal court would be arrested, imprisoned, exiled, or even executed. For these reasons all court officials were afraid of speaking out.

But courageous Hai Rui sent a petition to the emperor in February 1566 proposing a drastic reform. The petition stated:

> How would you compare yourself with Emperor Wen Di of the Han dynasty?[2] You did a fairly good job in your early years, but what has happened to you now? For nearly twenty years you have not appeared in the imperial court, and you have appointed many fools to the government. By refusing to see your own sons, you are mean to your own blood; by suspecting court officials, you are mean to your subordinates; and by living in the Western Park refusing to come home, you are mean to your wife. Now the country is filled with corrupt officials and weak generals; peasants begin to revolt everywhere. Although such things happened when you were enthroned, they were not as serious as they are today. Now Yan Gao has resigned [as Grand Minister], but there is still no sign of social reform. In my judgment you are much inferior to Emperor Wen Di.

The Jiajing emperor always compared himself with Emperor Yao, but Hai Rui said that he was even worse than Wen Di. No wonder he became angry with Hai Rui.

Hai Rui's petition continued:

> The dynasty's officials know that the people have been dissatisfied with you for some time. By engaging in occultism and searching for immortality, you have confused yourself. Your shortcomings are numerous: rudeness, short-temperedness, self-righteousness, and deafness to honest criticism. But worst of all is your search for immortality. . . .
>
> You should realize the impossibility of achieving immortality and repent past mistakes. You should attend the imperial court regularly and discuss national affairs with your court officials. This is the only way to

---

2. Traditionally regarded as a role model.

redeem yourself. By doing so you may still be able to make yourself useful to the country during your remaining years.

The most urgent problems today are the absurdity of imperial policies and the lack of clarity of official responsibilities. If you do not tackle these problems now, nothing will be accomplished.

After having finished reading Hai Rui's petition, the emperor threw it angrily on the floor and ordered the palace guard to arrest Hai Rui. Eunuch Huang Jin told the emperor: "It is said that Hai Rui already expects death, has bade farewell to his wife, prepared his funeral arrangements, and dispersed all his servants. Therefore he will not run away, and the arrest is quite unnecessary. He is very simple and straightforward in his nature and has a good reputation among the people. He is an honest official and never steals anything from the public."

When the emperor learned from the eunuch that Hai Rui was not afraid of death, the emperor began to wonder and picked up the petition from the floor and read it over again. However, he could not make up his mind what to do with Hai Rui. . . . One day he became so angry that he beat the imperial concubines. Some concubines complained, "He was scolded by Hai Rui and he tries to take it out on us."

The emperor then sent an investigator to find out who else had been conspiring with Hai Rui. Many colleagues tried not to get involved and avoided Hai Rui. Hai Rui stayed at home waiting to be arrested. . . .

Soon [however] the emperor became ill. He discussed with Grand Secretary Xu Jie the possibility of letting the crown prince succeed him and said, "What he [Hai Rui] said about me was right, but how could I go to court every day with this illness." He continued, "It was my own fault in getting this sickness, otherwise I could go to court every day to attend to state affairs. Then I would never have been scolded by him." Finally the emperor ordered the arrest of Hai Rui. Although Hai Rui was sentenced to death by the Ministry of Justice, the emperor never ratified the execution. Two months later the emperor died. The new emperor pardoned Hai Rui and restored him to his previous position as the director of census.

Many people supported Hai Rui's scolding of the emperor and sympathized with him. Hai Rui became very famous in his time. However, he was impeached again in 1586. This time many young scholars who had passed the civil service examination . . . courageously defended Hai Rui in court and said, "We have heard the name of Hai Rui since we were ten. Hai Rui is the greatest statesman of our time; he will be respected for thousands of years to come. His noble character is as high as the sky, very few people can compare with him." These were some of the typical praises he received from the young people of his day. When Hai Rui died, the people in Nanjing closed shops. When his body reached the Yangzi River, people, in white dress to mourn his death, filled both banks for more than a hundred miles. These actions manifested how great Hai Rui was and how he was respected by his fellow men.

[*People's Daily*, June 19, 1959; trans. adapted from Fan,
*The Chinese Cultural Revolution*, pp. 72–78]

# THE CULTURAL REVOLUTION

Despite its name, the "Great Proletarian Cultural Revolution" emerged not from the "proletariat" but from a power struggle at the top in which certain leaders, including Mao, sought to enlist the "masses" (especially students) in a campaign against moderate leaders then in control of the Party and state administration. The initial battle cry "To rebel is justified" was taken from an early speech by Mao (see p. 453), but "rebellion" came to mean almost anything, depending on whatever group was activated to engage in generalized "class struggle," and before long the movement deteriorated into an anarchy of cross-purposes and violent infighting.

The *Sixteen Points*, briefly excerpted here, are taken from a decision of the Party Central Committee, engineered by Mao, Lin Biao, and their cohorts in 1966. They are perhaps the closest thing to a coherent statement of Mao's original purposes in attacking "those in authority taking the capitalist road."

### THE *SIXTEEN POINTS*: GUIDELINES FOR THE GREAT PROLETARIAN CULTURAL REVOLUTION

## 1. A New Stage in the Socialist Revolution

The Great Proletarian Cultural Revolution now unfolding is a great revolution that touches people to their very soul and constitutes a new stage in the development of the socialist revolution in our country, a deeper and more extensive stage. . . .

Although the bourgeoisie has been overthrown, it is still trying to use the old ideas, culture and customs, and habits of the exploiting classes to corrupt the masses, capture their minds, and endeavor to stage a comeback. The proletariat must do just the opposite: it must meet head-on every challenge of the bourgeoisie in the ideological field and use the new ideas, culture, customs, and habits of the proletariat to change the mental outlook of the whole of society. At present our objective is to struggle against and crush those persons in authority who are taking the capitalist road, to criticize and repudiate the reactionary bourgeois academic "authorities" and the ideology of the bourgeoisie and all other exploiting classes, and transform education, literature, and art and all other parts of the superstructure that do not correspond to the socialist economic base, so as to facilitate the consolidation and development of the socialist system.

## 2. The Main Current and the Zigzags

The masses of the workers, peasants, soldiers, revolutionary intellectuals, and revolutionary cadres form the main force in this Great Cultural Revolution. Large numbers of revolutionary young people, previously unknown, have become courageous and daring pathbreakers. They are vigorous in action and intelligent. Through the media of big character posters and great debates, they argue things out, expose and criticize thoroughly, and launch resolute attacks on the open and hidden representatives of the bourgeoisie. . . .

Since the Cultural Revolution is a revolution, it inevitably meets with resistance. This resistance comes chiefly from those in authority who have wormed their way into the party and are taking the capitalist road. It also comes from the old force of habit in society. At present, this resistance is still fairly strong and stubborn. However, the Great Proletarian Cultural Revolution is, after all, an irresistible general trend. There is abundant evidence that such resistance will crumble fast once the masses become fully aroused. . . .

## 9. Cultural Revolutionary Groups, Committees, and Congresses

Many new things have begun to emerge in the Great Proletarian Cultural Revolution. The cultural revolutionary groups, committees, and other organizational forms created by the masses in many schools and units are something new and of great historic importance.

These cultural revolutionary groups, committees, and congresses are excellent new forms of organization whereby under the leadership of the Communist Party the masses are educating themselves. They are an excellent bridge to keep our party in close contact with the masses. They are organs of power of the Proletarian Cultural Revolution.

The cultural revolutionary groups, committees, and congresses should not be temporary organizations but permanent, standing mass organizations. They are suitable not only for colleges, schools, government, and other organizations but generally also for factories, mines, and other enterprises, urban districts, and villages.

It is necessary to institute a system of general elections, like that of the Paris Commune, for electing members to the cultural revolutionary groups and committees and delegates to the cultural revolutionary congress.

[Adapted from Selden, *The People's Republic of China*, pp. 550–556]

## QUOTATIONS FROM CHAIRMAN MAO ZEDONG

Mao replaced Peng Dehuai as defense minister with Lin Biao, another prominent general who had been with Mao since the early days of the revolution. Lin used his position to turn the army into a bastion of Mao loyalism, employing *Quotations from Chairman Mao*, or the *Little Red Book*, to inculcate the peasant recruits. When the Cultural Revolution started, the Red Guards adopted this book as their "bible," memorized it, and waved it in the air at huge rallies at Tiananmen Square.

— Be resolute, fear no sacrifice, and surmount every difficulty to win victory. [p. 102]

— Thousands upon thousands of martyrs have heroically laid down their lives for the people; let us hold their banner high and march ahead along the path crimson with their blood! [p. 102]

— Whoever wants to know a thing has no way of doing so except by coming into contact with it, that is, by living (practicing) in its environment. . . . If you want knowledge, you must take part in the practice of changing reality. If you want to know the taste of a pear, you must change the pear by eating it yourself. . . . If you want to know the theory and methods of revolution, you must take part in revolution. All genuine knowledge originates in direct experience. [p. 118]

— Unquestionably, victory or defeat in war is determined mainly by the military, political, economic, and natural conditions on both sides. But not by these alone. It is also determined by each side's subjective ability in directing the war. In his endeavor to win a war, a military strategist cannot overstep the limitations imposed by the material conditions; within these limitations, however, he can and must strive for victory. The stage of action for a military strategist is built upon objective material conditions, but on that stage he can direct the performance of many a drama, full of sound and color, power and grandeur. [p. 49]

— Who are our enemies? Who are our friends? This is a question of the first importance for the revolution. The basic reason why all previous revolutionary struggles in China achieved so little was their failure to unite with real friends in order to attack real enemies. A revolutionary party is the guide of the masses, and no revolution ever succeeds when the revolutionary party leads them astray. To ensure that we will definitely achieve success in our revolution and will not lead the masses astray, we must pay attention to uniting with our real friends in order to attack our real enemies. To distinguish real friends from real enemies, we must make a general analysis of the economic status of the various classes in Chinese society and of their respective attitudes toward the revolution. [p. 7]

— Historically, all reactionary forces on the verge of extinction invariably conduct a last desperate struggle against the revolutionary forces, and some revolutionaries are apt to be deluded for a time by this phenomenon of outward strength but inner weakness, failing to grasp the essential fact that the enemy is nearing extinction while they themselves are approaching victory. [pp. 44–45]

[From Schram, *Quotations from Chairman Mao*, pp. 7, 44–45, 49, 102, 118]

## WHAT HAVE SONG SHUO, LU PING, AND PENG PEIYUN DONE IN THE CULTURAL REVOLUTION?

The big character posters plastered over the walls of campuses, towns, and cities became a ubiquitous form of expression for those attacking the establishment. The most famous of these posters was put up on May 25, 1966, at Beijing University by Nie Yuanzi and six other philosophy instructors attacking the university authorities. Although the government tried to repress it, Mao had it broadcast on June 1 and the Beijing media carried it the next day. The poster's strident tone characterized writings during the Cultural Revolution.

At present, the people of the whole nation, in a soaring revolutionary spirit that manifests their boundless love for the Party and Chairman Mao and their inveterate hatred for the sinister anti-Party, anti-socialist gang, are making a vigorous and great cultural revolution; they are struggling to thoroughly smash the attacks of the reactionary sinister gang, in defense of the Party's Central Committee and Chairman Mao. But here in Beijing University the masses are being kept immobilized, the atmosphere is one of indifference and deadness, whereas the strong revolutionary desire of the vast number of the faculty members and students has been suppressed. What is the matter? What is the reason? There is something fishy going on. . . .

Why are you [top Beijing University officials cited in title] so afraid of big character posters and holding of big denunciation meetings? To counterattack the sinister gang that has frantically attacked the Party, socialism, and Mao Zedong's thought is a life-and-death class struggle. The revolutionary people must be fully aroused to denounce them vigorously and angrily, and to hold big meetings and put up big character posters, is one of the best ways for the masses to do battle. By "guiding" the masses not to hold big meetings, not to put up big character posters, and by creating all kinds of taboos, aren't you suppressing the masses' revolution, not allowing them to make revolution, and opposing their revolution? We will never permit you to do this! . . .

All revolutionary intellectuals, now is the time to go into battle! Let us unite, holding high the great red banner of Mao Zedong Thought, unite around the Party's Central Committee and Chairman Mao and break down all the various controls and plots of the revisionists; resolutely, thoroughly, totally, and completely wipe out all ghosts and monsters and all Khrushchevian counterrevolutionary revisionists, and carry the socialist revolution through to the end.

Defend the Party's Central Committee!

Defend Mao Zedong Thought!

Defend the dictatorship of the proletariat!

[Adapted from Benton and Hunter, *Wild Lily, Prairie Fire*, pp. 105–108]

## RED GUARD MEMOIRS

Although portrayed as a spontaneous movement among students, it is clear from the following account that the initiative came from above and surprised many middle-school and college students who were organized into units known as the Red Guards to form the vanguard of the Cultural Revolution. At massive rallies in Tiananmen Square in Beijing, Mao sanctioned their role in rooting out the "capitalist roaders" in party and government. These developments are reported by a student participant as recorded many years after the actual events.

At a school assembly the working group announced that we were now in revolution, the Cultural Revolution. We finally knew what was happening in our school. The working group then informed us about our new Revolutionary Committee, and asked each class to elect a Cultural Revolutionary Small Group to lead the campaign. . . . Thus the Cultural Revolution, which lasted ten years, entered my life. Important newspaper articles and Central Party documents were passed to our small group, and we in turn organized the students to study them. We learned that during the seventeen years of Communist Party control, China's culture, art, and education had been under the dictatorial command of "capitalist and revisionist black gangs." Later each student was issued a pamphlet, *Chairman Mao's Comments on Educational Revolution.* . . .

I was astonished to learn that our country was in such bad shape. Until then I hadn't suspected that the songs I sang, the movies I watched, and the books I read were unhealthy. I had thought my school a revolutionary one, maybe too revolutionary. Nevertheless, I swallowed what I was told and didn't raise a single negative question, not even to myself. I had been chosen leader of this revolution in my class. If I had problems in understanding these documents, how could I expect the rest of the class to do so? Besides, what experience and qualifications did I have to judge what Chairman Mao and the Central Committee deemed right and wrong?

My classmates tried to comprehend too. We all considered ourselves progressive youth, and we were determined to follow Chairman Mao and the Party center. If they thought this Cultural Revolution to be necessary, if they wanted us to participate, we would.

[Adapted from Zhai, *Red Flower of China*, pp. 61–62]

*The students quickly ignored the call to refrain from violence in the* Sixteen Points, *and teachers and intellectuals became one of their main targets. Many were maimed or killed by the students, while others committed suicide rather than face further torture and humiliation. Like the above account, this one was recorded many years after the events described.*

The list of accusations grew longer by the day: hooligans and bad eggs, filthy rich peasants and son-of-a-bitch landlords, bloodsucking capitalists and neo-bourgeoisie, historical counterrevolutionaries and active counterrevolutionaries, rightists and ultra-rightists, alien class elements and degenerate elements, reactionaries and opportunists, counterrevolutionary revisionists, imperialist running dogs, and spies. Students stood in the roles of prosecutor, judge, and police. No defense was allowed. Any teacher who protested was certainly a liar.

The indignities escalated as well. Some students shaved or cut teachers' hair into curious patterns. The most popular style was the yin-yang cut, which featured a full head of hair on one side and a clean-shaven scalp on the other. Some said this style represented Chairman Mao's theory of the "unity of opposites." It made me think of the punishments of ancient China, which included shaving the head, tattooing the face, cutting off the nose or feet, castration, and dismemberment by five horse-drawn carts.

At struggle meetings, students often forced teachers into the "jet-plane" position. Two people would stand on each side of the accused, push him to his knees, pull his head back by the hair, and hold his arms out in back like airplane wings. We tried it on each other and found it caused great strain on the back and neck.

[Adapted from Gao Yuan, *Born Red*, pp. 53–54]

WANG XIZHE, LI ZHENGTIAN, CHEN YIYANG, GUO HONGZHI:
"THE LI YI ZHE POSTER," NOVEMBER 1974

By 1968 it was clear that the Cultural Revolution had spun out of control, and Mao brought in the army to bring it to a halt. Thousands of young people whom Mao had a short time ago called upon to make revolution were now slaughtered by the military; millions more were sent down to the countryside to "learn from the peasants." Yet in the midst of the chaos of the Cultural Revolution what came to be known as the Thinking Generation had been born. Unable to find reliable guidance in the vague sayings of Mao, some Red Guards turned toward the works of Marx, Engels, and Lenin to discover the true nature of socialism. The wall poster put up in Guangzhou in 1974 and excerpted below reflects Marx's ideas about the role of democracy in a socialist society as well as the original goals of the Cultural Revolution as stated in the Sixteen Points. Notions of the party's responsibilities to the people expressed here would blossom in the "Democracy Wall" or " Beijing Spring" movement of the late seventies and early eighties. "Li Yi Zhe" is a composite pen name consisting of characters from three of four joint authors, one of whom, Wang Xizhe, went on to play a prominent role in that movement.

## Expectations for the Fourth National People's Congress

How is the soon-to-be-convoked Fourth National People's Congress going to reflect the Great Cultural Revolution, which people call China's "second revolution"? Law is the expression of the will of the ruling class. So how is the country's basic legal system that is to be promulgated — the new constitution — to express the will of the proletariat and the broad masses in China who have experienced the Great Cultural Revolution?

What are the popular masses thinking now? What are their demands? What sort of expectations do they have for the representative congress of the "people of the whole country"?

Legal System, Yes! A "System of Rites," No!

Our country was born from a semi-feudal, semi-colonial society into socialism. The traditions formed by several thousands of years of feudal despotism stubbornly maintain their strong hold over thought, culture, education, law, and virtually every other sphere of the superstructure. . . .

Under the conditions of proletarian dictatorship, how can the people's rights, under the centralized leadership of the Party, be protected in the struggle against the capitalist roaders and incorrect lines in the Party? This is the big topic facing the Fourth National People's Congress.

Needless to say, the Party's leadership should carefully listen to the masses' opinions, and it should be needless to note the people's own rights to implement revolutionary supervision over all levels of the Party's leadership. It is even more unnecessary to say that rebelling against the capitalist roaders is justified. Even though the masses' opinion might be incorrect or excessive, or even if they become discontented because of misunderstanding certain Party policies, is it justified to implement a policy of "suppress if persuasion fails and arrest if suppression fails"? Moreover, the fragrant flower and the poisonous weed, correct and incorrect, and revolutionary and counterrevolutionary, are not always easy to distinguish. It takes a long process and has to stand the test of time. Therefore, we should not be frightened by an open and honorable opposition so long as it observes discipline and plays no tricks and engages in no conspiracy.

The Fourth National People's Congress should enact regulations clearly in black and white that . . . will . . . protect all the democratic rights rightfully belonging to the masses.


## Limitation of Special Privileges

We are not utopian socialists. We recognize that in the present stage of our society there exist various types of differences, which cannot be completely destroyed by a decree alone. However, the law of the development of a socialist revolutionary movement should not itself widen these differences but eliminate them, above all prohibit such differences from expanding into economic and political privileges. Special privilege itself is fundamentally in opposition to the interests of the people. Why should we avoid condemning such privileges? . . . The Fourth National People's Congress should enact, in black and white, clauses limiting special privileges.

Guaranteeing the People's Right to Manage the Country and Society

"Who has given us our power?" The people have. Our cadres should not become officials and behave like lords, but should be servants of the people. But power can corrupt people most easily. When a person's status changes, it is most effective to test whether he is working for the interests of the majority or the minority. Whether he can maintain his spirit to serve the people depends, apart from his own diligence, mainly on the revolutionary supervision of the masses. And the mass movement is the richest source of the maintenance of the revolutionary spirit of the revolutionaries.

How should the masses' right of revolutionary supervision over the Party's and country's various levels of leadership be determined? And how should it be clearly established that when certain cadres (especially high-level cadres of the central organs) lose the trust of the broad masses of people, the people "can replace them any time"?

The Fourth National People's Congress should answer these questions.

[Adapted from Chan, Rosen, and Unger, *On Socialist Democracy*, pp. 74–80]

PART 7

*The Return to Stability and Tradition*

## Chapter 37

### DENG'S "MODERNIZATION" AND ITS CRITICS

The era following the death of Mao and the demise of the so-called Gang of Four is identified with the leadership of Deng Xiaoping and his policies proclaimed under the banner of "modernization." To the latter concept, problematical and contestable in almost any case, a special irony attaches here, after three decades of Maoist "liberation" and revolutionary struggle had failed to fulfill their modernizing goals. What remained to be done, and how, is the subject of the claims, proposals, and counterproposals put forward in the following by some of the leading actors and activists of this period.

In December 1978, veteran leader Deng Xiaoping and his allies gained control of the Party and government and began repudiating the policies of the Cultural Revolution while rehabilitating many of those purged during the last several decades. The new regime claimed it was returning, after Maoist deviations and distortions of Marxism, to orthodox or scientific socialism. It rejected class conflict and emphasized instead the building of the forces of production through the Four Modernizations of agriculture, industry, national defense, and science and technology. The modernization of these four sectors would then create the preconditions for bringing about true socialism, albeit at some vague point in the future. The regime, concurrently, began to emphasize its nationalist as well as socialist credentials, and later to portray itself as the protector of the Chinese cultural heritage.

In the early 1980s the agricultural communes were dismantled and land was leased to individual farm families; agricultural production, helped by a spate of good weather, sharply increased. The government at the same time retooled factories to meet pent-up consumer demand. The country was opened to the outside world, and foreigners were encouraged to bring capital, technical information, and managerial knowledge to China. The new government established four Special Economic Zones to absorb and experiment with foreign knowledge and technology. At the same time, it lessened its reliance on political campaigns and reduced the political pressure on the people. As long as they did not oppose the "socialist" system and the rule of the Chinese Communist Party, the Chinese could think what they wished. In a society where almost every aspect of people's lives had been controlled, this represented real change. Popular religion revived in the countryside, while cultural and intellectual life in the cities cautiously reappeared. Publishers poured out translations of foreign works, as well as new and old books by Chinese authors. The new regime seems to have been genuinely popular in its early years; people affectionately referred to Deng Xiaoping as "Old Deng," a term they rarely used for the venerated yet remote Mao Zedong.

The opening of the country and the relaxing of political control, however, created problems for Deng's regime. Many Chinese came to believe that life in the Western liberal democracies and Japan was much better than life in "socialist" China. Moreover, neighboring countries and territories such as Hong Kong, South Korea, Taiwan, and Singapore, which had decisively rejected socialism, flourished over the course of the 1980s while the Soviet Union and "socialist" bloc countries languished. Belief in the superiority of socialism was shaken. If countries with much the same cultural heritage and racial background as China had advanced so rapidly, they reasoned, why shouldn't China? Students and intellectuals, already disillusioned by the violence and contradictions of the Cultural Revolution, now had the chance to learn about foreign countries and different political and economic systems. Many came to wonder about the efficacy of the existing Chinese political and economic system. Some, moreover, came to see the regime's claims to preserve Chinese culture as really intended to block out cultural and intellectual influences from the outside world.

Increased contact with the outside world also now gave members of the Party and government increased opportunities for graft and corruption. The People's Republic of China had not yet succeeded in establishing institutions to handle this problem, and many of the Party's political campaigns going back to the early 1940s can be explained in part as attempts to wipe out corruption and curtail special privilege. The prestige of the Party and government, already badly shaken by the violent and seemingly arbitrary political campaigns of the past decades, plummeted. Moreover, since the new regime stressed the modernization of the country rather than revolutionary leadership and the building of socialism, the dominant role of the Party was now called into question. Despite efforts to bring younger and better-educated people into the Party and government, many Chinese saw members of the Party and government as elderly veterans of the Long March or uneducated people who got their positions through seniority rather than through merit. They did not seem equipped to lead China into the twenty-first century.

These developments led to a series of student movements, or "tides," over the course of the 1980s, which garnered increasing support from the urban population. Intellectuals moved from thinking about reforming socialism to considering how to establish liberal democracy and called for the release of activists imprisoned in the late 1970s and early 1980s. In the summer of 1988, government price reforms brought about high rates of inflation in China's cities, and this in turn created a wave of panic buying. Despite their new admiration for consumer goods and capitalism, urban Chinese were not willing to give up the safety net established for them by the party. In the fall the government slammed on the economic brakes, cutting back on reform. This move, while not entirely reassuring the populace, led to fears among students and intellectuals that reforms begun by Deng Xiaoping a decade before were now being retracted. All these developments culminated in the 1989 student movement and the Tiananmen Massacre of early June.

Through repression, the government managed to stifle dissent and curtail the student movement. At the same time, increased foreign investment led to an economic boom in certain parts of the country; attention was drawn, even by Deng, from making revolution to making money. While certain areas along the coast, such as the southern province of Guangdong, boomed, areas in the hinterland languished. With China rapidly becoming a nation of two unequal halves, migrants from depressed interior provinces crowded increasingly into the more dynamic coastal areas, seeking employment. Meanwhile the population, despite government efforts to curb it, continued to grow, while efforts to increase production and make money at all costs led to increased exploitation and degradation of the environment and to charges that the affluence of some was gained by collusion and corruption among entrepreneurs and bureaucrats.

# THE TURN TO STABILITY AND MODERNIZATION

ZHOU ENLAI: "REPORT ON THE WORK OF THE GOVERNMENT,"
DELIVERED ON JANUARY 13, 1975, AT THE FIRST SESSION OF THE FOURTH
NATIONAL PEOPLE'S CONGRESS OF THE PEOPLE'S REPUBLIC OF CHINA

In 1975 Prime Minister Zhou Enlai was already stricken with cancer and would die early the following year. This speech, given to the rubber-stamp legislature, is considered the clarion call to emphasize modernization rather than class struggle. The Four Modernizations referred to as the second stage became slogans of a national campaign.

Socialist revolution is the powerful engine for developing social productive forces. We must adhere to the principle of *grasping revolution, promoting production and other work, and preparedness against war*, and with revolution in command, work hard to increase production and speed up socialist construction so that our socialist system will have a more solid material foundation.

On Chairman Mao's instructions, it was suggested in the report on the work of the government to the Third National People's Congress that we might envisage the development of our national economy in two stages beginning from the Third Five-Year Plan: The first stage is to build an independent and relatively comprehensive industrial and economic system in fifteen years, that is, before 1980; the second stage is to accomplish the comprehensive modernization of agriculture, industry, national defense, and science and technology before the end of the century, so that our national economy will be advancing to the front ranks of the world.

We should fulfill or overfulfill the Fourth Five-Year Plan in 1975 in order to reinforce the foundations for completing the first stage before 1980 as envisaged above. In light of the situation at home and abroad, the next ten years are crucial for accomplishing what has been envisaged for the two stages. In this period we shall not only build an independent and relatively comprehensive industrial and economic system but march toward the splendid goal set for the second stage. With this objective in mind, the State Council will draw up a long-range ten-year plan, five-year plans, and annual plans. The ministries and commissions under the State Council and the local revolutionary committees at all levels down to the industrial and mining enterprises and production teams and other grass-roots units should all rouse the masses to work out their plans through full discussion and strive to attain our splendid goal ahead of time.

[From *Peking Review* 4 (January 24, 1975), p. 23]

## COMMUNIQUÉ OF THE THIRD PLENARY SESSION OF THE ELEVENTH CENTRAL COMMITTEE OF THE COMMUNIST PARTY OF CHINA, DECEMBER 22, 1978

Deng Xiaoping and his allies gained control of the party at the third plenary session of the Eleventh Party Congress. This document indicates that they intended to steer the country in a new direction, away from the class struggle and mass movements of the Cultural Revolution and toward the modernization of the economy. Though the rhetoric of revolutionary struggle is still used, the main thrust is to achieve stability.

The Eleventh Central Committee of the Communist Party of China held its third plenary session in Beijing between December 18 and 22, 1978. . . .

The plenary session unanimously endorsed the policy decision put forward by Comrade Hua Guofeng on behalf of the Political Bureau of the Central

Committee that, to meet the developments at home and abroad, now is an appropriate time to take the decision to close the large-scale nationwide mass movement to expose and criticize Lin Biao and the Gang of Four, and to shift the emphasis of our Party's work and the attention of the people of the whole country to socialist modernization. This is of major significance for fulfillment of the three-year and eight-year programs for the development of the national economy and the outline for twenty-three years, for the modernization of agriculture, industry, national defense, and science and technology and for the consolidation of the dictatorship of the proletariat in our country. The general task put forward by our Party for the new period reflects the demands of history and the people's aspirations and represents their fundamental interests. Whether or not we can carry this general task to completion, speed socialist modernization, and on the basis of a rapid growth in production improve the people's living standards significantly and strengthen national defense — this is a major issue that is of paramount concern to all our people and of great significance to the cause of world peace and progress. Carrying out the Four Modernizations requires great growth in the productive forces, which in turn requires diverse changes in those aspects of the relations of production and the superstructure [that are] not in harmony with the growth of the productive forces and requires changes in all methods of management, actions, and thinking that stand in the way of such growth. Socialist modernization is therefore a profound and extensive revolution. There is still in our country today a small handful of counterrevolutionary elements and criminals who hate our socialist modernization and try to undermine it. We must not relax our class struggle against them, nor can we weaken the dictatorship of the proletariat. But as Comrade Mao Zedong pointed out, the large-scale turbulent class struggles of mass character have in the main come to an end. Class struggle in socialist society should be carried out on the principle of strictly differentiating the two different types of contradictions and correctly handling them in accordance with the procedures prescribed by the Constitution and the law. It is impermissible to confuse the two different types of contradictions and damage the political stability and unity required for socialist modernization. The plenary session calls on the whole Party, the whole army, and the people of all our nationalities to work with one heart and one mind, enhance political stability and unity, mobilize themselves immediately to go all out, pool their wisdom and efforts, and carry out the new Long March to make China a modern, powerful socialist country before the end of this century. . . .

While we have achieved political stability and unity and are restoring and adhering to the economic policies that proved effective over a long time, we are now, in the light of the new historical conditions and practical experience, adopting a number of major new economic measures, conscientiously transforming the system and methods of economic management, actively expanding economic cooperation on terms of equality and mutual benefit with other countries on the basis of self-reliance, striving to adopt the world's advanced technologies and equipment, and greatly strengthening scientific and educational work to meet the needs of modernization. Therefore, there can be no doubt that our country's economic construction is bound to advance rapidly and steadily once again. . . .

The session points out that one of the serious shortcomings in the structure of economic management in our country is the overconcentration of authority, and it is necessary boldly to shift it under guidance from the leadership to lower levels so that the local authorities and industrial and agricultural enterprises will have greater power of decision in management under the guidance of unified state planning; big efforts should be made to simplify bodies at various levels charged with economic administration and transfer most of their functions to such enterprises as specialized companies or complexes; it is necessary to act firmly in line with economic law, attach importance to the role of the law of value, consciously combine ideological and political work with economic methods, and give full play to the enthusiasm of cadres and workers for production; it is necessary, under the centralized leadership of the Party, to tackle conscientiously the failure to make a distinction between the Party, the government, and the enterprise and to put a stop to the substitution of Party for government and the substitution of government for enterprise administration, to institute a division of responsibilities among different levels, types of work and individuals, increase the authority and responsibility of administrative bodies and managerial personnel, reduce the number of meetings and amount of paperwork to raise work efficiency, and conscientiously adopt the practices of examination, reward and punishment, promotion and demotion. . . .

The session held a serious discussion on the question of democracy and the legal system. It holds that socialist modernization requires centralized leadership and strict implementation of various rules and regulations and observance of labor discipline. Bourgeois factionalism and anarchism must be firmly opposed. But the correct concentration of ideas is possible only when there is full democracy. Since for a period in the past, democratic centralism was not carried out in the true sense, centralism being divorced from democracy and there being too little democracy, it is necessary to lay particular emphasis on democracy at present, and on the dialectical relationship between democracy and centralism, so as to make the mass line the foundation of the Party's centralized leadership and the effective direction of the organizations of production. In ideological and political life among the ranks of the people, only democracy is permissible and not suppression or persecution. . . . The constitutional rights of citizens must be resolutely protected, and no one has the right to infringe upon them.

In order to safeguard people's democracy, it is imperative to strengthen the socialist legal system so that democracy is systematized and written into law in such a way as to ensure the stability, continuity, and full authority of this democratic system and these laws; there must be laws for people to follow, these laws must be observed, their enforcement must be strict and lawbreakers must be dealt with. From now on, legislative work should have an important place on the agenda of the National People's Congress and its Standing Committee. Procuratorial and judicial organizations must maintain their independence as is appropriate; they must faithfully abide by the laws, rules, and regulations, serve the people's interests, keep to the facts, guarantee the equality of all people before the people's laws, and deny anyone the privilege of being above the law.

[From *Peking Review*, no. 52 (December 29, 1978), pp. 10–15]

## YU QIULI: "THE RELATIONSHIP BETWEEN POLITICS AND ECONOMICS"

In September 1979, after Deng Xiaoping's assumption of party leadership, the chairman of the State Planning Commission, Yu Qiuli, a vice premier of the State Council and a Politburo member, addressed the State Council on a basic redirection of economic policy. While reaffirming the inseparability of politics and economics, he reversed Mao's priority of "politics in command" and declared that economics should guide state policy and technical expertise [an "economic cabinet"] provide political leadership. Putting ideology aside in favor of pragmatism, he argued that Mao's China, following the Soviet model, had fallen far behind after 1949 in the economic competition with Taiwan and Japan, which followed the Western model.

1. The relationship between politics and economics cannot be severed because to do well in economics is to serve the purposes of politics. . . . From now on, we should break away from the bad habit of beginning every briefing with a political report before taking up the subject concerning business operations. People used a lot of political terms even at meetings called by departments in charge of business operations. . . .

2. There is nothing wrong with the "State Council's being not a political cabinet but an economic one." Let others say what they want, I see no harm in Jiang Jingguo's bringing in a large number of economic experts to form a Taiwan economic cabinet. Taiwan's economy is making rapid progress; the people there are living many times better than the people in any of our provinces, and Taiwan's per capita income is reported to be the forty-fourth in the world, putting Taiwan among the rich areas. It would not be a bad idea to learn from this economic cabinet. . . .

3. Why do we compare ourselves with Taiwan rather than with any other country? The economic situation in Taiwan during the 1950s differed little from that in any of our provinces, the only difference being that the area on their side continued to be ruled by the Nationalists while on our side we had a change of government. At first, they lived on American aid, later taking the Japanese route of economic development, while we, on the other hand, "leaned com-

pletely to one side" and followed the Soviet pattern of economic development. In the first decade, we did have some achievements. In the second decade, Sino-Soviet relations deteriorated; the Soviet Union tore up treaties, withdrew its experts, and suspended all kinds of assistance and cooperation projects. It was a time when we could have turned a misfortune into a blessing. For if we had turned back as soon as possible and opened wide our door to take in scientific and technical achievements and equipment from the advanced Western countries, instead of continuing to follow the Soviet pattern, the situation today would not be like this. . . . It is always more difficult to rebuild after destruction than to build up from nothing. The situation in Taiwan is just the opposite. While we were rapidly regressing, they suddenly forged ahead like a miracle. With one working in high gear and the other moving backward, the gap between us has become wider and wider. When our ostrich policy no longer worked, we had to admit that we have lost in this peaceful economic competition in which there was not even a whiff of gunpowder. One does not lose "face" in conceding defeat. Failure is the mother of success. There is no reason why we cannot win back the lost time if we would learn from past experiences.

[From *Xuexi zhiliao*, September 4, 1979; trans. adapted from *Issues and Studies* 16, no. 5 (January 1980): 88–90]

### "UPHOLD THE FOUR BASIC PRINCIPLES," SPEECH BY DENG XIAOPING, MARCH 30, 1979

Although the Deng regime put an end to the Maoist emphasis on political campaigns and class conflict, from early on it tried to set parameters on speech and actions. Despite these strictures, the eighties, as we shall see below, saw greater freedom for intellectuals than any period since the founding of the People's Republic in 1949.

The [Party] Center believes that in realizing the four modernizations in China we must uphold the four basic principles in thought and politics. They are the fundamental premise for realizing the four modernizations. They are [as follows]:

1. We must uphold the socialist road.
2. We must uphold the dictatorship of the proletariat.
3. We must uphold the leadership of the Communist Party.
4. We must uphold Marxism-Leninism and Mao Zedong Thought.

The Center believes that we must reemphasize upholding the four basic principles today because some people (albeit an extreme minority) have attempted to shake those basic principles. . . . Recently, a tendency has developed for some people to create trouble in some parts of the country. . . . Some others also deliberately exaggerate and create a sensation by raising such slogans as "Oppose starvation" and "Demand human rights." Under these slogans, they incite some people to demonstrate and scheme to get foreigners to propagandize their words and actions to the outside world. The so-called China Human Rights Organization has even tacked up big character posters requesting the American president "to show solicitude" toward human rights in China. Can we permit these kinds of public demands for foreigners to interfere in China's domestic affairs? A so-called Thaw Society issued a proclamation openly opposing the dictatorship of the proletariat, saying that it divided people. Can we permit this kind of "freedom of speech," which openly opposes constitutional principles?

[Trans. from *Deng Xiaoping wenxuan* 2:158–184 — RL]

## "BUILDING SOCIALIST SPIRITUAL CIVILIZATION," LETTER FROM LI CHANG, VICE PRESIDENT OF THE CHINESE ACADEMY OF SCIENCES, TO A MEMBER OF THE PARTY CENTRAL COMMITTEE, DECEMBER 1980

Like the Qing dynasty in the nineteenth century, the new regime hoped to open the country to the outside world without modifying its legitimating ideology. New technology or scientific advances were welcomed while Western cultural or political notions were considered threatening and undesirable. The regime therefore developed this concept of a socialist spiritual civilization in the hope of combating the inroads of what it called Western bourgeois material civilization.

Since the Fifth Plenary Session of the Eleventh Party Central Committee, inspired by the idea of "improving and strengthening the Party leadership," I have felt all along that, after the ten disastrous years of the "cultural revolution," there still exists within the Party the pernicious influence of the ultra-left line of the Gang of Four, remnants of the factional ideology of feudalism, selfish individualism of the bourgeoisie, anarchism of the petty bourgeoisie, and colonial ideas that worship things foreign. Under these influences, ideological demands inside and outside the Party have grown somewhat slack. . . . I feel that, along with the general goal of realizing the Four Modernizations, we should also consider putting forward a goal of "building socialist spiritual civilization." The phrase itself first appeared in Vice Chairman Ye's 1979 speech at the meeting in celebration of the thirtieth anniversary of the founding of the People's Republic of China.

I consider that the socialist spiritual civilization includes a concrete aspect (such as well-developed education and thriving science, literature, and art) as well as an ideological aspect (such as social ethics, traditions, and customs). For example, by ideals we mean dedication to the people's cause and building the socialist motherland, whereas moral concepts imply identification of individual interests with the interest of the people and, when the two fall into contradiction, subordination of personal interests to the overall interests of the people. Moral concepts also refer to democracy and unity, hard work and plain living, eagerness to acquire an education, attaching importance to the development of science, paying attention to personal and public hygiene, and being polite and courteous. . . .

It was wrong for Lin Biao and the Gang of Four to emphasize the primacy of the spiritual role. However, we should not overlook the fact that spirit can play a definite role.

[From *Beijing Review* 10 (March 9, 1981): 16–17]

OFFICE OF THE CCP DEHONG DAI NATIONALITY AND QINGBO AUTONOMOUS
ZHOU COMMITTEE: "SEVERAL QUESTIONS IN STRENGTHENING AND
PERFECTING THE JOB RESPONSIBILITY SYSTEMS OF AGRICULTURAL
PRODUCTION," NOVEMBER 7, 1980

The people's communes had been established during the heyday of the Great Leap Forward, and although they were modified in the early sixties, they remained the primary form of rural organization until the early eighties. At that time the new regime dismantled the communes and leased the land to the people of the communes, hoping that this would increase agricultural production. The farmers still had to sell a certain amount of grain to the state at fixed (albeit higher) prices but could now sell the surplus on the market for whatever price they could get. The new contracting arrangement came to be known as the responsibility system, and at least in the first few years, helped by a period of good weather, production rose. Note, however, that these moves toward free enterprise and a market economy are all clothed in the language of socialism and collectivization and concede nothing in respect to overall state control.

Owing to the shortcomings in the movement of collectivization, the ultra-left interruptions, and the fact that for a long period of time the Party had not shifted the emphasis of work to economic construction, the current material and technical bases for the collective economy are still comparatively weak. Meanwhile, there also are matters in need of improvement and perfection concerning systems and structure of the people's communes, the weakest link being the management and administrative work. For a long time there have been no significant improvements and breakthroughs in implementing the principle of distribution according to work and in perfecting the system of job responsibility for production. This has caused suppression of the peasants' socialist initiative as well as insufficient exertion of the superiority of collectivization. Because the collective economy has not been doing satisfactorily, people in a few backward and poverty-stricken localities have even less faith in agricultural collectivization. We must face these problems squarely and solve them aggressively and step by step. At present, it is necessary to regard improvement of management and administration, implementation of distribution according to work, and improvement and perfection of the system of job responsibility for production as the central link for further consolidation of the collective economy and for development of agricultural production. It is necessary to put in a lot of strenuous effort to grasp it tight and grasp it well. . . .

3. Under the moral encouragement of the Third Plenary Session, Party cadres and the masses of commune members have in the recent two years proceeded from actual conditions, liberated their thought and boldly explored, and established many forms of job responsibility systems for production, which can be generally divided into two categories: one is contracted work of small segments with payments according to fixed quotas, and the other is contracted work and production quotas with payments in accordance with actual production. Results of implementation indicate that most areas have increased production by acquiring some new experience. Especially noteworthy is the emergence of the system of job responsibility that gives contracts to specialized persons and gives payment in accordance with actual production, which is widely welcomed by commune members. This is a very good start. Leadership at various levels should sum up the positive and negative experiences, together with the broad masses, and help the communes and brigades perfect and improve the system of job responsibility to energetically push further the management work of the collective economy. . . .

5. The system of job responsibility, of giving contracts to specific persons and giving payments in accordance with actual production, is a system based on division of labor and cooperative work. Under the system, the labor forces [peasants] who are good in agriculture receive contracts for arable lands according to their ability, while those who are good in forestry, stock raising, sideline production, fishery, industry, commerce, and so on receive contracts of various trades concerned according to their ability. Contracts for production of fixed quotas in various trades are assigned to teams, to labor forces, or to households, according to the principle of facilitating production and benefiting management. All operations in the process of production are to be centralized whenever centralization is suitable, and decentralized whenever decentralization is good, by the production team. Centralized distribution [of payment] is made for the portions under fixed quotas, while rewards or penalties are given for production in excess of quotas or unfulfilled production. These are stipulated in the form of contracts for the current year or for the next several years.

This kind of system of production responsibility has many more merits than other forms of contracted production: it can satisfy the commune members' demand for calculating payments in accordance with production, stabilize the production team's position as the main economic entity, concretely consolidate both the mobilization of production initiative of individual commune members and the exertion of the superiority of centralized management as well as division of labor and cooperative work; it is favorable to the development of diversified business, popularization of scientific farming, and the promotion of production of commercial items; it is good for people to exert their talents, things to exert their usefulness, and land to exert its potential; it is favorable for the commune members to take care of their sideline business; and it is convenient for making arrangements for production to ensure a livelihood for the four categories of bereaved households . . . and the weak-labor households. This form is, on the one hand, applicable to areas currently undergoing difficulties while, on the other, it can be developed into a system of job responsibility that further divides specialties by an even higher degree and with more socialist characteristics.

[*Issues and Studies* 17, no. 5 (May 1981): 77–79]

## EARLY CRITIQUES OF THE DENG REGIME

### PUBLICATION STATEMENT, *BEIJING SPRING* MAGAZINE, JANUARY 1979

During the Beijing Spring period, roughly 1978 to 1981, unofficial journals and big character posters expressing all sorts of ideas flourished, free of government censorship. Most of them, subscribing to Marx-Leninism and the Communist Party, supported the new regime under Deng Xiaoping, which tolerated their existence because they were useful in its battle with political enemies opposed to Deng's emphasis on modernization of the economy and minimizing of class conflict. Once those enemies were vanquished, however, these publications were closed down and many of their editors and writers were punished by long jail sentences.

It was once predicted that the China giant would shake the world the moment it rose. In 1949 it rose, but over a long period of thirty years it has not yielded proper influence. It not only has failed to surpass the imperialist powers but has staggered along behind, hesitating and wavering. Finally, we realize that this great nation wears two tight shoes — ignorance and tyranny. This is why China fails to keep pace with the times and lacks the ability to stand in the front ranks of the nations in the world. Can it be that the Chinese people truly lack such ability?

To be rich and powerful, China must be built into a modern socialist power. This has long been the dream of the Chinese people. However, to stride toward this great ideal we must break down modern feudalism and modern superstition and gradually acquire socialist democracy and modern science.

On the basis of Marxism-Leninism, this publication supports the Chinese Communist Party, adheres to the socialist path, and follows Comrade Mao Zedong's policy of "a hundred flowers blossoming and a hundred schools of thought contending." As a comprehensive mass periodical, it fully exercises the democratic rights of speech and publication as provided by the Constitution. It will publish the appeals of the people and all kinds of articles of an exploratory nature.

The road of progress is arduous and tortuous, but the historical current of the people's desire for democracy and the nation's desire for wealth and power is irresistible. The fresh flowers of socialist democracy and science will brave blizzards and spring's chills and will bloom proudly. Baptized by the great and powerful April Fifth Movement, the Chinese people will, with an indomitable fighting spirit, welcome Beijing spring's hundred flowers.[1]

[Adapted from Seymour, *The Fifth Modernization*, p. 38]

WEI JINGSHENG: THE FIFTH MODERNIZATION — DEMOCRACY, 1978

Wei Jingsheng edited the journal *Exploration* during the Beijing Spring period and differed from most of his fellow editors and writers in warning that Deng Xiaoping and other members of the new reform faction could become dictators themselves without the implementation of democracy in China — what Wei dubbed the "fifth modernization." More than any writings of this period, his heralded the student and democracy movements of the mid- and late 1980s. After the following poster appeared on Beijing's Democracy Wall on December 5, 1978, he was arrested on trumped-up charges and served nearly fifteen years in prison. Upon his release in late 1993, Wei resumed his political activities and was re-arrested in April 1994 and sentenced to fourteen more years in prison. He was exiled to the United States in 1998.

Newspapers and television no longer assail us with deafening praise for the dictatorship of the proletariat and class struggle. This is in part because these were once the magical incantations of the now-overthrown Gang of Four. But more importantly, it's because the masses have grown absolutely sick of hearing these worn-out phrases and will never be duped by them again. . . .

After the arrest of the Gang of Four, the people eagerly hoped that Vice Chairman Deng Xiaoping, the possible "restorer of capitalism," would rise up again like a magnificent banner. Finally he did regain his position in the central leadership. How excited the people felt! How inspired they were! But alas, the old political system so despised by the people remains unchanged, and the democracy and freedom they longed for has not even been mentioned. . . .

But now there are people warning us that Marxist–Leninist–Mao Zedong Thought is the foundation of all things, even speech, that Chairman Mao was the "great savior" of the people, and that the phrase "without the Communist Party, there would be no new China" actually means "without Chairman Mao,

---

1. "April Fifth Movement" refers to a gathering of townspeople in Beijing's Tiananmen Square to commemorate the recently deceased Zhou Enlai and support his protege Deng Xiaoping.

there would be no new China." If anyone denies this point, the official notices make it clear that they'll come to no good end. There are even "certain people" who try to tell us that the Chinese people need a dictator and if he is more dictatorial than the emperors of old, it only proves his greatness. The Chinese people don't need democracy, they say, for unless it is a "democracy under centralized leadership," it isn't worth a cent. Whether you believe this or not is up to you, but there are plenty of recently vacated prison cells waiting for you if you don't.

But now there are those who've offered us a way out: if you take the Four Modernizations as your guiding principle, forge ahead with stability and unity, and bravely serve the revolution like a faithful old ox, you will reach paradise — the glory of communism and the Four Modernizations. Those kindhearted "certain people" have also told us that if we find this confusing, we should undertake a serious and thorough study of Marxist–Leninist–Mao Zedong Thought! If you're confused, it's because you don't understand it, and the fact that you don't understand only goes to show just how profound a theory it is! Don't be disobedient or the leadership of your work unit will be uncompromising! And so on and so on.

I urge everyone to stop believing such political swindlers. When we all know that we are being tricked, why don't we trust ourselves instead? The Cultural Revolution has tempered us and we are no longer so ignorant. Let us investigate for ourselves what should be done! . . .

What is true democracy? Only when the people themselves choose representatives to manage affairs in accordance with their will and interests can we speak of democracy. Furthermore, the people must have the power to replace these representatives at any time in order to prevent them from abusing their powers to oppress the people. Is this possible? The citizens of Europe and the United States enjoy just this kind of democracy and could run people like Nixon, de Gaulle, and Tanaka out of office when they wished and can even reinstate them if they want to, for no one can interfere with their democratic rights. In China, however, if a person so much as comments on the now-deceased "Great Helmsman" or "Great Man peerless in history" Mao Zedong, the mighty prison gates and all kinds of unimaginable misfortunes await him. If we compare the socialist system of "democratic centralism" with the "exploiting class democracy" of capitalism, the difference is as clear as night and day.

Will the country sink into chaos and anarchy if the people attain democracy? On the contrary, have not the scandals exposed in the newspapers recently shown that it is precisely due to an absence of democracy that dictators, large and small, have caused chaos and anarchy? The maintenance of democratic order is an internal problem that the people themselves must solve. It is not something that the privileged overlords need concern themselves with. Besides, they are not really concerned with democracy for the people but use it as a pretext to deny the people their democratic rights. Of course, internal problems cannot be solved overnight but must be constantly addressed during the development process. Mistakes and shortcomings are inevitable, but these are for us to worry about and are infinitely preferable to facing abusive overlords against whom we have no means of redress. Those who worry that democracy will lead to anarchy and chaos are just like those who worried that without an emperor China would fall into chaos following the overthrow of the Qing dynasty. Their recommendation was, Patiently suffer oppression! Without the weight of oppression, the roofs of your homes might fly off!

With all due respect, let me say to such people: We want to be the masters of our own destiny. We need no gods or emperors and we don't believe in saviors of any kind. We want to be masters of our universe, not the modernizing tools of dictators with personal ambitions. We want the modernization of people's lives. Democracy, freedom, and happiness for all are our sole objectives in carrying out modernization. Without this fifth modernization, all others are nothing more than a new promise.

Comrades, I appeal to you: Let us rally under the banner of democracy. Do not be fooled again by dictators who talk of "stability and unity." Fascist totalitarianism can bring us nothing but disaster. Harbor no more illusions; democracy is our only hope. Abandon our democratic rights and we shackle ourselves again. Let us have confidence in our own strength! We are the creators of human history. Banish all self-proclaimed leaders and teachers, for they have already cheated the people of their most valuable rights for decades.

I firmly believe that production will flourish even more when controlled by the people themselves because the workers will be producing for their own benefit. Life will improve because the workers' interests will be the primary goal. Society will be more rational because all power will be exercised by the people as a whole through democratic means.

I don't believe that all of this will be handed to the people effortlessly by some great savior. I also refuse to believe that China will abandon this goal because of the many difficulties it will surely encounter along the way. As long as people clearly identify their goal and realistically assess the obstacles before them, then surely they will trample any praying mantis that might try to bar their way. . . .

If the Chinese people want modernization, they must first put democracy into practice and modernize China's social system. Democracy is not merely an inevitable stage of social development, as Lenin claimed. In addition to being the result of productive forces and productive relations that have developed to a certain stage, democracy is also the very condition that allows for such development to reach beyond this stage. Without this condition, society will become stagnant and economic growth will face insurmountable obstacles. Therefore, as history tells us, a democratic social system is the premise and precondition for all development, or what we can also call modernization.

Without this premise and precondition, not only will further progress be impossible but it will be very difficult to maintain the development we have already achieved. . . .

Does democracy come about naturally when society reaches a certain stage? Absolutely not. An enormous price is paid for every tiny victory, so much so that even coming to a recognition of this fact requires sacrifices. The enemies of democracy have always deceived their people by saying that just as democracy is inevitable, so it is also doomed, and therefore it is not worth wasting energy fighting for.

But let us look at the real history, not that fabricated by the hired hacks of the "socialist government"! Every small twig of true and worthy democracy is stained with the blood of martyrs and tyrants, and every step taken toward democracy has been fiercely attacked by the reactionary forces. The fact that democracy has been able to surmount such obstacles proves that it is precious to the people and that it embodies all their aspirations. Thus the democratic trend cannot be stopped. The Chinese people have never feared anything; they need only recognize the direction to be taken and the forces of tyranny will no longer be invincible.

[From "Diwuge xiandaihua — minzhu ji qita," in *Wei Jingsheng qishilu*, pp. 37–39, 44–46, 47–48; trans. adapted from Wei, *The Courage to Stand Alone*, pp. 199–212 — KMT]

DEMOCRACY OR NEW DICTATORSHIP, *EXPLORATION*, MARCH 1979

Everyone in China knows that the Chinese social system is not democratic and that this lack of democracy has severely stunted every aspect of the country's social development over the past thirty years. In the face of this hard fact there are two choices before the Chinese people — either to reform the social system if they want to develop their society and seek a swift increase in prosperity and economic resources or, if they are content with a continuation of the Mao Zedong brand of proletarian dictatorship, then they cannot even talk of democracy, nor will they be able to realize the modernization of their lives and resources. . . .

Does Deng Xiaoping want democracy? No, he does not. He is unwilling to comprehend the misery of the common people. He is unwilling to allow the people to regain those powers usurped by ambitious careerists. He describes the struggle for democratic rights — a movement launched spontaneously by the people — as the actions of troublemakers who must be repressed. To resort to such measures to deal with people who criticize mistaken policies and demand social development shows that the government is very afraid of this popular movement.

We cannot help asking Mr. Deng what his idea of democracy is. If the people have no right to express their opinions and criticisms, then how can one talk of democracy? If his idea of democracy is one that does not allow others to criticize those in power, then how is such a democracy different from Mao Zedong's tyranny concealed behind the slogan "Democracy of the dictatorship of the proletariat"? . . .

The people should ensure that Deng Xiaoping does not degenerate into a dictator. After he was reinstated in 1975, it seemed he was unwilling to follow Mao Zedong's dictatorial system and would instead care for the interests of the people. So the people eagerly looked up to him in the hope that he would realize their aspirations. They were even ready to shed their blood for him — as the Tiananmen Square [April Fifth] incident showed. But was such support vested in his person alone? Certainly not. If he now wants to discard his mask and take steps to suppress the democratic movement, then he certainly does not merit the people's trust and support. . . . People entrusted with government positions must be controlled by and responsible to the people. According to the constitution, organizations and individuals in the administration must be elected by the people, empowered and controlled by an elected government under the supervision of the people and responsible to the people. Only then is there a legality for executive powers. . . .

Only a genuine general election can create a government and leaders ready to serve the interests of the electorate. If the government and its leaders are truly subject to the people's mandate and supervision, those two afflictions that leadership is prone to — personal ambition and megalomania — can be avoided.

[From Benton and Hunter, *Wild Lily, Prairie Fire*, pp. 181–184]

### WALL POSTER FROM THE APRIL FIFTH FORUM

This essay (March 1979) reflects the sentiment of Beijing Spring activists who found Wei Jingsheng's attitude toward the new regime too extreme but who tried nevertheless to establish a rational basis for public discourse.

An article titled "Democracy or New Dictatorship" in the March 25 *Exploration* has aroused argument and general concern. We differ with some of the main points made in the article. We present our view here to engender further discussion with that author. We also invite criticism and suggestions from the people. . . .

The *Exploration* article criticized "would-be autocrats" who "take advantage of people's gullibility" for their own petty ends. For example, in his March 16 talk to leading cadres of various central ministries and commissions, Vice-Chairman Deng Xiaoping attempted to use the people's previous confidence in him to oppose the democratic movement. He made various charges against the democratic movement, attempted to blame it for the failure of the Hua-

Deng regime to save China's economy and production, and tried once again "to make the people scapegoats for the failure of their policies." We doubt that this is correct. . . .

We wonder whether *Exploration* has evidence to sustain the view that Comrade Deng is "petty" and "a would-be autocrat." . . .

Lin Biao and the Gang of Four used to take a sentence or two [out of context] and use them to label people and oppress them. We must do everything we can to rid ourselves of this bad practice. Placing labels on people on the basis of a few sentences spoken is the wrong way to treat either a leader like Deng Xiaoping or a common person. . . .

Deng Xiaoping remains China's most powerful personage. If he really wants to suppress the democratic movement, he will have the support of many officials and could easily do so. But he has not done so, and the people are able to write what they wish and the publications are available at Democracy Wall. . . .

But no good end awaits anyone seeking to suppress the democratic movement. History will attest to that.

[Adapted from Seymour, *The Fifth Modernization*, pp. 201–203]

HU PING: "ON FREEDOM OF SPEECH," WRITTEN FOR HIS SUCCESSFUL 1980 CAMPAIGN TO BECOME BEIJING UNIVERSITY'S DELEGATE TO THE HAIDIAN DISTRICT PEOPLE'S ASSEMBLY

In the early 1980s the new regime began experimenting with free elections from the local level. Hu Ping, a Beijing University graduate student in European philosophy, ran for delegate to the county-level legislature and won. The government, however, did not allow him to assume his post.

The purpose of this article is to assert freedom of speech. At a time when there is absolutely no freedom of speech, it is certainly not possible to engage in such a novel endeavor. However, at a time of complete freedom of speech, it would not seem necessary to expound on it. This peculiarity often leads to a misunderstanding — that is, to the assumption that the question of freedom of speech is dependent on the will of those in power. This misunderstanding again leads to a neglect of any work or discussion of the theoretical side of this question and thus results in smothering completely any value and vitality in the principle of freedom of speech. This unfortunate misunderstanding is so deep-rooted that when this highly important and sensitive topic is brought up, many people take it to be a tiresome commonplace, the empty talk of scholarly nitwits. But when a country is without freedom of speech, the real reason is that its people lack a consciousness of freedom of speech. It is for this reason that it becomes a matter of the highest importance to clarify the inherent meaning of freedom of speech, its value and power, in the course of our work of perfecting and developing our country's socialist democracy and legal system.

Freedom of speech for our citizens is the first article in the list of the various political rights in our constitution. If a man loses the right to make known his own aspirations and ideas, he will of necessity sink to the status of slave or a mere tool. Of course, to have the right of free speech does not mean to have everything, but losing the right of free speech will definitely lead to losing everything. In the science of mechanics, everybody knows the highly important function of the fulcrum. Even though the fulcrum itself cannot perform any work, it is indispensable to make the lever work effectively. It is said that Archimedes, the discoverer of the principle of leverage, made the statement "Give me a fulcrum and I will move the world." In political life, isn't freedom of speech just like this fulcrum?

What is freedom of speech? It is freedom to make known various opinions, and this includes everything: good speech, bad speech, correct speech, and incorrect speech. If freedom of speech were to be limited to only the sphere outlined by those in power, then one might ask: Is there any country in the world, past and present, that did not have "freedom" of speech? In this sense, wouldn't the article of our sacred constitution on freedom of speech become a most useless piece of rubbish? . . .

We must point out in passing that some people consider it anarchism if "everyone is free to speak and act as he pleases." This amounts to equating freedom of speech with freedom of action. It is true that if everybody is free to do as he pleases, it may lead to a state of anarchy. However, if we extend our prohibition to preclude everybody from speaking as he pleases, that will lead to despotism. In our future opposition to any particular "ism," we must have a fairly distinct definition of it and not commit the same error as in the past when we opposed revisionism.

There is an ancient Chinese saying: "Do not condemn the speaker." What does it mean? Since it is only those in power who can condemn anybody else, and since those in power will of course not send their cohorts to prosecute someone who speaks the way they, the rulers, approve, it is clear that the saying "Do not condemn the speaker" especially affirms that no guilt should be attached to those who "sing a different tune." This again proves that our definition of freedom of speech above is absolutely correct.

[Adapted from *SPEAHRhead* 12/13 (Winter/Spring 1982): 36]

## WANG RUOSHUI: "DISCUSSING THE QUESTION OF ALIENATION"

The suppression of the Democracy Wall of the Beijing Spring movement did not silence debate on China's future. People both inside and outside of the party and the government continued discussion as the state periodically tightened and loosened its control over free expression.

Wang Ruoshui, an established intellectual older than the Democracy Wall activists, rejected both the Maoist interpretation and the new regime's Leninist interpretation of Marx, and instead sought to imbue Chinese socialism with a humanism seen as the heart of Marx's vision.

The question is quite complex. We cannot simply say that once a system of public ownership is established, all problems will be solved. It seems that originally Marx and Engels assumed that the root of all alienation was the system of private property and once society mastered the means of production, alienation would disappear. . . . From today's perspective, getting rid of private ownership and wiping out exploitation have indeed been an important issue, but this is not to say that, having done this, society is completely free of all problems and the people can enter an unfettered realm. No! There is still alienation because people can still fail to fully understand the laws of social development; there is still obscurantism, giving rise to problems and thereby leading to a certain loss of freedom. In my view, Chairman Mao had something to contribute here. He said, "Human history develops continuously from the realm of necessity to the realm of freedom. It will never end." This formulation is quite scientific and accords with dialectical materialism.

Therefore, in a socialist society, in addition to the possibility of alienation in thought and politics, alienation can also appear in the economy. Of course, this alienation is different from capitalist alienation, in that mainly it is created not by exploitation but by not understanding objective economic laws. In addition, problems with bureaucratism and the system itself still exist. . . . In some matters we frequently concern ourselves with the immediate or obvious result. It is good that we can foresee short-term results, but we frequently cannot predict the long-term effects. Yet the long-term consequences can slip out of our control and on the contrary harm people. . . . This is also alienation. The goal of socialist production is to satisfy the needs of the people; this should be very clear! Yet socialist society can also give rise to this kind of phenomenon, one-sidedly pursuing speed and one-sidedly developing heavy industry. The advantage of speed is that it quickly raises the people's standard of living. Only in this sense is it an advantage! Sacrificing the people's living standard for the sake of speed or heavy industry — speed for speed's sake or heavy industry for heavy industry's sake — results in great suffering, and the greater the enthusiasm, the greater the suffering. The fruits of labor do not benefit the people, but on the contrary cause them loss; this is also alienation. Due to this . . . , not understanding objective economic laws along with great blindness results in economic alienation. Exploitation is one type of alienation — admittedly a very important type — but it is not the only type. Therefore we can look at this question from a broader perspective and see that many social problems are actually problems of alienation. We must now overcome alienation by recognizing objective laws and mastering our own fate.

Raising this question of alienation now touches upon many new problems in our midst, and we must all reapply ourselves. In the past we did not pay enough attention to the early works of Marx. I think there were two reasons.

We felt they were unimportant and also too difficult to understand. It is true that they are difficult to understand, but they are not unimportant. We can now see the profundity of his thought on alienation. Actually, Marx in his later years also discussed alienation, and although he discussed it a little less, he nevertheless never abandoned this concept.

[From *Xinwen zhanxian*, no. 8 (1980): 8–12 — RL]

## WANG RUOSHUI: "IN DEFENSE OF HUMANISM"

A specter is haunting China's intellectual world — the specter of humanism.

In the last three years more than four hundred articles on the question of "humanity" have appeared, and among them quite a few explore the Marxist concept of humanism. . . . That the question of humanity inspired such strong interest, in my view, is not merely a reaction to the decade of domestic turmoil but also reflects the necessity of creating a highly civilized and highly democratic socialist society for a new era. In the process, when deviations arise, these must of course be corrected through discussion and criticism. However, some well-intentioned comrades fundamentally reject any call for humanism, considering it to be heretical. . . .

Consequently, I would like to argue in defense of humanism, especially Marxist humanism.

## What Is Humanism?

"Humanism is the ideology of the bourgeoisie" — If this statement means humanism was the ideology of the bourgeoisie, this is an objective, historical fact and there is nothing to dispute. If, however, this statement means that humanism can only be the ideology of the bourgeoisie, then it must be questioned. The meanings of these two statements cannot be confused; the second meaning cannot be inferred from the first.

Materialism was also the ideology of the bourgeoisie (and even of the slave-owner and feudal classes), and yet this has not prevented materialism from becoming the worldview of the proletariat. Indeed, there is a huge difference between Marxist materialism and old-style materialism, and yet this is the difference between one type of materialism and another, not materialism and idealism.

Can a similar distinction be made concerning humanism?

It depends on the content of this concept of humanism. If the concept of humanism is substantially and necessarily linked to the special class characteristics of the bourgeoisie (for example, "individualism" is this kind of concept), then humanism can only be the ideology of the bourgeoisie. Otherwise, such is not the case.

What is humanism? *Humanism* is a term borrowed from abroad, and many people in our country are not sure what it means precisely. Yet they judge it on the basis of this hazy understanding. Of course, the schools of humanism are numerous, and the various theories differ. However, there is still a generally accepted explanation. . . .

In essence, the term *humanism* at the earliest indicated the central intellectual theme of the Renaissance (this is humanism in the narrow sense, in general it is also translated as *renwen zhuyi* — the doctrine of humane learning); later it came to refer to all concepts or philosophical thought that placed primary importance on humanity, the value of humanity, the dignity of humanity, the interests or well-being of humanity, the development or freedom of humanity (this is humanism in the broader sense, which is discussed in this essay).

In my view, some of the comrades who evaluate humanism negatively may be starting with a mistaken conception of humanism. Humanism is a long-standing and well-established intellectual trend, going back at least six hundred years in the West. After the Renaissance, there was the humanism of the Enlightenment, the humanism of utopian socialism, the humanism of Feuerbach (*renbenxue*) and also the multifarious modern humanisms. . . . So many intellectual schools are all called "humanism" because they have a common principle. This common principle, simply put, is the value of humanity. This is the same as the many philosophical systems called "materialism" because they all recognize the "primacy of material substance." The understanding of the value of humanity by the different humanisms may differ greatly, but as long as they emphasize the value of humanity, then these differences are distinctions between different types of humanisms, and not differences between humanism and non-humanism or anti-humanism.

## Socialism Needs Humanism

In carrying out socialist modernization reconstruction today we need socialist humanism. What does this humanism mean to us?

- It means firmly abandoning the "total dictatorship" and cruel struggle of the ten years of internal chaos, abandoning the cult of personality that deified an individual and demeaned the people, and insisting that human equality, the personal freedom of citizens, and human dignity not be encroached upon in fact or in law.
- It means opposing the feudal notions of rank and special privilege, opposing capitalism's money-worshiping philosophy, opposing viewing people as commodities or mere tools; it means demanding that people be seen as people and valued not for their background, position, or property but for themselves.
- It means recognizing that people are the end, not only the end of socialist production, but the end of all work; it means constructing and realizing

socialist spiritual civilization's new social relations of mutual respect, mutual care, mutual aid, and friendly cooperation; it means opposing bureaucratism that neglects the people and extreme individualism that benefits oneself at the expense of others.

- It means emphasizing the people factor in socialist construction, enhancing the prominence and creativity of the working classes; it means emphasizing education, emphasizing the cultivation of talent, and emphasizing the complete development of humanity. . . .

Isn't this socialist humanism already existing in our practice, and isn't it increasingly developing? Why treat it as something strange and alien?

A specter haunts the intellectual world. . . .

"Who are you?"

"I am humanity."

[From *Wenhuibao*, January 17, 1983, p. 3 — RL]


## ASSESSING THE NEW POLICIES

### DENG XIAOPING: "BUILD SOCIALISM WITH CHINESE CHARACTERISTICS"

This excerpt is from a talk with the Japanese delegation to the second session of the council of Sino-Japanese nongovernmental figures, June 30, 1984. Although he did not always hold top positions in the party or government, Deng Xiaoping clearly led the nation from the late seventies to the late eighties. As the regime adopted more and more capitalist-style practices over that period, however, it was forced into an ideological corner. How could the Chinese Communist Party (CCP) introduce capitalist practices? It looked back to a more orthodox theory of development from capitalism to socialism to provide it with an ideological fig leaf. Since socialist revolution, according to this theory, could take place only in an advanced capitalist country, it was the task of the CCP to build up the forces of production that would eventually serve as the premise and basis for socialism.

People may ask, If China had taken the capitalist instead of the socialist road, could the Chinese people have liberated themselves and could China have finally stood up? The Nationalists took that road for more than twenty years and proved that it does not work. By contrast, the Chinese Communists, by adhering to Marxism and integrating Marxism with actual conditions in China in accordance with Mao Zedong Thought, took their own road and succeeded in the revolution by encircling the cities from the countryside. Conversely, if we had not been Marxists, or if we had not integrated Marxism with Chinese conditions and followed our own road, China would have remained fragmented, with neither independence nor unity. China simply had to adhere to

Marxism. If we had not fully believed in Marxism, the Chinese revolution would never have succeeded. That belief was the motive force. After the founding of the People's Republic, if we had taken the capitalist rather than the socialist road, we would not have ended the chaos in the country or changed its conditions — inflation, unstable prices, poverty, and backwardness. We started from a backward past. There was virtually no industry for us to inherit from old China, and we did not have enough grain for food. Some people ask why we chose socialism. We answer that we had to, because capitalism would get China nowhere. We must solve the problems of feeding and employing the population and of reunifying China. That is why we have repeatedly declared that we shall adhere to Marxism and keep to the socialist road. But by Marxism we mean Marxism that is integrated with Chinese conditions, and by socialism we mean socialism that is tailored to Chinese conditions and has Chinese characteristics.

What is socialism and what is Marxism? We were not quite clear about this before. Marxism attaches utmost importance to developing the productive forces. We advocate communism. But what does that mean? It means the principle of from each according to his ability, to each according to his needs, which calls for highly developed productive forces and overwhelming material wealth. Therefore, the fundamental task for the socialist stage is to develop the productive forces. The superiority of the socialist system is demonstrated by faster and greater development of the productive forces than under the capitalist system. One of our shortcomings since the founding of the People's Republic was that we neglected the development of the productive forces. Socialism means eliminating poverty. Pauperism is not socialism, still less communism. The superiority of the socialist system lies above all in its ability to increasingly develop the productive forces and to improve the people's material and cultural life. The problem facing us now is how China, which is still backward, is to develop the productive forces and improve the people's living standard. This brings us back to the point of whether to continue on the socialist road or to stop and turn onto the capitalist road. The capitalist road can only enrich less than 10 percent of the Chinese population; it can never enrich the 90 percent. That is why we must adhere to socialism. The socialist principle of distribution to each according to his work will not create an excessive gap in wealth. Consequently, no polarization will occur as our productive forces become developed over the next twenty to thirty years.

The minimum target of our Four Modernizations is to achieve a comparatively comfortable standard of living by the end of the century. . . . By a "comfortable standard" we mean that per capita GNP will reach U.S. $800. That is a low level for you, but it is really ambitious for us. China has a population of 1 billion now and it will reach 1.2 billion by then. If, when the GNP reached $1,000 billion, we applied the capitalist principle of distribution, it would not amount to much and could not help to eliminate poverty and backwardness.

Less than 10 percent of the population would enjoy a better life, while more than 90 percent remained in poverty. But the socialist principle of distribution can enable all the people to become relatively comfortable. This is why we want to uphold socialism. Without socialism, China can never achieve that goal.

However, only talking about this is not enough. The present world is an open one. China's past backwardness was due to its closed-door policy. After the founding of the People's Republic, we were blockaded by others, and so the country remained closed to some extent, which created difficulties for us. Some "left" policies and the Cultural Revolution in particular were disastrous for us. In short, the experience of the past thirty years or more proves that a closed-door policy would hinder construction and inhibit development. Therefore, the ideological line formulated at the Third Plenary Session of the Party's Eleventh Central Committee is to adhere to the principles of integrating Marxism with Chinese conditions, seeking truth from facts, linking theory with practice, and proceeding from reality. In other words, the line is to adhere to the essence of Comrade Mao Zedong's thought. Our political line focuses on the four modernizations, on continuing to develop the productive forces. Nothing short of world war would make us release our grip on this essential point. Even should world war break out, we would engage in reconstruction after the war. A closed-door policy would not help construction. There are two kinds of exclusion: one is directed against other countries; the other is directed against China itself, with one region or department closing its doors to the others. We are suggesting that we should develop a little faster — just a little, because it would be unrealistic to go too fast. To do this, we have to invigorate the domestic economy and open up to the outside. We must first of all solve the problem of the countryside, which contains 80 percent of the population. China's stability depends on the stability of the countryside with this 80 percent — this is the reality of China from which we should proceed. No matter how successful our work in the cities is, it will not mean much without the stable base of the countryside. Therefore, we must first of all solve the problem of the countryside by invigorating the economy and adopting an open policy so as to bring the initiative of 80 percent of the population into full play. We adopted this policy at the end of 1978, and after several years in operation it has produced the desired results. . . .

As for our relations with foreign countries, we shall pursue the policy of opening up still wider to the outside world. We have opened fourteen medium and large coastal cities. We welcome foreign investment and advanced techniques. Management is also a kind of technique. Will they undermine our socialism? Not likely, because the socialist economy is our mainstay. Our socialist economic base is so huge that it can absorb tens and hundreds of billions of dollars' worth of foreign funds without shaking the socialist foundation. Besides, we adhere to the socialist principle of distribution and do not tolerate economic polarization. Thus, foreign investment will doubtless serve as a major supplement to the building of socialism in our country. And as things stand now, this supplement is indispensable. Naturally, some problems will arise in the wake of foreign investment. But the negative aspects are far less significant than the positive use we can make of it to accelerate our development. It may entail a slight risk, but not much.

Well, those are our plans. We shall accumulate experience and try new solutions as new problems arise. In general, we believe the road we have chosen — building socialism with Chinese characteristics — is the right one and will work. We have followed this road for five and a half years and have achieved satisfactory results. We want to quadruple China's GNP by the end of the century. The pace of development so far exceeded our projections. And so I can tell our friends that we are even more confident now.

[From Deng, *Speeches and Writings*, pp. 95–98]

### CHEN YUN: SPEECH GIVEN AT THE CHINESE COMMUNIST NATIONAL REPRESENTATIVE CONFERENCE, SEPTEMBER 23, 1985

Chen Yun, a veteran party leader and specialist in economic affairs, had opposed Mao's Great Leap Forward during the late 1950s but by the mid-1980s found that the policies of the post–Cultural Revolution regime had moved too far in adopting capitalist practices. Chen's advocacy of a stable economy based upon agriculture and his rejection of commerce echo the views of conservatives throughout the imperial era (221 B.C.E. – 1912 C.E.).

We still must pay close attention to and master grain production. . . .

There are now some peasants who have no interest in growing grain, and we must pay attention to this problem. . . . Raising pigs and growing vegetables are looked upon with contempt since "industry is wealth." . . . The problem is that the voices yelling "industry is wealth" drown out those yelling "agriculture is stability."

Clothing and food for one billion people is a great economic problem for our country, and also a great political problem. The matter of "no grain means chaos" cannot be ignored.

In a socialist economy, there still must be proportionate planning.

We are a Communist party, and Communist parties work for socialism.

The current reform of the socialist economic system is the self-perfecting and development of the socialist system.

The reform of the economic system is meant to develop the productive forces and gradually improve the lives of the people. The rural reforms have already achieved noticeable results. As for the reforms of the urban economic system, the general direction is correct, while the concrete steps and measures are now being explored. We'll proceed step by step, summing up our experience as we go, and persevere in carrying out reform.

From the perspective of national work, the planned economy is the mainstay, while regulated markets remain supplementary. This notion is not obsolete.

Of course, planning includes command planning and guided planning. The two methods of planning are different, but both make planned use of various methods of economic regulation. The guided plan really is not the equivalent of market regulation. Market regulation — that is, no planning — carries out production only according to changes in market supply and demand — that is blind regulation.

The plan is the foundation of macroscopic control. Only having achieved macroscopic control can we profitably achieve microscopic [control] to prosper without chaos.

The resolution concerning the seventh five-year plan, which was passed at this meeting, proposed that the speed of industrial and agricultural development over the course of the five-year plan be divided into 7 percent and 6 percent [annual growth, respectively]. This speed is quite moderate and can be exceeded as we proceed, but there is no need to subjectively set even higher targets.

On August 2 when receiving foreign guests, Comrade Xiaoping, in discussing the excessive speed of industrial development in our country, said, "It sounds wonderful, but there are unhealthy aspects." I agree with him.

In 1984 total industrial output value increased 14 percent over the previous year; in the first half of this year it increased 22.8 percent over the same period last year. We cannot sustain this high rate of growth because our present energy sources, transportation and natural resources and the like are inadequate.

In the end, we must still steadily advance in accordance with proportionate planning; only then can we achieve the highest rate of speed. Otherwise, we will create all kinds of strains and loss of control and be unable to avoid redundancies, and the results will instead be slow. Haste makes waste.

Improving the Party's work style is still the great task of the entire Party.

In recent years [Party] Central has taken on the problem of the Party's work style. However, the mission of improving the Party's work style is still extremely important.

At present there definitely is a minority of Party members and party cadres, especially individual old Party members and old cadres, who are unable to uphold the principles of Party loyalty and have indulged in every harmful trend.

Serious violations of Party discipline and national laws such as counterfeiting medicines and alcohol have occurred throughout the Party.

That vast numbers of cadres, both inside and outside of the Party, and the masses are extremely dissatisfied about these matters should draw the serious attention of the whole Party. . . .

I hope that all high-level leading personnel, in disciplining their sons and daughters, should set an example for the whole Party. They should never allow them to use their family connections to gain power and profit and become privileged characters.

Strengthen thought and political work, and uphold the authority of the thought and political work department.

Recently, the secretariat has discussed the problem of strengthening thought and political work; in my view this is absolutely necessary. We are the ruling party and are currently in a new stage of development; how we effectively carry out intellectual construction and organization work is of great consequence.

At present, some people, including some members of the Communist Party, have forgotten the ideals of socialism and communism and have forsaken the goal of serving the people. Pursuing private advantage, they have become "money-mad," disregarding the interests of the nation and the masses, even violating the law and discipline. It's just like all those phenomena so frequently reported by the press — speculation and fraud, corruption and bribery, illicitly gained wealth and consorting with foreigners with no regard for national or individual dignity.

These problems are related to our letting up on thought and political work and weakening the function and authority of the thought and political work department; we should thereby draw a lesson.

All levels of party organization should conscientiously take on propaganda and political work.

[From *Chen Yun wenxuan* 3:349–353 — RL]


# NEW DEMANDS FOR CHANGE AND DEMOCRACY

## FANG LIZHI: DEMOCRACY, REFORM, AND MODERNIZATION

Fang Lizhi, an astrophysicist at Science and Technology University, Hefei, Anhui, became famous for his frank and trenchant criticism of the post–Cultural Revolution regime. Arguing from scientific method, he sought to analyze China's problems and debunk the ideological dogma of the regime. His ideas express the thinking of Chinese students and intellectuals during the 1980s and make a clear argument for more power and responsibility to be placed in the hands of intellectuals. Fang seeks an end to state control of intellectuals and the return of the freedom that intellectuals enjoyed during the May 4 period.

The following are excerpts from Fang's best-known speech, delivered to an audience of about three thousand students and faculty members at Shanghai's Tongji University on November 18, 1986. Many of the remarks in this speech were later singled out for criticism by the Communist Party as examples of bourgeois liberal thought.

Our goal at present is the thorough modernization of China. We all have a compelling sense of the need for modernization. There is a widespread demand for change among people in all walks of life, and very few find any reason for complacency. None feel this more strongly than those of us in science and academia. Modernization has been our national theme since the Gang of Four was overthrown ten years ago, but we are just beginning to understand what it really means. In the beginning we were mainly aware of the grave shortcomings in our production of goods, our economy, our science and technology, and that modernization was required in these areas. But now we understand our situation much better. We realize that grave shortcomings exist not only in our "material civilization" but also in our "spiritual civilization" — our culture, our ethical standards, our political institutions — and that these also require modernization.

The question we must now ask is, What kind of modernization is required? I think it's obvious to all of us that we need complete modernization, not just modernization in a few chosen aspects. People are now busy comparing Chinese and Western culture — including politics, economics, science, technology, education, the whole gamut — and there is much debate over the subject. The question is, do we want "complete Westernization" or "partial Westernization"? Should we continue to uphold the century-old banner of "using Western methods but maintaining the Chinese essence" or any other "cardinal principle"? Of course, this is not a new discussion. A century ago, insightful people realized that China had no choice but to modernize. Some wanted partial modernization, others wanted complete modernization, and thus they initiated a debate that continues down to the present day.

I personally agree with the "complete Westernizers." What their so-called complete Westernization means to me is complete openness, the removal of restrictions in every sphere. We need to acknowledge that when looked at in its entirety, our culture lags far behind that of the world's most advanced societies, not in any one specific aspect but across the board. Responding to this situation calls not for the establishment of a priori barriers but for complete openness to the outside world. Attempting to set our inviolable "essence" off-limits before it is even challenged makes no sense to me. Again, I am scarcely inventing these ideas. A century ago people said essentially the same thing: Open China up and face the challenge of more advanced societies head-on, in every aspect from technology to politics. What is good will stand up, and what is not good will be swept away. This prognosis remains unchanged.

Why is China so backward? To answer this question, we need to take a clear look at history. China has been undergoing revolutions for a century, but we are still very backward. This is all the more true since Liberation, these decades of the socialist revolution that we all know firsthand as students and workers. Speaking quite dispassionately, I have to judge this era a failure. This is not my opinion only, by any means; many of our leaders are also admitting as much, saying that socialism is in trouble everywhere. Since the end of World War II, socialist countries have by and large not been successful. There is no getting around this. As far as I'm concerned, the last thirty-odd years in China have been a failure in virtually every aspect of economic and political life.

Of course, some will say that China is a big, poor country, and therefore that progress has been hard to come by. Indeed, our overpopulation, our huge geographical area, and our preexisting poverty do contribute to our problems. This being the case, some say, we haven't done badly to get where we are today.

But these factors by themselves don't completely account for the situation. For every one of them you can find a counterexample. Take population, for example. While our population is the world's largest in terms of absolute numbers, our population density is not. China has about 750 persons depending on each square kilometer of arable land, while Japan has about twice that, some 1,500 persons per square kilometer. Why has Japan succeeded while China has not? Our initial conditions were not that different; after the war, their economy was nearly as devastated as ours. Why have we not prospered like Japan? Overpopulation alone does not explain this. . . .

We need to take a careful look at why socialism has failed. Socialist ideals are admirable. But we have to ask two questions about the way they have been put into practice: Are the things done in the name of socialism actually socialist? And, do they make any sense? We have to take a fresh look at these questions, and the first step in that process is to free our minds from the narrow confines of orthodox Marxism. . . .

I've always had the feeling, even though we claim that Marxism embraces all contributions to civilization down through the ages, that when you really get down to it, we're saying that only since Marx has anyone known the real truth. Sometimes even Marx himself is tossed aside, and all that counts is what's happened since Liberation. Everything else is treated very negatively. Anything from the past, or from other cultures, is denigrated. We are very familiar with this attitude. When a historical figure is discussed, there is always a disclaimer at the end: "Despite this person's contributions, he suffered from historical limitations." In other words, he wasn't quite of the stature of us Marxists.

This is typical. When scholars of other races or nationalities make great discoveries, we'll say that they've done some good things, but due to the limitations of their class background, thus-and-so. In one area after another, it is made to appear that only since Liberation have truly great things been accomplished. This is parochial and narrow-minded in the extreme. What became of embracing the contributions of other cultures? We see ourselves towering over the historical landscape, but the fact is, nothing can justify such a claim. Only religions view their place in history in this fashion. . . .

Democracy is based on recognizing the rights of every single individual. Naturally, not everyone wants the same thing, and therefore the desires of different individuals have to be mediated through a democratic process, to form a society, a nation, a collectivity. But it is only on the foundation of recognizing the humanity and the rights of each person that we can build democracy. However, when we talk about "extending democracy" here, it refers to your superiors "extending democracy" for you. This is a mistaken concept. This is not democracy.

"Loosening up" is even worse. If you think about it, what it implies is that everyone is tied up very tightly right now, but if you stay put, we'll loosen the rope a little bit and let you run around. . . . In democratic societies, democracy and science — and most of us here are scientists — run parallel. Democracy is concerned with ideas about humanity, and science is concerned with nature. One of the distinguishing features of universities is the role of knowledge; we do research, we create new knowledge to develop new products, and so forth. In this domain, within the sphere of science and the intellect, we make our own judgments based on our own independent criteria.

This is the distinguishing characteristic of a university. In Western society, universities are independent from the government, in the sense that even if the money to run the school is provided by the government, the basic decisions — regarding the content of courses, the standards for academic performance, the selection of research topics, the evaluation of results, and so on — are made by the schools themselves on the basis of values endemic to the academic community, and not by the government. At the same time, good universities in the West are also independent of big business. This is how universities must be. The intellectual realm must be independent and have its own values.

This is an essential guarantee of democracy. It is only when you know something independently that you are free from relying on authorities outside the intellectual domain, such as the government. Unfortunately, things are not this way in China. I have discussed this problem with educators. In the past, even during "the seventeen years" [1949 to 1966, the era before the Cultural Revolution], our universities were mainly engaged in producing tools, not in educating human beings. Education was not concerned with helping students to become critical thinkers, but with producing docile instruments to be used by others. Chinese intellectuals need to insist on thinking for themselves and using their own judgment, but I'm afraid that even now we have not grasped this lesson. . . .

Knowledge must be independent from power, the power of the state included. If knowledge is subservient to power, it is worthless. . . . When it comes to our fields of knowledge, we must think for ourselves and exercise our own judgment about what's right and wrong, and about truth, goodness, and beauty as well. We must refuse to cater to power. Only when we do this will Chinese intellectuals be transformed into genuine intellectuals and our country have a chance to modernize and attain real democracy. This is my message to you today.

[From *Bringing Down the Great Wall*, pp. 157–159, 161–162, 167, 171–173]

FANG LIZHI: "REFORM AND INTELLECTUALS," TALK GIVEN IN 1986

At present, the biggest problem of the reforms is the lack of theoretical studies. We are still in a country where ideology decides everything. If the theoretical problem[s] are left unsolved, the reforms have no hope of success. Also, no one has studied our economic problems from the viewpoint of modern economics. The level of discussion at our highest-level economic conferences is no more profound than everyday conversation, and it amounts to no more than the presentation of general problems. Among the older generation of revolutionaries, there is not one who understands economics.

I believe we intellectuals must have a strong sense of social responsibility. In this regard, European intellectuals are far more committed than those of America. They are conscious of a historical duty to pay attention to and discuss world affairs. They believe that anyone who merely understands his own occupation can be called a technician or specialist, but never an intellectual. Intellectuals must assume certain responsibilities and duties. We too must have this consciousness as intellectuals, since we hope at least that the Chinese nation will not be cast aside by history. . . .

Freedom, democracy, and human rights are [the] common heritage of humanity, and they do not belong only to the bourgeoisie. What I want to emphasize is this: freedom, democracy, and human rights have to be fought for; if we don't fight, they will never arrive on their own.

[From *China Spring Digest* 1, no. 2 (March/April 1987): 30–34]

FANG LIZHI: "THE SOCIAL RESPONSIBILITY OF TODAY'S INTELLECTUALS,"
SPEECH GIVEN AT BEIJING UNIVERSITY, NOVEMBER 4, 1985

As intellectuals, we are obligated to work for the improvement of society. Our primary task in this regard is to strive for excellence and creativity in our chosen professions. This requires that we break the bonds of social restraint when necessary. In keeping with Chinese tradition, creativity has not been encouraged over the past three decades. It is a shame that, as a result, China has yet to produce work worthy of consideration for the Nobel Prize. Why is this? We should reflect upon this question and take a good look at ourselves.

One reason for this situation is our social environment. Many of us who have been to foreign countries to study or work agree that we can perform much more efficiently and productively abroad than in China. . . . Foreigners are no more intelligent than we Chinese are. Why, then, can't we produce first-rate work? The reasons for our inability to develop to our [full] potential lie within our social system. Therefore all of us, when considering our social responsibility, should dedicate ourselves to the creation of a social environment that allows intellectuals to fully utilize their abilities and encourages productivity in their work. . . .

Lately the state has been promoting idealism and discipline. [Its] idea of idealism is simply that we should have a feeling of responsibility toward our society. Of course, our goal should be the improvement of society, but it shouldn't be some utopian dream a million years down the road. (Applause.) Scientists like myself, who study the universe, cannot see that far into the future. What is much more important is to identify problems that exist now and try to solve them and to identify problems that will beset us in the near future that we might be able to minimize or avoid. . . .

What is the real reason we have lost our ideals and discipline? The real reason is that many of our important party leaders have failed to discipline themselves. I will give you an example: There was recently an international symposium on particle accelerators. Both Taiwan and mainland China were represented. In my mind, of course, the participants should be scholars and experts who are directly involved in this kind of work. But in the Chinese delegation of over ten people there was only one from our university. Many of those sent had no qualifications in physics and no familiarity with accelerators. Is this considered "observing discipline"? Among those attending was Beijing vice-mayor Zhang Baifa. I have no idea what he was doing there. (Loud laughter.) If you are talking about discipline, this is an excellent example of what it is not. (Applause.) And this kind of breakdown of discipline is the same thing as corruption. (Loud applause.) In the future, as you learn more about our society, you will find that this sort of corruption is very commonplace. If we are really serious about strengthening discipline, we should start at the top. (Applause.) . . .

We Communist Party members should be open to different ways of thinking. We should be open to different cultures and willing to adopt the elements of those cultures that are clearly superior. A great diversity of thought should be allowed in colleges and universities. If all thought is simplistic and narrow-minded, creativity will die. At present, there are certainly some people in power who still insist on dictating to others according to their own narrow principles. They always wave the flag of Marxism when they speak. But what they are spouting is not Marxism. . . .

We must not be afraid to speak openly about these things. It is our duty. If we remain silent, we have failed to live up to our responsibility.

[From *China Spring Digest* 1, no. 2 (March/April 1987): 34–38]

## LI XIAOJIANG: "AWAKENING OF WOMEN'S CONSCIOUSNESS"

Although the Chinese Communist Party's commitment to improving the lot of Chinese women was never complete and less than claimed, it could point to a certain record of accomplishment. With the new emphasis on practicality in the eighties, however, the party and government lessened efforts to advance women. Some reforms inadvertently reduced women's access to education and participation in the workforce. As a result, some earlier gains were lost and new problems appeared. Li Xiaojiang, a professor of Chinese at Zhengzhou University and chair of the Women's Studies Research Center, analyzes the situation in 1988.

The "Report on Work" of the Thirteenth Party Congress clearly lays out the theory of the first stages of socialism: so-called reform, including reform of political structures, is intended first and foremost to advance the development of society's productive forces. The congress initiated improvements in economic efficiency in order to realize more quickly the transformation of our country from impoverishment, to relative comfort, to prosperity. It also attacked the bureaucracy of the political world, the dogmatism of the theoretical world, the egalitarianism of the economy, and the apathy of the individual. It proposed a realistic approach to reform and true economic competition. These goals, sought after but unrealized for many years, are well and good — but they threaten women. In the spirit of realism, we are impelled to face squarely the issue of biology and childbirth for women in social production. In actual economic competition, the facts that the quality of women as workers is inclined to be low and that they have a dual role evidently make women and the enterprises that employ them less competitive.

Reform has also eliminated life tenure for cadres and the "iron rice bowl" of industry. At precisely the same time that the limited tenure policy and the contract system were being implemented, much of the protection and many of the benefits for women in industry began to disappear one by one. As a result, the problems of "same work — different pay" and unequal promotions for men and women have arisen.

In 1988 a series of women's issues became even more pronounced. Not only women, but the many men whose interests are intertwined with women's and who are with women from morning to night, were affected, as well as all the families concerned about a daughter or a wife. Let us take a glimpse at the issues in the natural course of that one year.

*First quarter.* In the process of democratic elections for people's congresses at every level and for the Seventh National People's Congress, few female cadres were elected, highlighting the problem of women's participation in government.

*Second quarter.* With the simultaneous implementation of enterprise self-management and discretionary hiring and contract systems, women's social benefits, salary, employment, and promotions were all threatened, rendering women workers' problems more acute.

*Third quarter.* In job assignments for college graduates and those who failed to pass the college entrance examinations, employment problems for women surfaced anew. This directly endangered young women intellectuals' future prospects and development.

*Fourth quarter.* With the deepening of economic reform and the widespread pursuit in industry of peak work capacity, the increased vigor of enterprises and the increasingly tense double burden for women came into direct conflict. The call for "equal work — equal pay" causes women to face even more severe challenges in light of the actual work assignments and the disadvantaged position women encounter returning to work after childbirth. Under the circumstances, some women will inevitably decide to return to the home. But people will interpret this not as the will of society but as the conscious choice of women.

The travesty is that these pressures women endured then and continue to endure are never seen as social problems; they are construed as merely *individual problems.* Criticizing society as unfair is to no avail. The balance of justice has never been the moving force in the progress of history. If one is only willing to face reality, then one must see that the emergence of women's problems is actually a means for society to resolve many other social problems that emerged with reform (such as excess labor, labor productivity, and so on). Women have thus been the cornerstone in the development of society's productive capacity. Historically it has been so; in reality it is so. No wonder authoritative sociological publications are unwilling to print much on women's issues, for to speak excessively of women's liberation at this point would be to say that women's problems are obstructing society's reform and economic development. This means that Chinese women, who have worked hard all along to recognize their unity with society, cannot but acknowledge that women's issues in the midst of economic reform have been abandoned by society. There are truly women's problems, in that they have become sociologically insignificant.

## What Exactly Are the Issues?

Discussions of women's issues in the past were always about women enduring oppression, discrimination, and enslavement; these were the pernicious vestiges of feudalism and the product of capitalist exploitation. To put it bluntly, these were mostly the problems of working women and could be categorized as problems of class.

Today, however, just as issues of class in China and the world have receded, women's issues have gradually become more pronounced. They are reflected not only in the problems of women workers and of all women at work but also in the lives of women of every class and in every facet of women's lives. Especially in contemporary China, women's problems come from every direction, creating among those who concern themselves with women's issues a sense of crisis.

It is hard to deny, even for Chinese women accustomed to the catch phrase "Socialism liberates women," that the crisis objectively exists. If we use the obvious "equality of men and women" standard to measure women's actual plight, then Chinese women's liberation seems to be taking the road of regression. In the face of this "reverse tide," the long-parroted, never tested, never deeply researched theory of women's liberation appears exhausted. It is this weakness of conventional theory that compels us to face the reality of Chinese society and the reality of Chinese women, to investigate conscientiously all these earth-shattering women's issues.

[*Shehui kexue zhanxian* 4 (1988): 300–310; trans. adapted from Gilmartin et al., *Engendering China*, pp. 361–364]

# THE NEW AUTHORITARIANISM

Many intellectuals debated the merits of the "new authoritarianism" during the latter half of the 1980s. To its proponents it had some resemblances to what earlier was called "political tutelage" or "guided democracy," but its main emphasis was on the need for stability as a precondition for economic growth. We see in the excerpts below, a decade after Deng's opening to the outside world, the influence of Western political experience and philosophy and references to the Four Dragons — Hong Kong, Taiwan, South Korea, and Singapore. Wu Jiaxiang, a noted advocate of the new authoritarianism, was a researcher at the Investigation and Research Division of the Chinese Communist Party's Central Office at the time of the debate. Rong Jian, an important opponent of the new authoritarianism, was a doctoral student in the philosophy department of People's University in Beijing.

## WU JIAXIANG: "AN OUTLINE FOR STUDYING THE NEW AUTHORITARIANISM," MAY 1989

3. The development of human society cannot be without authority; authority provides stability. Similarly, it cannot be without liberty; liberty provides vitality. A stable and yet continuously changing society is a modern society in which authority and freedom are integrated. . . .

4. The fundamental program of the new authoritarianism is the market economy. Without a new authority, marketization cannot be accomplished, and without that, there can never be true democratic politics. . . .

5. The new authoritarianism is dedicated to forming the political power necessary to resolve major social problems and liberate society from crises during the stage of society's transformation. It has been said that China's most critical problem today is that the country is not clear on what its critical problems are. This is a clever saying but expresses poor judgment. In fact, China is already clear on its problems; the reason there has not been an effective resolution is that a sufficiently large and strong political power has not yet been amassed. There are two aspects to this political power that are necessary to solve society's problems: the government's power and the power of the masses. . . .

6. The new authoritarianism is most concerned about the form of the redis-

tribution of social power resources in a traditional society when the old authority
has declined or even collapsed. . . .

7. The new authoritarianism's "bible" is human equality. The realization of
this equality, however, is certainly not as relaxed, romantic, and poetic as is
perhaps envisioned by some radical democrats. . . . The hierarchy that authority
(the old one) created must be abolished by authority (the new one). There is
no other way.

8. The new authoritarianism holds a critical attitude toward Rousseau's theory of the general will and the theory of sovereignty. Rousseau's theory is a
politically malformed baby of French literary romanticism. If we were to follow
this theory, the result could only be a return to the traditional monarchical
autocracy or to a traditional government by gangs. An indivisible general will
and popular sovereignty is merely a fantasy in Rousseau's mind. In practical
politics, one either has an indivisible dictatorial power, a divisible checked-and-
balanced party politics, or warlord or gang politics in which each piece of
authority occupies a "mountaintop." . . .

9. China's new authoritarians are particularly concerned about how democratic politics can fit the conditions of a large country. As we all know, Aristotle,
Rousseau, and Montesquieu were all admirers of small countries. In their view,
democracy befits a smaller country, whereas autocracy is more suited to a large
country. . . . [The new authoritarianism] seeks to combine a powerful central
government with regional self-rule, and it is precisely in this sense that I call
the Federalists of the United States the American examples of new authoritarianism.

10. The new authoritarianism is not particularly picky about the form in
which society produces its new authority. It is almost impossible to have a design
or a set of rules for how the new authority of a society is to be produced. . . .

11. The new authoritarianism is, first and foremost, a political philosophy.
Its scope of study is restricted to the question of what kind of government strategy
and plan should the rulers have. It does not extend to how a good ruler may
be produced or how the ruler could maintain the position. In other words, it
explains what the new authority is and what it does but not how the new authority is obtained. Second, I believe the new authoritarianism is a philosophy
of history. From the perspective of the new authoritarianism, a typical history
of politics must go through the evolutionary stages — namely, the old authoritarian stage, the new authoritarian stage, and the liberal democratic stage. . . .

The fortunate societies are the ones that can successfully go through all three
stages; the unfortunate often interrupt the process of evolution. . . . China had
some problems: the muddleheadedness of the Qing monarchy plunged China
in modern times into a protracted stage of chaos in which there was no clear
idea of authority. It is more difficult to go from a stage of chaos to the new
authoritarian stage than to go directly from the stage of the old authoritarianism

to the new authoritarian stage. As soon as a normal process is interrupted, it is extremely easy to plunge history into a pitiable cycle of old authority and chaos with no authority, replacing each other repeatedly. Therefore, we can see that the new authoritarian stage is a stage that cannot be leapfrogged by any nation that seeks to realize modernization. Any attempt to do so would only bring about disaster. . . . History has demonstrated that the monarchical form was the ideal instrument . . . for going through the new authoritarian stage. It was able to minimize the crisis of the legitimacy and unity of the authority during the period of social transformation and was able to reduce the use of violence while enhancing the use of the government's prestige. Therefore, according to my theory, I do not consider the new authoritarianism to be merely a summation of the post–World War II political system in Latin America and the East Asian region; rather, I see it as a philosophical summation of a certain stage of development in the history of humanity as a whole.

[From Liu and Li, Xin quanwei zhuyi, pp. 47–53; trans. adapted from<br>Chinese Sociology and Anthropology 23, no. 3 (Spring 1991): 16–23]

RONG JIAN: "DOES CHINA NEED AN AUTHORITARIAN POLITICAL SYSTEM IN THE COURSE OF MODERNIZATION?" MAY 1989

China's reliance on political authoritarianism during the period of developing a liberated economy may appear, phenomenologically, to reflect that China, too, cannot bypass what seems to be a necessary and unavoidable stage in the progress toward modernization. This may well further confirm the resolve on the part of the highest level decision [makers] and policy makers in the reforms to carry out an intense concentration of power. In reality, the reforms have already shown signs of developing in this direction. Nevertheless, I believe that to carry out, under China's present conditions, a coexistence between political authoritarianism and a liberated economy would invite a confrontation with an ever-sharper contradiction than that which existed in those countries where modernization has already been completed or is being completed. The reasons are the following:

First, from the perspective of the progress of modernization in what were the nondeveloped countries, especially from the perspective of the Four Little Dragons in Asia, the premise of political authoritarianism is the thorough dualism between politics and economics. By "thorough," we mean the privatization of the ownership system (or socialization), the "marketization" of the economy, and the independence of the enterprises. On the other hand, it remains dubious as to whether this same dualism can become a reality in China . . . still saddled with a basic problem, namely, that the question of the system of ownership has not yet been resolved. . . .

Second, China's traditional system was based politically on an intense concentration of power. Even though this basis has suffered tremendous impact since the reforms began, it has become ossified but has not died and is still the greatest current roadblock to the liberalization of the economy. Clearly, we cannot use this kind of "political authoritarianism" to facilitate the development of the commodity economy. . . .

Third, in China's traditional system, the contradictions between "vertical strips and horizontal blocks" have existed for a long time; these are the contradictions between the center and localities. The reason for the long-term existence of such a contradiction is that the traditional system simply had not resolved the problem of the dualism between politics and economics. . . .

Fourth, . . . when the Four Little Dragons in Asia, as well as other developing countries, carried out their political authoritarianism, there was a close connection between that and the prevailing international conditions at the time. The state of the cold war created an excuse for every dictator to carry out autocratic government. But now the world has already moved into an age of moderation, and it is precisely in this general trend of moderation that a worldwide tide of democracy, especially that in the developing countries, has become the mainstream of the world. . . . Faced with such a worldwide democratic tide, China cannot be negligent and certainly cannot be immune from its influence. . . .

The fifth and most important issue is that the broad masses of the people, who have already spent forty years under the traditional system of management with its high degree of concentration of power and have also experienced the tempering of the economic reform and the last few years of democratic enlightenment, today have a greatly enhanced democratic consciousness. The clamor for political reform is rising by the day. . . . According to the historical experience of the democratization of the world, unless the people's democratic demands can be met and realized through normal means, they are bound to be vented through abnormal means, such as demonstrations, protests, strikes, and even violent behavior. . . .

From this argument, we may see that at the same time that China takes steps toward the unity of liberalizing the economy and democratizing politics, it must also carry out a thorough reform and transformation of the traditional, highly centralized political system and economic system. The essence of the reform should be the following: on the one hand, creating the social conditions for the liberal development of the economy and, on the other hand, creating the social conditions for the transition from political authoritarianism toward democratic politics.

[From Liu and Li, *Xin quanwei zhuyi*, pp. 113–131; trans. adapted from *Chinese Sociology and Anthropology* 23, no. 2 (Winter 1990/1991): 57–61]

### YAN JIAQI: "HOW CHINA CAN BECOME PROSPEROUS"

Yan Jiaqi, a researcher at the Chinese Academy of Social Sciences, led the discussion on political reform during the eighties and clearly admired the political structure of the Western liberal democracies. Note that the question of how China is to achieve wealth and power goes back to the self-strengthening movement of the 1860s, when it was also linked to domestic political reform. Like the self-strengthener Feng Guifen, Yan seeks to release the energies and enthusiasm of the Chinese people through political reform and to bring about wealth and power.

## Give Free Play to People's Initiative

China is at present engaged in a reform of its political and economic structures. However, if this reform cannot bring into full play the enthusiasm and initiative of individuals, then it is of little use. Each person comes to know politics through his personal experiences. A successful reform must be conducive to bringing into play the initiative of the individual. . . .

## Use Systems to Limit the Tenure of Leaders

China has a very long history. However, despite the differences among the political systems of the various dynasties, they were all built on the foundation of the "perfect man." Whenever Chinese society is faced with all sorts of serious problems, the only remedy that comes to the mind of the Chinese is to hope for the appearance of a morally upright and perfect leader, whose efforts will then change the status quo. For all the complexities of the "Cultural Revolution," its guiding idea is exceedingly simple — that is, China must search for a perfect leader in order to transfer the highest state power. The tremendous calamities caused by the "Cultural Revolution" shook this idea to its very foundations. As I see it, the starting point for China's political structural reform is to admit that no one is perfect. Since human beings have all kinds of defects and weaknesses, a system is needed to restrain them. . . .

## Democracy Is an Error-Correcting Mechanism

Though it promoted "big democracy," the Cultural Revolution actually was a period of the total destruction of democracy. To call the destruction of democracy "big democracy" was a great invention in human history. Therefore, I think there is a need today for clarifying the meaning of *democracy*, to prevent certain people from using the banner of "democracy" to trample on democracy. I believe the most important foundation for democratic politics is to recognize the imperfectibility of human nature — to err is human. In an organization or group that cannot fully agree on goals, opinions, or values, the adoption of democracy means the making of group decisions according to agreed-on procedures and the will of the majority. The practice of democracy often requires people to bow to mistakes. When a majority of the people realize that the original decisions were wrong, then they can be corrected according to procedures that are agreed on by most people and predetermined. . . . When a country or an area has such an error-correcting mechanism, it has democracy; when a political party or a social organization has this kind of error-correcting mechanism, it has democracy. There are various forms of decision making in human society; on questions where there are clear goals and no disagreements over values, decision making should be left to science, advisory groups, and think tanks. Consequently, on scientific questions, we will not resort to majority rule but will have to follow the dictates of truth constantly; on questions of democracy, however, we must be constantly ready to follow mistakes [made by the majority]. The premise of democracy, like those procedures of freedom of speech and freedom of the press, as I just related, is to recognize the imperfectibility of human nature, recognize that the decision makers possess different cultural levels and capabilities, recognize that people may freely express their opinions, desires, and emotions, and make or revise decisions through procedures.

## Change "Personal Rule" to "Legal Rule"

Whether to recognize "human imperfectibility" or not is also the foundation determining whether a country or area can establish "legal rule." The idea of legal rule is to establish the idea that laws are supreme; political parties, the government, enterprises, organizations, and individuals all have to obey the law without exception. . . . Not only the prosperity and stability of Hong Kong but that of the whole of China will depend on the constitution and laws guaranteeing the independent decision-making powers of each level of government, each enterprise, each organization, and each individual. Only in so doing can our society be full of vitality and efficiency and the initiative of each of us given full play.

## Use the Market to Regulate the Movement of Resources

China's prosperity has to rely not only on political and legal reforms but also on economic reforms. . . . The problem facing China's economic reform is how, in an economy dominated by public ownership, to establish an economy where the market determines resource flow, enterprises have self-development abilities, and the industrial structure is continuously renewed. Today, in some areas on the Chinese mainland, some industrial departments will develop the private economy on a larger scale while using the stock and responsibility systems to reform the traditional public ownership system. I think all these measures are extremely useful explorations.

## Using Law to Promote and Guarantee Reform

A major task facing China's political and economic structural reforms is to improve the legal system and imbue reform with the spirit of the rule of law. Use the law to promote reform; use the law to guarantee reform. I believe, if we do so, then China's prosperity will not be a very distant thing from us.

[From Bachman and Yang, *Yan Jiaqi and China's Struggle
for Democracy*, pp. 84–90]

## Chapter 38

TWENTIETH-CENTURY CHRISTIANITY IN CHINA

In keeping with the pattern of wars and political turmoil, broken by brief moments of peace and stability, the twentieth century has been a time of growth, suppression, resurrection, and revival for the Christian religion in China. In this short account the focus is on how leading Chinese Christians — Catholic and Protestant — responded to the encounter between Chinese culture and Christianity, as well as to the repressions of the Communist regime.

Christianity came late to China and remains a minority religion in Communist China, bearing some stigma of Western imperialism. But its followers could be found even among the top political leaders like Sun Yat-sen and Chiang Kai-shek, and the wives of these two were sisters from a strong Methodist family. Madame Sun, née Song Qingling (1893–1981), however, went on to hold high posts in the Communist Chinese government, and at her death the official press identified her posthumously as a member of the Chinese Communist Party.

To represent twentieth-century Chinese Christianity and the problem of cultural encounter between China and Christianity, we have two Catholics — Ma Xiangbo and John C. H. Wu (Jingxiong) — and three Protestants — Zhao Zichen (T. C. Chao), Wu Yaozong (Y. T. Wu), and Wang Mingdao, who held different views regarding cooperation with the government, as the Communist takeover in 1949 raised the burning issue of Christian collaboration with an atheistic regime.

The Protestants chosen, despite their own agreements and disagreements, were leaders of church institutions, whereas the Catholics selected here became known more for their own individual achievements than for their service to the institutional church. The Protestants sought to convert educated people, at a time when Catholic missionaries were working mainly with townspeople, peasants, and fisherfolk. Both, but especially the Protestants, gave special attention to the building up of new colleges and contributed significantly to the development of modern education, medical training, and studies in the humanities and social sciences.

Some Protestant leaders, like Wu Yaozong and Ding Guangxun (K. H. Ting), as individuals were already sympathetic to the Communist movement before 1949 and found it easier to collaborate with the new regime. Others were more reserved, like Zhao Zichen and Wang Mingdao, and they suffered for it, in a struggle that often found Christians pitted against one another. Catholics, on the other hand, loyal to Rome and unwilling to collaborate with the state, found themselves virtually silenced under the Communists. Eventually, however, some Catholic leaders decided to form a Patriotic Church in a move to consecrate more Chinese bishops with official approval. Others went underground or were condemned to long prison terms.

Among the individuals presented here, Ma made an impact, especially as an educator, during the twentieth-century part of his unusually long and fruitful life. His personal life as well as his public career mirrored the struggles of dedicated Chinese Christians in a society that often distrusted such religious dedication, while some in the Catholic Church were uncomfortable with his continued devotion to Chinese culture. Such struggles characterized the lives of many, if not most, Chinese Christian intellectuals in the contemporary period.

## MA XIANGBO

Ma Xiangbo (Joseph Ma, 1840–1939) was born to a prominent scholar-official family from Jiangnan that traced its genealogy to a great Yuan-dynasty scholar, Ma Duanlin (c. 1254–1324) (see chapter 19). In the late Ming dynasty, his ancestors were converted to Catholicism by Jesuit missionaries, who also converted the heads of other big families, like Xu Guangqi (1562–1633) of Shanghai and Yang Tingyun (1557–1627) of Qiantang (see chapter 27). His father was a Confucian teacher who turned his attention to the study of medicine and business. From early childhood, Ma and his siblings received a Chinese classical education in a private school, while being suffused with a Christian family atmosphere. In 1852 he passed the county-level government examination and could have become a provincial scholar in the old Chinese sense, but instead he enrolled in the Collège St. Ignace (Xuhui Middle School) in Shanghai, to receive a Western education from the Jesuits there. His decision in 1862 to enter the Society of Jesus and become a priest led him to continue Western studies, although he never abandoned Chinese studies. Eventually he learned Greek, Latin, French, English, Japanese, and other foreign languages and studied Western philosophy and theology, as well as mathematics, astronomy, and geography.

Ma's brilliance was early recognized by the Jesuits, who made him principal of Collège St. Ignace in 1871. However, the French Jesuits who started the school wanted to Westernize the curriculum further, whereas Ma maintained that students should continue to study Chinese subjects and to prepare for civil service examinations, in order to be able to serve their country. In 1876 he resigned from the Society of Jesus, hoping thereby to pursue other possibilities of service to society at large, but he discovered that while his broad-ranging knowledge equipped him for a wide range of activities, his close church connections tended to disqualify him for high government positions.

During the next twenty years, Ma served as an adviser or aide to Li Hong-zhang, a top official of the Manchu government, and was sent on missions to Korea, Japan, Europe, and America. Frustrated in this career as well, he returned to live with the Jesuits in 1898, devoting his time to interpreting Catholic Christianity to Chinese society and helping his religion to become more rooted in Chinese culture. This led to his translating the New Testament into classical Chinese and to his founding in 1903 of Aurora (Zhendan) Academy, later a university, in Shanghai, "to place a priority on science, to emphasize liberal arts, and to avoid any religious dispute." It was financed with a generous endowment from his own personal inheritance — a sign of Ma's determination that Christianity in China should be self-supporting, as well as self-propagating and self-administered. Thus he became an early advocate of the church's non-dependence on foreign support.

Nevertheless, Ma was unable to avoid disputes with the French Jesuits who staffed his academy and sought also to transform it into a French university, and the school consequently closed. Ma then turned his attention in 1905 to the founding of another institution: the Fudan ("A Revived Aurora") Institute. Chinese intellectuals, including Yan Fu and others, rallied to this cause, obtained the grounds, and raised the necessary funds.

Confronted also with difficult political choices at a tumultuous time, Ma next went to Japan in 1906 to join Liang Qichao's Society to Promote Constitutional Monarchy and became its general secretary. In 1911 he joined the republican cause and then became an adviser to the second president, Yuan Shikai, but he became disenchanted with Yuan's efforts to make Confucianism the state religion and to become emperor. He also argued strongly in favor of a democratic system of government along Western lines. Philosophically, he had emphasized the human conscience, called *liangxin*, which he identified with Wang Yangming's innate good knowing (*liangzhi*). Ma was briefly in charge of Beijing University and also helped in the founding of Furen Catholic University in Beijing, one of two prominent Catholic institutions of higher learning. He also championed the founding of a Chinese Academy of Humanities and Sciences, as a successor to the Hanlin, to be modeled on the French Academy. He gathered together in 1912 scholars like Liang Qichao, Yan Fu, and Zhang Binglin as founding members, with the aim of promoting classical learning and reviving traditional morality. Although it had little success in those turbulent times, the later Academia Sinica bears some marks of his vision.

In 1931, already advanced in age and living in Shanghai, he participated in the resistance movement against Japanese aggression. In 1937, at age ninety-eight, he was made a councilor of Chiang Kai-shek's government in Nanjing. That same year, as the Japanese invaders moved south, he and his family retreated to the interior, and he died on November 4, 1939, in Lang Son, Vietnam, while en route to Chongqing.

"I am a dog, and only know how to bark," Ma said of himself. "I've been barking for a hundred years, but I haven't yet awakened China."

RELIGION AND THE STATE

## Should a Head of State Preside Over Religious Ceremonies?

In the *Mencius*, Wan Zheng asks, "Was it the case that Yao gave the empire to Shun?"[1] Mencius believed that Yao could not give Shun the empire but could only make him the chief religious leader, so that the gods would benefit from his sacrifices, or make him the political leader, so that the people could live in peace. Clearly the empire was given to Shun by Heaven and by the people, not by Yao. In Zhu Xi's notes on the *Mencius*, he comments on the point that it was not Yao who bestowed the empire, saying the empire means all-under-Heaven, and all-under-Heaven cannot become the private possession of one man. If Heaven can bestow this, it must belong to Heaven; if the people can bestow it, it must belong to the people. . . .

What I want to discuss today is as follows: First, if one makes a broad investigation in both China and the outside world, does the state ruler also have responsibility for heading up religion? Second, if we consult both past and present experience, including all social orders that have lasted for a long time, should the state leader also assume religious leadership? . . .

If we look through China's classical records, from earliest times the state ruler did also undertake religious leadership. This cannot be denied. But if we investigate the situation in Europe and America [we see that] that was not the case. Even before the time that church and state were separated, religious cere-

---

1. *Mencius* 5A:5.

monies were presided over by someone other than the state ruler. If the state ruler wished to participate in religious ceremonies, he did so. If the people wished to participate, they did so. If we go back to the period before there was freedom of religious belief, even though the people were required to participate in religious ceremonies, still the state ruler did not have a primary responsibility for religious leadership. Even in countries that have a national church, this is mainly a matter of the state treasury's subsidizing religious ceremonies and religious leadership. In the cases where financial subsidy means that the state ruler exercises some control and regulation over the church, as with the Anglican Church in England, the Eastern Orthodox Church in Russia, and Islam among the Muslims, the state ruler may head the church, but as head [he] does not actually preside over religious ceremonies. As for countries like France and Italy, that have a national church, the state ruler is never made head of the church, let alone president over religious ceremonies. No wonder contemporary scholars of politics and religion strongly advocate the division of state and church. . . .

Freedom of religious belief means that everyone makes [his] own free choice in religious belief and does not suffer from governmental interference. Even less [does he] suffer from interference from other religions. Thus state rulers of Europe and America can be an example. No matter what religion, they do not take on religious leadership.

[Adapted from Hayhoe, *Ma Xiangbo*, pp. 241–244]

### RELIGION AND CULTURE

Today there are people who misunderstand the true nature of religion and say religion is a kind of fetter on human freedom or religion is a kind of narcotic for the masses. What in fact is the nature of religion? Let me give a clear explanation. Religion is the only solution to the problems of human life. . . .

What we call "religion" is nothing other than the problem of the relation between people and the Creator. The Western term *religion* has the meaning of "binding back together again." This notion of binding is linked to nature (*xing*) and law (*fa*), and to the Confucian notion of ritual. . . . Thus religion imposes certain restrictions precisely in order to show people a standard so they support what is best in others rather than the opposite. This will enable people to enjoy the true freedom they ought to enjoy and prevent them [from] having illusions about a false freedom that they should not have. No person has control over his birth or his death. If this is not all in the hands of the Creator, then who is in control? The reason we are at present opposing the violent actions of the Japanese is because we object to the freedom of the enemy army to kill at will and to freely expropriate the land needed to keep our people alive. Since they think they can freely decide on the life or death of our 450 million people, we therefore have the natural right to refuse to allow ourselves to be exploited and so we have had to go to war. This provides us an example to explain the problem of freedom.

Let me now turn to the second view, that religion is a narcotic of the people. . . .

In our religion, we know that Jesus Christ, in accordance with the prophecies of the holy prophets of the Old Testament, came from the Creator into the world as its Savior. The Creator himself has spoken and he does not use human persons to speak. Those who believe in Him are saved, and those who do not believe will suffer eternal punishment. This Savior was once nailed to the cross, and after He rose from the dead and prepared to return to heaven, He commanded His disciples to preach the gospel and convert people, with no special privileges or power. They carried the message to Europe, Africa, India, and China. After going to all of the Old World, they took the message to the New World, wherever the sun rises, wherever the moon shines, wherever boat or road can reach; no matter what race, no matter what region, there are already some converts. So we have to ask — if this person who was nailed to the cross was only a saint, would it be possible that nineteen hundred years later 329,274,398 people would have become His disciples? Millions and millions of believers trust in the Creator, trust in the Savior. These people believe in Him, respect and adore Him, and praise Him. Thus the Holy Cross has brought salvation to the whole world. Many people have given up their lives and their homes, have even suffered death in order to bear witness to this indisputable truth.

You will remember how Chinese historians associate Fang Xiaoru with "orthodox scholarship" (*zhengxue*) (see chapter 24) since he swore that he would defend the truth and cut out his own tongue and wrote in blood the word *usurper* (*chuan*) as a rebuke to the emperor. He remained faithful to the truth and did not bend.[2] Well, if we look at the history of the world, we can't count how many Fang Xiaorus there have been among Catholic believers, including men and women, old and young, noble and wealthy, distinguished and base, who have sacrificed themselves and shed their blood in order to be witness[es] to the principles of the church. . . .

To take another example, the national army is shedding its blood in resistance to Japan in order to show its loyalty to the country. It has won commendation for this. Then how can we say that these millions of believers, who have

---

2. [Original note of Ma Xiangbo:] Fang Xiaoru lived during the early part of the Ming dynasty. Because he opposed Ming Chengzu in his action of usurping the throne from his nephew Jian Wendi, he was put to death. At the same time all of his direct family, and all of his relatives, including ten different clans, were put to death. "Orthodox scholarship" refers to the Song Neo-Confucian scholarship of Zhu Xi.

shown their loyalty and respect to the Creator, who have shown absolute and unwavering commitment, are simply drugged? To be honest, opium, morphine, and other narcotics certainly can drug the body. For people, however, religion transforms human life through the truth; it causes human hearts to submit themselves gladly, so that they worship the Creator and exercise self-restraint in order to be socially responsible (*keji fuli*). They take the mind of the Savior as their own, and they follow the commands of the Creator. They sacrifice all that they have and go to the original Source, and so fulfill their purpose. It is certainly clear that there is not a trace of the narcotic in this!

[Hayhoe, *Ma Xiangbo*, pp. 272–277 — JC]

## ZHAO ZICHEN

Nearly half a century younger than Ma Xiangbo, Zhao Zichen (1888–1979), known to the world as T. C. Chao, was by consensus China's best-known Protestant thinker. Born to an affluent merchant family in Zhejiang, Zhao attended a Presbyterian school in Suzhou, Jiangsu, and then studied at the Methodist Suzhou (Dongwu) University. From 1914 to 1917 he studied theology at Vanderbilt University in the United States and then returned to teach theology at Suzhou University until he moved to Beijing in 1926. Zhao served as a professor and then became dean of the school of religion at Yanjing University in Beijing, and he was for almost three decades the leading spokesman of Christianity on campuses and among the educated.

At first a Methodist, he later became an Anglican, receiving ordination in 1941. In 1948 he was elected one of the six presidents of the World Council of Churches, although he later faded away in Communist China on account of his initial opposition to the Three-Self Movement (movement for self-administration, self-support, and self-propagation), which represented Protestant Christianity's effort — under Wu Yaozong (Y. T. Wu) — to cut its links with the West and work with the Communist government. In 1951–1952, Zhao came under severe attack by his colleagues and students for his allegedly halfhearted support of the movement, and his holy orders were revoked by his bishop. He suffered dreadfully also during the ten years of the Cultural Revolution — but this time from the enemies of Christianity and of all religion — and from rumors that were spread of his renunciation of his faith. With the reopening of China in the late 1970s, Zhao reemerged and reaffirmed his faith as a Christian thinker and theologian. By this time, however, the world's attention had shifted to the leaders of the Three-Self Movement, especially Ding Guangxun and Chen Zeming, both leftist sympathizers from early on.

The two articles below were written in the mid-twenties when Christianity was under severe attack by the forces of nationalism and communism.

PRESENT-DAY RELIGIOUS THOUGHT AND LIFE IN CHINA

To the casual observer the preponderance of irreligious literature and talk by intellectual and anti-religious people seems to show that China is at the present time a country that has dispensed with religion or at least thinks that religion is merely good for superstitious folks in limiting their conduct to proper social spheres. . . .

Deeper study, however, shows a different picture. It reveals that, in spite of the loud anti-Christian movement, which is a sign of the need for a deeper manifestation of religion, the Chinese people, the steady and respectable class of people, are searching for a satisfactory spiritual life. . . .

There have been attempts to make Confucianism into a religion. At least three things might be adduced to make such attempts for some people worth making. They are the worship of Heaven, the worship of ancestors, and the worship of Confucius himself as a kind of prophet of the religion, in which he is raised to a position of divinity essentially the same as the divine nature of Heaven. . . .

This attempt was defeated, not because Christians strenuously opposed it but mainly because the leaders of the new popular government took no interest and sometimes thought this sort of religious legislation was contrary to the spirit of the revolution that had just come to pass. . . .

The anti-Christian movement makes us think of two things — namely, are we, in following Jesus, politically unfit to be China's best citizens? Are we superstitious in our beliefs and practices? If the answer is in the affirmative and we are sure of it, then let us quit altogether and become anti-Christians as devoutly as we can. But if the answer is no, then it is our immediate duty to find the reality in our own experience and in our own life, in our clear-cut thinking and in our activities, to bear witness to the gospel of individual and social salvation.

The demands on Christianity are these. First, it must present to the thoughtful of today a religious life of power, thoroughly ethical, profoundly critical and discriminating and completely loyal to God. Second, it must become adjusted to its social and intellectual environment, so that from this time the religion of Christians should be an inner growth rather than an external imposition even in appearance. No religion brought into the country from outside can become indigenous unless it becomes a growth from within and makes its own natural and living adaptations and improvements. Third, there should be a reasonable interpretation of the deep religious experience of the believers, a Christian rationalism that is free, yet based upon the facts of the spiritual life. Fourth, those who believe must now work to Christianize and create a new community in China. Christianity stands for a redeemed and new humanity, in the form, at first, of a brotherhood, then of a society, and then of a nation that is a part of the whole of humanity. The Communists want society to become communistic; the workingmen want society to be the workingmen's society; anti-Christians and half-baked scientists want society to be one of atheism and rationalism without a foundation for it; but all will fail unless those who can do it make society a society of loving souls. The Christian, believing in God, must desire to have, and work hard for the realization of, a society that may be called the Kingdom of God. Then, finally, the times call aloud for the forthcoming of prophets, men and women who know God and who can transcend the sins of the times and have visions of the truth and of the future. Great opportunities are linked up with grave dangers. And the sin of Chinese Christians today lies in the fact that they are being led astray and they are not leading the times as they should. The clearest demand today is for a new leadership among Chinese Christians, which can transcend the times in thought and life and can lead.

## LEADERSHIP AND CITIZENSHIP TRAINING

The Christian college is facing a new intellectual situation, which requires a scholarly contact between Christian and non-Christian educators and which demands the participation of Christian educators in many of the national movements. The [Chinese] Renaissance has discovered for the nation the new individual, who has new aspirations for self-realization, through a systematization of the learning of the past, the organization of the conditions of human existence in the present, and the scientific actualization of the hopes for the future. The new individual must have a new nation, and hence the Renaissance and the patriotic movements have merged into each other, on the one hand to resist foreign, imperialistic encroachments on Chinese territory and resources, sovereign rights, and culture, and on the other hand to build up the new China from within rather than from without, in spite of foreign imperialistic propaganda working insidiously among the Chinese youths. The true leaders of such movements deeply realize that success depends upon intellectual guidance. So while "in the writings of the younger generation, there is a great deal of cheap iconoclasm and blind faddism . . . the saner and more far-sighted leaders are trying to inculcate into the people what they regard as the only safeguard against these dangers — namely, the historical and evolutionary point of view and a truly scientific attitude of life."[3] This, as we Christian educators see, is not enough, because without a transcendent faith in God, we believe, the historical and scientific spirit will not lead us very far in our national movements. We need intellectual leadership that is coupled with religious aspirations, and precisely here the Christian college must make its contribution.

This leads us to the third consideration — namely, the demand of the Christian movement as a whole for thorough Christian intellectual leadership. The

---

3. Hu Shih, "On the Chinese Renaissance," *Bulletins on Chinese Education*, p. 35.

Christian church and the Christian college are the two great forces of the Christian religion that reveal its true nature and express its true life. Whereas the church must, by its institutionalized forms and constituted authorities, conserve the religious values of life, the college, by virtue of its tasks of scientific experimentation and its academic freedom in the field of the humanities, counterbalances the conservative and crystallizing influence of the church and thus, by freely discovering new values and quietly and gradually replacing old values, creates at the same time a living, growing equilibrium for the Christian religion. The church gives support to educational institutions, so that in matters of theory the scholars may be preeminently qualified to judge without being restrained, while on the other hand the educational institutions help the church to adapt itself to new and unfamiliar environments. This, however, does not exhaust the relationship between the two organizations. In the history of the Christian movement, prophets have often been men of high intellectual attainment. As the growing complexities of life in modern times demand intellectual leadership in all spheres of activity, the prophets of the Christian movement will have to be men of great intellectual acumen and thorough education. . . .

Having briefly stated the demands for intellectual leadership made upon the Christian college by the growth of the educational work itself, by the rising of the new China, and by the necessities of the Christian movement, let us mention in passing the terrible need today for men to show the way to transcend the difficulties and wrong thinking of the times. *Leadership* means nothing else than that some prophets arise who can point the way out of the present unsatisfactory conditions of thought and life to a more satisfactory future. Leadership always implies a future for ourselves, who must transcend our own conditions, and for our race and nation, which, too, must outgrow the old limitations. When we say that we need leaders of new ideas, we express a desire for the coming of prophets who know the past so thoroughly that they will not be bound by it and who hold a faith in the future so strongly that they will reveal sufficient idealism to lead us toward the realization of cherished ideals.

[Adapted from Zhao, *China Today*, pp. 33, 38–39, 41, 47–49, 124–127  — JC]

## WU YAOZONG

Almost ten years younger than Zhao, Wu Yaozong (Y. T. Wu, 1893–1979) represented the leftist sympathizers among Chinese Protestants. Born into a struggling non-Christian family from Guangdong in southern China, he prepared himself to enter the customs service, enrolling in the Customs College of Beijing. After graduation in 1913, he returned south to take a position as customs officer, was transferred to Beijing in 1917, where he stayed at a YMCA hostel, and received baptism in 1918. He gave up his secular career two years later to join the YMCA staff, working chiefly with students. Like Zao Zichen, he perceived Christianity initially as a basis for a spiritual reconstruction of China, but eventually, in an age that saw the Russian Revolution and the Great Depression, Wu moved from social reform to social revolution.

In 1924 Wu studied theology at Union Theological Seminary in New York. He received a master's in philosophy in 1927 from Columbia University with a thesis on William James. He returned ten years later to do a thesis at Union Seminary that had special reference to John Dewey's pragmatism. As a prominent churchman in China, he traveled to several conferences abroad, before and after World War II. During the war he spent four years in Chengdu. In 1945, he began the journal *Tian Feng* (*Heaven's Wing*), which was to become in 1951 the official organ of the Three-Self Movement.

Wu was at first opposed to communism for what he termed its terror and brutality, and its alienness to the temperament of the Chinese people. Following the Mukden Incident of 1931, however, he found himself increasingly in agreement with the Communists on the need to resist foreign aggression and change the social order. When the Communists came to power in 1949, he sought to play a mediating role with the new government, in order to permit Christians to integrate in the new society.

In 1950, after three conversations with Zhou Enlai in Beijing, he concluded that Chinese Christianity must distance itself from foreign powers and influence. Thereupon he launched the Three-Self Movement, the declared purpose of which was to free Chinese Christianity from financial dependence on the capitalist West. He drafted a document called "The Christian Manifesto," which was published in 1950 over the signatures of forty prominent Protestant leaders. However, other leaders declined to become involved in collaboration with the government. Wang Mingdao was the best known of this group. Bitter struggles ensued among the Protestants, especially between Wang and the leaders of the Three-Self Movement. Then, during the Cultural Revolution, even the Three-Self Movement was attacked as a "conspiracy between Liu Shaoqi [denounced as a revisionist] and Wu Yaozong." All religious activities ceased, and many leaders were forced publicly to renounce their faith.

## THE PRESENT-DAY TRAGEDY OF CHRISTIANITY

This article by Wu Yaozong, which appeared in *Tian Feng* for April 10, 1948, more than a year before the Communist armies reached Shanghai, is in a sense the opening salvo of the Three-Self Movement.

A world revolution is developing before our eyes. No matter how we may fear and hate it, this revolution is already an undeniable fact. The opposition of the toilers, the struggles of ethnic minorities, and on the international scene the sharp opposition between democratic and anti-democratic forces, all these are inevitable phenomena of that world revolution. At the present stage the most important task of that revolution, negatively speaking, is to oppress peoples and enslave the world; and positively speaking, [it is] to unite all democratic forces in establishing a new society of freedom and equality, a society of no classes, where everyone works and everyone receives the results of his labors. . . .

At present the cause of the tragic situation in Protestantism is America, and this is because of the historical development. America is a newly developed capitalist power, which only since the Second World War has suddenly become the leading capitalist nation. Its establishment and later separation from the mother country were due partly to economic and political conflict and partly to difference of religious belief, but these two were interrelated. And so the spirit of American capitalism can be said to be the spirit of current Protestantism, and the individualism and freedom that capitalism preaches are the individualism and freedom that certain Protestant leaders preach. . . .

At this critical juncture the position of Chinese [Protestant] Christians is tragic. Chinese Christian tradition is primarily British and American. At present its relations with America are especially close. Most of its missionaries are American, and most of its leaders have been trained in America. Its institutions depend upon American support. Because of these relationships in faith and thinking, the Chinese Christian Church is practically a copy of American Christianity. . . .

The history of Christianity in China has not been all a favorable one. Of course there has been bandit and mob violence due to the superstition of the people — of that we are not now speaking. But since the May 4 movement, from 1922 to 1925, the anti-Christian movement in China has been led by intellectual elements. They said that Christianity is the opiate of the people, it is the running dog of imperialism, the forerunner of cultural aggression. . . .

The historic tragedy of Christianity is that in its history of the past hundred years it has unconsciously changed to become a conservative force. And now at the present stage it has become a reactionary force. . . . In the course of this tragedy of history, Christianity has not only not shown the insight of a prophet in opposing the forces of reaction but has almost made itself one with those forces. . . .

To avoid misunderstanding I will add one further word: When I speak of the tragedy of Christianity today, I do not wish to deny or obscure the fact that within the Christian Church there are many honorable persons and many noteworthy accomplishments. In China, and in the whole world, there are many devout Christians who devote themselves to constructive efforts. They do not seek renown but, accepting obscurity in their own little place in life, make an effective witness for their faith. . . . March 31, 1948.

[Adapted from Merwin, *Three-Self Movement*, pp. 1–5, 12–19 — JC]

## THE REFORMATION OF CHRISTIANITY

The influential Shanghai daily *Da Gong Bao* carried on July 16, 17, and 18, 1948, a serial by Wu Yaozong under the title "The Reformation of Christianity: On the Awakening of Christians."

I have not given up hope for Christianity. I have been a Christian for thirty-one years and am still a true Christian. During the past decade my Christian belief has been tried and cleansed, but I still keep and follow its essence. . . .

Can there be a reformation and rebirth of Christianity? I think there can. Christian faith itself has an inner life, the voice of God that Christ preached is endowed with a deep cosmology and outlook on life in ideals and motive power for living. It is the truth of life, and all truth is of revolutionary nature. . . .

First of all, I think Christianity will have to disassociate itself from the capitalist and imperialist order. This is not an easy undertaking, but it must be done. . . . Second, Chinese churches must carry out their former avowed principle of becoming self-governing, self-supporting, and self-propagating, and thus become really Chinese churches. . . . Christianity must learn that the present period is one of liberation for the people, the collapse of the old system, a time when the old dead Christianity must doff its shroud and come forth arrayed in new garments.

[Adapted from Merwin, *Three-Self Movement*, pp. 12–14 — JC]

### THE CHRISTIAN MANIFESTO

This document of May 1950 was worked out by the founding group of the Three-Self Movement in consultation with Premier Zhou Enlai.

Protestant Christianity has been introduced to China for more than 140 years. During this period it has made a not unworthy contribution to Chinese society. Nevertheless — and this was most unfortunate — not long after Christianity's coming to China, imperialism started its activities here; and since the principal groups of missionaries who brought Christianity to China all came themselves from these imperialistic countries, Christianity consciously or unconsciously, directly or indirectly, became related with imperialism. Now that the Chinese revolution has achieved victory, these imperialistic countries will not rest passively content in [the] face of this unprecedented historical fact in China. They . . . may also make use of Christianity to forward their plot of stirring up internal dissension and creating reactionary forces in this country. It is our purpose in publishing the following statement to heighten our vigilance against imperialism, to make known the clear political stand of Christians in New China, to hasten the building of a Chinese church whose affairs are managed by the

Chinese themselves, and to indicate the responsibilities that should be taken up by Christians throughout the whole country in national reconstruction in New China.

[Adapted from Merwin, *Three-Self Movement*, p. 19 —JC]

# WANG MINGDAO

Wang Mingdao (1900–1991) came from a working-class family and attended a primary school run by the London Missionary Society, becoming a Christian in his teens. He taught afterward in a Presbyterian school with the hope that the church would support his college and seminary education. However, conviction grew in him that baptism by sprinkling was inadequate, so in 1920 he got a second baptism by immersion. For this reason, and for his strong declarations of his religious views, he was discharged from his teaching duties at the Presbyterian school.

Thereafter, Wang studied the Bible incessantly, led Bible study groups, and decided in 1937 to set up his own ministry, with no overseas links, which he called the Christian Tabernacle. For the following decade, he also traveled throughout the country as a preacher, giving a mainly fundamentalist message about faith and the Bible. He was interrogated and cajoled by the Japanese invaders for refusing to join a pro-Japanese association of Christians and publish their political slogans in his periodical. Subsequently he took an uncompromising attitude to the Chinese Communist government and the Three-Self Movement that started in the early 1950s under Wu Yaozong's leadership. For this, he was the object of attack at a denunciation meeting called by the movement and was arrested as a counterrevolutionary in 1955 when he published a statement to explain his reasons for not joining the Three-Self Movement. Imprisoned in 1957, he was not released until 1979, when he was already seventy-nine years old. Eventually Ding Guangxun (K. H. Ting), who took over the Three-Self Movement and the China Christian Council after Wu Yaozong's death, acknowledged that Wang, who had no foreign ties and whose movement was independent of foreign support, had committed no crime deserving a long imprisonment.

## WE, BECAUSE OF FAITH

Wang Mingdao openly fought the Three-Self Movement. His opposition was based not on any political or social motive but purely on the fundamentalist-modernist conflict, since most of the Three-Self leaders were modernists. This pamphlet, "We, Because of Faith," was published in Beijing in June 1955. Shortly after, on August 8, the author was arrested and put in prison.

During the past thirty years the churches of China, like other churches through-out the world, have had within them a conflict of faith between fundamentalists and modernists. Fundamentalists believe in the fundamental doctrines: The Bible is the revelation of God; Christ . . . was born of a virgin; He performed many miracles; . . . He gave His life . . . for all Mankind; . . . after three days He rose bodily from death; . . . forty days later He was received into Heaven where He sits at the right hand of God; in the future He will come again to earth; . . . He will give [His disciples] transformed, spiritual, and immortal bodies; . . . He will exercise judgment on earth and finally set up His Heavenly kingdom.

But modernists evidently do not believe these essential doctrines. They do not come out into the open and deny the doctrines; they simply interpret them in a hazy and ambiguous way; they say that they believe but only express the truth in a different way from the fundamentalists. . . .

For thirty years I have constantly spoken and written against modernism. . . .

We will not unite in any way with these unbelievers, nor will we join any of their organizations. And even with true believers and faithful servants of God we can enjoy only a spiritual union. There should not be any kind of formal, organizational union, because we cannot find any teaching in the Bible to support it. . . . For our loyalty to God we are ready to pay any cost that is required. We shall shrink from no sacrifice. Misrepresentation and slander can never intimidate us.

Everyone has a mouth with which he can say what he pleases. But facts are facts forever. God sees them clearly and God's people see them clearly, no matter how others may twist them or malign us. We take our stand on Christian doctrine.

[Adapted from Merwin, *Three-Self Movement*, pp. 99–114 — JC]

## WU JINGXIONG: CHRISTIANITY AND CHINESE TRADITION

Wu Jingxiong (1899–1986) was a native of Ningbo, Zhejiang, and the son of a little-educated father who rose out of poverty to a relatively comfortable position as a local banker. Starting his studies at age six with a private tutor and trans-ferring to a primary school two years later, he eventually attended Baptist College in Shanghai and then transferred to law in 1916, first at Beiyang University in Tianjin and then at Methodist Comparative Law School in Shanghai. A brilliant student, he graduated in 1920, having also become a Methodist, and pursued further studies in law at Ann Arbor, Michigan, and later in international law at Paris and in Berlin. While in the United States, he developed a lifelong friendship with Chief Justice Oliver Wendell Holmes of the U.S. Supreme Court.

Back in Shanghai, Wu Jingxiong taught for a while, was made a judge in 1927, traveled to the United States to give lectures at Northwestern Law School and to do research at Harvard, and then returned home in 1930 to start a law practice in Shanghai. In 1937, at the beginning of the Sino-Japanese War, he became a Catholic, the fruit of his readings — of the scriptures and of John Henry Newman, William James, and others — and of his friendship with a Chinese Catholic family in Shanghai. He himself became the inspiration for some of his friends to convert to Catholicism, and he earned greater respect for the religion among intellectuals. After some time in Hong Kong, he escaped from Japanese occupation to go to Guilin and Chongqing, where, with encouragement from Chiang Kai-shek, he translated the Psalms and the New Testament into Chinese. In 1947 he was named the Chinese ambassador to the Vatican and delighted Pius XII with his brilliance and his family of twelve children. With the Communist takeover in 1949, Wu Jingxiong accepted a position as professor of Chinese philosophy at the University of Hawaii, and later he taught law at Seton Hall University. In 1966 he returned to Taiwan, and twenty years later, at age eighty-seven, he died.

A jurist as well as a comparative philosopher, he single-handedly drafted the first constitution of the Republic of China and the Chinese version of the United Nations charter. Although the course of political events prevented him from making an even larger contribution to his fellow countrymen, in his later years he pursued wide-ranging intellectual and religious interests and wrote about many aspects of both Western and Chinese culture, including Confucianism, Daoism, Chan Buddhism, and Tang poetry.

Blessed with a happy temperament, Wu usually saw the positive side of things, so that a sense of optimism pervades his writings and what he has to say about his own life.

## BEYOND EAST AND WEST

What a wonderful privilege it is to have been born in China in my generation! I was brought up as a child entirely in the atmosphere of the old tradition. To be steeped in the old tradition and later to come into contact with the spirit of Christianity makes one feel like a contemporary of the first Disciples of Christ, who had more or less fully lived their lives under the dominion of Law and were suddenly introduced into the Reign of Grace. Far be it from me to assert that my cultural and spiritual heritage was on a par with the Old Testament. What I do assert is that, in an analogical way, the three religions of China served as my tutors, bringing me to Christ so that I might find justification in faith (Gal. 3:24). Of course, every conversion is due to the grace of God; but there is no denying that in my case God used parts of the teachings of Confucius, Laozi, and Buddha as instruments to open my eyes to the Light of the world.

To begin with, to have lived under the moral tradition of old China has proved to me the absolute necessity of sanctifying and actual grace in order to live up, even imperfectly, to the lofty ideals of life. Speaking of the Mosaic Law, Saint Paul said, "Is the Law sin? By no means! Yet I did not know sin save through the Law. For I had not known lust unless the Law had said, 'Thou shalt not lust.' But sin, having found an occasion, worked in me by means of the commandment all manner of lust, for without the Law sin was dead" (Rom. 7:7–8). Now this was *exactly* what happened to me when I had read some of the moral books current in my childhood. They warned young folks against doing this and doing that. I do not know how they worked on others; as for me, they only served to stir up my curiosity and my passions, with the result that the more resolutions I made, the more often I broke them. I honestly believe that few persons are as bad as I am by nature; but speaking for myself, the Confessional has proved to me the only effective channel of medicinal grace, so effective as many a time to surprise myself. I am no longer surprised, knowing as I do the absolute veracity and power of the Divine Physician, Who said, "It is not the healthy who need a physician, but they who are sick" (Matt. 9:13).

[Wu, Beyond East and West, pp. 150–151 — JC]

THE LOTUS AND THE MUD

The much-mooted question of idealism and materialism I have solved with some satisfaction to my own mind. Ideals, like lotus flowers, can only grow from the mud of matter. A sculptor cannot dispense with the plastic material. Without it no bust can be made, whether that of Xishi or that of her ugly mimicker, Dongshi. On the other hand, I believe with equal conviction that matter alone does not constitute beauty. Otherwise all busts or even living persons would be equally beautiful — which, unfortunately, does not seem to be true. Only through a fit arrangement of material things can ideals be created, or at least be made to emerge. Even justice depends upon a harmonious distribution of material wealth.

Similar to this problem of idealism and materialism, but more fundamental still, is the problem of worldliness and otherworldliness. Is life a dream? Or is it real and earnest, as Longfellow would have it? Formerly I used to swing like a pendulum between the two extremes as most of my countrymen seem to do. But now I have gradually come to realize that life is a dream, but that something real and earnest may come out from a dream. And I have learned this from experience. It is thanks to my intensive participation in practical life that although I am by nature a stargazer, yet I seldom fall into wells. For life, especially in politics, is like tightrope walking. You have always to maintain your balance. A little slip may cause you to fall. Your superiors, your subordinates, your colleagues, your friends, and finally job seekers are all to be dealt with tactfully and yet with sincerity: with such tactfulness as to satisfy them, and with such sincerity as to satisfy yourself. You will often find yourself between the devil and the deep sea.

[Wu, *Beyond East and West*, pp. 190–191 — JC]

*Chapter 39*

REOPENING THE DEBATE ON CHINESE TRADITION

For all its strident iconoclasm, the Great Proletarian Cultural Revolution did not spring from any clear consensus on values or political direction. Indeed, the power struggles and factional infighting that marked the campaign betrayed great ideological confusion.

"Confucianism," though a prime target of attack, had long since been eclipsed educationally and politically — largely replaced by Western-style learning in the first decades of the century and then, post-1949, by a Marxist-Leninist-Stalinist ideology and curriculum in the schools. Except among a few remnants of the older generation, Confucianism was perceived negatively through the anti-Confucian diatribes of the New Culture and May 4 Movements. Thus, paradoxically, the ghost of Confucius had to be conjured up anew by the propagandists of the Cultural Revolution, and Confucian texts, long out of print, had to be reproduced so that they could be criticized.

## THE NEW CONFUCIANS

In the meantime, however, at home an inchoate popular Confucianism barely survived attacks on the family system, while abroad some serious study and reinterpretation of Confucianism was going on — especially in Hong Kong and Taiwan but also in Japan and, by now, in the West. On the mainland itself two threads of continuity persisted, though intangibly. Some survivors of the Maoist onslaught had, simply as leaders identified with moderate policies, begun to think of a return to Confucian ideas of "harmony," civility, and forbearance as an antidote to the violence of Maoist "class struggle" (meaning, really, political and ideological struggle). Theirs was a view born more out of hard experience, common sense, and practicality than out of any philosophical theory or deep knowledge of Confucianism. Contemporaneously, however, a few Confucian thinkers who lived into the Mao years held independent views that differentiated them from either pragmatists or their Communist fellow travelers.

One of these was the influential thinker and teacher Xiong Shili (1885–1968), who inspired a whole philosophical movement known as the New Confucians. Basing his teaching on the *Classic of Changes (Yijing)*, but incorporating elements of Buddhist idealistic philosophy and Daoism, he considered himself a latter-day exponent of Wang Yangming's Neo-Confucian teachings centering on the "humaneness that forms one body (substance) with Heaven-Earth-and-all-things." This original substance he also explained in terms of the *Changes'* concept of the Way as unceasing creativity ("production and reproduction"), the original mind in Buddhism and Neo-Confucianism, and Wang Yangming's doctrine of the unity of substance and function. Making no concessions to Marxism and Mao, he lived and worked quietly in the early years of the People's Republic, but his greatest influence was on thinkers who carried on as refugees in Hong Kong and Taiwan (represented herein by the Manifesto of 1957, pp. 551–558).

Another of these Confucians was the aforementioned Liang Shuming (1893–1988), whose independent version of Neo-Confucianism synthesized elements of Bergson, Buddhism, Daoism, and a homegrown communitarian tradition linked to the community compacts of Zhu Xi and Wang Yangming. Courted early by the Mao regime and made a member of the People's Republic Political Consultative Conference, he showed his independence as early as 1953 (when most people believed Mao could no do wrong) by criticizing the harshness of the CCP's agricultural policies and treatment of the rural areas. For this outspokenness he was subjected to repeated attacks by Mao and others, but he refused to compromise on his principles and later came to be respected in the Deng years as a thinker and teacher of genuine integrity.

A third but somewhat different case is represented by Feng Youlan (Fung Yu-lan, 1895–1990). Well known in the West for his *History of Chinese Philosophy*, Feng returned to Beijing after getting his doctorate at Columbia University under John Dewey and developed what he called the "New Rationalism" or the "New Philosophy of Reason or Principle" (*xinlixue*), linked more closely to Zhu Xi's school of Neo-Confucianism than to Wang Yangming's. He, too, remained in Beijing after 1949, but with the avowed purpose of synthesizing Confucianism with Marx-Leninism and the "new socialist reality," an effort at adaptation and compromise that proved highly problematical. Feng thought of his mission as showing the continued relevance of Confucianism to the modern scene, but his repeated attempts at Communist-style self-criticism eventually lost credibility, while his personal associations with people like Mao's wife, Jiang Qing, later discredited along with the Gang of Four, left Feng looking like an opportunist to some and a tragic figure to others. His apologia appears later in this chapter.

It cannot be said that any of these latter-day exponents of Confucianism have had great influence on contemporary Chinese thought on the mainland. Many younger Chinese, especially those once active in the Cultural Revolution, remain imbued with earlier forms of anti-Confucian "liberationism," and even critics of the Deng regime in the 1980s, whose dissent culminated in the Tiananmen demonstration of June 4, 1989, continued to see Confucianism as a reactionary ideology now appropriated by a repressive regime, rather than as a form of liberal humanism. They have not been much edified, least of all inspired, by the official movement to revive Confucianism as represented here in the final reading. To what extent the present regime will tolerate a more liberal reading of Confucianism, or rather keep its revival well within conservative bounds, remains unclear.

## XIONG SHILI

1. In discussing the "original substance," philosophers in general regard it as a thing separable from our heart-and-minds. They believe that, through rational means, it can be obtained from the outside. As a result, philosophers, through cogitation, depict a multiplicity of imagined [objective] realms and construct their theories of the "original substance" accordingly. Whether the materialist/idealist or the non-materialist/non-idealist version, it is, in essence, a reflection of the attitude of searching for something outside by guessing, each falsely trying to settle on a kind of substance. This is of course mistaken. Moreover, there are philosophers who deny "original substance" altogether and focus their attention exclusively on epistemology. This position can be said to have departed from philosophy. For the reason that philosophy can still maintain itself is precisely because ontology cannot be occupied by science. The purpose of epistemological inquiry is to help us to bear witness to substance; if we are determined not to recognize that there is original substance and spend all our energy working through epistemology, there can be no result to this kind of inquiry. How can this not be said to have departed from the philosophical position? This kind of falsehood is not different from what the worthies of old characterize as "the Way is near but we search for it from the difficult." This kind of mistake lies in our inability to recognize the original heart-and-mind through self-reflectivity. To put it simply, the mistake arises from our failure to understand the unity of the original source of all things and our true nature. (The so-called true nature here refers to the true heart-and-mind. Since it is the principle of our life, it is called true nature; since it is in command of the body, it is called original heart-

and-mind.) It is because we falsely imagine that the original substance of the cosmos exists outside, independent of our heart-and-minds, that we try to search for it through our quantitative intelligence. . . .

2. The "original substance" of all things in mysterious learning is so vast that there is nothing outside of it (this vastness is not contrasted with smallness); it is void (the so-called void does not mean "empty"; it is not meaningless, for, as lasting existence, it does not have visible traces), all-encompassing, complete, in possession of the tiniest and absolutely inexhaustible functions. In Confucian philosophy, the original substance of all things is referred to as the Great Change, which has no visible forms or traces. (The so-called Great Change is originally changeless, but it entails transformations and changes; since the changeless is seen through transformations and changes, it is called the Great Change.) If we say that the tiniest is a real thing and that since it is the tiniest it is the original source of everything (such as the heterodox teaching of "following the world" in India), then we only acknowledge matter as real; there is nothing that can be called the original substance. Many materialists claim that what we refer to as substance is a mystic idea, but it is not mystic. Truth presents itself in front of us. If there is some blockage in our heart-and-minds, we will not be able to recognize it. Some also criticize us as departing from the objective, independent real world in order to construct through random imagination a lofty, wondrous original substance, like the floating clouds in aerospace. Actually, while what we call original substance is not like the mundane real world clung to by false consciousness, we do not mean to say that the original substance is outside of all things. If it is indeed outside of all things, how can it be the original substance of all things? It should be noted that all things are manifestations of the original substance. It should not be perceived as a thing. Analogously, the waves are all manifestations of the ocean. We should not perceive waves separately as if they are discretely isolated waves. If we understand this, we can know that we and all things are intertwined inseparably into an undifferentiated whole. How can we draw a major rupture between our inner heart-and-minds and the outside realms? The materialists, without any basis, imagine an objective independent material world. This is a form of self-deception. I should note, however, that I am in full agreement with the Mahāyāna's successful critique of the theory of the tiniest matter. In summary, I deny the existence of the outer realm departing from the heart-and-mind. This is not to deny the existence of [objective] realms. Indeed, the heart-and-mind is manifest through encountering the [objective] realm. As soon as we refer to the heart-and-mind, we already posit the existence of an [objective] realm. If the [objective] realm is absent, the name of the heart-and-mind will not exist. Actually, the heart-and-mind and the [objective] realm is a developing totality laden with internal contradictions. From the perspective of mysterious learning, the totality in itself is not real, it is merely the manifestation of absolute functions.

[*Xin weishilun, yudi* ed., 1:3b–4a, 19b–20a — TWM]

3. The reason that the "original substance" is so constituted, in short, entails the following meanings: (1) The original substance provides myriad principles, contains myriad virtues, initiates myriad transformations, and is itself *dharma*-like pure and originally so. (The term *dharma*-like connotes the idea of self-completion without dependence; *pure* means no defilement, which suggests that evil is totally absent. *Originally so* means it is original and as such. It should be noted that the original substance is not that which originally did not exist and has come into being now and that, more emphatically, it is not put into a proper place out of conjecture. This is the reason that it is referred to as original. Since it can never be altered, it is depicted in such terms.) (2) The original substance is absolute. If it were dependent, it would not be named as the original substance of all phases of existence. (3) The original substance is imperceptible, formless, which means it is not spatial. (4) The original substance is everlasting, beginningless, and endless, which means it is not temporal. (The term *everlasting* does not carry temporal significance; we reluctantly employ the word *everlasting*.) (5) The original substance is complete, fully complacent without deficiency, and indivisible. (6) When we say that the original substance is changeless, the implication is that it entails transformations and changes; when we say that the original substance is changing and transforming, the implication is that it is changeless. It is extremely difficult to describe the original substance. Since the original substance manifests itself in immeasurable and boundless functions, which means that it is all phases of existence, it is changing. However, even though the original substance manifests itself in a multiplicity of functions or all phases of existence, its own nature is, in the last analysis, never altered. Its nature is always pure, steadfast, enduring; therefore it is said that it is changeless.

Someone may ask, What meanings does the original substance entail? The answer is, In short, there are four meanings: (1) The original substance is the source of myriad principles, the beginning of myriad virtues, and the initiator of myriad transformations. (*Initiator* means the root.) (2) The original substance is without opposites and, at the same time, with opposites; it is with opposites and, at the same time, without opposites. (3) The original substance is beginningless and endless. (4) The original substance manifests itself in limitless and inexhaustible great functions, thus it should be noted as changing. Yet, since the flowing of the great functions ultimately does not alter in the slightest the vitality, steadfastness, and other qualities of the original substance, it should be said to be changeless.

[*Tiyonglun*, p. 5]

4. I firmly believe that the cosmos is a cosmos of life. We should not say that the cosmos is just a bundle of matter. Human life is a life force. We should not say that life and heart-and-mind are derived from matter. Matter and life are the two natures of the same originality. Life guides and moves matter; matter

contains and supports life. However, matter as a thing is originally light, tiny and fluid. When it becomes crystallized into each real thing, it is often coarse and gigantic to the extreme, such as the immeasurable heavenly bodies in aerospace. The development of matter is extremely easy, extremely coarse and gigantic, clearly visible. It contains the qualities of consolidation and enclosure. This is the reason that although the great life force silently moves in the midst of all material universes, it does not easily reveal itself. Furthermore, we should know that it is necessary for the emergence of the great life force to transform matter into organism and to give rise to biological realities. Only then can life guide and move [its own dynamism] in the biological organisms so that it can express its superbly lofty and rich virtue. There is, however, something we cannot afford to ignore. We cannot measure and determine how many of the immeasurable material universes that fill aerospace, such as the countless heavenly bodies, seen from its various internal degrees of heat and the multifarious external relations, can provide the wholesome conditions for the birth and flourishing of biological beings. The most critical factors are the temperance of heat and weather and the production of nutrients. All these are difficult to obtain — the biological beings on earth that lead to the development of the highest human species. Must we search for such a marvelous thing in other heavenly bodies and discover beings that are comparable to the human species of the great earth? I emphatically will not lightly doubt that there is absolutely no chance of finding a comparable species elsewhere, but I do not feel the need to fantasize that we will find many cases of comparable species. If we search for the conditions necessary for biological beings among the countless heavenly bodies of the aerospace, they are probably difficult to find. Yet the question of a life force hidden in matter without visibly revealing itself belongs to a different domain. The countless heavenly bodies in aerospace are definitely not separate and isolated entities. Rather, they are interconnected into a great complete whole. Our great earth, among them, is ultimately the home of the great life force, which is vastly sufficient and real, dynamic and vital; it can also break through the consolidated and enclosed matter, shake the great void, radiate its light, enable numerous material universes to transform themselves into life universes with overflowing vitality, ceaseless self-renewal, and inexhaustible great beings. It is indeed wondrously beautiful!

[*Cunzhai suibi*, pp. 194–195 — TWM]

## MANIFESTO FOR A REAPPRAISAL OF SINOLOGY AND THE RECONSTRUCTION OF CHINESE CULTURE

This manifesto, a reaffirmation of the enduring values of Chinese culture in a time of extreme trial for the Chinese people, was the joint work of four leading intellectuals who went into exile in Hong Kong, Taiwan, and America in advance of the Communist takeover of the mainland. It was produced, on the initiative of Dr. Zhang Junmai (Carsun Chang) (see chapter 33), on the basis of an initial draft by Tang Junyi (known as T'ang Chün-i), dean of New Asia College in Hong Kong, and revised in consultation with the other subscribers to it, including Mou Zongsan and Xu Fuguan, as well as Zhang and Tang.

The manifesto begins with a strong rejoinder to certain Western critiques of Chinese civilization (here referred to as "Sinology") and proceeds to defend a Chinese spirituality embracing elements of Daoism and Buddhism along with a Confucian core, which have enabled the Chinese people to survive repeated challenges and catastrophes of the kind they were experiencing when the manifesto was drawn up in the 1950s. The statement gives an analysis of the weaknesses of modern Western civilization, including its obsession with rapid progress and unlimited expansion. Rejecting Mao's communism as un-Chinese, it proposes as an alternative and as a remedy for the excesses of the West, the perennial values of Chinese tradition.

Reproduced below is a much abridged version of this lengthy manifesto as rendered in English and published under the name of Carsun Chang.

## The Permanence of China's History and Culture

Why have China's history and culture endured? It cannot be explained away by Spengler's hypothesis that they have become stagnant since the Han dynasty. The fact is that they did not stop progressing. Some say it is due chiefly to the people's emphasis on the maintenance of the concrete daily life, and not like the West, devoting much time to idealism and utopias. Others attribute it to conservatism, the performance of activities in accordance with habitual procedures so that the national vitality is preserved on account of frugality. Yet others have the opinion that the reason may be found in the importance traditionally attached to having a large number of offspring, because of which the nation survived numerous catastrophes. These explanations, and many others, cannot, no doubt, be dismissed as entirely trivial. Yet, holding that a nation's culture is the expression of its spiritual life, we believe that the answer is to be sought for in its ideologies.

The aspiration for the eternal took shape very early in Chinese thought. In ancient religious teaching there was the saying that the "decree of heaven is not immovable" — in other words, that heaven, or God, is impartial, the decree falling on the virtuous. The Duke of Zhou understood this impermanence from the examples of Xia (1818–1766 B.C.E.) and Yin (1751–1111 B.C.E.),[1] and hence incessantly admonished the people to preserve and prolong its sociopolitical heritage. For this very reason, the Zhou dynasty lasted for some eight hundred

---

1. Current estimates date Yin (Shang) from the mid-sixteenth century to the mid-eleventh century, and Xia prior to the mid-sixteenth century. See vol. 1, ch. 1.

years, the longest in Chinese history. The philosophical presentation of this concept is first found in the *Classic of Changes*, the *Mean*, and the writings of Laozi. These might have been compiled during the period of the Warring States, when social and political conditions were most unstable. The later dynasties of Han, Tang, and Song all lasted for centuries because of this desire to attain permanence, which also explains why China's entire civilization has endured. Briefly speaking, this concept of seeking the permanent, as expounded in Daoism, is utilitarian, or "advancing by retreating." As Laozi put it, "That Heaven and Earth are lasting is because they do not last for themselves." Also, "The sage keeps himself behind and yet is in front; he forgets himself, and yet is preserved." It enjoins one to rise above subjective prejudices and extraneous exertions so as to preserve one's vitality in order to attain longevity. It also urges one to abate selfishness and desires, to embrace what is simple and natural, to attain the idea of the "void" so as to be quiescent, and to keep one's energy within limits in order to be able to come back to oneself constantly. This is the way to attain the origin of the vitality of life and at the same time to help preserve one's natural strength.

Confucians also taught man to control this vitality. However, in this case the motive is initially the establishment of *li* (rites) between man and man. Following [the Rites of] Zhou's "Li Regulations," they compared the virtues of a superior man with the qualities of jade. The characteristics of jade are its polished appearance and its firmness and solidity inside. With moral strength, one can accumulate all the vital energy of life. This is similar to what the *Mean* (*Zhongyong*) called the "strength of the South," which stressed "forbearance and gentleness in teaching others and even not to recompense for trespasses," thus preserving the vitality. Both of these point to the moral virtuousness a man should possess. This kind of virtuousness is able not only to preserve man's vitality within himself but also to manifest itself by penetrating through his body. That is, this virtuousness has also the function of keeping one in good health; as the saying goes, "Virtue nurtures the body." In Western ethical studies, discussion of morality is usually devoted to consideration of the regulations of human behavior, or the social or religious values of moral codes. Few writers have particularly stressed this thorough transformation of man's natural life by moral practices, so that his attitudes and manners manifest his inner virtues and enrich and illuminate this life. On the other hand, it is precisely what traditional Confucianism has greatly emphasized.

With regard to the conservation of China's national life, the emphasis on having many offspring should not be interpreted as a mere instinct of race preservation. Even during the Zhou dynasty, this emphasis was on self-consciousness motivated by the desire to perpetuate the ancestral lineage — a motivation that had religious, moral, and political connotations as well. Psychologically, this natural instinct is limited to the love between husband and wife and between parents and children. People need to rise above this natural tendency in order to acquire respect for parents and ancestors from whom they receive their life, and with it the fear that they might not receive ceremonial worship should they have no issue. This gave rise to the desire to perpetuate one's life down to thousands of generations, and also to the saying that "There are three unfilial things; of them the worst is lack of posterity." The explanation is to be sought in the pervading conception that in its unfathomable vastness *xin* (mind-and-heart) ought to reach up to thousands of epochs that had passed and down to myriads of generations to come.

Similarly, the desire of the Chinese people to preserve their civilization should not be understood as mere conservatism. In early Confucian thought, it was already considered unrighteous to destroy another state or to terminate another man's ancestral lineage. Confucians worked not only to keep intact the culture handed down by the Duke of Zhou but also to safeguard the varied traditions of the Xia and Yin dynasties. The dictum in the *Spring and Autumn Annals*, "to revive the perished state and restore the broken family," applied to all states, and not only to Lu, the native land of Confucius. At the same time, the purpose of the sage's extensive travels was clearly that the entire world might embrace the ways of Dao. Such is certainly neither provincial nor merely conservative. . . .

It is now clear why we can never accept the explanation of the Chinese emphasis on the preservation of their culture by means of racial instinct or conservatism. The real reason behind the discrimination against the barbarian tribes was simply that objectively China's culture was more advanced than theirs. For the same reason, the cream of the cultures of other nations has always been received and preserved by the Chinese. This is corroborated by their persistence in affirming the value of Buddhism, Christianity, and other Western doctrines despite the Communist denial. . . .

## Science and the Development of Chinese Culture

According to our understanding, the direction of progress to be taken should extend the attainment of moral self-realization to the fields of politics, of knowledge and of technology. In other words, China needs a genuine democratic reconstruction and scientific and technological skills. For this reason, China must embrace the civilization of the world; for this will enable her national character to reach higher planes of perfection and her spiritual life to achieve a more comprehensive development. . . .

The scientific spirit of the West originated in the Greek dictum of "knowledge for the sake of knowledge." This demands the suspension, at least temporarily, of all practical or moral activities, transcending evaluations and moral judgments to permit the intellect on the one hand to observe each phenomenon objectively and on the other to pursue rational inferences by means of which it may illuminate the laws of the universe and its categories of thought and logic. Such a spirit is precisely what was lacking in China's ancient philosophy so that theoretical science could not evolve, and the progress of her arts and technology was arrested. The privation of such a scientific spirit was the result chiefly of the obsession with the fulfillment of moral principles, which prevented any objective assessment of the world. There was no theoretical scientific knowledge to link together the inner moral cultivation, the "establishing of virtues," and the outward practical activities of tailoring nature to enrich life. . . .

The Chinese people must therefore endeavor to achieve self-realization as intellectuals, as well as moral beings. As we have demonstrated, this requires the temporary suspension of their moral consciousness in favor and in support of intellectual activities. . . . At the same time, it is necessary to have a proper balance between the two elements. It is precisely this harmony between morality and intellect that is the supreme function of man.

## Democratic Reconstruction and the Development of Chinese Culture

Apart from the aristocratic feudalism of the pre-Qin period (ended 222 B.C.E.), the sole form of government in China was monarchy, until 1911. In such a system the ultimate political powers lay in the ruler rather than the people, and because of this there arose many unsolved problems, such as the order of succession to the throne, the interim between two dynasties, and the status of the ministers. . . . In order to break through this situation the only way is to establish a democratic government.

That China should have as yet failed to do so does not mean that her political development does not tend toward democracy or that there is not the germ of democracy in the culture. Chinese monarchy was quite different from its Western counterpart, for Chinese political thought early identified popular will with the decree of Heaven. Whoever proclaimed himself ordained by Heaven to be the ruler must also respect and seriously consider the desires of the people. Accordingly, it was provided that he should carefully weigh the admonitions of his ministers, high or low, and the petitions of his subjects. [Reference is here made to institutions such as the court historian, censorate, examination system, etc.] . . . These all serve to offset the monarch's power and to bridge the gap between the central government and the populace, although their effectiveness depended ultimately solely on the personal integrity of the monarch, since there was no fundamental law or constitution to check him. It is therefore clear that the limitations on the powers of the ruler must be transferred from the ministers to the people outside the governmental structure if they are to be effectual. . . .

It then follows that a constitution must be drawn up, in accordance with the popular will, to be the basis of the exercise by the people of their political rights. Only thus may the people all attain moral self-realization, since self-realization demands, politically, the freedom both to ascend to and to retire from official positions.

## Our Understanding of China's Contemporary Political History

That constitutional democracy has not been realized despite the aspirations of the people has its sociological and ideological reasons. . . . Although they had inklings of the notions of rights and sovereignty of the people, most of the Chinese, having no clear idea of what democracy meant, regarded the establishment of the new Republic [in 1911] as just another dynastic changeover. Furthermore, there were few religious, economic, cultural, or scientific organizations and no class opposition. Unlike their Western counterparts, the early members of the parliament were largely intellectuals who had little social experience and who hardly represented the interests of any organization or class. . . .

Communism did not originate in China. Introduced into the country by intellectuals who dwelled in attics in the various foreign settlements, it has spread so widely only because China did suffer greatly from the imperialism and capitalism of the West. Communist premises were never accepted or demanded by the spiritual life of the people. . . .

There are five fundamental reasons why communism as a guiding principle of Chinese culture and politics cannot last. (1) Marx-Leninism denies the possibility of individualized human nature except insofar as it is determined by economics. In this attempt to annihilate all institutions of religion, art, literature, and morality, it is violating the common principles of all the world's higher civilizations. (2) It denies the individuality and rights of each human being. (3) The natural course of Chinese cultural history points toward humanity's political, intellectual, and technological, as well as moral, self-realization. . . . That is, freedom of thought and academic pursuit must be affirmed without qualification. (4) In striving for political self-realization, the Chinese cannot tolerate party dictatorship, just as they could not tolerate absolute monarchy. (5) In the Communist totalitarian system, there is no rule governing succession of leadership, so that on the death of a leader there are inevitably life-and-death struggles between the aspirants. . . . To avoid such an unpleasant situation the only means is popular election in accordance with a fundamental constitution, making for peaceful transfer of political power.

In view of these reasons, Communist totalitarianism is doomed, despite various temporary industrial and technological achievements. After all, Marxist-Leninism has no positive basis in Chinese culture. . . .

The future development of Chinese politics cannot be precisely predicted, but it is certain that Marxist-Leninism will be discarded eventually and the spiritual life of the nation will press forward toward the establishment of a democratic government.

## What the West Can Learn from Eastern Thought

It is clear that the formation of a world civilization is contingent upon cooperation on a high plane among the various cultures of the world. . . .

The strength of the West's cultural spirit lies in its ability to push ahead indefinitely. However, there is no secure foundation underlying this feverish pursuit of progress. Along with this pursuit of progress there is a feeling of discontentment and of emptiness. In order to fill this emptiness, the individual and the nation constantly find new ways for progress and expansion. At the same time external obstructions and an internal exhaustion of energy cause the collapse of the individual and the nation. . . . Chinese thought has always regarded "retreat" as more fundamental than "advance." Complementing the characteristically Western push for progress, this will provide a solid and secure foundation for Western civilization. . . .

The second element the West can learn from the East is all-round and all-embracing understanding or wisdom. . . . In Western science or philosophy, principles and universals are attained by intellect and are sharply enunciated and defined. They are abstract and cannot be applied to what is concrete, because the characteristics that are peculiar to each class and that are inexhaustible have been eliminated. Wisdom is needed to comprehend and to deal with all the unprecedented changes of life. This wisdom does not operate by adhering to universals, but by submerging universals in order to observe the changing conditions and peculiarities. . . .

The Western world is in great need of this wisdom if it intends to understand the nature of the different cultures and to have an authentic communication with them. In addition to their knowledge, technology, ideals, and God, they must above all search deeper for the source of life, the depth of personality, and the common origin of human culture in order to arrive at a true unity with mankind.

The third point that the West can learn from the East is a feeling of mildness and compassion. The Westerner's loyalty to ideals, his spirit of social service, and his warmth and love for others are indeed precious virtues, to which Eastern counterparts cannot measure up. However, the highest affection between men is not zeal or love, for with these emotions is often mingled the will to power and its acquisitive instinct. . . . Compassion, on the other hand, is the sympathetic consonance between the life-spirit of one's own and another's authentic being. Here there is also natural interflowing of true sympathy, which is partly directed outward and partly inward. The emotional flowback makes it possible to purge any desire to dominate or possess. . . .

Fourth, the West can obtain from the East the wisdom of how to perpetuate its culture. Contemporary Western culture is, it is true, at its height of brilliance, yet many observers have been concerned with its future, whether it will perish like ancient Greece and Rome. Culture is the expression of a people's spiritual life, and by the laws of nature all expression drains the energy of life. If this energy is exhausted, perishing is inevitable. To preserve its spiritual life, humanity needs a depth formed by a historical awareness that reaches both into the past and into the future, and this depth connects with the lifegiving source of the cosmos. . . . From this point of view, the West's chief concern with speed and efficiency constitutes a great problem. While the former easygoing attitude of the Chinese is not a suitable remedy in many aspects, yet the maximum rate of progress with which the West leads the world is not conducive to durability. . . . The West needs to develop a historical awareness with which to tap the lifegiving source. It will then come to appreciate the value of conservation of life-energy and the meaning of filial piety, and learn to fulfill the ancestral will in order to preserve and prolong its culture.

The fifth point the West can learn from the East is the attitude that "the whole world is like one family." Though there are many nations now, mankind will eventually become one and undivided. Chinese thought has emphasized this attitude. . . .

## What We Expect from World Thought

While the West can certainly learn from the East, we have also a few remarks to make concerning the intellectual development of China and of the world.

1. The expansion of Western civilization has brought the peoples into close contact and unfortunately has also produced much friction. What needs to be done now is for each nation crucially to reexamine and reevaluate its own culture, taking into consideration the future of mankind as a whole. In order to achieve coexistence of the various cultures and world peace, one must first, through a transcendental feeling that goes beyond philosophical and scientific research, attain an attitude of respect and sympathy toward other cultures and thereby acquire genuine compassion and commiseration toward mankind in adversity. . . .

2. In cultivating this feeling, it is evident that objective and scientific learning is inadequate. Man needs a different kind of learning, one that treats himself as a conscious, existential being. It is not theology; it cannot be the merely phenomenological study of ethics or mental hygiene. Rather it is a learning that applies understanding to conduct, by which one may transcend existence to attain spiritual enlightenment. . . .

3. The human existence as formed by "establishing Man as the Ultimate" is that of a moral being that, at the same time, attains a higher spiritual enlightenment; for this reason, it can truly embrace God, thereby attaining "harmony in virtue with Heaven." Hence, this human existence is simultaneously moral and religious existence. Such a man is, in politics, the genuine citizen of democracy; in epistemology, one who stands over and above the physical world.

Not being bound by his concepts, his intellectual knowledge does not contradict his spiritual apprehension. . . . Such should be the direction of the new movement.

[From Chang, *The Development of Neo-Confucianism*, 2:465–483]

## MOU ZONGSAN'S CONFUCIAN PHILOSOPHY

Mou Zongsan (Tsung-san) (1909–1995) is considered one of the premier Confucian scholars of his generation instrumental in founding the international movement called New Confucianism. He studied philosophy at Beijing University under Xiong Shili and later became known as the most creative systematic philosopher among the New Confucians. Along with Zhang Junmai (Carsun Chang), Tang Junyi, and Xu Fuguan, he was a cosigner of the 1957 *Manifesto for a Reappraisal of Sinology and the Reconstruction of Chinese Culture*.

Despite the complexity of his system, Mou succeeded in creating a new vision of the mainline of Confucian thought stretching from Confucius and Mencius to Cheng Hao of the Northern Song and down to Liu Zongzhou, the great Ming martyr to Confucian loyalty and perseverance.

Mou conceived of his own philosophic development in three stages. First, he began as a student of Western philosophy and logic with a special love for the thought of Kant and the other philosophers of the German Enlightenment. Next, he turned his attention to political philosophy and the philosophy of history, including provocative studies of Daoism. Third, Mou returned to a discussion of human nature, the moral mind-heart and the rise and development of Neo-Confucian thought from the Northern Song to the fall of the Ming dynasty. Mou also wrote studies of Western philosophy, Buddhism, and ethics.

Throughout his career Mou wrote about Chinese thought in the context of world philosophy, ranging from modern European phenomenology to a reevaluation of the history of Chinese Buddhist thought. He believed that Confucian thought had been correctly based on the intellectual intuition of the patterns and dynamics of the cosmos and that it was the task of modern Confucian intellectuals to disclose the logical and epistemological rationales for these claims in light of modern Western critiques of Chinese thought. Moreover, Mou affirmed the profound religious dimension of the Confucian search for sageliness as a form of spiritual self-cultivation. What he ultimately sought to create was a moral metaphysics.

### THE SENSITIVITY AND STEADFASTNESS OF HUMANENESS (*REN*)

In the following excerpt from chapter 5 of a series of public lectures on the nature of Chinese thought, titled *The Uniqueness of Chinese Philosophy*, Mou addresses the central Confucian ideal of humaneness, or *ren*. Set within his larger discussion of the connection of human nature and the Heavenly Way, Mou defines humaneness as sensitivity and steadfastness and as the ultimate human manifestation of creativity itself, the very core of the dynamic process of the Way of Heaven and earth.

The *qian* section of the *Classic of Changes* says, "The great man is someone whose virtue is consonant with Heaven and earth, his brightness with the sun and moon, his consistency with the four seasons and his prognostications of the auspicious and inauspicious with the workings of gods and spirits."[2] In order to become a "great person," one must join personal virtue with Heaven and earth, which is to say, the life-values of the individual must respond to the life-values of the universe in order to obtain a fundamental, unbreakable melding (or, we can say, a conciliation). What was cited in the first lecture as the virtue of Heaven and earth is certainly "the Heavenly Will mysteriously, unceasingly active" as representing the essence of endless creativity. The uniting virtue of the great person, Heaven and earth joined together have the unceasing essence of creativity. In modern terms, if one truly sees the life-value of the self, one has already embraced nonmaterial life-values; these nonmaterial life-values then become true life-values such that the person manifests the special characteristic of life. This true life-value is definitely a spiritual life-value and is not a worldly life-value and hence is somewhat analogous to what Jesus meant when he said, "I am the Way, the Truth, and the Life." The great person must also conjoin action with the spirits of auspicious and inauspicious fortune in a fashion that explains clearly how the life-values of the great person respond to both the dark and the light sides of the cosmos, both of which become mutually active in the world. In other words, it is necessary for the dark and light sides of humankind and the light and dark sides of the cosmos to be mutually interpenetrating and reconciled. The light and dark sides of the cosmos are commonly known by humankind; for example, the spirits, night and day, spring and summer are all recognized as the bright side of the cosmos, while demons, blackest night, fall and winter are all recognized as the dark side of the cosmos. Human life is like the cosmos because it has its dark and bright sides, as when we say that birth is bright and death is dark. In order to comprehend the totality of the idea of the cosmos, we must look at both the light and the dark sides of the cosmos; just as, in order to understand the idea of humaneness, we must also observe the life and the death of human beings. The "great person" must include the totality of the life-value of humaneness with the life-values in the cosmos in order to create unity. The essential natures of humaneness, wisdom, and sageliness are not disparate but are mutually connected with the Heavenly Will and the Heavenly Way.

Another question follows the explication of the function of humaneness,

---

2. See Lynn, *The Classic of Changes*, p. 138.

wisdom, and sageliness — what causes humaneness, wisdom, and sageliness to be capable of being mutually connected with the Heavenly Will and the Heavenly Way? That is, in what fashion can it create unity with the cosmos? The answer requires an explanation of the idea of the concept of humaneness. According to the general idea of the perspective on humaneness found in the *Analects*, we know how an individual person can become one who is humane or a sage and we can also learn why one who is humane and a sage can become unified with the cosmos. According to the interpretation of this lecturer, Confucius's idea of humaneness has two main characteristics:

1. Sensitivity. This is not the awareness of the senses or sense perception, but rather the sensitivity of sorrow, what the *Analects* says is the feeling of "unease," and what Mencius called the sorrowful mind-heart or the unbearable mind-heart. Having this sensitivity, then, a person can also have the four seeds of the mind-heart, but without that awareness, then one can speak of a numbness, as the Chinese saying has it, "numb and not humane," which points out the special characteristic of humaneness as being aware and not being numbed. A person can have a great knowledge of or sensitivity to affairs of money, wealth, and possessions, but can also be very insensitive and numb, even though he has an extremely brilliant talent and understanding. This is because the point of sensitivity is the moral mind-heart, and whoever has this sensitivity can perceive the four seeds of the moral mind-heart.

2. Steadfastness. This is the notion of steadfastness in the *Classic of Changes* wherein there is "steadfastly acting without tiring." The *Changes* says, "Heaven acts steadfastly, and the Noble Person, by his own strength, does not tire." "Heaven acts steadfastly" is a statement of the manifestation of the Heavenly Will, "mysteriously without ceasing." The Noble Person seeks the steadfast, endless action of Heaven-and-earth and understands that they also must emulate the steadfast, unceasing action of the Heavenly Way. This manifests our life-values as a responsive, penetrating sensitivity to demonstrate steadfastness, or in other words, to be one with Heaven, to manifest the creative nature, because the essential virtue of Heaven is the essence of creativity. The inclusive meaning of the word *steadfast* does not mean the persistence of muscular strength in physical cultivation, but rather is the pure spiritual strength of unceasing creativity.

To extrapolate from the explanation of these two points, we can explain the true nature of "humaneness [*ren*]" stating that "humaneness takes feeling to be human nature and benefiting as its function." Feeling as penetration is the greatly enhanced life-value (the spiritual side), and the process of this enlargement is without cessation, and therefore, this sensitive penetration must unite with all the other things in the cosmos. This is also to state that this is the ultimate extension of "[the great person] whose virtue is consonant with Heaven and earth, his brightness with the sun and moon, his consistency with the four seasons, and his prognostications of the auspicious and inauspicious with the workings of gods and spirits." The process of benefiting things by sensitive penetration acts in favor of humaneness by means of a warm empathy that can encourage and elicit the life-values of other people. This enriching function is quite like the sweet dew that moistens the plants. The function of humaneness is this very profound deepening; we must say that humaneness represents real life; and this real life must then be our real substance and this real substance must then also be our real subject; and the real substance must be our real self. Therefore, the idea and value of humaneness are already proclaimed. Confucius established the connection of humaneness's inner root to the Heavenly Way so that human nature and the Heavenly Way were not the subject of empty and idle chatter. If humaneness was empty and idle chatter without any internal content, the Heavenly Way would be high and far away, eternally unreachable by humankind. The humaneness of Confucius is really a verification of the Heavenly Will and the Heavenly Way.

[From Mou Zongsan, *Zhongguo zhexue de tezhi*, pp. 34–36 — JHB]

## FENG YOULAN: "CHINA — AN ANCIENT NATION WITH A NEW MISSION"

Feng Youlan (Fung Yu-lan, 1895–1990), along with Hu Shi (see chapters 32 and 33) one of two leading students of John Dewey, became known as a dominant figure in the study of Chinese philosophy from the 1930s on. His two-volume *History of Chinese Philosophy* in both Chinese and English was long regarded in China and abroad as the standard work on the subject. In 1949, when many other intellectuals went into exile abroad, he chose to remain in Beijing and endure the same experience under communism as his fellow countrymen, hoping to develop his own philosophy in a synthesis with the new form of Chinese Marxism. Despite repeated efforts to adapt, as well as successive attempts at self-criticism, he found it difficult to resolve his problems and complete his own work, but he continued to believe that traditional Chinese thought would form the basis of a modernized China.

Feng's lifetime work, summed up in his posthumous *Selected Philosophical Writings* of 1991, included studies in English reiterating his earlier views with relatively little modification. The following excerpts are taken from the concluding essay in the volume, as he summed up a life of "conflict and contradiction" on the occasion of his receiving an honorary degree from Columbia University in 1982. The final note recalls a passage from the *Classic of Odes* [here called the *Book of Poetry*]: "Although Zhou is an old nation, it has a new mission" — which is Professor Feng's understanding of the passage rendered in chapter 2: "Zhou is an old people, but its charge is new."

Although Feng's philosophical stance and his role contrast with that of the authors' of the manifesto reproduced above, who firmly rejected communism as un-Chinese, Feng's own survival strategy and persistence in reasserting Chinese values as the basis of the new mission of modernization exemplify the same spirit of determination and endurance as is expressed in the manifesto. In the end, his rejection of Maoist class struggle and strong reaffirmation of Confucian humanism and harmonious relations were such that the final volume of his *Collected Works* had to be published in Taiwan and Hong Kong, not on the mainland.

## Speech of Response Delivered at the Convocation of September 10, 1982, at Columbia University

I live in a period of conflict and contradiction between different cultures. My problem is how to understand the nature of this conflict and contradiction, how to deal with it, and how to adjust myself within this conflict and contradiction.

I first came to America at the end of what is known as the May 4 Movement, which was a climax to the conflict and contradiction of different cultures at that time. I came with these problems and I began to deal with them seriously. As I did so, my thought developed in three stages. In the first stage, I interpreted the difference of cultures in terms of geographical areas — that is to say, the difference of cultures is the difference between the East and the West. In the second stage, I interpreted the difference of cultures in terms of historical epochs — that is to say, the difference of cultures is the difference between the ancient and the modern. In the third stage, I interpreted the difference of cultures in terms of social development — that is to say, the difference of cultures is the difference between types of society.

In 1922 I presented a paper to the conference of the philosophy department, titled "Why China Has No Science." Later it was published in the *International Journal of Ethics*. In this paper I maintained that the difference between cultures is the difference between the East and the West. This in fact was the prevailing opinion at that time. However, as I further studied the history of philosophy, I found this prevailing opinion to be incorrect. I discovered that what is considered to be the philosophy of the East has existed in the history of philosophy of the West as well, and vice versa. I discovered that mankind has the same essential nature with the same problems of life. . . . My thesis, published in 1924 under the title A *Comparative Study of Life Ideals*, denied the then current interpretation of the conflict and contradiction between different cultures, [but] it did not provide a new interpretation in its place. Such a new interpretation, however, appeared implicitly in my later work A *History of Chinese Philosophy*. The book asserted that, strictly speaking, there had been no modern philosophy in China, but as soon as China would become modernized there would be a modern Chinese philosophy. This assertion implicitly suggests that what is called the difference between the cultures of the East and the West is, in fact, the difference between the medieval and the modern.

But what are the contents of these words *medieval* and *modern*? Later on I began to realize that the difference between the medieval and the modern is, in fact, a difference between types of society. In the Western countries, the transformation from one type of society into another took place one step earlier than in the Eastern countries. The key to the transformation has been the industrial revolution. Before the industrial revolution, the family was the basic unit of production. After the revolution, because of the introduction of machinery, production became enlarged in scope — that is, it was performed by large groups of people, not by separate families. In the forties, I wrote six books, one of them titled *China's Way to Freedom*, in which I proposed that this way consists of modernization and that the main content of modernization is an industrial revolution.

Then came the revolution in China, and with it the philosophy of Marxism. . . .

The intellectuals, encouraged by the victory of the revolution, made efforts to help build a new socialist society. My own effort was to revise my book *A History of Chinese Philosophy*. Only the first two volumes of the revised edition of this early work were published before I found the revision unsatisfactory to myself. I set out to revise the revision, but before it went to press I found that this newly revised edition needed to be done over again. . . . The source of my hesitation and vacillation is really a question of how to adjust to conflict and contradiction between different cultures. This question manifested itself in the further questions of how to inherit the spiritual heritage of the past. In the early fifties, I raised this question, the discussion of which was rather warm for a time.

The simplest way to make the adjustment is just to declare that the philosophy of the past was all for the sake of the exploiting classes. Thus there is nothing worthy to be inherited. The present should disregard the past and consider it nonexistent. The present should start from zero and build everything anew. . . . People holding this view do not understand that the present is a continuation and development of the past. The higher type of society supersedes the lower just as a steamship supersedes a rowboat. The steamship replaces the rowboat, but it is built and operated on the same general principles that apply to all ships, including the rowboat. The experience and the experiment of the rowboat are the bases of the steamship. In this sense the steamship is the development of the rowboat, and this is the real meaning of the word *development*. The process of the development is a dialectical movement. To use Hegelian terms, there are affirmation, negation, and negation of negation. In other words, there are thesis, antithesis, and synthesis. Such synthesis embraces all of the best in the thesis and antithesis. In this sense, the present should embrace all the best of the past. This is the natural way of adjustment of different cultures. . . .

Throughout Chinese history, after a great dynasty had unified the country and established a strong central government and after people of different nationalities were living together harmoniously, there usually appeared a new and very comprehensive philosophy. Such a philosophy, with its interpretations of nature, society, and man, reflected the unity of the country and, at the same time, served as a theoretical foundation for the structure of the society of the time and its spiritual content. Confucianism and Neo-Confucianism were such philosophies, and China today needs such a comprehensive philosophy to embrace all aspects of the new civilization and to be her guide.

Generally speaking, we in China today have Marxism and Mao Zedong Thought. Marxism will become Chinese Marxism, Mao Zedong Thought will further develop. . . . Mao Zedong Thought is defined as the unity of the universal principles of Marxism with the practice of the Chinese Revolution. . . . In the early stages of the revolution, the unity was well carried out. The theories by which the proletariat led the peasants in military insurrection and by which the village besieged the city are examples of this unity, and also of Chinese Marxism. Strategies based on these theories led the revolution to victory. In later stages, however, when the unity was not so well carried out and it was then further distorted by the intrigues of the "Gang of Four," there appeared the extreme leftist policy known as the Cultural Revolution, the results of which are well known. . . .

A system of philosophy is not a patchwork. Philosophy is a living thing. You can patch together ready-made parts to produce a machine but not a living thing, even such a living thing as a tiny insect or a blade of grass. You can only furnish nourishment to the living thing and let it absorb the nourishment itself. Under present circumstances, I feel I have a new task with the revised edition of my book A History of Chinese Philosophy. It should be not only a narration of the story of the past but also a nourishment for the philosophy of the future. . . .

I always recall one line that appears in the Book of Poetry of the Confucian classics. It reads, "Although Zhou is an old nation, it has a new mission." At the present time, China is an ancient nation that has a new mission, and that mission is modernization. My effort is to preserve the identity and individuality of the ancient nation, yet, at the same time, to promote the fulfillment of the new mission. People on the left appreciate my efforts to promote the fulfillment of the new mission but blame my effort to preserve the identity and individuality of the ancient nation. I understand their reasons and accept the applause as well as the blame. Applause and blame may cancel each other out. I shall go on according to my own judgment.

[From Selected Philosophical Writings, pp. 658–663]

## THE CONTINUING CRITIQUE OF TRADITION

In the 1980s debate over Chinese culture broke out once more in greater China. With the rise of the East Asian economies attributed to Confucian influences, and the widespread decline of morale and sense of anomie that followed the collapse of the Cultural Revolution, some intellectuals began to advocate the

revival of Chinese culture. The first hints appeared in the works of such prominent fiction writers as Wang Anyi, Han Shaogong, and Ah Cheng. In what
came to be known as "Chinese Culture Fever," issues related to culture were
debated in the prominent journal *Reading (Dushu)*, as well as in other forums.
However, many intellectuals, influenced by the sweeping attacks on Chinese
culture that had been made in the May 4 Movement, still saw in Chinese
culture the reasons why China, in their eyes, remained backward despite the
massive changes of the twentieth century. Just as the failure of the early Chinese
republic had contributed to the May 4 Movement, the perceived failure of the
People's Republic aroused further questioning as to the persistent debilitating
effects of Chinese culture. Of the writers below, Bo Yang (Guo Yidong) is from
Taiwan (though born and raised on the mainland), Sun Longji from Hong
Kong, and Su Xiaokang and Wang Luxiang from the mainland. All try to show
how tradition has stood in the way of new ideas from abroad.

Both Sun Longji's *The Deep Structure of Chinese Culture* and Bo Yang's *The
Ugly Chinaman* had become well known to mainland intellectuals by the mid-
1980s. An edited mainland version of *The Ugly Chinaman* circulated briefly
before it was banned. Su Xiaokang and Wang Luxiang's "River Elegy" was not
a book but a television documentary. By the summer of 1988, when the documentary was aired, about 90 percent of the Chinese people had access to television, and thus the documentary and the ideas contained in it reached an
unprecedentedly large audience. Eventually, however, the documentary was
criticized by powerful Chinese Communist Party figures like Wang Zhen and
finally banned.

Although this debate took place during a brief, relatively open period in the
PRC, the CCP's rejection of a critique of traditional Chinese culture is significant. By 1988 the Party, like the Nationalists in the late twenties, was already
moving away from its earlier condemnation of Chinese culture and instead
looking for traditional values that would be supportive of its rule. This had
become especially vital in the wake of the collapse of Marxist values and a
growing perception of a moral vacuum in Chinese society. Yet this attempted
return to tradition did little to enhance the popularity of the existing regime
among intellectuals already disenchanted with both it and tradition.

BO YANG: "THE UGLY CHINAMAN"

The sharply negative tone of the following essay reflects a sense of alienation and
despair in the wake of the Cultural Revolution, as well as a feeling that age-old weaknesses have persisted through revolutionary change. Underlying this is the widespread
presumption of the revolutionary ideology itself, much reinforced by Marxism, that
traditional China had been marked by unrelieved stagnation and was ripe for total
revolution. This expectation set the stage for later disillusionment over the failure of

the revolution to fulfill its promises, followed in this case by a sense of resignation to more modest limited goals.

[Concerning China] No other nation on earth has such a long history or such a well-preserved cultural tradition, a tradition that has in the past given rise to an extremely advanced civilization. Neither the Greeks nor the Egyptians of today bear any relationship to their ancient forebears, while the Chinese people of today are the direct descendants of the ancient Chinese. How is it possible for such a great people to have degenerated to such a state of ugliness? Not only have we been bullied around by foreigners; even worse, for centuries we've been bullied around by our own kind — from tyrannical emperors to despotic officials and ruthless mobs. . . .

## Chinese People Are the Same Everywhere

. . . I've asked a number of people from the mainland why they ended up in prison. The answer was invariably "I spoke the truth." And that's the way it is. But why does speaking the truth lead to such unfortunate consequences? My answer is that this is not a problem of any particular individual but rather of Chinese culture as a whole.

## The Scourge of Infighting

One of the qualities for which the Chinese people are notorious is a propensity for quarreling among themselves. . . . They squabble among themselves no matter where they are. Their bodies seem to lack those cells that enable most human beings to cooperate.

## The Inability to Admit Error

The Chinese people's inability to cooperate and their predilection for bickering among themselves are deep-rooted, harmful traits. These behavior patterns do not stem from an inherent weakness in the moral fiber of the Chinese people but rather from a "neurotic virus" that infects Chinese culture, making it impossible for us not to act in certain ways in given situations. We may be entirely aware of the fact that we quarrel among ourselves, yet it is beyond our control to stop it. "If the pot breaks, no one can have anything to eat; but if the sky falls there'll always be someone tall enough to prevent it from falling on me." This tendency toward internecine struggle is associated with a terrible reluctance to admit mistakes. . . .

Chinese people find it hard to admit their mistakes and produce myriad reasons to cover up for them. There's an old adage: "Contemplate errors behind closed doors." Whose errors? The guy next door's, of course! . . . Chinese people expend a great deal of effort in covering up their mistakes, and in so doing make additional ones. Thus it is often said that Chinese are addicted to bragging, boasting, lying, equivocating, and malicious slandering. For years people have been going on about the supreme greatness of the Han Chinese people and boasting endlessly that Chinese traditional culture should be promulgated throughout the world. But the reason why such dreams will never be realized is because they're pure braggadocio. I need not cite any further examples of boasting and lying, but Chinese verbal brutality deserves special mention. . . . And in matters of politics and money, or in power struggles of any kind, the viciousness can be out of all proportion. This raises the additional question: What makes Chinese people so cruel and base? . . .

## Stuck in the Mud of Bragging and Boasting

Narrow-mindedness and a lack of altruism can produce an unbalanced personality that constantly wavers between two extremes: a chronic feeling of inferiority and extreme arrogance. In his inferiority, a Chinese person is a slave; in his arrogance, he is a tyrant. Rarely does he or she have a healthy sense of self-respect. In the inferiority mode, everyone else is better than he is, and the closer he gets to people with influence, the wider his smile becomes. Similarly, in the arrogant mode, no other human being on earth is worth the time of day. The result of these extremes is a strange animal with a split personality.

## A Nation of Inflation

What makes the Chinese people so prone to self-inflation? Consider the saying: A small vessel is easily filled. Because of the Chinese people's inveterate narrow-mindedness and arrogance, even the slightest success is overwhelming. It is all right if a few people behave in this manner, but if it's the entire population or a majority — particularly in China — it spells national disaster. Since it seems as if the Chinese people have never had a healthy sense of self-respect, it is immensely difficult for them to treat others as equals: if you aren't my master, then you're my slave. People who think this way can only be narrow-minded in their attitude toward the world and reluctant to admit their mistakes.

## Only the Chinese Can Change Themselves

With so many loathsome qualities, only the Chinese people can reform themselves. Foreigners have a duty to help us, not in the realm of economics but through culture. The Chinese ship of state is so large and overcrowded that if it sinks many non-Chinese will be drowned as well.

One last point: China is seriously overpopulated. China's more than one billion mouths can easily devour the Himalayas. This should remind us that

China's difficulties are complex and call for awareness on the part of each and every Chinese person. Each one of us must become a discriminating judge and use our powers to examine and appraise ourselves, our friends, and our country's leaders. This, I believe, is the only way out for the Chinese people.

## Developing a Personal Sense of Judgment

In the last four thousand years, China has produced only one great thinker: Confucius. In the two and one-half millennia since his death, China's literati did little more than add footnotes to the theories propounded by Confucius and his disciples, rarely contributing any independent opinions, simply because the traditional culture did not permit it. The minds of the literati were stuck at the bottom of an intellectual stagnant pond, the soy-sauce vat of Chinese culture. As the contents of this vat began to putrefy, the resultant stench was absorbed by the Chinese people. Since the numerous problems in this bottomless vat could not be solved by individuals' exercising their own intelligence, the literati had to make do with following others' ways of thinking. If one were to place a fresh peach in a soy-sauce vat full of putrescent brine, it would eventually turn into a dry turd. China has its own particular way of transforming foreign things and ideas that enter within its borders. You say you've got democracy; well, we have democracy too. But the Chinese form of democracy is: You're the *demos* (people), but I've got the *kratos* (power). You've got a legal system; we've got one too. You've got freedom; so have we. Whatever you have, we have too. You've got pedestrian crossings painted on the street; we have too, but ours are there to make it easier for cars to run pedestrians over.

The only way to improve the situation of the Ugly Chinaman is for each of us to cultivate our own personal taste and judgment. . . . I have my freedom and rights, whether the government gives them to me or not. If we had the capacity to make proper judgments, we would demand elections and be rigorous in our selection of candidates. But without this capacity, we'll never be able to distinguish a beautiful woman from a pockmarked hag.

[Adapted from Barmé and Minford, *Seeds of Fire*, pp. 170–176 — RL]

### SUN LONGJI: "THE DEEP STRUCTURE OF CHINESE CULTURE"

The following critique of Chinese culture is dressed in voguish psychological terms (supposedly Western) and reflects "modernist" attitudes dismissive of traditional culture. However, it shows little actual familiarity with traditional Confucian values or discourse and seems unaware that much the same critique could be made of current attitudes from a Confucian standpoint.

Pervading this, as in the preceding and following pieces, is a strong sense of despair over China's decadence, most directly attributable to the failure of revolutionary expectations in the twentieth century, following the violent upheavals and relapses of 1911, 1949, and the Cultural Revolution. Also reflected here, however, are other ideological factors, both indigenous and foreign.

The traditional view of Chinese history tended to follow repeated cycles of dynastic rise and decline; thus in Huang Zongxi's analysis of China's troubles, his preface to *Waiting for the Dawn* (in 1662) cites Mencius's view that periods of order alternate with periods of disorder and then adds: "How is it that since the Three Dynasties there has been no order but only disorder?"

From the West, at the turn of the century, came views of human progress and evolution, but with these also strongly negative views, especially marked in Adam Smith, Hegel, and Marx, of traditional China as stagnant and unprogressive, caught in an endless degenerative process. Indeed, it became a fundamental "Marxist" assumption of Mao and the Chinese Communist Party that only a radical, violent upheaval could lift China out of this historical rut. The writers who follow here struggle to get their footing in the backwash of such crosscurrents and erosive tides.

Stagnation in China may be explained in terms of the deep structure of Chinese culture. China has been "ultrastable" for thousands of years, and even now it is a country that still seems to be insensitive and slow in responding to the outside world. Throughout the twentieth century and especially since the establishment of the People's Republic, Marxism has provided the dynamic [that has been] traditionally absent from Chinese culture. Nevertheless, the success of the Communist movement has largely depended on the fact that it developed during a period of transition, at a particular point in the cycle of order and disorder. After the Cultural Revolution, that Marxist-inspired motivation for action would appear to have died away. The Four Modernizations are no longer adequate to mobilize the hearts-and-minds of the people. In contrast, "stability and unity" are emphasized.

This tendency toward stagnation is also evident in the personality of every Chinese individual. A Chinese is programmed by his culture to be "Chinese." In other words, inbred cultural predispositions make the Chinese what they are and prevent them from being full-blown individuals. Dynamic human growth is an alien concept to the Chinese. Growth is seen as just a physical process. Maturity is to know how to play a proper role in bilateral social relationships. Normally, physical growth is accompanied by mental development, but the Chinese are held back by their own culture, and they generally exhibit serious tendencies toward oral fixation. In short, the Chinese do not fully experience the various stages of personality development. . . .

Disorganization of the self easily leads to a weakening of the will. In similar fashion, the rule of law is difficult to achieve in China because the Chinese do not enact appropriate legislation. They are too easily influenced by personal relationships or power. Today in the mainland when "the Party looks after everything for the individual," the disorganization of the self has reached a critical stage. At home, at school, at work, a man cannot organize things for himself. He is forever looked after by an overprotective mother.

Some people think that the present Chinese policy of one child per family will result in a highly individualistic generation. In fact, the opposite may happen. Chinese parents tend to encourage dependence in their children, and if they concentrate all their attention and concern on one child, the Chinese may become even more lacking in personal organization in the future. A man must be fully developed before his life can be a dynamic process; only then can he attain self-actualization in body and mind, can he organize and control his life, his work, his future, his thoughts, his conscience, his interpersonal relationships, and so on. Only to such a man are human rights important.

The majority of the Chinese are unsure of their own rights. They submit meekly to oppression and allow others to encroach on their rights. The meekness of the Chinese people makes them particularly receptive to authoritarianism.

[Adapted from Barmé and Minford, *Seeds of Fire*, pp. 136, 311 — RL]


SU XIAOKANG AND WANG LUXIANG: "RIVER ELEGY,"
A TELEVISION DOCUMENTARY

"River Elegy" is predicated on the imaginative notion that early China once partook of a seafaring Pacific civilization (identified with the sea and the blue sky), adventurous and open to the world like the civilization of Columbus and Magellan. In China, however, this was overtaken and hemmed in by a land-oriented continental culture (identified with the silt of the Yellow River delta), blocking access to the open sea and intercourse with the larger world. China thus became constricted, stagnant, and monolithic, in contrast to the dynamic, pluralistic West. Ironically, the reference herein to Adam Smith's analysis of the China problem reminds us of Smith's influence on Karl Marx's view that the stagnancy of Oriental civilization differentiated it from the dynamic development pattern of Western civilization. Thus an early Marxist (and very Eurocentric) perspective still dominates this critique by intellectuals of post-Maoist China. Not surprisingly, then, it concludes with an exhortation to revive the sweeping May 4 attack on Chinese tradition — the only rhetoric readily available for challenge to the status quo.


The ocean was originally the cradle of life. In all the Earth's traumatic changes and upheavals, it was the sea that once protected the lives of our ancestors. Later on, when human beings returned to the land, they could not adapt. In the process of forcing themselves to adapt to the continental environment, humankind created civilization.

The sphinxlike stone statues on Easter Island tell us that as far back as ten thousand years ago, there was an ancient and vital maritime civilization on the shores of the Pacific Ocean. The maritime tools that appear today [to be] so simple and primitive were the ones that brought humankind back to the sea from the land once again. What is the conviction that supported those primitive people in their attempt to cross this great ocean that even today's people find forbidding? Can we not hear the grand melody of the destiny of humanity echoing in the maritime, seafaring activities of these primitive people, as well as in the great voyages of Columbus and Magellan, which established new ages of human history?

It is precisely because of the continuous and unflagging existence of maritime life that human civilization came to be separated into two major elements — or continental civilization and the maritime civilization.

This country stands on the rim of the western Pacific Ocean. At the same time, it stands astride, mightily, the eastern part of the great Euro-Asian land mass. Its body is yellow, and the great river running through it like a spinal column is also yellow.

As we look at this ancient wooden boat, excavated from the Hemudu archaeological site, it is as if we can see that faraway fountainhead of Chinese civilization glimmering with the light of azure waves.

Yet as far back as the periods of prehistory that were still shrouded in myth, the inland civilization that came from the loess region of the middle stretches of the Yellow River was already continuously overcoming the lower stretches and the coastal areas. Even today we can hear the deep, muffled voices of the history of this period, in the sounds of the stories of the great battles of the Yellow Emperor with the Red Emperor and Chiyou.

Eventually, the Zhou people's conquest of the Shang people proved that this force that came from the heartland was an irresistible one. The epic battles in the late Warring States period, in which the state of Qin defeated and conquered the state of Chu, represent and symbolize how the yellow civilization that fed on wheat, fought with chariots, and was influenced by the nomadic tribes and by the culture of Persia eventually overcame and defeated the azure civilization that fed on rice, fought with ships on the water, and was influenced by the cultures of Southeast Asia and the Pacific. . . .

The recession of the azure laid down a destiny for the nation and the civilization. . . .

The unending azure waves of the Pacific Ocean have always beckoned this ancient nation that slept on the continent. Occasionally they might stir up for a while and send sailing ships to venture out on their waters, even as far as the Persian Gulf and the Arabian Peninsula. Yet, in the end, the attraction of the azure ocean would prove to be much weaker, after all, than the magnetism of the yellow earth.

The mysterious power that provided this yellow civilization with an amazing and tremendous centripetal force was the fact that the Confucian culture gradually attained supremacy on this land.

Confucian thought, as a whole system, expressed the ideals and boundaries of the life of a continental, inland civilization. In the heyday of the oriental feudal society of the Orient, this system had the clear advantage of rationality. Its unitarian ideology, however, also weakened the possibility for the development of pluralism. The elements of the maritime civilization that had been rich and abundant in ancient life deteriorated into a few feeble streams . . . that disappeared instantly.

Nonetheless, while the continental civilization was flourishing in the land of China, another azure civilization of the sea was cropping up, a bit more quietly perhaps, along the shores of the Mediterranean Sea.

Back in the time of ancient Greece, at the same time that Athens' sea power emerged, so too did its democratic ideas, and thus maritime power led to a democratic revolution.

The Western bourgeois revolution in modern times was also predicated, socially, on the opening of the sea lanes of the European nations. The galleons that navigated between sea and sky starting in the fifteenth century not only raised the curtain on world trade and colonial activity, they also conveyed the hopes of science and democracy. With these ships, puny as they were, the color azure symbolized the destiny of the modern world.

The vast markets of the Orient, and of the "New World" of the Americas, made Europe rich almost overnight.

To cross the great oceans, large, sturdy, yet carefully and intricately constructed ships were required. Mathematics and physics were needed for the building of these ships, and technological sciences were also needed. In 1636 Galileo published his work *Dialogue on the New Science*. It was in a shipbuilding factory that this "dialogue" took place.

Britain was the first to obtain great profit from overseas trade, which promoted the primitive accumulation of capital as well as the popularization of the ideas of freedom. It was in Britain that the first bourgeois revolution, led by Oliver Cromwell, took place. In 1651 Cromwell's government, in turn, promulgated the Navigation Act; in 1690 John Locke published his *Two Treatises on Government*. The theory of free trade became the slogan of, and the principle to serve, the bourgeoisie.

Capitalism, churning the wheels of the industrial revolution and free trade, began to bring about tremendous leaps in history, and so began the dual historical chorus of science and democracy.

All this was closely related to the ocean.

What was China doing at the time?

When Magellan was sailing around the globe, the Jiajing emperor of the Ming dynasty formally "closed" China to the outside world because of a quarrel with a Japanese tribute-bearer.

In 1776 Adam Smith published his famous book *The Wealth of Nations*. In this book he declared that China's history and civilization had stagnated. He said: "The stagnation is due to China's disregard for overseas trade; to close up the country is bound to lead to national suicide."

Unfortunately, not a single Chinese ear heard these ominous words in time. . . .

Even today, in the 1980s, in the great debate over "the craze for Chinese culture," people still seem to be caught in this century-old and unresolved controversy over the relative strengths of Chinese and Western cultures. Whether people seem to hold illusions of "wholesale Westernization" or whether they one-sidedly wish for the appearance of "the third age of the flowering of Confucian civilization," everything seems to still be marking time in the same spot; nothing seems to have really changed. No wonder younger scholars today lament: A tremendous cultural heritage has become nothing but a tremendous cultural burden; a great sense of cultural superiority has turned into a great sense of cultural guilt. This must be considered a major psychological obstacle in the course of China's modern cultural progress.

The difficulty of reform and change lies perhaps in the fact that we are constantly worrying over "whether the Chinese will remain Chinese." We do not seem to have realized that in the last two or three centuries in the West, having gone through the Renaissance, the Reformation, and the Enlightenment, the Western Europeans have not worried about whether after these reforms they would remain Italians or Germans or Frenchmen. It is only in China that this has always been the greatest concern.

Perhaps this is precisely the deepest aspect of this yellow civilization, and also its shallowest aspect. . . .

This great yellow earth cannot teach us what a scientific spirit really is.

The ruthless Yellow River cannot teach us a true awareness of democracy. . . .

It may well be that Confucian culture had all sorts of ancient "marvels," but for thousands of years now it has failed to produce a national spirit or enterprise, or an order based on the rule of law, or even a mechanism for cultural self-renewal. Instead, it has been moving constantly toward decline; it has formed a horrible suicidal mechanism that continues to destroy its own finest people, kill off its own inner vital elements, and stifle this nation's best and brightest year after year, generation after generation. Even if it did possess those ancient wonders, they can no longer save it from going down in today's flames.

History has proven that if we were to carry out the construction of modernization according to the model of governance of a continental culture, even if we were able to absorb some of the fruits of modern technology — and indeed it should be possible for us to launch a few satellites and test a few atom bombs — we would nonetheless still be unable to endow this nation fundamentally with some powerful and new cultural vitality. . . .

It was back in 1919 that for the first time in Chinese history the May 4 Movement unfurled the banners of Science and Democracy, and did so in a thorough and uncompromising spirit. Since then, Western culture and ideology, including Marxism, have been widely propagated in China. Yet this radical cultural current failed to wash away the sedimentation of feudalism in politics, or in the economy, or even in the Chinese people's character. In the last several decades, sometimes this sedimentation would rise to the top, and at other times there has simply been a frozen sheet of ice.

It seems that many things in China need to begin again, with the May 4 Movement as the starting point. . . .

The character of an autocratic government lies in its mysteriousness, its despotism, and its arbitrariness. On the other hand, it should be the character of a democratic government to be transparent, to honor the people's opinions and to be scientific.

We are now moving from murkiness to transparency. We have already moved from being closed to openness.

[Adapted from Xie Xuanjun and Yuan Zhiming, trans., "Heshang" ("River Elegy"), pp. 78–88 — RL]

### LI ZEHOU: "A REEVALUATION OF CONFUCIANISM"

A prominent contributor to the debate over Chinese tradition in the 1980s was Li Zehou (b. 1930), a professor at the Chinese Academy of Social Sciences who took a less dim view of Chinese culture than the authors of "River Elegy" and believed that Confucius himself could be exonerated from the misappropriation of his teaching in later Chinese history. Thus while he, like most other heirs of the New Culture and the May 4 Movement, concurred in their condemnation of the later tradition, he nevertheless saw in Confucius's teaching itself elements of a perennial humanism that could be sifted out of the later dross and adapted to modern needs.

In explaining the historical contexts in which Confucianism was embedded, Li originally spoke of it in terms of the pseudo-Marxist, unilinear path of historical development — from primitive communalism to slave and feudal and on to capitalist and socialist societies — which became the orthodox view after 1949, and one rarely questioned by those educated in the Stalinist ideology installed by Mao. Subsequently Li backed away from these references to slave and feudal society, but he still held to the idea that some of the values of primitive communal society survived in Confucianism.

Though its roots thus lay in an ancient social system, still, as a "cultural-psychological" construct shaped by Confucius, the tradition, according to Li, has outlasted the monarchial system and endured as the essential ingredient of Chinese culture, still applicable to China's situation today.

A way of understanding Confucius in a more or less correct perspective might be based upon the view that the Spring and Autumn period marked a social transition. The present writer thinks that Confucius's philosophy is the epitome of the nature of the clans-tribes living in these periods of change and that it is a cultural-psychological structure, which, by virtue of its relatively stable and independent features, has since persisted and continued to develop down to the present day.

## Characteristics of Rites

No one can deny that Confucius did all he could throughout his life to uphold and defend the Zhou dynasty ethical code. In the *Analects* Confucius repeatedly expounds rites and rules of human conduct — evidence that he was grieved by the violation of the traditional rites and rules of human conduct; he urged the people to restore and observe in every way possible the Zhou dynasty ethical code.

What, then, is the Zhou dynasty ethical code?

It is generally accepted that the Zhou dynasty ethical code was a set of decrees, institutions, regulations, rules of etiquette, and the like promulgated in the early years of the Zhou dynasty. On the one hand, the code clearly and strictly stipulated orders and positions of the rulers and the ruled, of the elite and the lowly, of seniors and juniors. However, the rites and rules of human conduct that had been shared by many clan members had by now become a monopoly serving the interests of a few nobles. On the other hand, the base of the social structure continued to be characterized by clans and primitive collectives, so those rites and rules of human conduct retained certain features of primordial democracy of a humanitarian nature. It is clear that filial piety and brotherhood presupposed reverence for elders. I subscribe to the idea of Yang Kuan, that "the wine-drinking ceremony was not merely a banquet in honor of elders but partook of the nature of a patriarchal council that had an important political position and function in its own right in ancient China."[3] It was exactly via such primitive ceremonial activities that the ancient clans and tribes were able to gradually organize and unite themselves for living purposes and productive efforts according to generally accepted modes, creating a regular social order so that their society could exist and their life could endure. They were equal in importance to the laws that followed in later periods. The rites were many and of various categories, but they all originated from and centered around ancestor worship.

The so-called Zhou dynasty ethical code was characterized by the primitive rites of worship of ancestors, which were gradually reformed, systematized, and amplified so that they eventually crystallized into a set of unwritten laws (a system of rites). The backbone of such unwritten laws was a hierarchy based upon the sanguinity of patriarchy. And enfeoffment, hereditary rights, the "nine-square" [well-field] land system, the patriarchal clan-rule institution, and other

---

3. Yang Kuan, *A New Approach to Ancient Chinese History*, p. 297.

political and economic systems were the extension and continuation of such laws.

However, Confucius lived in an age in which the rites and the ceremonies had begun to lose their vitality and were decaying. A social ideology coupled with a political theory — as advocated by scholars of the Legalist school — gained ascendancy, openly defending oppression and exploitation. In this period of turbulent changes Confucius stood unswervingly on the conservative side. Politically he upheld the ruling order of rites as against law and punishment, and economically he tried to preserve the old social and economic order, preferring a society with all people being equally poor to a society tending to polarization of rich and poor, which was a threat to the existence of the communal system and the old ruling order.

Confucius defended the Zhou dynasty ethical code — he was being conservative and was going against the tide of history. But he was against ruthless oppression and exploitation and championed the cause of ancient clan rule with its comparative moderation, showing the democratic and plebeian side of his thinking. It was on this contradictory and complex foundation that he built up his philosophy of humaneness (*ren*).

## The Structure of Humaneness

Most scholars in China agree that the main idea of Confucius is humaneness, not rites. Confucius was the first to use humaneness as indicative of the nucleus of his system of thinking. What, then, is "humaneness"?

The four factors that constitute the ideological pattern and the structure of humaneness are (1) the basis in consanguinity, (2) the psychological principle, (3) humanism, (4) individuality, and practical rationalism as the overall feature.

1. Whenever Confucius talked about humaneness he was interpreting rites; and so humaneness, as it is understood by posterity, is closely associated with his defense of rites. Rites, as previously stated, are based on consanguinity and characterized by the clan hierarchy, which it is the ultimate goal of humaneness to safeguard.

2. "Ceremonies come from without." Rites were originally a whole set of unwritten laws, ceremonies, proprieties, and shamanistic practices bearing upon the people. At the same time, the rites were subjected to new interpretations from various standpoints — for instance, the rites should not be formalities to be blindly obeyed; they should contain in themselves justifiable features. The rites as a political-social order are based on human nature, which consists in the senses of taste, color, sound, and likes and dislikes. Government has very much to do with the senses and the emotions. If that is the case, then the question arises: What is human nature?

In conformity with the spirit of reinterpreting and redefining the rites, Confucius ascribed the traditional three years of mourning to human love between parents and children, basing his observation on human psychology. Thus, he also correlated consanguinity and filial piety and fraternity and traced filial piety to love between parents and children. He was all the while trying to transform the rites and ceremonies, which were external restraining forces, into an internal aspiration of humans, trying to promote what was rigid and compulsory to the level of what would be a conscious ideal in the people's daily life.

What is most worthy of notice is that Confucius never did attempt to lead internal human emotions toward external objects of worship or to direct them toward mysticism. Instead, he boiled human relationships down to love between parents and children as the core of all human emotions. He integrated what would have been three elements of religion — conception, emotion, ceremony — into secular ethics and common psychology, thus dispensing with the necessity of setting up an edifice of theology. This fact makes it possible for us to say that Confucianism, though it is not a religion, has religious functions — a nonreligion playing the role of a religion, a unique phenomenon in the history of world culture.

Confucianism integrates ideas, emotions, and ceremonies with the ethical-psychological system, which in itself is based on the normal aspirations of normal men.

3. Associated as it was with the psychological principle, humaneness was externally colored by certain democratic traces and humanitarian ideas dating back to the primitive clan system.

Humaneness was closely related to the interests of the whole of society based on the clan-tribe system. This factor imposed social obligations upon the individual taking the relationship and social intercourse between man and man as the essence of human nature and the criterion of humaneness.

4. Extrinsically, humaneness was associated with, and restricted by, humanism. Intrinsically, humaneness brought into relief individuality with its initiative and independence.

The rites lost their mysterious and authoritative functions. The rites ceased to be the privilege of clan oligarchs such as witches, kings, prime ministers, princes, and historians, but became a historical responsibility or a paramount duty for every member of the clan. This was a great step forward in boosting individual personality and inducing personal initiative, independence, and the sense of historical responsibility.

Perfection of personality presupposes learning and education and acquisition of historical and practical knowledge.

The practical rationalism of Confucianism ruled out mysticism or fanaticism and instead adopted a realistic and reasonable attitude toward explaining and treating traditional institutions, at the same time one full of emotion and feeling; it disapproved of asceticism or hedonism and instead sought to guide, satisfy, and regulate human sentiments and desires; it rejected nihilism or egoism and instead strove for a balance between the pursuit of humanism and the cultivation of individuality.

This rationalism is characterized by an emphasis on practice. In other words, Confucianism does not lay store by speculative theorizing for its own sake. Polemics and rhetoric do not solve philosophical problems. Speculative or abstract thinking or debating seldom avails anything. What is important for humans is how to live their life in a practical and reasonable way.

Consanguinity, psychology, humanism, and individuality combine to form an organic whole of an ideological pattern characterized by practical rationalism. This pattern is an organic whole in the sense that its factors are mutually restricting, mutually balanced, and internally sufficient to produce adjustment and development.

In Confucianism we find an active and positive attitude toward living, a conformity with rationalism, a preference for practicality over polemics, a dominance of human affairs over references to gods and ghosts. Confucianism harmonizes human groups, allows for a reasonable and moderate satisfaction of the desires and passions, avoids fanaticism and blind submission, thereby forming an unconscious collective prototype phenomenon of a national cultural-psychological structure. Confucianism is almost synonymous with Chinese culture.

## Weak and Strong Points of Confucianism

Although cultural phenomena like material advance, spiritual progress, language, and so on may bear a certain kind of nonclass nature, none of them is separable from society and history, and each must be a historical product, though not necessarily a product of a certain class or class struggle. Often enough, in matters of cultural inheritance, class nature is not the only, and not even the principal, determining factor.

In the hands of different Confucian scholars serving the interests of their respective classes or political ideologies, Confucianism often went off at a tangent. The Confucius that the May 4 movement in 1919 destroyed was just the Confucius that Confucians from the Han dynasty to the Qing dynasty had identified with monarchy. This is just as Li Dazhao said: "We are launching an attack not upon Confucius himself but upon the Confucius whom the past successive emperors have molded into a political idol and authority — not upon Confucius himself but upon the Confucius whom the emperors have invested with a tyrannical soul."[4]

---

4. Li Dazhao, *Selected Works* (Beijing, 1959), p. 80.

This Confucius who represented the traditional superstructure and ideology through the advocacy of despotic monarchy, asceticism, and a rigid hierarchy naturally became the target of the bourgeois democratic revolution. In this connection we may refer to Lu Xun, who pointed out certain defects in the Chinese national character and sharply criticized them. In *The True Story of Ah Q 3*,[5] he exposed and denounced his hero's insensitivity to pain and suffering, narrow-mindedness, reconciliation with oppression, slavish mentality, contentment with poverty, conservatism, and so-called moral self-salvation and spiritual civilization. These characteristics do not come from the class nature of a particular ruling class. In essence, they are problems about the cultural-psychological structure. Though they cannot be directly or completely attributed to Confucius, they are related to Confucianism. That is why Lu Xun frequently aimed his attacks at Confucius.

Apart from the weak points of the cultural-psychological structure, we come now to the strong points of this structure. Where does the strength of the Chinese nation lie? The strength that has for thousands of years enabled the Chinese nation to survive all external aggression and internal disasters and yet to preserve, to develop, and to glorify the Chinese nation? Among them are the constituents of what is best in the Chinese legacy. The humanistic spirit and the personality ideal that originated from the democratic system in the clans, the rational attitude that emphasized the realities of human life, the optimistic and active spirit — these have all helped to affect, educate, and mold numberless men and women into eminent figures with lofty ideals and heroic deeds.

Nevertheless, the weak points of the Confucian structure of humaneness, as against its strong points, must be quickly eliminated — especially the effects of small-scale production and the vestiges of autocracy — so that China will get rid of her present poverty and backwardness. Only then can China, with the good aspects of the tradition of humaneness, refined and practiced by a large population, hope to make her contributions to mankind.

[From *Zhongguo shehui kexue* 1:2 (1980); trans. Liu Qizhong]

---

*A major aim of Li's three-volume* Essays on the History of Chinese Thought *is to trace Mao Zedong's thought back to currents in traditional Chinese philosophy and to show that not only Mao but most progressive Chinese intellectuals in the early twentieth century were still to a great extent influenced by traditional, antimodern ideas and values. Li's thesis is that Maoism has little to do with Marx and much more with tradition. These traditional elements impede China's modernization by putting up obstacles against capitalism, democracy, the rule of law, and large-scale industrialization based upon science and technology. Mao's brand of voluntarism, according to Li, compounds the fundamental fallacies of traditional Chinese thought, which encouraged him to launch ill-conceived and destructive mass campaigns such as the Great Leap Forward*

---

5. See Lu Xun, *Selected Works*, 1:102–154.

*and the Cultural Revolution. This "voluntarism" he identifies with long-standing Chinese misconceptions about the unlimited power of the ruler's purified moral will to transform the environment directly and instantaneously, without the support of a technological infrastructure. This tendency toward voluntarism and subjectivism culminated in Wang Yangming's activist brand of Neo-Confucianism, which, in Li's view, inspired Kang Youwei, Tan Sitong, Mao, and other twentieth-century Chinese intellectuals.*

*Furthermore, Li argues, Confucianism shared a fundamental stress on "asceticism" and frugality with the outlook of Mohism, which emphasized limited consumption and egalitarian distribution. In this respect, Mao's vision of the New Society accorded with traditional egalitarian ideals about the simple life in the unspoiled ancestral village. Moreover, Mao's call for the intense pursuit of moral and ideological purity as a precondition for the realization of the ideal society had a certain resemblance to Confucian ideas of how the sage can draw as if on cosmic power to transform the whole of reality immediately, by the pure strength of his moral will.*

*The thought of the young Mao, Li argues, still moved within the orbit of a traditional Chinese holism, although the moving force of the cosmos, in Mao's view, was not the harmonious complementarity of opposites but "motion" and "conflict," accomplished by means of convulsive mobilizational campaigns aimed at changing people's ideology (by molding the strength and direction of their willpower) rather than by science, technology, democracy, and the rule of law. This was combined with ideas current in Wang Yangming's school of Neo-Confucianism, according to which both knowledge of external reality and action aimed at changing external reality were spontaneous and unmediated: since man can know the essential principles of the universe merely by introspection, knowledge is a matter of intuition, unmediated by practice, and action that is inspired by the good force of the cosmos does not need technology, as its effect is instantaneous. In Li's view, Chinese holism contributed to an exaggerated belief in the divine powers of the sage ruler to control the universe solely by means of moral willpower. Thus Mao himself succeeded in taking the place in popular imagination traditionally occupied by the shaman and his reincarnations (the Chinese emperor and the moral hero), who are able to summon the good power of the cosmos by the force of their purified moral will, spreading its blessings over the entire community.*

*Through his teacher and later father-in-law Yang Changji, Mao was introduced to the philosophy of Wang Yangming, and Mao's early writings, according to Li, are clearly influenced by Wang's subjectivism and voluntarism.*

## Wang Yangming and Mao

Characteristic of the school of Wang Yangming is the great stress on the dynamic nature of subjective practice (moral behavior), i.e., the unity of knowledge and action. "Knowledge that is true and genuine is action, action that is conscious and discriminating is knowledge." This means that ethics is entirely reduced to the self-conscious action of the individual. "Knowledge" is necessarily "action"; "innate knowledge" automatically becomes action, and conscious action is identical to knowledge. That is to say, man's true existence lies in the "innate knowledge" [expressed in] activity and only in this activity can man achieve his noumenal existence. . . . [48]

In Wang Yangming's doctrine of the unity of knowledge and action, there is not much place left for epistemology; in a certain sense, it can even be said that epistemological questions have been eliminated. The so-called extension of knowledge is not about knowledge at all but is about moral feeling.

From the beginning, starting with Lu Xiangshan, there had been a strong emphasis on "being one's own master," "self-reliance and self-respect," the doubting of canonical authority and the opposition to blind obedience . . . and this characteristic became even more important and significant with Wang Yangming and his followers. . . .

[This] emphasis on subjectivity and willpower influenced, to a greater or lesser extent, many men of strong purpose and lofty ideals in later generations, such as Kang Youwei, Tan Sitong, the young Mao Zedong, and Guo Moruo, who used it as a spiritual weapon or support in their battle against the old society, the old order, and the old customs. The . . . aspect of individual moral cultivation, the steeling of the will, and the spirit of militancy . . . became a factor of real significance. [48]

Although Liu Shaoqi's *How to Be a Good Communist* and Neo-Confucianism are diametrically opposed to each other, are they really dissimilar in the way in which they establish the subjective will and a sense of moral responsibility? . . . Is there really no continuity here in regard to national tradition? . . . Is it unrelated to the Chinese nation's establishment of a subjective volitional structure in terms of a high regard for moral courage and character, the desire to control the feelings by means of principle, self-restraint, and firm determination? . . . In his youth, Mao Zedong earnestly studied Neo-Confucianism with his teacher Yang Changji and even spoke approvingly of Zeng Guofan. . . . He paid attention to self-improvement, the steeling of the will, and attached great importance to ideals, spiritual values, and moral achievements. Could all this have had no influence upon his later activities and ideology? [51–52]

[Li, *Sixiangshi*, pp. 48, 51–52 — WLC]

## GU MU: CONFUCIANISM AS THE ESSENCE OF CHINESE TRADITION

In October 1989, not long after the crackdown at Tiananmen Square earlier in June, an elaborate celebration of the 2540th anniversary of Confucius's birthday was held in Beijing by the Confucius Foundation, which had been set up in 1983 with the support of the Deng regime. Among the dignitaries present was the president of the People's Republic and general secretary of the Communist Party, Jiang Zemin, who spent two hours recollecting his own Confucian upbringing at home and giving his blessing to what was said by Gu Mu, a prime architect of Deng's economic modernization program who served as the honorary chairman of the foundation and of this event.

In his keynote speech Gu Mu claimed the time-honored Confucius as China's own and characterized Chinese culture as quintessentially Confucian (skipping over the Party's earlier anti-Confucian stance and the virulent attacks on Confucius during the Cultural Revolution). By relying on the Confucian values of harmony and social discipline as the criteria for excluding decadent libertarian influences from the West, Gu would have China screen out the spiritual pollution that was responsible for the alleged unbridled disorders of Tiananmen Square. Understood as a call for compliance with direction from above, such harmony and discipline would yield the stability needed for economic progress. Nothing was said about the "harmony without conformity" spoken of by Confucius, much less the kind of political remonstrance advocated by Mencius.

By this time an established regime, Deng's government no longer invoked Marxist revolutionary morality and class struggle (as in the Cultural Revolution) to guard the gates against Western liberal decadence, but instead leaned toward a conservative brand of Confucianism to buttress the status quo — yet not without a bow to such progressive trends from the West as environmentalism and ecology!

Subsequently an International Confucius Foundation was set up, which has joined in sponsoring meetings both in China and abroad (Singapore) along the lines proposed in this speech, usually participated in by officials and businessmen along with scholars.

The following excerpts are taken from the official English text of Gu's speech:

The Chinese nation has had a long history and brilliant ancient culture. For a long period of time in human history, the Chinese culture, with the Confucian school of thought as the mainstream, glittered with colorful splendor. . . .

Culture serves both as the emblem of the level of civilization of a nation or a country and the guidance for its political and economic life. To promote prosperity and peace for a nation and for mankind in general, it is necessary to develop a compatible culture. In this regard, a proper attitude toward the traditional national culture is very important. It is inadvisable either to be complacent about the past or to discard the past and the tradition. The correct attitude is to inherit the essence and discard the dross.

The Chinese people are working hard to build socialist modernization and a prosperous and strong socialist country. In order to reach this goal, we must develop and improve our new culture, which, we believe, should be national, patriotic, scientific, and democratic. This calls for inheriting and reforming the traditional culture of our nation and parallel efforts to courageously and yet selectively assimilate the advanced cultures of the outside world, merging the two into an integral whole.

As for the attitude toward the traditional culture and foreign cultures, there is no doubt that the traditional culture should be kept as the mainstay. . . .

As is known to all, the idea of harmony is an important component of the Chinese traditional culture. As early as the last years of the West Zhou dynasty three thousand years ago, ancient scholars elucidated the brilliant idea of "harmony making for prosperity." Later Confucius and the Confucian school put forward the proposition of "harmony above all" and established theories on the coordination of interpersonal relations, the protection of the natural environment, and the maintenance of ecological balance. These thoughts not only made positive contributions to the prosperity of ancient Chinese society but also have profound practical significance for the survival and development of mankind today.

[Keynote speech, 2540th Anniversary of Confucius's Birthday,
Beijing, October 1989]

# BIBLIOGRAPHY

Titles of collections that appear repeatedly in the list are cited as follows:

CSJC *Congshu jicheng*. 1,384 titles in 2,000 vols. Shanghai: Commercial Press, 1935–1937.

SBBY *Sibu beiyao*. 537 titles in 1,327 *ce*. Shanghai: Zhonghua shuju, 1927–1935.

SBCK *Sibu congkan*. 1st ser. 323 titles in 2,102 *ce*. Shanghai: Commercial Press, 1920–1922, reprinted in 1929. 3d ser. Shanghai: Commercial Press, 1935.


Bachman, David, and Dali L. Yang. *Yan Jiaqi and China's Struggle for Democracy.* Armonk, N.Y.: M. E. Sharpe, 1991.

Barmé, Geremie, and John Minford, eds. *Seeds of Fire: Chinese Voices of Conscience.* New York: Noonday, 1989.

*Beijing Review*, Beijing, vol. 22, no. 1 (Jan. 1979).

Benton, Gregor, and Alan Hunter, eds. *Wild Lily, Prairie Fire: China's Road to Democracy, Yan'an to Tian'anmen, 1942–1989.* Princeton: Princeton University Press, 1995.

Bernard, Henri, S. J. *Matteo Ricci's Scientific Contribution to China.* Westport, Conn.: Hyperion, 1973.

Bo Yang. "The Ugly Chinaman." In Barmé and Minford, *Seeds of Fire*, pp. 168–176.

Brandt, Conrad, Benjamin Schwartz, and John K. Fairbank. *A Documentary History of Chinese Communism.* Cambridge: Harvard University Press, 1952.

Chan, Anita, Stanley Rosen, and Jonathan Unger. *On Socialist Democracy and the Chinese Legal System: The Li Yizhe Debates.* Armonk, N.Y.: M. E. Sharpe, 1985.

Chang, Carsun. *The Development of Neo-Confucianism.* 2 vols. New York: Bookman, 1962.

Chao, T. C., et al. *China Today Through Chinese Eyes*. 2d ser. London: Student Christian Movement, 1927.

Chard, Robert. "Master of the Family: History and Development of the Chinese Cult to the Stove." Ph.D. diss., University of California, Berkeley, 1990.

Chen Duxiu. "Jianshe di wenxue geminglun." *Xin qingnian* 4, no. 4 (April 1918).

———. "Kongzi zhi dao yu xiandai shenghuo." *Xin qingnian* 2, no. 4 (December 1916).

———. "Rensheng zhenyi." *Xin qingnian* 4, no. 2 (February 1918).

———. "Wenxue geminglun." *Xin qingnian* 2, no. 6 (February 1917).

Chen Hongmou. *Chen Wengong gong shudu*. 1936 ed.

———. *Jiaonü yigui*. 1936 ed.

———. *Peiyuantang oucun gao*. 1896 ed.

———. *Xueshi yigui*. 1879 ed. (Preface dated 1769.)

Chen Yun. Speech given at the Chinese Communist National Representative Conference, September 23, 1985. In *Chen Yun wenxuan*, vol. 3. Beijing: Renmin chubanshe, 1995.

Chiang Kai-shek. *China's Destiny*. Authorized translation by Wang Chung-hui. New York: Macmillan, 1947.

———. *Zongzai yanlun xuanji*. Geming shijian yanjiuyuan ed. 5 *juan*. Taipei, 1952.

*Chouren zhuan*. *See* Ruan Yuan

Chu Chengbo. *Jianzheng tang zhegao*. 2 *juan*. 2 *ce*. 1905.

"Communiqué of the Third Plenary Session of the Eleventh Central Committee of the Communist Party of China, December 22, 1978." *Peking Review*, no. 52 (December 29, 1978): 6–16.

Compton, Boyd, ed. and trans. *Mao's China: Party Reform Documents, 1942–1944*. Seattle: University of Washington Press, 1966.

Cui Shu. *Kaoxinlu tiyao*. CSJC ed.

*Cunzhai suibi*. *See* Xiong Shili

*Da Qing lichao shilu* (*Veritable Records of Successive Reigns of the Qing Dynasty*). Mukden: Manzhouguo guowuyuan, 1937–1938. Facsimile ed., Taipei: Hualien and Huawen, 1964.

*Dai Dongyuan ji*. *See* Dai Zhen

Dai Fengyi, comp. *Guoshan miaozhi*. N.p., 1897.

Dai Zhen. *Dai Dongyuan ji*. SBBY ed.

Dean, Kenneth. *Taoist Ritual and Popular Cults of Southeast China*. Princeton: Princeton University Press, 1993.

de Bary, Wm. Theodore. *Learning for One's Self*. New York: Columbia University Press, 1991.

———, trans. *Waiting for the Dawn: A Plan for the Prince. Huang Tsung-hsi's Ming-i tai-fang lu*. New York: Columbia University Press, 1993.

Deng Xiaoping. "Build Socialism with Chinese Characteristics." In *Speeches and Writings*. 2d expanded ed. Oxford: Pergamon Press, 1987.

———. *Deng Xiaoping wenxuan* (*Selected Works of Deng Xiaoping*). 2 vols. Beijing: Renmin chubanshe, 1994.

———. "Uphold the Four Basic Principles." In *Deng Xiaoping wenxuan* (*Selected Works of Deng Xiaoping*), 2:158–184.

*Dictionary of Ming Biography*. Ed. L. Carrington Goodrich and Chaoying Fang. 2 vols. New York: Columbia University Press, 1976.

Ding Ling. *I Myself Am a Woman: Selected Writings of Ding Ling*. Ed. Tani E. Barlow with Gary J. Bjorge. Boston: Beacon Press, 1989.

———. "Thoughts on March 8." In Ding Ling, *I Myself Am a Woman*, trans. Gregor Benton, pp. 316–321.

*Documents of the Three-Self Movement*. Comp. Wallace C. Merwin. New York: National Council of Churches of Christ in the U.S.A., Division of Foreign Missions, Far Eastern Office, 1963.

*Dongxi wenhua ji qi zhexue*. *See* Liang Shuming

Ewell, John W., Jr. "Re-Inventing the Way: Dai Zhen's 'Evidential Commentary on the Meanings of Terms in Mencius' (1777)." Ph.D. diss., University of California, Berkeley, 1990.

Fan, K. H., ed. *The Chinese Cultural Revolution: Selected Documents*. New York: Grove Press, 1968.

Fang Lizhi. *Bringing Down the Great Wall: Writings on Science, Culture, and Democracy in China*. Ed. and trans. James R. Williams. New York: Knopf, 1991.

———. "Democracy, Reform, and Modernization." In *Bringing Down the Great Wall*, trans. James R. Williams.

———. "Reform and Intellectuals." Speech given sometime in 1986. *China Spring Digest* 1, no. 2 (March/April 1987): 30–34.

———. "The Social Responsibility of Today's Intellectuals." Speech given at Beijing University, November 4, 1985. *China Spring Digest* 1, no. 2 (March/April 1987): 34–38.

Fang Yizhi. *Tongya*. 2 *ce*. In *Fang Yizhi quanshu*. Shanghai: Guji chubanshe, 1988.

Feng Guifen. *Jiaobin lu kangyi*. Jinhe guangren tang ed. 1 *ce*, 1883, 126 leaves; 2 *ce*, n.d., 126 leaves.

Fung Yu-lan. *Selected Philosophical Writings*. Beijing: Foreign Languages Press, 1991.

Gallagher, Louis J., trans. *China in the Sixteenth Century*. New York: Random House, 1953.

Gamble, Sidney. *Chinese Village Plays*. Amsterdam: Philo Press, 1970.

Gao Yuan. *Born Red: A Chronicle of the Cultural Revolution*. Stanford: Stanford University Press, 1987.

Ge Maochun et al. *Wuzhengfu zhuyi sixiang ziliao xuan* (*Selected Materials on Anarchist Thought*). Beijing: Beijing daxue chubanshe, 1984.

Gilmartin, Christina, Gail Hershatter, Lisa Rafel, and Tyrene White, eds. *Engendering China: Women, Culture, and the State*. Cambridge: Harvard University Press, 1994.

Goldman, Merle. "The Party and the Intellectuals." In MacFarquhar and Fairbank, *The Cambridge History of China*.

Gong Zizhen. *Gong Zizhen quanji*. Beijing: Zhonghua shuju, 1959.

Goodman, David S. G. *Beijing Street Voices: The Poetry and Politics of China's Democracy Movement*. London: Marion Boyars, 1981.

Grant, Beata. "The Spiritual Saga of Woman Huang." In David Johnson, ed., *Ritual Opera, Operatic Ritual: "Mu-lien Rescues His Mother" in Chinese Popular Culture*. Berkeley: Chinese Popular Culture Project, 1989.

Gu Jiegang and Luo Gence. *Gushi bian*. 6 vols. Beijing and Shanghai: Poshe and Kaiming shudian, 1926–1938.

Gu Mu. Keynote speech for the 2540th anniversary of Confucius's birth, October 5, 1989, Beijing Confucius Foundation.

Gu Yanwu. *Qiugulu*. In Zhu Jirong, ed., *Xingsu caotang jinshi congshu*. 4 *ce*. 1888.

———. *Rizhilu jishi*. 32 *juan*. SBBY ed.

———. *Tinglin shiwen ji*. SBCK ed. 1st ser.

*Guangxu chao Donghualu*. Ed. Zhu Shoupeng. 5 vols. Beijing: Zhonghua, 1958.

Guo Moruo. *Moruo wenji*. Vol. 6. Shanghai: Xin wenyi chubanshe, 1955.

———. "Ode to Stalin." Unpublished translation by Chaoying Fang.

*Guoshan miaozhi*. *See* Dai Fengyi

*Gushi bian*. *See* Gu Jiegang

*Haiguo tuzhi*. *See* Wei Yuan

Han Yi [pseud.]. "Huaijia lun" ("Destroying the Family"). *Tianyi bao* (*Natural Justice*), no. 4, July 25, 1907. Reprinted in Zhang Nan and Wang Renshi, eds., *Xinhai geming qianshi nianjian shilun xuanji*, 2B:916–917.

Hayhoe, Ruth, ed. *Ma Xiangbo and the Mind of Modern China, 1840–1939*. Armonk, N.Y.: M. E. Sharpe, 1996.

He Zhen. "Lun nüzi dangzhi gongchan zhuyi" ("What Women Should Know About Communism"). *Tianyi bao* (*Natural Justice*), nos. 8–10 (October 30, 1907, combined ed.). Reprint. Tokyo: Daiyasu, 1966, pp. 229–232.

———. "Nüzi fuzhou lun" ("Women's Revenge"). *Tianyi bao* (*Natural Justice*), no. 3 (July 10, 1907): 7–23. Reprint. Tokyo: Daiyasu, 1966.

*Hengbao* (Macao), no. 7 (June 28, 1908). Reprinted in Ge Maochun et al., *Wuzhengfu zhuyisixiang ziliao xuan*, ch. 34.

"Heshang" ("River Elegy"). Trans. Xie Xuanjin and Yuan Zhiming. *Chinese Sociology and Anthropology* 24, no. 2 (Winter 1991/1992).

Hong Liangji. *Hong Liangji nianpu*. Reprint. Hong Kong: Zhongwen, 1973.

———. *Juanshi geji*. 2 vols. Reprint. Taipei: Wenhai, 1977.

Hu Ping. "On Freedom of Speech." *SPEAHRhead* 12/13 (Winter/Spring 1982): 35–37.

Hu Shi. *Hu Shi wencun*. Taipei: Yuantong, 1953.

Hu Shih. "On the Chinese Renaissance." *Bulletins on Chinese Education*.

Huang Zongxi. *Mingyi daifanglu*. Selections from de Bary, *Waiting for the Dawn*.

*Huangchao jingshi wenbian*. 120 *juan*. Comp. Wei Yuan. 1827 ed.

Huc, Evariste-Régis. *The Chinese Empire: Forming a Sequel to the Work Entitled "Recollections of a Journey Through Tartary and Thibet."* London: Longmans, 1855. Reprint. Port Washington, N.Y.: Kennikat Press, 1971. (First published in Paris, 1853–1854.)

Hudson, G. F., ed. and trans. *Let a Hundred Flowers Bloom: The Complete Text of "On the Correct Handling of Contradictions Among the People."* New York: Tamiment Institute, 1957.

Ji Yun. "How China Proceeds with the Task of Industrialization." *People's Daily*, May 23, 1953. In Selden, *The People's Republic of China*, pp. 290–293.

Jiang Jingguo. *Jiang Jingguo xiansheng wenji*. 28 vols. Taipei: Xingzheng yuanxin wenju, 1991.

Jiang Tingfu. "Jianguo yu zhuanzhi." *Duli pinglun*, no. 81 (December 1933).

———. "Kaiming yu zhuanzhi." *Duli pinglun*, no. 80 (December 1933).

*Jianzheng tang zhegao*. *See* Chu Chengbo

*Jiaobinlu kangyi*. *See* Feng Guifen

*Jiaonü yigui*. *See* Chen Hongmou

Johnson, David. "Mu-lien in pao-chüan." In David Johnson, ed., *Ritual and Scripture in Chinese Popular Culture*. Berkeley: Chinese Popular Culture Project, 1995.

Jordan, David K. "Folk Filial Piety in Taiwan: The Twenty-four Filial Exemplars." In Slote, *The Psycho-cultural Dynamics of the Confucian Family*. Seoul: International Cultural Society of Korea, 1986.

*Juanshi geji. See* Hong Liangji

Kang Youwei. *Kongzi gaizhi kao*. Wanmu caotang congshu ed. 5 *ce*. Beijing, 1920.

———. *Lunyu zhu*. Wanmu caotang congshu ed. 20 *juan*. 1917.

———. *Wuxu zougao*. 1 *ce*. Japanese ed. 1911.

———. *Yingchao tongchou quanjuzhe*. In *Wuxu zougao*.

*Kao xin lü tiyao. See* Cui Shu

*Kongzi gaizhi kao. See* Kang Youwei

Lagerwey, John. *Taoist Ritual in Chinese Society and History*. New York: Macmillan, 1987.

Legge, James. *The Chinese Classics*. 5 vols. Oxford: Clarendon Press, 1893–1895. Reprint. Hong Kong: Hong Kong University Press, 1979.

———. "Imperial Confucianism." *China Review* 6 (July 1877): 149–150.

Li Chang. "Building Socialist Spiritual Civilization." *Beijing Review*, no. 10 (March 9, 1981): 16–17.

Li Fuqun. "Report on the First Five-Year Plan for Development of the National Economy of the People's Republic of China in 1953–1957, July 5 and 6, 1955." In Selden, *The People's Republic of China*, pp. 295–299.

Li Jinghan and Zhang Shiwen, eds. *Dingxian yangge xuan*. Dingxian: Zhonghua pingmin jiaoyu cujinhui, 1933. Reprint. Taipei: Orient Culture Service, 1971.

Li Xiaojiang. "Gaige yu Zhongguo nüxing qunti yishi de juexing" ("Economic Reform and the Awakening of Chinese Women's Collective Consciousness"). *Shehui kexue zhanxian* (*Social Science Battlefront*), no. 4 (1988): 300–310. Trans. S. Katherine Campbell, adapted from Gilmartin et al., *Engendering China*, pp. 360–382.

Li Zehou. "A Reevaluation of Confucius." *Zhongguo shehui kexue* (*Social Sciences in China*), no. 2 (1980).

———. *Zhongguo gudai sixiang shi lun*. Beijing: Renmin chubanshe, 1985.

Li Zhizao. "Tianzhu shiyi." In *Tianxue chuhan*, microfilm copy of the 1629 ed. in the National Library in Beijing.

Liang Qichao. *Xinmin shuo*. Chung-hua shu-chü ed. Taiwan: Zhonghua shuju, 1959.

———. *Yinbing shi heji*. Comp. Lin Zhijun. 40 vols. Shanghai, 1936.

Liang Shuming [Liang Sou-ming]. *Dongxi wenhua ji qi zhexue*. Comp. Chen Zheng and Luo Changpei. Shanghai: Commercial Press, 1922.

———. *Xiangcun jianshe lilun*. Zouping, 1937. Reprint. Taipei, 1971.

Liu Binyan. *A Higher Kind of Loyalty: A Memoir of China's Foremost Journalist*. New York: Pantheon, 1990.

Liu Huiqun. "Qiju mulianxi zongheng tan." In Hunan sheng xiqu yanjiusuo et al., eds., *Mulianxi xueshu zuotanhui lunwen xuan*. N.p.: Hunansheng xiqu yanjiusuo, 1985 [?].

Liu Jin and Li Lin. *Xin quanwei zhuyi* (*The New Authoritarianism*). Beijing: Beijing jingji yanjiusuo chubanshe, 1989.

Liu Shaoqi. *How to Be a Good Communist*. New York: New Century, 1952.

———. *On Inner-Party Struggle*. Beijing: Foreign Languages Press, n.d.

Liu Shipei. "Wuzhengfu geming yu nongmin geming" ("Anarchist Revolution and Peasant Revolution"). In *Hengbao*, no. 7 (June 28, 1908). Reprinted in Ge Maochun et al., *Wuzhengfu zhuyi sixiang ziliao xuan*, pp. 158–162. Beijing: Beijing daxue chubanshe, 1984.

Lu Xun. *Selected Works*. Trans. Yang Xianyi and Gladys Yang. 2d ed. 4 vols. Beijing: Foreign Languages Press, 1980.

Lu Zhuangzhang. *Yimu liaoran chujie*. In *Pinyin wenzi shiliao congshu*. Beijing: Wenzi gaige chubanshe, 1956.

*Lunyu zhu. See* Kang Youwei

Luo Longji. "Women yao shemayang de zhengzhi zhidu?" ("What Kind of Political System Do We Want?"). *Xinyue* 2, no. 12 (1930): 4–13.

Lynn, Richard John, ed. and trans. *The Classic of Changes: A New Translation of the I Ching as Interpreted by Wang Pi*. New York: Columbia University Press, 1994.

Ma Xiangbo. "Religion and the State" and "Religion and Culture." In Hayhoe, *Ma Xiangbo and the Mind of Modern China*.

MacFarquhar, Roderick. *The Hundred Flowers Campaign and the Chinese Intellectuals*. New York: Praeger, 1960. Reprint. New York: Octagon Books, 1974.

MacFarquhar, Roderick, Timothy Cheek, and Eugene Wu, eds. *The Secret Speeches of Chairman Mao: From the Hundred Flowers to the Great Leap Forward*. Cambridge, Mass.: Council on East Asian Studies, 1989.

———, and John K. Fairbank. *The Cambridge History of China*. Vol. 14. Cambridge: Cambridge University Press, 1987.

Mair, Victor. "Language and Ideology in the Written Popularizations of the Sacred Edict." In David Johnson et al., eds., *Popular Culture in Late Imperial China*. Berkeley: University of California Press, 1984.

Mann, Susan. "*Fuxue* (*Women's Learning*), by Zhang Xuecheng (1738–1801): China's First History of Women's Culture." *Late Imperial China* 13, no. 1 (June 1992): 40–62.

Mao Zedong. "Leaning to One Side." In Selden, *The People's Republic of China*, pp. 176–177.

———. *Let a Hundred Flowers Bloom: The Complete Text of "On the Correct Handling of Contradictions Among the People."* Ed. and trans. G. F. Hudson. New York: Tamiment Institute, 1957.

———. "On the Correct Handling of Contradictions Among the People." In Mao, *Let a Hundred Flowers Bloom*, pp. 14–49.

———. "The Question of Agricultural Cooperation." In Schram, *The Political Thought of Mao Tse-tung*, pp. 343–346.

———. "Remarks at the Beidaihe Conference, August 1958." In MacFarquhar, Cheek, and Wu, *The Secret Speeches of Chairman Mao*, pp. 397–441.

———. *Report from Xunwu*. Ed. and trans. Roger R. Thompson. Stanford: Stanford University Press, 1990.

———. *Selected Works of Mao Tse-tung*. Vols. 1 and 2, London: Lawrence and Wishart, 1954. Vols. 3 and 4, New York: International Publishers, 1954, 1956.

———. "Stalin Is Our Commander." *People's Daily*, December 20, 1939. In Schram, *The Political Thought of Mao Tse-tung*, pp. 426–429.

Mao Zedong (attrib.). Chinese Communist Party Central Committee directive, June 1943.

Merwin, Wallace C., comp. *Documents of the Three-Self Movement*. New York: National Council of the Churches of Christ in the USA, Division of Foreign Missions, Far Eastern Office, 1963.

Michael, Franz. *The Taiping Rebellion — History and Documents*. 3 vols. Seattle: University of Washington Press, 1971.

Mou Zongsan. *Zhongguo zhexue de tezhi*. Taipei: Xuesheng shuju, 1984.

Nee, Victor. *The Cultural Revolution at Peking University*. New York: Monthly Review Press, 1969.

Nivison, David. *The Life and Thought of Chang Hsüeh-ch'eng*. Stanford: Stanford University Press, 1966.

Office of the CCP Dehong Dai Nationality and Qingbo Autonomous Zhou Committee. "Several Questions in Strengthing and Perfecting the Job Responsibility Systems for Agricultural Production." *Issues and Studies* 17, no. 5 (May 1981): 74–83.

Palace Museum Archives. Taipei: Memorial of 1763, QL 015160 *Tianxue chuhan*.

*Peking Review*, Peking (Beijing), vols. 1–21 (1958–1978).

*Peiyuantang shugao*. *See* Chen Hongmou

Peng Dehuai. "Letter of Opinion," *Selections from People's Republic of China Press* 4032 (36b, p. 7). Trans. adapted from Selden, *The People's Republic*, pp. 476–480.

*Pianxue shugao*. *See* Xu Guangqi

Price, Francis Wilson, trans. *San min chu i: The Three Principles of the People by Sun Yat-sen*. Shanghai: Commercial Press, 1929.

"Publication Statement." *Beijing Spring* Magazine, January 1979. In Seymour, *The Fifth Modernization*, p. 38.

*Qiugulu*. *See* Gu Yanwu

*Quanshan yishu*. *See* Wang Fuzhi

*Renxue*. *See* Tan Sitong

"Report of the Propaganda Bureau of the Central Committee on the Cheng Feng Reform Movement," April 1942. In Compton, *Mao's China*, pp. 1–8.

"River Elegy." *See* "Heshang."

*Rizhilu jishi*. *See* Gu Yanwu

Rong Jian. "Does China Need an Authoritarian Political System in the Course of Modernization?" In Liu Jin and Li Lin, *Xin quanwei zhuyi (The New Authoritarianism)*, pp. 113–131. Trans. adapted from Rosen and Zou, "The Chinese Debate on the New Authoritarianism (I)."

Rosen, Stanley, and Gary Zou. "The Chinese Debate on the New Authoritarianism (I)." *Chinese Sociology and Anthropology* 23, no. 2 (Winter 1990/1991): 46–68.

———. "The Chinese Debate on the New Authoritarianism (II)." *Chinese Sociology and Anthropology* 23, no. 3 (Spring 1991): 16–23.

Ruan Yuan. *Chouren zhuan*. CSJC ed.

Sa Mengwu et al. "Zhongguo benwei di wenhua jianshe xuanyan." *Wenhua jianshe* 1, no. 4 (January 1935).

*San Min Chu I*. *See* Sun Yat-sen

Schram, Stuart R., ed. *The Political Thought of Mao Tse-tung*. New York: Praeger, 1972.

———. *Quotations from Chairman Mao Tse-tung*. New York: Bantam Books, 1967.

Selden, Mark, ed. *The People's Republic of China: A Documentary History of Revolutionary Change*. New York: Monthly Review Press, 1979.

Seymour, James D., ed. *The Fifth Modernization*. Stanfordville, N.Y.: Human Rights Publishing Group, 1980.

Shen Xue. "Shengshi yuanyin" ("Original Sounds for a Flourishing Age"). In *Pinyin wenzi shiliao congshu*. Beijing: Wenzi gaige chubanshe, 1956.

Shen Yunlong, ed. *Jindai Zhongguo ziliao congkan*. Taipei: Wenhai, 1971.

"Shibao fakanci" (Inaugural Statement to *Shibao*). *Shibao*, June 12, 1904.

*Sishu jizhu. See* Zhu Xi

Slote, Walter H., ed. *The Psycho-cultural Dynamics of the Confucian Family: Past and Present*. Seoul: International Cultural Society of Korea, 1986.

Song Shu. *Jingxiang lou congshu*. Ser. 1, no. 18 (1928).

———. *Liuzhai beiyi*. In *Song Shu ji* 1:135–136. Beijing: Zhonghua, 1993.

Su Xiaokang and Wang Luxiang. "Heshang" ("River Elegy"). Beijing: Xiandai chuban-she, 1988.

Su Yu, ed. *Yijiao congbian*. Collected in Shen Yunlung, ed., *Jindai Zhongguo ziliao congkan*. Taipei: Wenhai, 1971.

Sun Longji. "The Deep Structure of Chinese Culture." In Barmé and Minford, *Seeds of Fire*, pp. 136, 311.

Sun Yat-sen. *San Min Chu I: The Three Principles of the People*. Ed. L. T. Chen. Trans. Frank W. Price. Shanghai: Commercial Press, 1927.

———. *Zhongshan quanshu*. 4 vols. Shanghai: Sanmin tushu gongsi, 1946.

*Taiping tianguo congshu*. Comp. Xiao Yishan. Ser. 1. 10 vols. Shanghai, 1936.

Tan Sitong. *Renxue*. In Chen Naiqian, ed., *Tan Liuyang quanji*. 6 *ce*. Shanghai, 1924.

Teng, Ssu-yu, and John K. Fairbank. *China's Response to the West*. Cambridge: Harvard University Press, 1954.

Thompson, Laurence G. *The One-World Philosophy of K'ang Yu-wei*. London: Allen and Unwin, 1958.

Thompson, Roger R. *Mao Zedong: Report from Xunwu*. Stanford: Stanford University Press, 1990.

*Tianxue chuhan. See* Li Zhizao

*Tianyibao* (*Natural Justice*), no. 3 (July 10, 1907): 7–23. Tokyo: Daiyasu, 1966.

———, no. 8–10 (October 10, 1907, combined ed.): 229–232. Tokyo: Daiyasu, 1966.

"Tianzhujiao Rujiao tongyi kao." *See* Zhang Xingyao

*Tianzhujiao tongjuan wenxian xubian*. Ed. Wu Xiangxiang. Taipei: Xuesheng shuju, 1966.

*Tinglin shiwen ji. See* Gu Yanwu

*Tiyong lun. See* Xiong Shili

*Tongya. See* Fang Yizhi

"Wall Poster from the April Fifth Forum." In Seymour, *The Fifth Modernization*, pp. 201–203.

Wang Fuzhi. *Quanshan yishu*. Taipingyang shudian ed., 1933.

Wang Ruoshui. "Tantan yihua wenti" ("Discussing the Question of Alienation"). *Xinwen zhanxian* (*Journalism's Frontline*), no. 8 (1980).

———. "Wei rendao zhuyi bianhu" ("In Defense of Humanism"). *Wenhuibao*, January 17, 1983, p. 3.

Wang Shiwei. "Wild Lily" and "Political Leaders, Artists." In Benton and Hunter, *Wild Lily, Prairie Fire*, pp. 69–75, 75–78.

Wang Tao. *Taoyuan wenlu waibian*. 6 *ce*. Hong Kong, 1883.

Wang Xizhe, Li Zhengtian, Chen Yiyang, and Guo Hongzhi. "The Li Yizhe Poster." In Anita Chan, Stanley Rosen, and Jonathan Unger, *On Socialist Democracy and the Chinese Legal System*, pp. 74–80.

Wang Zhao. *Guanhua heshang zimu*. In *Pinyin wenzi shiliao congshu*. Beijing: Wenzi gaige chubanshe, 1956.

Watson, Burton, trans. *The Complete Works of Chuang Tzu*. New York: Columbia University Press, 1968.

Wei Jingsheng. *The Courage to Stand Alone: Letters from Prison and Other Writings*. Ed. and trans. Kristina M. Torgeson. New York: Viking Penguin, 1997.

———. "Democracy or New Dictatorship." In Benton and Hunter, *Wild Lily, Prairie Fire*, pp. 181–184.

———. "Diwuge xiandaihua — minzhu ji qita" ("The Fifth Modernization: Democracy"). In Xie Dinghua, *Wei Jingsheng qishilu*, pp. 37–48. Taipei: Lianya chubanshe, 1981. Translation adapted from *The Courage to Stand Alone*, pp. 199–212.

Wei Yuan. *Haiguo tuzhi (Illustrated Gazetteer of the Maritime Countries)*. 1876 reprint of the 100 *juan* ed. 24 *ce*.

———. *Wei Yuan ji*. 2 vols. Beijing: Zhonghua, 1983.

*Wei Yuan ji*. *See* Wei Yuan

*Wenshi tongyi*. *See* Zhang Xuecheng

*Wenshi tongyi xinbian*. *See* Zhang Xuecheng

"What Have Song Shuo, Lu Ping, and Peng Peiyun Done in the Cultural Revolution?" In Benton and Hunter, *Wild Lily, Prairie Fire*, pp. 105–108.

Wu, John C. H. *Beyond East and West*. New York: Sheed and Ward, 1951.

Wu Han. "Hai Rui Scolds the Emperor." *People's Daily*, June 19, 1959. In Fan, *The Chinese Cultural Revolution*, pp. 72–76.

Wu Jiaxing. "An Outline for Studying the New Authoritarianism." In Liu Jin and Li Lin, *Xin quanwei zhuyi (The New Authoritarianism)*, pp. 47–53. Trans. in Stanley Rosen and Gary Zou, "The Chinese Debate on the New Authoritarianism (II)," *Chinese Sociology and Anthropology* 23, no. 3 (Spring 1991): 16–23.

*Wuxu zougao*. *See* Kang Youwei

*Wuzhengfu zhuyi sixiang ziliao xuan*. *See* Ge Maochun

*Xiangcun jianshe lilun*. *See* Liang Shuming

*Xinhai geming qianshi nianjian shilun* xuanji. *See* Zhang Nan

*Xinmin congbao*.

*Xinmin shuo*. *See* Liang Qichao

*Xinweishilun*. *See* Xiong Shili

Xiong Shili. *Cunzhai suibi*. Taipei: Erhu Publishers, 1993.

———. *Tiyonglun*. Shanghai: Longmen lianhe, 1958.

———. *Xin weishilun*. Yudi ed. Taipei: Lianya chubanshe, 1981.

Xu Guangqi. *Pianxue shugao*. In Wu Xiangxiang, *Tianzhujiao tongjuan wenxian xubian* 1:21–28, 36. Taipei, 1966.

Xue Fucheng. *Yongan quanji*. 12 *ce*. 1888.

*Xueshi yigui*. *See* Chen Hongmou

*Yan Fu yi*. 5 vols. Ed. Wang Ji. Beijing: Zhonghua, 1986.

———. "On Strength." In *Yan Fu yi*, 1:15–32.

Yan Jiaqi. "How China Can Become Prosperous." Speech given at the Da Gong Bao anniversary gathering in early 1988. Trans. in David Bachman and Dali L. Yang, *Yan Jiaqi and China's Struggle for Democracy*, pp. 83–90.

Yang Guangxian. *Bu deyi (I Could Not Do Otherwise)*. 1929 photolithographic ed. reprinted in Wu Xiangxiang, ed., *Tianzhujiao tongjuan wenxian xubian*, 3:1909–1092, 1121–1123.

Yang Kuan. *A New Approach to Ancient Chinese History*. Beijing: Zhonghua Publishing House, 1964.

Ye Dehui. "The Superiority of China and Confucianism." In Su Yu, ed., *Yijiao congbian*.

*Yijiao congbian. See* Zhu Yixin

*Yingchao tongchou quanjuzhe. See* Kang Youwei

*Yongan quanji. See* Xue Fucheng

Yu Qiuli. "The Relationship Between Politics and Economics," *Xuexi ziliao*, September 4, 1979. Trans. Yun-hua Kao, *Issues and Studies* 16, no. 5 (January 1980): 88 — 90.

Zeng Guofan. *Zeng Wenzheng gong quanji, Yishu hangao*.

*Zeng Wenzheng gong quanji, Yishu hangao. See* Zeng Guofan

Zhai Zhenhua. *Red Flower of China: An Autobiography*. New York: Soho Press, 1992.

Zhang Binglin. See Zhang Taiyan.

Zhang Boxing. *Zhengyi tang quanshu*. Zhengyi xueyuan ed. Fuzhou, 1866.

Zhang Junmai, Ding Wenjiang, et al. *Rensheng guan*. In *Kexue yu rensheng guan*. Vol. 1. Shanghai, 1923.

———. *Xuanxue yu kexue*. In *Kexue yu rensheng guan*. Vol. 2. Shanghai, 1923.

Zhang Nan and Wang Renshi, eds. *Xinhai geming qianshi nianjian shilun xuanji* (A Selection of Polemical Writings from the Decade Preceding the Revolution of 1911). Beijing: Sanlian shudian, 1963.

Zhang Taiyan. *Zhang Taiyan quanji (The Complete Works of Zhang Binglin)*. 5 vols. Shanghai: Renmin chubanshe, 1982.

———. *Zhang Taiyan xuanji: Zhushiben. (The Selected Works of Zhang Binglin: Annotated Edition)*. Shanghai: Renmin chubanshe, 1981.

*Zhang Wenxiang gong quanji. See* Zhang Zhidong

Zhang Xingyao. "Tienzhujiao Rujiao tongyi kao." Manuscript in the former Xujiahui Library collection (Shanghai), preface dated 1715, pp. 1a–2b.

Zhang Xuecheng. *Wenshi tongyi*. SBBY ed.

———. *Wenshi tongyi xinbian*. Ed. Cang Xiuliang. Shanghai: Shanghai guji chubanshe, 1993.

Zhang Zhidong. *Zhang Wenxiang gong quanji*. 229 *zhuan*. Beijing, 1928.

*Zhengyi tang quanshu. See* Zhang Boxing

*Zhongguo Guomindang shi gao*. Ed. Zou Lu. Shangwu yinshuguan, 1947; reproduced in *Minguo congshu*, vols. 25–26. Shanghai: Shanghai shudian, 1989.

*Zhongshan quanshu. See* Sun Yat-sen

*Zhongyong zhangzhu. See* Zhu Xi

Zhou Enlai. "Report on the Work of the Government." Delivered on January 13, 1975, at the First Session of the Fourth National People's Congress of the People's Republic of China. *Peking Review*, no. 4 (January 24, 1975): 2–25.

Zhu Xi. *Zhongyong zhangzhu*. In *Sishu jizhu*. Zhongguo zixue mingzhu jicheng ed.

Zhu Yixin. In Su Yu, ed., *Yijiao congbian*.

*Zongzai yanlun xuanji. See* Chiang Kai-shek

# INDEX

Translated selections from the Chinese sources are indicated by *italics*.

Prince, 6–8; On Ministership, 8–10; On Law, 10–12; Establishing a Prime Minister, 12–14; Schools, 14–17; Selection of Scholar-Officials, 17

Wang Anshi, 251

Wang Anyi, 565

Wang Can, 358

Wang Fuzhi, 28–35; 4, 39, 43, 67, 194, 281, 309; life and career of, 26; Zhang Zai's thought and, 26–27; problems of Ming China and, 27–28; cosmology of, 28–29; "revision" of orthodox Neo-Confucianism in, 29–30; concept of material force in, 29–30; understanding of history in, 30–32; distinctions between gentleman and mean man, Chinese and barbarians in, 32–35

Wang Gen, 261

Wang Luxiang, 565

Wang Mang, 251, 392

Wang Mingdao, 527, 528, 537; background of, 540; Three-Self Movement and, 540. *See also* We, *Because of Faith*

Wang Shiwei. *See* "Political Leaders, Artists"; "Wild Lily"

Wang Sitong, 42

Wang Tao, 250–252, 263, 264; journalism and, 252, 299. *See also* "Reform"

Wang Xianqian, 274

Wang Xizhe, 479

Wang Xizhi, 63

Wang Yangming, 19, 21, 27, 29, 42, 50, 51, 67, 185, 261–262, 382, 546, 580; Li Zehou on Mao and, 579–581

Wang Yangming and Mao (Li Zehou), 580–581

Wang Yangming school, 20, 36, 41, 370

Wang Zhao, 307–308

Wang Zhen, 565

Wanli emperor, 147

Warlords, 330, 397

Warring States period (479–221 B.C.E.), 32, 365, 552, 571

Wars of the Roses, 335

Waseda University, 370

*Water Margin* (*Shuihu zhuan*) (Shi Naian), 357, 358, 362, 364, 540

The Way, 244; Wang Fuzhi on, 29; Gong Zizhen on "guests" and, 184; instruments and, 252, 253; Western institutions and, according to Kang Youwei, 264

"The Way of Confucius and Modern Life" (Chen Duxiu), 353–356

Way of Governance, 181–182

Way of the Grand Commonality of Complete Peace and Equality. *See* Grand Commonality

Way of the Sages: Kang Youwei on change, 264

*Wealth of Nations* (Adam Smith), 255, 572

Wealth and power [for the state] (*fuqiang*): Wei Yuan on, 190–191

Wei Jingsheng, 497, 501. *See also* Democracy or New Dictatorship; The Fifth Modernization

Wei Shou, 53

Wei Yuan, 156, 157, 179, 201, 213, 309; role of scholar-official in, 188–195; ideas on governance of, 188–192; governance and profit in, 192–194; institutional progress in, 194–195; tribute rice transport and salt monopoly in, 197, 198; statecraft publications of, 206–212. *See also* Anthology of Qing Statecraft Writings; *Anthology of Qing Statecraft Writings*, preface to; *Criteria* for Anthology of Qing Statecraft Writings; *Illustrated Gazetteer of the Maritime Countries*; *Military History of the Qing Dynasty*, preface to; *The Silent Gourd*

Wei Zhongxian, 15 n38

*Weishu*, 53

Well-field system, 21, 22, 24, 265, 318, 319, 364

Wen, King (Zhou dynasty), 13 n31, 146, 209, 243, 267, 365

Wendi (Emperor Wen) (Han dynasty), 194–195, 472

*Wenshi tongyi* (Zhang Xuecheng), 52

The West: Gong Zizhen on resistance to, 180; tributary relations and, 200; earliest Chinese publications on, 206–207; Wei Yuan on policy toward, 207; Taiping movement and, 216, 218; China's inadequacies and, 234; Xue Fucheng on Chinese imitation of, 243; Yan Fu on,

List of permissions *(continued from page iv)*

OTHER WORKS IN THE

COLUMBIA ASIAN STUDIES SERIES

# TRANSLATIONS FROM THE ASIAN CLASSICS

*Reflections on Things at Hand: The Neo-Confucian Anthology*, comp. Chu Hsi and Lü Tsu-ch'ien, tr. Wing-tsit Chan 1967

*The Platform Sutra of the Sixth Patriarch*, tr. Philip B. Yampolsky. Also in paperback ed. 1967

*Essays in Idleness: The Tsurezuregusa of Kenkō*, tr. Donald Keene. Also in paperback ed. 1967

*The Pillow Book of Sei Shōnagon*, tr. Ivan Morris, 2 vols. 1967

*Two Plays of Ancient India: The Little Clay Cart and the Minister's Seal*, tr. J. A. B. van Buitenen 1968

*The Complete Works of Chuang Tzu*, tr. Burton Watson 1968

*The Romance of the Western Chamber (Hsi Hsiang chi)*, tr. S. I. Hsiung. Also in paperback ed. 1968

*The Manyōshū*, Nippon Gakujutsu Shinkōkai edition. Paperback ed. only. 1969

*Records of the Historian: Chapters from the Shih chi of Ssu-ma Ch'ien*, tr. Burton Watson. Paperback ed. only. 1969

*Cold Mountain: 100 Poems by the T'ang Poet Han-shan*, tr. Burton Watson. Also in paperback ed. 1970

*Twenty Plays of the Nō Theatre*, ed. Donald Keene. Also in paperback ed. 1970

*Chūshingura: The Treasury of Loyal Retainers*, tr. Donald Keene. Also in paperback ed. 1971; rev. ed. 1997

*The Zen Master Hakuin: Selected Writings*, tr. Philip B. Yampolsky 1971

*Chinese Rhyme-Prose: Poems in the Fu Form from the Han and Six Dynasties Periods*, tr. Burton Watson. Also in paperback ed. 1971

*Kūkai: Major Works*, tr. Yoshito S. Hakeda. Also in paperback ed. 1972

*The Old Man Who Does as He Pleases: Selections from the Poetry and Prose of Lu Yu*, tr. Burton Watson 1973

*The Lion's Roar of Queen Śrīmālā*, tr. Alex and Hideko Wayman 1974

*Courtier and Commoner in Ancient China: Selections from the History of the Former Han by Pan Ku*, tr. Burton Watson. Also in paperback ed. 1974

*Japanese Literature in Chinese*, vol. 1: *Poetry and Prose in Chinese by Japanese Writers of the Early Period*, tr. Burton Watson 1975

*Japanese Literature in Chinese*, vol. 2: *Poetry and Prose in Chinese by Japanese Writers of the Later Period*, tr. Burton Watson 1976

*Scripture of the Lotus Blossom of the Fine Dharma*, tr. Leon Hurvitz. Also in paperback ed. 1976

*Love Song of the Dark Lord: Jayadeva's Gītagovinda*, tr. Barbara Stoler Miller. Also in paperback ed. Cloth ed. includes critical text of the Sanskrit. 1977; rev. ed. 1997

*Ryōkan: Zen Monk-Poet of Japan*, tr. Burton Watson 1977

*Calming the Mind and Discerning the Real: From the Lam rim chen mo of Tson-kha-pa*, tr. Alex Wayman 1978

*The Hermit and the Love-Thief: Sanskrit Poems of Bhartrihari and Bilhana*, tr. Barbara Stoler Miller 1978

*The Lute: Kao Ming's P'i-p'a chi*, tr. Jean Mulligan. Also in paperback ed. 1980

*A Chronicle of Gods and Sovereigns: Jinnō Shōtōki of Kitabatake Chikafusa*, tr. H. Paul Varley 1980

*Among the Flowers: The Hua-chien chi*, tr. Lois Fusek 1982

*Grass Hill: Poems and Prose by the Japanese Monk Gensei*, tr. Burton Watson 1983

*Doctors, Diviners, and Magicians of Ancient China: Biographies of Fang-shih*, tr. Kenneth J. DeWoskin. Also in paperback ed. 1983

*Theater of Memory: The Plays of Kālidāsa*, ed. Barbara Stoler Miller. Also in paperback ed. 1984

*The Columbia Book of Chinese Poetry: From Early Times to the Thirteenth Century*, ed. and tr. Burton Watson. Also in paperback ed. 1984

*Poems of Love and War: From the Eight Anthologies and the Ten Long Poems of Classical Tamil*, tr. A. K. Ramanujan. Also in paperback ed. 1985

*The Bhagavad Gita: Krishna's Counsel in Time of War*, tr. Barbara Stoler Miller 1986

*The Columbia Book of Later Chinese Poetry*, ed. and tr. Jonathan Chaves. Also in paperback ed. 1986

*The Tso Chuan: Selections from China's Oldest Narrative History*, tr. Burton Watson 1989

*Waiting for the Wind: Thirty-six Poets of Japan's Late Medieval Age*, tr. Steven Carter 1989

*Selected Writings of Nichiren*, ed. Philip B. Yampolsky 1990

*Saigyō, Poems of a Mountain Home*, tr. Burton Watson 1990

*The Book of Lieh Tzu: A Classic of the Tao*, tr. A. C. Graham. Morningside ed. 1990

*The Tale of an Anklet: An Epic of South India--The Cilappatikāram of Iḷaṅkō Aṭikaḷ*, tr. R. Parthasarathy 1993

*Waiting for the Dawn: A Plan for the Prince*, tr. and introduction by Wm. Theodore de Bary 1993

*Yoshitsune and the Thousand Cherry Trees: A Masterpiece of the Eighteenth-Century Japanese Puppet Theater*, tr., annotated, and with introduction by Stanleigh H. Jones, Jr. 1993

*The Lotus Sutra*, tr. Burton Watson. Also in paperback ed. 1993

*The Classic of Changes: A New Translation of the I Ching as Interpreted by Wang Bi*, tr. Richard John Lynn 1994

*Beyond Spring: Tz'u Poems of the Sung Dynasty*, tr. Julie Landau 1994

*The Columbia Anthology of Traditional Chinese Literature*, ed. Victor H. Mair 1994

*Scenes for Mandarins: The Elite Theater of the Ming*, tr. Cyril Birch 1995

*Letters of Nichiren*, ed. Philip B. Yampolsky; tr. Burton Watson et al. 1996

*Unforgotten Dreams: Poems by the Zen Monk Shōtetsu*, tr. Steven D. Carter 1997

*The Vimalakirti Sutra*, tr. Burton Watson 1997

*Japanese and Chinese Poems to Sing: The Wakan rōei shū*, tr. J. Thomas Rimer and Jonathan Chaves 1997

*A Tower for the Summer Heat*, Li Yu, tr. Patrick Hanan 1998

*The Classic of the Way and Virtue: A New Translation of the Tao-te ching of Laozi as Interpreted by Wang Bi*, tr. Richard John Lynn 1999

*The Four Hundred Songs of War and Wisdom: An Anthology of Poems from Classical Tamil, The Puranāṉūru*, eds. and trans. George L. Hart and Hank Heifetz 1999

*Original Tao: Inward Training (Nei-yeh) and the Foundations of Taoist Mysticism*, Harold D. Roth 1999

*Lao Tzu's Tao Te Ching: A Translation of the Startling New Documents Found at Guodian*, Robert G. Henricks 2000

*Mistress and Maid (Jiaohongji) by Meng Chengshun*, tr. Cyril Birch 2001

# MODERN ASIAN LITERATURE SERIES

*Modern Japanese Drama: An Anthology,* ed. and tr. Ted. Takaya. Also in paperback ed. 1979

*Mask and Sword: Two Plays for the Contemporary Japanese Theater,* by Yamazaki Masakazu, tr. J. Thomas Rimer 1980

*Yokomitsu Riichi, Modernist,* Dennis Keene 1980

*Nepali Visions, Nepali Dreams: The Poetry of Laxmiprasad Devkota,* tr. David Rubin 1980

*Literature of the Hundred Flowers,* vol. 1: *Criticism and Polemics,* ed. Hualing Nieh 1981

*Literature of the Hundred Flowers,* vol. 2: *Poetry and Fiction,* ed. Hualing Nieh 1981

*Modern Chinese Stories and Novellas, 1919–1949,* ed. Joseph S. M. Lau, C. T. Hsia, and Leo Ou-fan Lee. Also in paperback ed. 1984

*A View by the Sea,* by Yasuoka Shōtarō, tr. Kären Wigen Lewis 1984

*Other Worlds: Arishima Takeo and the Bounds of Modern Japanese Fiction,* by Paul Anderer 1984

*Selected Poems of Sō Chōngju,* tr. with introduction by David R. McCann 1989

*The Sting of Life: Four Contemporary Japanese Novelists,* by Van C. Gessel 1989

*Stories of Osaka Life,* by Oda Sakunosuke, tr. Burton Watson 1990

*The Bodhisattva, or Samantabhadra,* by Ishikawa Jun, tr. with introduction by William Jefferson Tyler 1990

*The Travels of Lao Ts'an, by Liu T'ieh-yün,* tr. Harold Shadick. Morningside ed. 1990

*Three Plays by Kōbō Abe,* tr. with introduction by Donald Keene 1993

*The Columbia Anthology of Modern Chinese Literature,* ed. Joseph S. M. Lau and Howard Goldblatt 1995

*Modern Japanese Tanka,* ed. and tr. by Makoto Ueda 1996

*Masaoka Shiki: Selected Poems,* ed. and tr. by Burton Watson 1997

*Writing Women in Modern China: An Anthology of Women's Literature from the Early Twentieth Century,* ed. and tr. by Amy D. Dooling and Kristina M. Torgeson 1998

*American Stories,* by Nagai Kafū, tr. Mitsuko Iriye 2000

*The Paper Door and Other Stories,* by Shiga Naoya, tr. Lane Dunlop 2001

# STUDIES IN ASIAN CULTURE

*The Ōnin War: History of Its Origins and Background, with a Selective Translation of the Chronicle of Ōnin,* by H. Paul Varley 1967

*Chinese Government in Ming Times: Seven Studies,* ed. Charles O. Hucker 1969

*The Actors' Analects (Yakusha Rongo),* ed. and tr. by Charles J. Dunn and Bungō Torigoe 1969

*Self and Society in Ming Thought,* by Wm. Theodore de Bary and the Conference on Ming Thought. Also in paperback ed. 1970

*A History of Islamic Philosophy,* by Majid Fakhry, 2d ed. 1983

*Phantasies of a Love Thief: The Caurapañcāśikā Attributed to Bilhaṇa,* by Barbara Stoler Miller 1971

*Iqbal: Poet-Philosopher of Pakistan,* ed. Hafeez Malik 1971

*The Golden Tradition: An Anthology of Urdu Poetry*, ed. and tr. Ahmed Ali. Also in paperback ed. 1973

*Conquerors and Confucians: Aspects of Political Change in Late Yüan China*, by John W. Dardess 1973

*The Unfolding of Neo-Confucianism*, by Wm. Theodore de Bary and the Conference on Seventeenth-Century Chinese Thought. Also in paperback ed. 1975

*To Acquire Wisdom: The Way of Wang Yang-ming*, by Julia Ching 1976

*Gods, Priests, and Warriors: The Bhṛgus of the Mahābhārata*, by Robert P. Goldman 1977

*Mei Yao-ch'en and the Development of Early Sung Poetry*, by Jonathan Chaves 1976

*The Legend of Semimaru, Blind Musician of Japan*, by Susan Matisoff 1977

*Sir Sayyid Ahmad Khan and Muslim Modernization in India and Pakistan*, by Hafeez Malik 1980

*The Khilafat Movement: Religious Symbolism and Political Mobilization in India*, by Gail Minault 1982

*The World of K'ung Shang-jen: A Man of Letters in Early Ch'ing China*, by Richard Strassberg 1983

*The Lotus Boat: The Origins of Chinese Tz'u Poetry in T'ang Popular Culture*, by Marsha L. Wagner 1984

*Expressions of Self in Chinese Literature*, ed. Robert E. Hegel and Richard C. Hessney 1985

*Songs for the Bride: Women's Voices and Wedding Rites of Rural India*, by W. G. Archer; eds. Barbara Stoler Miller and Mildred Archer 1986

*A Heritage of Kings: One Man's Monarchy in the Confucian World*, by JaHyun Kim Haboush 1988

# COMPANIONS TO ASIAN STUDIES

*Approaches to the Oriental Classics*, ed. Wm. Theodore de Bary 1959

*Early Chinese Literature*, by Burton Watson. Also in paperback ed. 1962

*Approaches to Asian Civilizations*, eds. Wm. Theodore de Bary and Ainslie T. Embree 1964

*The Classic Chinese Novel: A Critical Introduction*, by C. T. Hsia. Also in paperback ed. 1968

*Chinese Lyricism: Shih Poetry from the Second to the Twelfth Century*, tr. Burton Watson. Also in paperback ed. 1971

*A Syllabus of Indian Civilization*, by Leonard A. Gordon and Barbara Stoler Miller 1971

*Twentieth-Century Chinese Stories*, ed. C. T. Hsia and Joseph S. M. Lau. Also in paperback ed. 1971

*A Syllabus of Chinese Civilization*, by J. Mason Gentzler, 2d ed. 1972

*A Syllabus of Japanese Civilization*, by H. Paul Varley, 2d ed. 1972

*An Introduction to Chinese Civilization*, ed. John Meskill, with the assistance of J. Mason Gentzler 1973

*An Introduction to Japanese Civilization*, ed. Arthur E. Tiedemann 1974

*Ukifune: Love in the Tale of Genji*, ed. Andrew Pekarik 1982

*The Pleasures of Japanese Literature*, by Donald Keene 1988

*A Guide to Oriental Classics*, eds. Wm. Theodore de Bary and Ainslie T. Embree; 3d
   edition ed. Amy Vladeck Heinrich, 2 vols. 1989

# INTRODUCTION TO ASIAN CIVILIZATIONS

Wm. Theodore de Bary, General Editor
*Sources of Japanese Tradition*, 1958; paperback ed., 2 vols., 1964
*Sources of Indian Tradition*, 1958; paperback ed., 2 vols., 1964; 2d ed., 2 vols., 1988
*Sources of Chinese Tradition*, 1960; paperback ed., 2 vols., 1964; 2d ed., 2 vols., 1999
*Sources of Korean Tradition*, ed. Peter H. Lee and Wm. Theodore de Bary; paperback
   ed., vol. 1, 1997
*Sources of Chinese Tradition*, 1999; 2d ed., vol. 1, compiled by Wm. Theodore de Bary
   and Irene Bloom; vol. 2, compiled by Wm. Theodore de Bary and Richard Lufrano

# NEO-CONFUCIAN STUDIES

*Instructions for Practical Living and Other Neo-Confucian Writings by Wang Yang-ming*,
   tr. Wing-tsit Chan 1963
*Reflections on Things at Hand: The Neo-Confucian Anthology*, comp. Chu Hsi and Lü
   Tsu-ch'ien, tr. Wing-tsit Chan 1967
*Self and Society in Ming Thought*, by Wm. Theodore de Bary and the Conference on
   Ming Thought. Also in paperback ed. 1970
*The Unfolding of Neo-Confucianism*, by Wm. Theodore de Bary and the Conference on
   Seventeenth-Century Chinese Thought. Also in paperback ed. 1975
*Principle and Practicality: Essays in Neo-Confucianism and Practical Learning*, eds. Wm.
   Theodore de Bary and Irene Bloom. Also in paperback ed. 1979
*The Syncretic Religion of Lin Chao-en*, by Judith A. Berling 1980
*The Renewal of Buddhism in China: Chu-hung and the Late Ming Synthesis*, by Chün-
   fang Yü 1981
*Neo-Confucian Orthodoxy and the Learning of the Mind-and-Heart*, by Wm. Theodore
   de Bary 1981
*Yüan Thought: Chinese Thought and Religion Under the Mongols*, eds. Hok-lam Chan
   and Wm. Theodore de Bary 1982
*The Liberal Tradition in China*, by Wm. Theodore de Bary 1983
*The Development and Decline of Chinese Cosmology*, by John B. Henderson 1984
*The Rise of Neo-Confucianism in Korea*, by Wm. Theodore de Bary and JaHyun Kim
   Haboush 1985
*Chiao Hung and the Restructuring of Neo-Confucianism in Late Ming*, by Edward T.
   Ch'ien 1985
*Neo-Confucian Terms Explained: Pei-hsi tzu-i*, by Ch'en Ch'un, ed. and trans. Wing-tsit
   Chan 1986
*Knowledge Painfully Acquired: K'un-chih chi*, by Lo Ch'in-shun, ed. and trans. Irene
   Bloom 1987
*To Become a Sage: The Ten Diagrams on Sage Learning*, by Yi T'oegye, ed. and trans.
   Michael C. Kalton 1988
*The Message of the Mind in Neo-Confucian Thought*, by Wm. Theodore de Bary 1989